P9-BBV-110

World Development Report 1993
Investing in Health

Published for the World Bank
Oxford University Press

Oxford University Press

OXFORD NEW YORK TORONTO DELHI
BOMBAY CALCUTTA MADRAS KARACHI
KUALA LUMPUR SINGAPORE HONG KONG
TOKYO NAIROBI DAR ES SALAAM
CAPE TOWN MELBOURNE AUCKLAND
and associated companies in
BERLIN IBADAN

*Manufactured in the United States of America
First printing June 1993*

*The maps that accompany the text have been prepared solely for the
convenience of the reader; the designations and presentation of material in
them do not imply the expression of any opinion whatsoever on the part of
the World Bank, its affiliates, or its Board or member countries concerning
the legal status of any country, territory, city, or area, or of the authorities
thereof, or concerning the delimitation of its boundaries or its national
affiliation.*

*The map on the cover, which shows the
eight demographic regions used in the analysis in this Report,
seeks to convey an impression of the general improvement
in health experienced worldwide during the past forty years.*

*ISBN 0-19-520889-7 clothbound
ISBN 0-19-520890-0 paperback
ISSN 0163-5085*

*Text printed on recycled paper that conforms to
the American National Standard for Permanence of Paper
for Printed Library Materials, Z39.48-1984*

Foreword

World Development Report 1993, the sixteenth in this annual series, examines the interplay between human health, health policy, and economic development. The three most recent reports—on the environment, on development strategies, and on poverty—have furnished an overview of the goals and means of development. This year's report on health, like next year's on infrastructure, examines in depth a single sector in which the impact of public finance and public policy is of particular importance.

Countries at all levels of income have achieved great advances in health. Although an unacceptably high proportion of children in the developing world—one in ten—die before reaching age 5, this number is less than half that of 1960. Declines in poverty have allowed households to increase consumption of the food, clean water, and shelter necessary for good health. Rising educational levels have meant that people are better able to apply new scientific knowledge to promote their own and their families' health. Health systems have met the demand for better health through an expanded supply of services that offer increasingly potent interventions.

Yet developing countries, and especially their poor, continue to suffer a heavy burden of disease, much of which can be inexpensively prevented or cured. (If the child mortality rate in developing countries were reduced to the level that prevails in high-income countries, 11 million fewer children would die each year.) Furthermore, increasing numbers of developing countries are beginning to face the problems of rising health system costs now experienced by high-income countries.

This Report advocates a three-pronged approach to government policies for improving health in developing countries. First, governments need to foster an economic environment that enables households to improve their own health. Growth policies (including, where necessary, economic adjustment policies) that ensure income gains for the poor are essential. So, too, is expanded investment in schooling, particularly for girls.

Second, government spending on health should be redirected to more cost-effective programs that do more to help the poor. Government spending accounts for half of the $168 billion annual expenditure on health in developing countries. Too much of this sum goes to specialized care in tertiary facilities that provides little gain for the money spent. Too little goes to low-cost, highly effective programs such as control and treatment of infectious diseases and of malnutrition. Developing countries as a group could reduce their burden of disease by 25 percent—the equivalent of averting more than 9 million infant deaths—by redirecting to public health programs and essential clinical services about half, on average, of the government spending that now goes to services of low cost-effectiveness.

Third, governments need to promote greater diversity and competition in the financing and delivery of health services. Government financing of public health and essential clinical services would leave the coverage of remaining clinical services to private finance, usually mediated through insurance, or to social insurance. Government regulation can strengthen private insurance markets by improving incentives for wide coverage and for cost control. Even for publicly financed clinical services, governments can encourage competition and private sector involvement in service supply and can help improve the efficiency of the private sector by generating and disseminating key information. The combination of these measures will improve health outcomes and contain costs while enhancing consumer satisfaction.

Significant reforms in health policy are feasible, as experience in several developing countries has shown. The donor community can assist by financing the transitional costs of change, especially in low-income countries. The reforms outlined in this Report will translate into longer, healthier, and more productive lives for people around the world, and especially for the more than 1 billion poor.

The World Health Organization (WHO) has been a full partner with the World Bank at every step of the preparation of the Report. I would like to record my appreciation to WHO and to its many staff members at global and regional levels who facilitated this partnership. The Report has benefited greatly from WHO's extensive technical expertise. Starting from the Report's conception, WHO participated actively by providing data on various aspects of health development and systematic input for many technical consultations. Perhaps WHO's most significant contribution was in a jointly sponsored assessment of the global burden of disease, which is a key element of the Report. I look forward to continued collaboration between the World Bank and WHO in the discussion and implementation of the messages in this Report. The United Nations Children's Fund (UNICEF), bilateral agencies, and other institutions also contributed their expertise, and the

World Bank is grateful to them as well. Specific acknowledgments are provided elsewhere in the Report.

Like its predecessors, *World Development Report 1993* includes the World Development Indicators, which offer selected social and economic statistics on 127 countries. The Report is a study by the Bank's staff, and the judgments made herein do not necessarily reflect the views of the Board of Directors or of the governments they represent.

Lewis T. Preston
President
The World Bank

May 31, 1993

This Report has been prepared by a team led by Dean T. Jamison and comprising José-Luis Bobadilla, Robert Hecht, Kenneth Hill, Philip Musgrove, Helen Saxenian, Jee-Peng Tan, and, part-time, Seth Berkley and Christopher J. L. Murray. Anthony R. Measham drafted and coordinated contributions from the Bank's Population, Health, and Nutrition Department. Valuable contributions and advice were provided by Susan Cochrane, Thomas W. Merrick, W. Henry Mosley, Alexander Preker, Lant Pritchett, and Michael Walton. Extensive input to the Report from the World Health Organization was coordinated through a Steering Committee chaired by Jean-Paul Jardel. An Advisory Committee chaired by Richard G. A. Feachem provided valuable guidance at all stages of the Report's preparation. Members of these committees are listed in the Acknowledgments. Peter Cowley, Anna E. Maripuu, Barbara J. McKinney, Karima Saleh, and Abdo S. Yazbeck served as research associates, and interns Lecia A. Brown, Caroline J. Cook, Anna Godal, and Vito Luigi Tanzi assisted the team. The work was carried out under the general direction of Lawrence H. Summers and Nancy Birdsall.

Many others inside and outside the Bank provided helpful comments and contributions (see the Bibliographical note). The Bank's International Economics Department contributed to the data appendix and was responsible for the World Development Indicators. The production staff of the Report included Ann Beasley, Stephanie Gerard, Jane Gould, Kenneth Hale, Jeffrey N. Lecksell, Nancy Levine, Hugh Nees, Kathy Rosen, and Walton Rosenquist. The support staff was headed by Rhoda Blade-Charest and included Laitan Alli and Nyambura Kimani. Trinidad S. Angeles served as administrative assistant. John Browning was the principal editor, and Rupert Pennant-Rea edited two chapters.

Preparation of this Report was immensely aided by contributions of the participants in a series of consultations and seminars; the subjects and the names of participants are listed in the Acknowledgments. The consultations could not have occurred without financial cooperation from the following organizations, whose assistance is warmly acknowledged: the Canadian International Development Association, the Danish International Development Agency, the Edna McConnell Clark Foundation, the Norwegian Ministry of Foreign Affairs, the Rockefeller Foundation, the Swiss Development Cooperation, the U.S. Agency for International Development, the Overseas Development Administration of the United Kingdom, and the Environmental Health Division and the Special Programme for Research and Training in Tropical Diseases of the World Health Organization. The World Health Organization and the United Nations Children's Fund contributed to the preparation of the statistical appendices. Three academic institutions—the Harvard Center for Population and Development Studies, the London School of Hygiene and Tropical Medicine, and the Swiss Tropical Institute—provided important support for the preparation of the Report.

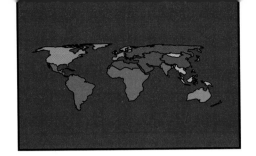

Contents

Tables

Appendix tables

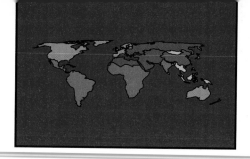

Definitions and data notes

Selected terms related to health, as used in this Report

Child mortality. The probability of dying between birth and age 5, expressed per 1,000 live births. The term *under-five mortality* is also used.

Median age at death. The age below which half of all deaths in a year occur. This measure is determined both by the age distribution of the population and by the age pattern of mortality risks. It does not represent the average age at which any group of individuals will die, and it is not directly related to life expectancy.

Total fertility rate. The number of children that would be born to a woman if she were to live to the end of her childbearing years and bear children at each age in accordance with prevailing age-specific fertility rates.

Externality. A spillover of benefits or losses from one individual to another.

Intervention (in health care). A specific activity meant to reduce disease risks, treat illness, or palliate the consequences of disease and disability.

Allocative efficiency. The extent of optimality in distribution of resources among a number of competing uses.

Technical efficiency. The extent to which choice and utilization of input resources produce a specific health output, intervention, or service at lowest cost.

Cost-effectiveness (in health care). The net gain in health or reduction in disease burden from a health intervention in relation to the cost. Measured in dollars per disability-adjusted life year (see next two entries).

Global burden of disease (GBD). An indicator developed for this Report in collaboration with the World Health Organization that quantifies the loss of healthy life from disease; measured in disability-adjusted life years.

Disability-adjusted life year (DALY). A unit used for measuring both the global burden of disease and the effectiveness of health interventions, as indicated by reductions in the disease burden. It is

calculated as the present value of the future years of disability-free life that are lost as the result of the premature deaths or cases of disability occurring in a particular year. (See Box 1.3 and Appendix B for further details.)

Population-based health services. Services, such as immunization, that are directed toward all members of a specific population subgroup.

Tertiary care facility. A hospital or other facility that offers a specialized, highly technical level of health care for the population of a large region. Characteristics include specialized intensive care units, advanced diagnostic support services, and highly specialized personnel.

Country groups

For operational and analytical purposes the World Bank's main criterion for classifying economies is gross national product (GNP) per capita. Every economy is classified as low-income, middle-income (subdivided into lower-middle and upper-middle), or high-income. Other analytical groups, based on regions, exports, and levels of external debt, are also used.

Because of changes in GNP per capita, the country composition of each income group may change from one edition to the next. Once the classification is fixed for any edition, all the historical data presented are based on the same country grouping. The income-based country groupings used in this year's Report are defined as follows.

• *Low-income economies* are those with a GNP per capita of $635 or less in 1991.

• *Middle-income economies* are those with a GNP per capita of more than $635 but less than $7,911 in 1991. A further division, at GNP per capita of $2,555 in 1991, is made between lower-middle-income and upper-middle-income economies.

• *High-income economies* are those with a GNP per capita of $7,911 or more in 1991.

• *World* comprises all economies, including economies with sparse data and those with less than 1 million population; these are not shown separately in the main tables but are presented in Table 1a in the technical notes to the World Development Indicators (WDI).

Demographic regions

For purposes of demographic and epidemiological analysis, this year's Report (including its health data appendices but not the WDI) groups economies into eight demographic regions, defined as follows:

• *Sub-Saharan Africa* comprises all countries south of the Sahara including Madagascar and South Africa but excluding Mauritius, Reunion, and Seychelles, which are in the Other Asia and islands group.

• *India*

• *China*

• *Other Asia and islands* includes the low- and middle-income economies of Asia (excluding India and China) and the islands of the Indian and Pacific oceans except Madagascar.

• *Latin America and the Caribbean* comprises all American and Caribbean economies south of the United States, including Cuba.

• *Middle Eastern crescent* consists of the group of economies extending across North Africa through the Middle East to the Asian republics of the former Soviet Union and including Israel, Malta, Pakistan, and Turkey.

• *Formerly socialist economies of Europe (FSE)* includes the European republics of the former Soviet Union and the formerly socialist economies of Eastern and Central Europe.

• *Established market economies (EME)* includes all the countries of the Organization for Economic Co-operation and Development (OECD) except Turkey, as well as a number of small high-income economies in Europe.

These eight regions fall into two broad demographic groups. The first consists of the FSE and EME, where relatively uniform age distributions are leading to older populations. The other six regions are referred to as *demographically developing,* in the sense that their age distributions are younger but aging. The demographically developing economies correspond approximately to the low- and middle-income economies. Figure 1 of the Overview depicts these regional groups. Table A.10 of Appendix A lists all economies by demographic region and indicates their mid-1990 population. Appendix tables A.3 through A.9 provide demographic and health data by economy within these regions for economies with populations greater than 3 million.

The regional grouping of economies in the WDI differs from that used in the main text of this Report. Part 1 of the table "Classification of economies" at the end of the WDI lists countries by the WDI's income and regional classifications.

Low-income and middle-income economies are sometimes referred to as developing economies. The use of the term is convenient; it is not intended to imply that all economies in the group are experiencing similar development or that other economies have reached a preferred or final stage of development. Classification by income does not necessarily reflect development status. (In the WDI, high-income economies classified as developing by the United Nations or regarded as developing by their authorities are identified by the symbol †.) The use of the term "countries" to refer to economies implies no judgment by the Bank about the legal or other status of a territory.

Analytical groups

For some analytical purposes, other overlapping classifications that are based predominantly on exports or external debt are used, in addition to income or geographic groups. Listed below are the economies in these groups that have populations of more than 1 million. Countries with sparse data and those with less than 1 million population, although not shown separately, are included in group aggregates.

• *Fuel exporters* are countries for which exports of petroleum and gas accounted for at least 50 percent of exports in the period 1987–89. They are Algeria, Angola, Brunei, Congo, Gabon, Islamic Republic of Iran, Iraq, Libya, Nigeria, Oman, Qatar, Saudi Arabia, Trinidad and Tobago, Turkmenistan, United Arab Emirates, and Venezuela.

• *Severely indebted middle-income economies* (abbreviated to "Severely indebted" in the WDI) are twenty-one countries that are deemed to have encountered severe debt-servicing difficulties. These are defined as countries in which, averaged over 1989–91, either of two key ratios is above critical levels: present value of debt to GNP (80 percent) or present value of debt to exports of goods and all services (200 percent). The twenty-one countries are Albania, Algeria, Angola, Argentina, Bolivia, Brazil, Bulgaria, Congo, Côte d'Ivoire, Cuba, Ecuador, Iraq, Jamaica, Jordan, Mexico, Mongolia, Morocco, Panama, Peru, Poland, and Syrian Arab Republic.

• In the WDI, *OECD members*, a subgroup of high-income economies, comprises the members of the OECD except for Greece, Portugal, and Turkey, which are included among the middle-income economies. In the main text of the Report, the term ''OECD countries'' includes *all* OECD members unless otherwise stated.

Data notes

- *Billion* is 1,000 million.
- *Trillion* is 1,000 billion.
- *Tons* are metric tons, equal to 1,000 kilograms, or 2,204.6 pounds.
- *Dollars* are current U.S. dollars unless otherwise specified.
- *Growth rates* are based on constant price data and, unless otherwise noted, have been computed with the use of the least-squares method. See the technical notes to the WDI for details of this method.
- *The symbol* / in dates, as in ''1988/89,'' means that the period of time may be less than two years but straddles two calendar years and refers to a crop year, a survey year, or a fiscal year.
- *The symbol* .. in tables means not available.
- *The symbol* — in tables means not applicable. (In the WDI, a blank is used to mean not applicable.)
- *The number* 0 or 0.0 in tables and figures means zero or a quantity less than half the unit shown and not known more precisely.

The cutoff date for all data in the WDI is April 30, 1993.

Historical data in this Report may differ from those in previous editions because of continuous updating as better data become available, because of a change to a new base year for constant price data, or because of changes in country composition of income and analytical groups.

Economic and demographic terms are defined in the technical notes to the WDI.

Acronyms and initials

AIDS	Acquired immune deficiency syndrome
ARI	Acute respiratory infection
BCG	Bacillus of Calmette and Guérin vaccine (to prevent tuberculosis)
DALY	Disability-adjusted life year
DPT	Diphtheria, pertussis, and tetanus vaccine
EPI	Expanded Programme on Immunization (immunization against diphtheria, pertussis, tetanus, poliomyelitis, measles, and tuberculosis)
EPI Plus	EPI with additional components: immunization against hepatitis B and yellow fever and, where appropriate, vitamin A and iodine supplementation
GBD	Global burden of disease
GDP	Gross domestic product
GNP	Gross national product
HIV	Human immunodeficiency virus
HMO	Health maintenance organization
NGO	Nongovernmental organization
OECD	Organization for Economic Cooperation and Development (Australia, Austria, Belgium, Canada, Denmark, Finland, France, Germany, Greece, Iceland, Ireland, Italy, Japan, Luxembourg, Netherlands, New Zealand, Norway, Portugal, Spain, Sweden, Switzerland, Turkey, United Kingdom, and United States)
STD	Sexually transmitted disease
UNDP	United Nations Development Programme
UNICEF	United Nations Children's Fund
UNPF	United Nations Population Fund
WHO	World Health Organization

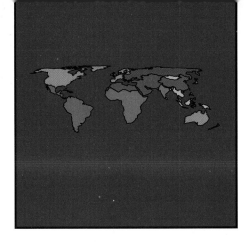

Overview

Over the past forty years life expectancy has improved more than during the entire previous span of human history. In 1950 life expectancy in developing countries was forty years; by 1990 it had increased to sixty-three years. In 1950 twenty-eight of every 100 children died before their fifth birthday; by 1990 the number had fallen to ten. Smallpox, which killed more than 5 million annually in the early 1950s, has been eradicated entirely. Vaccines have drastically reduced the occurrence of measles and polio. Not only do these improvements translate into direct and significant gains in well-being, but they also reduce the economic burden imposed by unhealthy workers and sick or absent schoolchildren. These successes have come about in part because of growing incomes and increasing education around the globe and in part because of governments' efforts to expand health services, which, moreover, have been enriched by technological progress.

Despite these remarkable improvements, enormous health problems remain. Absolute levels of mortality in developing countries remain unacceptably high: child mortality rates are about ten times higher than those in the established market economies. If death rates among children in poor countries were reduced to those prevailing in the rich countries, 11 million fewer children would die each year. Almost half of these preventable deaths are a result of diarrheal and respiratory illness, exacerbated by malnutrition. In addition, every year 7 million adults die of conditions that could be inexpensively prevented or cured; tuberculosis alone causes 2 million of these deaths. About 400,000 women die from the direct complications of pregnancy and childbirth. Maternal mortality

ratios are, on average, thirty times as high in developing countries as in high-income countries.

Although health has improved even in the poorest countries, the pace of progress has been uneven. In 1960 in Ghana and Indonesia about one child in five died before reaching age 5—a child mortality rate typical of many developing countries. By 1990 Indonesia's rate had dropped to about one-half the 1960 level, but Ghana's had fallen only slightly. Table 1 provides a summary of regional progress in mortality reduction between 1975 and 1990. (Figure 1 illustrates the demographic regions used in Table 1 and frequently throughout this Report.)

In addition to premature mortality, a substantial portion of the burden of disease consists of disability, ranging from polio-related paralysis to blindness to the suffering brought about by severe psychosis. To measure the burden of disease, this Report uses the disability-adjusted life year (DALY), a measure that combines healthy life years lost because of premature mortality with those lost as a result of disability.

There is huge variation in per person loss of DALYs across regions, mainly because of differences in premature mortality; regional differences in loss of DALYs as a result of disability are much smaller (Figure 2). The total loss of DALYs is referred to as the global burden of disease.

The world is facing serious new health challenges. By 2000 the growing toll from acquired immune deficiency syndrome (AIDS) in developing countries could easily rise to more than 1.8 million deaths annually, erasing decades of hard-won reductions in mortality. The malaria parasite's increased resistance to available drugs could lead to

Figure 1 Demographic regions used in this Report

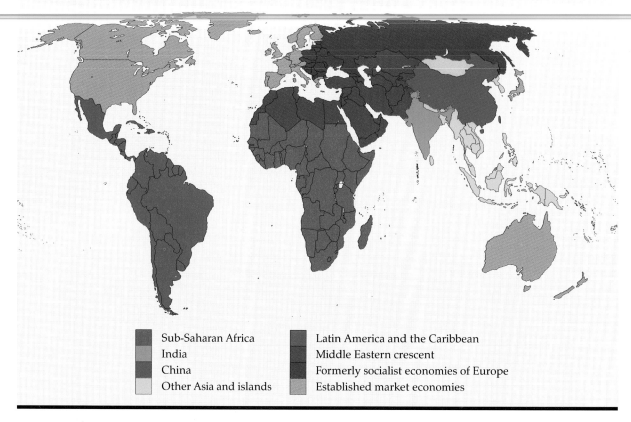

■ Sub-Saharan Africa	■ Latin America and the Caribbean
■ India	■ Middle Eastern crescent
■ China	■ Formerly socialist economies of Europe
■ Other Asia and islands	■ Established market economies

Table 1 Population, economic indicators, and progress in health by demographic region, 1975–90

Region	Population, 1990 (millions)	Deaths, 1990 (millions)	Income per capita — Dollars, 1990	Income per capita — Growth rate, 1975–90 (percent per year)	Child mortality 1975	Child mortality 1990	Life expectancy at birth (years) 1975	Life expectancy at birth (years) 1990
Sub-Saharan Africa	510	7.9	510	−1.0	212	175	48	52
India	850	9.3	360	2.5	195	127	53	58
China	1,134	8.9	370	7.4	85	43	56	69
Other Asia and islands	683	5.5	1,320	4.6	135	97	56	62
Latin America and the Caribbean	444	3.0	2,190	−0.1	104	60	62	70
Middle Eastern crescent	503	4.4	1,720	−1.3	174	111	52	61
Formerly socialist economies of Europe (FSE)	346	3.8	2,850	0.5	36	22	70	72
Established market economies (EME)	798	7.1	19,900	2.2	21	11	73	76
Demographically developing group[a]	4,123	39.1	900	3.0	152	106	56	63
FSE and EME	1,144	10.9	14,690	1.7	25	15	72	75
World	5,267	50.0	4,000	1.2	135	96	60	65

Note: Child mortality is the probability of dying between birth and age 5, expressed per 1,000 live births; life expectancy at birth is the average number of years that a person would expect to live at the prevailing age-specific mortality rates.
a. The countries of the demographic regions Sub-Saharan Africa, India, China, Other Asia and islands, Latin America and the Caribbean, and Middle Eastern crescent.
Source: For income per capita, World Bank data; for other items, Appendix A.

a doubling of malaria deaths, to nearly 2 million a year within a decade. Rapid progress in reducing child mortality and fertility rates will create new demands on health care systems as the aging of populations brings to the fore costly noncommunicable diseases of adults and the elderly. Tobacco-related deaths from heart disease and cancers alone are likely to double by the first decade of the next century, to 2 million a year, and, if present smoking patterns continue, they will grow to more than 12 million a year in developing countries in the second quarter of the next century.

Health systems and their problems

Although health services are only one factor in explaining past successes, the importance of their role in the developing world is not in doubt. Public health measures brought about the eradication of smallpox and have been central to the reduction in deaths caused by vaccine-preventable childhood diseases. Expanded and improved clinical care has saved millions of lives from infectious diseases and injuries. But there are also major problems with health systems that, if not resolved, will hamper progress in reducing the burden of premature mortality and disability and frustrate efforts to respond to new health challenges and emerging disease threats.

• *Misallocation.* Public money is spent on health interventions of low cost-effectiveness, such as surgery for most cancers, at the same time that critical and highly cost-effective interventions, such as treatment of tuberculosis and sexually

The disease burden is highest in poor countries, but disability remains a problem in all regions.

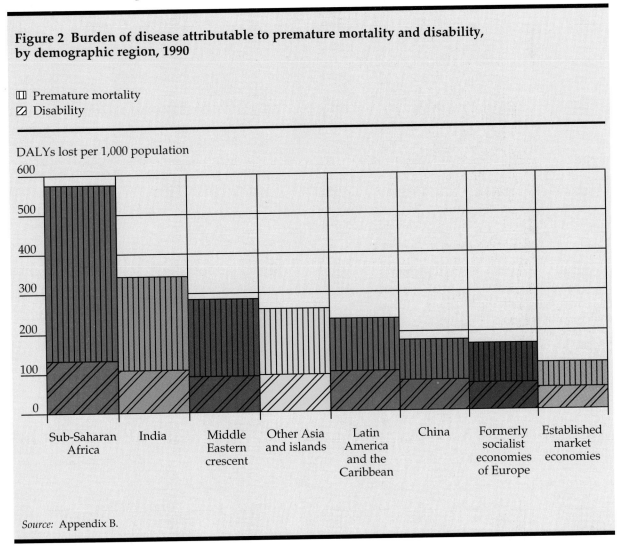

Figure 2 Burden of disease attributable to premature mortality and disability, by demographic region, 1990

▥ Premature mortality
▨ Disability

DALYs lost per 1,000 population

Source: Appendix B.

transmitted diseases (STDs), remain under-funded. In some countries a single teaching hospital can absorb 20 percent or more of the budget of the ministry of health, even though almost all cost-effective interventions are best delivered at lower-level facilities.

• *Inequity.* The poor lack access to basic health services and receive low-quality care. Government spending for health goes disproportionately to the affluent in the form of free or below-cost care in sophisticated public tertiary care hospitals and subsidies to private and public insurance.

• *Inefficiency.* Much of the money spent on health is wasted: brand-name pharmaceuticals are purchased instead of generic drugs, health workers are badly deployed and supervised, and hospital beds are underutilized.

• *Exploding costs.* In some middle-income developing countries health care expenditures are growing much faster than income. Increasing numbers of general physicians and specialists, the availability of new medical technologies, and expanding health insurance linked to fee-for-service payments together generate a rapidly growing demand for costly tests, procedures, and treatments.

World health spending—and thus also the potential for misallocation, waste, and inequitable distribution of resources—is huge. For the world as a whole in 1990, public and private expenditure on health services was about $1,700 billion, or 8 percent of total world product. High-income countries spent almost 90 percent of this amount, for an average of $1,500 per person. The United States alone consumed 41 percent of the global total—more than 12 percent of its gross national product (GNP). Developing countries spent about $170 billion, or 4 percent of their GNP, for an average of $41 per person—less than one-thirtieth the amount spent by rich countries.

In the *low-income countries* government hospitals and clinics, which account for the greatest part of the modern medical care provided, are often inefficient, suffering from highly centralized decision-making, wide fluctuations in budgetary allocations, and poor motivation of facility managers and health care workers. Private providers—mainly religious nongovernmental organizations (NGOs) in Africa and private doctors and un-licensed practitioners in South Asia—are often more technically efficient than the public sector and offer a service that is perceived to be of higher quality, but they are not supported by government policies. In low-income countries the poor often lose out in health because public spending in the sector is heavily skewed toward high-cost hospital services that disproportionately benefit better-off urban groups. In Indonesia, despite concerted government efforts in the 1980s to improve health services for the poor, government subsidies to health for the richest 10 percent of households in 1990 were still almost three times the subsidies going to the poorest 10 percent of Indonesians.

In *middle-income countries* governments frequently subsidize insurance that protects only the relatively wealthy—a small, affluent minority in the case of private insurance in South Africa and Zimbabwe and, in Latin America, the larger industrial labor force covered by compulsory public insurance (so-called social insurance). The bulk of the population, especially the poor, relies heavily on out-of-pocket payments and on government services that may be largely inaccessible to them. In Peru, for example, more than 60 percent of the poor have to travel for more than an hour to obtain primary health care, as compared with less than 3 percent of the better-off. The quality of care is also low: drugs and equipment are in short supply; patient waiting times are long and medical consultations are short; and misdiagnoses and inappropriate treatment are common.

In the *formerly socialist economies,* where governments have historically been responsible for both the financing and the delivery of health care, health care is free in principle, and wide coverage of the population has been achieved. This has led to greater apparent equity. But in reality, better-off consumers make informal out-of-pocket payments to get better care: about 25 percent of health costs in Romania and 20 percent in Hungary, for example, are under-the-table payments for pharmaceuticals and gratuities to health care providers. Inefficiency is also widespread because the government-run health system is highly centralized, bureaucratic, and unresponsive to citizens. Governments have been slow to regulate workplace safety and environmental pollution and have failed to mount effective campaigns against unhealthy personal behaviors—especially alcohol consumption and cigarette smoking. In recent years real government spending for health has fallen dramatically in the course of the transition to more market-oriented economies. The public sector has suffered from serious shortages of drugs and equipment and a lack of skills to manage changing health institutions. The consequences have been declining staff morale and falling quality of care.

The roles of the government and of the market in health

Three rationales for a major government role in the health sector should guide the reform of health systems.

- Many health-related services such as information and control of contagious disease are *public goods*. One person's use of health information does not leave less available for others to consume; one person cannot benefit from control of malaria-carrying mosquitoes while another person in the same area is excluded. Because private markets alone provide too little of the public goods crucial for health, government involvement is necessary to increase the supply of these goods. Other health services have large *externalities*: consumption by one individual affects others. Immunizing a child slows transmission of measles and other diseases, conferring a positive externality. Polluters and drunk drivers create negative health externalities. Governments need to encourage behaviors that carry positive externalities and to discourage those with negative externalities.

- Provision of cost-effective health services to the poor is an effective and socially acceptable approach to *poverty reduction*. Most countries view access to basic health care as a human right. This perspective is embodied in the goal, "Health for All by the Year 2000," of the conference held by the World Health Organization (WHO) and the United Nations Children's Fund (UNICEF) at Alma-Ata in 1978, which launched today's primary health care movement. Private markets will not give the poor adequate access to essential clinical services or the insurance often needed to pay for such services. Public finance of essential clinical care is thus justified to alleviate poverty. Such public funding can take several forms: subsidies to private providers and NGOs that serve the poor; vouchers that the poor can take to a provider of their choice; and free or below-cost delivery of public services to the poor.

- Government action may be needed to compensate for problems generated by *uncertainty* and *insurance market failure*. The great uncertainties surrounding the probability of illness and the efficacy of care give rise both to strong demand for insurance and to shortcomings in the operation of private markets. One reason why markets may work poorly is that variations in health risk create incentives for insurance companies to refuse to insure the very people who most need health insurance—those who are already sick or are likely to become

ill. A second has to do with "moral hazard": insurance reduces the incentives for individuals to avoid risk and expense by prudent behavior and can create both incentives and opportunities for doctors and hospitals to give patients more care than they need. A third has to do with the asymmetry in information between provider and patient concerning the outcomes of intervention; providers advise patients on choice of treatment, and when the providers' income is linked to this advice, excessive treatment can result. As a consequence of these last two considerations, in unregulated private markets costs escalate without appreciable health gains to the patient. Governments have an important role to play in regulating privately provided health insurance, or in mandating alternatives such as social insurance, in order to ensure widespread coverage and hold down costs.

If governments do intervene, they must do so intelligently, or they risk exacerbating the very problems they are trying to solve. When governments become directly involved in the health sector—by providing public health programs or financing essential clinical services for the poor—policymakers face difficult decisions concerning the allocation of public resources. For any given amount of total spending, taxpayers and, in some countries, donors want to see maximum health gain for the money spent. An important source of guidance for achieving value for money in health spending is a measure of the cost-effectiveness of different health interventions and medical procedures—that is, the ratio of costs to health benefits (DALYs gained).

Until recently, little has been done to apply cost-effectiveness analysis to health. This is, in part, because it is difficult. Cost and effectiveness data on health interventions are often weak. Costs vary between countries and can rise or fall sharply as a service is expanded. Some groups of interventions are provided jointly, and their costs are shared. Nonetheless, cost-effectiveness analysis is already demonstrating its usefulness as a tool for choosing among possible health interventions in individual countries and for addressing specific health problems such as the spread of AIDS.

Just because a particular intervention is cost-effective does not mean that public funds should be spent on it. Households can buy health care with their own money and, when well informed, may do this better than governments can do it for them. But households also seek value for money, and governments, by making information about cost-effectiveness available, can often help im-

Box 1 Investing in health: key messages of this Report

This Report proposes a three-pronged approach to government policies for improving health.

Foster an environment that enables households to improve health

Household decisions shape health, but these decisions are constrained by the income and education of household members. In addition to promoting overall economic growth, governments can help to improve those decisions if they:

• Pursue economic growth policies that will benefit the poor (including, where necessary, adjustment policies that preserve cost-effective health expenditures)

• Expand investment in schooling, particularly for girls

• Promote the rights and status of women through political and economic empowerment and legal protection against abuse.

Improve government spending on health

The challenge for most governments is to concentrate resources on compensating for market failures and efficiently financing services that will particularly benefit the poor. Several directions for policy respond to this challenge:

• Reduce government expenditures on tertiary facilities, specialist training, and interventions that provide little health gain for the money spent.

• Finance and implement a package of public health interventions to deal with the substantial externalities surrounding infectious disease control, prevention of AIDS, environmental pollution, and behaviors (such as drunk driving) that put others at risk.

• Finance and ensure delivery of a package of essential clinical services. The comprehensiveness and composition of such a package can only be defined by each country, taking into account epidemiological conditions, local preferences, and income. In most countries public finance, or publicly mandated finance, of the essential clinical package would provide a politically acceptable mechanism for distributing both welfare im-

provements and a productive asset—better health—to the poor.

• Improve management of government health services through such measures as decentralization of administrative and budgetary authority and contracting out of services.

Promote diversity and competition

Government finance of public health and of a nationally defined package of essential clinical services would leave the remaining clinical services to be financed privately or by social insurance within the context of a policy framework established by the government. Governments can promote diversity and competition in provision of health services and insurance by adopting policies that:

• Encourage social or private insurance (with regulatory incentives for equitable access and cost containment) for clinical services outside the essential package.

• Encourage suppliers (both public and private) to compete both to deliver clinical services and to provide inputs, such as drugs, to publicly and privately financed health services. Domestic suppliers should not be protected from international competition.

• Generate and disseminate information on provider performance, on essential equipment and drugs, on the costs and effectiveness of interventions, and on the accreditation status of institutions and providers.

Increased scientific knowledge has accounted for much of the dramatic improvement in health that has occurred in this century—by providing information that forms the basis of household and government action and by underpinning the development of preventive, curative, and diagnostic technologies. Investment in continued scientific advance will amplify the effectiveness of each element of the three-pronged approach proposed in this Report. Because the fruits of science benefit all countries, internationally collaborative efforts, of which there are several excellent examples, will often be the right way to proceed.

prove the decisions of private consumers, providers, and insurers.

Government policies for achieving health for all

This Report focuses primarily on the relation between policy choices, both inside and outside the health sector, and health outcomes, especially for the poor. Box 1 summarizes the Report's three key messages for government policy and notes the im-

portance of continued investment in scientific advance.

• Since overall economic growth—particularly poverty-reducing growth—and education are central to good health, governments need to pursue sound macroeconomic policies that emphasize reduction of poverty. They also need to expand basic schooling, especially for girls, because the way in which households, particularly mothers, use information and financial resources to shape their dietary, fertility, health care, and other life-style choices has a powerful influence on the health of household members.

• Governments in developing countries should spend far less—on average, about 50 percent less—than they now do on less cost-effective interventions and instead double or triple spending on basic public health programs such as immunizations and AIDS prevention and on essential clinical services. A minimum package of essential clinical services would include sick-child care, family planning, prenatal and delivery care, and treatment for tuberculosis and STDs. Low-income countries would have to redirect current public spending for health and increase expenditures (by government, donors, and patients) to meet needs for public health and the minimum package of essential clinical services for their populations; less reallocation would be needed in middle-income countries. Tertiary care and less cost-effective services will continue, but public subsidies to them, if they mainly benefit the wealthy, should be phased out during a transitional period.

• Because competition can improve quality and drive down costs, governments should foster competition and diversity in the supply of health services and inputs, particularly drugs, supplies, and equipment. This could include, where feasible, private supply of health care services paid for by governments or social insurance. There is also considerable scope for improving the quality and efficiency of government health services through a combination of decentralization, performance-based incentives for managers and clinicians, and related training and development of management systems. Exposing the public sector to competition with private suppliers can help to spur such improvements. Strong government regulation is also crucial, including regulation of privately delivered health services to ensure safety and quality and of private insurance to encourage universal access to coverage and to discourage practices—such as fee-for-service payment to providers reimbursed by a ''third-party'' insurer—that lead to overuse of services and escalation of costs.

Improving the economic environment for healthy households

Advances in income and education have allowed households almost everywhere to improve their health. In the 1980s, even in countries in which average incomes fell, death rates of children under age 5 declined by almost 30 percent. But the child mortality rate fell more than twice as much in

The poor suffer far higher levels of mortality at all ages than do the rich.

Figure 3 Infant and adult mortality in poor and nonpoor neighborhoods of Porto Alegre, Brazil, 1980

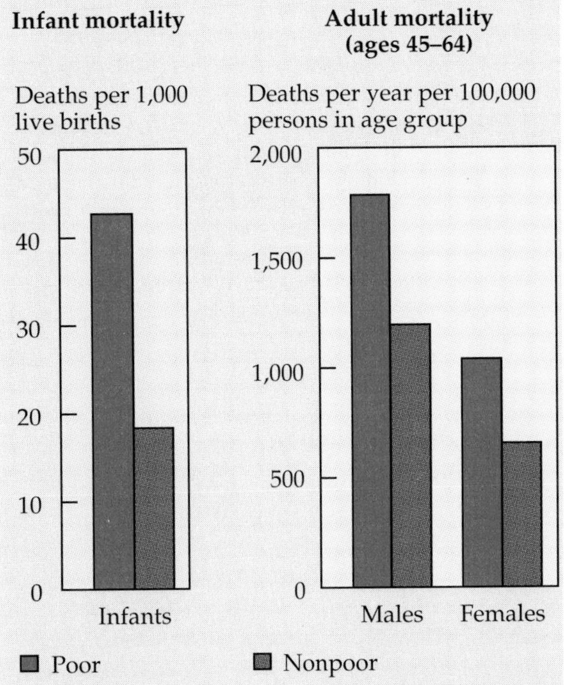

Note: Poor neighborhoods were defined according to specific criteria. They are, broadly, squatter settlements with substandard housing and infrastructure.
Source: Barcellos and others 1986.

countries in which average incomes rose by more than 1 percent a year. Economic policies conducive to sustained growth are thus among the most important measures governments can take to improve their citizens' health.

Of these economic policies, increasing the income of those in poverty is the most efficacious for improving health. The reason is that the poor are most likely to spend additional income in ways that enhance their health: improving their diet, obtaining safe water, and upgrading sanitation and housing. And the poor have the greatest remaining health needs, as Figure 3 illustrates for Porto Alegre, Brazil. Government policies that promote equity and growth together will therefore be better for health than those that promote growth alone.

In the 1980s many countries undertook macro-economic stabilization and adjustment programs designed to deal with severe economic imbalances and move the countries onto sustainable growth paths. Such adjustment is clearly needed for long-run health gains. But during the transitional period, and especially in the earliest adjustment programs, recession and cuts in public spending slowed improvements in health. This effect was less than originally feared, however—in part because earlier expenditures for improving health and education had enduring effects. As a result of this experience, most countries' adjustment programs today try to rationalize overall government spending while maintaining cost-effective expenditures in health and education. Despite these improvements, much is still to be learned about more efficient ways of carrying out stabilization and adjustment programs while protecting the poor.

Policies to expand schooling are also crucial for promoting health. People who have had more schooling seek and utilize health information more effectively than those with little or no schooling. This means that rapid expansion of educational opportunities—in part by setting a high minimum standard of schooling (say, six full years) for all—is a cost-effective way of improving health. Education of girls and women is particularly beneficial to household health because it is largely women who buy and prepare food, maintain a clean home, care for children and the elderly, and initiate contacts with the health system. Beyond education, government policies that support the rights and economic opportunities of women also contribute to overall household well-being and better health.

Investing in public health and essential clinical services

The health gain per dollar spent varies enormously across the range of interventions currently financed by governments. Redirecting resources from interventions that have high costs per DALY gained to those that cost little could dramatically reduce the burden of disease without increasing expenditures. A limited package of public health measures and essential clinical interventions is a top priority for government finance; some governments may wish, after covering that minimum for everyone, to define their national essential package more broadly.

Public health

Government action in many areas of public health has already had an important payoff. Immuniza-

tions are currently saving an estimated 3 million lives a year. Social marketing of condoms to prevent transmission of human immunodeficiency virus (HIV) has proved highly successful in Uganda, Zaire, and elsewhere. Information on the risks of smoking, and taxes on both tobacco and alcohol, are changing behavior in some countries—although mostly, so far, in the richer countries.

Governments need to expand these efforts and to move forward with other promising public health initiatives. Several activities stand out because they are highly cost-effective: the cost of gaining one DALY can be remarkably low—sometimes less than $25 and often between $50 and $150. Activities in this category include:
- Immunizations
- School-based health services
- Information and selected services for family planning and nutrition
- Programs to reduce tobacco and alcohol consumption
- Regulatory action, information, and limited public investments to improve the household environment
- AIDS prevention.

Intensified government support is required to extend the Expanded Programme on Immunization (EPI), which currently protects about 80 percent of the children in the developing world against six major diseases at a cost of about $1.4 billion a year. Expanding EPI coverage to 95 percent of all children would have a significant impact on children in poor households, who make up a disproportionately large share of those not yet reached by the EPI. Other vaccines, particularly those for hepatitis B and yellow fever, could be added to the six currently included in the EPI, as could vitamin A and iodine supplements. In most developing countries such an ''EPI Plus'' cluster of interventions in the first year of life would have the highest cost-effectiveness of any health measure available in the world today.

A second high priority for governments should be to provide inexpensive and highly efficacious medications to treat school-age children afflicted with schistosomiasis, intestinal worm infections, and micronutrient deficiencies. Treatment of these conditions through distribution of medications and micronutrient supplements in schools would greatly improve the health, school attendance, and learning achievement of hundreds of millions of children, at a cost of $1 to $2 per child per year. In addition to treatment, schoolchildren can be taught by their teachers or by radio about the human body and about avoiding risks to health—for example, from smoking or unsafe sex.

Governments need to encourage healthier behaviors on the part of individuals and households by providing information on the benefits of breast-feeding and on how to improve children's diets. Programs in Colombia, Indonesia, and elsewhere show the potential for success. Information on the benefits of family planning and on the availability of family planning services is also critical. Government dissemination of this information can take a number of creative forms, as the effective use of radio drama and folk theater in Kenya and Zimbabwe demonstrates.

Measures to control the use of tobacco, alcohol, and other addictive substances—through information campaigns, taxes, bans on advertising, and, in certain cases, import controls—can help substantially to reduce chronic lung disease, heart disease, cancer, and injuries. Unless smoking behavior changes, three decades from now premature deaths caused by tobacco in the developing world will exceed the expected deaths from AIDS, tuberculosis, and complications of childbirth combined.

Governments must do more to promote a healthier environment, especially for the poor, who face greatly increased health risks from poor sanitation, insufficient and unsafe water supplies, poor personal and food hygiene, inadequate garbage disposal, indoor air pollution, and crowded and inferior housing. Collectively, these risks are associated with nearly 30 percent of the global burden of disease. To help the poor improve their household environments, governments can provide a regulatory and administrative framework within which efficient and accountable providers (often in the private sector) have an incentive to offer households the services they want and are willing to pay for, including water supply, sanitation, garbage collection, clean-burning stoves, and housing. The government has a vital role in disseminating information about hygienic practices. It can also improve the use of public resources by eliminating widespread subsidies for water and sanitation that benefit the middle class. Government legislation and regulations to increase security of land tenure for the poor would encourage low-income families to invest more in safer, healthier housing.

A special challenge for concerted public health action is to reduce the spread of AIDS. The AIDS epidemic has already become a dominant public health concern in many countries. Although HIV, the virus that causes AIDS, has only recently be-gun to spread through human populations, it has so far caused 2 million deaths and infected about 13 million individuals. Some parts of the developing world are already heavily infected: in Sub-Saharan Africa an average of one in forty adults has the virus, and in certain cities the rate is one in three. In Thailand one adult in fifty is infected. More than 90 percent of the infected individuals are in their economically most productive years, ages 15–40. They will be developing AIDS and dying over the next decade. Projections of the future course of the epidemic are gloomy: conservative estimates from WHO are that by 2000, 26 million individuals will be HIV-infected and 1.8 million a year will die of AIDS. By destroying individuals' immune systems, HIV will also vastly worsen the spread of other diseases, especially tuberculosis. In highly affected areas demand for AIDS treatment will overwhelm capacity for clinical treatment and cause a deterioration of care for other illnesses.

What governments need to do is clear: intervene early, before a major epidemic gets under way. Countries as diverse as Bangladesh, Ghana, and Indonesia share the preconditions for rapid transmission of HIV—substantial numbers of prostitutes and high rates of prevalence of other STDs, such as syphilis, gonorrhea, and chancroid, which facilitate the spread of the AIDS virus. Strong public action is required to reduce HIV transmission. Particularly important are efforts targeted to high-risk groups: information to promote change in sexual behavior; distribution of condoms; and treatment for other STDs. Early reduction in HIV transmission by high-risk individuals is very cost-effective, but later in an AIDS epidemic the cost-effectiveness of interventions declines substantially. Current expenditures on AIDS prevention in developing countries—totaling less than $200 million a year—are woefully inadequate. Five to ten times this level of spending is needed to deal with the emerging epidemic.

Essential clinical services

The components of a package of essential clinical services of high cost-effectiveness will vary from country to country, depending on local health needs and the level of income. At a minimum, the package should include five groups of interventions each of which addresses very large disease burdens. The five groups are:

• Services to ensure pregnancy-related (prenatal, childbirth, and postpartum) care; strength-

9

ened efforts could prevent most of the almost half-million maternal deaths that occur each year in developing countries.

• Family planning services; improved access to these services could save as many as 850,000 children from dying every year and eliminate as many as 100,000 of the maternal deaths that occur annually.

• Tuberculosis control, mainly through drug therapy, to combat a disease that kills more than 2 million people annually, making it the leading cause of death among adults.

• Control of STDs, which account for more than 250 million new cases of debilitating and sometimes fatal illness each year.

• Care for the common serious illnesses of young children—diarrheal disease, acute respiratory infection, measles, malaria, and acute malnutrition—which account for nearly 7 million child deaths annually.

These clinical interventions are all highly cost-effective—often costing substantially less than $50 per DALY gained.

A minimal package of essential clinical services would also include some treatment for minor infection and trauma and, for health problems that cannot be fully resolved with existing resources, advice and alleviation of pain. The provision of hospital-based emergency care other than the interventions mentioned above would depend on day-to-day capacity and availability of resources. This emergency care includes, for example, treatment of most fractures, as well as appendectomies. Depending on resource availability and social values, some countries may define their essential clinical package to include a much broader range of interventions than this minimum. At modest increases in spending, relatively cost-effective measures for the treatment of some common noncommunicable conditions could be included. Examples are low-cost protocols for treatment of heart disease using aspirin and antihypertensive drugs; treatment for cervical cancer; drug treatment of some psychoses; and removal of cataracts.

Many health services have such low cost-effectiveness that governments will need to consider excluding them from the essential clinical package. In low-income countries these might include heart surgery; treatment (other than pain relief) of highly fatal cancers of the lung, liver, and stomach; expensive drug therapies for HIV infection; and intensive care for severely premature babies. It is hard to justify using government funds for these medical treatments at the same time that much more cost-effective services which benefit mainly the poor are not adequately financed.

Widespread adoption of an essential clinical package would have a tremendous positive impact on the health of people in developing countries. If 80 percent of the population were reached, 24 percent of the current burden of disease in low-income countries and 11 percent of that in middle-income countries could be averted (Table 2). The estimated impact of implementing the minimum clinical services is more than twice that for the public health package outlined above; when combined with the public health package, the share of current illness that could be eliminated rises to perhaps 32 percent for low-income countries and 15 percent for middle-income countries. This reduction in disease is equivalent, in terms of DALYs

Table 2 Estimated costs and health benefits of the minimum package of public health and essential clinical services in low- and middle-income countries, 1990

Group	Cost (dollars per capita per year)	Cost as a percentage of income per capita	Approximate reduction in burden of disease (percent)
Low-income countries *(Income per capita = $350)*			
Public health	4.2	1.2	8
Essential clinical services[a]	7.8	2.2	24
Total	12.0	3.4	32
Middle-income countries *(Income per capita = $2,500)*			
Public health	6.8	0.3	4
Essential clinical services[a]	14.7	0.6	11
Total	21.5	0.9	15

a. The estimated costs and benefits are for a *minimum* essential package of clinical services, as defined in the text. Many countries may wish, if they have the resources, to define their essential clinical package more broadly.
Source: World Bank calculations.

gained, to saving the lives of more than 9 million infants each year.

Paying for the package

The most sophisticated facility required to deliver the minimum elements of the essential clinical package is a district hospital. Providing services in lower-level facilities allows costs to be contained at modest levels for minimal versions of the essential clinical package. The cost is about $8 per person each year in low-income countries and $15 in middle-income countries. The cost differences are the result of distinct demographic structures, epidemiological conditions, and labor costs in the two settings. When the cost of the public health interventions described above is added, total costs rise to $12 per capita in low-income countries and $22 per capita in middle-income countries.

Adoption of the package in all developing countries would require a quadrupling of expenditures on public health, from $5 billion at present to $20 billion a year, and an increase from about $20 billion to $40 billion in spending on essential clinical services. In the poorest countries governments typically spend about $6 per person for health and total health expenditures are about $14 per person. There, paying for an essential package will require a combination of increased expenditures by governments, donor agencies, and patients and some reorientation of current public spending for health. In middle-income countries, where public spending for health averages $62 per person, the $22 cost of the package is financially feasible if the political commitment exists for shifting existing resources away from discretionary services with lower cost-effectiveness toward public health programs and essential clinical care. These major changes cannot be made overnight, but it is important to start and complete them as swiftly as possible, before interest groups and bureaucratic inertia undermine reform.

A critical question in designing an essential clinical package is the extent of government financing. Should governments pay for everyone, or only for the poor? The main problem with universal government financing is that it subsidizes the wealthy, who could afford to pay for their own services, and thus leaves fewer government resources for the poor. A policy requiring those who can pay all or part of their own costs to do so may make sense on equity grounds, but it also has disadvantages. Often, the administrative costs of targeting are high, and exclusion of wealthy and middle-income

groups can lead to erosion of political support for the essential package and to decreased funding and lower quality of care. Furthermore, problems of cost escalation and access to insurance on the part of high-risk groups can complicate private finance. For these reasons, in most member countries of the Organization for Economic Cooperation and Development (OECD), governments finance (or mandate the financing of) comprehensively defined essential packages for virtually all their citizens.

In low-income countries, where current public spending for health is less than the cost of an essential package, some degree of targeting is inevitable. If the wealthy are already opting out of government-financed services because of the higher quality and convenience of privately financed services, targeting is fairly easy. Community-financing schemes, whereby patients at local health centers and pharmacies pay modest fees, are another option that can help both to improve the quality of care and, when fees are retained and managed locally, to sustain services. A large number of countries in Africa have had some early success with community financing as part of the Bamako Initiative led by UNICEF and WHO. Nonetheless, experience to date suggests that introduction of user fees at levels that do not discourage the poor is likely to be more useful for improving technical efficiency (for example, by facilitating drug supply) than for raising substantial revenues on a nationwide basis.

Reforming health systems: promoting diversity and competition

Ensuring basic public health services and essential clinical care while the rest of the health system becomes self-financed will require substantial health system reforms and reallocations of public spending. Only by reducing or eliminating spending on discretionary clinical services can governments concentrate on ensuring cost-effective clinical care for the poor. One way to do so is by charging fees to affluent patients who use government hospitals and services. In Chile, Kenya, Lesotho, and other countries governments are increasing user fees for the wealthy and for those covered by insurance and are strengthening the legal and administrative systems for billing patients and collecting revenues.

Promoting self-financed insurance, thus eliminating large and inequitable subsidies to the more affluent groups who are covered by insurance, would also help to free government funds for public health programs and essential clinical care. Subsidies in the form of tax relief for contributions to private insurance are equal to nearly a fifth of total government spending for health in South Africa. In Latin America subsidies to the social insurance systems are widespread and include tax relief, direct transfers to cover the operating deficits of social security health funds, and matching government funds for employee payroll contributions. Where these subsidies benefit only the better-off in society, they need to be scaled back.

Reforms entail shifting new government spending for health away from specialized personnel, equipment, and facilities at the apex of health systems and "down the pyramid" toward the broad base of widely accessible care in community facilities and health centers. Very few cost-effective interventions depend on sophisticated hospitals and specialized physicians—all the services contained in the minimum essential clinical package proposed in this Report can be provided by health centers and district hospitals. Yet specialized facilities everywhere absorb a large amount of public resources, a problem that has frequently been exacerbated by donor investments in tertiary care facilities. In the 1980s Papua New Guinea, to correct overconcentration of resources on higher-level facilities, limited public spending on hospitals to 40 percent of the recurrent budget of the Ministry of Health—well below the level in most developing countries.

Governments need to use more effective policies for financing training (including use of national service mechanisms) to help meet the need for primary care providers, particularly nurses and midwives, and for public health, health policy, and management personnel. At the same time, governments should limit or eliminate subsidies for specialist training. Increased government support for health information systems and operations research would help to guide public policies for health. Estimates of the national burden of disease along the lines of the global burden of disease methodology used in this Report, and local information on the cost-effectiveness of different interventions, would enable governments to establish health priorities.

In every developing country decisive steps are needed to correct the pervasive inefficiency of clinical health programs and facilities and especially of government services. Clinics and outreach programs operate poorly because of shortages of drugs, transport, and maintenance. Hospitals keep patients longer than necessary and are poorly organized and managed. Countries pay too much for drugs of low efficacy, and drugs and supplies are stolen or go to waste in government warehouses and hospitals.

In the short term, reforms in pharmaceutical usage offer the greatest gains in efficiency. Governments that have introduced competition in the procurement of drugs have typically achieved savings of 40 to 60 percent. Governments can also develop national essential drug lists, consisting of a limited number of inexpensive drugs that address the important health problems of the population. Many countries have such lists, but not all use them to guide the selection and procurement of drugs for the public sector. New treatment protocols and alternative uses of facilities can also raise efficiency. Outpatient surgery can replace some procedures customarily performed on an inpatient basis, at considerable savings.

In the long run, decentralization can help to increase efficiency when there is adequate capacity and accountability at lower levels of the national health system. Some countries, such as Botswana and Ghana, have delegated a wide range of management responsibilities to regional and district-level offices of the ministry of health; others, including Chile and Poland, have devolved authority and resources to local government agencies. Their experience provides evidence that success is possible—but also that hasty and unplanned decentralization, sometimes purely in response to political pressures, can create new problems.

Greater reliance on the private sector to deliver clinical services, both those that are included by a country in its essential package and those that are discretionary, can help raise efficiency. The private sector already serves a large and diverse clientele in developing countries and often delivers services of higher quality without the long lines and inadequate supplies frequently found in government facilities. In many countries private doctors and pharmacies face unnecessary legal and administrative barriers, and these need to be removed. But the tendency for profit-making providers to overprescribe drugs, procedures, and diagnostics needs to be countered; encouraging the for-profit sector to move away from fee-for-service to prepaid coverage (through, for example, encouraging health maintenance organizations) is one feasible approach.

Governments could also subsidize private health care providers who deliver essential clinical services to the poor. This is already beginning to happen and needs to go further. In many African countries, including Malawi, Uganda, and Zambia, governments subsidize the operating expenditures of church hospitals and clinics in rural areas and the training of their health personnel. In Bangladesh, Kenya, Thailand, and other countries, governments, with assistance from donors, are supporting the work of traditional birth attendants in safe pregnancy and delivery care and of traditional healers in controlling infectious diseases such as malaria, diarrhea, and AIDS.

Regulation is an essential element of government efforts to encourage private health care suppliers. In most countries, governments have an important role to play in ensuring the quality of private sector health care—through accreditation of hospitals and laboratories, licensing of medical schools and physicians, regulation of drugs, and reviews of medical practices. Some countries in which the government's ability to regulate is particularly weak could explore self-regulation for health care providers, while building up government capacity. In Brazil experiments with self-regulation for local hospital associations and medical ethics boards are now under way.

Government regulation of insurance is equally important. In some countries part of the population is denied insurance because of selection bias under private voluntary insurance. In the United States millions of people with high health risks—and thus high need for health insurance—are unable to obtain affordable coverage. Some types of insurance schemes also seem to contribute to pushing up health care costs; this is particularly true of third-party systems and of systems that reimburse hospitals and physicians item by item for any and all services performed. In both the Republic of Korea, which relies on universal social insurance, and the United States, which uses mostly private insurance, health care already absorbs an unusually high share of GNP—and costs are still rising. During the 1980s, for example, health expenditures in Korea increased from 3.7 to almost 7 percent of GNP, in large part because of expansion of third-party insurance coverage combined with fee-for-service provider compensation.

To eliminate selection bias and expand insurance coverage, governments can require insurers to pool risks across large numbers of people. To control costs, governments have a number of options for limiting payments to health providers. One approach is to encourage prepayment of a fixed amount for each person, as is now done in private health maintenance organizations and in the British National Health Service. Another is for insurers jointly to negotiate uniform fees with doctors and hospitals, as is done in Japan's social insurance system and Zimbabwe's private medical aid insurance system; or insurers themselves can set fixed payments for specified medical diagnoses, as in Brazil. Yet a third approach, which has been tested on a limited scale in the United States, is "managed competition." This scheme pursues the three objectives of cost-effective health spending, universal insurance coverage, and cost containment simultaneously through tightly regulated competition among companies that provide a specified package of health care for a fixed annual fee. Each of these approaches has proved workable, but each also has its limits and disadvantages. There are no simple answers for health policymakers.

An agenda for action

Adoption of the main policy recommendations of this Report by developing country governments would enormously improve the health status of their people, especially poor households, and would also help to control health care spending (Table 3). Millions of lives and billions of dollars could be saved. Implementation of the public health and essential clinical care packages, pursuit of economic growth strategies that reduce poverty, and increased investment in schooling for girls would have the largest payoffs in averting deaths and reducing disability. Scaling back public spending for tertiary care facilities, specialist training, and clinical care with lower cost-effectiveness would help to increase the effectiveness of health spending. So would encouragement of competition in delivery of health services and regulation of insurance and of provider payment systems.

These recommendations will facilitate progress toward the goal contained in the declaration from the historic 1978 Alma-Ata conference: "The attainment of all peoples of the world by the year 2000 of a level of health that will permit them to lead a socially and economically productive life." Continued momentum toward this goal was provided by the 1990 World Summit for Children. Almost 150 countries have now signed commitments to specific goals for their countries to improve the health of children and women (Box 2). These goals include reduction of child mortality rates by one-third (or to 70 per 1,000 births, whichever would be less) over the course of the decade of the 1990s,

Table 3 Contribution of policy change to objectives for the health sector

Government objectives and policies	Improving health outcomes	Reaching the disadvantaged	Containing costs
Foster an enabling environment for households to improve health			
Pursue economic growth policies that benefit the poor	Favorable	Favorable	No impact expected
Expand investment in education, particularly for females	Very favorable	Favorable	No impact expected
Promote the rights and status of women through political and economic empowerment and legal protection against abuse	Somewhat favorable	Somewhat favorable	Somewhat favorable
Improve government investments in health			
Reduce government expenditures for tertiary care facilities, specialist training, and discretionary services	No impact expected	Somewhat favorable	Very favorable
Finance and ensure delivery of a public health package, including AIDS prevention	Favorable	Somewhat favorable	Somewhat favorable
Finance and ensure delivery of essential clinical services, at least to the poor	Very favorable	Very favorable	Somewhat favorable
Improve the management of public health services	Somewhat favorable	Somewhat favorable	Favorable
Facilitate involvement by the private sector			
Encourage private finance and provision of insurance (with incentives to contain costs) for all discretionary clinical services	Somewhat favorable	No impact expected	Very favorable
Encourage private sector delivery of clinical services (including those that are publicly financed)	Somewhat favorable	Somewhat favorable	Favorable
Provide information on performance and cost	Somewhat favorable	Somewhat favorable	Somewhat favorable

■ Very favorable   ■ Favorable   ☐ Somewhat favorable   ☐ No impact expected

reduction of maternal mortality rates by half, eradication of polio, and major reductions in morbidity and mortality from several other diseases. Commitments to specific improvements in education, nutrition, water supply, and sanitation were also made. These commitments underscore the political potential of action agendas for improving health.

The relevance of the main recommendations of this Report varies from one setting to another. In low-income countries renewed emphasis on basic schooling for girls, strengthening of public health programs, and support for expanded public financing of essential clinical services should be at the top of the policy agenda. In most middle-income countries these policies are still germane, but reducing public subsidies for insurance and discretionary care would also yield large benefits and should therefore be a key element of policy change. In the formerly socialist economies there are two particularly crucial policy areas—improving the management of government health services and developing sustainable health-financing systems that maintain universal coverage while encouraging competition among cost-conscious suppliers.

Box 2   The World Summit for Children

The declaration and plan of action adopted at the World Summit for Children, held in New York in 1990, incorporate a politically salient agenda for health. The summit focused, in particular, on the needs of children and women but was set in the broader context of human and community goals. The seventy-one heads of state who attended and the seventy-seven more who subsequently signed the declaration committed their countries to developing national programs of action (NPAs) for achieving these goals. To date, about eighty-five countries have drawn up NPAs, and another sixty are in the process of preparing them.

NPAs typically cover, among other concerns, primary health care, family planning, safe water, environmental sanitation, nutrition, and basic education. Because of their concentration on the welfare of children, NPAs are able to transcend political differences. They offer a means of mobilizing the whole of civil society—neighborhood and civic associations, religious groups and professional bodies, businesses, voluntary agencies, organized labor, and universities—in the cause of investment for health.

NPAs are being integrated into national development planning. They set forth measurable, attainable goals—to be met by 2000 or earlier—that are adapted to the realities of the country. By quantifying the resources required to achieve these goals, NPAs help to identify the changes that are needed in national bud-

gets and external aid if priorities for human development are to be met. The health goals of the summit's plan of action include:

- The eradication of polio by 2000
- The elimination of neonatal tetanus by 1995
- A 90 percent reduction in measles cases and a 95 percent reduction in measles deaths
- Achievement (by 2000) and maintenance of at least 90 percent immunization coverage of one-year-old children, as well as universal tetanus immunization for women of childbearing age
- A halving of child deaths caused by diarrhea and a one-quarter reduction in the incidence of diarrheal disease
- A reduction by one-third in child deaths caused by acute respiratory infections
- Virtual elimination of vitamin A deficiency and iodine deficiency disorders
- A reduction in the incidence of low birth weight (2.5 kilograms or less) to no more than 10 percent
- A one-third reduction from 1990 levels in iron deficiency anemia among women
- Access for all women to prenatal care, trained attendants during childbirth, and referral for high-risk pregnancies and obstetric emergencies.

The agenda for action of the children's health summit is broadly consistent with the messages of this Report.

At first glance, it might appear that adoption of this Report's major recommendations will be easy. To reach most people living in the developing world with the minimum package of cost-effective public health and essential clinical services, about half of current government expenditures on other, more discretionary care would have to be redirected. But in reality, change will be difficult, since an array of interest groups may stand to lose—from suppliers of medical services to rich beneficiaries of public subsidies to protected drug companies. Many of the changes will take years to implement because they mean a major redirection of public resources and require the development of new institutional capabilities.

A number of developing countries have already shown in recent years that broad reforms in the health sector are possible when there is sufficient political will and when changes to the health system are designed and implemented by capable planners and managers. Zimbabwe has imposed a decade-long moratorium on new investments in

central hospitals and has concentrated on improving health centers and other district-level infrastructure. Tunisia has converted eleven large government hospitals to semiautonomous institutions with strong incentives for improved performance. During the 1980s Chile delegated responsibility for its entire primary clinical care system to local governments and fostered more public and private competition in health service delivery and in insurance. Costa Rica and Korea achieved universal health coverage through social insurance.

The international community can do more to support health policy reforms. In 1990 donors disbursed about $4.8 billion of assistance for health, or about 2.5 percent of all health spending in developing countries. The share of total development aid for health declined slightly in the 1980s, from 7 to 6 percent, despite widespread calls for increased investment in human resource development, including health. As an immediate first step, donors need to restore this share to its former level. A more substantial increase can be easily justified, given the importance of health in reducing poverty and the large gap between current and needed spending for public health programs and minimum clinical services. An additional $2 billion a year from donors would meet about one-quarter of the costs of stabilizing the AIDS epidemic ($500 million) and one-sixth of the extra resources needed to provide the public health and clinical care package for low-income countries ($1.5 billion of the $10 billion required).

Increased external assistance for health research that focuses on the major health problems of developing countries—such as the search for new antimalarial drugs and new or improved vaccines—could have a very high payoff and would build on the comparative advantage of donor countries in conducting scientific research. That most health research benefits many countries further justifies donor support, particularly through such effective internationally collaborative mechanisms as the Special Programme for Research and Training in Tropical Diseases.

Donors and developing country governments can also do much to improve the effectiveness of aid for health. This is especially important in low-income Africa, where aid already accounts for an average 20 percent of health spending—and for over half in Burundi, Chad, Guinea-Bissau, Mozambique, and Tanzania. Even in other developing regions, where aid amounts to 2 percent or less of health expenditures, better targeting and management of this assistance can catalyze policy change.

Redirecting donor money from hospitals and specialist training to public health programs and essential clinical care—especially for tuberculosis control, the EPI Plus program, AIDS prevention, and reduction of tobacco consumption—would be a significant contribution to policy reform. So would support for capacity-building. Countries that are willing to undertake major changes in health policy should be strong candidates for increased aid, including donor financing of recurrent costs. An increasing number of donors, among them the World Bank, are now supporting this kind of broad sectoral reform. Stronger donor coordination, especially at the level of individual developing country clients, would improve the positive impact of aid on health, as shown by the experience of Bangladesh, Senegal, and Zimbabwe.

The benefits to the developing world from adopting sound policies for health are enormous. There is great potential for change during the closing years of this decade as more countries encourage broad political participation and public accountability, as levels of education and knowledge improve, and as understanding of human biology, public health, and health care systems increases. If the right policy choices are made, the payoff will be high. The momentum of past reductions in the burden of infectious disease in developing countries can be maintained and accelerated. The AIDS epidemic can be slowed or reversed. The emerging problems of noncommunicable disease in aging populations can be managed without rapid increases in health expenditures. In the end, this will translate into longer, healthier, and more productive lives for people around the world, especially the more than 1 billion now living in poverty.

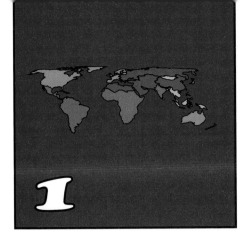

Health in developing countries: successes and challenges

On October 22, 1977, Ali Maow Maalin, a twenty-three-year-old cook living in the town of Merca, Somalia, developed a fever and rash that was subsequently diagnosed as smallpox. Vaccination teams immediately descended on Merca and within three weeks had vaccinated more than 50,000 people. They also began an intensive search for other cases in Merca and along the road and footpaths leading to it. By December 29 the World Health Organization (WHO) had removed Merca from its list of potential outbreaks of smallpox and had initiated a two-year surveillance for the disease throughout the Horn of Africa. It turned out, however, that Mr. Maalin had experienced the world's last case of smallpox. He survived, and WHO's twelve-year-long Intensified Smallpox Eradication Programme was brought to a triumphant end.

In 1967, the year when the program began, somewhere between 1.5 million and 2 million people died from smallpox. Perhaps half a million more were blinded, and more than 10 million were seriously and permanently disfigured. In the early 1950s the toll from smallpox had been three or four times greater. Then more and more countries undertook vaccination programs, and by the time the global program began, the disease had been virtually eradicated in 125 countries. Even so, the cost of smallpox vaccination, quarantine programs, and treatment totaled more than $300 million in 1968 alone. The eradication program, by contrast, cost $300 million over the whole of its twelve-year life and has therefore saved hundreds of millions of dollars a year in direct, measurable costs, as well as unquantifiable amounts of human suffering.

Few investments of any kind generate human and financial benefits on that scale. Yet in many ways the Intensified Smallpox Eradication Programme exemplifies the potential of today's medicine. Around the world, the past half century has seen startling improvements in health. Progress in drugs, vaccines, epidemiological knowledge, and organizational experience continually expands the range of options for tomorrow. Tools and methods for combating and eliminating much of the remaining burden of disease are now affordable, even by the poorest countries. Good policy, however, is essential for achieving good health. Some countries have made full use of the potential of medicine; others have barely tapped it, despite heavy spending. This Report draws from this varied experience lessons that will assist policymakers in realizing the enormous potential returns from their countries' investments in health.

Why health matters

Good health, as people know from their own experience, is a crucial part of well-being, but spending on health can also be justified on purely economic grounds. Improved health contributes to economic growth in four ways: it reduces production losses caused by worker illness; it permits the use of natural resources that had been totally or nearly inaccessible because of disease; it increases the enrollment of children in school and makes them better able to learn; and it frees for alternative uses resources that would otherwise have to be spent on treating illness. The economic gains are relatively greater for poor people, who are typically most handicapped by ill health and who stand to gain the most from the development of underutilized natural resources.

Gains in worker productivity

The most obvious sources of gain are fewer work days lost to illness, increased productivity, greater opportunities to obtain better-paying jobs, and longer working lives. To take a classic example, leprosy is a disease that affects people in the prime of life, with peak incidence rates among young adults. As many as 30 percent of those affected may be seriously deformed, and their working lives will be shortened as well. A study of lepers in urban Tamil Nadu, India, estimates that the elimination of deformity would more than triple the expected annual earnings of those with jobs. The prevention of deformity in all of India's 645,000 lepers would have added an estimated $130 million to the country's 1985 GNP. This amount is the equivalent of almost 10 percent of all the official development assistance received by India in 1985. Yet leprosy accounted for only a small proportion of the country's disease burden, less than 1 percent in 1990.

Healthier workers earn more because (as research in Bangladesh has demonstrated) they are more productive and can get better-paying jobs. In Côte d'Ivoire daily wage rates are estimated to be 19 percent lower, on average, among men who are likely to lose a day of work per month because of illness than among healthier men.

When illness strikes, an individual's lost output and earnings often go undetected in economic statistics because they are borne by the household. In many developing countries unemployment (or disability) insurance is rare, and healthier members of the household work harder or longer to make up for the loss in income. In a sample of 250 Sudanese households, each of which lost, on average, forty working hours per year because of malaria alone, this extra work made up for 68 percent of the lost agricultural labor. Similar findings have come from research in Paraguay and Colombia.

In the long run, the benefits of improved health are also likely to influence the way work is organized and carried out. With a healthy work force, employers can reduce the costs of building slack into their production schedules, invest more in staff training, and exploit the benefits of specialization. Similar gains are likely among farmers, who often hedge against sickness by being risk-averse; they forgo higher output in return for less vari-

ability in their income. In Paraguay, for example, farmers in malarious areas choose to grow crops that are of lower value but that can be worked outside the malaria season.

Improved utilization of natural resources

Some health investments raise the productivity of land. In Sri Lanka the near-eradication of malaria during 1947–77 is estimated to have raised national income by 9 percent in 1977. The cumulative cost was $52 million, compared with a cumulative gain in national income over the thirty-one years of $7.6 billion, implying a spectacular benefit-cost ratio of more than 140. Areas previously blighted by mosquitoes became attractive for settlement; migrants moved in, and output increased. In Uganda massive migration to fertile but underexploited land followed the partial control of river blindness (onchocerciasis) in the 1950s. The Onchocerciasis Control Programme, conducted in eleven countries of the Sahel, is a more recent example of the same benefits (see Box 1.1).

Benefits in the next generation through education

There is no question that schooling pays off in higher incomes. Four years of primary education boosts farmers' annual productivity by 9 percent on average, and workers who do better at school earn more. Studies in Ghana, Kenya, Pakistan, and Tanzania indicate that workers who scored 10 percent above the sample mean on various cognitive tests have a wage advantage ranging from 13 to 22 percent; in Nepal farmers with better mathematical skills are more likely to adopt profitable new crops.

Poor health and nutrition reduce the gains of schooling in three areas: enrollment, ability to learn, and participation by girls. Children who enjoy better health and nutrition during early childhood are more ready for school and more likely to enroll. A study in Nepal has found that the probability of attending school is only 5 percent for nutritionally stunted children, compared with 27 percent for those at the norm.

Health and nutrition problems affect a child's ability to learn. Nutritional deficiencies in early childhood can lead to lasting problems: iron deficiency anemia reduces cognitive function, iodine deficiency causes irreversible mental retardation, and vitamin A deficiency is the primary cause of blindness among children. Older children are subject to other kinds of disease. In a recent study in

Box 1.1   Controlling river blindness

Onchocerciasis, or river blindness as it is more commonly known, is caused by a parasitic worm which produces millions of larvae that move through the body, causing intense itching, debilitation, and eventually blindness. The disease is spread by a small, fiercely biting blackfly that transmits the larvae from infected to uninfected people.

The goals of the Onchocerciasis Control Programme (OCP), set up in 1974 and covering eleven Sahelian countries, are to control the blackfly by destroying its larvae with insecticides sprayed from the air. The environmental impact of the insecticides is continuously monitored by an independent ecological committee, in cooperation with the national governments. The committee has full authority to screen insecticides and to approve or reject their use. The program has also collaborated with the pharmaceutical industry to develop for human use a drug, ivermectin, that safely and effectively kills the larvae in the body. Ivermectin, however, has little impact on the adult worm and so must be supplemented with vector control by aerial spraying. The producer of ivermectin, Merck & Co., has committed itself to provide the drug free of charge as long as it is needed to combat river blindness.

The OCP's four sponsoring agencies—the Food and Agriculture Organization, the United Nations Development Programme (UNDP), the World Bank, and WHO—through a steering committee chaired by the World Bank, make broad policy decisions and oversee operations. WHO has executive responsibility through a team of entomologists, epidemiologists, field staff, and pilots; 97 percent of the staff are nationals of the participating countries. The World Bank organizes the finances and manages them through a trust fund. It also supports socioeconomic development in the areas affected by the disease.

The program is widely regarded as a great success. It protects from river blindness about 30 million people, including more than 9 million children born since the OCP began, at an annual cost of less than $1 per person. More than 1.5 million people who were once seriously infected have completely recovered. It is estimated that the program will have prevented at least 500,000 cases of blindness by the time it is wound up around the end of the century. And it is already freeing approximately 25 million hectares of previously blighted land for resettlement and cultivation, boosting agricultural production.

The estimated cost of the OCP during the whole of its existence, from 1974 to 2000, is about $570 million. Its estimated internal rate of return is in the range of 16 to 28 percent (depending on the pace at which the newly available land is settled, the incremental output added by the new land, the income level of the OCP area, and the productivity growth rate that is projected). These estimated benefits do not include the program's favorable effects on income distribution; its main beneficiaries are subsistence farmers whose incomes are well below average.

Jamaica children with moderate whipworm infection scored 15 percent lower before treatment than uninfected children in the same school. When retested after treatment, those same children did almost as well as the uninfected children.

In a sample of children in a poverty-stricken area of northeast Brazil, inadequately nourished children lagged 20 percent behind the average gain in achievement score over a two-year period. The same study also shows the harm done by a simple and easily remedied handicap: children with bad eyesight lagged 27 percent behind the average gain over the two years. Both groups had below-average promotion rates and above-average dropout rates. In China a child at the twentieth percentile in height-for-age (a sign of poor health) averages about one-third of a year behind the grade normally reached by children of that age. In Thailand children whose height-for-age is 10 percent below average are 14 percent lower in grade attainment.

Girls are particularly liable to suffer from iodine or iron deficiency—reasons why fewer of them complete primary school. Other health-related reasons include dropping out as a result of pregnancy and parental concern about sexual violence. In societies where girls' education is given lower priority than boys', girls miss school because they have to stay home to look after sick relatives.

Reduced costs of medical care

Spending that reduces the incidence of disease can produce big savings in treatment costs. For some diseases the expenditure pays for itself even when all the indirect benefits—such as higher labor productivity and reduced pain and suffering—are ignored. Polio is one example. Calculations for the Americas made prior to the eradication of polio in the region showed that investing $220 million over fifteen years to eliminate the disease would prevent 220,000 cases and save between $320 million

Box 1.2   The economic impact of AIDS

The AIDS epidemic, through its effects on savings and productivity, poses a threat to economic growth in many countries that are already in distress. World Bank simulations indicate a slowing of growth of income per capita by an average 0.6 percentage point a year in the ten worst-affected countries in Sub-Saharan Africa. In Tanzania, where income per capita has already fallen 0.2 percent a year in recent years, the estimated slow-down ranges between 0.1 and 0.8 percentage point, depending on the assumptions used. In Malawi, which has had a recent growth rate of 0.9 percent a year, the simulated reduction ranges from 0.3 to 0.5 percentage point. These calculations include the effect of the epi-demic on population growth, which will slow slightly in severely affected countries.

The heavy macroeconomic impact of AIDS comes partly from the high costs of treatment, which divert resources from productive investments. Tanzanian cli-nicians estimate that, on average, an HIV-infected adult suffers 17 episodes of HIV-related illnesses prior to death and a child suffers 6.5 episodes. Depending on how much medical care a patient gets, in the typical developing country the total cost per adult death ranges from 8 to 400 percent of annual income per cap-ita; the average is about 150 percent of annual income per capita.

That AIDS kills so many skilled adults adds to its economic impact. At a large hospital in Kinshasa, for example, more than 1 percent per year of the health personnel, including highly trained staff, become in-fected (through sexual rather than occupational con-tact). Among the (largely male) employees at a Kin-shasa textile mill, managers had a higher infection rate than foremen, who in turn had a higher rate than workers. The cost of replacing skilled workers will be substantial. A study of Thailand estimates that through 2000 the cost of replacing long-haul truckers lost to AIDS will be $8 million, and another study, of Tan-zania, projects the cost of replacing teachers at $40 mil-lion through 2010.

The death of an adult can tip vulnerable households into poverty. Even in Tanzania, where the government pays a large share of health costs, a World Bank study shows that affected rural households in 1991 spent $60—roughly the equivalent of annual rural income per capita—on treatment and funerals. The study also showed that the effects of losing an adult persist into the next generation as children are withdrawn from school to help at home. School attendance of young people ages 15–20 is reduced by half if the household has lost an adult female member in the previous year.

and $1.3 billion (depending on the number of peo-ple treated) in annual treatment costs. The pro-gram's net return, after discounting at even as much as 12 percent a year, was calculated to be between $18 million and $480 million.

AIDS is another example. Although it remains much less common in the developing world than diseases such as malaria, its economic impact per case is greater for two reasons: it mainly affects adults in their most productive years, and the in-fections resulting from it lead to heavy demand for expensive health care (Box 1.2). For example, be-cause individuals with AIDS are typically more prone to pneumonia, diarrhea, and tuberculosis, the cost of medical care is high even though there is no effective treatment as yet for the disease it-self. Research in nine developing and seven high-income countries suggests that preventing a case of AIDS saves, on average, about twice GNP per capita in discounted lifetime costs of medical care; in some urban areas the saving may be as much as five times GNP per capita. Calculations for India show that, given prevailing transmission patterns, each currently HIV-positive person infects one

previously uninfected person every four years. At this rate, there will be six HIV-positive persons in 2000 for every one today. If the transmission rate could be slowed to one every five years, that num-ber could be reduced to only four infected persons in 2000 for every one today. The corresponding reduction in medical costs, after discounting at 3 percent a year, amounts to $750 by 2000 for each currently HIV-positive person in India, for a total saving of $750 million. Similar calculations for Thailand suggest savings of $1,250 per currently HIV-positive person, for a potential total of $560 million.

Health investments and poverty

The goal of reducing poverty provides a different but equally powerful case for health investments. The adverse effects of ill health are greatest for poor people, mainly because they are ill more of-ten, but partly because their income depends ex-clusively on physical labor and they have no sav-ings to cushion the blow. They may therefore find it impossible to recover from an illness with their human and financial capital intact.

The health consequences of poverty are severe: the poor die younger and suffer more from disability. In Porto Alegre, Brazil, adult mortality rates in poor areas in the late 1980s were 75 percent higher than in rich areas, and in São Paulo rates were two to three times higher for nonprofessionals than for professionals. In the late 1970s among Kenyan families in which the mother had no schooling, the probability of dying by age 2 averaged 184 per 1,000 in regions where half of the families lived below the poverty line but 100 per 1,000 in regions where only one-fifth of the families lived in poverty. The poor are exposed to greater risks from unhealthy and dangerous conditions, both at home and at work. Malnourishment and the legacy of past illness mean that they are more likely to fall ill and slower to recover, especially as they have little access to health care.

When a family's breadwinner becomes ill, other members of the household may at first cope by working harder themselves and by reducing consumption, perhaps even of food. Both adjustments can harm the health of the whole family. If free health care is not available, the costs of treatment may drive a household deeper into debt. Although ill health is only one of many factors that can cause financial distress, its potential for disaster means that it should be explicitly recognized in formulating policies. Investments to reduce health risks among the poor and provision of insurance against catastrophic health care costs are important elements in a strategy for reducing poverty.

Spending on health is a productive investment: it can raise incomes, particularly among the poor, and it reduces the toll of human suffering from ill health. Good health, however, is a fundamental goal of development as well as a means of accelerating it. Targeting health as part of development efforts is an effective way to improve welfare in low-income countries. Evidence gathered over the past thirty years indicates that in health, unlike income, the gap between poor and rich countries has been narrowing.

Putting the effects together

The detrimental effects of poor health on individuals and households and on the use of resources suggest that better health should lead to better economic performance at the national level. A number of analyses have found a positive relationship between growth of income per capita and the initial national educational stock. A similar analysis carried out for this Report examines the relation

of growth in income per capita between 1960 and 1990 in about seventy countries to the initial level of national income, the initial educational level, and an indicator of initial health status (the child mortality rate, used in this Report to mean the risk of dying by age 5 per 1,000 live births). The health status indicator is found to be a highly significant predictor of economic performance. For the average country in the sample, the annual growth rate of income per capita is 1.40 percent and the child mortality rate is 116 per 1,000. An otherwise average country with a child mortality rate of 106 would have a growth rate of income per capita of 1.55 percent, whereas one with a child mortality rate of 126 would have a growth rate of 1.26 percent.

Not surprisingly, the health status variable is strongly correlated with educational stock, but the significant association between income growth and health remains strong and of similar magnitude across time periods and for a range of model formulations. Although it is possible that unobserved factors such as government capacity to implement effective policies could explain the apparent association, the data do suggest that better health means more rapid growth.

The record of success

Mortality started to decline in Europe, North America, and Australasia about two centuries ago, but slowly at first. A century ago life expectancy in the United States, then the world's richest country, was only forty-nine years, and child mortality was about 180 per 1,000. The rate of improvement accelerated in the first half of this century; by 1950 life expectancy in the United States had increased to sixty-six years, and child mortality had fallen to 34 per 1,000. Progress was also being made in developing countries: in Chile, for example, life expectancy increased from thirty-seven years in 1930 to forty-nine in 1950, and child mortality fell from 350 to 209 per 1,000.

Mortality transitions since 1950

Health conditions around the world have improved more in the past forty years than in all previous human history. Life expectancy at birth in developing countries increased from forty to sixty-three years, and child mortality fell from 280 to 106 per 1,000. In a high-income country life expectancy is more than seventy-five years; in a low-mortality developing country it is seventy years or

Child mortality has fallen sharply in the past thirty years, with particularly rapid declines in parts of Asia and Latin America.

Figure 1.1 Child mortality by country, 1960 and 1990

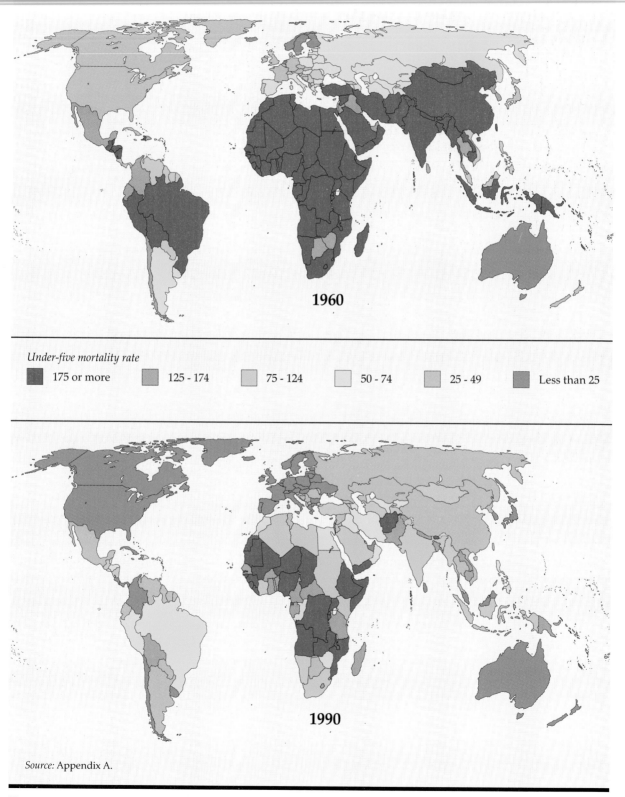

Under-five mortality rate

| ■ 175 or more | ▨ 125 - 174 | ▨ 75 - 124 | ▨ 50 - 74 | ▨ 25 - 49 | ▨ Less than 25 |

Source: Appendix A.

more; and in Sub-Saharan Africa, the region where least progress has been made, it is about fifty years.

Much of what is known about the decline in mortality in the developing world since 1950 is limited to the mortality of children and has come from a series of standardized, internationally funded demographic surveys. Enormous reductions in child mortality occurred almost everywhere around the world between 1960 and 1990 (Figure 1.1). For example, child mortality in Chile dropped from 155 to 20 per 1,000, in Tunisia from 245 to 45, and in Sri Lanka from 140 to 22.

The statistics for adult mortality in the developing world are much less satisfactory than those for child mortality. Approximate estimates for all developing countries suggest that the adult mortality rate (defined as the probability of dying between ages 15 and 60 per 1,000 persons reaching age 15) fell from about 450 in 1950 to about 230 in 1990. In Chile, a country with excellent statistics, the rate dropped from 466 in 1930 to 152 in 1990.

The decline in mortality has accelerated over the past thirty years. In the 1960s child mortality fell by approximately 2 percent a year in about seventy developing countries for which estimates are available. The annual decline increased to more than 3 percent in the 1970s and to more than 5 percent in the 1980s. This result could be skewed by changes in the mix of countries with reliable data; there were, however, twenty-one countries with a continuous series of acceptable estimates of child mortality from the early 1960s to the late 1980s, and for this group as a whole the fall in child mortality averaged 3 percent a year in the 1960s but 6 percent a year in the 1980s. In seventeen of the twenty-one the pace of decline increased over the period.

Regional patterns

The extent of success has varied significantly between regions. Between 1950 and 1990 all eight demographic regions used for this Report enjoyed increases in life expectancy at birth, but China and the Middle Eastern crescent did particularly well (see Figure 1.2). Sub-Saharan Africa showed the slowest improvement, with life expectancy increasing only from thirty-nine to fifty-two years—although even this compares well with European experience in the nineteenth century. (It took England and Wales more than half a century to raise life expectancy by a similar amount.) The formerly socialist economies of Europe showed a rapid improvement in the 1950s and 1960s, but the rise was much slower in the 1970s and 1980s.

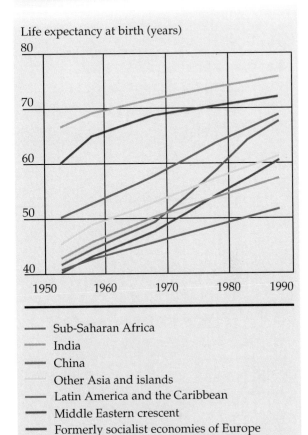

Figure 1.2 Trends in life expectancy by demographic region, 1950–90

Life expectancy at birth (years)

— Sub-Saharan Africa
— India
— China
  Other Asia and islands
— Latin America and the Caribbean
— Middle Eastern crescent
— Formerly socialist economies of Europe
  Established market economies

Source: Appendix A.

There are strong parallels between the pattern of mortality decline in the high-income countries and the accelerated progress of developing countries over the past forty years. In both groups the control of communicable diseases, particularly those of childhood, accounts for most of the gains. (The term "communicable diseases," in the analyses for this Report, includes deaths from maternal and perinatal causes.) Progress against noncommunicable diseases—primarily those of the circulatory and respiratory systems, which principally affect adults—has been much slower. In both Chile (from 1930 to 1987) and England and Wales (over the longer period 1891 to 1990) mortality from communicable disease fell to less than 5 percent of its initial level, whereas mortality from noncommuni-

23

Figure 1.3 Age-standardized female death rates in Chile and in England and Wales, selected years

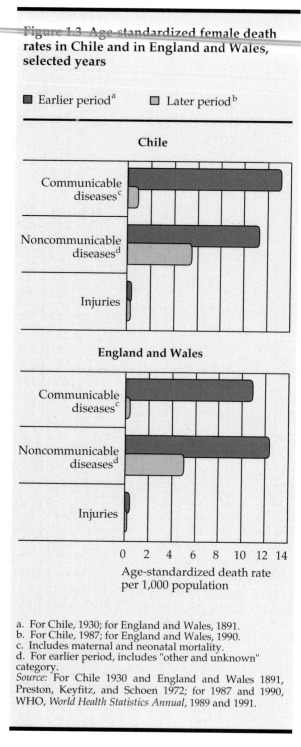

Figure 1.4 Change in female age-specific mortality rates in Chile and in England and Wales, selected years

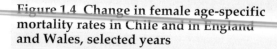

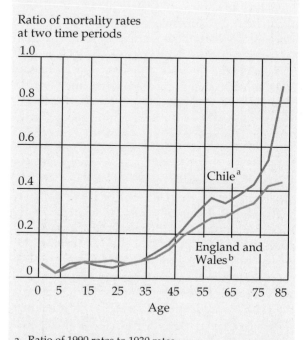

a. Ratio of 1990 rates to 1930 rates.
b. Ratio of 1981 rates to 1891 rates.
Source: For Chile 1930 and England and Wales 1891, Preston, Keyfitz, and Schoen 1972; for Chile 1990, World Health Organization data; for England and Wales 1990, United Nations, *Demographic Yearbook*, 1991.

a. For Chile, 1930; for England and Wales, 1891.
b. For Chile, 1987; for England and Wales, 1990.
c. Includes maternal and neonatal mortality.
d. For earlier period, includes "other and unknown" category.
Source: For Chile 1930 and England and Wales 1891, Preston, Keyfitz, and Schoen 1972; for 1987 and 1990, WHO, *World Health Statistics Annual*, 1989 and 1991.

cable disease fell much less rapidly (Figure 1.3). One result of this change is that mortality risks have fallen much faster for children than for

adults. In Chile, for example, mortality risks up to age 30 fell by more than 90 percent between 1930 and 1990; the decline was at least 60 percent at ages 30–70, but above age 70 the gains were much smaller (Figure 1.4). The age pattern of mortality decline in Chile over sixty years is strikingly similar to the pattern in England and Wales during the ninety years from 1891 to 1981.

The only exception to this broad similarity between industrial and developing countries has been in the formerly socialist economies. In these countries child mortality has continued to decline, as has the mortality of women, albeit more slowly. The mortality of adult men, on the other hand, has stopped declining in the past two decades and has actually started to increase. This excess male mortality is largely the result of extremely high death rates from cardiovascular disease, associated with heavy smoking and drinking.

Measuring the burden of disease

The health improvements of the past few decades have done much to enhance human welfare, both directly and indirectly. But much more remains to be done. Communicable (and largely preventable) diseases are still common. Health systems also have to cope with the aging of populations, which leads to an increased burden of the more expensive noncommunicable diseases. New illnesses, such as AIDS, have emerged. One simple statistic gives a sense of the remaining burden of disease: about 12.4 million children under age 5 died in 1990 in the developing world. Had those children faced the mortality risks of children in the established market economies, the number of deaths would have been cut by more than 90 percent, to 1.1 million.

Any discussion of health policy must start with a sense of the scale of health problems. These problems are often assessed in terms of mortality, but that indicator fails to account for the losses that occur this side of death because of handicap, pain, or other disability. A background study for this Report, undertaken jointly with the World Health Organization, measures the global burden of disease (GBD) by combining (a) losses from premature death, which is defined as the difference between actual age at death and life expectancy at that age in a low-mortality population, and (b) loss of healthy life resulting from disability. The GBD is measured in units of disability-adjusted life years (DALYs). Worldwide, 1.36 billion DALYs were lost in 1990, the equivalent of 42 million deaths of newborn children or of 80 million deaths at age 50. Premature deaths were responsible for 66 percent of all DALYs lost and disabilities for 34 percent. In the developing world 67 percent of all DALY loss was a result of premature death; in the established market economies and the formerly socialist economies of Europe the figure was only 55 percent. Table 1.1 shows the GBD broken down by sex, category of disease, and type of loss (premature death or disability). The three categories of disease used are the group of communicable diseases, noncommunicable diseases, and injuries.

The derivation and interpretation of the GBD are explained in Box 1.3. The results of research on the GBD challenge the belief that the war against infectious and parasitic diseases has been won. Di-

Table 1.1 Burden of disease by sex, cause, and type of loss, 1990
(millions of DALYs)

Sex and outcome	Disease category		
	Communicable[a]	Noncommunicable	Injuries
Male			
Premature death	259	152	70
Disability	47	146	39
Female			
Premature death	244	135	33
Disability	74	142	20

Note: DALY, disability-adjusted life year.
a. Includes maternal and perinatal causes.
Source: Appendix B.

arrhea, childhood diseases such as measles, respiratory infections, worm infections, and malaria account for one-quarter of the GBD. The burden of these largely preventable or inexpensively curable diseases of children is far larger in Sub-Saharan Africa (43 percent of all DALYs lost) than anywhere else, although it is still substantial in India (28 percent), Other Asia and islands (29 percent), and the Middle Eastern crescent (29 percent). For adults too, communicable diseases are far from trivial: sexually transmitted diseases (STDs) and tuberculosis together contribute 7 percent of the GBD.

Even as broad a measure as the GBD does not capture all the consequences of disease or injury. It excludes the social costs of disfigurement, such as that arising from river blindness or leprosy, and of dysfunction—for example, marital breakups resulting from obstetric fistula (permanent damage to the reproductive tract incurred during delivery). And some health-related factors are likely to be underreported. A clear example is violence against women, much of which goes undetected—but not unsuffered.

Comparisons of absolute numbers of DALYs lost may be misleading because the sizes and age structures of the populations at risk are not the same. The effects of population size can be allowed for by expressing the 1990 burden per 1,000 population. Figure 1.5 shows the resulting rates by sex and regional group. This index is 259 for the world as a whole, but it varies widely among regions. Sub-Saharan Africa loses 574 DALYs for every 1,000 population, more than twice the global average. India, the Middle Eastern crescent, and Other Asia and islands all have values between 250 and 350. For China, the formerly socialist economies of Europe, and Latin America and the Caribbean, the figures are between 150 and 250. The burden per

Box 1.3 Measuring the burden of disease

Most assessments of the relative importance of different diseases are based on how many deaths they cause. This convention has certain merits: death is an unambiguous event, and the statistical systems of many countries routinely produce the data required. There are, however, many diseases or conditions that are not fatal but that are responsible for great loss of healthy life: examples are chronic depression and paralysis caused by polio. These conditions are common, can last a long time, and frequently lead to significant demands on health systems.

To quantify the full loss of healthy life, the World Bank and the World Health Organization undertook a joint exercise for this Report. Diseases were classified into 109 categories on the basis of the *International Classification of Diseases* (ninth revision). These categories cover all possible causes of death and about 95 percent of the possible causes of disability. Using the recorded cause of death where available, and expert judgment when records were not available, the study assigned all deaths in 1990 to these categories by age, sex, and demographic region. For each death, the number of years of life lost was defined as the difference between the actual age at death and the expectation of life at that age in a low-mortality population. For disability, the incidence of cases by age, sex, and demographic region was estimated on the basis of community surveys or, failing that, expert opinion; the number of years of

healthy life lost was then obtained by multiplying the expected duration of the condition (to remission or to death) by a severity weight that measured the severity of the disability in comparison with loss of life. Diseases were grouped into six classes of severity of disability; for example, class 2, which includes most cases of leprosy and half the cases of pelvic inflammatory disease, was given a severity weight of 0.22, and class 4, which includes 30 percent of cases of dementia and 50 percent of those of blindness, was assigned a severity weight of 0.6. The death and disability losses were then combined, and allowance was made for a discount rate of 3 percent (so that future years of healthy life were valued at progressively lower levels) and for age weights (so that years of life lost at different ages were given different relative values). The value for each year of life lost, shown in the left-hand panel of Box figure 1.3, rises steeply from zero at birth to a peak at age 25 and then declines gradually with increasing age. These age weights reflect a consensus judgment, but other patterns could be used—for example, uniform age weights, with each year of life having the same value, which would increase the relative importance of childhood diseases.

The combination of discounting and age weights produces the pattern of DALYs (disability-adjusted life years) lost by a death at each age. As the right-hand panel of Box figure 1.3 shows, the death of a newborn

Box figure 1.3 Age patterns of age weights and DALY losses

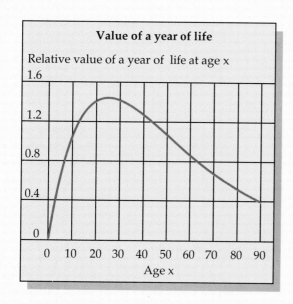

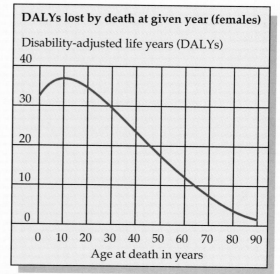

Source: World Bank data.

Box table 1.3 Distribution of DALY loss by cause and demographic region, 1990
(percent)

Cause	World	Sub-Saharan Africa	India	China	Other Asia and islands	Latin America and the Caribbean	Middle Eastern crescent	Formerly socialist economies of Europe	Established market economies
Population (millions)	5,267	510	850	1,134	683	444	503	346	798
Communicable diseases	45.8	71.3	50.5	25.3	48.5	42.2	51.0	8.6	9.7
Tuberculosis	3.4	4.7	3.7	2.9	5.1	2.5	2.8	0.6	0.2
STDs and HIV	3.8	8.8	2.7	1.7	1.5	6.6	0.7	1.2	3.4
Diarrhea	7.3	10.4	9.6	2.1	8.3	5.7	10.7	0.4	0.3
Vaccine-preventable childhood infections	5.0	9.6	6.7	0.9	4.5	1.6	6.0	0.1	0.1
Malaria	2.6	10.8	0.3	*	1.4	0.4	0.2	*	*
Worm infections	1.8	1.8	0.9	3.4	3.4	2.5	0.4	*	*
Respiratory infections	9.0	10.8	10.9	6.4	11.1	6.2	11.5	2.6	2.6
Maternal causes	2.2	2.7	2.7	1.2	2.5	1.7	2.9	0.8	0.6
Perinatal causes	7.3	7.1	9.1	5.2	7.4	9.1	10.9	2.4	2.2
Other	3.5	4.6	4.0	1.4	3.3	5.8	4.9	0.6	0.5
Noncommunicable diseases	42.2	19.4	40.4	58.0	40.1	42.8	36.0	74.8	78.4
Cancer	5.8	1.5	4.1	9.2	4.4	5.2	3.4	14.8	19.1
Nutritional deficiencies	3.9	2.8	6.2	3.3	4.6	4.6	3.7	1.4	1.7
Neuropsychiatric disease	6.8	3.3	6.1	8.0	7.0	8.0	5.6	11.1	15.0
Cerebrovascular disease	3.2	1.5	2.1	6.3	2.1	2.6	2.4	8.9	5.3
Ischemic heart disease	3.1	0.4	2.8	2.1	3.5	2.7	1.8	13.7	10.0
Pulmonary obstruction	1.3	0.2	0.6	5.5	0.5	0.7	0.5	1.6	1.7
Other	18.0	9.7	18.5	23.6	17.9	19.1	18.7	23.4	25.6
Injuries	11.9	9.3	9.1	16.7	11.3	15.0	13.0	16.6	11.9
Motor vehicle	2.3	1.3	1.1	2.3	2.3	5.7	3.3	3.7	3.5
Intentional	3.7	4.2	1.2	5.1	3.2	4.3	5.2	4.8	4.0
Other	5.9	3.9	6.8	9.3	5.8	5.0	4.6	8.1	4.3
Total	100.0	100.0	100.0	100.0	100.0	100.0	100.0	100.0	100.0
Millions of DALYs	1,362	293	292	201	177	103	144	58	94
Equivalent infant deaths (millions)	42.0	9.0	9.0	6.2	5.5	3.2	4.4	1.8	2.9
DALYs per 1,000 population	259	575	344	178	260	233	286	168	117

*Less than 0.05 percent.
Note: DALY, disability-adjusted life year; STD, sexually transmitted disease; HIV, human immunodeficiency virus.
Source: World Bank data.

baby girl represents a loss of 32.5 DALYs; a female death at age 30 means the loss of 29 DALYs; and a female death at age 60 represents 12 lost DALYs. (Values are slightly lower for males.) The sum across all ages, conditions, and regions is referred to as the global burden of disease (GBD). More details on the GBD are presented in Appendix B.

The global burden measures the present value of the future stream of disability-free life lost as a result of death, disease, or injury in 1990. It is thus based on events that occurred in 1990 but includes the loss of disability-free life in future years. This Report expresses the burden in three distinct ways: as the number of DALYs, as a percentage of some larger aggregate (such as the percentage of total loss attributable to a specific disease), and in relation to population size in 1990. This last measure calls for careful interpretation because all future loss is expressed in relation to the current population, and the measure can easily exceed

one year per person. A baby who died in 1990 contributed about thirty-two years (the discounted value of about eighty years of expected life) to the burden but counted as one in the population. To take an extreme case, if the entire population of the world were to be killed in one year, the burden per 1,000 population in that year would exceed 20,000 DALYs. There is therefore no absolute scale with which the GBD per 1,000 population can be compared; the only comparisons that make sense are those between categories—of regions, risk factors, disease groups, or sex. Box table 1.3 shows the GBD by cause and demographic region.

The approach used to compute the GBD can also be used to track improvements in a nation's health over time by following changes in the national burden of disease. Preliminary plans for initial national assessments have been developed for Costa Rica, South Africa, and Andhra Pradesh State in India.

Figure 1.5 Disease burden by sex and demographic region, 1990

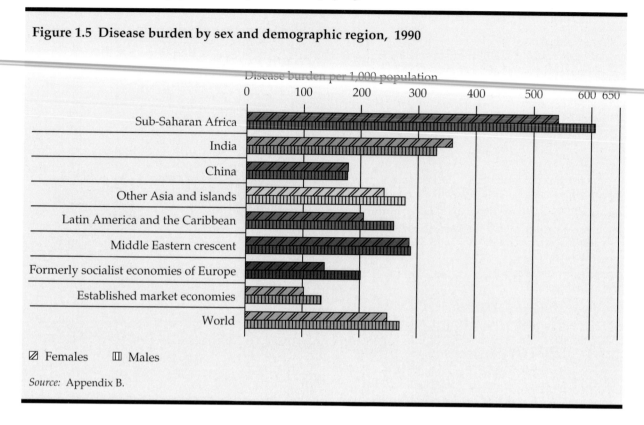

Females   Males

Source: Appendix B.

1,000 population for the established market economies is easily the lowest, at 117. It turns out that these broad rankings are not significantly affected by differences in age distributions between regions.

Females have about a 10 percent lower disease burden per 1,000 population than males for the world as a whole. They lose fewer DALYs from premature mortality, but their DALY loss from disability is about the same as for males. Within the disability category, however, the female disease burden from the group of communicable causes is considerably higher than that for males, partly because of a substantial toll from maternal causes but also because of the much greater female burden associated with STDs. Effective interventions exist for much of this excess female burden. For all causes together, the female advantage ranges from more than 30 percent in the formerly socialist economies, where adult mortality is much higher for men than for women, to negative in India, where females suffer a disadvantage of 8 percent. Both India and China show a female disadvantage in disease burden per 1,000 population, and, not coincidentally, both countries also have large num-

bers of "missing" (and presumed dead) women in relation to the expected population balance between the sexes. In China illegal female infanticide (and, in the recent past, illegal sex-selective abortion) is thought to be the main reason.

Table 1.2 Burden of five major diseases by age of incidence and sex, 1990
(millions of DALYs)

	Age (years)					
Disease and sex	*0–4*	*5–14*	*15–44*	*45–59*	*60+*	*Total*
Diarrhea						
Male	42.1	4.6	2.8	0.4	0.2	50.2
Female	40.7	4.8	2.8	0.4	0.3	48.9
Worm infection						
Male	0.2	10.6	1.6	0.5	0.1	13.1
Female	0.1	9.2	0.9	0.5	0.1	10.9
Tuberculosis						
Male	1.2	3.1	13.4	6.2	2.6	26.5
Female	1.3	3.8	10.9	2.8	1.2	20.0
Ischemic heart disease						
Male	0.1	0.1	3.6	8.1	13.1	25.0
Female	**	**	1.2	3.2	13.0	17.5

** Less than 0.05 million.
Note: DALY, disability-adjusted life year.
Source: World Bank data.

The figures on disease burden by age (Table 1.2) suggest how health officials should target their programs. More than 80 percent of the DALY loss from diarrhea is a result of infections in children under age 5. Worm infections are concentrated among children ages 5–14. More than half the burden of tuberculosis is borne by the 15–44 age group. More than 60 percent of the burden of ischemic heart disease falls on the population over age 60.

The higher the disease burden, the higher the proportion attributable to the communicable group of causes (Figure 1.6). Sub-Saharan Africa has the highest disease burden per 1,000 population, and 71 percent of this is from the communicable disease group, whereas in Latin America (a medium-burden region) the figure is 42 percent and in the established market economies it is only 10 percent. Noncommunicable diseases show the opposite pattern, accounting for 19 percent of the total burden in Sub-Saharan Africa, 43 percent in Latin America, and 78 percent in the established market economies. Despite these marked differences in relative burden, however, the absolute rates of loss for both groups are highest in Sub-Saharan Africa and lowest in the established market economies. The pattern is plain: as health improves, the burden from all types of disease declines, but the distribution of the burden shifts dramatically from a preponderance of communicable disease to a preponderance of noncommunicable disease.

Despite the sharp improvements in health around the world, the GBD calculations show that a large burden of premature mortality and disability still remains, particularly in the world's poorer regions. There are inexpensive and effective ways to eliminate the share caused by communicable diseases (other than maternal and perinatal conditions), which is roughly 35 percent of the world burden and more than 60 percent in Sub-Saharan Africa. The remaining 65 percent of the world burden is less responsive to such measures, and reducing it will require changes in the behavior and life-styles of adults.

Challenges for the future

New health challenges will emerge over the next few decades. Some are certain: these involve the significant increase in noncommunicable diseases arising from the continuing demographic transition. Others are less certain: the spread of HIV and the increase in AIDS deaths; the increasing num-

The share of communicable diseases in the disease burden declines as mortality rates fall.

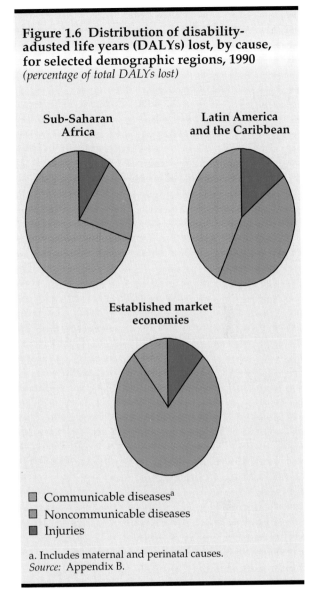

Figure 1.6 Distribution of disability-adusted life years (DALYs) lost, by cause, for selected demographic regions, 1990
(percentage of total DALYs lost)

a. Includes maternal and perinatal causes.
Source: Appendix B.

ber of drug-resistant disease strains; and the continued use of health-damaging substances such as tobacco. Although nobody can forecast the impact of these challenges with any precision, reasonable projections are possible. For example, outside the established market economies the number of deaths attributable to smoking is expected to increase from 1.7 million in 1990 (40 percent of which were in the formerly socialist economies of Europe) to more than 3 million by 2005 and to about 4.5 million by 2015. Other challenges are potentially important but not forecastable: possible ex-

Worldwide, fertility and mortality declines go hand in hand.

Figure 1.7 Trends in life expectancy and fertility in Sub-Saharan Africa and Latin America and the Caribbean, 1960–2020

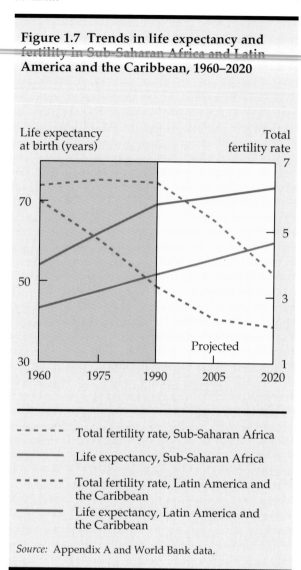

Total fertility rate, Sub-Saharan Africa

Life expectancy, Sub-Saharan Africa

Total fertility rate, Latin America and the Caribbean

Life expectancy, Latin America and the Caribbean

Source: Appendix A and World Bank data.

amples are the emergence of new microbes as devastating as HIV and the inadvertent spread of biological agents developed for use in war.

This section reviews predictions concerning three major challenges in the light of their contribution to the GBD: the aging of populations, AIDS, and drug-resistant strains of disease.

Aging populations

The mortality decline that has occurred almost everywhere has usually been accompanied by steep falls in fertility. The overall transition from high mortality and high fertility to low mortality and low fertility is essentially complete in the high-income countries and has almost been completed in China and Latin America. Even in Sub-Saharan Africa fertility seems to be starting to decline.

The systematic relationship between gains in life expectancy and reductions in fertility is expected to continue into the next century. Figure 1.7 shows this relationship for two developing regions at different stages of the transition, Latin America and Sub-Saharan Africa. The projected changes for Sub-Saharan Africa are substantial, but they are similar in magnitude to those that have already occurred in Latin America. In much of the developing world the decline in death rates has preceded the decline in birth rates by two decades or more, resulting in temporarily high rates of population growth of 3 or even, occasionally, 4 percent a year. (By contrast, in the established market economies and the formerly socialist economies of Europe birth and death rates declined more or less

Box figure 1.4 Evolving patterns of age distribution and mortality in England and Wales and in Latin America and the Caribbean

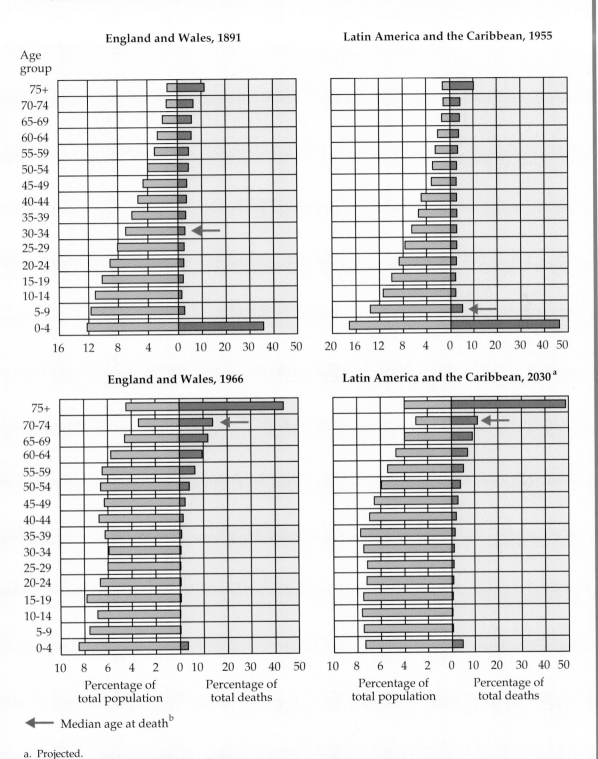

England and Wales, 1891

Latin America and the Caribbean, 1955

England and Wales, 1966

Latin America and the Caribbean, 2030 [a]

Age group

75+
70-74
65-69
60-64
55-59
50-54
45-49
40-44
35-39
30-34
25-29
20-24
15-19
10-14
5-9
0-4

Percentage of total population

Percentage of total deaths

← Median age at death [b]

a. Projected.
b. The age below which half of all deaths in a year occur.
Source: For England and Wales 1891, Preston, Keyfitz, and Schoen 1972; for England and Wales 1966, United Nations, *Demographic Yearbook*, 1978; for Latin America and the Caribbean, 1955 and 2030, World Bank data.

in tandem beginning in the late nineteenth century, and population growth rates rarely exceeded 2 percent a year.)

These demographic changes are having, and will continue to have, dramatic effects on age distributions in developing countries. As fertility declines, age structures in these countries are evolving toward the existing patterns in the established market economies and the formerly socialist economies (see Box 1.4). The proportion of the population age 65 and over is expected to increase from 4 percent in 1990 to 9 percent by 2030 (in absolute numbers, from 184 million to 678 million). As a result, the burden from noncommunicable dis-

All regions will experience the health transition, but the timing will differ.

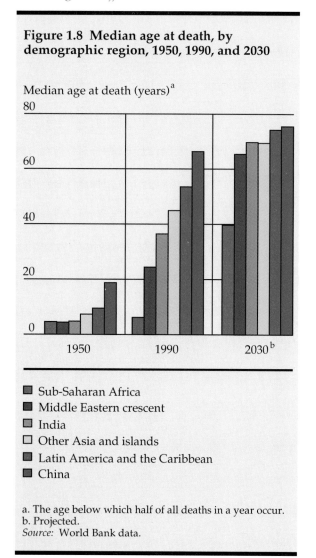

Figure 1.8 Median age at death, by demographic region, 1950, 1990, and 2030

Median age at death (years)[a]

- ■ Sub-Saharan Africa
- ■ Middle Eastern crescent
- ■ India
- □ Other Asia and islands
- ■ Latin America and the Caribbean
- ■ China

a. The age below which half of all deaths in a year occur.
b. Projected.
Source: World Bank data.

eases will increase sharply, both absolutely and proportionately. At the same time, the challenge of communicable diseases of the young will persist. Despite declines in fertility, the number of births each year in developing countries will rise somewhat, from 127 million in 1990 to 145 million in 2020, before decreasing to 142 million in 2030. The number of children under age 5 will increase more rapidly, from 552 million in 1990 to 682 million in 2030. These changes, which took a century to complete in today's high-income countries, are occurring within fifty years or less in parts of the developing world.

In judging the importance of the health problems of the young in comparison with those of the elderly, one useful guide is the median age at death. For all six regions of the developing world, the median was below 20 in 1950, indicating the dominance of the health problems of children. By 1990 the median had risen close to age 60 in China and in Latin America but was scarcely above 5 in Sub-Saharan Africa and was still below 25 in the Middle Eastern crescent (see Figure 1.8). By 2030, assuming that current trends continue, the median age at death will have risen above 60 in all regions except Sub-Saharan Africa, where it will still be close to 40.

The message from these population projections is that health services must plan for a modest increase in child-related demands over the next forty years. At the same time, the numbers of the elderly, with very different health needs, will be rising sharply. The pace of demographic change has been, and is expected to continue to be, faster in the developing world than it was in the high-income countries, and the problems of adaptation are therefore greater. Because treatments for noncommunicable diseases are often expensive, there is a danger that these diseases will absorb resources needed to combat communicable diseases (which will still be widespread). This kind of dilemma has already been noted in World Bank studies in Brazil and China.

HIV and AIDS

More than 80 percent of the estimated 8.8 million people infected with HIV in 1990 lived in developing countries. There the disease is primarily one of heterosexual adults, with substantial perinatal infection of young children. Of the eight demographic regions used in this Report, only the formerly socialist economies, the Middle Eastern crescent, and China have little recorded spread of

Table 1.3 Evolution of the HIV-AIDS epidemic

Region	HIV incidence (millions)		HIV prevalence (millions)		AIDS-related deaths (millions)	
	1990	2000[a]	1990	2000[a]	1990	2000[a]
Demographically developing group[b]	1.6	2.5	7.4	25	0.3	1.7
Sub-Saharan Africa	1.1	1.0	5.8	12	0.3	0.9
Asia[c]	0.3	1.3	0.4	9	**	0.6
EME and FSE[d]	0.1	**	1.4	1	0.1	0.1
Total	1.7	2.5	8.8	26	0.4	1.8

** Less than 0.05 million.
Note: Incidence refers to new infections in a given year; prevalence refers to the total number of persons infected.
a. Conservative estimates.
b. The countries of the demographic regions Sub-Saharan Africa, India, China, Other Asia and islands, Latin America and the Caribbean, and Middle Eastern crescent.
c. India, China, and the demographic region Other Asia and islands.
d. EME, established market economies; FSE, formerly socialist economies of Europe.
Source: World Health Organization data.

the virus. Spread of the virus may be about to occur even in these three regions. It takes six to ten years, on average, for an HIV-infected adult to develop AIDS. Thus, regardless of future changes in transmission of the virus, there will certainly be an increasing number of AIDS cases over the next few years.

It is difficult to predict the future course of the epidemic because so little is known about the dynamics of HIV transmission. WHO has projected that in 2000, 2.5 million people will be newly infected with HIV, HIV prevalence will have reached 26 million, and AIDS deaths will total 1.8 million (see Table 1.3). These estimates are conservative, since they assume that the rate of new infections in Africa will slow somewhat and that new transmission will be concentrated in India and in the Other Asia and islands region. If no effective interventions to slow transmission are introduced, the total number of deaths may be twice as large, in which case AIDS would be responsible for 8 percent of the global burden of disease by 2000 instead of the 3.5 percent implied by the estimates in Table 1.3. If, however, sexual behavior changes dramatically over the next decade, even the conservative projections given here may prove too pessimistic. Relatively modest reductions in numbers of casual sexual partners, or in the prevalence of STDs—or, alternatively, substantial increases in condom use—could reduce transmission significantly. Early (and still tentative) findings from Thailand are encouraging; perhaps behavior really will change.

Opinions differ concerning the effects of AIDS on population growth. The variables needed to model the epidemic—including baseline rates of infections, behavioral risk factors, efficacy of trans-

mission, incubation periods, survival times, and the role of such factors as STDs—are not well quantified, and accurate projections are therefore impossible. In the African communities that are most severely affected, early assessments predicted absolute declines in population. Later views suggest that population growth will continue, albeit at a reduced rate. Trial projections for Sub-Saharan Africa, based on a high assumption of HIV prevalence of 60 million infections worldwide in 2000, suggest a reduction in life expectancy by 2010 of about six years, in comparison with a low-HIV model, and a 25 percent increase in adult mortality. The effect on population growth would still be modest: a reduction of about 0.25 percentage point a year, to an annual rate of 2.7 rather than 2.95 percent in 2005–10. In areas such as Thailand where fertility and mortality rates are much lower than in Sub-Saharan Africa, AIDS may well contribute to actual population declines over a period of thirty years or more.

Drug-resistant diseases

Microbes evolve as a result of natural mutation, which throws up new threats, and of drug therapy–induced selection, which fosters drug resistance. Two major new threats have arisen in this century: the influenza virus responsible for the 1918–19 worldwide epidemic, and HIV.

The evolution of drug resistance, partly driven by incomplete or inadequate treatment, is more gradual and less dramatic but no less serious. The everyday bacteria responsible for pneumonias and diarrheas have become resistant to the older antibiotics and will gradually do the same with the newer antibiotics developed over the past few dec-

Figure 1.9 Life expectancy and income per capita for selected countries and periods

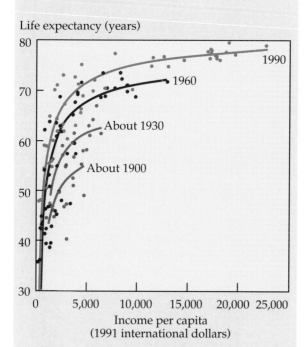

Life expectancy (years)

Income per capita
(1991 international dollars)

Note: International dollars are derived from national currencies not by use of exchange rates but by assessment of purchasing power. The effect is to raise the relative incomes of poorer countries, often substantially. For illustrative country comparisons and a more detailed explanation, see Table 30 in the World Development Indicators.
Source: Preston, Keyfitz, and Schoen 1972; World Bank data.

emerging. In the developing world the diseases for which drug resistance is already a major issue (respiratory infections, tuberculosis, STDs, and malaria) accounted for almost one-fifth of the GBD in 1990.

This steady evolution of drug-resistant microbes poses challenges for research and for health care. Better understanding of infectious agents is needed as a basis for the development of new therapies. Health providers must consider the effects of drug use on the evolution of resistant microbial strains. Basic scientific advances can contribute to tracking resistance, as recently shown by developments in identifying drug-resistant strains of tuberculosis. There is little reason to hope for permanent success in humanity's struggle against infection; investments in scientific research and vigilance on the part of public health authorities will remain indispensable.

These problems arising from microbial evolution are most severe in Sub-Saharan Africa. If efforts to control the spread of HIV fail, by 2000 an additional 1 million people in the region will be dying from AIDS each year. Most of them will be young adults who would otherwise have gone on to live healthy lives. If malaria develops resistance to all available drugs, the number of people it kills every year could increase sharply, from the expected 1.5 million deaths in 2000 to 2.3 million. Sub-Saharan Africa might also suffer from a tuberculosis epidemic, driven partly by drug resistance and partly by the spread of the disease by people with HIV. Extrapolation of current trends indicates an annual total of 8.5 million premature deaths in Sub-Saharan Africa by the end of the century. But it is all too easy to project a figure as high as 11.5 million, accompanied by a sharp reduction in life expectancy.

Lessons from the past: explaining declines in mortality

Three factors have been important in the dramatic and unprecedented mortality declines of the past hundred years and in the still more dramatic declines in developing countries since World War II. These factors are income growth, improvements in medical technology, and public health programs combined with the spread of knowledge about health.

Income growth

Increased income allows people, particularly the poor, to buy more food, better housing, and more

ades. Tuberculosis resistant to the standard mix of antibiotics is becoming more common in the industrial world, and it kills many of those who contract it. Chloroquine-resistant malaria has now spread to practically all endemic areas, and although new drug therapies are available, widespread resistance even to several of these is being reported. Malaria has thus reemerged as a significant health risk in urban areas that had been free of it for several decades. Resurgence of the disease has been abetted by the reduced effectiveness of vector control, which is partly attributable to the increasing resistance of mosquitoes to standard insecticides. Resistant strains of many STDs are also health care. Throughout the twentieth century life expectancy has been strongly associated at the national level with income per capita, as seen in Figure 1.9. Life expectancy rises rapidly with income at low levels of income, particularly when income per capita is less than $3,000 (1991 purchasing power dollars). The figure shows, however, that the relationship has shifted upward over each thirty-year period, so that more health is realized for a given income. For example, in 1900 life expectancy in the United States was about forty-nine years and income per capita in 1991 dollars was about $4,800. In 1990 that income per capita would be associated with a life expectancy of about seventy-one years. This upward shift shows that health depends on more than income alone.

Improvements in medical technology

Before the 1930s medical technology had little to offer humanity, with the exception of smallpox inoculation, the use of which was widespread in Europe from the late eighteenth century onward, and diphtheria antitoxin, discovered in 1894. Starting in the 1930s, with the introduction of antibacterial drugs and new vaccines, a wide range of effective interventions has become available to counter most communicable diseases.

The effect of these technological improvements on health has depended on other factors, such as income gains for the poor, increased schooling, and public policies that affect health systems. As a result, outcomes have varied widely by country, even within the same region. For example, in the early 1980s child mortality was three times higher in Mali than in Botswana, six times higher in Bolivia than in Chile, and five times higher in Bangladesh than in Sri Lanka. Between the early 1960s and the early 1980s child mortality fell 20 percent in Bangladesh but 65 percent in Sri Lanka, 10 percent in Uganda but 50 percent in Kenya, and 10 percent in Haiti but nearly 80 percent in Costa Rica. Some countries have clearly made better use of the available technology than others.

Public health and the spread of knowledge

The introduction of public health measures—particularly clean water, sanitation, and food regulation—certainly contributed to the decline in child mortality in the late nineteenth century and to the accelerated decline in the early twentieth century. The geographic distribution of mortality declines suggests, however, that until people began to understand the sources of poor health, such public health measures were responsible for only a small part of the progress made. In the late nineteenth century Robert Koch showed that the bacterium *M. tuberculosis* causes tuberculosis, and people began to understand about germs. They took simple precautions—preparing food and disposing of waste hygienically, eliminating flies, and quarantining sick family members—that had far-reaching benefits. Recent research has shown that child mortality differed little by education or even by income in the United States in the last decade of the nineteenth century but that differences widened sharply as child mortality fell in the early twentieth century. The implication is that affluence and education made little difference until scientific knowledge showed households how to reduce the dangers to their health. Since better-educated individuals acquire and use new information more quickly, this emphasis on knowledge helps to explain the large differences in child mortality by mother's education observed in developing countries today.

The potential for effective action

The recent declines in mortality in the developing world have been sharper than the earlier declines in the high-income countries and more influenced by technical advances. To take one example, Sri Lanka achieved a remarkable decrease in mortality after World War II; the crude death rate fell from 21.5 per 1,000 in 1945 to 12.4 in 1950. Some 23 percent of that drop has been attributed to the malaria eradication program, which mainly involved spraying of insecticide from the air. The same approach also did much to control yellow fever, onchocerciasis, and many other diseases. Widespread use of newly available antibiotics against conditions such as yaws in Africa helped to reduce STDs and (probably) acute respiratory infections. Improvements in water and sanitation curbed the spread of disease, particularly in towns and cities. Whereas at the beginning of this century child mortality rates in today's high-income countries were much higher in urban than in rural areas, the opposite has been true of the developing world since 1950.

Vaccination, too, has produced dramatic results, including the eradication of smallpox and the elimination of paralytic polio in the Western Hemisphere. About 80 percent of the world's children are now vaccinated against the main infectious diseases of childhood, thanks largely to the Expanded Programme on Immunization (EPI) sponsored by WHO and UNICEF. It is estimated that the EPI prevented the deaths of 2.6 million children in 1990 alone. Substantial benefits have also come from simple curative measures such as oral rehydration to avert death from diarrhea and a short course of drugs for curing tuberculosis. But there is much more still to be done: in 1990 childhood deaths from diarrhea and immunizable diseases alone accounted for 12 percent of the GBD.

The march of science has increased both the range of inexpensive clinical treatments and practices and the potential performance of health systems. It is now possible to treat at low cost tuberculosis, STDs, many respiratory infections, and risky deliveries, which together accounted for more than 20 percent of the GBD in 1990. Epidemiological advances are giving governments and households warning of the enormous health toll from smoking. But if the full benefits of scientific advances are to be realized, parallel developments are needed to empower households so that they can put the advances into practice. The key developments are schooling, particularly of girls; income growth, particularly of the poor; and a flexible, responsive health system able to provide the necessary preventive and curative care. The policies needed to achieve these developments are the subject of the remainder of this Report.

Households and health

What people do with their lives and those of their children affects their health far more than anything that governments do. But what they can do is determined, to a great extent, by their income and knowledge—factors that are not completely within their control. In every society, moreover, the capabilities, income, and status of women exert a powerful influence on health. Because of these interrelations, government actions, through their effects on the conditions facing households and individuals, can be important to people's health. Especially in the poorest countries, policies that accelerate income growth and reduce poverty make it possible for people to afford better diets, healthier living conditions, and better health care. Policies to expand educational opportunities, particularly for girls, help households achieve healthier lives by increasing their access to information

Economic growth and investments in human resources interact to improve well-being.

Figure 2.1 Mutually reinforcing cycles: reduction of poverty and development of human resources

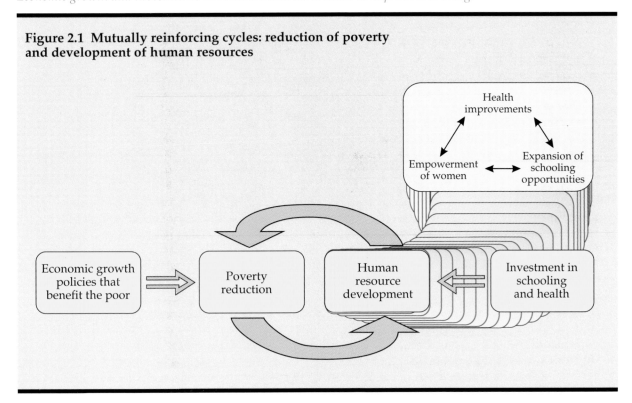

and their ability to make good use of it. The same goes for policies that work to ensure effective and accessible health services for all. When all these policies are combined, they create a virtuous cycle in which reduction of poverty and improvements in health reinforce each other (Figure 2.1).

Household capacity: income and schooling

Within the household, health improves rapidly as people escape from poverty and low education (Box 2.1). Beyond the household, every society's health services are affected by its national income,

---

Box 2.1 Progress in child health in four countries

In the 1960s a child born in the developing world had a 77 percent chance of surviving the first five years of life. About thirty years later, the chances of survival have improved to 89 percent. How much did income growth and expansion of schooling contribute to this gain? What was the role of other factors, such as progress in science and medicine? Some answers to these questions emerge from data on child survival from seventy-five industrial and developing countries for the period between 1960 and 1987 (see note to Appendix table A.3). This box reviews the results for four countries with different income levels—Costa Rica, Côte d'Ivoire, Egypt, and Japan (see Box table 2.1 and Box figure 2.1).

In all four countries, part of the gain in child health depends on the initial levels in 1960 of schooling in the population and of income per capita. Because schooling and income per capita produce health benefits that often persist through time, health in a population may be improved simply by maintaining initial levels of schooling and income. In Costa Rica, where in 1960 income per capita was relatively high and schooling was already widespread, initial conditions accounted for 58 percent of the gain in child health between 1960 and 1987. In Côte d'Ivoire and Egypt, where the levels of schooling and income per capita were modest in 1960, initial conditions contributed only about one-fifth to one-quarter of the gains. In Japan, too, these initial conditions contributed a fifth of the gains in child health, but this is not surprising in a country where a baby's chance of survival was already very good in 1960.

In reality, of course, income and schooling have improved in all these countries, and these improvements contributed to further gains in child survival. In Côte d'Ivoire educational improvements did the most for child health, accounting for 66 percent of the gains between 1960 and 1980. For Egypt, by contrast, the figure was only 21 percent. A comparison between Côte d'Ivoire and Egypt is illuminating. The probability of surviving the first five years of life started at similar levels in both countries and improved at comparable rates. In both, too, the responsiveness of child survival to income per capita and to the schooling of adults was comparable. In Côte d'Ivoire, however, adult schooling started from much lower levels than in Egypt but increased five times faster. Income per capita in Côte d'Ivoire was nearly twice Egypt's in 1960 but then grew

only 60 percent as fast. Thus, improvements in schooling were most significant in Côte d'Ivoire, whereas in Egypt growth in income per capita accounted for fully half of the gain in child health.

Costa Rica and Japan followed the same pattern as Egypt: growth of income per capita contributed substantially more to child health gains than did educational improvements. Technical progress (estimated using the passage of time as a proxy), however, was important in Japan, whereas in Costa Rica and Egypt it mattered less than improvements in education. Except in Japan, where people were already quite well educated in 1960, the analysis probably underestimated the contribution of schooling because it dealt with the schooling of all adults rather than of women alone. Child health is particularly affected by maternal education, and the number of years of schooling received by younger women is likely to have risen much faster between 1960 and 1987 than was the case for the adult population as a whole.

Box table 2.1 Child health, income per capita, and schooling in Costa Rica, Côte d'Ivoire, Egypt, and Japan, 1960–87

Indicator	Costa Rica	Côte d'Ivoire[a]	Egypt	Japan
1960				
Child survival[b]	0.89	0.72	0.74	0.96
Income per capita (1987 international dollars)[c]	2,160	1,021	557	2,701
Average schooling of adults (years)	4.0	0.2	3.0	10.7
Average annual percentage change, 1960–87				
Child survival[b]	0.4	0.8	0.6	0.1
Income per capita	2.3	3.2	5.2	5.3
Schooling of adult population	2.0	11.8	2.4	0.2
Elasticity of child survival with respect to:				
Income per capita[d]	0.04	0.06	0.06	0.02
Schooling of adult population[d]	0.03	0.04	0.04	0.02

a. Data refer to 1960–80.
b. Child survival refers to the probability of surviving from birth through age 5.
c. Income is adjusted for differences in purchasing power parity.
d. Elasticities denote the percentage change in the probability of surviving from birth through age 5 corresponding to a 1 percent change in the indicated variable.
Source: Lau and others, background paper.

and its ability to acquire and apply new scientific knowledge depends on the level of schooling in the population.

The influence of income on health

The higher a country's average income per capita, the more likely its people are to live long and healthy lives. Of course, this effect tapers off as income rises: a doubling of income per capita (adjusted for purchasing power parity) from, say, $1,000 in 1990 corresponds to a gain of eleven years in life expectancy, whereas a doubling from

Box figure 2.1 Gains in child health, 1960–87, and share contributed by various factors

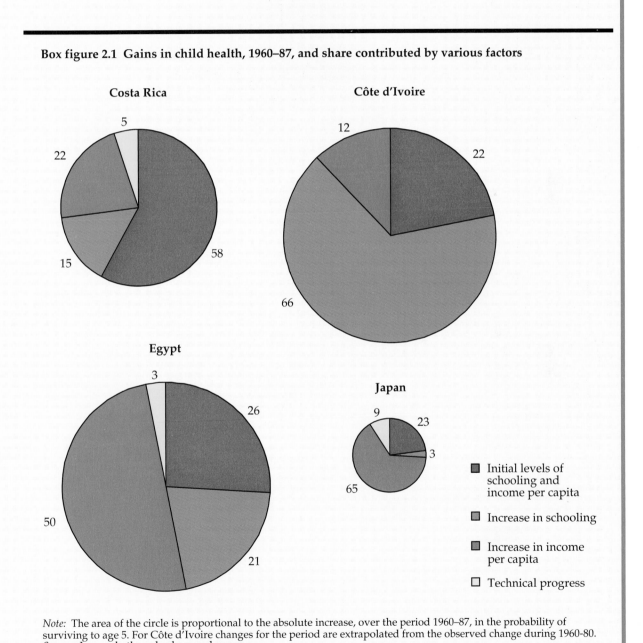

Note: The area of the circle is proportional to the absolute increase, over the period 1960–87, in the probability of surviving to age 5. For Côte d'Ivoire changes for the period are extrapolated from the observed change during 1960-80.
Source: Lau and others, background paper.

Within the same city, health status is worse in poorer areas.

Figure 2.2 Child mortality in rich and poor neighborhoods in selected metropolitan areas, late 1980s

■ Poor neighborhoods
□ Rich neighborhoods

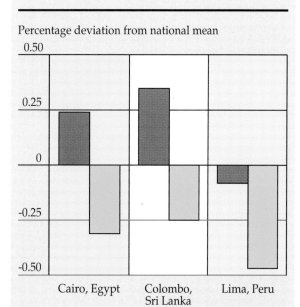

Percentage deviation from national mean

Note: Child mortality indexes for each neighborhood are calculated by dividing the observed number of deaths among children of women in the sampled households of a neighborhood by the expected number (given the distribution of women by the length of time they have been bearing children and the national average child mortality levels at each duration of childbearing). Percentage deviations from the national average are obtained by subtracting 1 from a neighborhood's index and multiplying the result by 100. Neighborhoods in each city were ranked according to the proportion of houses with concrete floors. Poor neighborhoods were the lowest 25 percent in this ranking; rich neighborhoods were the top 25 percent.
Source: Calculated from data from national Demographic and Health Surveys.

$4,000 is matched by a gain of only four years (see Figure 1.9 in Chapter 1). Income growth has more impact in poor populations because additional resources buy basic necessities, particularly food and shelter, that yield especially large health benefits.

Because poverty has a powerful influence on health, it is not just income per capita that is relevant; the distribution of income and the number of people in poverty matter as well. In industrial countries life expectancy depends much more on income distribution than on income per capita, and it has been rising faster in countries with improving income distribution. Japan and the United Kingdom had similar income distributions and life expectancies in 1970, but they have diverged since then. Japan now has the highest life expectancy in the world and a highly egalitarian income distribution. In the United Kingdom, where income disparity has widened since the mid-1980s, life expectancy is now more than three years shorter than in Japan.

In developing countries the number of people in poverty is an especially important reason for differences in health. One study looked at twenty-two developing countries with comparable data on poverty (defined as the share of the population consuming less than $1 a day at 1985 purchasing power parity prices) and found that variation in the prevalence of poverty and in per capita public spending on health is important in explaining cross-country variation in life expectancy. Differences in income per capita became unimportant once those two factors were taken into account. This does not mean that income growth is irrelevant to increased life expectancy; rather, its main effect lies in how much it reduces poverty and supports public health services. In the twenty-two countries, roughly one-third of the effect of economic growth on life expectancy came through poverty reduction and the remaining two-thirds through increased public spending on health. In Sri Lanka an increase in per capita public spending on health was twenty-two times more effective in reducing infant mortality than was the same increase in average income.

Within countries, too, health correlates strongly with poverty. In India, Indonesia, and Kenya child mortality is higher in states or provinces with larger proportions of poor people. Within cities, there are large differences in child survival between rich and poor neighborhoods (Figure 2.2). And children in poor families are less healthy. In Madurai, the second largest city in India's Tamil Nadu State, children ages 2–9 in the poorest households were more than twice as likely to suffer from serious physical or mental disabilities as children from slightly better-off families.

Poor people are vulnerable to disease not only because of poor living conditions but often also for work-related reasons. In Adana, Turkey, the risk of malaria is significantly greater among migrant workers than for the local population; the average

40

number of anopheline mosquito bites per person was five times greater in the tents of these workers than in the houses of village residents. In Sri Lanka one of the commonest causes of pesticide poisoning is leaky knapsack sprayers; surveys show that although farmers are aware of the risks involved, they continue to use broken equipment because they cannot afford to replace or repair it.

The distribution of income within households also affects health. Increasing women's access to income can be especially beneficial for the health of children. In Brazil income in the hands of the mother has a bigger effect on family health than income controlled by the father. In Jamaica households headed by women eat more nutritious food than those headed by men; they also spend more of their income on child-centered goods and significantly less on alcohol. In Côte d'Ivoire a doubling of household income under women's control reduces the share of alcohol in the family budget by 26 percent and the share of cigarettes by 14 percent. In Guatemala it takes fifteen times more spending to achieve a given improvement in child nutrition when income is earned by the father than when it is earned by the mother. Although a working mother may breastfeed less and have less time for child care—both of which could be detrimental to her children's health—evidence from numerous developing countries suggests that this harm can be offset by the health benefits that her earnings bring.

Because fewer people live in poverty as average incomes rise, there is generally a strong link between incomes and health status. Across countries, more than 75 percent of the difference in health is associated with income differences. Indeed, this relation is not merely associative but causal and structural: income growth leads directly to better health. In a sample of fifty-eight developing countries, a 10 percent increase in income per capita, all else being equal, reduced infant and child mortality rates by between 2.0 and 3.5 percent and increased life expectancy by a month. This estimate reflects the total impact of income on health; it includes effects working directly through income (such as food consumption), as well as indirectly through factors that are themselves mainly determined by income (access to safe water and sanitation, availability of physicians, and so on). Studies based on individual households corroborate the cross-country results. A 10 percent advantage in income reduces infant mortality by between 1 and 2 percent in Nigeria, Sri Lanka, Thailand, and several Latin American

Child mortality falls faster in countries where income per capita is growing rapidly.

Figure 2.3 Declines in child mortality and growth of income per capita in sixty-five countries

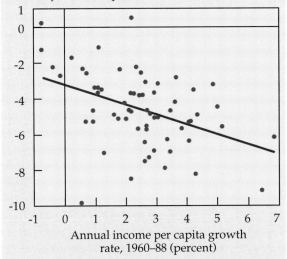

Annual rate of change in child mortality, 1970–88 (percent)

Annual income per capita growth rate, 1960–88 (percent)

Note: Child mortality refers to the probability of dying between birth and age 5; the period over which the rate of mortality decline is averaged differs from the period used for income per capita growth to take account of lags in the relation between the two rates.
Source: World Bank data.

countries and by as much as 4 to 8 percent in Côte d'Ivoire and Ghana.

These findings highlight the costs to health of slow economic growth. Child health has been improving everywhere, but gains are much less rapid in countries with slow income growth (Figure 2.3). During the 1980s the economic performance of developing countries was mixed, with income per capita constant or falling, and in some countries the incidence of poverty rose (Table 2.1). Had economic growth been as fast in the 1980s as in the period between 1960 and 1980, in 1990 alone an estimated 350,000 infant deaths, or 6 percent of total infant deaths, would have been averted in developing countries (excluding India and China). In Africa and Latin America, where average growth was 2.5 percentage points slower during the 1980s, the saving in babies' lives in 1990 would

Table 2.1 Poverty and growth of income per capita by developing region, 1985 and 1990, and long- and medium-term trends

Region	Head-count index of poverty[a]		Annual percentage change in income per capita	
	1985	1990	1970–92	1982–92
All developing countries	30.5	29.7	1.7	0.8
Sub-Saharan Africa	47.6	47.8	−0.2	−1.1
East Asia	13.2	11.3	5.3	6.3
South Asia	51.8	49.0	2.0	3.0
Eastern Europe	7.1	7.1	1.2	1.7
Middle East and North Africa	30.6	33.1	0.1	−1.6
Latin America and the Caribbean	22.4	25.2	1.1	−0.2

Note: Regional data on annual change in income per capita refer to unweighted country averages. The regions used in this table are as defined in the World Development Indicators, except for Eastern Europe, which includes Albania, Bulgaria, Hungary, Poland, Romania, the former Czechoslovakia, and the former Socialist Federal Republic of Yugoslavia. Disaggregated data for the last two are not yet available.
a. Estimated share of the population consuming less than $32 per person per month at 1985 purchasing power parity prices.
Source: For poverty index, World Bank 1993c; for change in income per capita, World Bank data.

have been as much as 7 and 12 percent, respectively. Latin America's recession in 1983 is estimated to have caused 12,000 additional deaths of babies, or 2 percent of all infant deaths in that year. And because slow economic growth hampers poverty reduction and constrains spending on health, schooling, and other services, it is highly likely that the health of the poor suffered disproportionately in the 1980s.

The influence of schooling on health

Households with more education enjoy better health, both for adults and for children. This result is strikingly consistent in a great number of studies, despite differences in research methods, time periods, and population samples.

MATERNAL SCHOOLING AND CHILD HEALTH. In most households women have the main responsibility for a broad range of activities that affect health. They manage household chores, keep the house clean, process foods and prepare meals, feed and care for young children, and look after the sick. Women's own health and their efficiency in using available resources have an important bearing on the health of others in the family, particularly children. A study of children under 10 in

Bangladesh, for example, found that over a period of two years following the death of a mother, mortality rates, in comparison with those of children with living mothers, were twice as high for boys and three times as high for girls.

Education greatly strengthens women's ability to perform their vital role in creating healthy households. It increases their ability to benefit from health information and to make good use of health services; it increases their access to income and enables them to live healthier lives. It is not surprising, therefore, that a child's health is affected much more by the mother's schooling than by the father's schooling. Data for thirteen African countries between 1975 and 1985 show that a 10 percent increase in female literacy rates reduced child mortality by 10 percent, whereas changes in male literacy had little influence. Demographic and Health Surveys in twenty-five developing countries show that, all else being equal, even one to three years of maternal schooling reduces child mortality by about 15 percent, whereas a similar level of paternal schooling achieves a 6 percent reduction. The effects increase when mothers have had more education; in Peru, for example, seven or more years of maternal schooling reduces the mortality risks nearly 75 percent, or about 28 percent more than the reduction for the same level of paternal schooling (Figure 2.4). Countries that in 1965 had achieved near-universal enrollment for boys but much less for girls had about twice the infant mortality in 1985 of countries with a smaller boy-girl gap.

The advantages that a mother's schooling confers on her children's health are felt even before birth. In developing countries better-educated women marry and start their families later, diminishing the risk to child health associated with early pregnancies. Educated women also tend to make greater use of prenatal care and delivery assistance. In a study in Lima that controlled for service availability and socioeconomic status, 82 percent of women with six or more years of education sought prenatal care, compared with only 62 percent for women with no education.

Following birth, the children of educated mothers continue to enjoy other health-enhancing advantages: better domestic hygiene, which reduces the risk of infection; better food and more immunization, both of which reduce susceptibility to infection; and wiser use of medical services. A study of women in Bangladesh documented how educated women kept their homes and children tidier and cleaner than uneducated women and

Figure 2.4 Effect of parents' schooling on the risk of death by age 2 in selected countries, late 1980s

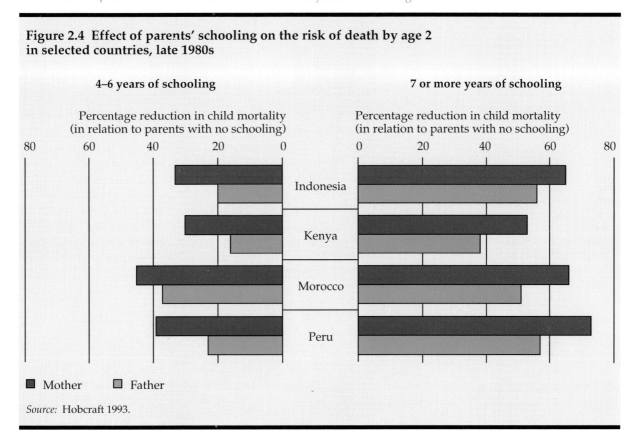

4–6 years of schooling

Percentage reduction in child mortality
(in relation to parents with no schooling)

7 or more years of schooling

Percentage reduction in child mortality
(in relation to parents with no schooling)

■ Mother   ■ Father

Source: Hobcraft 1993.

expressed a preference for water from tanks or tubewells at home rather than from canals or rivers. In Brazil, India, and Nigeria better-educated households are willing to pay 6 to 50 percent more than other households for improved water supplies.

Educated mothers are also better at getting information on health and acting on it. In Brazil the child health benefits of a father's education work mostly through his income, whereas almost all the effect of maternal education comes from learning about health through newspapers, television, and radio. In Thailand mothers with primary education were 30 percent more likely than mothers with no education to treat childhood diarrhea with oral rehydration therapy or a homemade solution of salt and sugar; this figure rose to 90 percent for mothers with secondary or higher education. Similar results have been reported in countries as diverse as Burundi, Colombia, Ghana, Morocco, and Nigeria. And well-educated mothers often manage to reduce the damage that poverty does to health. Among poor rural households in Côte d'Ivoire, for

example, 24 percent of the children of mothers with no education were stunted, compared with only 11 percent of children of mothers with some elementary schooling. Educated women are an important part of the reason for the impressive health achievements of China, Costa Rica, India's Kerala State, and Sri Lanka, despite relatively low incomes.

SCHOOLING AND ADULT HEALTH. Personal habits and life-style choices affect adult health enormously. Because educated people tend to make choices that are better for their health, there is often a strong relation between schooling and health. A study of U.S. life expectancy at age 25 found that between the highest and the lowest levels of education, the difference was about six years for white men and about five years for white women. These differences—which may partly reflect differences in income associated with education—have persisted since the 1960s.

The same pattern occurs in developing countries. Surveys in Côte d'Ivoire, Ghana, Pakistan,

Figure 2.5 Schooling and risk factors for adult health in Porto Alegre, Brazil, 1987

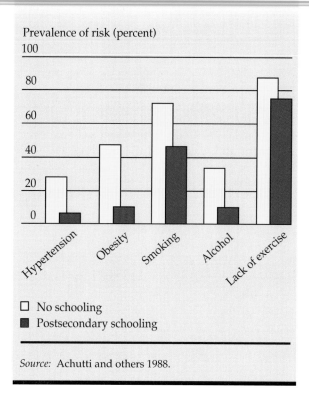

Prevalence of risk (percent)

- ☐ No schooling
- ■ Postsecondary schooling

Source: Achutti and others 1988.

ample, when the AIDS epidemic began, infection was initially concentrated among well-educated elites, but these same groups were the first to change their life-styles as information became available about the disease and its prevention. In Brazil between 1982 and 1985, 79 percent of those infected had completed postsecondary education; by the late 1980s this group's share of cases had fallen to 33 percent. Even more striking is the way that well-educated people have changed their behavior on smoking. In the United Kingdom the proportion of smokers among adults declined between 1958 and 1975 by 50 percent among the most educated but hardly changed among the least educated. In the United States between 1974 and 1987 the smoking habit declined nine times faster in the highest education group than in the lowest. The corresponding difference was twofold in Canada and threefold in Norway.

Policies to strengthen household capacity

Because people's ability to improve their own health depends so much on income and education, the policy conclusions are clear: governments should work to boost economic growth, reduce poverty, expand schooling (particularly for girls), and help strengthen women's ability to care for their families. This section deals with each of these points in turn.

Promoting growth and reducing poverty

During the 1980s the pattern of economic growth in developing countries was very uneven. Income per capita grew at more than 6 percent a year in East Asia but remained constant or fell in many other countries. The disappointing record reflected the impact of adverse external shocks as well as poor domestic policies. Nonetheless, some economies grew rapidly despite the external shocks, showing that a great deal can be done by developing countries themselves.

Because it is difficult to reduce poverty without economic growth, establishing sound economic policies for growth is one of the most valuable things a government can do. Development strategies also need to emphasize broadly based growth to give the poor better income-earning opportunities and better access to a range of social services. To protect the most vulnerable members of society, it is appropriate for governments to make transfers and other special arrangements.

and Peru show that respondents whose parents were educated were more likely to have living parents than those with uneducated parents. In Peru 72 percent of the educated fathers of respondents ages 25–29 were still alive at the time of the survey, compared with only 55 percent of the uneducated fathers. In Jamaica education had a bigger influence on adult health than did income, particularly before age 50. Death rates for specific diseases also show educational differentials. In Russia death from coronary heart disease was two to three times more common for the poorly educated than for those with higher education. In Brazil those who were illiterate or who had only primary schooling were about five times more likely to have high blood pressure than those with postsecondary schooling. The first group was also substantially more inclined to obesity, alcohol and tobacco consumption, and lack of exercise (Figure 2.5).

The advantages of education continue to show up when new types of health risk appear. For ex-

POLICY REFORM AND ADJUSTMENT LENDING. As a consequence of the economic crisis of the early 1980s, many developing countries changed their economic policies. They adopted macroeconomic reforms intended to achieve price stability and sustainable internal and external monetary balance and made microeconomic and institutional reforms to promote the efficient use of resources and faster economic growth. These changes typically involved cuts in public spending, the opening of the economy to competition, liberalization of prices, measures to improve the efficiency of public expenditure, and the development of a sound financial system and other institutions needed in a well-functioning market economy.

To support these reforms, the World Bank and the International Monetary Fund have extended adjustment lending. The purpose of this lending is to cushion an economy during the transitional phase to its new growth path. Adjustment lending is therefore essentially an investment in a more productive future. It has been central to the reforms in Latin America and Sub-Saharan Africa and important in other regions as well. Its role will continue in the 1990s: it is already a major channel of assistance for the formerly socialist economies; it is being used for the first time in India; and it has both old and new clients in other parts of the world.

Nonetheless, adjustment lending remains controversial. Does it really raise long-term growth? Do the poor suffer as a consequence of such adjustment policies as cuts in public spending and liberalization of food and other prices? How is health affected? The answers to these questions are complicated because adjustment lending is neither necessary nor sufficient for policy reform. Some of the most dramatic "adjustment" reforms took place without adjustment lending (as in Chile and Viet Nam), and some countries that received adjustment loans did little or nothing to pursue reforms (for example, Tanzania and Zambia). In addition, because a country's economic performance is affected by many factors, it is hard to isolate the part played by adjustment lending.

Despite these difficulties, World Bank studies on the impact of adjustment lending are revealing. The research looked at countries in the "intensive adjustment lending" group (which includes countries that received at least two structural adjustment loans or three sectoral adjustment loans by 1990, with the first loan started by mid-1986) and found that in general they did achieve faster growth than in other countries. All else being

equal, middle-income countries in the "intensive" group boosted their growth rates during 1986–90 by an estimated average of about 4 percentage points a year over what would probably otherwise have occurred. The low-income countries, especially in Sub-Saharan Africa, did less well; for them, the benefit was 2 percentage points.

Since health is helped by economic recovery and faster long-term growth, adjustment lending, by facilitating economic progress, benefits health in the long run. When a government has to adjust—in response to economic shocks or to rectify mistaken past policies—the whole society, poor and nonpoor, may suffer short-run reductions in employment and wages. But the resulting fall in income is caused not so much by policies associated with adjustment lending as by the necessity for the country to curb its consumption; without adjustment loans, even greater decreases in consumption would probably have been necessary. Nonetheless, adjustment lending can take five or more years to bear fruit, and the transition can be painful because incomes may fall in the short run. Evidence from Sub-Saharan Africa and Latin America suggests that economic downturns are associated with less favorable child mortality outcomes than would be predicted from long-term trends. In countries where child mortality rates are declining over time, for example, adjustment lending would be associated, in the short run, with a slower rate of decline. To minimize such adverse effects, some countries have begun to use resources, including adjustment loans, to support nutrition programs for vulnerable children, as well as basic health and other social services targeted to the poor.

ADJUSTMENT LENDING AND PUBLIC EXPENDITURE ON HEALTH. Because cuts in government spending are usually central to an adjustment program, health spending is likely to be reduced. In many countries early cuts were indiscriminate and failed to preserve those elements of the health system with the strongest long-term benefits for health. Drugs were often cut more heavily than personnel because it is difficult to lay off public employees. Côte d'Ivoire's experience illustrates the mistakes that occurred in some early programs of economic adjustment. With real income per capita falling 19 percent between 1980 and 1984, the government cut public spending, among other measures. Health expenditure dropped in real terms by 12 percent between 1981 and 1984. But personnel costs were not cut; instead public expenditures on medicines and materials absorbed the reduction,

Figure 2.6 Deviation from mean levels of public spending on health in countries receiving and not receiving adjustment lending, 1980–90

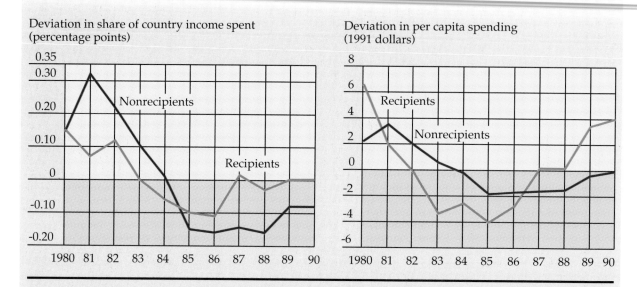

Deviation in share of country income spent
(percentage points)

Deviation in per capita spending
(1991 dollars)

Note: Recipients of adjustment lending include countries that received two structural adjustment loans or three or more adjustment operations, all effective by June 1990, with the first operation effective in or before June 1986. Data were available for the following countries in this group: Bolivia, Brazil, Chile, Costa Rica, Kenya, Republic of Korea, Mauritius, Mexico, Pakistan, Philippines, Turkey, and Uruguay. Nonrecipients are countries that had not received adjustment lending by June 1990. Data were available for Burkina Faso, Dominican Republic, Egypt, El Salvador, Guatemala, Liberia, Malaysia, and Papua New Guinea.
Source: Yazbeck, Tan, and Tanzi, background paper.

shrinking in real terms by more than one-third during the first half of the 1980s. In rural clinics, already precarious supplies of basic consumables became even scarcer.

The implications for child health looked grim. Cross-sectional data show that the nutritional status of Ivorian children is strongly related to the availability of drugs in the community. All else being the same, the difference in height-for-age (a measure of long-run nutritional status) of children in communities lacking basic medicines and those in well-supplied communities was equivalent to more than one-third of the difference between the average child in Côte d'Ivoire and in the United States. The health of children from poor families suffers even more when drugs are unavailable. Since 1990 the government has begun putting more resources into nonwage health inputs: their share of the health budget rose from 20 percent in 1991 to 24 percent in 1993. Health services, par-

ticularly in rural areas, have been improving as a result.

Various studies have assessed the effect of adjustment programs on public spending on health. Most have found that central government expenditure on health in countries with adjustment lending programs did not suffer more than elsewhere; this result, however, is not definitive because state and local governments are often responsible for a substantial share of public spending on health. More comprehensive data available for twenty countries during 1980–90 show that in both countries with and without adjustment loans, public spending on health as a percentage of total country income declined in the early 1980s in relation to the average for the decade. In 1985–90, however, health spending recovered much faster in countries with adjustment programs. Similarly, per capita public spending on health also recovered faster in such countries (Figure 2.6). Unfortunately, the data are not good enough to allow any judgment on whether adjustment programs directly helped to ensure that public spending on health was efficient. (And, as this Report will show, not all health spending deserves to be protected; some of it is inefficient and regressive.)

Expanding and improving schooling

In general, developing countries have made much progress in expanding schooling since the 1960s, but the trends conceal some shortcomings. In the poorest countries, especially in Africa, many children never go to school at all. In Mali, for example, fully 77 percent of all school-age children never go to school—a figure that has remained largely unchanged since 1980. Of those who do go to school, many often enroll late—thus missing the benefits of early learning opportunities—and leave before

they complete even the first few years of basic education. Fewer than 60 percent of first-graders in the lowest-income countries and about 70 percent of those in the lower-middle-income countries reach the last year of primary school.

Enrollments are particularly low in isolated rural areas, for lower socioeconomic groups, and for girls. In developing countries as a group, about 10 percent of boys ages 6–11 do not enroll; for girls in the same age group the figure is 40 percent. Especially in poor countries, the gaps can be substantial, as Figure 2.7 illustrates for India. But Sri Lanka's experience shows that this gender gap is not an inevitable consequence of poverty.

Leaving aside the gaps in enrollment, education in many countries is inadequate. Even children who complete primary school fail to acquire basic literacy and numeracy skills and scientific understanding. These weaknesses in the education system reduce the potential impact of schooling on

Substantial male-female gaps in schooling persist in some low-income countries.

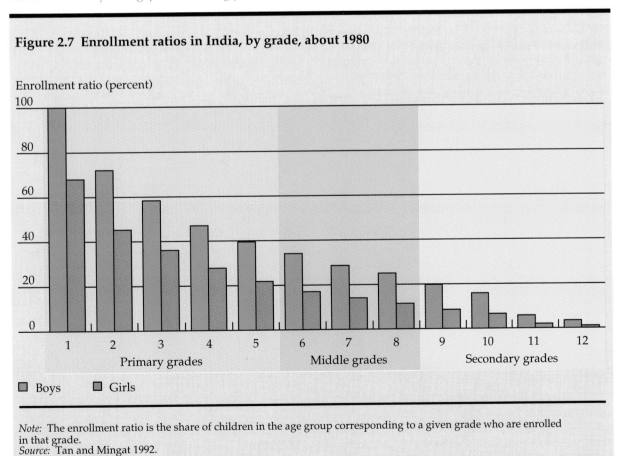

Figure 2.7 Enrollment ratios in India, by grade, about 1980

Note: The enrollment ratio is the share of children in the age group corresponding to a given grade who are enrolled in that grade.
Source: Tan and Mingat 1992.

health. More important, they also reduce parents' willingness to enroll their children, thus perpetuating a vicious cycle of poor schooling and poor health. In India, for example, more than 40 percent of parents in a nationwide survey cited either ''not interested in education/further study'' or ''failure'' as the main reason for not sending their children to school.

Much more needs to be done to extend education in developing countries. Government support for schooling at the lower levels and for girls is especially justified: the benefits for society are large, and poor families in low-income countries typically undervalue the benefits of sending children to school or are unaware of them. In addition, for such families the opportunity costs of sending children to school are often high. A policy priority is to ensure that every child receives a minimum quantity of schooling—say, 5,000 hours, or roughly six full years of schooling. This would be consistent with the aims of the 1990 World Conference on Education for All, sponsored by the United Nations Educational, Scientific, and Cultural Organization (UNESCO), UNICEF, the UNDP, and the World Bank. Most pupils in developing countries currently receive much less than 5,000 hours of schooling in the primary grades (because of pupil and teacher absences caused by sickness, among other factors). In India no more

than a third of girls reach this level, and in China and Latin America only 60 percent do. Achieving 5,000 hours of schooling for all children will thus require significant and sustained policy effort in large parts of the world. To reinforce the effects of school expansion on health, it may be useful to include health topics in school curricula (see Box 2.2).

Incomplete enrollments reflect the combined influence of weak demand for education (which is partly caused by low achievement) and inadequate schooling opportunities. To overcome these obstacles requires a combination of policies. Governments can do more to ensure that lower levels of schooling receive priority in the allocation of public spending. In some countries, current levels of resources for primary schooling are insufficient to support even minimal conditions for instruction. In India public spending per primary pupil in relation to income per capita averages only one-third that in Korea, basically because much more of India's public expenditure on education goes to higher education. In Burkina Faso, Mali, Mauritania, and Niger one-quarter of the education budget is for higher education, and between 60 and 80 percent of that quarter is devoted to scholarships and other forms of student aid. This, it can be argued, is inefficient, and it is also extremely regressive because most of the benefits of higher education are captured privately in the form of increased earnings and because students tend to come from higher-income families.

On its own, spending more resources for primary schools is not enough. Whatever is spent must also be used efficiently.

Although the health and nutrition of school-age children are not normally thought of as education issues, in fact they do affect a child's school attendance and performance. Allocating resources to address health problems in this population can often be an efficient way to improve schooling. (Specific interventions are discussed in Chapter 4.) Teachers and pedagogical materials are the main school inputs at lower levels of schooling (with teacher salaries absorbing the bulk of spending). Efficient use of these inputs is thus crucial, particularly in countries where rapid population growth threatens to reverse progress in expanding enrollments. In Mauritania, for example, if spending per pupil and the share of primary schooling in total government expenditure remain constant, the enrollment ratio in primary schools is projected to drop from 51 percent in 1988 to 45 percent by 2000. To forestall such regress, maximizing the learning gain per unit cost and making the correct tradeoffs between unit costs and coverage are of particular importance. A recent World Bank–sponsored review found expenditures on nonsalary inputs such as textbooks and interactive radio instruction to be most cost-effective in improving learning outcomes.

In some circumstances it may also be right to spend more to lower the barriers to schooling for girls and other disadvantaged groups. This can be done in many ways: through scholarships (used in Bangladesh to encourage girls to go to secondary school); by offering free textbooks or fee-exemptions; or by siting schools close to pupils' homes so that parents are less worried about their daughters' safety. In Pakistan, for example, girls are as likely to enroll as boys when there is a school in the village but are 10 percent less likely to do so when the school is nearby but not in the village. In several African countries distance education—whereby radio and correspondence materials replace classroom teachers as the principal medium of instruction—has sometimes helped to overcome the physical barriers to schooling for girls.

Empowering women

In addition to education, other policies can enhance women's capacity to improve their health and that of their families. Removing discrimination—in the labor market, in access to credit, in property law, and so on—can boost women's earnings and financial security, which (as an earlier section has shown) can promote family health. And women need to be healthy themselves to fulfil their roles as mothers and household managers. They have specific health needs, including protection against violence. More than one-third of the global burden of disease for women ages 15–44, and over one-fifth of that for women ages 45–59, is caused by conditions that afflict women exclusively (maternal mortality and morbidity and cervical cancer) or predominantly (anemia, sexually transmitted diseases, osteoarthritis, and breast cancer). Most of these problems can be addressed cost-effectively, but health services in many developing countries have typically focused narrowly on women as mothers.

What is lacking is a strategy for engaging women in health care from adolescence onward. Often this failing occurs because health services are insensitive to the cultural needs of women: in many Middle Eastern countries, for example, most physicians are men, but there is a strong belief that women should not be seen after puberty by men who are not part of their family. Inconvenience is another deterrent; in many countries individual health services (for example, prenatal care and immunizations) are offered on different days, meaning that women have to return repeatedly with their children. The solution is often as feasible as it is clear: to provide child health services, prenatal care, treatment of sexually transmitted diseases, and family planning services jointly at convenient times. The Bangladesh Women's Health Coalition and the Chilean Institute of Reproductive Medicine, for example, offer integrated family planning services at the same time as child health services, and Thailand is experimenting with mobile health clinics to reach women in their homes.

The design of health services must also be sensitive to the stigmas surrounding certain diseases, especially any that are sexually transmitted or physically disfiguring. Women are more likely to seek treatment for sexually transmitted diseases if health centers offer multiple services, with privacy in consultations, so that it is not obvious why a person is visiting the center. Diseases that damage the skin (such as leprosy, onchocerciasis, and leishmaniasis) have severe psychological implications for girls and women, reduce their marriage prospects, and may lead to marital separation. In Colombia and India women tend to seek treatment

Box 2.3 Violence against women as a health issue

Data from many industrial and developing countries reveal that anywhere between one-fifth and more than half of women surveyed say they have been beaten by their partners. Often, this abuse is systematic and devastating. In Papua New Guinea, for example, 18 percent of all urban wives surveyed had sought hospital treatment for injuries inflicted by their husbands. In the United States domestic violence is the leading cause of injury among women of reproductive age; between 22 and 35 percent of women who visit emergency rooms are there for that reason.

Research has shown that battered women run twice the risk of miscarriage and four times the risk of having a baby that is below average weight. In some places violence also accounts for a sizable portion of maternal deaths. In Matlab Thana, Bangladesh, for example, intentional injury during pregnancy—motivated by dowry disputes or shame over a rape or a pregnancy outside wedlock—caused 6 percent of all maternal deaths between 1976 and 1986. Research from the United States indicates that battered women are four to five times as likely to require psychiatric treatment as nonbattered women and are five times as likely to attempt suicide. They are also more prone to alcohol abuse, drug dependence, chronic pain, and depression.

Rape and sexual abuse also damage women's health and are widespread in all regions, classes, and cultures. In Seoul 17 percent of women report being victims of attempted or actual rape. In one study of U.S. women a history of rape or assault was a stronger predictor of how many times women sought medical help and of the severity of their health problems than was a woman's age or unhealthy habits (such as smoking). In addition to physical injury and emotional trauma, rape victims run the risk of becoming pregnant or contracting sexually transmitted diseases, including AIDS. A rape crisis center in Bangkok reports that 10 percent of its clients contract STDs as a result of rape and 15 to 18 percent become pregnant, a figure consistent with data from Korea and Mexico. In countries where abortion is restricted or illegal, rape victims often resort to unsafe abortions, greatly increasing the danger of infertility or even death.

Another form of violence against women and girls is female genital mutilation, popularly known as female circumcision. An estimated 85 million to 114 million women in the world today have experienced genital mutilation. The practice is reported in twenty-six African countries, among minorities in India, Malaysia, and Yemen, and among some immigrant populations in Western countries. If current trends continue, more than 2 million girls will be at risk of genital mutilation every year.

Clitoridectomies account for 80 to 85 percent of cases worldwide. Infibulation, which involves removal of more tissue, is more common in eastern Africa. These initiation rituals pose a health risk to girls and women and are a threat to their psychological, sexual, and reproductive well-being. The consequences of both procedures can include hemorrhage, tetanus, infection, urine retention, and shock. Infibulation carries the added risk of long-term complications because of the repeated cutting and stitching at marriage and with each childbirth, and it can limit a woman's choice of contraceptive method.

---

for leprosy later than men do, when patches have already reached the face and hands; they are reluctant to ask for help when the first patches appear, on the buttocks. Again, sensitivity is needed to encourage women to come forward.

The same is true of another category of danger to women's health: domestic violence and rape. Violence against women is widespread in all countries in which it has been studied (see Box 2.3). Although this has only recently been viewed as a public health issue, it is a significant cause of female morbidity and mortality, leading to psychological trauma and depression, injuries, sexually transmitted diseases, suicide, and murder. Rape and domestic violence cause a substantial and roughly comparable level of disease burden per capita to women in developing and industrial countries. These problems account for about 5 per-

cent of the total disease burden among women ages 15–44 in developing countries, where the burden from maternal and communicable causes still overwhelms that from other conditions. In industrial countries, where the total disease burden is much smaller, this share rises to 19 percent. By damaging a woman's physical, mental and emotional capacity to care for her family, domestic violence and rape also hurt the health of other family members, particularly young children.

This is an issue with complex economic, cultural, and legal roots, and it is therefore not easily dealt with by public policies. Prevention will require a coordinated response on many fronts. In the short to medium term, the right measures include training health workers to recognize abuse, expanding treatment and counseling services, and enacting and enforcing laws against battering and rape. In the long term, much depends on changing cultural beliefs and attitudes toward violence against women. In Africa women's groups have worked to break the practice of female circumcision, partly by informing people of its severe consequences for health. In the United States the American Medical Association launched a major campaign in 1991 to educate the public and physicians about family violence. Research shows that even health professionals often fail to identify cases of battering. Recently, the U.S. Joint Commission on Hospital Accreditation issued new standards requiring all hospitals to develop protocols and train their staffs to respond to different forms of abuse. In Colombia the Ministry of Health has begun to document the scale of the problem in its most recent Demographic and Health Survey. These efforts come on the heels of almost two decades of organizing efforts by women around the world; in Latin America alone there are now nearly 400 separate organizations working to reduce violence against women.

What can be done?

Around the world, much has already been done to enable people to live longer, healthier lives. The achievements of the past point to the requirements of the future—above all, to economic growth and the expansion of schooling and health services. According to World Bank projections, income per capita in Sub-Saharan African countries will grow by only 0.8 percent a year over the next ten years. Even this modest increase will bring about a decline in the infant mortality rate of between 2 and 4 percent. In South Asia, where faster growth—3.3 percent a year—is projected, infant mortality declines of 15 percent can be expected.

These benefits can be powerfully reinforced by better education and health services. In Africa increasing female literacy rates by 10 percent is likely to lower the infant mortality rate by an estimated 10 percent. In India and Kenya two maternal deaths and about forty-five infant deaths would be averted for every 1,000 girls provided with one extra year of primary schooling. Even in poor countries governments can enhance people's ability to improve their own health by expanding schooling opportunities for all children—with special efforts to encourage parents to enroll their daughters—and by widening access to health services, particularly for women and children. Such investments pay off in better health and provide a foundation for future economic growth.

3

The roles of the government and the market in health

World spending on health totaled about $1,700 billion in 1990, or 8 percent of global income. Of this, governments spent more than $1,000 billion, or nearly 60 percent. Of the $170 billion spent on health in the developing countries of Africa, Asia, and Latin America, governments spent half the total amount—2 percent of those regions' GNP. In the established market economies, where total health spending was almost $1,500 billion, governments spent just over $900 billion—more than 5 percent of GNP (Table 3.1). The sheer size of these expenditures on health makes it critical to understand the impact of government policies on people's health. But governments profoundly influence health in less direct ways, through their policies toward education, water supply, sanita-

tion, and other sectors important for health, as well as through regulation of health systems, health providers, and insurers. Governments further affect health by their impact on household income and educational levels (as discussed in Chapter 2), by financing public health services, and by providing care directly. What governments do varies enormously from country to country, but every government plays an important role.

Three economic rationales justify and guide a government role in health. They are discussed in greater detail in ''The rationales for government action,'' below.

• The poor cannot always afford health care that would improve their productivity and well-being. Publicly financed investment in the health

Table 3.1 Global health expenditure, 1990

Demographic region	Percentage of world population	Total health expenditure (billions of dollars)	Health expenditure as percentage of world total	Public sector health expenditure as percentage of regional total	Percentage of GNP spent on health	Per capita health expenditure (dollars)	Ratio of per capita spending (SSA = 1)
Established market economies	15	1,483	87	60	9.2	1,860	78.9
Formerly socialist economies of Europe	7	49	3	71	3.6	142	6.0
Latin America	8	47	3	60	4.0	105	4.5
Middle Eastern crescent	10	39	2	58	4.1	77	3.3
Other Asia and islands	13	42	2	39	4.5	61	2.6
India	16	18	1	22	6.0	21	0.9
China	22	13	1	59	3.5	11	0.5
Sub-Saharan Africa	10	12	1	55	4.5	24	1.0
Demographically developing countries	78	170	10	50	4.7	41	1.7
World	100	1,702	100	60	8.0	329	13.7

Note: SSA, Sub-Saharan Africa.
Source: Appendix table A.9.

of the poor can reduce poverty or alleviate its consequences.

• Some actions that promote health are pure public goods or create large positive externalities. Private markets would not produce them at all or would produce too little.

• Market failures in health care and health insurance mean that government intervention can raise welfare by improving how those markets function.

Any potential benefits from greater public sector involvement in health must be weighed against the risk that governments will in fact make matters worse. For example, to satisfy special interest groups, governments may adopt policies that reduce the general welfare. Even when they choose correct policies, they may fail to implement them properly.

Governments have a responsibility to spend well, to get "value for money," whenever they devote public resources to health. This means allocating resources so as to obtain the most improvement in health per public dollar, taking into account the private market's response to public sector spending. Because private health care markets can also fail to achieve value for money, government policy has a role in providing information and incentives to improve the allocation of resources by the private sector. In most of the world a great deal of additional health could be obtained from a relatively small number of cost-effective interventions that could be delivered at modest cost and with little need for high-level facilities or medical specialties.

Health expenditures and outcomes

Chapter 1 showed how greatly health status differs among populations. Life expectancy ranges from forty years or less in some countries of Sub-Saharan Africa to seventy-five or more in the established market economies. In Sub-Saharan Africa half of all deaths occur under age 5; in the established market economies half occur after age 74. Child mortality rates exceed 200 per 1,000 in several African countries but are below 20 in the richest countries. The burden of disease is five times higher, per capita, in the worst-off than in the healthiest regions.

Three factors help to explain these huge differences. The first is human behavior. Chapter 2 showed that both health and the capacity to improve health are related to income and education and to the changes in behavior that wealth and

education bring. The second factor is the amount and effectiveness of expenditure in the health system. The third factor is the range of diseases present, which is determined largely by climate and geography. Effective health policy takes account of different disease prevalences but is not simply determined by them.

Differences in health spending are an obvious starting point in the search for an explanation of differences in health. In 1990 total annual health spending ranged from less than $10 per person in several African and Asian countries to more than $2,700 in the United States. There was also considerable variation within regions. In Africa, Tanzania spent only $4 per capita for health in 1990, while Zimbabwe spent $42 per person. In Asia, Bangladesh spent $7 per person each year, as against $377 in Korea. Since the share of GNP devoted to health tends to rise with income, rich countries differ from poor ones even more in health expenditure than in income.

But health spending alone cannot explain all the variation in health among countries. Nor can income and education, or even spending, income, and schooling taken together. Figure 3.1 illustrates the discrepancies. The vertical axis shows how far life expectancy in a country differs from the value predicted on the basis of that country's income and average schooling. France, Haiti, Singapore, and Syria have almost exactly the life expectancy predicted. China, Costa Rica, Honduras, and Sri Lanka, in the top half of the figure, all achieve five years or more of life beyond what would be expected. Egypt, Ghana, Malawi, Uganda, the United States, and Zambia, in the bottom half of the figure, all have a life expectancy about five years lower than expected, given their levels of income and education.

The horizontal axis of Figure 3.1 shows how far total health spending differs from the value predicted by income and education. Egypt, Morocco, Paraguay, Singapore, and Syria, in the left half of the figure, spend relatively little. France, Haiti, India, Mozambique, and the United States, in the right half, spend more than expected.

At any level of income and education, higher health spending should yield better health, all else being equal. But there is no evidence of such a relation. Countries are scattered in all quadrants of the figure. The countries that appear in the upper-left quadrant obtain better health for less money. China, for instance, spends a full percentage point less of its GNP on health than other countries at the same stage of development but obtains nearly

Figure 3.1 Life expectancies and health expenditures in selected countries: deviations from estimates based on GDP and schooling

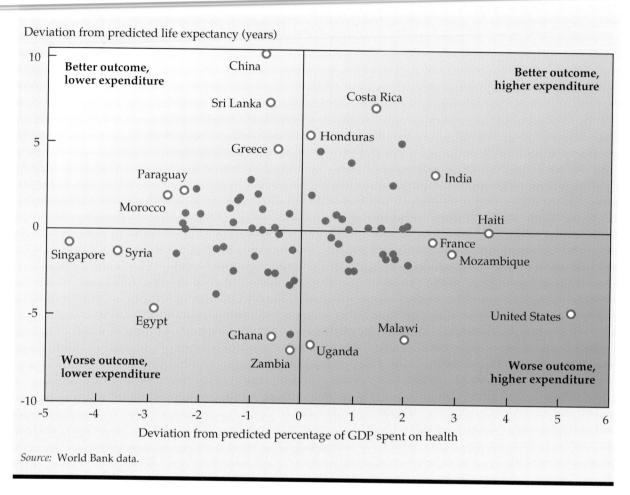

Source: World Bank data.

ten years of additional life expectancy. Singapore spends about 4 percent less of its income on health than others at the same level of development but achieves the same life expectancy. Other countries, of which Costa Rica and India are examples, obtain relatively good health results but also spend relatively more. (In the case of India health spending is low and health status is poor, but even lower spending and worse status would be expected for a country with such low levels of income and schooling.) Egypt and Zambia, by contrast, get poor health for a lower-than-predicted level of spending. Finally, it is possible both to spend more than predicted on health care and still achieve unexpectedly poor results. The United States is an extreme case, spending 5 percent more of GNP

than predicted to achieve several years less of life expectancy than would be typical for its high income and high educational level.

Analyses using other measures of health status, such as child mortality, yield similar results. This raises obvious and important questions. What accounts for these large deviations? How much is attributable to the characteristics of health systems? How can public policy help to provide better health outcomes for a given national effort?

The rationales for government action

Public policy in health is successful if it leads to increased welfare through better health *outcomes*, greater *equity*, more consumer *satisfaction*, or lower total *cost* than would occur in the absence of public action. Of course, the pursuit of one or more of these objectives does not by itself justify government intervention. There must be a basis for believing that the government can achieve a better outcome than private markets can. There are three broad reasons why that belief may be true: one centers on poverty and the equitable distribution of health care and the other two involve market failures.

Reduction or alleviation of poverty provides a straightforward rationale for public intervention in health. Success in reducing poverty requires two equally important strategies: promoting the use of the most important asset of the poor—their labor—and increasing their human capital through access to basic health care, education, and nutrition. As Chapter 1 showed, investment in the health of the poor raises their educability and productivity. It gives them both the assets they need to lift themselves from poverty and the immediate welfare gain of relief from physical suffering. Furthermore, in most societies providing health and education for the poor commands a degree of political assent that is altogether lacking for transfers of income or of assets such as land. Investing in the health of the poor is an economically efficient and politically acceptable strategy for reducing poverty and alleviating its consequences, as *World Development Report 1990* emphasized.

If "the poor" are all those living on less than $1 (in real purchasing power) per day, they can typically neither afford much health care nor borrow to pay for it. Simply transferring small amounts of income to poor people would create relatively little additional demand for health care. But because the poor are more sensitive to the price of medical care and also suffer a greater burden of disease than the nonpoor, access to free or low-cost care can produce large increases in their consumption of health care.

To ensure that subsidized health services actually reach the poor, however, may require restrictions, particularly on the kind of care that is paid for by the public sector. Offering free care of all kinds to everybody typically leads to rationing of services—geographically or according to quality. Such universal programs may not reach the poor or improve their health. They may, however, command more political support than targeting, and they more easily address the problems of insurance markets that are discussed below. Who should receive free care depends on the prevalence of poverty and on the country's capacity to finance care: spending more can translate into more services for the poorest or the same services for more people, including the less poor. In practice, very poor countries must target if they are to offer the poor any meaningful health care.

Public goods and externalities are forms of market failure that may justify government intervention. The key characteristic of public goods—which may be products or services—is that one individual can use them or benefit from them without limiting others' consumption or benefit. As long as somebody pays, everybody benefits—which makes it difficult or impossible to find anybody altruistic enough to pay. Many public health interventions, such as wide-area control of disease vectors and radio-based health information campaigns, are nearly pure public goods for which only the government can ensure provision. Another public good, new scientific information, has contributed enormously to the rapid improvements in health during this century. Its continued creation will depend at least in part on governments. The right choice of interventions and the proper level of provision of any public good require careful analysis of the health benefits in relation to the costs. Prices provide no indication of what benefits are worth because private markets do not supply public goods. Nonprofit nongovernmental organizations (NGOs) may supply such goods but cannot fully substitute for government action.

Externalities, or spillovers of benefits or losses from one individual to another, characterize cases in which a private market might function but would produce too much or too little. For example, curing an individual of tuberculosis also prevents transmission of the disease. But an individual's demand to be cured of tuberculosis (or of mild or asymptomatic sexually transmitted disease) is probably not affected by consideration of the risk to others. If the externality is not taken into account, treatment will be priced too high in private markets, and too little treatment will be given. Subsidies for treatment are therefore justified. An example of negative externalities is a person's use of antibiotics, which may, by increasing microbial resistance to a drug, reduce the drug's value to others and increase their risks.

Failures in markets for health care and health insurance provide a third rationale for government action to improve efficiency and, in the case of failures in the market for health insurance, to improve equity. One source of market failure, "adverse selection," arises because individuals face different risks. Customers who know themselves to be at high risk are motivated to buy more insurance and are more likely to use it. So it is in the insurer's interest to find out who the high-risk customers are and either to exclude them or to compensate for their greater risk by charging them higher premiums. (Higher prices for all customers would reduce demand by low-risk people and therefore push prices still higher.) Defensive efforts to obtain valuable information about risks add to the cost of insured health care without improving health outcomes.

Adverse selection presents a serious problem for risks existing at the time insurance is taken out, but an even more complex problem arises from the fact that an initially low-risk person may become high-risk later in life. In principle, there should be insurance available specifically against this likelihood of increased risk, or else insurance should cover a person's entire lifetime, with sharing of risks that may arise in the distant future, as well as of current ones. Neither solution is easy to implement because of the extreme uncertainty; insurance can cover known risks but not uncertainty about risks.

Another problem is the tendency of consumers to use more of a service when its marginal cost to them decreases. Insurance reduces or eliminates the marginal cost of health care to consumers. So, providing insurance does not simply shift the way a given amount of health care is paid for but increases the amount of care demanded.

Because the financial cost of disease is reduced, people may take less care of their health, leading to more illness and more subsequent demand for care. Or they may protect their health more by way of health care, paid for by insurance, and less through their own behavior. Passing costs on to others such as insurers because one does not bear the full consequences of one's actions is called "moral hazard." It arises because of uncertainty and because insurers cannot fully monitor consumers' behavior and make them responsible for their decisions. Moral hazard also results when providers induce demand for services that neither they nor consumers will pay for.

Both adverse selection and moral hazard have more pernicious effects in markets for health insurance than in markets for insurance on houses or cars. Risks to houses are higher in areas prone to earthquakes or hurricanes, but they are easy to determine, and insurers respond by charging higher premiums in those areas. Similarly, car insurance premiums are higher for young drivers and other identifiable groups at greater risk of vehicular accidents.

There is some moral hazard in the markets for house and vehicle insurance. The extreme form is when somebody burns down a house to collect the insurance or abandons a car and reports it as stolen. But unlike consumption of too much health care, these actions are crimes, with penalties that may greatly exceed the value of the asset. In any case, the insurer's potential liability is limited to the (easily determined) market value of the asset.

All the limitations on moral hazard and adverse selection are weaker in health insurance. It is harder to identify individual risks, and still harder to attribute them to behavioral choices. There is no market value for the human body and no possibility of abandoning one that is worn out and acquiring a new one. The lack of a natural limit on costs (since the asset being insured, the body, has no price with which costs can be compared) distinguishes health from other insurable risks.

The difficulties in insurance markets carry over directly into markets for health care. If people have "too much" health insurance, they will have an incentive to use "too much" health care at too high prices. Unfortunately the difficulty of judging health care risks and the impossibility of placing a value on a living body make it impossible to determine how much is "too much" in health care and health insurance. Nor is making a consumer pay more for health care a sure way of reducing only "unnecessary" demand.

Failures of information make matters even worse. A patient who knew the likely outcome and the cost to him or her of every possible treatment might yet be able to choose rationally between gains and costs. But patients do not have such knowledge, and the medical professional generally knows far more than the customer. This asymmetry of information means that the provider not only provides services but also decides what services should be provided. The result is a potential conflict of interest between what the provider stands to gain from selling more services and his or her duty to do what is best for the patient. The patient is at even more of a disadvantage when sick and unable to make decisions or when decisions must be made quickly because of threats to life.

The same potential for consumption of unnecessary services can arise any time a supplier is better informed than a customer. It is a notorious problem in car repair and home improvement services. But in these sectors the insurer has more opportunity to supervise the service provider, and the insurer may decide simply to replace the item rather than to repair it. Health insurers have no replacement option. They may try to review professionals' recommendations before agreeing to pay for services, but health professionals often disagree about expected medical outcomes, and waiting for a second opinion may cause pain, suffering, and increased risk for the patient.

These problems constitute the market failure peculiar to health: expenditure on medical care can be extremely high, yet not all justified care is provided and much care of doubtful value is paid for. Some people are denied insurance, while others may be overprotected. Those who do not pay the full costs of treatment may take poorer care of their own health than they could. Many of the extra costs are paid by society as a whole.

The market for health care goods and services can also fail through imperfect competition among providers, which allows excess profits, inefficient use of resources, poor quality, and too little production. Sometimes governments themselves artificially stifle competition. For example, governments may prohibit or interfere unduly with the operation of private health care providers, particularly NGOs. Governments often also protect domestic producers of drugs and vaccines. In Bangladesh tetanus vaccine produced domestically at government insistence had such low potency that its use in 1989–92 risked thousands of lives before it was replaced with imported vaccine.

Economies of scale in production—which occur when a single large producer is much more efficient than many small ones—also lead to noncompetitive situations. In many parts of the world hospitals and specialists face little or no competition because of economies resulting from large-scale operation. Such situations may call for regulation of the private market.

The three rationales for government intervention in the health sector—provision of public goods, reduction of poverty, and market failure—correspond roughly to three different kinds of services. First, the services classified as public goods, and some of those characterized by large externalities, constitute what is known as "public health." Public health includes those services provided to the population at large or to the environment, such as spraying to control malaria. It also typically includes some services such as immunizations that are not public goods but that carry substantial externalities.

Second, the inclusion of health care as part of a strategy for combating poverty justifies public financing of "essential" clinical or individual services. These are highly cost-effective services that would greatly improve the health of the poor.

Since poor people typically cannot buy such care for themselves, there is a straightforward case for public finance. Public health measures and essential clinical care together constitute a package of health care that might justifiably be financed by general revenues, with perhaps some contribution from user fees. This strategy is also compatible with the argument that basic health care is a fundamental right. Although most of the population may be able to pay for such care, the government has a responsibility to ensure that the poor, too, can exercise their right—at least to the extent that society can afford.

Third, the rationale that the government should intervene in health care markets because of significant market failures applies particularly to the regulation of health care and health insurance. The government cannot finance all medical care for which insurance might be desirable without worsening the tendency toward higher costs and risking de facto rationing of health care, which particularly hurts the poor. Beyond a well-defined package of essential services, therefore, the role of the government in clinical services should be limited to improving the capacity of insurance and health care markets to provide discretionary care—whether through private or through social insurance (earmarked taxes such as social security or other mandated arrangements). Of course, the range of services included in the nationally defined essential package will vary substantially from country to country. To provide equitable access for the poor, to address problems of adverse selection, and to contain costs, the governments of almost all OECD countries have made available a comprehensive essential package with public (or publicly mandated) financing. Poorer countries must, of necessity, define their essential packages more narrowly.

Governments can further improve how markets function by providing information about the cost, quality, and outcome of health care. Simply by defining an essential clinical package, the public sector provides valuable guidance on what is and what is not cost-effective. This distinction may then influence the design of private or social insurance packages and the behavior of individual providers or patients. Information on the relative cost-effectiveness of different discretionary procedures is similarly valuable and might be used by insurers and providers to reduce costs and attract clients.

Neither theory nor experience points to a general rule on the extent to which the public sector should provide health care directly, as distinct from financing it. Governments might have to

Box 3.1 Paying for tuberculosis control in China

Tuberculosis kills or debilitates more adults than any other single infectious agent. Without appropriate treatment, 60 percent of those with the full-blown disease will die. In China, it is estimated, more than 360,000 people—most of them poor peasants—die of tuberculosis every year. Tuberculosis is best prevented by curing infectious persons early in the course of disease, thus interrupting transmission to others. Well-run programs can cure 80 to 90 percent of patients; poorly administered programs cure 30 percent or less, leading to larger numbers of sustained cases of infection and related deaths and to new infections.

China made substantial progress against tuberculosis during the 1960s and 1970s, using standard long-term (twelve to eighteen months) antibiotic therapy that was essentially free of charge. Since the early 1980s, however, infection rates in about half the country's provinces have stagnated or increased, despite the adoption of an improved short-course (six to eight months) therapy. Much of the trend is attributable to changed health-financing policies and, in particular, to the government's decision that health facilities should be encouraged to charge patients for virtually all services. Starting in 1981, health institutions had to earn much of their operating costs from sales of drugs and services. Although base salaries were still funded from the public budget, workers' bonuses, housing, and retirement benefits depended in part on institutional income from service provision. Managers' investment budgets were also linked to revenues from fees. A few public health services such as immunizations remained partially subsidized, but tuberculosis diagnosis and treatment were not, despite drug costs of $30 to $80 per treatment.

Charging tuberculosis patients had perverse effects. When doctors and institutions expected to be reimbursed by insurance, they provided excessive diagnostic tests and examinations during treatment and dispensed higher-cost antibiotics that should have been reserved for the most resistant cases. Daunted by the costs, many low-income victims failed to enter treatment or dropped out early. There were no incentives to ensure that patients completed treatment or were cured. Because health system records showed very high rates of cure for those who completed treatment, the government remained largely unaware of the deteriorating situation. The direct cost to the health system of a poorly functioning program was nil, but the indirect costs to the economy—and the personal costs to patients and their families—were enormous.

An estimated 1 million to 1.5 million additional tuberculosis cases remained infectious during the 1980s because treatment was no longer free. Tens of millions of new infections were produced, and many of those infected will fall victim to the disease later in life. The development of drug-resistant strains was also accelerated. Given appropriate policies, many of the more than 3 million persons who died of tuberculosis in China during the decade could have been saved, and the risk of infection for society could have been halved.

China, having recognized the problems caused by charging for tuberculosis therapy, has begun a major national tuberculosis-control effort that provides subsidies for treatment and appropriate incentives for providers of care. Early results of this policy show dramatic increases in the number of cases cured.

---

supply a package of essential health services directly where private care would not be feasible without high subsidies—for example, in lightly populated, very poor areas. (In many parts of the developing world an alternative method of providing such services is to subsidize an NGO.) In most circumstances, however, the primary objective of public policy should be to promote competition among providers—including between the public and private sectors (when there are public providers), as well as among private providers, whether nonprofit or for-profit. Competition should increase consumer choice and satisfaction and drive down costs by increasing efficiency. Government supply in a competitive setting may improve quality or control costs, but noncompetitive public provision of health services is likely to be inefficient or of poor quality.

In some circumstances market failure may impose only slight welfare losses, and the benefit of correcting it may be outweighed by the costs of government action. In other cases the losses from failure to take account of positive externalities and supplier-induced demand can be enormous. Policy toward tuberculosis control in China provides an example: elimination of some free health care and introduction of profit incentives in the provision of health services dramatically reduced treatment rates, reversing progress against the disease and causing much needless suffering (Box 3.1).

Failures of government intervention can arise, however, even when government action might be sound policy.

• Governments may misjudge how an intervention will work in practice. Governments have only partial control over how private actors respond, and those responses can undermine the intended objective. Since 1971 physicians' fees in all provinces of Canada have been set by negotiation with provincial governments, and fees are no longer rising faster than the general price level. To protect their incomes, particularly during the inflationary period 1971–75, physicians carried out a greater number of procedures. This reaction was strongest where real fees fell the most. The saving in government expenditure was therefore much less than had been anticipated.

• Governments may not have the capacity to administer or implement policies well. Indeed, they may suffer from corruption and from sheer incompetence. The examples of two donor-financed public hospitals, each with 500 to 600 beds, in two Latin American countries illustrate the problem. One was simply too large to administer and operate and therefore could not be used at more than 60 percent of capacity. The other was so badly designed that it could not accommodate more than one-third the planned number of patients.

• Governments are vulnerable to special interests both within and outside the health system. By financing the training of unneeded physicians, by paying for low-value discretionary services for better-off patients, and by protecting domestic industries, governments help create the interests that later impede good policy, especially when quick responses are needed to meet changing circumstances or new opportunities. Even when society as a whole would gain, public action may fail because it does not overcome the resistance of those who would lose as a result.

Perhaps the most fundamental problem facing governments is simply how to make choices about health care. Too often, government policy has concentrated on providing as much health care as possible to as many people as possible, with too little attention to other issues. If governments are to finance a package of public health measures and clinical services, there must be a way to choose which services belong in the package and which will be left out. (The next section describes a measure of cost-effectiveness for health interventions that helps with this choice.) If financing is public but provision is private, governments must decide how to subsidize private care. The question of incentives to providers raised by that issue also applies to paying for publicly provided care—to the "internal market" in the public sector. And if governments are to influence the market for discretionary services, they must decide what instruments are most appropriate for affecting the behavior of insurers, providers, and patients. This raises the question of how far the government should itself act as an insurer, through social insurance, and how far it should regulate private insurers. Each of these decisions involves tradeoffs among the objectives of health policy: better health outcomes, lower costs, more equity, and greater consumer satisfaction with the health system as a whole and with individual care.

Value for money in health

No matter how health services are organized and paid for, what they actually provide are health *interventions*: specific activities meant to reduce disease risks, treat illness, or palliate the consequences of disease and disability. Debates about whether health services should concentrate on "vulnerable groups" such as children, pregnant women, or the elderly, or about the relative roles of hospitals versus health centers, or about preventive versus curative activities, are at bottom debates concerning the proper mixture of interventions. In health, as in every other sector, customers want value for the money spent on such interventions—whether they pay directly or indirectly, in their roles as taxpayers or as buyers of health insurance.

Knowing the cost-effectiveness of a health intervention—the net gain in health (compared with doing nothing) divided by the cost—can be extremely useful for both public and private decisions. Governments can generate such information, and they can use it in two ways. First, they can use it in determining whether a particular public sector intervention is cost-effective: this means judging the improvement in health compared with what would have happened through private decisions in the absence of public action. (Chapter 4 addresses these issues for public health measures and Chapter 5 for the public finance of essential clinical services.) Second, they can supply information about the outcomes and costs of different health interventions to consumers, providers, and insurers, and this knowledge can increase the value per health dollar spent in the private sector, including what is spent on discretionary services. Private providers have no more incentive than public providers to measure health outcomes, but they do face greater incentives to know their costs. Cost information alone can promote allocative efficiency, as the experience of a Brazilian nonprofit maternal and child hospital demonstrates (Box

Box 3.2 Cost information and management decisions in a Brazilian hospital

The Instituto Materno-Infantil de Pernambuco (IMIP) is a private, nonprofit hospital founded in 1960 to serve the metropolitan area of Recife. In 1992 it received the first UNICEF award to a "child-friendly" hospital in Brazil in recognition of its work, particularly in the promotion of breastfeeding. IMIP depends for 95 percent of its revenue on contracts from the Instituto Nacional de Assistência Médica e Previdência Social (INAMPS) of Brazil's Ministry of Health. Annual spending runs about $6 million.

Starting in 1989, IMIP organized an accounting system that divides services according to eleven cost centers for final output. Administrative, laundry, food, radiology, laboratory, transport, and other nonfinal services were assigned to these final outputs in proportion to their measured or estimated use.

IMIP must match its average costs to average revenues determined by the price schedule of INAMPS, which is organized by treatment groups rather than by individual services. Losses in any cost center must be offset by surpluses elsewhere. Gravely ill children are referred to the hospital from all over northeast Brazil, and there are three infant deaths per day among them. To reduce mortality, IMIP created a pediatric intensive care unit. The treatments provided, however, cost much more than INAMPS would pay. And mortality did not decline. Even without cost-effectiveness calcu-

lations, it was evident that closing the intensive care unit (except for newborns) and strengthening other services would save a greater number of children's lives. In particular, since the children who died in the hospital typically arrived very sick and often severely malnourished, it appeared more cost-effective to try to find high-risk children and treat them earlier. The strategy used was to expand the network of small community health posts in the slum neighborhoods of Recife. IMIP opened the first such posts in 1983; by 1986 infant mortality in those neighborhoods had fallen from 147 to 101 per 1,000 births.

The experience of IMIP illustrates three lessons about cost-effective delivery of essential care. One is that allocative efficiency can be improved without complete information: medical professionals know much about outcomes and often need only to know more about costs. A second lesson is that autonomy facilitates such changes: since private facilities generally have much more autonomy than public ones, this is an argument for more public finance of private provision or for decentralization of public systems. The third lesson is that even prices that are not based on cost-effectiveness criteria can guide decisions about what care to provide. It is more useful for government to set those prices correctly than to try to make all the allocative choices.

3.2). By estimating costs for "cost centers" and relating them to outputs, the hospital discovered that its pediatric intensive care unit would drain resources from other departments, given the prices the government paid for various services. The decision was made to limit the intensive care unit to newborns; community-level health posts appeared more cost-effective for other cases.

Measuring the cost-effectiveness of health interventions

Given a common currency for measuring cost and a unit for measuring health effects, different interventions can be compared by what it costs to achieve one additional year of healthy life. Outcomes are measured in the same unit of disability-adjusted life years (DALYs) used to estimate the burden of disease. Nonhealth burdens, such as income lost because of disease, are not included in the measure. The ratio of cost and effect, or the unit cost of a DALY, is called the cost-effectiveness of the intervention; the lower that number, the greater the value for money offered by the intervention. This approach avoids assigning a dollar

value to human life, as would be necessary if costs and gains were to be put in the same units.

Only in the past decade have costs and effectiveness been systematically estimated for a wide range of health care interventions—although the first such calculations had been made many years earlier. Only a small share of the thousands of known medical procedures has been analyzed, but the approximately fifty studied would be able to deal with more than half the world's disease burden. Just implementing the twenty most cost-effective interventions could eliminate more than 40 percent of the total burden and fully three-quarters of the health loss among children.

The cost and effectiveness estimates used in this Report are based, as far as possible, on actual conditions in developing countries. Some fixed costs of operating a health system that cannot be attributed to particular interventions are not considered, but the costs of intervention-specific capacity are taken into account. Costs are assessed at market prices. For inputs that cannot be traded internationally (such as semiskilled labor), costs will be lower in developing countries. For drugs, most equipment, and high-level manpower, costs are likely to be equal across countries, leaving aside the effects of tariffs or other barriers. Indirect costs, such as patients' costs of travel to treatment or the income they forgo, can be substantial for some interventions and perhaps particularly for women. Because these costs are difficult to determine, they were largely ignored; more study is needed of how these barriers affect the utilization of health services.

For some common health service packages such as immunizations, costs are computed on a joint basis rather than separately for each intervention in the package. The estimates do not represent an unattainable ideal; they assume that medically correct procedures are followed and that reasonable care is taken as to quality, but they also allow for incomplete coverage or compliance. Whenever possible, actual experience is used to guide estimates of such things as how many patients will fail to complete a course of treatment. Future gains from current interventions are discounted at 3 percent per year, which has little effect on the ranking of interventions the effects of which are felt quickly, although it does reduce measured gains from interventions when the health effects are felt only in the long run.

This Report found huge differences in both the cost and the effectiveness of various health interventions. Figure 3.2 presents both dollar costs and gains in DALYs for each of forty-seven different interventions. Higher points represent interventions that are more effective in improving health; points farther to the right represent lower-cost interventions. Some interventions cost more than $10,000 per person benefited, while others cost less than $1. Some interventions add more than ten years of healthy life; for others the gain is equivalent to only a few hours or days of full health. Both axes are scaled in logarithms so that the diagonal lines show equal cost-effectiveness ratios in dollars per DALY. These ratios vary widely, from as little as $1 to as much as $10,000. Higher lines represent more cost-effective interventions. Four specific interventions illustrate extreme combinations of cost and health gain: vitamin A supplementation in areas where the risk of blindness from vitamin deficiency is high (very low cost, high gain), chemotherapy for tuberculosis (high cost, very high gain), environmental control of dengue (low cost, low gain), and treatment of childhood leukemia (very high cost, moderately high gain).

Because interventions can differ so much in cost-effectiveness, making allocative decisions badly in either the public or the private sector costs lives. An expenditure of $100,000 on chemotherapy for tuberculosis could directly save about 500 patients. It would also prevent them from infecting others, for a total gain of about 35,000 DALYs. The same expenditure on management of diabetes would also benefit 500 patients but would save only 400 DALYs; each patient would gain less than one healthy year from a year of treatment, and there would be no benefit from reducing incidence. Insisting on value for money is not only fully consistent with compassion for the victims of disease, it is the only way to avert needless suffering.

The results of cost-effectiveness analysis confirm the value of the primary health care interventions included in programs to reduce childhood malnutrition and mortality, chiefly from infectious diseases. Several hitherto neglected interventions are also very cost-effective: chemotherapy against tuberculosis, integrated prenatal and delivery care, mass programs to deworm children, provision of condoms along with information and education to combat AIDS, and measures against smoking, such as education, consumer taxes on tobacco products (an effective deterrent for adolescents who are not yet addicted), and prohibition of smoking in public places. Many of the most cost-effective health interventions are preventive in character. But not all preventive measures are cost-effective: spraying to control the mosquitoes that carry dengue is an example of relatively poor value for money. At the same time, a small number of neglected but cost-effective clinical (mostly curative) interventions could eliminate a substantial fraction of the burden of disease in many countries.

In general, most cost-effective interventions can be performed outside hospitals. By treating a small number of severe cases of disease, however, hospitals can sometimes improve health at a lower cost per DALY than lower-level facilities—provided that clinics or health posts treat most cases and refer to hospitals only those requiring more sophisticated care.

Complications in the use of cost-effectiveness

Both the cost and the effectiveness of an intervention can be affected by the incidence and prevalence of the disease and the probability of dying from it. Preventive interventions are less cost-effective for relatively rare diseases because more people have to be reached to prevent one case. The fatality rate matters because preventing or controlling a disease saves more lives if there is a high

Figure 3.2 Benefits and costs of forty-seven health interventions

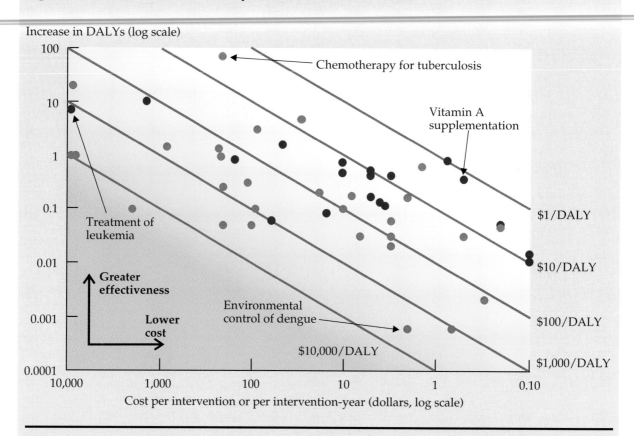

Increase in DALYs (log scale)

Cost per intervention or per intervention-year (dollars, log scale)

Target:
● Children under age 15
● Adults age 15 or older[a]

Note: DALY, disablility-adjusted life year. Interventions are specific activities intended to reduce disease risks, treat illness, or palliate the consequences of disease and disability; an intervention-year is an intervention repeated throughout the year rather than provided only once.
a. Includes some interventions that benefit all age groups.
Source: Jamison and others forthcoming; World Bank data.

probability of dying. Immunization in an environment in which children are undernourished and many die from preventable diseases is more cost-effective than if children are otherwise healthy and face little risk of dying. (Box 3.3, on measles and tuberculosis, illustrates these issues.) Fortunately, differences in cost-effectiveness between one intervention and another are often much larger than either the variation from one locale to another or the uncertainty in the estimates. Where this is not the case, as exemplified by malaria, detailed local

information is needed to judge which interventions should have priority. National or regional assessments are also important for estimating the expenditure levels required and the probable impact on the national burden of disease.

If providing an intervention did not impose any fixed costs in infrastructure and program administration, then a low cost per DALY saved would suffice to justify the intervention. In practice, there may be substantial fixed costs to share over a number of interventions, and administrative capacity

Box 3.3   Cost-effectiveness of interventions against measles and tuberculosis

The costs and effects of measles vaccination were estimated for a model urban area based on data from Lagos and Kinshasa. Data from Matlab, Bangladesh, were used to model measles in rural areas. In each area, 36,400 cases of measles were assumed to occur in the absence of vaccination, with 1,452 urban deaths and 806 rural deaths. All the health damage from measles comes from deaths, each of which costs thirty DALYs. The simulations considered three different strategies: no vaccination, immunization at nine months (the earliest age at which the standard vaccine is effective) with 60 percent coverage, and nine-month vaccination plus efforts to increase coverage to 80 percent, which raises supervision costs by 10 percent. For the last strategy, incremental as well as average costs were calculated to highlight the effect of raising coverage. Costs were related to each of three effects: cases averted, deaths averted, and DALYs gained. Box table 3.3 shows the results.

Measles strikes later in childhood in rural areas, so cases are easier to prevent. But because earlier cases (in urban areas) cause more deaths, the cost per death averted or per DALY is higher. In both urban and rural areas, the marginal cost of raising coverage exceeds the average cost of the lower-coverage strategy, but the higher-coverage approach continues to be extremely cost-effective. Similar calculations were made for chemotherapy for tuberculosis, for both a standard course of treatment (twelve to eighteen months) and a short course (six to eight months), each with and without hospitalization. Using data from Malawi, Mozambique, and Tanzania, the average incremental cost (marginal cost plus the average cost attributable to the fixed costs of the tuberculosis control program but excluding other fixed costs of the health system) was estimated at about $80 to $110 per cure for ambulatory treatment, and $160 to $300 when hospitalization was required. Cost per death directly averted was in the range of $75 to $275, but cost per total death averted, taking account of the interruption of transmission, can be as low as $20 and never exceeds $100. These very low costs translate into costs per DALY saved of about $1 to $3, making chemotherapy for tuberculosis one of the most cost-effective of all interventions. These costs do not vary with the annual rate of infection. The cost-effectiveness of BCG vaccine, by contrast, is extremely sensitive to infection rates; the vaccine is cost-effective only when the risk of infection is high.

Box table 3.3   Health costs and gains from measles immunization

Item	Urban, by percentage vaccinated		Rural, by percentage vaccinated	
	60	80	60	80
Cases prevented (thousands)	10.7	14.2	16.2	22.6
Total cost per case prevented (dollars)	17	18	11	12
Incremental cost (dollars)	—	22	—	15
Deaths averted (thousands)	0.4	0.6	0.4	0.5
Total cost per death averted (dollars)	432	462	525	561
Incremental cost (dollars)	—	552	—	670
DALYs gained (thousands)	12.3	16.4	10.2	13.5
Total cost per DALY (dollars)	15	16	18	19
Incremental cost (dollars)	—	19	—	23

Source: Foster, McFarland, and John forthcoming.

may be limited. Spending on interventions that are very cost-effective but resolve very small disease burdens could waste resources by making it difficult to deal with diseases that impose much larger burdens. Priority should go to those health problems that cause a large disease burden *and* for which cost-effective interventions are available (Box 3.4). If a particular health problem causes the loss of many healthy life years but there are no means—or only very costly means—for dealing with it, then it should be a priority not for health care but for research on development of cost-effective interventions.

Since only relative ranking is possible, the attractiveness of an intervention also varies according to what other health problems and treatments are locally prevalent. Oral rehydration therapy is an example: in environments in which child mortality is low, it is much less cost-effective than immunization because it may have to be given repeatedly during a child's first few years, but as mortality rises it becomes more cost-effective. In general, the cost-effectiveness ratio varies not only with local conditions but also with the degree to which an intervention penetrates or covers a population. Cost-effectiveness is also influenced by the presence of other interventions that might affect costs (through sharing of joint costs) or outcomes. Sometimes combining two interventions, one preventive and one curative, is the appropriate way to deal with a particular disease, as is the case for tuberculosis and malaria. Some treatment for malaria is necessary because preventive measures do not protect everyone; even if treatment is more costly, both interventions should be applied.

In exceptional circumstances it may be worth paying high marginal costs to extend coverage of an intervention to the entire population because the disease can be eradicated permanently (as has occurred with smallpox and may now be possible with polio). The gains in such cases include not only the DALYs saved at the margin from the last people immunized but all the healthy years that would otherwise be lost to the disease in the future. A similar argument holds if a low-cost intervention that has to be applied continually is replaced by one with large initial costs but permanent effects, such as sanitation to reduce the need for treating many fecally borne diseases.

An important limitation on the use of cost-effectiveness analysis of resource allocation in health is that a number of interventions with important health consequences also affect income or welfare in other ways. Chemotherapy for tuberculosis has no value beyond the DALY gain associated with curing tuberculosis, but investing in girls' schooling has both important consequences for health (as documented in Chapter 2) and for income and status later in life. Similarly, family planning, in addition to its health benefits, permits family choice about the number and spacing of children; improved water supply and sanitation create amenity and time-saving benefits; increased food consumption allows higher levels of physical activity; and improved road safety reduces property damage and saves lives. For some of these interventions (for example, family planning and girls' schooling) the cost per DALY is sufficiently low to make them attractive on health grounds alone; other benefits only strengthen the case. For other interventions the cost per DALY gained may be too high to justify investment on health grounds alone, but consumer willingness to pay for non-health benefits means that costs to the health system can be low. Many water and sanitation investments are in this category.

Using cost-effectiveness to select health interventions for public financing does not necessarily mean spending the most resources where the burden of disease is greatest. Instead, it means concentrating on the interventions that offer the greatest possible gain in health per public dollar spent. The relevant comparison is usually not with a situation in which nothing is done but with the situation created by privately financed health interventions. The most justified public measures will therefore combine a strong rationale for public action with a cost-effective health intervention. Because individuals differ in how they value the present in relation to the future and in how they judge the seriousness of different health conditions, a uniform ceiling on what the government pays to gain one DALY may leave some people with more publicly financed care than they would choose and some with less. But of all possible uniform criteria by which to judge what interventions to pay for, cost-effectiveness appears to yield the most efficient distribution of health resources.

Data limitations

Cost-effectiveness analysis requires data on expenditures for particular interventions and on outcomes—information that health facilities and systems, particularly those in the public sector, typically do not collect. Such information could promote substantial gains in efficiency, but it will take considerable time and effort for most public systems in developing countries to learn how to gather and use it. Budgets often disaggregate only by inputs, not by programs, and costs per consultation or per bed-day mix many different interventions. Outcomes are seldom quantified. For interventions the cost-effectiveness of which vary greatly with local conditions, there is no substitute for information on both costs and results.

Health policy and the performance of health systems

All governments subscribe to the view that the state must ensure the provision of certain basic public health services. But few achieve this goal—even for immunization, which is probably the health intervention that has received the greatest government attention and donor support and that

has the most easily measured output. Coverage in many regions remains incomplete. Immunization against measles and against diphtheria, pertussis, and tetanus has reached 90 percent or more in Chile, China, Cuba, Korea, and Saudi Arabia, but it is still below 50 percent in some Asian and many Sub-Saharan African countries. Many of the other components of an adequate public health package scarcely exist.

As far as clinical services are concerned, the principal government failing in most countries is the attempt to provide everything to everybody, with no distinction between more and less essential care and more or less needy patients. For some health services provided by the public sector, the system of provision is so grossly inefficient that it is unlikely to be cost-effective no matter what interventions the system tries to provide. Such inefficiencies have been criticized so clearly and for so long that it is evident they will only be overcome by radical changes in the organization of health care—such as a shift in the government's role from providing care to financing care and stimulating competition among providers. These changes will in turn require a clear distinction between essential and discretionary spending and a new determination by governments to achieve value for money in health services. There is no other equitable way to control government spending.

Most governments also perform poorly in regulating markets for private services, including insurance. As recent research in Brazil has shown, the quality of medical care could be substantially improved at low cost if government discharged this role better. The rapid growth and almost total lack of regulation of private insurance in such countries as Brazil and Korea present another challenge for which governments are ill-prepared.

Allocation of spending to cost-effective services

There are no calculations of how many years of healthy life are currently saved by health systems. Nonetheless, it is clear that many of them perform much worse than they might. Many governments spend too much on sophisticated hospital services of low cost-effectiveness and too little on essential public health and clinical services. The share of public expenditures for health absorbed by tertiary and secondary care hospitals, for example, is as high as 70 to 75 percent in Jordan and Venezuela. Tertiary care hospitals alone may consume 30 to 50 percent of the health budget. Only a quarter of government spending, and often less, is devoted

Table 3.2 Actual and proposed allocation of public expenditure on health in developing countries, 1990
(dollars per capita)

| Package component | Spending under the proposed package | | | Estimated actual spending, all developing countries | Contents |
	Low-income countries[a]	Middle-income countries[b]	All developing countries		
Public health	4	7	5	1	EPI Plus; school health programs; tobacco and alcohol control; health, nutrition, and family planning information; vector control; STD prevention; monitoring and surveillance
Essential clinical services (minimum package)	8	15	10	4–6	Tuberculosis treatment; management of the sick child; prenatal and delivery care; family planning; STD treatment; treatment of infection and minor trauma; assessment, advice, and pain alleviation
Total, public health and minimum essential clinical services	12	22	15	5–7	
Discretionary clinical services[c]	−6	40	6	13–15	All other health services, including low-cost-effectiveness treatment of cancer, cardiovascular disease, other chronic conditions, major trauma, and neurological and psychiatric disorders
Total	6	62	21	21	

Note: Current spending on essential clinical services is estimated to be 20–30 percent of total public expenditure on health on the basis of estimates in World Bank health sector reports. The numbers reported should be regarded as approximations.
a. Estimated for an income level of $350 per capita.
b. Estimated for an income level of $2,500 per capita.
c. Estimated residually. The negative number for low-income countries reflects total spending below the cost of the package.
Source: World Bank calculations; World Bank sector reports on Ghana (1989), India (1992), Indonesia (1991), Jamaica (1989), Jordan (1989), Mexico (1989), Nigeria (1991), Pakistan (1992), Turkey (1990), and Venezuela (1992).

to cost-effective public health measures and essential clinical care, delivered mainly in health centers and communities. In many countries the share of public spending devoted to these basic services has been falling in recent years. In Brazil 64 percent of public spending on health in 1965 was for preventive and public health activities, but by the mid-1980s the share had dropped to 15 percent, and hospitals absorbed fully 70 percent of expenditure. The resulting weakness of the primary care network leads patients to seek care in hospitals; up to 80 percent of the cases crowding hospital emergency rooms could be treated as effectively, but more cheaply, at the primary level.

In the world as a whole, almost half the existing disease burden is from communicable diseases, nutritional disorders, and maternal and perinatal causes. It is primarily these problems that an ap-

propriate package of cost-effective care would address. Even the best-designed care package could not prevent all the health damage from these diseases because of the low cost-effectiveness of some interventions and the increasing marginal costs of even the best ones. Still, because of the size of the burden and the low cost per DALY of the interventions, it is reasonable to conclude that public expenditure on health should initially be concentrated on those conditions. What this implies for the distribution of spending by type of input or level of facility is less clear, but it probably means that facilities above the district hospital level should account for only a small share of the total, primarily for dealing with referrals.

Table 3.2 illustrates the degree of misallocation of health spending by comparing estimated actual expenditure with what would be spent for a package of health services designed to address most effectively the burden of disease in the developing world. This package consists of public health services that would cost just over $4 per capita in poor countries (with average income per capita of $350) and a minimum package of essential clinical services that would cost about $8 per capita more. In middle-income countries (with average income per capita of $2,500), the same package of public health measures and essential clinical services would cost about 80 percent more, or $22 per person. This difference partly reflects different epidemiological conditions, but input costs, particularly salaries, would also be higher in middle-income countries. Many countries will define the essential clinical package much more broadly than the minimum discussed here. Even in relatively poor countries, targeting public finance of essential services to the poor would allow creation of a broader and more generous package. Such a package can be built up by adding interventions in order of decreasing cost-effectiveness until the additional health gain is judged not to be worth the cost, given the country's resources. To ensure political support and to deal with problems of market failure and equity, countries may choose to finance the essential package universally from public, or publicly mandated, sources.

Governments in developing countries spend an estimated $21 per capita on health, for a total of about $84 billion. It is estimated that only a little more than $1 per person, or a total of $5 billion, goes for cost-effective public health measures. To buy the package described here, countries would need almost to quintuple what they spend on public health. About $4 to $6 per capita, or $17 billion to $25 billion total, goes for clinical services delivered through lower-level facilities or classified as primary health care. These services commonly include many of those in the essential clinical care package, but they are usually not delivered to the entire population. And this expenditure includes some less cost-effective services that should be regarded as discretionary. Paying for a minimum package of essential clinical care would require expenditure of an additional $16 billion to $24 billion, doubling the current expenditure level. If total spending did not change, this would imply a reduction by about half in what is now spent on discretionary services.

For some countries, paying for the proposed package of services poses a severe challenge. In fact, in the poorest countries total current public spending of $6 per person is about $6 short of the cost of the package. Total per capita spending, including private spending, is about $14, about the same as the proposed package. This means that either substantial private resources will have to be used or additional government resources will be needed; even if all public expenditure on discretionary services were eliminated, current government spending on health would not meet the costs of the package.

Since the minimum package would cost only about $60 billion for all developing countries together, the task is to reallocate resources in middle-income countries and to find additional resources of about $10 billion in low-income countries. The $8 to $10 per capita needed in extra spending on public health measures and essential clinical services is less than the $13 to $15 per capita now spent, on average, on discretionary or nonessential clinical services. In fact, spending on these less cost-effective services is now roughly double the amount that countries spend on the recommended package of public health measures and essential clinical care. The right combination of reallocation and additional expenditure would allow governments to achieve a large improvement in overall health.

Table 3.3 indicates how large this gain could be. Properly allocated, an expenditure of only $12 per person in low-income countries (excluding China) would be enough to reduce the disease burden by almost one-third. This is 226 million DALYs, equivalent to 7.0 million infant deaths per year. In middle-income countries the proposed package could deal with only 15 percent of the disease burden, despite the higher expenditure per person. The total reduction in ill health in middle-income countries would be about 45 million DALYs, the equivalent of 1.4 million infant deaths per year. The smaller gain in these countries reflects the fact that they have already eliminated much of the burden from easily controlled communicable diseases. A large part of the remaining burden is caused by chronic disease and disability.

It is assumed that the disease burden would decline by the same share in China as in a middle-income country because China has already substantially reduced the burden from the diseases addressed by the package. About 30 million DALYs could be gained, the equivalent of 930,000 infant deaths prevented. The cost per capita would be the same as in low-income countries.

Full coverage with the minimum package would cost an estimated $22 billion in low-income countries, $14 billion in China, and $26 billion in middle-income countries. The total cost would be about $62 billion, or $15 per person in the develop-

Table 3.3 Total cost and potential health gains of a package of public health and essential clinical services, 1990

Country group and package component	Cost per capita (dollars)	Total cost (billions of dollars)	Reduction in disease burden Percent	Reduction in disease burden Millions of DALYs
Low-income countries[a]	12	22	32	226
Public health	4	8	8	57
Essential clinical services	8	14	24	170
China[b]	12	14	15	30
Public health	4	5	4	8
Essential clinical services	8	9	11	22
Middle-income countries[c]	22	26	15	45
Public health	7	8	4	12
Essential clinical services	15	18	11	33
All developing countries	15	62	25	301
Public health	5	21	6	77
Essential clinical services	10	41	19	225

a. Estimated from data for Bangladesh, Egypt, India, Indonesia, Pakistan, and Sub-Saharan Africa.
b. China is shown separately because its cost per capita is assumed to be that of a low-income country but its percentage reduction in disease burden is assumed to be that of a middle-income country.
c. Estimated from data for Latin America and the Caribbean, Other Asia and islands except for Indonesia and Bangladesh, and the Middle Eastern crescent except for Egypt and Pakistan.
Source: World Bank calculations.

ing world as a whole. This figure includes what countries are already spending on the services in the package, estimated at $20 billion to $30 billion. The incremental cost would therefore be only $30 billion to $40 billion a year.

The gain in health would be about 300 million DALYs, which is equivalent to 9.3 million infant deaths. Universal application of the package would therefore yield about the same health gain as eliminating nearly all the infant deaths in the world today. These gains could be achieved for an average cost of about $50 per DALY for the public health measures and about $100 per DALY for the minimum package of essential clinical services. The cost per DALY of the interventions in the package ranges from less than $5 to more than $200; average costs also reflect those public health measures that do not improve health directly but that are essential to the functioning of a health system.

In both low-income and middle-income countries the marginal cost per DALY would be less than the average cost because all the fixed costs of infrastructure are included in these estimates and there would be spare capacity for producing small additional amounts of most services. Because of joint costs, it is difficult to separate the cost per DALY for every intervention in the package.

In middle-income countries the package could be entirely financed by reallocating current public spending. In poor countries there would be a shortfall of about $10 billion a year, which could be

covered by a combination of greater public spending, increased donor contributions, and more private expenditure by those able to pay. Shifting some part of the cost to higher-income consumers—for example, through private or social insurance—would allow for an expansion of the package or a reduced burden of public expenditure.

There are several reasons why developing countries fail to allocate sufficient resources to cost-effective health interventions. Health providers often lack incentives to provide cost-effective services. Doctors' pay, promotion, and professional recognition are enhanced by specialization and by the use of expensive new medical technology—not by serving as public health doctors or district medical officers in poor rural areas. Badly designed government salary schedules and price systems may exacerbate this trend. In China hospitals currently have a strong incentive to use new diagnostic and therapeutic technologies, for which full costs can be charged, instead of older and less expensive technologies for which government-set prices are far below actual costs.

Consumer demand for cost-effective services is often weak. This may reflect lack of information. In rural Africa, for example, goiter and impaired mental abilities from iodine deficiency have in many places become accepted as the normal state of affairs. Low demand may also reflect deficiencies in supply. Most cost-effective interventions can be delivered at primary care sites, but in poor countries such as Burkina Faso and Mali, more than half of the population lives more than 10 kilometers from the nearest primary care center.

At a more fundamental level, the distribution of political power explains much of the misallocation of government resources for health. The urban population is better organized than rural groups and more vocal in demanding health facilities and services. Similarly, middle-class workers in wage employment, who frequently belong to powerful trade unions, are more effective than self-employed farmers and workers in the informal sector in lobbying for government-subsidized health benefits. Health professionals are also often better organized than the population they serve, and in promoting their own interests they may make the health system less efficient. Despite these problems, many countries have succeeded in dramatically improving the health of their people. This success can be accelerated, as newly available information makes it clear how costly misallocation is and how much health can be gained for relatively modest levels of spending.

Equity in health status, utilization, and finance

Data on health status, physical access to health services, consumption of health care, the distribution of the financial burden of health care spending, and public expenditures for health all tell the same story of severe inequities in developing countries. In Bangladesh, for example, the infant mortality rate for the urban poor (13.4 percent) is nearly twice the urban average (6.8 percent) and about 50 percent higher than the average rate for the entire country (10 percent). In China, despite remarkable overall progress in health (infant mortality fell from 20 percent in 1950 to 4.6 percent in 1982), there is considerable geographic variation, which is strongly related to income. Poor regions such as Yunnan, Xinjiang, and Tibet have infant mortality rates of more than 7 percent, compared with less than 2 percent in more affluent Beijing, Guangdong, Shanghai, and Tianjin. To take another example, in Kenya the probability of a child's dying before age 2 varied among ethnic groups from 7.4 to 19.7 percent, and in Cameroon these probabilities ranged from 11.6 to 20.5 percent.

The poor also have considerably worse access to health care. A number of surveys show that low-income households, especially in rural areas, have to travel considerably farther or longer to reach the first level of referral services, usually a primary health care center or doctor's office. In Indonesia in 1991, for example, rural households in the top income decile were three times more likely to live in a village with a health center than those in the bottom decile.

Partly because of difficulties in access, the poor in developing countries generally consume fewer health services. Household surveys from Sub-Saharan Africa and Latin America demonstrate clearly that among people who report themselves to be sick, those in urban areas seek and obtain medical care more often than those in rural areas, and the wealthy contact a care provider more often than do the poor. The differences can be large: in Côte d'Ivoire in the mid-1980s, for example, an urban household was nearly twice as likely to seek care as a rural household (60 versus 36 percent), and within the rural population a family in the top income quintile was almost twice as likely to seek care as a family in the bottom quintile (44 versus 23 percent).

A study of Peru showed similar inequalities among geographic regions and educational groups. There was little variation in self-declared illness, but the likelihood of obtaining medical care when sick was nearly three times higher in some parts of the country than in others. Regional differences in immunization rates were highest for uneducated mothers, whose children were only one-third as likely to be fully immunized as the children of women with secondary schooling. The 36 percent of all the self-declared sick who lived in the capital city accounted for 53 percent of all Ministry of Health ambulatory consultations, 41 percent of hospital admissions, and 47 percent of all public expenditure attributable to care for individual patients. At the other extreme was Piura, a poor mountainous region with 10 percent of the sick but only 4 percent of public spending and of consultations.

Inequity in public spending for health both accounts for and reflects marked inequalities in access to and utilization of care. In Indonesia, for example, despite significant investments in lower-level health facilities in the 1980s, only 12 percent of public spending for health in 1990 went for services consumed by the bottom 20 percent of households, while the top 20 percent obtained 29 percent of the government subsidy. This bias in favor of the wealthy was mainly a result of the distribution of government spending for hospital inpatient and ambulatory care, services that were used more frequently by the rich. Much more unequal situations can be found in many countries that concentrate government spending even more on high-level facilities.

The few countries in which public spending on health is biased toward the poor show that government policies can help reduce inequities in access and health status. In Malaysia the government has followed a pro-poor policy since the 1970s, with the lowest-income groups receiving a larger share of public subsidies for health than the middle class and the wealthy. Similarly, in Costa Rica government spending for health has continued to favor the poor, despite economic shocks and a major adjustment program in the 1980s that entailed cuts in public expenditure. In 1988 about 30 percent of government spending for health went to the poorest 20 percent of households and just over 10 percent of spending to the richest 20 percent. The poverty-oriented pattern of public spending for health in Costa Rica can be explained largely by the high degree of coverage by the social security health system (the entire population is covered in principle, even though only 63 percent of the working population contributes) and the relatively equal access to and quality of care enjoyed by all Costa Ricans. It also helps that the wealthy get most of their outpatient care from the private sector.

Consumer satisfaction with health care

How satisfied people are with their own health and their health care can be only partly explained by objective criteria; subjective expectations matter. People can also be pleased with their own health care and dissatisfied with their country's health system as a whole. A comparison of ten OECD countries with different health systems found that in eight countries public satisfaction was related to the level of spending. Canada, with the second-highest expenditure, had the highest satisfaction rating, and people were generally better satisfied with the costlier health systems of France, Germany, and the Netherlands than with the lower-spending systems in Australia, Italy, Japan, and the United Kingdom. Both very high expenditure and great dissatisfaction were found in the United States. The study also showed that having a unified national health system did not guarantee a high level of satisfaction. In most countries 30 to 50 percent of those polled supported "fundamental changes" in the health system. In Italy and the United States many people thought that such changes would not suffice and that the health system should be "completely rebuilt."

Household surveys systematically show that people choose whether to seek care and which provider to consult on the basis of many factors—hours of service, travel time or cost, waiting time, availability of doctors or of drugs, and how patients are personally treated. The time required to get care can be valued according to local wages and treated as a cost of service together with money payments. On this basis, free public medical care often is more costly than unsubsidized private care for which patients do not have to travel so far or wait so long. It is not surprising that, under these circumstances, even poor people express their dissatisfaction with public services by paying for a great deal of private outpatient care. In both El Salvador and the Dominican Republic residents of the poorest quintile of the capital city obtain more than half their ambulatory care from private physicians. Although the price of private care to the poorest quintile is, on average, half that for patients in the richest quintile, it is still fifteen times higher than Ministry of Health fees. Differences in waiting time—one hour for private patients as against two and a half hours at Ministry of Health facilities—account for much of this effect.

Sensitivity to price and travel time is also found in rural Peru and Côte d'Ivoire. But private hospital care is still much too expensive for the poor; even those who use private doctors go to public hospitals. The excessive use of hospital care in relation to ambulatory services often seen in public health systems partly reflects dissatisfaction with the high cost in time and the perceived poor quality of ambulatory care. In the absence of incentives to improve lower-level facilities and service, this overuse reinforces the tendency to concentrate resources on hospitals, urban areas, and less cost-effective interventions.

The importance of public satisfaction with a health care system raises two issues for the package of publicly financed services proposed here. First, it suggests that quality can be maintained only if coverage is broad enough. Services designed only for the poor will almost inevitably be low in quality and will not receive the political support necessary for adequate provision. This is a difficult political issue because it may be hard to maintain equity and control costs if coverage is universal. The proper balance between more care for fewer people and the same amount of care for more people depends on ensuring that the poor have access to the same quality of care as everyone else and on limiting public finance to cost-effective services for which there is a sound rationale. Second, reform of public provision alone, important as it may be, may have much less effect on health outcomes, costs, and satisfaction than reforms that also try to stimulate competition and improve people's access to a variety of providers.

Matching means and ends

The objectives of a health system are to improve outcomes, control costs, increase equity, and satisfy users. Policy instruments, however, do not correspond to individual objectives. What governments actually do is build facilities, buy equipment and supplies, hire and train people, set fees or other service conditions, regulate providers and insurers, disseminate information, determine overall policy, and maintain surveillance of disease conditions or other variables. Misallocation and inequity are caused by mistakes in deciding what facilities to build, where to locate them, how to staff them, and what services to provide. If governments spend too much on tertiary care, for example, not only can they not adequately finance more cost-effective care, but they also cannot provide equitably what care they do offer because facilities will inevitably be geographically concentrated.

One of the principal responsibilities of government is to match the available instruments of policy—the levers the public sector actually controls—to the objectives. Much of governments' failure to achieve better health outcomes derives not from the wrong choice of objectives but from the wrong choice of instruments—in particular, from too much reliance on direct provision of care and central control of health facilities and too little use of the financial, informational, and regulatory instruments at the disposal of the government. These instruments are particularly important for improving performance in the private market. When governments pay for health care in addition to regulating it, they have a further responsibility to provide value for money by ensuring that public resources go first to cost-effective public health and essential clinical services so as to buy the largest health gain possible.

Public health

Health services interact with households in two fundamentally different ways. *Public health programs* strike against health problems of entire populations or population subgroups. Their objective is to prevent disease or injury and to provide information on self-cure and on the importance of seeking care. *Clinical services* respond to demand from individuals. They generally seek to cure or to ease the pain of those already sick. This chapter discusses public health; Chapter 5 turns to clinical services.

Public health programs work in three ways: they deliver specific *health services to populations* (for example, immunizations), they promote healthy *behavior,* and they promote healthy *environments.* Governments play a leading role, and provision of information through public education is a central feature of most programs, especially those designed to change behavior. But difficult choices have to be made about the best use of public money. The Expanded Programme on Immunization (EPI), described below, is highly cost-effective, at about $25 per DALY gained, but not all programs offer such good value for money. This chapter examines six particularly cost-effective public health services in the realms of population-based services (including immunization), nutrition, fertility, tobacco and other drugs, the household and external environment (including control of insect vectors of disease), and AIDS. Public health packages in developing countries should include components in most or all of these six areas.

Population-based health services

In 1979 the World Health Organization declared that smallpox had been eradicated. It then initi-

ated, in collaboration with UNICEF, a global effort to prevent a range of childhood diseases by immunization. The EPI now reaches about 80 percent of children in developing countries and averts an estimated 3.2 million deaths a year at a cost of $1.4 billion a year.

Population-based health services such as the EPI rely on personnel with limited training to provide drugs, vaccines, or specific health services directly to specific populations—in schools, at worksites, or in households. Government finance for such programs is justified because the objective is usually to provide services to all in a community, because the services create externalities or indirect benefits, and because the diseases they typically combat are particular problems for the poor. Three types of interventions are immunization, mass treatment for worms and other infections, and screening and referral. Information, education, and communication are critical to many such programs, both to attract participation and to achieve durable change in behavior.

Immunization

Vaccines to prevent tuberculosis, measles, diphtheria, pertussis, tetanus, and polio have revolutionized preventive medicine over the past two decades. Costs are less than $10 per DALY gained for measles immunization and less than $25 for a combination of polio plus DPT (diphtheria, pertussis, and tetanus). These vaccines, together with BCG immunization against tuberculosis and leprosy and immunization of pregnant women against tetanus, form the EPI.

As a result of the EPI, the proportion of children immunized rose from less than 5 percent in 1977 to

20 to 30 percent by 1983. By 1990 coverage with polio, DPT, and measles vaccines had reached approximately 80 percent of all children, and about 35 percent of pregnant women were receiving tetanus toxoid. The lowest vaccine coverage is reported in Sub-Saharan Africa.

Had vaccination coverage remained at the low levels of the 1970s, as many as 120 million DALYs a year (the equivalent of 23 percent of the global burden of disease among children under age 5 in 1990) would be lost to diseases preventable by the EPI. At current levels of vaccination coverage, these diseases cause a loss of 55 million DALYs, or 10 percent of the disease burden among children under age 5 (Table 4.1).

The cost of fully immunizing a child in low-income countries is about $15, with a range of $6 to more than $20, depending on the prices of labor and other local inputs. Reducing the number of contacts needed to immunize each child fully could cut costs dramatically, by as much as 70 percent if only one contact instead of the current five were needed. This prospect depends on the success of ongoing research efforts. Technical improvements in the cold chain (by which vaccines are kept refrigerated until use), good administration, widespread deployment of delivery teams, and effective social mobilization efforts can also contribute to dramatic cost reductions. In the Gambia the cost of immunizations fell from $19 in 1982 to $6 in 1988. Costs also depend on the immunization strategy: campaigns achieve high initial coverage, but routine services are more cost-effective. In Ecuador campaigns cost $66 per DALY gained compared with $30 for routine services. Because many countries lack the infrastructure to deliver vaccines routinely in remote rural areas, campaigns continue to be justified. In areas with better infrastructure, routine services make more sense.

An ambitious current goal, established in 1988 by WHO's governing body, the World Health Assembly, is to eradicate polio by 2000. Current trends suggest that even if eradication is not achieved on that schedule, it will be soon thereafter. And substantial success has already been achieved: there has been no naturally occurring case of polio in the Western Hemisphere since August 1991.

Two extensions to the EPI appear to be justified. First, coverage should be extended, probably to 95 percent of all children born. The costs of expanding coverage are relatively high, but so are the gains. Those not covered at present often lack any health services and are disproportionately vulnerable to the diseases. Second, it makes sense to include additional items in the package: hepatitis B and yellow fever vaccines for selected countries and vitamin A and iodine supplements in regions where deficiency of these micronutrients is highly prevalent. If micronutrients are not delivered through the EPI, some other vehicle must be found for reaching very young children. Adding these two vaccines and two micronutrients to the EPI (EPI Plus) would improve health substantially, particularly in the poorest households, for a modest increase of about 15 percent in the cost of reaching each child with complete services (vaccine and micronutrients). Table 4.2 summarizes the estimated costs and health benefits of the EPI Plus cluster in two different settings. Total annual costs range between $2.2 billion and $2.4 billion for EPI Plus, or less than 2 percent of the public health expenditure of developing countries. Expanding coverage from 80 to 95 percent would probably

Table 4.1 Burden of childhood diseases preventable by the Expanded Programme on Immunization (EPI) by demographic region, 1990

Region	Burden (millions of DALYs per year)	Share of the total burden in children under age 5 (percent)	Burden per 1,000 children under age 5 (DALYs)
Sub-Saharan Africa	23	15	242
India	16	12	137
China	1	3	8
Other Asia and islands	7	10	81
Latin America and the Caribbean	1	3	18
Middle Eastern crescent	7	10	86
Formerly socialist economies of Europe	*	*	1
Established market economies	*	*	1
World	55	10	87

* Less than 1.
Note: The EPI includes immunizations for pertussis, polio, diphtheria, measles, tetanus, and tuberculosis. These estimates exclude the burden from tuberculosis because most of it falls on adults.
Source: Calculated from Murray and Lopez, background paper.

Table 4.2 Costs and health benefits of the EPI Plus cluster in two developing country settings, 1990

Costs and benefits	Low-income countries (high mortality and fertility)	Middle-income countries (low mortality and medium fertility)
Cost per capita (dollars)	0.5	0.8
Cost per fully immunized child (dollars)	14.6	28.6
Cost per DALY gained (dollars)	12–17	25–30
Cost per DALY gained as a percentage of income per capita[a]	0.14	0.03
Potential health gains as a percentage of the global burden of disease	6.0	1.0

Note: Figures are based on 95 percent coverage.
a. Income per capita in 1990 was assumed to be $350 for low-income countries and $2,500 for middle-income countries.
Source: World Bank data and authors' calculations.

increase annual costs by between $500 million and $750 million. In low-income countries the increase in coverage would reduce by about 6 percent the global disease burden.

Mass treatment for parasitic worm infection

The most common intestinal worms—roundworms, hookworms, and whipworms—each infect between 170 million and 400 million school-age children annually. Schistosomiasis infection, also caused by parasitic worms, affects almost 100 million school-age children annually. The immediate effects of infection—including failure to thrive, anemia, and impaired cognition—can now be rapidly reversed by low-cost, single-dose oral therapy. Studies of single-course treatment of schoolchildren with hookworm or schistosomiasis in Kenya, with worm-induced disease in India, and with trichuriasis in the West Indies showed remarkable spurts in growth and development in all the populations studied, including the large percentages of children with asymptomatic infections. And treatment also appears to have improved cognitive development.

Curing worm infections is simple with inexpensive modern drugs such as albendazole and praziquantel because it is not necessary to determine which species are present. Furthermore, the high level of safety of these drugs has led WHO to develop protocols for their use on a mass basis (where a high prevalence of infection exists) and by providers who are not medically trained—a combination that makes for high cost-effectiveness. Treatment usually cures the current infection, but in endemic areas children will inevitably become reinfected. A return to pretreatment levels of infection typically takes about twelve months for roundworm and whipworm and twenty-four months or more for hookworm. Rates of reinfec-

tion can be reduced by environmental improvements, especially sanitation, but where this is impractical or unaffordable, it is cost-effective to repeat the therapy at regular intervals.

The benefits of individual treatment can be significantly enhanced by community-wide treatment which, by lowering the overall levels of contamination of the environment with infective stages of the worms, slows the rate of reinfection. Treatment programs targeted at the most heavily infected group (school-age children) reduce infection immediately both among those treated and in the rest of the population. Treatment through schools also allows delivery at relatively low cost: a program in Montserrat was estimated to cost less than $1.50 per person for a cycle of eight treatments. A program managed by a nongovernmental organization in Jakarta initially cost $0.74 per capita per year, but after expansion to almost 1,000 schools the costs fell to $0.26. Such programs are extremely cost-effective, at $15 to $30 per DALY gained. In light of this cost-effectiveness and the burden of disease addressed, the Rockefeller Foundation and the UNDP are initiating a major program to document and explore the potential of school-based health interventions that focus on deworming and provision of micronutrient supplements.

Mass screening and referral

Mass screening for disease control involves the examination of asymptomatic individuals to identify and treat those affected by disease. Although this method has been used to control some infectious diseases, such as tuberculosis, it is mostly used for noncommunicable diseases. Mass screening makes sense for highly prevalent diseases that can be cured by early treatment, especially when latency periods span many years. An example is cervical cancer, which is the leading cause of death from cancer among women in developing countries, accounting for 150,000 deaths each year. Screening with Papanicolaou (Pap) smears is common in industrial countries, but attempts to replicate those efforts in developing countries have rarely been successful. Such programs could, however, be made cost-effective by the use of a simplified design that targets women over 35, screens only every five to ten years, and uses inexpensive outpatient treatment (such as freezing abnormal cells) for severe precancerous conditions. When backed up with good follow-up services, such interventions are cost-effective, at $150 to $200 per DALY gained.

Diet and nutrition

Eating well is necessary for good health. Either directly or in association with infectious diseases, inadequate diets account for a large share of the world's disease burden, including as much as a quarter of that among children. Much of this suffering stems from poverty-related underconsumption of protein and energy, but equally important are deficiencies of key micronutrients—iodine, vitamin A, and iron—from which children and women suffer disproportionately. Increasing the incomes of the poor is the most effective means of reducing protein-energy malnutrition, but governments can play an effective direct role through nutrition education, measures to increase consumption of micronutrients, and reduction in diarrheal and parasitic infections among children. Public action is also essential for preventing crop failures from leading to famines.

Malnutrition and ill health

Low height for a given age, or stunting, is the most prevalent symptom of protein-energy malnutrition; approximately 40 percent of all two-year-olds in developing countries are short for their age (see Appendix table A.6). The prevalence of stunting may be as high as 65 percent in India; it is more than 50 percent in Asia other than India and China and about 40 percent in China and Sub-Saharan Africa. Stunted children are often also underweight or have low weight for their age. Wasting (low weight for a given height) is less prevalent—11 percent or less worldwide except in India, where it reaches 27 percent.

Diets must contain both energy and protein. Because little is known about the relative importance of adding energy or protein to an initially poor diet, the effect of deficiencies in either or both components is combined under the term "protein-energy malnutrition." Foods rich in protein, such as soybeans and animal products, tend to be relatively costly per unit of energy, and low-cost sources of energy such as cassava tend to be expensive per unit of protein. Because food takes up much of a poor household's budget, choosing the protein-energy balance that is right for health can be difficult.

Protein-energy malnutrition raises the risk of death and may reduce physical and mental capacity. Worldwide, about 780 million people are estimated to be energy deficient according to WHO standards. It is not known how many of them are also protein deficient, or how many people who get enough energy may still suffer from shortage of protein. Exploratory studies of the determinants of human growth suggest that at the margin, the importance of additional protein may be greater than is recognized. Malnutrition is not synonymous with hunger because people who have become accustomed to a deficient diet may not consider themselves hungry. If malnutrition is widespread in the community, underweight and lethargic children look normal to parents who do not know how healthy children behave.

Iron deficiency is the most common micronutrient disorder. It reduces physical productivity and children's capacity to learn in school. By reducing appetite, it may diminish children's intake and growth. Women suffer especially because menstruation and childbearing raise their need for iron, and anemia, a shortage of iron in the blood, increases the risk of death from hemorrhage in childbirth. The problem is worst in India, where 88 percent of pregnant women are anemic. Almost 60 percent of women are anemic in other parts of Asia, but the proportion does not exceed 40 percent in China, Africa, or Latin America. Anemia affects 15 percent of pregnant women in the established market economies.

Iodine deficiency causes mental retardation, delayed motor development, and stunting, as well as neuromuscular, speech, and hearing disorders. It is the leading preventable cause of intellectual impairment in the world. Cretinism from iodine deficiency affects about 5.7 million people, and lack of iodine causes another 20 million to be mentally retarded.

Vitamin A deficiency causes varying degrees of vision loss and is the primary cause of acquired blindness in children. It also increases the severity

Table 4.3 Direct and indirect contributions of malnutrition to the global burden of disease, 1990

(millions of DALYs, except as specified)

Type of malnutrition	Sub-Saharan Africa	India	China	Other Asia and islands	Latin America and the Caribbean	Middle Eastern crescent	Formerly socialist economies	Established market economies	World
Direct effects									
Protein-energy malnutrition	2.2	5.6	1.7	0.9	1.0	1.0	0.2	0.2	12.7
Vitamin A deficiency	2.2	4.1	1.0	2.5	1.4	0.5	0.0	0.0	11.8
Iodine deficiency	1.7	1.4	1.0	1.3	0.5	1.4	0.0	0.0	7.2
Anemia	1.0	4.5	2.7	2.3	1.0	1.5	0.4	0.6	14.0
Total direct	7.0	15.5	6.3	7.0	3.9	4.5	0.6	0.9	45.7
Total DALYs per 1,000 population	13.8	18.3	5.6	10.3	8.9	8.9	1.7	1.1	8.7
Indirect effects (minimum estimate)									
Mortality from other diseases attributed to mild or moderate underweight[a]	23.6	14.9	3.3	8.0	2.4	8.0	0.0	0.0	60.4
Mortality from other diseases attributed to vitamin A deficiency[b]	13.4	14.0	1.0	7.0	1.8	2.0	0.0	0.0	39.1

a. Based on the global burden of disease (GBD) attributable to deaths from tuberculosis, measles, pertussis, malaria, and diarrheal and respiratory diseases in children under age 5; in developing countries 25 percent of those deaths are attributed to mild or moderate underweight.
b. Based on estimated deaths attributable to vitamin A deficiency in the age groups 6–11 months and 1–4 years. These account for, respectively, 10 and 30 percent of all such deaths in high-risk countries and for 3 and 10 percent of all such deaths in other countries. Thirty lost DALYs are attributed to each child death; losses are redistributed to the regional classification used in this Report.
Source: For GBD calculations, Appendix B; for estimate of mortality from underweight, Pelletier 1991; for estimate of mortality from vitamin A deficiency, Humphrey, West, and Sommer 1992.

Box 4.1 Women's nutrition

Women suffer more than men from iron deficiency anemia, from stunting caused by protein-energy malnutrition, and from iodine deficiency. The largest gap is for iron deficiency anemia, which affects 458 million adult women but 238 million men. About 450 million women are stunted because of protein-energy malnutrition, compared with 400 million men. Iodine deficiency also affects substantial numbers of women, probably more than for men. Corneal lesions and blindness caused by vitamin A deficiency afflict both sexes equally, but deficiency as such is twice as common for girls as for boys. Women's nutritional problems are worst in South Asia, where prevalences of anemia, protein-energy malnutrition, and vitamin A deficiency are the highest in the world and where, as a result of widespread discrimination, girls and women suffer disproportionately.

Small pelvic size among stunted women increases the risk of maternal and infant mortality, as does maternal anemia. Iodine-deficient mothers give birth to more infants with cretinism and other congenital abnormalities. A significant proportion of pregnancies end in poor maternal or infant health as a direct consequence of maternal malnutrition.

Iodine and vitamin A deficiencies tend to be localized rather than widely distributed and could be virtually eliminated through targeted, sporadic interventions, given a reasonable health infrastructure and a high level of political will. Anemia and protein-energy malnutrition, by contrast, affect much larger numbers of women and require more continuous intervention. Distribution of a regular supply of ferrous sulfate tablets can prevent or cure anemia among pregnant and lactating women. Such efforts should include all women of reproductive age, certainly where the prevalence of anemia among women in general exceeds 50 percent. To reduce protein-energy malnutrition, much must be done outside the health sector toward making more food available to households, increasing employment opportunities for women, decreasing the time and energy costs of women's home production, and reducing discrimination against women and girls.

of and mortality from a variety of infections, especially measles and diarrhea. WHO calculates that 13.8 million children have some degree of eye damage because of vitamin A deficiency; of these, 250,000 to 500,000 go blind every year, and two-thirds of the blinded children die. Both vitamin A and iodine deficiency are particularly common in Asia and Sub-Saharan Africa.

These four diseases of malnutrition caused a direct loss of almost 46 million DALYs in 1990, or 3.4 percent of the global burden of disease (Table 4.3). (The estimates do not include the health damage from deficiencies of other micronutrients. Calcium deficiency may be the most important of these; it causes bone deformities and slows skeletal growth in children, and it may contribute to osteoporosis in the elderly.) The estimated burden is slightly larger for females than males because anemia affects mostly women ages 15–44 (Box 4.1); anemia accounts for 1.3 percent of the total female disease burden but for 24 percent among women in the reproductive ages. Children under 5 are the principal victims of vitamin A deficiency, iodine deficiency, and protein-energy malnutrition. The nutritional disease burden for young children is 32 million DALYs, or 6 percent of their total burden of illness.

The total impact of malnutrition on health is much larger, however, because mild or moderate protein-energy malnutrition and micronutrient deficiencies (as well as overconsumption of energy, fat, salt, and sugar) are risk factors for illness and death. Studies in Asia and Africa consistently show that mild to moderate stunting or underweight in children raises the risk of death (Figure 4.1), contributing to 25 to 50 percent of childhood mortality. The greatest risk occurs for children in their second year, after they are weaned. Malnourished children die principally from measles, diarrheal and respiratory disease, tuberculosis, pertussis, and malaria. Child deaths from these diseases cost 231 million DALYs, making the total burden attributable to malnutrition at least one-fourth that amount, or 60 million DALYs.

Vitamin A deficiency, too, raises the risk of death from other causes. Of the 8 million deaths of children with vitamin A deficiency that occur each year, between 1.3 million and 2.5 million might be prevented by eliminating the vitamin deficiency, for a gain of 39 million to 74 million DALYs. Damage from being underweight and from vitamin A deficiency cannot be added together because many children suffer from both problems. Nonetheless,

Childhood mortality drops sharply as nutritional status improves.

Figure 4.1 Child mortality (in specific age ranges) and weight-for-age in Bangladesh, India, Papua New Guinea, and Tanzania

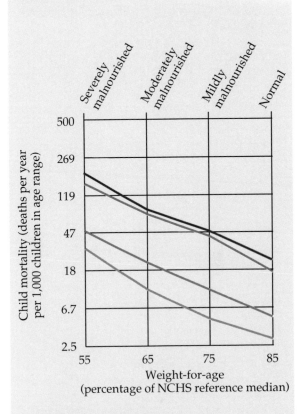

— Tanzania, 6–30 months
— Papua New Guinea, 6–30 months
— Matlab, Bangladesh, 12–59 months
— Punjab, India, 12–36 months

Note: NCHS, (U.S.) National Center for Health Statistics. The vertical axis shows the child mortality rate, CMR, in log-odds ratio form, $\log[CMR/(1000 - CMR)]$. Thus, for a child in Punjab weighing 60 percent of the reference median, the probability of dying between 12 and 36 months is 18 per 1,000.
Source: Pelletier 1991.

the total direct and indirect damage from malnutrition is at least 20 to 25 percent of the disease burden in children.

Links between nutrition and growth in childhood persist into adulthood. Both height and weight affect the risk of adult mortality. For men and women at all ages, greater height is associated with greater survival. Stunted adults are at particularly high risk of cardiovascular disease and obstructive lung disease. If the relative risk of death associated with stunting is the same in low-income countries as for richer populations, approximately 300,000 adult female deaths between the ages of 15 and 59 can be attributed to stunting.

Sources of malnutrition

Both food consumption and communicable disease affect nutritional status by way of a "malnutrition-infection complex." Food consumption depends both on people's capacity to acquire food and on their knowledge of how to choose a nutritious diet. For infants the chief determinant of nutritional status is whether they are exclusively breastfed for at least the first four to six months of life. In southern Brazil infants who were not breastfed were eighteen times as likely to die from diarrhea and three times as likely to die from respiratory illness as breastfed babies, both because they got less to eat and because of increased risk of infection. After six months children need solid food even if they are still breastfed. The composition and hygiene of this food are crucial to continued good health.

INCOME AND FOOD SECURITY. Chronic malnutrition is mostly a consequence of poverty. Higher income allows people to buy a more balanced diet, as well as better hygiene and medical care. In Indonesia during 1984–87 rising incomes translated into reduced malnutrition in nearly all fifty-two regions of the country. The fraction of families eating less than 2,200 calories per person per day—an energy intake adequate for only light physical activity—declined only 2 percentage points, but the decline was 9 percentage points at 1,800 calories and 26 percentage points at 1,400 calories. Conversely, increases in food prices in Côte d'Ivoire during the 1980s reduced the weight of both children and adults. Nutrition is also affected by who in the household controls the money; women's income is more likely than men's to be spent on better nutrition.

Chronic food insecurity for poor people is often made worse by seasonal fluctuations in availability and prices. In India and the Philippines temporal variation in children's food intake is greatest among poor households, and severely malnourished children are more likely to die during that part of the year when malnutrition is most prevalent. Small variations in diet can be fatal to children already at risk.

The extreme form of this risk is widespread famine as a result of a breakdown in food production, food distribution, or the flow of income with which people buy food. Famines occurred in China in 1959–61, in Bangladesh in 1974, in Ethiopia and the Sahel in 1973–74, in Ethiopia and Somalia in the 1980s, and in Somalia and Sudan in the early 1990s. As many as 30 million people are believed to have died in the Chinese famine and hundreds of thousands in the recent famines in Sub-Saharan Africa. A relatively small number of people die from outright starvation; many die of infectious diseases, to which people weakened by hunger are especially susceptible.

Public action is critical in preventing a food crisis from becoming a famine. A combination of actions is required to ensure that food is available in famine areas (through both market and nonmarket mechanisms) and to sustain the incomes of vulnerable households (through public employment or other transfers). This is particularly difficult when there is a breakdown in order: the major African famines of the past decade were mostly associated with war.

Hunger and crowding into refugee camps facilitate the spread of infectious disease and raise the risk of death from it, particularly when such camps are first established. Control of communicable disease is as crucial as the provision of food or of money to buy food. Even when refugee populations are protected from starvation, they are often exposed to micronutrient deficiencies because they are dependent on just a few foodstuffs. In recent years there have been outbreaks of scurvy (vitamin C deficiency) in Ethiopia and Somalia, pellagra (niacin deficiency) among Mozambican refugees in Malawi, and beri-beri (thiamine deficiency) among Cambodian refugees in Thailand. In nonfamine conditions these diseases make no contribution to the world's burden of disease.

Beyond ensuring food distribution and controlling the diseases that can easily become epidemics in conditions of social and sanitary breakdown, governments have two overriding responsibilities in famines. The first is to recognize the early signs of trouble and act before large numbers of people have become destitute. The second is to allow free flow of information about conditions during the famine so that relief agencies and others can react. Hiding the extent of a disaster only makes it worse.

of MSG in Indonesia cut child mortality by 30 percent. Whenever a food consumed by the target population can be fortified at reasonable cost, fortification can provide the same benefits as promoting changes in diet and may be quicker and easier.

MICRONUTRIENT SUPPLEMENTATION. Supplying micronutrients separately from food requires regular, sometimes frequent, contact with the target population. This may make it more difficult to sustain high coverage. It may also make supplements more costly than fortification of foods—although micronutrient supplementation can be added at very low marginal cost to immunization programs or school-based deworming programs. Vitamin A can be given in capsules at intervals of one week to six months, reducing the risk of blindness substantially. Vitamin A supplementation can reduce mortality from measles and diarrheal disease by about 30 percent but has little effect on deaths from respiratory disease.

Iodine can also be provided as a supplement to diets. Oral doses of iodized oil protect for two to four years, and injectable oil protects for three to five years. Side effects are usually not serious and occur mostly in older adults. Supplements for women of reproductive age prevent mental retardation in their children and reduce the risks of infant mortality. Iron deficiency is the most difficult micronutrient shortage to combat by supplementation: tablets must be taken every day, and they often cause side effects. Because these problems limit compliance, supplements are usually given only to pregnant women, who suffer most from anemia. When the principal cause of iron deficiency is infection with hookworm and other parasites, however, iron supplements are also given to all those treated for a limited period after deworming.

FOOD SUPPLEMENTATION. Programs that provide food instead of micronutrient supplements are harder to implement effectively. Inadequate targeting, replacement of food from the normal diet, or lack of attention to other causes of malnutrition often mean that the food is wasted. With proper targeting and attention to changing behavior, however, some supplementation programs have been made to work. A program in Tamil Nadu, India, achieved remarkable gains by distributing food only when children's growth faltered, while providing information to mothers continuously through highly motivated community nutrition workers (Box 4.2). This success came despite eco-

nomic stagnation. There was no improvement in districts not participating in the program. A large-scale program in Chile substantially reduced childhood malnutrition while increasing the use of the public health system. In many countries free meals for schoolchildren may have little effect on their nutritional status but improve school attendance and performance. In general, food supplementation works best when it is used to motivate and educate mothers to care for their children's health, when it can be concentrated within a crucial interval (during pregnancy, for example), or when it provides additional, nonnutritional benefits.

FOOD PRICE SUBSIDIES. Letting people buy basic foodstuffs more cheaply can, in theory, increase intake of particular foods, but there are often practical problems in targeting subsidies to needy households. Targeting by locale or by commodities eaten primarily by poor people is more efficient than wasteful general subsidies but less precise than targeting according to specific needs. Inefficiencies in administration can eat up much of the potential benefit. One large urban subsidy program in Brazil has often sold food for nearly the same price as private markets, despite a nominal 20 percent price reduction. When such waste is avoided, targeted subsidies can effectively transfer income to poor households. As with direct transfers of income or of food, subsidies are more likely to improve nutrition and health when they are combined with nutrition education and related health interventions. Unless that is done, subsidies are not cost-effective.

There is a strong case for government intervention to improve health by improving nutrition, but not for interfering generally in food markets, except in extraordinary conditions such as famine. Government action in nutrition has often been wasteful because it has duplicated what private markets do and has paid too little attention to the causes of poverty and to cost-effective measures that improve families' knowledge and capacity to feed themselves adequately. Reductions in mortality, blindness, mental impairment, and anemia can make fortification and supplementation extremely cost-effective, comparable to the best control measures for other diseases (Table 4.4). A year of healthy life can be bought for less than $10 with some micronutrient interventions and for less than $100 with programs that provide food supplements sparingly and combine them with behavioral change and health care. Improved adult health, more productive schooling, higher in-

Table 4.4 Cost-effectiveness of nutrition interventions

Intervention	Target group	Approximate cost (dollars)	
		Per death averted	Per DALY saved
Iron supplementation	Pregnant women	800	13
Iron fortification	Entire population	2,000	4
Iodine supplementation	Women of reproductive age	1,250	19
Iodine supplementation	Entire population	4,650	37
Iodization of salt or water	Entire population	1,000	8
Vitamin A supplementation[a]	Children under age 5	50	1
Vitamin A fortification	Entire population	154	4
Food supplementation	Children under age 5	1,942	63
Food supplementation	Pregnant women[b]	733	24

a. Semiannual mass dose.
b. Deaths averted and DALYs saved are for fetal deaths.
Source: Pinstrup-Andersen and others forthcoming; Levin and others forthcoming.

Fertility has been declining worldwide, but at different paces.

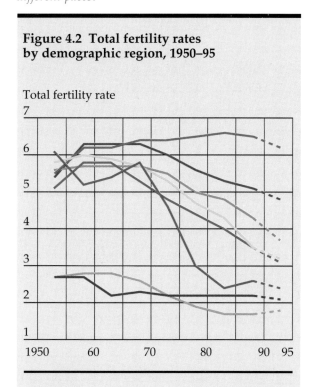

Figure 4.2 Total fertility rates by demographic region, 1950–95

Total fertility rate

- Sub-Saharan Africa
- India
- China
- Other Asia and islands
- Latin America and the Caribbean
- Middle Eastern crescent
- Formerly socialist economies of Europe
- Established market economies

Note: Dotted lines represent projected values.
Source: World Bank data.

comes, and other benefits that come with good childhood nutritional status strengthen the case for appropriate nutrition interventions.

Fertility

All pregnancies and births carry some health risks to the mother and the child. But the risks are higher when women have health problems (such as high blood pressure, heart disease, malaria, or diabetes) that could be aggravated by pregnancy, when pregnancies come too early or too late in a woman's reproductive life, when they are too closely spaced or are unwanted, and when they occur to high-parity women (for example, those who have already had four or more babies).

The use of family planning services by couples is an effective means of avoiding many of these fertility-related health risks, and it enables families to achieve their fertility goals. In many parts of the world, fertility has been falling over time as the use of family planning spreads (Figure 4.2). Governments can do much to help couples by promoting family planning as a socially acceptable practice, by providing information on the health effects of fertility regulation, by teaching couples about effective methods of contraception, and by removing restrictions on the marketing of contraceptives. Subsidies may be justified in low-income populations, in rural areas, and for programs targeted to young people. Nongovernmental organizations and the private sector will often have a large role in service provision. Ensuring access to safe abortion can complement family planning services in improving health.

Fertility patterns and health

Births to very young women elevate the health risks to both mother and child. Births that are too

Figure 4.3 Risk of death by age 5 for fertility-related risk factors in selected countries, late 1980s

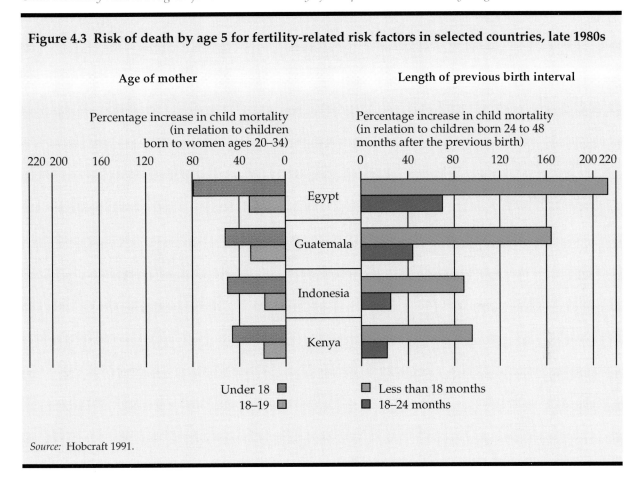

Source: Hobcraft 1991.

closely spaced increase the risk of child mortality; births at older ages and higher parities are riskier to mothers, as are unwanted pregnancies that lead to unsafe abortion or to neglect of prenatal care.

THE TIMING OF BIRTHS AND CHILD HEALTH. Short birth intervals pose substantial risks to child health throughout the first five years of life (Figure 4.3). In Kenya, for example, infants born within eighteen months of the birth of a previous child are more than twice as likely to die as those born after a longer interval. In Egypt the risks are more than triple. Babies born to teenage women are also at greater risk of dying. In Indonesia, for example, babies born to mothers age 18 and under are 50 percent more likely to die than those born to women ages 20–24.

Surveys taken in twenty-five developing countries in the 1980s show that, on average, nearly 35 percent of births occur within twenty-four months of the previous birth and that many women wish

to avoid such births. If the closely spaced births were delayed until mothers wanted them, overall child mortality in those countries might be reduced by more than 20 percent. The reduction could be as large as 30 percent in Brazil, Colombia, Ecuador, Peru, and Tunisia, where between 40 and 50 percent of births are spaced too closely.

CHILDBEARING AND MATERNAL HEALTH. Each year about 430,000 women in developing countries die from complications associated with childbearing. In the absence of obstetric care, women who have a birth before age 18 are three times as likely to die in childbirth as those who have a birth between ages 20 and 29; for women over 34, the risk of maternal mortality is five times as high. First births are often riskier than second or third births, but as parity rises thereafter, the risk of maternal mortality also climbs. In Jamaica the risk increases by 65 percent after the third birth. In Kenya, the Philippines, and Zimbabwe 30 to 60 percent of pregnant women are estimated to be at elevated risk of death on account of either age or parity.

Maternal deaths also arise from unsafe abortion. Almost 30 percent of pregnancies end in abortion, for a total of about 55 million induced abortions in the world each year; 25 million of these are performed under unsafe conditions. The damage to maternal health arises mainly from infection (the long-run consequences of which include ectopic pregnancy, chronic pain, and infertility), hemorrhage, damage to the cervix or uterus, and reaction to anesthesia and the drugs used to induce abortion. About 60,000 women a year are estimated to die from unsafe abortions (see Appendix table B.8); other estimates range as high as 200,000. Treatment of abortion-related complications can consume significant resources. In Brazil in 1988 about 2 percent of all hospital admissions in the publicly financed, privately provided health system were for abortion-related complications, and the costs amounted to about 6 percent of all spending on obstetrics and 1 percent of all hospital spending in that system.

Better health through family planning services

Family planning services can help women reduce the health risks from mistimed and unwanted pregnancies. In low-income populations and in rural areas there is a strong case on equity grounds for the government to subsidize and organize the provision of family planning services, using public as well as nongovernmental and private channels as appropriate. In these settings subsidized family planning services are often the most effective way of transmitting family planning information to the poor. They can also be an efficient means of improving the welfare of poor families, especially when private medical care is unavailable. For both reasons, family planning services are part of the minimum essential clinical package discussed in the next chapter. Special efforts are also appropriate for addressing the needs of adolescents, both because they tend to be particularly uninformed about reproductive health risks and because they often misjudge the consequences of early childbearing.

Beyond providing subsidized services to specific populations, the government also has a role in ensuring access to family planning services for those able and willing to pay. Encouraging better services and availability of more contraceptive methods requires various changes, including removal of price controls and bans on contraceptive advertising, easing of restrictions on the importa-

tion of contraceptives, and abandonment of unnecessary prescription requirements. Experience in the formerly socialist economies of Europe has shown that all such constraints reduce contraceptive use and often damage maternal and child health. Demand for many contraceptive supplies and services can be met by private doctors and commercial outlets, especially in towns and, for some methods (such as condoms), in rural areas as well.

Use of contraceptives is the best way to avoid unwanted pregnancies, but it is not foolproof. For women who wish to terminate their pregnancies, access to safe abortion as a complement to contraceptive services is also important to women's health.

REACHING LOW-INCOME AND RURAL POPULATIONS. The health infrastructure in poor countries is often limited in its ability to reach highly dispersed populations in rural areas. In rural Uganda, for example, travel time to the nearest family planning facility averages one hour, whereas it is only fifteen minutes in rural Thailand. Long waits at the facility are another problem; a study of clinics in several Latin American countries found that waiting times for initial visits averaged one hour and twenty minutes. In many countries rural women have no access to family planning fieldworkers who can provide information and simple services. In Guatemala, for example, 86 percent of rural women live in communities without a family planning fieldworker; in Egypt the figure is only 33 percent. Community-based strategies have been used with success in some countries to reach low-income women. In Colombia, Zaire, and Zimbabwe community-based-distribution (CBD) workers serve the dual purpose of spreading information about family planning and providing the most isolated populations with family planning methods—primarily barrier methods, such as condoms and foaming tablets, but also oral contraceptives.

Family planning services provided through community-based distribution are a highly cost-effective means of improving maternal and child health. In countries where both mortality and fertility are still relatively high, the cost per child death averted is extremely low. In Mali, for example, it averages about $130, which corresponds to a mere $4 to $5 per DALY gained. In other countries, such as Colombia, Mexico, and Thailand—where mortality and fertility are substantially lower—CBD family planning services cost no more than

$25 per DALY gained and thus remain highly cost-effective.

REACHING YOUNG PEOPLE. In developing countries childbearing among teenage women (ages 15–19) is common. Surveys in the 1980s in Liberia, Mali, and Uganda show that more than one in five teenage women had had at least one child or was pregnant at the time of the interview. In Latin American and Caribbean countries 16 percent of all births in 1992 were to teenage mothers. Adolescent pregnancies are often unintended and tend to be more prevalent among low-income women. In both Ghana and Kenya, for example, about 40 percent of married teenagers who have had children said their first pregnancies were unintended; among unmarried teenagers the proportion of unintended births rose to 58 percent in Ghana and 77 percent in Kenya. A 1986 study of Brazilian women showed that 65 percent of those who became mothers before age 20 came from poor families (that is, those with household income below the national median), in contrast to 48 percent for women who delayed childbearing.

Family life education in schools and other venues can help teenagers make informed choices about sexual behavior and the prevention of sexually transmitted disease (STD). Family planning services are needed to help sexually active adolescents prevent pregnancies. And programs to help teenagers cope with unintended pregnancies, especially premarital ones, can be especially valuable. In Jamaica the Women's Center Program has had some success in helping young mothers to complete their schooling after childbirth and to avoid another mistimed pregnancy.

IMPROVING SERVICES AND ENCOURAGING GREATER VARIETY IN METHODS. The quality of family planning services in developing countries has been improving, but more can be done. Providing good counseling to clients is important, in part because women's contraceptive needs change over the reproductive life cycle. Temporary methods are more appropriate earlier in the cycle, while permanent methods are more appropriate toward the end. And certain methods are more or less suitable depending on the duration of protection desired and on whether the woman is breastfeeding. Competent advice offered with sensitivity can help clients choose the right method at each stage and use it effectively while also addressing their concerns about possible side effects. Dissatisfaction with services and contraceptive failure often cause women to discontinue contraceptive use. In Thailand and Colombia, where the programs offer good services, about 6 percent of users quit each year for these reasons; in Paraguay as many as 18 percent of users discontinue annually.

There is considerable scope for broadening the range and quality of contraceptive methods. India, for example, has for a long time heavily emphasized sterilization and offered attractive financial incentives to both clients and providers. A nationwide survey in 1986–87 showed that among nonsterilized couples seeking a temporary method of contraception, nearly 75 percent of those who wanted intrauterine devices (IUDs) reported failure to get them, 67 percent reported failure to get contraceptive pills, and 40 percent reported not being able to get condoms. In China, where steel-ring IUDs have been in widespread use, the government, because of concern about the risk to women's health, recently decided to switch to the safer Copper-T IUDs. In some countries the range of available methods is constrained because public sector providers are required to use products on an essential drug list and the list mistakenly excludes some contraceptive methods. Other constraints on method availability include excessively restrictive medical screening requirements, unnecessary or duplicative approval procedures, packaging and labeling requirements that perform no useful function but increase costs, and import restrictions or tariffs. A study in Indonesia that surveyed a group of women eighteen months after they started using contraceptives found that, all else being the same, women who failed to get their contraceptive method of choice were more than three times as likely to have discontinued use as women who did receive their preferred method.

Providing an appropriate mix of contraceptive methods can also help to reduce the spread of STDs and human immunodeficiency virus (HIV). Linking the provision of family planning services with screening programs for STDs requires a clinical setting in which positive diagnoses may be followed up with treatment. The discussions of AIDS in this chapter, below, and in Chapter 5 address this point in more detail.

ENSURING ACCESS TO SAFE ABORTION. In 1990 about 40 percent of the world's population lived in countries where induced abortion was permitted on request, 25 percent lived where it was allowed only if the woman's life was in danger, and the remaining 35 percent lived in places where abortion laws varied in strictness between these ex-

Figure 4.4 Maternal mortality in Romania, 1965–91

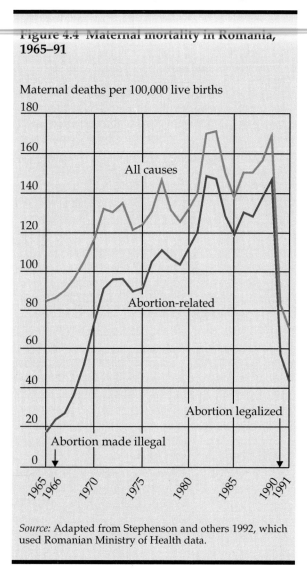

Maternal deaths per 100,000 live births

Source: Adapted from Stephenson and others 1992, which used Romanian Ministry of Health data.

maternal mortality rate had risen by nearly 40 percent above the level in 1965 (Figure 4.4). Before 1966 Romania's maternal mortality rate was similar to the rates in other Eastern European countries. By 1989 it was at least ten times the rate of almost any other European country. In 1990 Romania's new government legalized abortion, and the decline in maternal mortality was immediate and even sharper than its rise following the ban: only one year after abortion was legalized, maternal mortality had fallen to just 40 percent of the 1989 level. The percentage of all maternal deaths caused by abortion dropped from nearly 90 percent before the ban on abortion was lifted to just over 60 percent in 1990.

COSTS AND POTENTIAL GAINS IN HEALTH. Family planning services, particularly when delivered through community-based distribution, are among the most cost-effective means of improving maternal and child health. There is much scope for improving services in developing countries, where more than one women in five who wants to avoid pregnancy is not using contraception. In Bolivia, Ghana, Kenya, Liberia, and Togo at least one in three women ages 15–49 falls into this category. Lack of access to family planning services is one reason for not using them—although it is certainly not the only one. The cost of supplying family planning services to women without access (numbering an estimated 120 million in the developing world) is estimated at about $2 billion annually for developing countries as a whole. Selective allocation of public resources to address the needs of these women, particularly those in poor families, would be a cost-effective means of promoting their well-being, as well as that of their children. Satisfying the expressed wish of women to space or limit future births might each year avert as many as 100,000 maternal deaths and 850,000 deaths among children under 5.

Reducing abuse of tobacco, alcohol, and drugs

Decisions about the use of tobacco, alcohol, and other drugs are among the most important health-related choices that individuals can make. Because individual options are limited by the strongly addictive character of these substances, and because addiction is often established in adolescence, decisions about the control of tobacco and other addictive substances are among the most important health-related choices that societies can make collectively. In many populations prolonged cigarette

tremes. In countries where abortion is illegal, women resort to clandestine, and often unsafe, abortions at high risk to their health. Legalizing abortion is inadequate for protecting maternal health when problems with access continue. In India, for example, abortion is legal but not readily available, and many women continue to rely on unsafe abortion, with detrimental effects to their health.

Romania's experience is the most striking example of the impact of abortion laws on maternal health. In 1966 the government banned abortion and contraception and took steps to enforce the law. The consequences were dramatic: by 1970 the smoking is already the greatest single cause of premature death. Alcohol and other drugs also contribute to disease and disability. The damage from substance abuse is not limited to the individuals involved; others also suffer indirectly because of drunk driving, fires, passive smoking, and drug-related crime and violence.

Several sorts of government policy can be used to discourage consumption of tobacco, alcohol, and other drugs. Educating the public about the harmful effects of these substances is essential. Appropriate action will often involve special emphasis not only on reaching school-age children but also on helping adults to escape from addiction. Tax policies on tobacco and alcohol have also reduced consumption, especially by discouraging use by young adults before they become addicted. Governments can ban all direct or indirect advertising or promotion of tobacco goods or trademarks and could do the same for alcohol.

Tobacco

Tobacco is in legal use everywhere in the world, yet it causes far more deaths than all other psychoactive substances combined. About 3 million premature deaths a year (6 percent of the world total) are already attributable to tobacco smoking. If current trends continue, deaths from tobacco worldwide are projected to reach 10 million a year, or more than 10 percent of total deaths, by the second quarter of the next century. Tobacco is already responsible for 30 percent of all cancer deaths in developed countries, including deaths from cancers of the lung, oral cavity, larynx, esophagus, bladder, pancreas, and kidney. Even more people die from tobacco-related diseases other than cancer, including stroke, myocardial infarction, aortic aneurysm, and peptic ulcer. In countries where smoking has long been widespread, tobacco use is now responsible for about 30 percent of all male deaths in middle age. Smoking also harms the health of others. Among nonsmokers, exposure to environmental tobacco smoke increases the risk of lung cancer. And the babies of mothers who smoke weigh, on average, 200 grams less at birth than those of nonsmokers.

Per capita consumption of tobacco is decreasing slowly in industrial countries and has remained relatively unchanged in the formerly socialist economies. By contrast, per capita tobacco consumption is rising in many developing countries among both men and women and is expected to increase by about 12 percent between 1990 and 2000 (see Appendix table A.6). In China the increase in consumption from 500 billion cigarettes in 1978 to 1,700 billion in 1992 has produced smoking patterns that, if they persist, will eventually result in about 2 million deaths a year from tobacco. Similar consumption patterns exist in several other countries. If, as now, about one-third of the world's young adults become regular cigarette smokers and, as in industrial countries, more than one-third of them die prematurely because of the habit, then, of the 120 million who reach adult life each year, more than 10 percent—more than 12 million a year—will die prematurely because of tobacco. On current smoking patterns, the chief uncertainty is not whether mortality from tobacco will reach 12 million a year in the second quarter of the next century, but exactly when it will do so.

Largely because of the long delay between cause and full effect, people tend to misjudge the hazards of tobacco. When a generation of young adults begins to smoke, they do not witness the high mortality associated with their behavior until they reach middle age. The best-documented example of this delay is that of men in the United States, among whom the main increase in smoking took place before 1945. In 1945 smoking was common but lung cancer rare, as in developing countries today. Over the next forty years (1945–85) the smoking habit did not change greatly among young men in the United States, but lung cancer in this population rose sharply (Figure 4.5). Among U.S. nonsmokers lung cancer remained approximately constant at a low level during 1965–85, but among smokers the rates increased twentyfold. In 1985 tobacco caused the large majority (110,000) of all lung cancer deaths, among both males and females, in the United States, as well as an even larger number (290,000) of deaths from other diseases, for about 20 percent of 2 million U.S. deaths. About half of those killed by tobacco were still in middle age (35–69) and thereby lost almost twenty-five years of nonsmoker life expectancy.

Effective discouragement of addiction to tobacco involves slow social changes that take place over many years. Public education is central to this process. In China, the United Kingdom, and the United States, autonomous national action groups such as Action on Smoking and Health have helped sustain serious efforts to alert people to the hazards of tobacco consumption and, through legal action, to protect the public from the harmful health effects of the habit. Governments can contribute to the efforts of citizen groups by, for example, requiring prominent health warnings on ciga-

Figure 4.5 Trends in mortality from lung cancer and various other cancers among U.S. males, 1930–90

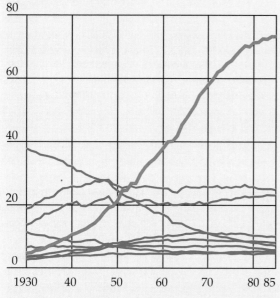

Deaths per 100,000 males[a]

▬ Lung cancer
▬ Various other cancers

Note: Other cancers shown include leukemia and cancers of the bladder, esophagus, pancreas, liver, prostate, stomach, and colon and rectum.
a. Adjusted to the age structure of the U.S. population in 1970.
Source: Boring, Squires, and Tong 1993.

rette packages and advertisements, as well as by targeting of clear messages not only to school-age children but also to adults. Reaching adults is important because over the next few decades it is those who are already smoking who will account for nearly all of the tens of millions of deaths per decade caused by tobacco. Some countries go further by banning commercial promotion of tobacco goods and tobacco trademarks and by placing restrictions on public smoking. Singapore has been in the forefront of public activism in Asia: it has prohibited advertising (since 1971), issued strong warnings on health effects, and created smoke-free zones. Tobacco consumption per adult appears to have fallen between 1975 and 1990. China, with 300 million smokers, is following a similar path: in 1992 it banned most tobacco advertising, mandated health education for youths, prohibited smoking in many public places, and required progressive reduction of tar levels. In support of countries' efforts to discourage tobacco consumption, the World Bank in 1992 set forth a new policy on tobacco (Box 4.3).

Tobacco has traditionally been taxed, although probably because it is a good source of revenue rather than for the health gains. Taxation reduces consumption, especially among the young. In industrial countries a 10 percent price increase reduces consumption by about 4 percent in the general population and about 13 percent among adolescents. Besides having few resources, most adolescent smokers probably have not been smoking long enough to be fully addicted and so tend to be more price sensitive than other smokers. In India cigarette sales declined by 15 percent after the excise tax on most of the popular cigarette brands more than doubled in 1986. In Papua New Guinea a 10 percent increase in the tobacco tax reduced consumption by 7 percent.

Alcohol and illegal drugs

Alcohol-related diseases affect 5 to 10 percent of the world's population each year and accounted for about 3 percent of the global burden of disease in 1990. Of the 2 million alcohol-related deaths that occur worldwide each year, about 50 percent stem from cirrhosis of the liver, about 35 percent from cancer of the liver or esophagus, 10 percent from alcohol dependence syndrome, and 5 percent from injuries caused by motor vehicles. The problems caused by alcohol abuse consume scarce medical resources and extend beyond the damage that drinkers do to themselves. In many Latin American countries in the 1980s, 20 percent of all hospital and emergency room admissions were alcohol-related. In Papua New Guinea more than 85 percent of fatal road accidents in the 1980s involved either drunk drivers or drunk pedestrians. Within households, drinking often leads to assault and injury, although the scale of the problem is hard to quantify.

Alcohol consumption is stable in the industrial world but is on the rise in many developing countries. Between 1960 and 1981 annual beer consumption per capita rose from 12 liters to 135 liters in Gabon and from 3 liters to 20 liters in Côte d'Ivoire. Total world production of beer nearly doubled between 1970 and 1989, far surpassing population growth, with much of the increase occurring in developing regions.

As with alcohol, abuse of illegal drugs causes serious health and social problems. Individuals run the risk of death from infectious, circulatory, respiratory, and digestive diseases, as well as from violence, overdose, and AIDS. Users of cocaine, especially in the form of "crack," often suffer acute cardiovascular problems that require emergency room services, and the babies of pregnant users of cocaine are often born with severe health problems.

Reliable data on trends and patterns in illegal drug use are scarce. Users typically fall in the age group 15–44, although most are in their mid-twenties. In the past decade the production and consumption of illicit drugs, especially cocaine, appear to have increased considerably worldwide. In some developing countries the use of psychoactive drugs such as inhalants is also a serious problem.

Taxes and judicial penalties have been used to discourage alcohol abuse. A 1982 U.S. study indicated that an increase in the liquor tax of about $3.50 (at 1991 prices) per gallon equivalent of pure alcohol would lower demand enough to reduce the incidence of liver cirrhosis by 5 percent in the short run and perhaps twice as much in the long run. In industrial countries mandatory license sanctions on drunk drivers are estimated to decrease traffic fatalities by about 10 percent; the imposition of a minimum legal drinking age and the assessment of relatively large mandatory fines (that is, about one to two months' wages) are estimated to reduce traffic fatalities by about 5 percent. Mandatory jail sentences for drunk driving have also been weakly effective. The effect of information campaigns concerning alcohol consumption has not been quantified, but there is evidence that in countries where alcohol is legal but commercial promotion is not, per capita alcohol consumption is 30 percent lower than elsewhere and deaths from motor vehicle accidents are 10 percent fewer. As a successful alcohol rehabilitation program in south India demonstrates, community efforts are generally more effective than medical interventions in helping individuals to overcome alcohol dependence, in part because of the importance of sustained encouragement, which is more easily offered by the community than by health service institutions.

Prohibition is a common approach to drug abuse. In the United States prohibition as an approach to control of alcohol failed early in this century. It appears to be having, at best, limited success in controlling use of other drugs now. In other settings, including Malaysia and Singapore, prohibition coupled with a mandatory death penalty for drug trafficking appears to have been more effective. The successes achieved in controlling the use of alcohol and tobacco—through restrictions on promotion and access, high taxation, rehabilitation of addicts, and public education—may also be relevant for efforts against other drugs. For alcohol and tobacco, past successes with these measures should spur efforts toward full implementation.

Environmental influences on health

The environment in which people live has a huge influence on their health. For poor people and poor regions, it is the household environment that carries the greatest risks to health. By providing information, reducing poverty, and facilitating and stimulating private sector action, governments can deploy potent mechanisms to improve this environment. Potential health gains from these efforts total nearly 80 million DALYs a year in developing countries. Other government actions, designed to ameliorate or remedy unsafe conditions in the workplace and pollution of the ambient environment, could save 36 million and 8 million DALYs a year, respectively. Finally, feasible reductions in the toll taken by road traffic injuries could avert the loss of 6 million DALYs a year.

The household environment

Poor households generally live in a domestic environment with high health risks caused by poor sanitation and inadequate water supply (often compounded by poor hygiene), inadequate garbage disposal and drainage, heavy indoor air pollution, and crowding. The diseases associated with poor household environments occur mainly in developing countries, where they account for nearly 30 percent of the total burden of disease (Table 4.5). Modest improvements in household environments would avert almost a quarter of this burden, mostly as a result of reductions in diarrhea and respiratory infections.

WATER AND SANITATION. About 1.3 billion people in the developing world lack access to clean and plentiful water, and nearly 2 billion people lack an adequate system for disposing of their feces (Figure 4.6). Feces deposited near homes, contaminated drinking water (sometimes caused by poorly designed or maintained sewerage systems), fish from polluted rivers and coastal waters, and agricultural produce fertilized with human waste are all health hazards. Water quantity is as important as water quality. Washing hands after defecation and before preparing food is of particular impor-

Table 4.5 Estimated burden of disease from poor household environments in demographically developing countries, 1990, and potential reduction through improved household services

Principal diseases related to poor household environments[a]	Relevant environmental problem	Burden from these diseases in developing countries (millions of DALYs per year)	Reduction achievable through feasible interventions (percent)[b]	Burden averted by feasible interventions (millions of DALYs per year)	Burden averted per 1,000 population (DALYs per year)
Tuberculosis	Crowding	46	10	5	1.2
Diarrhea[c]	Sanitation, water supply, hygiene	99	40	40	9.7
Trachoma	Water supply, hygiene	3	30	1	0.3
Tropical cluster[d]	Sanitation, garbage disposal, vector breeding around the home	8	30	2	0.5
Intestinal worms	Sanitation, water supply, hygiene	18	40	7	1.7
Respiratory infections	Indoor air pollution, crowding	119	15	18	4.4
Chronic respiratory diseases	Indoor air pollution	41	15	6	1.5
Respiratory tract cancers	Indoor air pollution	4	10[e]	*	0.1
All the above		338	—	79	19.4

* Less than one.
Note: The demographically developing group consists of the demographic regions Sub-Saharan Africa, India, China, Other Asia and islands, Latin America and the Caribbean, and Middle Eastern crescent.
a. The diseases listed are those for which there is substantial evidence of a relationship with the household environment and which are listed in Appendix B. Examples of excluded conditions are violence related to crowding (because of lack of evidence) and guinea worm infection related to poor water supply (not listed in Appendix B).
b. Estimates derived from the product of the efficacy of the interventions and the proportion of the burden of disease that occurs among the exposed. The efficacy estimates assume the implementation of improvements in sanitation, water supply, hygiene, drainage, garbage disposal, indoor air pollution, and crowding of the kind being made in poor communities in developing countries.
c. Includes diarrhea, dysentery, cholera, and typhoid.
d. Diseases within the tropical cluster most affected by the domestic environment are schistosomiasis, South American trypanosomiasis, and Bancroftian filariasis.
e. Based on very inadequate data on efficacy.
Source: Appendix tables B.2 and B.3 and authors' calculations.

Figure 4.6 Population without sanitation or water supply services by demographic region, 1990

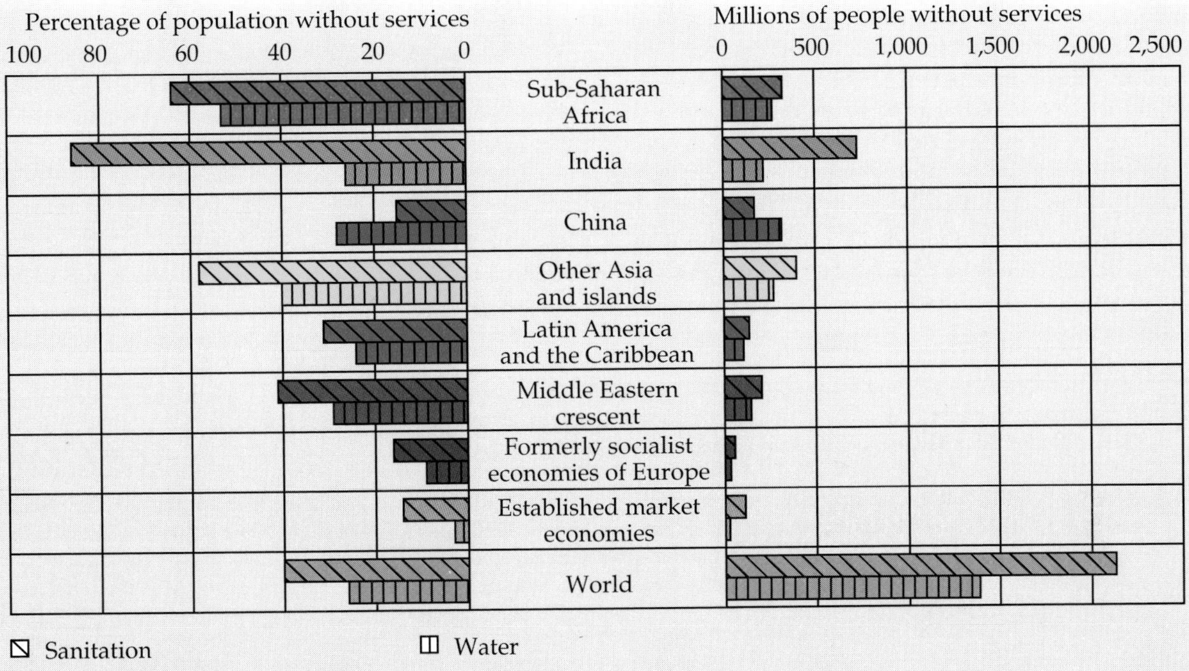

Percentage of population without services

Millions of people without services

☒ Sanitation ☐ Water

Note: Coverage is defined in accordance with local standards.
Source: World Health Organization data.

tance in reducing disease transmission, but without abundant water in or near the home, hygiene becomes difficult or impossible. The lack of water supply and sanitation is the primary reason why diseases transmitted via feces are so common in developing countries. The most important of these diseases, diarrhea and intestinal worm infections, account for an annual burden of 117 million DALYs, or 10 percent of the total burden of disease in developing countries. In addition, an inadequate water supply increases the risk of schistosomiasis, skin and eye infections, and guinea worm disease (Box 4.4).

INDOOR AIR POLLUTION. Indoor air pollution, which *World Development Report 1992* identified as one of the four most critical global environmental problems, probably exposes more people worldwide to important air pollutants than does pollution in outdoor air. Whereas air in such cities as Delhi, India, and Xian, China, contains a daily average of 500 micrograms per cubic meter of total

suspended particulates, smoky houses in Nepal and Papua New Guinea have peak levels of 10,000 or more. Rural people in developing countries may receive as much as two-thirds of the global exposure to particulates. Women and young children suffer the greatest exposure.

Indoor air pollution contributes to acute respiratory infections in young children, chronic lung disease and cancer in adults, and adverse pregnancy outcomes (such as stillbirths) for women exposed during pregnancy. Acute respiratory infections, principally pneumonia, are the chief killers of young children, causing a loss of 119 million DALYs a year, or 10 percent of the total burden of disease in developing countries. Data from the Gambia, Nepal, South Africa, the United States, and Zimbabwe suggest that reducing indoor air pollution from very high to low levels could potentially halve the incidence of childhood pneumonia.

Adults can suffer chronic damage to the respiratory system from indoor pollution. Studies in China, India, Nepal, and Papua New Guinea have

Box 4.4 After smallpox: slaying the dragon worm

Guinea worm disease, or dracunculiasis ("infection with a little dragon"), was endemic from ancient times in a belt stretching from West Africa through the Middle East to India and Central Asia. It has been successfully eliminated from the Central Asian republics and from Iran, where the last case was seen in the 1970s, and it has spontaneously disappeared from most of the Middle East and from several African countries, such as the Gambia and Guinea. There are now probably fewer than a million cases worldwide.

The disease does not kill people, but it causes pain and disability to its victims for several weeks in the year as the 60-centimeter-long female worm emerges from a blister, usually on the leg. In some cases the disability is permanent. The worms usually emerge in the early rainy season, the time when the incapacitated victims would otherwise be planting and weeding their crops. Children whose parents are stricken by guinea worm are more likely to be malnourished in the following year.

Because dracunculiasis can only be caught by drinking infected water, improving the water supply is an important preventive measure. Health education is also essential. Villagers need to be persuaded to stay

out of sources of drinking water when they have guinea worm blisters on their legs and to filter their water with a cloth if they do not have a safe water source.

Eradication of dracunculiasis by the end of 1995 has been adopted as an international goal. Pakistan may have achieved eradication in 1992, and Cameroon, India, and Senegal may do so in 1993. Between 1987 and 1992 cases reported per year fell from 653,000 to 201,000 in Nigeria, from 180,000 to 33,000 in Ghana, and from 17,000 to 900 in India. In general, these advances have been achieved through "vertical" programs—that is, programs specific to dracunculiasis. The eradication of the disease from the poor, sparsely populated endemic countries in West Africa will, however, require integrated programs in which the resources available for guinea worm control are shared with other activities, such as immunization. A by-product of guinea worm eradication will be community-based surveillance systems, which can be used by communities to monitor and improve their own health and by public health workers to combat other diseases, such as polio.

---

shown that up to half of adult women (few of whom smoke) suffer from chronic lung and heart diseases. Nonsmoking Chinese women exposed to indoor coal smoke (which is especially harmful) have a risk of lung cancer similar to that of men who smoke lightly. Comprehensive improvement in indoor air quality in the developing countries might avert a loss of 24 million DALYs each year by reducing the burden of acute respiratory infections and chronic respiratory diseases by 15 percent and of respiratory tract cancers by 10 percent (Table 4.5).

HOUSING. In many cities 30 to 60 percent of the population live in overcrowded and deteriorating shanties, tenements, and boardinghouses. Crowding is associated with increased airborne infection and personal violence. Poor structures lead to greater exposure to heat, cold, noise, dust, rain, insects, and rodents. And housing locations are often unhealthy because of, for example, poor drainage.

POLICIES FOR IMPROVING THE HOUSEHOLD ENVIRONMENT. The most powerful forces for reducing domestic risks to health are rising incomes and increased education for household members. Higher incomes make it possible for people to af-

ford the household improvements, including better water and sanitation services, that they desire. As people acquire more education, their hygiene improves, and their responsiveness to public information programs increases. To support households' efforts, governments have an important role in setting and enforcing appropriate environmental standards and disseminating information on, for example, the health benefits of good hygiene and the effects of exposure (especially of babies) to smoke. Governments should also concentrate on strengthening security of tenure (which is essential for encouraging households to invest in their housing) and on establishing a legal, regulatory, and administrative framework that facilitates responsive, accountable, and efficient provision, often by private suppliers, of services that people want and are willing to pay for. And they should refrain from supplying services directly and from granting indiscriminate, widespread subsidies. Such subsidies are often captured by wealthier consumers, go for improvements that households would make anyway, or encourage consumption patterns that are detrimental to health. (For example, subsidies for coal used in cooking lead to more indoor air pollution than would be the case with cleaner liquid or gas fuels.)

Past experience in water and sanitation illustrates the limitations of direct government provision of household services. Despite technical progress in developing affordable engineering solutions to the problems of water, sanitation, drainage, and housing, the delivery and maintenance of these services, especially by governments, have been disappointing. At the end of the International Drinking Water Supply and Sanitation Decade (the 1980s), most people in the poorer regions of the world still lacked sanitation, and the number of urban residents without water had not been reduced.

Supply-side failures are largely caused by inefficient and unresponsive public sector monopolies which, in the water sector, typically provide subsidized services at between one-third and two-thirds of the full economic cost. Massive public investments, often supported by the donor community and the World Bank, have been made in public or quasi-public agencies responsible for the delivery and maintenance of household services. The net result has often been bloated public agencies with low accountability to their customers and few incentives for improving efficiency; a middle class that is increasingly well served with subsidized services; a

poorer class that receives little or no service; and a ripe environment for political patronage.

The poor usually miss out on both services and subsidies. They suffer the substantial health consequences described in Table 4.5 and pay high prices for inadequate services. In Lima poor people may pay $3 for a cubic meter of contaminated water collected by bucket from a private vendor, while the middle class pays 30 cents per cubic meter for treated water provided on tap in their houses by the publicly subsidized water company.

Broadly based subsidies are not necessary for ensuring access to safe water and sanitation. In most urban communities households are willing to pay the full costs of water service and often the full cost of sanitation services. Willingness to pay for water may be high in rural areas as well, but what people can afford is commonly not enough to cover the high costs of supply. Subsidy may be justified in such situations. But the rationale should be primarily one of redistribution: a society may choose to provide cheap water or other services to the poor as one of many alternative means of improving their welfare. Health benefits alone do not generally provide a rationale for public subsidy of water and sanitation (see Box 4.5).

Box 4.5 The costs and benefits of investments in water supply and sanitation

People want safe water and good sanitation and are willing to pay for these services, especially for plentiful water in or very near the home. Improvements in water supply raise productivity through savings in the fuel used to boil polluted water and, even more important, through the time and energy savings for women who have to collect water from distant sources. Provision of public handpumps in Imo State, Nigeria, reduced the median time that each household spent on water collection in the dry season from six hours a day to forty-five minutes. In Lesotho, not an especially dry country, the benefits in time saved alone are sufficient to justify investments in rural water supply. Sanitation improvements have high amenity value, making possible a cleaner and more pleasant environment.

The costs of water supply and sanitation services vary by technology, population density, the hydrologic and geologic environment, and design standards. Design standards for water supply can range from one handpump per 250 people, supplying 20 liters per person per day, to multiple-tap in-house connections that supply several hundred liters of fully treated water per person per day. Design standards for sanitation can vary from a pit latrine to flush toilets connected to a sewerage system, with downstream treatment prior to

discharge. The cost of water and sanitation services can range from $15 per person per year for simple rural systems to $200 for full-fledged urban systems. Poor households cannot afford the design standards of industrial countries, but such standards are not necessary on health grounds. Completely eliminating fecal bacteria requires expensive chlorination, but low concentrations present little health hazard and should be tolerated.

If households pay the total cost of water and sanitation services because of the productivity and amenity benefits, substantial health gains are an added bonus achieved at no cost per DALY gained. When willingness to pay is much less than costs, it is usually a mistake to justify subsidies on the basis of health benefits alone. First, such subsidies compromise the demand-driven approach to service provision (that is, provision of services that people want and are willing to pay for); lack of accountability and inefficiency are the inevitable consequences. And second, if publicly financed investments in these services are being considered for health reasons, it should be noted that such investments generally cost more per DALY gained than other health interventions recommended in this Report.

Diseases transmitted by insect vectors account for losses of 44 million DALYs worldwide each year (35 million in Sub-Saharan Africa), or 3 percent of the world burden (12 percent in Sub-Saharan Africa). Although widespread application of insecticides is helping to control river blindness in West Africa (see Box 1.1) and Chagas' disease in South America, it is no longer the mainstay of vector control against other diseases. Emphasis has shifted to a range of targeted biological, physical, and behavioral approaches supported by insecticides when necessary. Two examples are given here.

Impregnated bednets

Bednets impregnated with a pyrethroid insecticide of low mammalian toxicity form lethal traps for mosquitoes attracted by the carbon dioxide and body odor emitted by the occupants. In Sichuan Province, China, up to 2.25 million nets—already owned by nearly all householders—have been treated each year since 1987. If nothing else, the cost is much lower than spraying the same houses with DDT. In Emei County, Sichuan, the number of malaria cases had been steady at about 4,000 between 1980 and 1986. After bednet treatment began, the number declined steadily, to 352 in 1991. In the Gambia a combination of net treatment and chemoprophylaxis, carried out by primary health care personnel, reduced overall child mortality by 63 percent.

Polystyrene beads

The application of polystyrene beads to pit latrines has proved successful in reducing the breeding of *Culex* mosquitoes and the transmission of filariasis. The beads form a floating layer that discourages egg laying and suffocates any mosquito larvae that do hatch. In the town of Makunduchi (population 12,000) in Zanzibar, Tanzania, a combination of polystyrene-bead application and mass drug treatment of the population between January 1988 and June 1989 virtually eliminated biting by infective mosquitoes, and the proportion of people infected by filariasis fell from 50 to 10 percent. By January 1993 the proportion of people infected had fallen to 3 percent. The polystyrene bead layers remained intact and effective for several years and were disrupted only by exceptional flooding.

In Zanzibar Town researchers are studying whether it is better to make beads freely available so that householders can apply them to their own pits or to have trained teams identify and treat all pits requiring treatment. In Dar es Salaam polystyrene beads are being used to control *Culex* nuisance biting and thereby increase public acceptance of house spraying against the *Anopheles* vectors of malaria. The effectiveness of the *Culex* control measures is evidenced by declining sales of mosquito coils in local shops. In Madras, India, polystyrene beads are being applied to water tanks to control the local vectors of malaria and dengue; the quality of the water is not affected.

An important policy issue, on which there is an apparent tension between health objectives and the demand-driven approach advocated here and in *World Development Report 1992*, concerns the sequencing and packaging of investments in water and sanitation. Given the patterns of household choice, a demand-driven approach will usually mean that provision of water supply services precedes that of sanitation services. It is frequently argued that this sequence would produce few health benefits because rapid increases in water use can overwhelm existing waste disposal capacity and because health benefits are maximized only when households utilize both better water and better sanitation services. These arguments are plausible, but experiences in many countries suggest that close adherence to the demand-driven approach remains appropriate in most places, including low-income settings. First, where rapid increase in water use is likely to cause environmental and health problems in the absence of household

sanitation services—as in urban areas—the demand for improved sanitation has invariably risen automatically as the demand for water services is satisfied. Second, where the demand-driven approach has not been followed, service provision has almost always been characterized by inefficiency and lack of accountability. For the provision of water supply and wastewater collection services, therefore, the demand-driven approach should be compromised only in rare circumstances.

Households are less willing to pay for the cost of trunk sewers and treatment of excreta and wastewater. Because these investments benefit the whole community and are important for environmental quality and health, there is potentially a case for using public funds to finance them. A few other situations may also justify direct government action or subsidies. Householders tend to undervalue such investments as areawide pollution abatement, vector control involving actions within households (see Box 4.6), and research and development. There may thus be grounds for public subsidy or other interventions in these areas. It will often be difficult to disentangle environmental and health benefits, and judgments will be necessary concerning the use of public funds.

Large institutional and cultural shifts are needed to create an efficient system for allocating scarce public and private resources to improve the household environment. Many developing countries have inherited—and then elaborated on—the former colonial powers' worst traditions of public sector inertia and professional inflexibility. Encouragingly, however, private sector involvement is increasing rapidly in both industrial and developing countries. SODECI, the privately run utility in Abidjan, is considered one of the best-run water companies in Africa. EMOS, the utility that serves Santiago, has used private sector contracts for such functions as meter reading, pipe maintenance, billing, and vehicle leasing and is one of the most efficient utilities in Latin America. The role of community organizations and NGOs may also be significant, particularly in drainage and sanitation improvements. In cities such as Karachi and São Paulo, community groups have significantly accelerated the provision of low-cost water supply and sanitation services to poor households, as well as helping to maintain and manage local services.

The occupational environment

Many women work in the home and thus suffer disproportionately from the health risks in the household environment just described. Both men and women may also encounter health risks in workplaces outside the home. A burden of 36 million DALYs, or 3 percent of the global burden of disease, is caused each year by preventable injuries and deaths in high-risk occupations and by chronic illness stemming from exposure to toxic chemicals, noise, stress, and physically debilitating work patterns (Table 4.6).

The International Labour Office has estimated that the cost of occupational injuries and associated production losses in a sample of industrial countries is between 1 and 4 percent of GNP. In developing countries this proportion is likely to be greater because accident rates tend to be higher. Rates of fatal occupational injuries among construction workers, for example, are more than ten times higher in Kenya and Thailand than in Finland. Agriculture, which employs more than half of all adults in most developing countries, is among the world's most dangerous occupations. Not only do agricultural workers suffer injuries, but they are also exposed to disease-carrying animals and to poisonous agrochemicals. Health risks are high in other sectors as well. Miners, construc-

Table 4.6 Estimated global burden of disease from selected environmental threats, 1990, and potential worldwide reductions through environmental interventions

Type of environment and principal related diseases[a]	Burden from these diseases (millions of DALYs per year)	Reduction achievable through feasible interventions[b] (percent)	Burden averted by feasible interventions (millions of DALYs per year)	Burden averted per 1,000 population (DALYs per year)
Occupational	318	—	36	7.1
Cancers	79	5	4	0.8
Neuropsychiatric	93	5	5	0.9
Chronic respiratory	47	5	2	0.5
Musculoskeletal	18	50	9	1.8
Unintentional injury	81[c]	20	16	3.1
Urban air	170	—	8	1.7
Respiratory infections	123	5	6	1.2
Chronic respiratory	47	5	2	0.5
Road transport (motor vehicle injuries)	32	20	6	1.2
All the above	473[d]	—	50	10.0

a. The diseases shown are those for which there is substantial evidence of a relationship with the particular environment and which are listed in Appendix B.
b. Estimates derived from the product of the efficacy of the interventions and the proportion of the global burden of disease that occurs among the exposed. All estimates of efficacy are speculative and assume the implementation of known, feasible, and affordable interventions in the circumstances encountered in developing countries.
c. Computed by subtracting motor vehicle injuries (32 million DALYs) from all unintentional injuries (113 million DALYs).
d. Adjusted for double counting.
Source: Appendix tables B.2 and B.3 and authors' calculations.

tion workers, migrant workers, and child laborers all suffer increased risk of disease because of their occupations. Small workplaces may have especially low standards of safety, yet such risks are often overlooked by government agencies and trade unions alike. A survey of companies in Samud Prakhan, Thailand, found that smaller plants, with fewer than fifty workers, had substantially lower levels of sanitation, health services, safety provisions, and environmental control measures than larger enterprises. Workers suffered more than twice as much noise and a third more lead fumes and vapors. And they experienced significant work-related health problems: 22 percent had lead poisoning or absorption, 27 percent had upper respiratory symptoms, and 6 percent had chronic obstructive pulmonary disease, even though most workers were below age 30.

Alleviating occupational risk depends on safety education for workers and managers, use of appropriate equipment and technology, and sound management practices. Governments can encourage these initiatives through legislation and regulation, financial incentives, investment in education, and research and development. Where worker organizations are strong, they have played a major role in identifying and reducing occupational risks. Tripartite agreements between workers, employers, and governments can lead to speedy progress.

The ambient environment

Radiation and pollution of air and water are additional health hazards. Since there is no market for clean air and water, government action is frequently justified.

AIR POLLUTION. Many cities suffer from air pollution caused by industry, power plants, road transport, and domestic use of coal. About 1.3 billion urban residents worldwide are exposed to air pollution levels above recommended limits. Air quality in the established market economies has generally improved in the past two decades. But in many developing countries and in the formerly socialist economies, air quality has deteriorated because of rising industrial activity, increasing power generation, and the congestion of streets with poorly maintained motor vehicles that use leaded fuel.

Air pollution damages the human respiratory and cardiorespiratory systems in various ways. The elderly, children, smokers, and those with chronic respiratory difficulties are most vulner-

able. Under the assumption that achievable reductions in urban air pollution can prevent 5 percent of all infectious and chronic respiratory disease, these reductions could avert a burden of 8 million DALYs each year, or 0.6 percent of the global burden of disease (Table 4.6). Local impacts and the effects on especially vulnerable groups can be much greater (Box 4.7).

Lead poisons many systems in the body and is particularly dangerous to children's developing brains and nervous systems. Airborne lead concentrations are high in polluted urban environments, where lead comes mainly from the exhaust of vehicles burning leaded gasoline. Elevated lead levels in children have been associated with impaired neuropsychologic development as measured by loss of IQ, poor school performance, and behavioral difficulties.

WATER POLLUTION. Newly industrialized countries, as well as many industrial countries, have polluted or are polluting their rivers, lakes, and coastal waters with a variety of chemical and biological wastes of both industrial and domestic origin. The practice of letting raw wastewater from industry and residential areas flow into rivers or the sea is common but unwise. Investment in preventing it may be justified because of the possibly severe local health consequences (as illustrated in Box 4.8) and because generalized water pollution, by reducing the number of water sources available for domestic supply, can foreclose cost-effective options for responding to demand for domestic services.

RADIATION. Individuals are exposed to natural background ionizing radiation and to radiation used for medical and dental diagnosis. Only a tiny amount of additional radiation comes from safely operated nuclear power stations or other installations (roughly one-thousandth of the background dose for those living within 50 kilometers of a nuclear power station). Current evidence suggests that the health effects of this radiation on the general population are extremely small or nonexistent. Accidents and occupational risks to workers in nuclear industries and to miners of radioactive ores, however, are different matters. The consequences of the nuclear power plant accident at Chernobyl, Ukraine, in 1986 have yet to be fully documented but are undoubtedly large. (The risk of such accidents is particularly high in the formerly socialist economies because of their large number of poorly designed nuclear facilities.) Standards and safe-

Box 4.7 Air pollution and health in Central Europe

Contrary to expectations, public ownership and centrally planned economies have neither controlled pollution nor brought health benefits to the populations of the formerly socialist economies. The countries of this region face a variety of serious environmental health threats, of which the greatest are particulates and gases in air, lead in air and soil, and nitrates and metals in water. A substantial gap in health status between these countries and those of Western Europe has opened up since the early 1960s: life expectancy is roughly five years shorter in the formerly socialist economies, and mortality rates in middle-aged males are roughly double. There has been considerable speculation among scientists and the public in Central Europe about how much of this health gap is attributable to environmental pollution.

Air pollution is the environmental factor that has had the greatest negative effect on health in Central Europe. Of the many air pollution "hotspots" throughout the region, the worst-affected area is the "Black Triangle," which covers northern Bohemia and Moravia, Silesia, and Saxony and has a population of roughly 6.5 million. In August 1991 the three governments involved—the Czech Republic, Germany, and Poland—and the Commission of the European Communities formed a Working Group for Neighbourly Cooperation on Environmental Issues to deal with the extremely high levels of air pollutants in the area.

The overall effect of air pollution on mortality in the Czech Republic has been estimated using data on the distribution of the population, the ambient levels of particulates and sulfur dioxide, and the relationship between excess mortality and pollution. This relationship is derived from studies in Canada, the United Kingdom, and the United States that indicate excess mortality of 1 percent for every 10 micrograms per cubic meter of particulates and sulfur dioxide. These estimates suggest air pollution causes up to 3 percent of total mortality in the Czech Republic and is responsible for roughly 9 percent in the gap in mortality rates between the Czech Republic and Western Europe. Similar estimates have been obtained for Silesia in Poland.

The effect of air pollution on mortality is greater for certain causes of death in specific age groups. A recent study of postneonatal respiratory mortality showed a rate 2.4 times higher in the most polluted districts of the Czech Republic than in the least polluted, after adjusting for a battery of socioeconomic factors. An increase in particulates of 25 micrograms per cubic meter was associated with an increase in postneonatal respiratory mortality of 58 percent.

The contribution of air pollution to morbidity in the Czech Republic is likely to be considerably greater than the effect on mortality and to have larger economic consequences through health expenditures, lost schooling, and lost productivity. Children in heavily polluted areas may suffer twice the rates of respiratory morbidity of those in clean areas. Overall, air pollution may be responsible for up to one-quarter of all respiratory morbidity in Czech children.

"Hotspots" of lead exposure exist throughout the formerly socialist economies. Average blood levels of more than 25 micrograms per deciliter in children have been reported in, for example, Pribram, Czech Republic, and Katowice, Poland. In comparison with normal levels, these higher levels could double the proportion of children requiring special education and halve the proportion in the exceptionally gifted group (IQ greater than 130).

---

guards against accidents and occupational hazards have been greatly improved, but risks may remain, and continued research and vigilance are required. Putative links of certain cancers with exposure to radon in houses and with electromagnetic fields created by high-voltage cables are being investigated in several industrial countries.

GLOBAL THREATS. Depletion of the atmospheric ozone layer and global warming pose potential threats of unknown magnitude to health. International agreements are limiting or will limit the release of chlorine compounds that can harm the ozone layer and of the greenhouse gases that contribute to global warming. The societies that will suffer least from these global changes are those that are wealthier (and therefore able to invest in appropriate coping strategies) and healthier. The best preparation at the national level for these uncertain future events is therefore to pursue sound economic and health policies in the medium term.

IMPROVING THE AMBIENT ENVIRONMENT. Improving health is only one of several reasons why societies may choose to invest in a cleaner environment. The policies and actions needed to clean up the air in a given city or area will depend on the origins of the pollution at that site. In most cities in developing countries motor vehicles are a significant source of air pollution and need to be specifically targeted. A few cities in the developing world, among them Bangkok and Mexico City, are pursuing systematic policies to reduce motor vehicle emissions, and their experience will be valuable

Box 4.8 Pollution in Japan: prevention would have been better and cheaper than cure

In the 1950s and 1960s Japan experienced a period of rapid industrialization and economic growth, but little attention was paid to the environmental consequences. The result was high levels of pollutants in the air, water, and soil in some areas and several infamous outbreaks of disease. Strong corrective action was taken in the 1970s and 1980s to redress the severest problems. Three conclusions emerge from the examples given below: allowing the release of toxic substances into the environment can lead to serious health consequences and economic losses; prevention, as Japan is now doing, is less costly than cleaning up; and taking corrective action now is less costly than allowing problems to persist.

Case 1: sulfur dioxide in the air

Between 1956 and 1973 one of Japan's largest petrochemical complexes was constructed at Yokkaichi City. By 1960 air pollution was causing local concern, and by 1963 one-hour average sulfur dioxide levels exceeded 2,800 micrograms per cubic meter, far above WHO's suggested maximum of 350 micrograms per cubic meter. In 1967 local residents successfully sued six companies, claiming medical costs and compensation for lost income. Seven percent of the total population of the district were certified to have been medically affected by ambient air pollution. Increasingly stringent pollution measures were introduced starting in 1970, and by 1976 sulfur dioxide levels were in compliance with local standards.

Air pollution control costs since 1971—including technical installations and their operation, monitoring, and creation of environmental buffer zones—have been $114 million a year. Without this investment, however, medical expenses and compensation would have been more than $160 million a year.

Case 2: mercury in the water

At the turn of the century Minamata was a scenic coastal town of 12,000 people who made their living from wood products, oranges, and fish. In 1908 a fertilizer plant was established that eventually became the Chisso Corporation, one of Japan's largest manufacturers of chemicals. By the 1920s compensation for damage to fisheries had already become an issue, and

in 1956 patients with a severe neurological affliction, later to be called Minamata disease, were observed. In 1968, following extensive research, the disease was linked to the ingestion of seafood containing high concentrations of methyl mercury, a compound discharged into Minamata Bay by the Chisso Corporation as a by-product of the manufacture of acetaldehyde. The discharge of methyl mercury peaked in 1959; it ended in 1968 when the company ceased production of acetaldehyde, but by then the floor of the bay and its aquatic life had become heavily contaminated. Starting in 1974, 1.5 million cubic meters of polluted sediment were dredged and removed.

By 1991, 2,248 people (1,004 of whom had died) had been certified as suffering from Minamata disease and were eligible for compensation. An additional 2,000 people are pursuing claims for compensation. Had discharge of mercury continued, the estimated annual costs of the damage, including patient treatment and compensation, sediment dredging, and losses to fisheries, would have been $97 million a year. If acetaldehyde production had continued, pollution abatement through in-plant waste recycling would have cost only $1 million a year.

Case 3: cadmium in the soil

In the late 1940s a disease characterized by extreme generalized pain, kidney damage, and loss of bone strength appeared in the Jinzu River Basin. The disease, which primarily afflicted women, was called *itai-itai* ("It hurts, it hurts!") after the cries of the sufferers. Two decades of research led, in 1968, to the conclusion that the cause was chronic cadmium poisoning, which was traced to the effluent from the Mitsui Mining and Smelting Company located in the upper reaches of the basin. The route for the cadmium poisoning was from river water to irrigation water to soil to rice. By 1991, 129 people had been certified as *itai-itai* sufferers, and 116 of them had died.

A major program of soil restoration was initiated in 1979. By 1992, 36 percent of the contaminated area of 1,500 hectares had been treated. Had the further release of cadmium not been prevented, the annual costs from medical compensation, agricultural losses, and soil restoration would have been $19 million a year. The costs of prevention were $5 million a year.

in designing the next generation of programs. Successful policies include incentives and regulations to improve fuel quality, enhance engine performance and maintenance, and reduce traffic volume. Most industrial countries and an increasing number of developing countries have set limits on

lead levels in gasoline and are using price differentials to encourage consumers to switch to lead-free products. Lead concentrations in the air have fallen by 50 percent or more in response to these measures, and average blood lead levels in urban areas have also declined substantially.

Clean technologies and practices can reduce local industrial pollution levels even as output expands. To encourage adoption of such technologies, governments need to pursue policies that improve the efficiency with which energy is used. Such policies include the elimination of subsidies for power generation and, in many countries, for vehicle fuels and coal. Efficient reforms help reduce pollution while raising a country's economic output. Policy options are described in full in *World Development Report 1992*.

The road transport environment

Motor vehicle crashes are responsible for an increasing burden of injury and death in developing countries. Each year throughout the world road traffic injuries cause a loss of 32 million DALYs, or more than 2 percent of the global burden of disease (Table 4.6). Men suffer roughly twice the burden from road traffic injuries as women. The young and the old are particularly vulnerable, as are drivers of nonmotorized vehicles and pedestrians. The number of road fatalities and injuries in developing countries is rising rapidly with urbanization and growth in the volume of traffic. Road fatalities in Africa increased fourfold between 1968 and 1988, whereas in Europe they declined by more than 20 percent during the same period.

A multipronged approach to road safety can reduce crashes at reasonable cost. Public investment in improved road infrastructure and highway operation systems, remedial action at known "blackspots" with high accident rates, and expanded public transport systems all make a difference. Legislation, financial incentives, and programs of road safety education can improve driver behavior, reduce traffic speeds, promote use of seat belts, improve vehicle safety, and reduce drunk driving. The insurance and legal liability systems may also offer powerful incentives for road safety. A carefully designed package of measures such as those mentioned above can, over time, reduce road fatalities and injuries by at least one-fifth, thus preventing the loss of at least 6 million DALYs a year worldwide (Table 4.6). Several countries, including Kenya and Malaysia, have set more ambitious targets for reductions in deaths and injuries over the next decade.

AIDS: a threat to development

Historians will look back on the latter half of this century as having had one great medical triumph, the eradication of smallpox, and one great medical tragedy, AIDS. Unknown prior to 1981, AIDS now dominates public health programs and health services in several countries and may come to dominate in many more. The human immunodeficiency virus (HIV) that causes AIDS is transmitted through sexual intercourse. Like other STDs, it can also be transmitted by contact with contaminated blood (notably from transfusions) and from mother to child during the perinatal period. Casual transmission from person to person does not occur. In developing countries more than 85 percent of infections occur through heterosexual intercourse. There is no cure, and discovery of a vaccine is unlikely before 2000. Action is needed now to combat the spread of the disease.

Why AIDS is a special case

AIDS deserves special attention because failure to control the epidemic at an early stage will result in far more damaging and costly consequences in the future.

• *The HIV epidemic is bad and is getting worse.* An estimated 9 million people worldwide carried the HIV virus in 1990; as many as 26 million could be infected by 2000, according to WHO estimates (see Table 1.3 in Chapter 1). AIDS will then contribute about 3.3 percent to the global burden of disease, and 1.8 million people will die of AIDS each year. Given the short time it takes infection rates to double in many developing countries and the rapid spread of the disease to countries that previously had low numbers of infections, total figures in 2000 may be two or three times higher than the above projections.

More than 80 percent of those infected lived in developing countries in 1990; by 2000 this will increase to an estimated 95 percent. In Thailand one in fifty adults is infected. In Sub-Saharan African one in forty adults is already infected, and in certain cities of Africa the prevalence of infection is as high as one in three. In some of these high-prevalence communities AIDS is already starting to reverse long-term declines in child mortality.

• *The cost-effectiveness of interventions drops sharply when infections cross from high-risk groups to the general population.* Since there is no vaccine or cure for AIDS, primary prevention is the only way to fight the disease. In the absence of adequate preventive action, AIDS spreads rapidly in the "core" groups (such as sex workers and their clients), followed by a slower and then accelerating

Early intervention against AIDS prevents spread of the disease to the general population.

Figure 4.7 Simulated AIDS epidemic in a Sub-Saharan African country

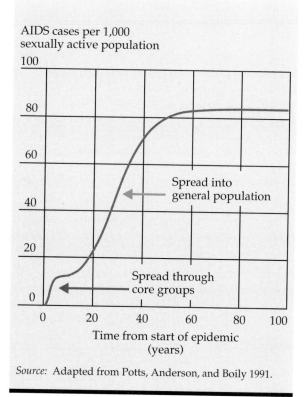

AIDS cases per 1,000 sexually active population

Spread into general population

Spread through core groups

Time from start of epidemic (years)

Source: Adapted from Potts, Anderson, and Boily 1991.

spread in the general population (Figure 4.7). Early and effective targeting of HIV interventions is critical because these interventions diminish in cost-effectiveness as the infection moves out of the high-risk, high-transmission core groups. The large number of new sexual contacts in the core groups means that each HIV case avoided in this group can avert more than ten times as many additional infections as can a case avoided in the general population.

• *AIDS has catastrophically costly consequences.* AIDS, affecting as it does mainly people in the economically productive adult years, has powerful negative economic effects on households, productive enterprises, and countries (see Box 1.2 in Chapter 1). Because so many of its victims are heads of households or parents, AIDS devastates families. Heavily infected countries have found their health systems burdened with costly cases of AIDS-related opportunistic infections. If the AIDS epidemic continues unchecked, the accelerated de-

mand for health care for AIDS patients will crowd out the needs of other patients. Furthermore, the number of tuberculosis cases is increasing dramatically as a direct result of HIV, and the presence of HIV worsens problems with other sexually transmitted diseases. (STDs both facilitate HIV transmission and are harder to treat in HIV-infected individuals.)

• *Prevention of AIDS involves sensitive and politically charged issues.* Preventing HIV infection often necessitates working with socially marginalized groups (including, in many cultures, homosexuals), and with people who pursue illegal activities such as drug use or prostitution. In addition, an effective preventive program must reach out to inform young people frankly about sexual practices and risks. These activities offer little political benefit and may be highly controversial. Strong government will and commitment are therefore essential to effective programs, the more so because the seven-to-ten-year lag between HIV infection and the development of AIDS makes it tempting for countries and individuals to put off dealing with AIDS issues until it is too late to avert a widespread epidemic.

Prevention: an absolute necessity

A combination of strategies, backed up with adequate resources, is required for stemming the spread of AIDS. Crucial elements in these strategies are providing information on how to avoid infection, promoting condom use, treating other sexually transmitted diseases, and reducing bloodborne transmission. These measures are especially cost-effective when targeted at the relatively few people in the core groups. Unless effective preventive action is taken, the number of new HIV infections can be expected to grow, especially in parts of Asia. But a comprehensive AIDS prevention program could check the growth of the disease (Figure 4.8).

Current annual worldwide expenditure on AIDS prevention is about $1.5 billion a year. Perhaps less than $200 million of this is spent in developing countries, where 85 percent of all infections occur. Among developing countries Thailand spends the most for AIDS prevention, with 1992 spending of $45 million, more than 75 percent of which was from government funds. Total AIDS spending on prevention in all Sub-Saharan Africa was only twice this amount, with a mere 10 percent from government funds. A recent study for WHO's Global Program on AIDS suggested that comprehensive AIDS and STD prevention services for all developing countries would cost $1.5 billion to $2.9 billion a year. This is ten to fifteen times current spending, but it would yield enormous benefits. The estimated number of new adult HIV infections averted by such spending between 1993 and 2000 would be about 9.5 million—4.2 million in Africa, 4.2 million in Asia, and 1.1 million in Latin America.

Groups to be targeted

Preventive efforts must reach populations with diverse needs: people at particularly high risk of acquiring and transmitting HIV infection (core groups), young people, and women. Preventive programs for the population at large are less cost-effective than targeted programs but are needed to increase awareness and understanding of AIDS and STDs, reduce discrimination against infected persons, and prepare the way for subsequent interventions when levels of infection rise. Monogamy might be encouraged as part of public information efforts to curb the spread of HIV, but it cannot be the only strategy; even where it is the societal norm, not all individuals adhere.

High-risk groups may include sex workers, migrants, members of the military, truck drivers, and drug users who share needles. For these groups, prevention of sexual transmission essentially means education on safer sex, promotion of condom use, and prevention and treatment of STDs. It is important not simply to provide information on condoms but also to ensure their availability and to empower members of the core group, especially female sex workers, to use them. Brothel managers and clients must also be persuaded of the need to change their behavior; experience from Zaire and other countries shows that promotion of condoms to male clients substantially improves the success of programs targeted at sex workers. Areas of high STD prevalence warrant aggressive attempts to control STDs through condom promotion, case management and counseling, notification of partners, and surveillance. These can be provided through a wide spectrum of health institutions such as family planning clinics and primary health centers.

Young people, both in and out of school, need comprehensive education on reproduction and reproductive health issues. To be most effective, education must begin before the onset of sexual activity (ages 12–14 in many countries) and must be targeted at boys as well as girls. Reaching boys is

Effective prevention can markedly slow the rate of new infection with HIV.

Figure 4.8 Trends in new HIV infections under alternative assumptions, 1990–2000: Sub-Saharan Africa and Asia

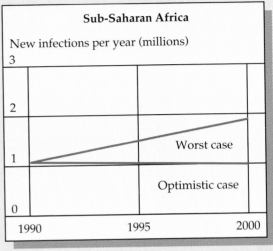

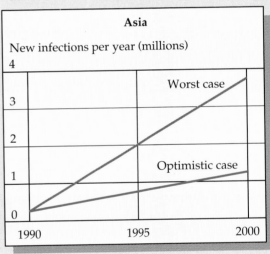

Note: Asia includes China, India, and Other Asia and islands.
Source: World Health Organization and World Bank data.

particularly important because men so often dominate the sexual relationship. The curriculum should be sensitive to local cultural conditions but should provide explicit, honest explanations of sexuality, gender issues, safe sexual practices, STDs and HIV, safe motherhood, and family planning. All potential behavioral choices, including abstinence and condom use, should be presented. There is no evidence to support the objection that providing sex education encourages promiscuity. In societies in which it is unacceptable for teachers to provide sex education, the task can be delegated to qualified voluntary groups.

Women are biologically more susceptible to acquiring HIV infection through heterosexual intercourse than are men, and social factors often add to the risks. In Uganda, for example, more than 60 percent of infected persons are women. Preventive efforts addressed to women, especially those of childbearing age, can protect both maternal and child health. In many African countries AIDS and HIV-related illnesses are already among the top ten causes of childhood mortality. At present there is no way to prevent HIV transmission from an infected woman to her fetus; about 30 percent of the babies of infected women are born with the infection. Most such babies survive their first year but succumb to opportunistic infections during their second or third year. The uninfected children of infected mothers are also at increased risk of dying because they are likely to lose one or both of their parents. The only strategy for fighting childhood AIDS is to target preventive efforts to women of childbearing age.

Babies can contract HIV through breast milk, creating difficult tradeoffs between the risk of infection and the benefits of breastfeeding for child health. Recent studies suggest that the risk is substantial (about 30 percent) for babies breastfed by mothers who develop an HIV infection after childbirth; the risk for babies of women who are infected prenatally is smaller, although still significant. Randomized controlled studies are under way in Haiti, Kenya, and Rwanda to determine the risks more accurately. In the meantime, in areas where the primary causes of infant deaths are infectious diseases and malnutrition, breastfeeding should probably continue to be recommended. In areas where a safe alternative to breastfeeding exists, testing of pregnant women would provide an opportunity to advise those infected about the health risk of breastfeeding for their babies.

Specific preventive interventions

Widespread experience with national AIDS control programs in industrial and developing countries is already on hand. It suggests some areas in which action needs to be taken and provides important lessons for programs to control AIDS.

PROVIDING INFORMATION. Informing people about the steps they can take to protect themselves against HIV infection is central to any strategy for combating AIDS. Individuals need to know that the risk of infection can be minimized by reducing the number of new sexual partners they have, by choosing partners of lowest risk, by avoiding contact with contaminated blood, by using condoms and refraining from risky sexual practices such as anal sex, and by avoiding or seeking treatment for cofactors such as STDs. Intravenous drug users can lower their risks by using clean needles. In communities where the HIV virus is present, people should be aware that unprotected sex is safe only with a person known unequivocally to be uninfected—for example, someone who has not yet been sexually active and has no other risk factors (such as intravenous drug use or transfusion) or who has recently undergone HIV testing and has been found to be uninfected.

ENCOURAGING CONDOM USE. Condom use is effective in slowing the spread of both HIV and STDs and needs to be encouraged in all risky sexual encounters. Programs to promote condom use in highly vulnerable groups such as clients of sex workers are cost-effective. One such program targeted to low-income sex workers in Nairobi reduced the mean annual incidence of gonorrhea from 2.8 episodes per woman in 1986 to 0.7 episode in 1989. The program averted an estimated 6,000 to 10,000 new HIV infections a year at an approximate cost of $0.50 per DALY gained. Community-wide interventions are also being tried with success. In Zimbabwe a community intervention estimated to cost $85,000 successfully reached more than 1 million persons, distributed more than 5.7 million condoms, and reduced STDs in the general population by 6 to 50 percent in different areas. The intervention also changed behavior among sex workers: the proportion reporting condom use with their last client rose to 72 percent, from only 18 percent before the intervention.

Social marketing is another strategy for promoting condom use. In Zaire distribution outlets—from pharmacies to traditional healers and from nightclubs to street vendors—were saturated with condoms. Condom sales rose from 20,000 in 1987 to 18.3 million in 1991. Consumer research indicates that 90 percent of the condoms were bought by men and that about 60 percent were intended for casual sex. Estimates suggest that the program averted about 25,000 HIV infections in 1991 alone.

REDUCING BLOOD-BORNE TRANSMISSION. Blood transfusions account for less than 5 percent of HIV transmission worldwide, but transfusion with infected blood almost always leads to infection. Measures for preventing transmission of HIV through blood transfusions include reducing the need for transfusions, eliminating payments for donated blood (because paid donors tend to have a higher risk of HIV), and screening donors. Effective early treatment of health problems, combined with education for health care providers about the proper indications for transfusion, can cut the need for transfusions by more than 50 percent. Public health programs such as helminth control in schools, iron supplementation, prenatal care, and malaria control can reduce the severity of existing anemia and thus diminish the need for transfusions. When transfusion is unavoidable, blood donors can be screened to ensure a supply of uninfected blood. The cost-effectiveness of blood screening varies dramatically depending on the prevalence of HIV. To maintain the population's overall confidence in the medical community, however, blood screening has been advocated even where HIV prevalence is low. When blood banks exist, screening adds only about 5 percent to the total cost of each unit of transfused blood.

INTEGRATING AIDS PREVENTION AND STD SERVICES. Wide availability of STD services is crucial for fighting AIDS because HIV transmission is facilitated by the genital lesions and inflammation associated with STDs. Treatment of STDs is often highly cost-effective in its own right. It becomes even more cost-effective when the benefits of reduced HIV transmission are added. Curing each case of gonorrhea in a core group saves 120 DALYs, at a cost well below $1 per DALY gained if the benefits of fewer secondary cases and reduced risk of HIV transmission are included.

Because many STDs are asymptomatic (especially in women), infected individuals may have little motivation to be tested and treated. Even for those with symptoms, charges for clinical services may reduce access to treatment and therefore increase the spread of STDs. In Nairobi, for example, the introduction of fees at the main STD clinic reduced attendance by 60 percent among men and 35 percent among women. Subsidizing STD services therefore makes sense as part of an AIDS control program. Another good strategy is to combine STD and family planning services; screening for asymptomatic STD infections in family planning clinics has revealed infection rates as high as 20 percent.

TESTING AND SCREENING. Voluntary HIV testing provides individuals with useful information about themselves and their partners. Studies suggest that counseling and testing can help individuals and couples adopt safer sexual behavior. The once-prohibitive cost of testing has been declining sharply; a couple can now be screened for less than $2 (excluding the cost of counseling). The test, however, is not always reliable because there is a short period during which HIV may not be detected in a newly infected person; furthermore, a negative test result is no guarantee of continuing risk-free behavior. As a result, testing is currently most useful for couples within or planning a long-term relationship. Governments need to ensure that testing remains voluntary and anonymous, meets quality standards, and is accompanied by appropriate counseling or information.

SURVEILLANCE. Public health surveillance for HIV is critical in areas where extensive spread of the virus has not yet occurred. Countries that establish a timely and reliable system of surveillance are able to give policymakers early warning of an impending spread of the virus. Useful activities include regular surveillance for HIV and syphilis in a few prenatal clinics and in centers serving clients at high risk of infection, such as sex workers and patients with STDs.

Several of the preventive interventions discussed above have been incorporated in the Indian government's National AIDS Control Project, launched in 1992 with the assistance of the World Bank and WHO. The Indian program emphasizes promoting public awareness about AIDS, promoting health in core groups through NGOs, controlling STDs, improving the safety of blood supplies, strengthening surveillance and institutional capabilities for control of HIV-AIDS, and encouraging the humane treatment of people with AIDS or HIV infections.

Care of AIDS patients

In 1992 developing countries spent about $340 million to care for AIDS patients. Although this is only a small fraction of the $4.7 billion spent by industrial countries to care for their AIDS patients, it is still nearly twice the amount spent on AIDS prevention in the developing world. If spending per patient remains constant, the amount spent on the care of AIDS patients in developing countries will more than triple, to $1.1 billion in 2000. To date, many AIDS control programs have not developed guidelines for the cost-effective provision of care for AIDS patients. Antiviral drugs such as azidothymidine (AZT) are enormously expensive, have severe side effects, and may, at best, delay the onset of AIDS and prolong life to some extent. One year of AZT costs more than $3,000, a prohibitively high figure. Treatment options in many low-income nations are therefore limited to alleviation of pain and management of the opportunistic infections—most commonly, tuberculosis, diarrhea, and candidiasis—that afflict HIV-infected persons. Strategic planning can greatly reduce costs through the use of a small number of less-expensive drugs and outpatient or community treatment where possible. Basic care, including outpatient treatment of opportunistic infections, can cost $200 to $400 per DALY gained, a substan-

tial sum. Palliative home care, by contrast, costs between $30 and $75 per DALY gained, but it may be a substantial burden to the family. Uganda's innovative activities have made it possible to provide caring responses, at modest cost, to those afflicted (Box 4.9).

The need for national and international action

At present, most national AIDS programs are inadequate, despite international attention and the significant effort by WHO to help design and implement plans for controlling AIDS. Most programs use only the resources available to ministries of health, are too standardized, and neglect the control of STDs. AIDS has to be approached as a national development issue. National leadership is crucial; the most effective programs, such as Thailand's, pursue strategies that involve many agencies, in and outside government, in an atmosphere of openness and frankness (Box 4.10).

Box 4.9 Coping with AIDS in Uganda

By June 1992 Uganda had reported 33,971 AIDS cases; the true number may be between 100,000 and 300,000, and it is estimated that 1 million to 1.5 million Ugandans are infected with HIV. In Kampala more than 30 percent of all pregnant women are infected, and in many parts of the country AIDS is the most common cause of admission and death among hospitalized adults. With this immense burden, care of infected individuals and management of the social consequences of infection are perceived to be as important as prevention of further cases of HIV.

In response, a variety of innovative activities have been undertaken. In 1987 the first AIDS clinic was opened, with a small staff, a few drugs, and little outside support. The clinic recently enrolled its 8,000th patient. Patients regard the care they get there as much higher in quality than that available elsewhere. The founder of the clinic, Dr. Ely Katabira, and another physician at the national teaching hospital have produced a 104-page manual on AIDS care that recommends simple diagnostic and treatment strategies for AIDS; for example, nine relatively inexpensive drugs used in combination with tuberculosis therapy can achieve a high degree of relief for patients with AIDS.

Also in 1987 sixteen Ugandans who were personally affected by AIDS (because of their own infection or that of a family member) set up a new voluntary organization, The AIDS Support Organization (TASO), to provide emotional support for AIDS sufferers. Twelve of the founding members have since died of AIDS, but

TASO has grown to include ninety-seven counselors, three supervisors, and six trainers in eight locations. Services, which reach more than 30,000 people a year, include counseling, condom education and distribution, home care, income-generating activities, feeding programs, and payment of orphans' school fees.

In 1990, to address the demand for personal testing, Uganda's first anonymous HIV testing and counseling center was established. The enormous demand has made individual pretest counseling impossible, but group counseling has become popular. Individual post-test counseling continues to be offered, and HIV-positive patients are referred to TASO for further support. AIDS awareness in Uganda is so high that many people assume they are infected. Couples who are tested and found to be negative report they are more motivated to be monogamous, and a small follow-up study found that such clients have fewer casual sex partners and use condoms regularly. Additional centers have been established in other areas, as well as an executive testing center for businessmen and parliamentarians uncomfortable about being served in the busy public clinic. High demand indicates that Ugandans want to know whether they are infected, particularly before embarking on important life events such as marriage. Uganda's experience demonstrates that an AIDS-testing program in a country with a high prevalence of heterosexual transmission can have a more positive influence on behavior than results from the industrial world would indicate.

Box 4.10 HIV in Thailand: from disaster toward containment

As late as 1988 Thailand and the rest of Asia were considered to be relatively free of HIV infection, leading senior Thai health experts to conjecture that Asians might be less susceptible to the disease. That year, however, an explosive HIV epidemic started its march through Thailand, affecting all levels of society. Today it is estimated that 2 percent of sexually active adults, or 400,000 to 600,000 people, are infected. Without effective prevention, by 2000 the number infected may be as high as 2 million to 4 million.

Faced with the HIV epidemic, Thai officials have moved quickly from complacency to action. Thailand, they realized, could not sustain its 10 percent annual growth of GNP in the presence of a huge AIDS epidemic. Indeed, in 1991 researchers projected that the aggregate direct and indirect cost of AIDS could be as high as $8 billion over the next decade and that AIDS could have negative effects on tourism, foreign investment, and labor remittances from abroad. They argued, however, that a major preventive effort, with the goals of reducing numbers of sexual partners by at least one-half, doubling condom use, and treating STDs, could mean 3.5 million fewer infections and more than $5 billion in savings by 2000.

AIDS prevention is now being accorded the highest priority in Thailand, and a national AIDS prevention and control committee chaired by the prime minister has been formed. In 1992 the cabinet approved the establishment of the AIDS Policy and Planning Coordination Bureau in the office of the permanent secretary of the prime minister. The multisectoral bureau coordinates the planning and budgeting of AIDS activities among fourteen ministries, international funding agencies, and local sources of support. The bureau also facilitates the planning of joint activities with private businesses and NGOs.

Thailand's strategy has led to a broad consensus within the country on the importance of taking action. Spending for AIDS prevention was $28 million in 1991 and $45 million in 1992. To monitor the epidemic, Thailand has established the world's most comprehensive national HIV surveillance system, which reports twice a year on HIV prevalence in all risk groups in all provinces of the country. Acknowledging that commercial sex is ingrained in Thai society and will remain so in the short run, the government has decided to mandate and enforce a policy of 100 percent condom use at the brothels. This ensures that brothels cannot compete for customers seeking condom-free sex. Preliminary evidence shows very high rates of condom use, with demand increasing from 10 million a year to about 120 million a year and reductions in the incidence of STDs.

The prime minister's office is launching national campaigns through the mass media in 1993–94 to promote changes in the sexual culture and the sexual norms of the population. Only time will determine whether intervention has been prompt and effective enough to halt the further spread of HIV.

No single strategy in the fight against AIDS will meet the needs of every country. Three main criteria can guide the choice of priorities from the range of HIV-AIDS interventions listed above. These criteria are current HIV prevalence, risk of future spread, and existing AIDS burden. Strategies for different countries and regions within countries fall into four main groups.

• Areas with little HIV and few STDs (for example, rural areas of northern China and North Africa) should emphasize comprehensive reproductive health education for youth, with some attention to AIDS prevention among high-risk groups, and should establish a sensitive HIV surveillance system.

• Areas at high risk of an epidemic from early spread of HIV or having a high rate of STDs (for example, Yunnan Province in China and Surabaya, Indonesia) should undertake massive, targeted preventive activities for high-risk groups, including sex workers, supplemented by general education and by testing of the blood supply.

• Areas with an HIV epidemic but as yet little disease (for example, Thailand, and urban areas of India) need to develop AIDS prevention programs for the entire population while continuing to target high-risk groups. Voluntary HIV testing and counseling and preparation for the care of AIDS patients should also begin.

• Finally, areas with a major epidemic and a high disease burden (for example, Uganda and Zambia) have to combine a broadly based preventive strategy with attention to care for AIDS patients (see Box 4.9).

Nongovernmental organizations can play a vital role in prevention, care, and community support programs, using their credibility and access to reach those at highest risk, such as intravenous drug users and sex workers. Such groups have been highly effective in using social marketing to reach individuals at the grass-roots level, particularly by initiating peer education and media programs that reinforce behavior change and work to modify the perceived social norms. A recent

Table 4.7 Costs and health benefits of public health packages in low- and middle-income countries, 1990

Country group and component of package	Annual cost (dollars)			Disease burden averted (percent)[a]
	Per participant	Per capita	Per DALY	
Low-income (income per capita = $350)				
EPI Plus	14.6	0.5	12–17	6.0
School health program	3.6	0.3	20–25	0.1
Other public health programs (including family planning, health, and nutrition information)[b]	2.4	1.4	—[c]	—[c]
Tobacco and alcohol control program	0.3	0.3	35–50	0.1[d]
AIDS prevention program[e]	112.2	1.7	3–5	2.0
Total	—	4.2 (1.2)	—	8.2
Middle-income (income per capita = $2,500)				
EPI Plus	28.6	0.8	25–30	1.0
School health program	6.5	0.6	38–43	0.4
Other public health programs (including family planning, health, and nutrition information)[b]	5.2	3.1	—[c]	—[c]
Tobacco and alcohol control program	0.3	0.3	45–55	0.3[d]
AIDS prevention program[e]	132.3	2.0	13–18	2.3
Total	—	6.8 (0.3)	—	4.0

Note: Numbers in parentheses refer to per capita cost as a percentage of income per capita.
a. Although costs are estimated for 100 percent coverage, the health benefits are based on 95 percent coverage for EPI Plus and 80 percent coverage for the school health, AIDS prevention, and tobacco and alcohol programs.
b. Includes information, communication, and education on selected risk factors and health behaviors, plus vector control and disease surveillance and monitoring.
c. The health benefits from information and communication and from disease surveillance are counted in the other public and clinical services in the health package. The health benefits from vector control are unknown.
d. Calculation of the potential disease burden averted through this program assumes no change in the prevalence of smoking and alcohol consumption; if such prevalence were to rise, the potential benefits would be larger.
e. Exludes treatment of STDs, which are in the clinical services package; see Table 5.3.
Source: Authors' calculations.

needs-assessment study conducted in a number of developing countries showed that the full potential of NGOs was not being realized for lack of financial, managerial, and technical support. Planning is under way for a program to provide innovative mechanisms for simple and flexible assistance to nongovernmental groups working on AIDS.

The world must do more to deal with the global challenge of AIDS. No country is immune from a future HIV epidemic, and the costs of delay are high. A global coalition is needed that will encourage and assist governments to take bold action before it is too late. Without a substantial increase in political commitment and leadership—as well as additional resources to support the $1.5 billion to $2.9 billion needed annually for effective prevention of AIDS—the HIV epidemic could cause a health disaster and an enormous setback for development.

The essential public health package

Public health programs that address the problems described above can produce substantial health gains at modest cost. Local conditions vary, but an essential public health package is likely to include:

• The Expanded Programme on Immunization, including micronutrient supplementation

• School health programs to treat worm infections and micronutrient deficiencies and to provide health education

• Programs to increase public knowledge about family planning and nutrition, about self-cure or indications for seeking care, and about vector control and disease surveillance activities

• Programs to reduce consumption of tobacco, alcohol, and other drugs

• AIDS prevention programs with a strong STD component.

This public health package would yield large benefits at low cost (Table 4.7). In low-income countries it would avert more than 8 percent of the burden of disease at a cost of just $4 per capita (1.2 percent of income per capita), while in middle-income countries it might avert 4 percent of the burden of disease at a cost of $7 per capita (0.3 percent of income per capita). Because it is difficult to quantify the health gains from the activities under "Other public health programs," the corresponding cost per DALY is not estimated.

Provision of information is needed in every aspect of the program. Information should cover the benefits of healthy eating, contraceptive use, and hygienic practices in the household; the health effects of smoking and of alcohol and drug abuse; and prevention of HIV infections. Some public health measures will involve providing services in clinics, including family planning and STD-related services. These are included in the essential package of clinical measures discussed in the next chapter. Health will also be served if governments do less in a number of areas—if they avoid intervening in food markets, cut indiscriminate subsidies for water and sanitation, remove most restrictions on contraceptive services, and abolish subsidies on fuels. Appropriate government regulatory action on the ambient environment, occupational conditions, and road safety can also safeguard people's health.

5

Clinical services

This chapter analyzes the roles of the public and private sectors in paying for and delivering clinical services. It examines in depth an important conclusion of Chapter 3: that governments have a fundamental responsibility for ensuring universal access to an essential package of clinical services, with special attention to reaching the poor (Table 5.1). The choice of services to be included in such a package for each country will be strongly influenced by information on the distribution of disease and the relative cost-effectiveness of clinical interventions. A minimum package of clinical services could reduce the present burden of disease by about one-quarter in low-income countries and by about one-tenth in middle-income countries. This package is affordable—but only if governments carry out significant health-financing reforms that will affect the allocation of public funds and the roles of insurance and of user charges.

Only by reducing or eliminating spending on clinical services that are outside the nationally defined essential package can governments concentrate on ensuring essential clinical care for the poor. Two key ways to reallocate government spending are to increase cost recovery, especially by charging the wealthy for services in government hospitals, and to promote unsubsidized insurance for middle- and upper-income groups. Governments can avoid the explosive increases in health expenditures that many countries are now confronting by encouraging competition among providers and prepayment for care, generating and disseminating information on providers' costs and insurers' products, and, in some cases, setting limits on compensation of physicians and hospitals.

Although both the public and the private sectors have important roles in the delivery of clinical services, government-run health systems in many developing countries are overextended and need to be scaled back. This can be done through legal and administrative changes designed to facilitate private (NGO and for-profit) involvement in provision of health services, by public subsidies to NGOs for supplying the essential package, and by curtailment of new investments in public tertiary hospitals. At the same time, the efficiency of public sector health services can be greatly enhanced through decentralization and improved management of government hospitals and programs.

Public and private finance of clinical services

Around the world, clinical services are financed through four main channels. Two—out-of-pocket payments and voluntary insurance—are private. The other two are public: compulsory insurance (sometimes known as social insurance) that is either publicly managed or heavily regulated by governments, and funding from general government revenues.

In the poorest countries total health expenditure may be as low as $2 per person a year, and more than half of this comes from private sources, mainly in the form of out-of-pocket payments. Insurance mechanisms in those countries are weak, and the amount of government revenues devoted to health is low. As incomes increase, so do both the percentage of income spent on health (as shown in the upper panel of Figure 5.1) and the share of health spending that comes from public sources (illustrated in the lower panel). In the for-

Table 5.1 Rationales and directions for government action in the finance and delivery of clinical services

Area	Conditions that may call for government action: market failure and poverty	Directions for government action
Essential clinical services	Failure to treat, for example, tuberculosis and STDs creates risks for the general population. Public financing can help offset the additional external costs to society. Poor people have limited ability to save or borrow to meet unexpected and uninsured health expenses. Families, including children, can fall into poverty because of ill health.	*Finance* essential clinical services by reallocating current government spending. In low-income countries this may mean increasing public expenditures for health. *Require* through legislation that social insurance or mandated private insurance cover an essential package. *Encourage* more private and NGO provision of essential services, through appropriate legislation and targeted public subsidies.
Clinical services outside the essential package	In insurance markets selection bias leads to lack of coverage for high-risk groups. "Moral hazard," by insulating patient and provider from the cost implications of their decisions, results in overuse of services. The asymmetry of information between patient and provider can cause suppliers to induce excess demand.	*Reduce or eliminate* subsidization of clinical services outside the essential package. Subsidies for public provision of services at less than cost and tax relief for employer and employee health insurance payments often cover services with low cost-effectiveness and primarily benefit the wealthy. *Legislate* compulsory social insurance or mandated private insurance, or define the national essential package comprehensively. *Limit* government involvement in delivery of nonessential services and encourage competition in service delivery by government, NGOs, and the private sector. *Regulate* private insurance by, for example, requiring community risk-rating and forbidding the rejection of high-risk consumers. *Define* the exact content of prepaid packages of care to serve as the products bought and sold in the insurance market. *Encourage* the use of prepayment or salary-based approaches to provider compensation. *Foster* improvements in the quality of private provision by encouraging self-regulation of hospitals, medical schools, and physicians and by disseminating performance indicators.

merly socialist economies and the established market economies (excluding the United States) public spending accounts for a full three-quarters of total health expenditure.

In addition to the four sources of health financing, there are three ways of organizing clinical health services: public, private nonprofit, and private for-profit. All national health systems use at least two of the twelve possible combinations of financing method and health service organization, and sometimes the different combinations serve sharply differentiated populations. Even so, it is possible to group countries according to income level and the predominant system of providing health care. A principal distinction is whether in-

surance pays for much care and, if so, what is the dominant type of insurance (Table 5.2).

In *low-income countries* private out-of-pocket payments account for more than half of the mere $2 to $40 per person spent each year for health care. Most of this sum goes for doctors' fees, payments to traditional healers, and drugs. NGOs, particularly those related to religious institutions, make important contributions to the provision of health services in many low-income countries. In Tanzania and Haiti NGOs operate nearly half of the hospitals, and in Cameroon and Uganda they manage 40 percent of health facilities. In Ghana and Nigeria about a third of all hospital beds are located in mission hospitals. Government spend-

As countries get richer, they spend more of their income on health, and the public share grows larger.

Figure 5.1 Income and health spending in seventy countries, 1990

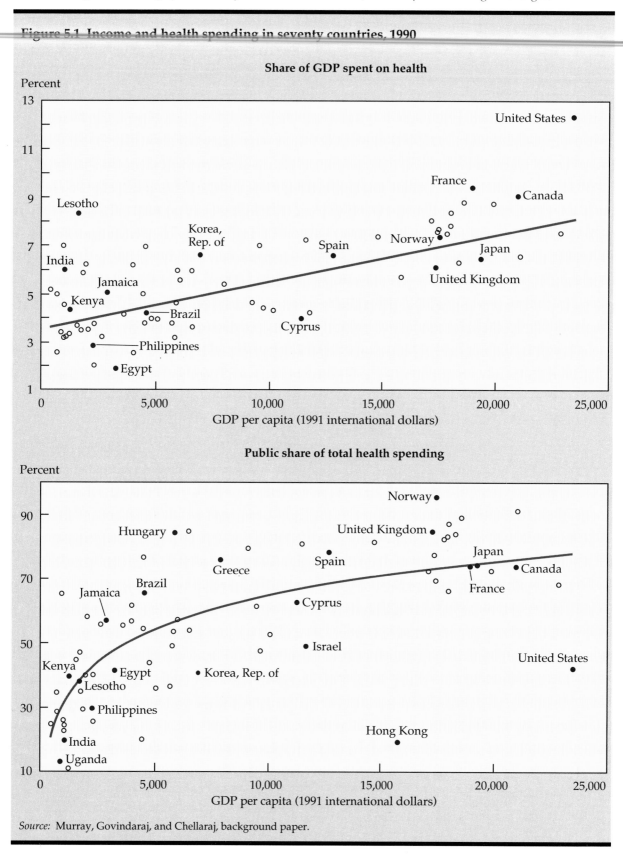

Share of GDP spent on health

Percent

(scatterplot with vertical axis labeled 13, 11, 9, 7, 5, 3, 1 and horizontal axis GDP per capita (1991 international dollars) labeled 0, 5,000, 10,000, 15,000, 20,000, 25,000; labeled points: United States, France, Canada, Lesotho, Korea, Rep. of, Spain, Norway, Japan, India, United Kingdom, Jamaica, Kenya, Brazil, Cyprus, Philippines, Egypt)

Public share of total health spending

Percent

(scatterplot with vertical axis labeled 90, 70, 50, 30, 10 and horizontal axis GDP per capita (1991 international dollars) labeled 0, 5,000, 10,000, 15,000, 20,000, 25,000; labeled points: Norway, Hungary, United Kingdom, Japan, Canada, Greece, Spain, France, Brazil, Jamaica, Cyprus, Kenya, Israel, Egypt, United States, Lesotho, Korea, Rep. of, Philippines, Hong Kong, India, Uganda)

Source: Murray, Govindaraj, and Chellaraj, background paper.

110

Table 5.2 Clinical health systems by income group

Country group and 1990 per capita income (dollars)	Health expenditure, 1990		Main characteristics	Examples
	As share of GNP (percent)	Dollars per capita		
Low-income (100–600)[a]	2–7	2–40	High private spending for traditional medicine and for drugs Public services financed from general revenues Little insurance	Bangladesh, India, Pakistan, most Sub-Saharan African countries
Middle-income (600–7,900) Private insurance	2–7	20–350	Government services for middle- and low-income groups financed from general revenues Private insurance and private provision for affluent (less than 10 percent of population)	South Africa, Zimbabwe
Social insurance	3–7	20–400	Public health and clinical care for low-income groups financed from general revenues Social insurance for wage labor force, with mixed provision	Costa Rica, Republic of Korea, Turkey
Formerly socialist economies of Europe (650–6,000)	3–6	30–200	Public services (which are low in quality or collapsing) financed from general revenues Large underground market in privately provided services	Czech Republic, Poland, Slovak Republic, republics of former U.S.S.R.
Established market economies, excluding United States (5,000–34,000)	6–10	400–2,500	Universal or near-universal coverage through general revenue financing or compulsory social insurance Use of capped third-party payments and global budgets	France, Germany, Japan (social insurance); Norway, Sweden, United Kingdom (general tax revenues)
United States (22,000)	12	2,800	Combination of private voluntary insurance and use of general revenue from taxes Unregulated and open-ended fee-for-service compensation High administrative costs associated with health provision and insurance	United States

a. Although China is a low-income country, its health system is closer to that of a middle-income country with social insurance.
Source: For expenditure, Appendix table A.9.

ing from general tax revenues generally amounts to less than half of the 2 to 7 percent of GNP allocated to health services. There is little or no insurance.

Until recently, China was an important exception among low-income countries. There, between 1960 and 1980, state enterprises provided health care directly to their workers or contracted with government hospitals to do so. Rural communes were required to earmark a portion of their financial resources for health services for all their members. By the late 1970s insurance covered virtually all the urban population and 85 percent of the rural population—a unique achievement for a low-income developing country. Since the elimination of communal agriculture and the liberalization of industry in the early 1980s, however, these forms of health insurance and service delivery have

weakened considerably. The rural population increasingly relies on a system of government-provided health care financed in part out of general revenues, but with substantial cost recovery through user charges, not unlike systems prevailing in other low-income countries.

In the *middle-income countries* there are two major types of health systems, distinguished by whether the government or the private sector provides health insurance. Health spending, at $20 to $400 per capita, is higher than in low-income countries, and both public and private managerial capacity is stronger. In countries with private insurance, such as South Africa and Zimbabwe, the government uses general revenues to pay for health care for middle- and low-income groups, while upper-income households (less than 20 percent of the population) use private insurance to pay for private physicians and hospitals or for private rooms in government hospitals.

In countries with social insurance, mandatory contributions from employees and employers, and sometimes government funds, finance insurance for part of the population, including most middle-class workers. Health care for the poor is financed from general revenues. This is the system that prevails in Korea, Turkey, and most of Latin America.

In the *formerly socialist economies* of Eastern Europe and the Soviet Union, general revenue financing with government provision of health services was until recently the only officially recognized form of health care. Public spending on health now accounts for 3 to 6 percent of GNP in these countries, or $30 to $200 per capita. Prior to the period of political and economic liberalization in the late 1980s, private payments were frequently made for ''public'' health services (for example, gratuities were given physicians in government hospitals), and drugs often leaked from the public sector into private markets. Since the political and economic reforms that swept across these countries in the late 1980s, the health systems there have been in crisis. Dwindling public funding and deteriorating government services have created strong pressures for new forms of public and private insurance.

The *established market economies*, with the exception of the United States, rely on one of the two types of public financing for more than three-quarters of their health expenditures, which range from $400 to $2,500 per person per year. Norway, Sweden, and the United Kingdom use general tax revenues to pay for health services that are provided directly by the government. In France, Germany, and Japan, among others, social insurance is the dominant mode of financing. The United States, with annual health spending of about $2,800 per capita, has a bewildering combination of systems, including voluntary private employment-based insurance, compulsory insurance for federal workers with each employee having a choice of alternative insurers and packages, and full public finance and provision for veterans. A single-payer approach financed from general revenue is used at the federal level for health care for the elderly (Medicare) and at the state level for the poor (Medicaid).

Selecting and financing the essential clinical package

A basic responsibility accepted by governments almost everywhere is to ensure access to a package of essential clinical services. But what should be the content of this package? Although political considerations will inevitably affect the decision, the most important factors in selecting the essential package should be the relative cost-effectiveness of interventions, the size and distribution of the health problems affecting the population, and the resources available.

Defining the essential package

A patient's health needs often require several interrelated interventions. A child with fever and diarrhea may require treatment for both acute respiratory and gastrointestinal infections. A pregnant woman needs to receive both prenatal and delivery care. For this reason, it makes sense to group certain interventions when analyzing their costs and benefits. Five groups, or clusters, of clinical interventions are likely to be important in every country's essential clinical package: prenatal and delivery care; family planning services; management of the sick child; treatment of tuberculosis; and case management of sexually transmitted diseases (STDs). The first two groups are often discussed under the umbrella of ''safe motherhood'' activities, but for the purposes of cost and benefit estimates they are presented separately here. All five sets of interventions are highly cost-effective; each costs $50 or less per DALY in low-income settings and $150 or less per DALY in middle-income settings. Moreover, they deal with widespread health problems that affect the poor.

Details on the health problems that these five groups of clinical interventions help to resolve, on ways of delivering the interventions efficiently to patients, and on the cost-effectiveness of the interventions are given in Boxes 5.1 through 5.4. The problems addressed are among the largest afflicting developing countries. Four preventable or easily treatable infectious diseases of children account for nearly 7 million child deaths annually. Unsafe childbirth is responsible for half a million maternal deaths each year. Tuberculosis kills more than 2 million people annually, making it the leading cause of death among adults. More than 250 million new cases of debilitating and potentially fatal STDs occur each year.

In addition to these five groups of clinical interventions, in any realistic setting an essential package would have to include treatment of minor infection and trauma, as well as advice and alleviation of pain for health problems that cannot be fully resolved with existing resources and technol-

Box 5.1 Making pregnancy and delivery safe

Under optimal conditions, about 990 of every 1,000 pregnancies that reach the seventh month of gestation conclude with a healthy newborn and a healthy mother. For most women in the developing world, however, childbirth is unsafe. About one in 50 women in developing countries dies as a consequence of complications of pregnancy and childbirth, compared with only one in 2,700 in the established market economies. Maternal mortality has profound consequences within the household; the chances of dying for children under 5 increase by up to 50 percent when the mother dies.

In 1987 the international health community, including the World Bank, WHO, the United Nations Population Fund (UNPF), and agencies in forty-five countries, launched the Safe Motherhood Initiative. The prime goal is to reduce by half the number of maternal deaths by 2000. The health programs recommended under the initiative include family planning and pregnancy-related care, prenatal care, and delivery care. (Family planning and abortion services are discussed more fully in Chapter 4.) The marginal cost-effectiveness of pregnancy-related care varies with circumstances, but the World Bank has estimated that the average cost per DALY is between $30 and $110, the equivalent of less than $2,000 per death averted.

The extension of prenatal, delivery, and postpartum care to 80 percent of the world's population would reduce by 40 percent the burden of disease associated with unsafe childbirth, at a cost of between $90 and $255 per birth attended, or $4 to $9 per capita. A reasonable program of pregnancy-related care would include three components:

• *Information, education, and communications* designed to create demand for clinical services, alert women and others to danger signs that may occur during pregnancy and childbirth, and mobilize communities for transport of women with complications to district hospitals

• *Community-based obstetrics* with trained nurse-midwife staff to provide prenatal care, including tetanus toxoid immunization, treatment for syphilis, provision of micronutrients (iron, folate, and iodine), and detection of complications of pregnancy and delivery; normal delivery, including prophylactic application of antibiotics against gonorrheal ophthalmia; obstetric first aid, including sedatives for early eclampsia (pregnancy-related seizures) and manual removal of the placenta; effective early referral of severe complications; and safe abortion.

• *District hospital facilities* to provide essential obstetric services (cesarean section, anesthesia, blood replacement, manual procedures, and monitoring of labor) and neonatal resuscitation (aspiration of secretions and assisted respiration with oxygen).

The emphasis given the different components will depend on local conditions. At one extreme are districts where resources are limited and women are highly isolated. Here, high priorities would be prenatal care aimed mainly at correcting micronutrient deficiencies and infections such as STDs and malaria. At the other extreme are urban and periurban areas where referral centers are overwhelmed with normal deliveries and the quality of care is typically low; here, health centers should be improved so that they can deal with normal births, and the quality of hospital care should be enhanced to provide better treatment of obstetric complications.

---

ogies. Hospital capacity would be sufficient to handle some emergency care, including most fractures and infrequently needed procedures such as appendectomies. Local discretion in the provision of these services would depend on the availability of inputs and on day-to-day capacity. This "limited care" and the five groups of interventions together constitute a *minimum package of essential clinical services*. Efficient delivery of these essential services requires a well-functioning district health system consisting of health posts and health centers as the first point of patient contact and district hospitals as referral facilities, with the two levels linked by emergency transport.

Governments must ensure that publicly provided facilities have the necessary inputs—drugs, supplies, facilities, equipment, and properly trained staff—to deliver essential services and that inputs for services outside the nationally defined package are not supplied. A district hospital with about one bed per 1,000 population served is needed to provide inpatient and specialized outpatient care, but the hospital would have to perform only basic surgery. No higher-level hospital is required for delivery of the minimum package. Although doctors are needed for supervising essential clinical care and handling more complicated cases, most of the services in the minimum package can be delivered by nurses and midwives. A ratio of fully qualified nurses to physicians of between 2 and 4 to 1 (estimates vary to accommodate the availability of physicians and nurses in different regions) and 0.1 to 0.2 physician per 1,000 population would be adequate. Although

Box 5.2 Integrated management of the sick child

Four groups of infectious disease—diarrheal diseases, acute respiratory infections (ARIs), measles, and malaria—account for more than half of the 12.7 million deaths every year of children under age 5. In the developing world measles alone causes 860,000 deaths in children under age 5 and accounts for 6 percent of DALYs lost in that age group. Malaria causes 4 percent of the disease burden in the under-five group. Sick children taken by their mothers to health centers for diarrheal disease and for ARIs such as pneumonia often receive inappropriate diagnosis and treatment, leading to unnecessary complications and deaths.

Whereas preventing diarrheal diseases and ARIs has proved difficult and is probably not cost-effective, case management in community-based programs is feasible and extremely effective. WHO and UNICEF have recently begun to support national programs on the Integrated Management of the Sick Child. This initiative builds on more than fifteen years of experience with case management of diarrheal diseases, mainly by oral rehydration therapy (ORT), and about seven years of research on and program implementation of case management of ARIs.

In Nepal a controlled intervention trial that relied exclusively on indigenous community health workers (CHWs) to detect and treat pneumonia without hospitalization led to a 28 percent reduction in the risk of death from all causes by the third year of service. Additional benefits were obtained from the reduction in deaths caused by diarrhea and measles. Other research on similar community-based strategies for children under age 5 indicates decreases of approximately 50 percent in infant mortality from ARIs. In Egypt the use of ORT has in some areas led to a reduction of 50 percent in mortality from diarrhea and 40 percent in overall mortality among children ages 1 month to 5 years. The experience with these two disease clusters can be expanded to include children with malaria, measles, and malnutrition. Evidence that malaria and pneumonia overlap in their clinical presentation and can be treated with the same antibiotic strengthens the case for treating several diseases together.

Under the integrated management approach, the sick child is initially assessed by means of a limited range of questions and observation of easily recognized symptoms. The child's nutritional and immunization status is measured, and immunization is given if needed. The child's condition is classified according to disease grouping and severity guidelines, which are used as a basis for treatment and possible referrals. The final step is to give the mother advice on follow-up care.

The core of the package is to train primary health care providers to diagnose diseases and prescribe the appropriate treatment at the health center level or refer immediately to a district hospital those cases with complications. An adequate supply of antibiotics, antimalarial drugs, and other drugs is critical for success. The integrated cluster of treatments, including hospital services, would cost between $30 and $100 per DALY saved. Since the walk-in component accounts for approximately 60 to 70 percent of the reduction in the disease burden, district hospitals are not indispensable for starting the program, but their presence and proper functioning add substantial health benefits. If high rates of health service use can be achieved, child deaths in high-mortality communities, according to WHO estimates, could be reduced by between 50 and 70 percent. This fact and the relatively low technology involved make the management of the sick child a high priority in countries with child mortality rates of more than thirty deaths per 1,000 children under age 5.

---

many developing countries can already deliver the minimum package, some low-income nations would require additional investments in personnel, equipment, and facilities.

In developing countries with the financial resources and political will to go beyond the minimum clinical package, a more comprehensive set of services could cover other interventions with slightly lower cost-effectiveness than those in the minimum package. This set might include a number of interventions for chronic disease, such as use of oral hypoglycemics or insulin to control diabetes, medical treatment for schizophrenia and manic-depressive illness, screening and treatment for breast and cervical cancer, measures (for example, use of aspirin and of simple antihypertensive

drugs) to reduce the risk of cardiovascular disease in high-risk individuals, and inexpensive management of angina and heart attacks. Other treatments that might fit into an expanded package include hernia repair, meningitis treatment for children, management of gastrointestinal ulcers, cataract removal, and treatment of moderately severe injuries and of complications of diabetes. Given the large contribution of disability to the burden of disease, inclusion of low-cost rehabilitative measures will often be a priority for interventions beyond the minimum essential package. These interventions—most of which respond to conditions that will become increasingly common with the epidemiological transition documented in Chapter 1—can cost as little as $200 to $300 per

DALY. Including them and other interventions of similar cost-effectiveness would reduce the current disease burden by 5 to 10 percent.

Many health procedures have such low cost-effectiveness that governments should exclude them from the essential clinical package. In low-income countries these might include heart surgery; treatment (other than pain relief) of highly fatal cancers of the lung, liver, and stomach; expensive drug therapies for HIV infection; and intensive care for severely premature babies. It is difficult to justify using government funds for these medical treatments when much more cost-effective services that benefit mainly the poor are not receiving adequate financing.

Several developing countries that have been highly successful at improving the health status of their populations have emphasized access to an essential package of services in their allocation of public spending on health. In Botswana and Zimbabwe the rapid decline in infant mortality and rise in life expectancy during the 1980s were strongly influenced by government action to expand the health infrastructure and by the use of general tax revenues to finance an array of public health and clinical services. Some key services that were initially left out of the package but are now being incorporated include vitamin A supplementation and improved control of STDs. Similarly, dramatic health gains in Costa Rica in the 1970s were largely brought about by new basic public health and clinical services, financed almost entirely by the Ministry of Health and the national social security agency. The remarkable improvements in health status in China, Kerala State in India, and Sri Lanka are attributable in part to gov-

---

Box 5.3 Treatment of sexually transmitted diseases

Sexually transmitted diseases (STDs) are extremely common infections: according to a 1990 estimate by WHO, there are more than 250 million new cases each year worldwide. These diseases have severe and often irreversible consequences that disproportionately affect women, who bear 80 percent of the total DALYs lost to STDs (excluding HIV). Women are more likely than men to acquire STDs because of the greater efficiency of male-to-female transmission for most STD pathogens, the lack of female-controlled preventive methods, and, in many settings, gender power dynamics that limit women's ability to determine the conditions under which sexual intercourse occurs. Women are less likely than men to obtain care for STDs because the majority of infected women are asymptomatic and those with symptoms may be deterred by fear of social stigma. Since STDs also inflict a heavy burden of illness on men, and since men are responsible for much STD transmission, disease control measures, to be effective, must be targeted to both sexes.

Because STDs increase the efficacy of transmission of HIV, controlling these infections is one of the most important interventions for containing the spread of AIDS. But even in the absence of AIDS, STDs cause substantial morbidity and mortality. They usually affect people in the 15–44 age group, the most economically productive ages. One of the main causes of neonatal morbidity and mortality in some countries is congenital syphilis. Because treatment is simple (one to three injections of penicillin) and inexpensive, screening and treatment for syphilis during prenatal care has been recommended for the minimum package. Depending on the prevalence of disease, on whether the person affected is a member of a "core" group and hence likely to transmit syphilis to others, and on the case-detection strategy used, curing a case of syphilis can cost as little as $0.10 or as much as $40 per DALY. In Zambia a syphilis treatment demonstration project for pregnant women achieved a two-thirds reduction in stillbirths, low birth weights, and neonatal deaths associated with syphilis, even though attendance, screening, and treatment were not optimal. The cost was $12 per adverse outcome prevented, or less than $1 per DALY. In a similar program in Kenya prevention of one neonatal death cost $50. Unfortunately, in most countries a comprehensive program of perinatal syphilis screening has not been implemented.

Effective interventions exist for other STDs, but lack of simple, appropriate, rapid, and inexpensive diagnostics for use in the field have made these measures much more difficult and expensive to implement. Consequently, when resources are limited, such interventions must be targeted specifically to core groups to be cost-effective. In these groups, case management of chlamydia (a bacterial infection of the reproductive tract) and gonorrhea can be highly cost-effective ($10 to $40 per DALY), as can treatment of chancroid in areas where it is common. Much of the cost of intervention for these diseases is related to diagnosis. Calculations suggest that if prevalence of an STD is more than 10 percent, treating everyone in the risk group may be more cost-effective than screening. This, however, does not take into account the problems of widespread use of the antibiotics used to treat STDs, including adverse reactions, development of microbial resistance, and change in microbial flora.

Box 5.4 Short-course treatment of tuberculosis

Tuberculosis (TB) kills or debilitates more adults ages 15–59 than any other disease and is responsible for about 2 to 4 percent of the burden of disease. It is the single leading cause of death in developing countries, accounting for about 2 million deaths a year, or approximately 5 percent of all deaths and 25 percent of preventable adult deaths in those countries. More women of childbearing age die from TB than from causes associated with pregnancy and childbirth. More than half of the world's population is infected with the TB bacillus. People who are malnourished or have another severe illness are at particular risk for TB, as are those infected with HIV. The relationship between TB and HIV is highly significant, as each person infected with HIV and TB could infect twelve other persons with TB per year.

Annual incidence rates of all forms of clinical TB vary from 50 to 260 per 100,000 in the developing world; more than half of these cases are infectious (sputum-smear-positive). For most forms of TB, 50 to 60 percent of those infected will die if untreated. All ages are at risk, but the peak is in young adulthood. In Sub-Saharan Africa the annual risks of infection remain high, partly because of poverty and overcrowding (which are risk factors for TB) and partly because any decrease in the annual risk of infection is offset by the HIV epidemic. In India and Sub-Saharan Africa TB is the leading cause of death and the biggest contributor to the disease burden; it is responsible for about 8 to 11 percent of the DALYs lost in the 15–59 age group.

There are two effective approaches to treating TB: short-course chemotherapy, which uses three to five drugs over six to eight months, and the "standard" course of two to three drugs taken over twelve to eigh-

teen months. Drugs for the short course cost about $50 to $80 per patient. Those for the standard course cost only $10 to $15, but the cost per death averted is higher because only 30 percent of patients complete treatment and are cured, as against 60 percent for the short course. Other benefits of the short course include a smaller number of resistant organisms and less need for expensive retreatment. (This discussion applies to the treatment of sputum-smear-positive TB. Once other forms of TB have been identified, treatment costs should be similar except for serious forms of smear-negative TB.)

Walk-in treatment is less expensive than hospitalization, but if this care cannot be closely monitored (as in many rural areas), hospitalization may be more cost-effective. The program described is modeled on passive case investigation, assuming that a person with TB will have symptoms such as cough and weight loss and will seek care and that infected persons discovered by active searches will be less likely to continue treatment than those who seek care. Although the BCG vaccination is important in TB control for children, its effectiveness in adults is still under investigation.

The cost of treatment is less than $10 per DALY in all chemotherapy scenarios. It is estimated that tuberculosis treatment of infectious (smear-positive) individuals prevents one to four new cases by stopping transmission. The positive externalities of short-course chemotherapy explain in part the extremely favorable cost-effectiveness and justify government intervention. Because the cost of drugs, at $50 to $80 per patient, is probably too high for the poor, public subsidy is especially warranted for low-income households.

---

ernment policies that emphasized the financing of cost-effective clinical services directed especially at the rural poor.

Benefits, costs, and financing of the essential clinical package

Widespread adoption of the minimum clinical package would have a tremendous positive effect on the health of people in developing countries. If 80 percent of the population were reached, 24 percent of the current burden of disease in low-income countries and 11 percent in middle-income countries could be averted (Table 5.3). When the minimum clinical package is combined with the public health package outlined in Chapter 4, the share of current illness that could be eliminated rises to approximately 32 percent in low-income countries and 15 percent in middle-income coun-

tries. This reduction in the burden of disease would be equivalent to saving the lives of more than 9 million infants each year.

Delivery of the minimum clinical package would cost an average of about $8 per person each year in low-income countries and about $15 in middle-income countries. Approximately half of these amounts would be for prenatal and delivery care alone. When the cost of selected public health interventions is added, total costs rise to $12 per capita in low-income countries and $22 in middle-income countries. The differences are the result of different demographic structures, epidemiological conditions, and labor costs in the two settings.

In low-income countries, where governments typically spend about $5.50 per person for health and where total health expenditures are about $14 per person (Figure 5.2), the affordability of the

Table 5.3 Estimated costs and health benefits of selected public health and clinical services in low- and middle-income countries, 1990

Country group and package	Annual cost (dollars)[a]			Per capita cost as share of income per capita (percent)	Disease burden averted (percent)[b]
	Per case or per participant	Per capita	Per DALY		
Low-income (per capita income = $350)					
Public health package[c]	—	4.2	—	1.2	8
Minimum essential package of clinical services	—	7.8	—	2.2	24
Short-course chemotherapy for tuberculosis	500	0.6	3–5		1
Management of the sick child	9	1.6	30–50		14
Prenatal and delivery care	90	3.8	30–50		4
Family planning	12	0.9	20–30		3
Treatment of STDs[d]	11	0.2	1–3		1
Limited care[e]	6	0.7	200–350		1
Total, public health and clinical services	—	12.0	—	3.4	32
Middle-income (per capita income = $2,500)					
Public health package[c]	—	6.8	—	0.3	4
Minimum essential package of clinical services	—	14.7	—	0.6	11
Short-course chemotherapy for tuberculosis	275	0.2	5–7		1
Management of the sick child	8	1.1	50–100		4
Prenatal and delivery care	255	8.8	60–110		3
Family planning	20	2.2	100–150		1
Treatment of STDs[d]	18	0.3	10–15		1
Limited care[e]	13	2.1	400–600		1
Total, public health and clinical services	—	21.5	—	0.9	15

Note: Figures assume coverage of 80 percent of the population.
a. Average costs.
b. Marginal benefits.
c. Includes EPI Plus; school health including deworming, micronutrient supplementation, and health education; information on health, nutrition, and family planning; tobacco and alcohol control programs; monitoring and surveillance; vector control; and programs for prevention of AIDS.
d. Benefits were calculated assuming an AIDS epidemic comparable to that in Sub-Saharan Africa today.
e. Limited care includes assessment, advice, alleviation of pain, treatment of infection and minor trauma, and treatment of more complicated conditions as resources permit.
Source: World Bank calculations.

Because the poorest countries spend far less on health than do middle-income countries and the public share is smaller, they have fewer resources available for reallocation.

Figure 5.2 Public financing of health services in low– and middle–income countries, 1990

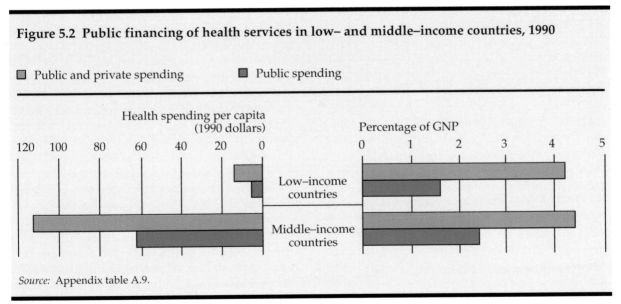

Source: Appendix table A.9.

$12 minimum package is problematic. Paying for the package would require an increase in public spending for health (part of which could be financed by donors in the short term), as well as a reorientation of current government expenditure for health from discretionary to essential care. In middle-income countries, where public spending for health averages about $62 per person, the $22 minimum package is financially feasible if there is adequate political commitment to shift existing resources in the direction of public health and essential clinical care. Indeed, upper-middle-income countries can afford public finance of an essential package that goes well beyond this minimum.

Who should pay for the essential clinical package? There are strong efficiency arguments for direct financing by developing country governments of the selected public health interventions discussed in Chapter 4. A number of the essential clinical services, including treatment of tuberculosis and STDs, have large positive externalities. What is more important is that the poor are disproportionately affected by the disease burden of the conditions listed in Table 5.3 and that, because of larger family sizes, they would benefit disproportionately from prenatal, delivery, and childhood services. Public finance of a basic package of services is an effective mechanism for reaching the poor.

The main problem with universal government financing of an essential package is that it leads to public subsidies to the wealthy, who could afford to pay for their own services, with the result that fewer government resources go to serve the poor. A policy of concentrating public resources on services for the poor and requiring others to pay all or part of their own costs makes sense on equity grounds but also has some disadvantages. Often, the administrative costs of targeting are high, and the exclusion of wealthy and middle-income groups can erode political support for the essential package, causing a decline in funding and quality of care. Furthermore, problems of cost escalation and access to insurance on the part of high-risk groups—discussed in Chapter 3—can complicate reliance on private finance. Perhaps for these reasons, most member governments of the OECD finance (or mandate finance of) comprehensively defined essential packages for virtually all their citizens.

In low-income countries, where current public spending for health is less than the cost of an es-

sential package, some degree of targeting is almost inevitable. In countries where the wealthy do not use government-financed services because of the greater quality and convenience of privately financed services, targeting may be fairly easy. In other cases, however, user charges will have to be applied selectively, relying on means testing and other targeting devices (see Box 5.5). Special amenities in teaching hospitals, for example, can be priced at or above cost, since they will be consumed exclusively by the wealthy. User charges can help generate additional revenues for the essential package, amounting to perhaps 10 to 20 percent of total government spending for health. Finally, directing donor funding to public health and essential clinical care can significantly expand the total resource basket available for the minimum package.

User charges for public health services in developing countries have sparked much debate since the World Bank endorsed the concept in 1987 in a policy study on health financing. Critics argue that fees restrict access to care, especially for the poor. Yet many developing countries, particularly in Sub-Saharan Africa, have been forced to rely increasingly on fees to supplement strained budgets. Studies on the effect of user fees are inconclusive and contradictory. One reason is that some researchers have failed to calculate the true cost to patients of treatment at government clinics. People often pay dearly for supposedly "free" health care. Recent household surveys in India, Indonesia, and Viet Nam indicate that each visit to a government health center actually costs patients two to three times the amount of the low official fees. Bribes aside, the indirect costs such as transport and the opportunity cost of time spent seeking care are substantial.

Since patients are already paying for supposedly free or low-cost health care, new user fees, when accompanied by a reduction in indirect costs and improvement of services, may increase utilization. Recent studies in four African countries—Benin, Cameroon, Guinea, and Sierra Leone—indicate that this is the case and, encouragingly, that the poor benefited most from these changes. Since facilities used fees to fund services not previously available locally, poor patients avoided costly travel, and the actual cost of care declined. Studies indicate that user fees amounting to less than 1 percent of annual household income have little impact on the utilization of health services, even by the poor. Because higher fees do decrease utiliza-

Box 5.5 Targeting public expenditure to the poor

When public spending on health is not targeted to the poor—as often happens, according to numerous studies—no other source of funds is likely to compensate. Which targeting mechanisms work best in practice will depend on their impact on demand, their administrative costs, their technical and managerial requirements, and the level of political support. In countries where incomes are too low for a minimum essential package to be provided universally, there are four main mechanisms for targeting the essential package of services:

• Assess *individuals* seeking services on the basis of income, nutritional status, or other criteria and, depending on the assessment, provide services from the essential clinical package free of charge or according to a sliding scale of fees. In evaluating income, direct measurements or proxies (such as housing characteristics) can be used, but this tends to be more administratively costly than other mechanisms.

• Subsidize essential clinical services for easily identified *subgroups* of the population (for example, all those living in certain low-income regions or neighborhoods or all children in public schools). Where social insurance mechanisms (usually financed through payroll taxes) exist, they generally tend to cover the rela-

tively well-off. Targeting public finance to those not participating in social insurance will reach the poor, and administration will be relatively simple. In countries with established social insurance mechanisms, this targeting mechanism will often prove best.

• Let individuals *self-target*. The essential services are available free of charge to all, but the program is designed in such a way as to deter the better-off from using them. Time costs, stigma, and fewer amenities associated with services are the usual mechanisms for encouraging self-targeting. Unfortunately, these same characteristics may discourage the poor as well as the better-off. Low-income working mothers, for example, may find that the time, for themselves and their children, involved in using subsidized services is an insurmountable obstacle.

• Target by *type of service*. Offer free of charge, or subsidize heavily, services that are needed disproportionately by the poor. This sort of targeting mechanism is inherent in much of the essential package of clinical services. Prenatal and delivery services, management of the sick child, and STD and tuberculosis treatment are all services that, if universally available, would especially benefit the poor.

---

tion, reducing charges or exempting the poor from the fees may be warranted.

In middle-income countries, where a significant part of the population may be covered by private or social insurance, governments can target public monies to essential clinical services for the poor by legally defining and mandating that the national essential package be covered in all insurance policies, thereby freeing government resources to target the poor. Surprisingly, emerging managed care institutions in developing countries often fail to cover benefits that would be in such an essential package. In the 1980s in Brazil, for example, many health maintenance organizations failed to include immunizations and family planning in the basic benefits package for their clienteles.

Insurance and finance of discretionary clinical services

Public financing of a national essential clinical package can be justified because the package creates positive externalities and reduces poverty. The case for government financing of discretion-

ary clinical health care—services outside the essential package—is far less compelling. In fact, governments can promote both efficiency and equity by reducing—or, when possible, eliminating—public funding for these services. Doing so requires recovering the cost of discretionary services provided in government health facilities and cutting subsidies to private and public insurance schemes that finance discretionary care. By reducing spending on these services, governments can concentrate public expenditure where it will do the most good—in public health and cost effective clinical services.

Out-of-pocket payments are the main source of financing for discretionary care in low-income countries. They remain substantial in middle-income countries, but insurance becomes increasingly important as incomes rise. Because, except for the very rich, out-of-pocket financing cannot cover expensive care or deal with catastrophic illness, widespread financing of discretionary care is possible only through insurance. Countries have two main options for meeting a growing demand and need for insurance. One is to move toward the current U.S. system, which relies substantially on private voluntary insurance. The other is to follow the examples of Canada, Japan, and most European countries, where general government revenues or social insurance cover the cost of relatively comprehensive essential packages, leaving only a small discretionary residual for private insurance.

Government policy can improve the functioning of insurance markets in three ways. It can strive to eliminate unfair subsidies to insurance. It can work to maximize the population covered by insurance by preventing selection bias—the tendency of insurers to discriminate against bad health risks. And it can help to eliminate another potential problem with insurance: the explosive increases in health care costs that are closely associated with fee-for-service payment of health providers by third-party insurers.

Redirecting public funding from discretionary care

There is substantial scope in the developing world for redirecting current public spending away from discretionary services. Cost recovery in government hospitals, especially from the wealthy and insured, is one important mechanism. Even in low-income countries, where insurance may account for less than 5 percent of total health spending, as in Ethiopia, Kenya, Lesotho, Pakistan, and the Philippines, a combination of limited private insurance and the ability of upper-income groups to pay makes it feasible for governments to charge for discretionary care delivered in public hospitals. In Kenya the government is currently attempting to recover the cost of caring for the insured at the national referral hospital in Nairobi. In Lesotho charges in the private ward of the central hospital in Maseru were increased in 1990 to recover costs from wealthier patients.

In middle-income countries insurance becomes more important as a mechanism for financing discretionary services. In South Africa private insurance covers about 15 percent of the population and accounts for more than a third of total health spending. In Brazil, even though everyone is eligible for publicly financed health services, about a fifth of the population is also privately insured. Social insurance, in which payroll deductions are earmarked for health care, is widespread in middle-income countries, especially in Latin America. Such payroll taxes account for a quarter or more of national health spending in Costa Rica, Korea, and Panama (Table 5.4). In countries with broader insurance coverage there is even greater potential for cost recovery than in poorer countries. Public hospitals in Chile are now being encouraged to charge, particularly for patients who have private insurance.

Table 5.4 Social insurance in selected countries, 1990
(percent)

Group and country	Share of population covered by social insurance	Social insurance as share of public sector health expenditure	Social insurance as share of total health expenditure	Health expenditure as share of GNP
Low-income				
India	5	9	2	6.0
Kenya	10	7	4	4.3
Indonesia	13	17	6	2.0
Middle-income				
Dominican Rep.	6	9	6	3.7
Ecuador	9	11	7	4.1
Colombia	15	18	8	4.0
Paraguay	18	24	13	2.8
Philippines	38	12	6	2.8
Panama	50	55	43	7.1
Turkey	58	26	14	4.0
Costa Rica	82	85	62	6.5
Korea, Rep. of	90	50	25	6.6
High-income				
Germany	75	76	63	8.0
Japan	100	64	56	6.5
France	100	95	71	8.9
Netherlands	100	94	73	7.9

Source: World Bank data; Mesa-Lago 1991; de Geyndt 1991; Vogel 1990; Brotowasisto and others 1988; Ikegami 1992; Hurst 1992; and Solon and others 1992.

The other way to redirect government spending away from discretionary care is to phase out public subsidies to insurance. These subsidies, which are large and widespread, take the form of both direct budgetary transfers to insurance institutions and tax concessions for employers' and employees' insurance contributions. They benefit the better-off and are therefore regressive.

In Latin America governments in Guatemala, Honduras, Mexico, Nicaragua, and Venezuela contribute a percentage of individual workers' wages to social security sickness and maternity funds. In Chile and Uruguay the government covers the operating deficits of the funds, and in Colombia and El Salvador it pays directly for a part of the cost of social security health services and administration. Private insurance in South Africa and Zimbabwe receives large public subsidies in the form of tax deductions for employer and employee contributions. Fees to insured patients using government hospitals in Zimbabwe are set at perhaps a third to a quarter of actual costs, providing another subsidy to the better-off.

Once subsidies to private and public insurance are established, they are extremely difficult to eliminate. Recipients—generally the better-off—view them as an important benefit. The current debate in the United States over reducing the employer tax deduction for contributions to medical insurance illustrates this strong political resistance. To date, very few developing countries have successfully cut subsidies. An exception is Zimbabwe, where major political shifts—national independence and the advent of a democratically elected government in 1980—led to a significant scaling back of tax breaks for medical aid premiums. The Chilean government is actively considering eliminating the existing tax concession for employers' contributions to social insurance.

Subsidies to insurance systems that cover only part of the population are invariably regressive, but subsidies can be progressive when insurance has become universal. At that point, public subsidies end up benefiting mainly those outside the formal labor force, notably the elderly and the poor. Examples of progressive subsidies are the 30 percent of national social insurance funding that the Korean government contributes on behalf of low-income households and the 20 percent of Japan's social insurance spending that derives from government budget transfers for retirees and the poor. Governments could provide equally progressive, targeted subsidies to buy regulated private health insurance for the poor, but there is no experience with such arrangements in developing countries.

Eliminating unequal access to clinical care under insurance

A serious problem with relying on insurance to pay for discretionary care in developing countries is that individuals and groups often have unequal access to insurance coverage. The problem is especially acute with voluntary private insurance because of selection bias. When insurers rate individual risks, they often either refuse to insure the sick and elderly or make insurance prohibitively expensive for these clients because their expected costs are so high. They also commonly exclude many health conditions that should ideally be covered. In Brazil, for example, where government regulation of insurance is weak, private insurers frequently refuse to enroll persons who are poor health risks, and they fail to cover costly risks such as HIV-AIDS. In South Africa and Zimbabwe private health insurance schemes known as medical aid societies have historically covered entire industries and occupational groups, but the recent marketing of individual insurance policies has introduced discrimination based on risk. Selection bias is an important reason for the incomplete insurance coverage in the United States, where 37 million people, or about 15 percent of the population, are uninsured.

Very few countries, developing or industrial, have managed to eliminate selection bias under private insurance, even though it could theoretically be done by prohibiting insurers from rating individuals' health risks and requiring them to rate only large groups, or "communities," in which high risks are spread over a large number of people to minimize the cost effect of the risks. Eliminating selection bias is easier with social insurance because contributions are compulsory and are normally a fixed percentage of wages for all employees regardless of their number of dependents or their individual health risks. The snag is that since compulsory insurance generally uses employment-based contributions, it is able to achieve broad coverage only when most of the economically active population is in the formal labor force.

Where only part of the population is covered by insurance, as in most developing countries, access to clinical services for the uninsured poor can be much more difficult than for insured, better-off people. The quality of care, including essential clinical services, may also be vastly inferior for the poor. In low-income Africa the wealthy consult private doctors for their clinical care while the poor are often forced to use understaffed government health centers that lack the most basic drugs and equipment. In much of Latin America middle-class families receive better care in hospitals and clinics belonging to the social security agency than the poor are given in the badly deteriorated facilities run by the ministry of health.

One way to eliminate these disparities would be to put all health facilities under a single administration and open them to all. Few countries have taken on this politically and administratively difficult task. Costa Rica, in which the social security agency manages all government hospitals, is a rare exception. Another solution is for the government to focus spending on the poor by investing heavily in the infrastructure (facilities, equipment, and transport) needed to improve essential clinical care for the poor and spending substantially more on the associated personnel and drugs. By focusing investments on peripheral health units (health centers, subcenters, and health posts) and on staff for these facilities, Malaysia and Zimbabwe have successfully upgraded separate clinical services targeted to the poor.

Containing the costs of clinical care

Escalating health spending is perceived as a crisis when it begins to crowd out other sectors of the economy or to raise the cost of labor, threatening a country's international competitiveness. This is currently happening in the United States and to a varying extent in other high-income countries (Box 5.6), and it is about to happen in several middle-income developing countries, including Chile and Korea.

The sources of excess health costs and growth of costs are complex and much debated. Health services have a high labor content, and their productivity has grown slowly in comparison with that of other areas of the economy. In the United States relatively high levels of underlying morbidity and greater amenities in hospitals are part of the reason, but inefficiencies are also important. Two types of inefficiency stand out: high administrative costs and unnecessary use of an ever-expanding array of sophisticated and ever more costly technologies for diagnostic tests and surgical pro-

---

Box 5.6 Containing health care costs in industrial countries

In 1990 the United States devoted 12.7 percent of its GNP to health, as against 9.1 percent in Canada, 8.9 percent in France, 8.0 percent in Germany, 6.5 percent in Japan, and 6.1 percent in the United Kingdom. The 2.7 percent annual increase in the health-to-GNP ratio for the United States during the 1980s was the highest among the OECD countries. U.S. health expenditures of $2,800 per person in 1990 were nearly $1,000 above the average for the OECD countries. The price of health care services in relation to other goods and services also rose much more rapidly in the United States (2.2 percent per year) than in the other OECD countries.

An important factor in explaining the rapid growth in health care costs in the United States is that doctors and hospitals are paid predominantly on a fee-for-service basis. Countries experiencing moderate spending growth (Canada and Japan) also use fee-for-service for outpatient physician care but have devised other ways of controlling expenditures: a uniform fee structure and aggressive peer review of doctors' spending patterns in Japan and fixed overall budgets for hospitals in Canada. Countries with low levels of spending (the United Kingdom) or low recent growth of costs (Den-

mark, Germany, and Sweden) set overall limits on payments to both doctors and hospitals. In the latter group, the method of limiting payments to doctors varies widely: capitation in Britain, fee-for-service in Germany, and salaries in Sweden. In Germany, as a means of controlling expenditure, fees are reduced if the volume of services exceeds the anticipated level. In general, the OECD countries that have contained costs better have greater government control of health spending and a larger public sector share of total health expenditures. This is also the case in eleven developing countries with income per capita of more than $6,000. In the poorer countries there is no apparent link between the public and private shares of health expenditure and the proportion of income devoted to health.

In the U.S. health insurance system, with its large numbers of insurers reimbursing providers at different rates, administrative costs absorb about 15 percent of health expenditures, compared with 5 percent or less in the other OECD countries. If the United States reduced its administrative outlays to the level in these other countries, a total of $80 billion annually could be saved, equivalent to about a third of total health spending for all developing countries combined.

cedures. These two kinds of inefficiency appear to be closely linked to basic features of the U.S. health system. Open-ended fee-for-service compensation for health providers encourages the development of new equipment, drugs, and procedures and leads to exploding costs because neither providers nor patients have strong incentives to hold down utilization or spending. A complex system of multiple insurance institutions and other payers, each with its own procedures, raises administrative overheads substantially.

The findings concerning health cost escalation in the United States and other industrial countries are especially relevant for middle-income developing countries. Those countries are under pressure from medical professionals, manufacturers, and consumers to use new medical technologies, and they face difficult policy choices related to insurance institutions and compensation of providers. Korea's problems with escalating health expenditures parallel those of the United States and may hold important lessons for other developing countries.

The Korean social insurance system is a nationwide network of "sickness funds" covering occupational and regional groups. Worker payroll contributions are compulsory. All Koreans are covered, and the government subsidy to extend coverage to the elderly and indigent is highly progressive. As in the United States, Korea's health providers are predominantly private—72 percent of physicians and 80 percent of hospital beds are in this category—and they are paid on a fee-for-service basis. There is little control of the acquisition of medical technologies. Korea already has more sophisticated new medical equipment, such as imaging machines and lithotripters (used to treat kidney stones), per capita than either Canada or Germany. During 1989–91 spending for medical devices and diagnostic products grew by more than 20 percent a year. As in Japan, physicians often sell the drugs they prescribe, and insurance reimburses the cost of nonprescription drugs, which creates strong incentives to overprescribe and overuse drugs. Prescription pharmaceuticals now account for 36 percent of health spending, one of the highest shares anywhere. Finally, the administrative costs associated with the more than 300 independent insurance funds are 10 to 20 percent of operating expenses, which is similar to the administrative burden of private insurance in the United States.

All these causes contributed to a dramatic increase in health spending in the past decade, far outstripping Korea's robust overall economic growth. The share of GNP devoted to health rose from 3.7 percent in 1980 to 6.6 percent in 1990. By 1990 Korea was spending $377 per capita for health, putting it 50 percent above the expected level for its income.

To control health care costs, countries need to limit payments to health care providers (Table 5.5). One approach is to pay a fixed amount for each person, as is now done by health maintenance organizations in Brazil and the United States and by the British National Health Service. Another method, used in several OECD countries, is to give each hospital or network of physicians a fixed total budget (Box 5.7).

Insurers may jointly negotiate uniform fees for physicians, as is done by Japan's social insurance system and by Zimbabwe's private insurance system. They can also set fixed payments for specified medical procedures or standard per diem payments for hospital stays. Brazil's social insurance system, for example, is paying standard fees for hospital care according to a modified version of the system of diagnostic-related groups that was developed in the United States for Medicare, the government-funded system for the elderly. Chile's public health system is introducing comparable internal prices for its hospitals.

As worldwide experience amply demonstrates, there is no perfect insurance system: every country's insurance institutions have their problems. But there are two important generalizations: third-party insurance leads to cost escalation, and, in general, social insurance and regulated private insurance with community rating avoid selection bias far better than voluntary private insurance. It is difficult to achieve wide coverage of the population in most developing countries, and without wide coverage, public subsidies to insurance will inevitably be regressive. Countries, whether they use social or private insurance, are finding it extremely hard to eliminate these deeply entrenched subsidies. Once widespread insurance coverage is achieved, costs can easily spin out of control unless provider compensation is tightly regulated or determined in ways that give incentives for cost containment. Developing country governments must be prepared to deal forthrightly with this difficult set of interlocking issues.

Delivery of clinical services

Policies related to the delivery of health services in developing countries should have two main objectives. The first is to improve access to essential

Table 5.5 Strengths and weaknesses of alternative methods of paying health providers

Payment method	Strengths	Weaknesses
Fee for service	Provider's reward closely linked to level of effort and output Allows for easy analysis of provider's practice	Tends to cause cost inflation Creates incentives for excessive and unnecessary treatment
Per case (for example, using diagnostic-related groups)	Provider's reward fairly well tied to output Gives provider incentive to minimize resource use per individual treated	Technical difficulty of forcing all cases into standard list can lead to mismatch between output and reward Providers may misrepresent diagnosis in order to receive higher payment
Capitation (per patient under continuous care)	Administratively simple; no need to break down physician's work into procedures or cases Facilitates prospective budgeting Gives provider incentive to minimize cost of treatment Allows for consumer clout if patient can select own provider	Gives provider incentive to select patients based on risk and to reject high-cost patients May create incentives for provider to underservice accepted patients Difficult to analyze provider's practice
Salary (straight payment per period of work)	Administratively simplest Facilitates prospective budgeting	Loss of patient influence over provider behavior unless patient choice links provider salary to patient satisfaction Can easily create incentives for provider to underservice patient and to reduce productivity

Source: Adapted from Reinhardt 1989.

clinical services, especially for the poor. The second is to increase the efficiency with which services are delivered. In the public sector inefficiency is widespread. Clinics and outreach programs operate poorly because of shortages of drugs, transport, and maintenance. Hospitals are poorly organized and managed and keep patients longer than necessary. Countries pay too much for drugs of low efficacy, and drugs and supplies are stolen or go to waste in government warehouses and hospitals. Although the problems are many and deep, appropriate government policies can do much to reduce or eliminate these kinds of inefficiency.

Most countries have mixed systems of both public and private delivery of clinical services and both public and private financing. The type of financing a country chooses does not dictate the kind of health delivery system it should have, or the other way around. Some countries, such as Botswana, Malaysia, Sweden, and the United Kingdom, have mainly public financing and public delivery; some, including Brazil and Korea, have public financing and private delivery; and still others, such as the Philippines, the United States, and Zaire, rely primarily on private financing and private delivery.

The private health sector typically serves a diverse clientele, and it typically delivers services that are perceived to be high in quality and more responsive to consumer demand than the government's. But there are also examples of highly efficient public sector health centers and district hospitals (for example, in Chile, China, Sri Lanka, and Zimbabwe), and there are circumstances in which it is impossible or too costly to persuade the private sector to deliver care—particularly in geographically remote or extremely poor areas.

The existence of alternative suppliers, both public and private, creates pressure for improved performance. In developing countries where the public system has a near-monopoly on health care delivery, a mixed system that exposes the public services to competition is likely to be more efficient and to improve quality of care. Furthermore, in countries where government health services are

---

Box 5.7 Health care reform in the OECD

The OECD countries face persistent difficulties in the financing and delivery of health services. Problems include inequitable access to services, gaps in insurance coverage, unacceptably rapid increases in health expenditure, inefficiency, and poor quality. These difficulties are partly the result of circumstances outside the control of governments—for example, demographic and technological change. To some extent, however, they arise from flaws in the design of the financing, payment, and regulation systems for health care. During the 1980s most OECD countries initiated moderate or major reforms of their health care systems to correct these flaws.

Three principal types of reforms can be distinguished. Several countries, including Ireland, the Netherlands, and Spain, have taken steps to *extend eligibility* for public medical care, bringing the last remaining groups of their populations into the public system of coverage for basic medical care. Despite widespread calls for privatization of finance, no country has reduced its commitment to public coverage.

Many governments have taken important initiatives to contain costs, through increased cost sharing or through supply-side reforms. Belgium, France, Germany, and the Netherlands have set fixed budgets for hospital expenditure. Virtually all the OECD countries greatly reduced the rate of growth of health expenditures during the 1980s. The biggest exception was the United States. Those countries that still relied to some extent on the reimbursement of patients for medical bills, with no connection between insurers and providers, were less successful in containing costs than those in which insurers had direct contracts or in which a public agency was both public insurer and health provider.

Probably the most important reforms of the 1980s involved the introduction of *improved incentives and regulations* for providers and insurers, with the aim of raising the productivity of rationed resources. There has been some convergence of systems toward contracting between public insurers and private providers. Belgium and France have introduced tighter contracts into their reimbursement systems, and the United Kingdom has moved away from its integrated National Health Service and toward more autonomous and competitive physicians and hospitals. Other countries reformed the contractual model itself by emphasizing consumer choice, active informed purchasing rather than passive funding by third parties, and managed competition among providers. These reforms are most marked in Germany, but elements of such changes have also been implemented in Belgium and the Netherlands in the form of mixed payment systems that combine budgetary caps with work-related payment of providers.

Finally, the Netherlands and the United Kingdom have embarked on differing experiments to introduce competition within their public systems. In the Netherlands it is envisaged that consumers will be able to choose among quasi-public sickness funds and private insurers, with a central health care fund taking income-related premiums and paying out risk-related premiums to the competing insurers. This amounts to a sophisticated health voucher scheme. In the United Kingdom part of the hospital budget is given to large (competing) general practices, which will enable general practitioners to purchase certain hospital services on behalf of their patients. Since the reforms were introduced only recently in the United Kingdom and are being carried out gradually in the Netherlands, it is not yet possible to evaluate them fully. There are, however, already signs that general practitioner ''fundholders'' in the United Kingdom are using their new purchasing power to negotiate a higher quality of hospital services for their patients.

Table 5.6 Policies to improve delivery of health care

Provider and policy	Potential impact on		
	Allocative efficiency	Technical efficiency	Reaching the poor
Public sector			
Protect nonsalary recurrent spending	Moderate	Moderate	Significant
Complete the district health delivery infrastructure	Significant	No significant impact	Moderate
Retain fees at point of collection	No significant impact	Moderate	Moderate
Decentralize financial resources and operational authority	Modest	Moderate	Modest
Subcontract ancillary services to private sector	No significant impact	Moderate	No significant impact
Improve drug selection, procurement, and use	Modest	Significant	Modest
Nongovernmental organizations			
Legalize and simplify registration	No significant impact	Modest	Moderate
Provide government subsidies (per case, per diem, or block grants) for essential clinical services	Significant	No significant impact	Moderate
Subsidize training for district health workers	Moderate	Modest	Moderate
Private (for–profit) sector			
Remove legal barriers to practice	No significant impact	Modest	No significant impact
Promote health maintenance organizations	Moderate	Modest	No significant impact
Establish managed competition among suppliers	Modest	Moderate	No significant impact
Regulate private hospitals and physicians	No significant impact	Moderate	No significant impact
Provide public subsidies for essential clinical services and selected public health interventions	Moderate	No significant impact	Modest

■ Significant ■ Moderate ☐ Modest ☐ No significant impact

both overextended and excessively concentrated on discretionary care at the expense of essential services for the poor, the public system needs to be scaled back. This means reducing public investment in tertiary care facilities and specialist training and, in some cases, transferring discretionary care facilities to the private sector. At the same time, governments have to improve the equity and efficiency of their remaining health programs and facilities, through selective and progressive user charges, decentralization, managerial incentives, and better information systems. The key policies for improving delivery of clinical services by government, NGO, and private for-profit providers are shown in Table 5.6.

Delivering the essential package

In a competitive health system, people seeking health services can choose from a diversity of providers—public, private nonprofit, and private for-profit. As developing countries move toward such a competitive system, they face a wide range of policy options that can improve the delivery of the essential clinical package.

THE PUBLIC SECTOR. For many countries an important step in improving access to government-provided essential clinical services is to complete the basic district health infrastructure by building health centers and health posts and training more nurses, midwives, and other providers of primary care. Provision of good-quality housing for rural health workers as part of the district health infrastructure can improve efficiency by encouraging staff to move to rural areas. Zimbabwe doubled the number of its rural health centers, from 500 to more than 1,000, during the period 1980–90 with the goal of making essential clinical services available within 8 kilometers of home for the whole population. When housing for rural physicians and nurses was added to the district health program in the mid-1980s, the effect on staff recruitment and retention was enormous: vacancy rates for physicians and nurses in the areas with new housing fell to zero, as against 20 to 30 percent elsewhere.

Government recurrent spending for primary care inputs other than salaries is particularly vulnerable to budget cuts. When revenue shortfalls occur—or tertiary care hospitals overspend—services in peripheral facilities and communities often suffer. In countries such as Chad, Haiti, Mozambique, and Nepal there are widespread reports of health centers that have staff but few or no drugs and of mobile health teams with little or no gasoline for their vehicles. Under these circumstances technical efficiency falls to near zero—governments continue to pay staff salaries, but virtually no meaningful health services can be delivered.

Protecting the nonsalary part of the budget is extremely difficult but critical. In Senegal the government is currently committed to increasing its budgetary allocation for drugs and medical supplies by 10 percent a year in real terms during 1992–96. Mauritania has set targets for annual government spending on drugs and other nonsalary operating expenditures for its thirteen predominantly rural health regions. Countries can also protect nonsalary spending by introducing more flexibility into their hiring arrangements. In India the Ministry of Health is planning to hire 8,000 workers for a leprosy control project on a per diem basis rather than engage them as civil servants with virtual lifetime guarantees of employment.

Another policy for ensuring adequate spending on essential clinical services for the poor is to allow primary care facilities to retain user charges and spend these revenues on drug supplies and incentive bonuses for health workers. In Cameroon when fees were introduced in a group of rural health centers and the revenues collected were used to replenish drug supplies, utilization of the centers—especially by low-income families—increased substantially. The percentage of sick people living near those centers who sought care rose by more than 25 percent compared with the areas where fees were not charged, demonstrating that user fees can actually increase services for the poor.

NONGOVERNMENTAL ORGANIZATIONS. Private nonprofit institutions, both local and foreign, provide a significant share of health services in developing countries, delivering essential clinical services to low-income households in the poorest countries. NGOs provide a third or more of all clinical care in Cameroon, Ghana, Malawi, Uganda, and Zambia. They own a quarter of the health facilities in Bolivia's three largest cities, and they supply more than 10 percent of clinical services in India and Indonesia. Although it is difficult to compare the performances of NGO and government health facilities, recent data from Africa suggest that NGOs are often more efficient than the public sector. In Uganda physicians in church mission hospitals treated an average of five times as many patients as physicians in government facilities, and NGO nurses attended more than twice as many patients as their government counterparts. Governments that have excluded NGOs or heavily restricted their operations have seen essential services deteriorate. When Mozambique decided after independence in 1975 to ban NGO health activities in favor of government-run facilities, a wide range of health services in rural areas suddenly disappeared. Where such bans or barriers to NGO activity exist, they should be removed.

Beyond this, there are important opportunities for governments to form constructive partnerships with NGOs to deliver essential clinical services. One approach being followed in Sub-Saharan Africa and in some states of India is to incorporate NGO health centers into the network of public facilities by nominating appropriately located NGO hospitals as district (first level of referral) hospitals. The NGOs are expected to provide a range of public health and clinical services and to perform specific districtwide functions such as health planning, supervision of lower-level clinics and community activities, and maintenance of emergency transport. In return, the government pays some of the NGOs' costs.

This kind of government-NGO collaboration takes a variety of forms. In Lesotho nine of the country's eighteen health service areas (districts) are headed by a church mission hospital that carries out comprehensive health planning and management for its entire area. In Zimbabwe government funds for rural health improvement are being used to expand mission ("designated district") hospitals and to purchase ambulances for the NGOs. Ministries of health pay the salaries of nursing staff in mission hospitals in Zaire and most of the recurrent costs of NGO facilities in Botswana. Government donation of free vaccines and contraceptives to NGO health providers has also become a common way to target public subsidies to specific health intervention programs.

THE PRIVATE SECTOR. In recognition of the growing importance of the modern private sector in developing countries' health systems, some governments have begun to encourage private practitioners to deliver essential services. In India several states and nonprofit groups are working with the private sector—including the country's 1 million semiqualified urban and rural medical practitioners—to improve the quality and effectiveness of basic care. Some innovative approaches are being tried: private distribution outlets are being stocked with condoms and oral rehydration solution to make both more widely available, and the Indian Rural Medical Association is trying to improve the skills of rural private practitioners through education on such subjects as family planning, immunization, and oral rehydration. In Mali, one of the world's poorest countries, the local medical school has started a program to train graduates to set up private practices in small towns of 15,000 to 50,000 inhabitants. Although experience is recent, a number of physicians have already established successful private practices in these towns, and they have demonstrated that small-town families are prepared to pay for good care. The average outpatient visit costs $2 and a normal delivery $8.

In Africa and Asia traditional medicine remains an important part of the health care system, sometimes accounting for more than 10 percent of total spending. The number of traditional healers—including herbalists, bonesetters, faith healers, and traditional birth attendants—is typically many times larger than the number of medical physicians. The ratio of traditional to modern health practitioners has been estimated at nine to one in Sri Lanka, seventeen to one in Indonesia, twenty-five to one in Ghana, and twenty-eight to one in Nigeria. Under these circumstances there may be opportunities for governments to improve the delivery of essential health services by using traditional practitioners. Successful examples include the use of traditional healers to screen for malaria and to distribute antimalarial drugs in Thailand, to promote modern contraceptives in Kenya, and to distribute condoms to reduce HIV and STD transmission in Uganda and Zimbabwe. Traditional birth attendants have also been enlisted to improve pregnancy outcomes in many countries, including Bangladesh (Box 5.8).

Making delivery of clinical services more efficient

There are many routes by which developing countries can improve the efficiency of clinical services. Policies to increase the efficiency of government health services through decentralization and better hospital management could have an especially large positive effect, as could policies for strengthening government regulation of a more competitive private sector.

DECENTRALIZATION. A policy that can improve both efficiency and responsiveness to local needs is decentralization of the planning and management of government health services. In Africa some central ministries of health have given provincial and district offices responsibility for planning, day-to-day management of funds, personnel, training, maintenance, and other functions. Many problems have arisen: local governments or local offices of the central health ministry have not had the capacity to plan and manage health activities; devolution of responsibility has not always been accompanied by allocation of the needed funds; and local officials have not necessarily been accountable to their constituents. There have been some successes, however, that offer lessons for other countries.

Box 5.8 Traditional medical practitioners and the delivery of essential health services

Many simple health activities do not require extensive professional training or major facilities and equipment. Health workers based in clinics or in their own communities play an important role in delivering these services. The millions of community-based traditional health practitioners have enormous potential as public health workers and providers of essential clinical services if governments can give them the appropriate training, information, and incentives.

Thus far, the experience with modern-traditional collaboration has been mixed. A number of projects have failed because of poorly designed training and inadequate supervision, and many governments need to do more to curb unnecessary and dangerous practices by traditional healers. But there have also been instructive successes.

• An evaluation of workers participating in a volunteer program for detection of malaria in northern *Thailand* found that the performance of volunteers who were traditional healers was superior to that of other volunteers. The program, which began in 1961, had by 1988 more than 40,000 malaria-control volunteers distributed across 34,000 Thai villages. Volunteers trained by the Ministry of Health are expected to examine villagers, take blood samples, prepare smears to be sent to the district malaria clinic for analysis, and treat fever. They also provide malaria-related education to the villagers. In comparison with alternatives such as paid outreach workers, the volunteers improve case detection and save the government considerable expense.

A WHO study found that traditional healer volunteers in Thailand were more active in pursuing and identifying malaria cases than other volunteers and that they tended to remain in the program longer because their service enhanced their standing in the community. Villagers indicated that they felt more confident about having someone they already knew as the village traditional healer draw their blood and administer treatment.

• In western *Kenya* the African Medical and Research Foundation (AMREF) has trained male and female traditional health practitioners who live in remote villages to dispense drugs and some types of contraceptives. Since the project began, the share of women of reproductive age using modern contraception in six pilot sites has risen from less than 10 percent to more than 25 percent. The Kenyan government has asked AMREF to expand the project.

• In *Bangladesh* a program to train and support midwives to work with traditional birth attendants helped to lower maternal mortality rates by 60 percent over a ten-year period. The results of the program indicate that, given adequate support systems, community-based services could bring about a substantial decline in maternal mortality.

• In Ghana, until recently, decisions on health spending were highly centralized, with inflexible expenditure levels set by the Ministry of Health for specific "vertical" programs such as immunization, control of tuberculosis and leprosy, and family planning. In the late 1980s the ministry agreed to delegate financial authority to health teams in each of the country's 110 districts. Unfortunately, most district health officials did not know the procedures for obtaining and accounting for funds. To remedy this problem, members of the district health management teams were given training that enabled them to make more timely budgeting and spending decisions, and expenditure levels increased as much as fivefold. In districts where earmarked funds from the center were pooled and reallocated according to local priorities, technical efficiency improved because of joint planning of work schedules and sharing of transport for outreach services and supervision.

• In Botswana, although secondary and tertiary health care is the responsibility of the central Ministry of Health, the government has devolved responsibility for primary care to local district councils. The process began on a pilot basis in 1973 and was gradually expanded to cover the entire country. To support decentralization, the Ministry of Health funded the creation of district health teams consisting of a medical officer, a public health nurse, and a health inspector. The central government continues to finance, through annual block grants, most of the recurrent primary care expenditures of the district councils, and the councils' proposals for capital spending are included in the ministry's investment budget. But the day-to-day management of primary care centers, including purchases of supplies and hiring of personnel, is in the hands of the councils.

Those countries that have gone furthest in decentralization have devolved responsibility for health services—including implementation of government health programs and management of government health facilities—to subnational levels of government. Such devolution has been going on for many years in some large developing countries with federal systems of government (for example, Brazil, India, Mexico, and Nigeria), but it is also becoming increasingly common in a number of other Latin American countries and in the formerly socialist economies.

The gradual devolution of Chile's health system over the past decade suggests that success can be achieved through a measured process accompanied by training and institutional development. Chile began the progressive decentralization of its publicly provided health services in 1979, when twenty-six health service areas (HSAs) were established to cover the country's thirteen administrative regions. Each HSA was given responsibility (and, to go with it, additional personnel and a share of the health budget) for managing all the government health facilities in its area. The second step in decentralization was taken in 1987, when management of the primary care network (consisting of more than 2,500 urban and rural clinics, rural health posts, and rural medical stations as well as about 14,000 health personnel) was transferred to the local government or municipalities. The HSAs were responsible for monitoring the municipalities' actions. In a third phase of the decentralization process, scheduled to begin in late 1993, the central Ministry of Health will withdraw completely from service provision, leaving this task entirely to the HSAs, which will enter into formal performance contracts with the ministry.

But not all decentralization has been a success. Countries such as Colombia that have devolved responsibility in a short period of time, without the requisite financial resources and institutional capacity at lower levels of government, have found that decentralization can be counterproductive, aggravating existing inefficiencies and inequities in the health system. In Brazil the municipality of Rio de Janeiro refused to accept responsibility for all the "decentralized" federal health facilities within its borders on the grounds that federal budget transfers to the municipality were inadequate.

IMPROVEMENT OF HOSPITAL MANAGEMENT. Low rates of hospital utilization in developing countries point to significant inefficiencies in the use of buildings and equipment (to which scarce capital has been devoted). Most common medical conditions can be treated in relatively simple facilities. In a well-run hospital system district hospitals would have the highest turnover rates and the shortest stays, while tertiary hospitals would have the lowest turnover rates and the longest stays. Some countries, including China and Fiji, have ef-

ficient systems that conform to the expected pattern. But in others, such as Indonesia, Jamaica, and Lesotho, there are no significant differences between the different types of hospitals. In Papua New Guinea the ideal pattern is reversed: the low turnover rate for district hospitals implies that the hospitals either have too many beds or offer such poor services that patients go directly to higher levels. The shorter average stay at the tertiary hospital suggests that many patients who do not require tertiary care are treated there.

Disparities in average length of stay across hospitals with a similar mix of cases are another indication of substantial inefficiencies. Data from Latin America for 1980–85 show that average stays in hospitals run by ministries of health varied from five days in Colombia to thirteen days in Uruguay, and stays in social insurance hospitals varied from five days in Mexico to twelve days in Peru. In public hospitals in Argentina the average length of stay ranged from eight to twenty-seven days. In Malawi average stays in six government hospitals with a similar case mix varied from five to thirteen days.

To remedy these inefficiencies, major steps to improve the organization and management of public hospitals are required. One approach would be to delegate responsibility for health service delivery to individual public institutions, but doing so will require changes in accounting and management practices. Government health budgets are now often highly aggregated, covering all facilities and programs in a given district, region, or even country. This prevents any detailed analysis of spending and services. Tracking costs should become part of the responsibility of the facility manager and the district management team. Cost analysis would make it easy for these managers to monitor areas of over- or underfunding and for higher-level officials to compare cost profiles and unit costs.

Some countries have converted public hospitals into semiautonomous foundations or public enterprises in order to improve performance by granting greater budgetary and management autonomy. These foundations or parastatals are under fewer restrictions than public facilities in managing their budgets and sometimes in hiring and firing. They can recover costs and collect charitable donations. The Tunisian government, for example, has converted eleven large public hospitals into semiautonomous entities over the past two years and will convert another ten in the next few years. Under the new arrangement, each hospital manages its own operational budget and is free to reassign funds across budget categories as needed. To ensure accountability, the hospital is required to operate within its annual budget and to provide to the Ministry of Health detailed reports about services provided and unit costs. Autonomy in personnel matters is more limited. All staff except the general manager are still governed by civil service regulations. The hospital management cannot fire employees, but it can ask the ministry to reabsorb staff and can use contracted personnel instead. The effect of these reforms will be fully assessed over the next few years, but some gains in efficiency are already apparent. One of the first hospitals converted has fully contracted out all food, cleaning, and security functions and now obtains services of much higher quality, at similar or even lower unit cost.

Elsewhere too, an increasing body of evidence suggests that the technical efficiency of government health facilities can be improved by contracting out ancillary services. In Venezuela, for example, Health Ministry hospitals contract out maintenance of large equipment, and social security hospitals frequently contract for laundry, gardening, food services, and security, as well as for maintenance. This arrangement has several advantages. It can be less costly than publicly provided services; services can be of better quality; and they can be more reliable (because less subject to strikes and other industrial action).

COMPETITION AND REGULATION. Competition among health providers in developing countries can improve the quality of services as perceived by patients and thus increase consumer satisfaction. This applies to the poor as well as the rich: competition among private physicians in the slums of Bombay, for example, is intense, with private practitioners offering convenient evening hours, short waiting times, and readily available drugs to win patients from other private practitioners and from public clinics.

It is much less clear, however, whether competition among suppliers of health services always leads to greater efficiency. In fact, the contrary sometimes happens, especially when competition among private providers is combined with third-party reimbursement of fees paid for services. Excessive tests, procedures, and drugs are supplied, and costs increase. This supplier-induced inefficiency takes place because most patients are unable to judge the value of specific services or to compare prices among suppliers—all the more so

when they are already sick or have a pressing health problem—and because, in the case of third-party reimbursement, they do not bear the full cost of the services they consume.

Governments can encourage efficiency-promoting competition among suppliers of health services by requiring them to offer a standard package of services at a price fixed in advance. Consumers can then pick the supplier that offers the most attractive combination of price, service, and quality, with competition spurring suppliers to improve quality and reduce costs. This is the basic approach taken in "managed competition" proposals for health care reform in the United States (Box 5.9). Although managed competition requires a high degree of government administrative capacity to set the rules and to monitor provider performance, it may be relevant in some middle-income developing countries.

As developing countries take steps to encourage a diversified system of health service delivery, including use of NGOs and private providers, they will also need to strengthen their governments' capacity to regulate the private sector. Regulations are required to ensure that quality standards are met, that financial fraud and other abuses do not take place, that those entitled to care are not denied services, and that confidentiality of medical information is respected. Regulation can be carried out in a number of ways: by inspecting private health facilities; by accrediting medical schools; by licensing physicians, nurses, and other health professionals; and by prohibiting certain insurance practices such as exclusion of prior medical conditions. When the government allocates funds to NGOs, reimburses private providers under public insurance schemes, or subcontracts with the private sector for ancillary services such as catering and laundry, it can require an independent audit of these private contractors.

In practice, few developing countries have established such regulatory mechanisms, but the situation may be changing. In Brazil, where social insurance finances the bulk of health care, and private hospitals and physicians provide 80 percent of hospital services and half of all outpatient care, important regulatory changes are now under discussion. These include comprehensive accreditation of facilities by state governments, standard licensing examinations for medical school graduates, and the inclusion of representatives of citizens' groups and consumer advocacy organizations in medical ethics boards, which are currently composed exclusively of physicians. The private

"Managed competition," which has attracted widespread interest in the United States, refers to a health services purchasing strategy designed to promote competition and to reward those health care providers with the best performance in terms of cost, quality, and patient satisfaction. The strategy is designed to address the fundamental problems of the current health care financing and delivery system in the United States. There, health care coverage is mainly employment-based and is far from universal: approximately 37 million people under age 65 lacked insurance coverage in 1990. Costs are increasing rapidly; if current trends continue, spending is expected to grow from 12 to 18 percent of GNP by 2000. Under third-party insurance, provider reimbursement methods often create financial incentives to provide more care. Insurers seek profits by excluding higher-risk individuals rather than by aggressively pursuing greater efficiency in providing health services. A major indirect cost of the system is reduced labor mobility as a result of the risks of exclusion from insurance at a new place of employment.

Under managed competition, a health insurance purchasing cooperative (HIPC) would be formed to organize purchasers of health care within a region. The HIPC would establish standards for the region's health plan by, for example, defining a basic benefit package of comprehensive health services, and would contract with eligible providers for this basic package. During the annual open-enrollment period the HIPC would provide information about the price of the basic package from different providers and about the quality of care offered. Equity would be improved by requiring providers to open their rolls to all consumers, regardless of risk. Universal coverage would be achieved through public subsidies to those not otherwise covered so that they could purchase packages. Standardi-

zation would enable consumers to choose among competing packages in an informed and more price-conscious way. One example of "managed competition" is the California Public Employees Retirement System, which operates like the proposed HIPC, arranging health coverage and managing competition on behalf of almost 1 million state employees and retirees and their families.

Analysts expect that over time competition would force third-party insurers to drop out or move in the direction of managed care networks because these networks can use financial incentives and management tools to achieve efficient care. Indeed, insurers are already shifting in this direction: nearly half of all health insurers now offer some sort of plan involving managed care. Competition would also give health care providers clear incentives to become more efficient. One question about the managed competition model is whether it would work in rural areas and areas of low population density, and, if not, what alternatives would be best. Another concern is the cost of extending universal coverage.

Although this proposal was developed to respond to the particular problems of the U.S. system, it has relevance elsewhere. The Netherlands, which is introducing choice of insurer under a universal social health insurance scheme, faces the same challenges regarding control of risk-selection behavior on the part of insurers. Chile has, since 1981, encouraged the growth of private prepaid health insurance schemes, known as ISAPREs. (Box 7.2 provides details on these plans.) Problems have come up with Chile's reforms, however: the lack of a standard package has limited effective competition, and weak regulation has allowed private insurers to deny coverage to high-risk individuals.

Brazilian Association of Hospitals is debating the establishment of its own accreditation system, and the medical association in São Paulo has begun a voluntary pilot effort to certify hospitals in that state on the basis of adherence to norms, assessment of patient data, and patient satisfaction surveys. Qualifying examinations for licensing physicians are being tested in another state where, at present, all medical school graduates are automatically licensed for life, without requirements for continuing education or recertification. And the Federal Council of Medicine has proposed legislation that would expand its authority to monitor the quality of health care and to discipline poorly performing doctors and hospitals.

Reorienting clinical services and beyond

It is a fundamental responsibility of governments everywhere to ensure access to a package of essential clinical health care, with special attention to the poor. Utilization of a minimum package defined by its high cost-effectiveness would reduce the total burden of illness in developing countries dramatically, by an average of 25 percent. Such a package is affordable in low-income countries if governments reallocate current health expenditures and increase public spending and if they implement policies that encourage selective payments directly from better-off patients and from existing insurance schemes. Middle-income countries could easily pay for the minimum package, using the resources currently devoted to health, and might wish to enrich the package by adding services.

Government efforts to improve health insurance should be aimed at increasing the portion of the population covered, reducing subsidies for insurance that benefit primarily the wealthy and the middle class, and controlling health care spending financed from insurance. This will require stronger regulation of private insurance and policies to expand compulsory social insurance based on payroll taxes. It also means shifting provider payment away from open-ended fee-for-service methods to prepayment through capitation and preset budgets for hospitals.

Greater diversity and competition in the supply of health services can do much to improve the delivery of an essential clinical package and raise the technical efficiency of doctors, hospitals, and other providers. Key government measures include strengthening legal and financial support to NGOs that provide health services and creating a positive environment for the private sector combined with important regulatory safeguards against abuse. Gains in technical efficiency can be achieved through a combination of careful decentralization of government health services and improved management of public hospitals.

These efforts to reorient government recurrent spending toward essential clinical care and to promote diversity and competition in the supply of health services must be accompanied by changes in longer-term investments in health inputs—facilities and equipment, health personnel, pharmaceutical management systems, health information, and health research infrastructure. Policies to bring about this reorientation are taken up in Chapter 6.

Health inputs

In recent decades developing countries have invested heavily in health. Often with help from donors, they have constructed hospitals and buildings and purchased equipment to fill them. They have educated doctors, nurses, and other health care professionals. And they have set up new systems to supply drugs, research, and information. Worldwide, the number of hospital beds rose between 1960 and 1980 from 5 million to almost 17 million, which more than doubled the per capita supply. The number of physicians increased more than fivefold between 1955 and 1990, from 1.2 million to 6.2 million. Such investments have created new opportunities, but they have also led to problems.

Once built, hospitals are extremely difficult to close. Once trained, physicians create pressure to be employed. In virtually every developing country, facilities, equipment, human resources, and drugs are skewed toward the top of the health system pyramid (Figure 6.1). Yet the cost-effective public health and clinical interventions discussed in preceding chapters of this Report are best delivered at the level of the district hospital or below. That they are often delivered through tertiary hospitals simply increases costs without improving quality. This problem is found in poor countries in which the principal tertiary teaching hospital in the capital city consumes a large proportion of the total resources available for health. It is also found in cities such as London, where numerous specialized teaching hospitals absorb large amounts of resources while failing to address the most common and pressing health problems of city residents.

In many countries public investments are concentrated unduly on tertiary services, and public spending subsidizes high-end facilities, equipment, and human resources for private markets. The challenge for public policy is to redress the balance and so permit the efficient delivery of public health and essential clinical services. Where cost containment of health spending is a concern, public policy can play a useful role in limiting the growth of both public and private investments in specialist training, equipment, and tertiary facilities. For some inputs, such as buildings and human resources, changes will necessarily be slow. For others, such as pharmaceuticals, a new policy can alter inputs rapidly. This chapter suggests how to set about these tasks. It also assesses how public support for information and research can help improve health sector performance today and create new health systems and technologies for tomorrow.

Reallocating investments in facilities and equipment

Investments to support delivery of essential clinical services are best directed at health centers and district hospitals and at improving access in underserved areas. Some public investments in tertiary facilities are needed to support research and training, but at levels well below current levels of public financing in most countries. Investments in specialized facilities can be left largely to the private sector, and public subsidies, where they exist, can often be greatly reduced. Redirecting public spending toward lower-level facilities is difficult politically, but some countries are moving in this direction. In Papua New Guinea, for example, public spending on hospitals has for the past decade been limited to 40 percent of the Ministry of

Figure 6.1 The health system pyramid: where care is provided

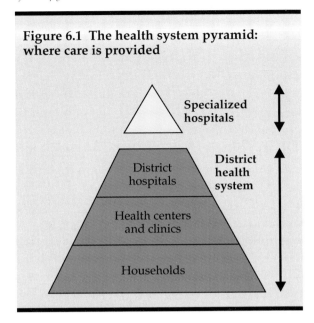

Health's recurrent budget, which is well below the average in most developing countries.

Facilities

Tertiary hospitals provide the most specialized and sophisticated services and are where most clinical research, education, and training take place. They are usually located in large urban areas. One step down the health hierarchy are district hospitals, which are typically located in towns or smaller cities serving rural areas but are valuable in large cities too. District hospitals generally have 100 to 400 beds, serve 50,000 to 200,000 inhabitants, and include departments of medicine, surgery, pediatrics, obstetrics and gynecology, and dentistry. They also provide basic anesthesia, radiology, and clinical laboratory services. The district hospital is the first level of referral from health centers and provides complementary services such as basic surgery. It mainly offers inpatient care but also typically provides some outpatient care, day surgery (in which the patient is operated on and discharged on the same day), and emergency services not available at health centers. In many cities that have grown rapidly over the past twenty years, periurban areas do not have enough health centers and district hospitals. In some African capitals one extremely large tertiary public hospital serves the whole city—an example is Zambia's University Teaching Hospital of Lusaka, with 1,835 beds.

Hospitals absorb the bulk—40 to 80 percent—of public spending on health in developing countries. Industrial countries have much higher health expenditures and more chronic disease problems, but the share allocated to hospitals is slightly smaller, 35 to 70 percent. Figure 6.2 shows the marked variations in hospital supply across the eight demographic regions used in this Report, from about eleven beds per 1,000 population in Central and Eastern Europe to less than one bed per 1,000 population in India. In most developing countries more than 60 percent of all hospital beds are public. The data used in Figure 6.2 unfortunately fail to distinguish between tertiary and district-level hospitals. The minimum package of essential clinical services described in Chapter 5 requires about one district hospital bed per 1,000 population. Given that some of India's and Sub-Saharan Africa's hospital beds are devoted to care outside the essential package, there is likely to be a shortage of district-level hospital beds in parts of those regions.

In some countries the underfunding of lower-level facilities has been exacerbated by the creation of multiple levels of outpatient facilities (health posts, dispensaries, and rural health centers), none of which functions well. At the same time, tertiary care hospitals are crowded with patients who could be treated in less costly and more accessible district hospitals or health centers. A study in Chad, for example, revealed that 71 percent of all central hospital consultations were for problems that could have been treated at lower-level facilities. An obvious way to reduce spending without sacrificing any health gains is to make full use of existing lower-level facilities. Measures for achieving this include charging a higher fee to patients who go straight to tertiary facilities without referrals, except in emergencies, and making a referral from the primary care provider a mandatory condition for specialized services. At the same time, however, the quality and responsiveness of services at lower-level facilities need to be improved.

INCENTIVES AND INVESTMENT DECISIONS. Public sector budgetary procedures often obscure the real costs of investments in health facilities and bias them toward high-profile investments in large hospitals. Major investments, including donor-financed projects, may be approved by a government body that does not have to face the recurrent costs of operating the facility. Regions can argue

Figure 6.2 Hospital capacity by demographic region, about 1990

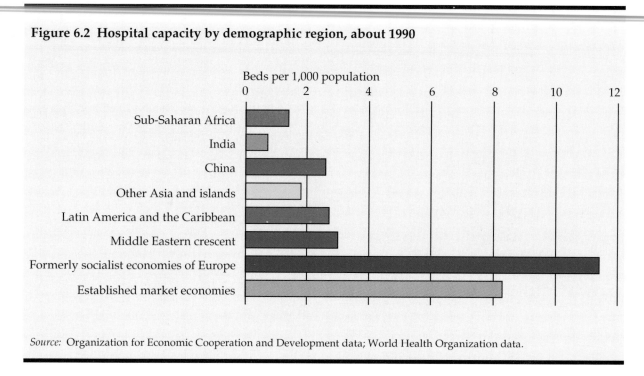

Source: Organization for Economic Cooperation and Development data; World Health Organization data.

for new facilities without having to weigh the budgetary consequences if federal-state resource transfers, instead of following predictable and transparent funding formulas (such as population-based schemes), are heavily politicized.

International assistance has frequently exacerbated the problem of unsustainable health investments. Donor assistance, particularly for tertiary facilities and teaching hospitals, has sometimes been provided even if the incremental recurrent costs from these investments are too high. Too many donor-financed hospitals have opened only partially, not at all, or at the expense of existing facilities. In Rwanda, for example, a 200-bed hospital was completed in 1991 but has not yet opened because of the difficulty of financing its high recurrent costs, which are estimated at about 15 percent of the Ministry of Health's already tightly constrained budget. In Chad, where external assistance amounts to about 30 percent of national income, a national development plan proved useful for screening out inappropriate donor financing. Two new hospital construction proposals that were found to conflict with the plan are being reconsidered.

In the private sector, financial incentives drive investment decisions. Health maintenance organizations (HMOs) in the United States have incentives for providing care efficiently. As a result, they operate with much less hospital infrastructure than the health system overall. Large HMOs (with hospitals) have about 1.5 hospital beds per 1,000 members—well below the average of 8 beds per 1,000 for established market economies and 5 for the United States overall and slightly below regional averages for China and Latin America. Evidence indicates that quality of care in HMOs is maintained even with significantly lower levels of hospitalization and hospital infrastructure. Privately financed health insurance with unconstrained fee-for-service payment, by contrast, provides no incentives to rationalize physical capacity.

DUPLICATION OF HEALTH FACILITIES IN THE PUBLIC SECTOR. Excess public facilities in urban areas are a problem in many countries. The historical growth of hospitals, especially in capital cities, has led to a proliferation of specialist tertiary services that are often linked to medical education and research. Another cause of duplication is the public provision of health services to different subgroups of the population, each with its own hospitals and health centers. In Poland, for example, parallel health systems exist for workers and their families in the railway, mining, police, and military sectors and for prisoners; another set of facilities serves the general population. This can result in excess capacity, with no facilities achieving economies of scale.

There are two solutions for duplication: creating internal markets and instituting central or regional planning linked to health budgets. If effective internal markets are created within the public sector, money will follow patients—and patients, together with their general practitioners, will have a choice as to which hospital to use. The availability of good information about quality and price will help efficient providers of specialist services to prosper, while less-efficient hospitals will close. The alternative is rationalization of services by central or regional planning. In the largely publicly financed health systems of the Nordic countries, health resources are allocated by region. Each region of about 350,000 inhabitants elects representatives who make decisions about health care spending. These representatives have incentives to avoid duplication of services and to capture economies of scale in service delivery. If left to individual hospitals, decisionmaking for large investments will tend to reflect the interests of that hospital, not the region. Multiple hospitals will want to provide specialized, ''prestige'' services, leading to overinvestment.

EQUITY CONSIDERATIONS. For the rural poor, lack of physical infrastructure is the largest obstacle to use of health services. Distance to health facilities limits people's willingness and ability to seek care, particularly when transport is limited. There is a heavy urban bias in the distribution of health facilities. Large cities are much better served by both public and private health infrastructure than would be expected from their roles of serving urban populations and providing referral services for the surrounding population. (Referral hospitals are needed for only a small proportion—no more than 10 percent—of total hospitalizations.) Wealthier regions also have better access to infrastructure. In India the richer states of Maharashtra and Gujarat have 1.5 and 1.1 beds, respectively, per 1,000 population; the poorer states of Bihar and Madhya Pradesh have only 0.3 and 0.4 bed, respectively, per 1,000 population. Public investments need to address inequities in the present distribution of health infrastructure. Donors have an important role in this regard, especially where a significant proportion of investment is donor financed.

PRODUCTIVITY. The potential for improving the productivity of installed hospital capacity is large. In addition to the financing and management reforms discussed in Chapter 5, efficiency gains can be achieved by taking the following measures, which will need to be supported by investments in training and infrastructure:

• Convert some acute care hospital capacity to less costly extended or chronic care facilities for patients who require less-intensive care for long-term recovery and for rehabilitation of chronic conditions. Extended care facilities operate at a lower cost per bed-day than acute care hospitals. In the absence of such lower-level facilities, patients occupy high-cost acute care beds.

• Perform outpatient diagnostic tests before admitting the patient to the hospital.

• Support home care as an alternative to long-term hospitalization for some ailments.

• Modify treatment protocols—for example, reduce unnecessary surgeries, perform low-risk deliveries at maternity centers, and treat tuberculosis patients and many surgical cases on an outpatient basis. In Cali, Colombia, costs per procedure for day surgery are less than 30 percent of the cost of traditional treatment in hospital. Outpatient surgery has grown rapidly in many industrial countries but is used much less in developing countries.

MAKING THE TRANSITION. The 1985 earthquake in Mexico City destroyed about 20 percent of public hospital capacity. The Ministry of Health chose to concentrate reconstruction and new construction in low-income periurban areas that had hitherto been poorly served, and six new 144-bed district hospitals were built in these areas. But such possibilities for rapidly reconfiguring capacity toward lower-level facilities and underserved areas are seldom available. The alternative is to reduce or refrain from public investment in tertiary hospitals while simultaneously increasing investment and operating budgets for health centers and district hospitals. Over time, the tertiary hospitals can be operated on a self-financing basis, or they can be closed, converted to chronic care facilities or district hospitals if these are needed, or even sold to the private sector. But in most countries this process will necessarily be slow.

Equipment

Developing countries account for about $5 billion, or 7 percent, of the $71 billion spent each year on medical equipment worldwide. This global estimate includes medical and dental supplies, surgical instruments, electromedical and X-ray equipment, diagnostic tools, and implanted products.

The ability of the medical equipment industry to develop new health care technologies has vastly exceeded the capacity of purchasers to evaluate the clinical value and the cost-effectiveness of such innovations. At present, approximately 6,000 distinct types of medical devices (equipment, supplies, and reagents) and more than 750,000 brands, models, and sizes, produced by perhaps 12,000 manufacturers worldwide, are on the market.

Efficiency losses from poor selection and maintenance of medical equipment can be very large. WHO estimates that less than half of all medical equipment in developing countries is usable. In Brazil an estimated 20 to 40 percent of the $2 billion to $3 billion worth of public sector medical equipment is not working. A study of twelve Kenyan hospitals in 1984 found that sterilizers operated for an average of two years instead of the six expected and that incubators lasted only two years rather than eight. Equipment failed prematurely because maintenance budgets were only about 1 percent of the value of the capital stock (10 percent might be considered optimal). In Viet Nam 39 percent of urban health centers and 29 percent of urban polyclinics surveyed in 1991 lacked a working sterilizer—a critical piece of equipment for developing countries that have to reuse such supplies as syringes.

Investments in medical equipment can be rationalized by controlling the purchase of expensive, sophisticated equipment and rejecting most donated medical equipment, new or used. To contain costs, Belgium, France, and Portugal directly control the acquisition of state-of-the-art medical technologies by both the public and the private sectors. In Canada major capital acquisitions require prior approval by the provincial or territorial ministry of health on the basis of a needs assessment and other factors. Alternatively, governments can encourage public hospitals to make tough choices by limiting their budgets. Even assuming that donated equipment meets local equipment requirements, very little of it ever becomes operational, for a variety of reasons, including missing or damaged parts, lack of disposable inputs and of user and service manuals, and problems with power supply. Standardization of equipment could simplify management and maintenance and reduce inventory costs. Purchasing decisions could be analyzed on a life-cycle cost basis. In many cases improving maintenance to increase operating life and reduce downtime of equipment is more efficient than buying new equipment.

Because of the many products on the market and the speed of change, carrying out technology assessments can be extremely costly. The international community could help by developing and disseminating information on the availability, effectiveness, and prices of equipment and on user guidelines. Essential equipment lists could be developed along the lines of the essential drug lists already used by many countries.

Equipment procurement would also benefit from greater use of competitive buying. Purchasing is commonly restricted to local distributorships, and some countries also heavily protect local industry. These policies reduce competition and can easily double the purchase price of equipment. Developing countries can cut costs by adopting competitive purchasing methods or by purchasing equipment from international agencies—such as UNICEF, Equipment for Charity Hospitals Overseas (ECHO), and the International Dispensary Association—that offer procurement services for some medical equipment at competitive prices.

There are several reasons for government involvement in the development of health infrastructure. The government itself, as a provider of health services, may finance and use infrastructure. It may also intervene to compensate for market failures that can lead to greater investment, particularly in specialized health inputs, than is socially optimal. Finally, the government has a role in undertaking technology assessment of medical equipment, which is a costly public good.

To reduce both capital and recurrent costs without sacrificing quality of care, governments can:

• Reallocate public spending toward the facilities and equipment required for providing public health programs and essential clinical services.

• Improve the efficiency of installed capacity by considering alternative uses of facilities, as well as new diagnostic and treatment protocols. (Examples are the conversion of some costly acute care capacity to less costly extended care beds and treatment of some surgeries on an outpatient basis.) Such reconfiguration may require modest new investment.

• When cost containment is a concern, consider controls on the purchase of expensive, specialized technologies, whether by public or by private providers.

• Support and disseminate technology assessments to purchasers.

• Reduce or eliminate subsidies to private investors in facilities and equipment.

Addressing imbalances in human resources

Nearly all countries face the same fundamental problems with human resources in the health sector. There are not enough primary care providers and too many specialists. Health workers are concentrated in urban areas. Training in public health, health policy, and health management has been relatively neglected. Medical training is subsidized even though physicians may earn high incomes and many work in the private sector.

There are several ways in which governments can do something about these problems. Public sector pay and employment policies can be improved to be more competitive with the private sector and to relate pay to performance. Career development paths and in-service training are needed to retain staff, especially in managerial positions. Policies on accreditation and licensing can be used to limit enrollments in training programs, to shape curricula (all physicians might spend time in rural practice during their medical training or be required to pass examinations in public health), and to set minimum standards for providers. Education finance policies can be used to curtail education opportunities for physicians and specialists and to expand them for workers in primary care, public health, health policy, and management. But where oversupply is greatest, as for specialist physicians, the only effective solution may be to set quotas for training, or at the very least for publicly subsidized training.

Improving the balance between primary care providers and specialists

A central role in delivery of most cost-effective health interventions belongs to primary care providers, a category that can include physicians, nurses, nurse practitioners, or midwives, depending upon how the jobs are defined. Nonphysician primary care providers have many advantages. They cost less to train (data from Myanmar, Pakistan, and Sri Lanka indicate that between 2.5 and 3 nurses can be trained for the cost of training one physician), and they receive lower salaries. They are easier to attract to rural areas and usually communicate more effectively with their patients. In Sub-Saharan Africa, where the few local physicians are concentrated in urban hospitals, nurses often function as primary care providers. China,

too, has long relied on graduates of three-year (instead of five-year) medical schools to meet the needs of rural areas.

In some countries tasks traditionally performed by physicians have been successfully delegated to lower-level primary care providers as a way of improving the efficiency of health services. By specializing in certain common procedures (as midwives specialize in deliveries, for example), such providers may become better at their tasks than a generalist physician. Surgical technicians in Mozambique perform hysterectomies and cesarean sections and remove ectopic pregnancies. Some nongovernmental organizations (NGOs) in Bangladesh use graduate nurses to do sterilizations, and in Thailand public sector nurse-midwives perform this procedure. In these cases, evaluations indicate no differences in outcomes compared with procedures done by physicians. Ophthalmic clinical officers, who are not physicians, have performed cataract surgery in Kenya on a pilot basis, and evaluations indicate acceptable results. Africa has only one ophthalmologist per 1 million people; without the use of nonphysician services, many patients would not be able to get cataract surgery.

The distribution of nurses and physicians by region is shown in Figure 6.3. Appropriate staffing ratios depend heavily on the organization and financing of care and the specific tasks health personnel carry out. Health maintenance organizations in the United States, for example, operate with about 1.2 physicians per 1,000 enrollees, compared with about 4.5 in the fee-for-service sector. Evaluations of health outcomes and user satisfaction indicate that these savings in resources do not come at the expense of quality. Sub-Saharan Africa has the fewest physicians and nurses of any region, which is an obstacle to the delivery of the public health interventions and essential clinical services described in Chapters 4 and 5 because some of the existing personnel are providing other services. The public health and minimum essential clinical interventions require about 0.1 physician per 1,000 population and between 2 and 4 graduate nurses per physician. Given resource constraints, however, the relatively high ratio of nurses to physicians in Sub-Saharan Africa is a good sign. There is no optimal level of physicians per capita or optimal nurse-to-physician ratio, but a rule of thumb is that nurses should exceed physicians by at least two to one. (The ratio is five to one in Africa but well under two to one in China, India, Latin America, and the Middle Eastern crescent.)

Figure 6.3 Supply of health personnel by demographic region, 1990 or most recent available year

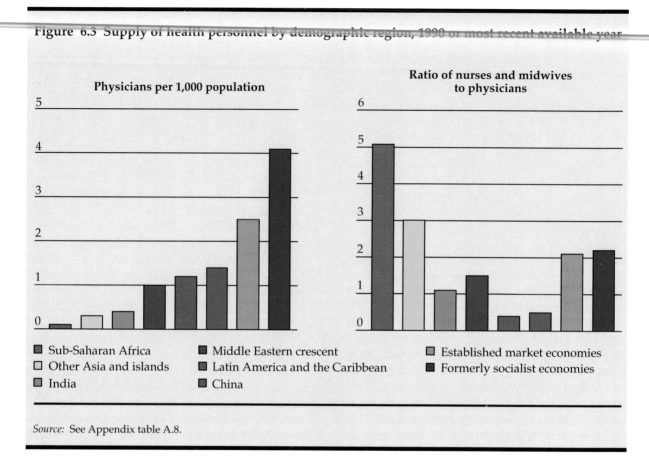

Source: See Appendix table A.8.

PHYSICIAN OVERSUPPLY. During the 1960s and 1970s many governments encouraged, primarily through subsidies to education, rapid expansion in physician training to meet the need for primary care providers. In many countries the excess of physicians in relation to nurses and of specialists in relation to other physicians has created problems. By the early 1980s the established market economies, Latin America, and parts of Asia were having trouble absorbing growing numbers of physicians. These policies have been costly, and it will take many years to correct the imbalances.

Mexico illustrates the problems. Medical enrollments in 1970 stood at about 29,000 in twenty-seven schools. Within ten years there were 93,000 in fifty-six schools. Many of the schools offered highly subsidized or free tuition, and some of the largest had open enrollment policies. At the same time, health services were growing only modestly. In 1960 there were 20,600 physicians in Mexico; by 1990 there were 166,000. A survey of physicians in major cities in 1986 revealed that 7 percent were unemployed, another 11 percent were working in

nonmedical jobs, and 11 percent were in low-income medical jobs or were seeing very few patients—which is a concern because the physicians may not see enough patients to maintain their competence. The quality of medical education also declined with the rapid growth in medical schools. Furthermore, the expansion of medical training did nothing to solve the problem of attracting physicians to rural areas. In 1983 an interinstitutional body was created, with representatives from the ministries of health and education, health care institutions, and universities. This group has, by agreement, reduced enrollments and contained the number of medical schools. More recently, the government has begun publishing average examination scores of medical school graduates by school to provide information on educational quality for prospective students and employers.

Other countries responded to physician oversupply by restricting medical immigration (Canada and the United Kingdom), by reducing working hours (Denmark), and by indirectly promoting outmigration of medical personnel. The last two

Box 6.1 International migration and the global market for health professionals

Over the past several decades, large numbers of physicians and nurses have migrated across national borders. WHO estimates that 14,000 nurses did so in the early 1970s and that in 1972 more than 140,000 physicians (or 6 percent of the total) resided outside the countries in which they were born or had been trained. Over the past half century the main flow of physicians and nurses has been from developing to industrial countries. Developing countries donate a full 56 percent of all migrating physicians and receive less than 11 percent. The principal donating countries for physicians are India and the Philippines. More than 90 percent of the nurses who migrate go to North America, Europe, and the high-income countries of the western Pacific, while only about 7 percent go to developing countries. Migrating nurses come overwhelmingly from the Philippines, which exports each year 2,000 to 3,000 nurses, many of whom go to North America. In 1970 more Filipino nurses were registered in Canada and the United States than in the Philippines, and the trend has continued to the present. Other major countries of origin for migrating nurses are Australia, Canada, the United Kingdom, and certain West Indian countries.

Consequences

The migration of health professionals has both positive and negative effects. It can help alleviate shortages in the receiving countries, and large remittances or tax revenues from overseas workers can improve the standard of living in the countries of origin. (The Philippines received an estimated $680 million from expatriate workers in all fields in 1986, and an estimated $8 billion in remittances went to developing countries as a group in 1975.) On the negative side, the net outflow of trained human resources can cause shortages of health workers. In Jamaica vacancy rates of more than 50 percent in nursing positions, in large part because of massive migration of nurses, have forced the Ministry of Health to close whole wards and to reduce the services offered in many facilities. In addition, emigrating health workers deprive their own countries of the benefits of (often state-financed) investments in their education. For example, the 111 registered nurses who resigned from government service in Jamaica in 1990 took with them nearly $1.7 million in government investment in training and education.

Policy responses

In an attempt to alter the patterns of migration, many countries have changed their immigration and licensing laws and regulations. During the 1980s, for example, the United States, to address its own nursing shortage, changed its policy on immigration of nurses, making it relatively easy for nurses wishing to come to the United States to obtain a visa. This had a profound effect on a number of neighboring countries. In the Philippines during the same period it became increasingly difficult for registered nurses to obtain travel documents because of the enormous outflow of nurses from that country.

Short-term immigration restrictions, however, may have only a limited effect. Other possibilities for encouraging health professionals to remain in their home countries include reforming education finance to require that individuals repay some or all of the costs of state-financed training, through student loans or enforced service bond requirements. And publicly financed opportunities for overseas training could be restricted because of its tendency to lead to outmigration.

---

solutions waste valuable resources (see Box 6.1). In some countries the government can limit enrollments in medical schools directly. Egypt has reduced medical enrollments by half since 1982; in France the Ministry of Health used quotas to cut new enrollments from about 11,000 in 1975 to less than 5,000 in 1989. In other countries, such as Germany and Mexico, universities have autonomy in determining enrollments, and cuts must be made through consensus or through education finance policies.

CURTAILING SPECIALIST TRAINING. Most governments will need to limit not only total enrollments but also the training of medical specialists. High numbers of specialists tend to increase the frequency of unnecessary and often risky procedures. This, in turn, pushes up health care costs and reduces the quality of care. The United States has the highest number of cardiologists and cardiac operating suites per capita in the world and correspondingly higher rates of surgery—a significant proportion of which is inappropriate.

While practice guidelines and incentive structures can be important policy tools for curbing overuse of procedures, training fewer cardiologists would also help. A classic U.S. study showed that a 10 percent increase in surgeons would bring about a 3 to 4 percent increase in surgical operations—the phenomenon of "supplier-induced demand."

Even when specialists function as generalists, they have more costly styles of practice, ordering more tests and procedures. Analysis of geographic variation in expenditures in the United States indicates that expenditures on physician services are unrelated to the total number of physicians per capita but are related to the ratio of primary care physicians to specialists. Many OECD countries limit the number of specialist training opportunities. This policy instrument is increasingly relevant for middle-income countries interested in cost containment. Subsidized medical education has already led to overproduction in some middle-income developing countries such as Chile, where 75 percent of all physicians are specialists, and Venezuela, where about 55 percent of all physicians employed in the public sector are specialists. In contrast, only 25 to 50 percent of physicians in Belgium, France, Germany, and the Scandinavian countries are specialists, and regulatory bodies and committees determine the number to be trained.

Few, if any, specialists are needed to deliver the cost-effective clinical interventions discussed in Chapter 5, even with a modest expansion in content beyond the minimum essential package. Some specialists are required for services outside the essential package. The overall proportion of physician generalists to specialists is an important indicator for governments to monitor, but this information is not at present readily available in many countries. A reasonable benchmark for the maximum proportion of specialists to physicians in developing countries might be 25 percent, which is about the lowest proportion found in the established market economies. In many developing countries the proportion could be much lower, given the epidemiological characteristics of the population and the smaller share of the population using clinical services beyond the essential package. Public regulation and rationing of specialist training, in addition to the elimination of training subsidies, may be needed to achieve this.

CONTENT OF TRAINING. Primary care training should include, at a minimum, the skills necessary to provide the essential clinical services discussed in Chapter 5. In fact, however, basic curricula in medical schools often fail adequately to cover some of these services, such as family planning services and the proper diagnosis and treatment of sexually transmitted diseases (STDs). For more than two decades there have been calls to stop training health professionals in high-technology tertiary institutions and to expose them thoroughly to health problems and practice at the grass-roots level. But progress has been extremely slow. The fifty-five member institutions of the international Network of Community-Oriented Educational Institutions for Health Sciences have adopted curriculum reforms that emphasize community-based and problem-based learning. The goal is to produce graduates whose competencies and experience correspond closely to community health needs. Significantly larger proportions of graduates from these schools have followed careers in primary care. Similar reform efforts have taken place in nursing education. In Nigeria, Senegal, and Uganda (for basic nurse training) and in Thailand (for public health nurse practitioners) the nursing curriculum has been oriented more toward community settings and preventive services.

Attracting primary care providers to underserved areas

Health providers are concentrated in urban areas. Professional isolation, lack of additional work opportunities, substandard housing, and other disamenities often make staffing rural health facilities difficult. If public sector wages cannot be increased, other methods must be found to increase the attractiveness of rural posts. Many countries require a period of rural service following publicly financed medical training. Canadian provinces have used many incentives, including differential pay scales, settlement allowances, payment of expenses for continuing education, and provision of scholarships for later study in return for a certain number of years of service.

In some settings lack of female health providers is an obstacle to utilization of health services. In Egypt, for example, most physicians are male, but cultural beliefs constrain women from being seen after puberty by men who are not family members. Even when trained, female primary care providers are hard to attract to underserved areas because of security concerns and the importance of living with their families. The Aga Khan Development Network in Pakistan, recognizing this problem, has trained women to work in their own communities as lady health visitors.

Community health workers can complement the work of primary care providers in rural areas. Burkina Faso, the Gambia, Ghana, and other countries have trained large numbers of community health workers as part of the national strategy for primary health care; in many other settings much smaller programs have been set up by NGO groups. Evaluations sometimes show disappointing results: community health workers have often had little impact on health service utilization and

Box 6.2 Community health workers

Over the past twenty years many countries have experimented with the use of community health workers (CHWs) to provide primary health care. Several African countries introduced CHW programs in the 1970s as a way of extending primary health care services at low cost nationwide. Health workers' responsibilities typically include providing education on sanitation, nutrition, family planning, child health, and immunizations, in addition to carrying out some basic health interventions. They can also be valuable as a referral point between health centers and the community. Regrettably, CHW programs have had mixed results. Studies have shown that in the Gambia and Indonesia traditional birth attendants who were not backed up by skilled services were unable to decrease the risk of maternal mortality.

A Jamaican program, launched in 1977, that used CHWs in primary health care efforts is an example of a well-intentioned effort gone awry. Problems emerged from the beginning, with the selection of personnel. CHWs generally demonstrate greater dedication when they serve the communities in which they live. Unfortunately, too few CHWs were recruited from the target communities, and workers who lived elsewhere had to be enlisted. Inability to recruit male volunteers limited the success of family planning and STD-prevention programs. The CHWs—a large group—sought and obtained civil service benefits, including a set salary structure and promotional opportunities. In 1985 salaries for briefly trained CHWs were to be equivalent to two-thirds those of registered nurses with three years' training. Health center buildings were altered to serve as bases for CHW operations. Shortages of higher-level staff prompted many health centers to substitute CHWs for nurses, even though the workers lacked the necessary training. CHWs became increasingly linked to the health system, but their availability to the community diminished. The program has since been greatly reduced.

Other efforts have been more successful. Perhaps the largest scale NGO-run community health worker program is the Pastoral da Criança, operated by the Catholic Church in Brazil. This program, initiated in 1983, receives strong support from the Ministry of Health and some technical and financial support from UNICEF and from the Bernard Van Leer Foundation and other NGOs. It now has 47,000 CHWs throughout Brazil. An estimated 1.5 million children were enrolled in the program in 1992. CHWs provide health education to low-income mothers regarding the importance of prenatal care, good diet during pregnancy, breast-feeding, proper weaning, immunizations, and management of diarrhea, and they monitor the growth of infants and young children. The training process for CHWs follows a central guideline but is adapted to fit the characteristics of different regions. Special care is given to the training programs for illiterate volunteers, and supervision of CHWs is closely integrated with continuing education and motivational support. An evaluation carried out in 1990 found that health and nutritional indicators for young children enrolled in the program were significantly better than indicators from similar communities in which the Pastoral da Criança had no activities.

Community health workers are also central to the successful Aga Khan Health Service primary health care programs in remote mountainous areas of rural Pakistan. The CHWs—volunteers selected by the villagers—collect epidemiological information, provide health education, identify problems, and provide simple treatment and referrals. They are backed up by mobile teams of physicians and nurses.

---

health indicators (Box 6.2). These same evaluations point to four necessary (but difficult) conditions for success: community health workers must be well trained, well supervised, well provided with logistical support, and linked to well-functioning district health systems for referral when needed.

Increasing training in public health, management, policy, and planning

Improvements in health systems performance can be facilitated by training adequate numbers of policymaking and management personnel, including public health specialists, policy analysts, hospital managers, and drug management specialists.

These skills are in short supply in most developing countries. Public health often receives little attention in basic medical curricula, specialty training is often inadequate, and courses in public health schools may be too academic and not relevant to local problems and needs. In Sub-Saharan Africa, where public health capacity is weakest, fewer than 100 people receive specialty training in public health annually. Some countries are exploring and implementing multidisciplinary training programs that include management and communication techniques as well as the traditional public health sciences. An innovative example of public health training designed to produce future leaders is the Union School of Public Health in Beijing, established in 1989 to stimulate public health training in the entire country. The school offers a master's degree in public health and draws students and teachers both from health disciplines and from economics, management, and the social and environmental sciences. Training is based on problem solving, and more than half of the educational experience is in the form of community service. In Zimbabwe, under a new public health training program, students spend 75 percent of their time in the field.

Health policy and planning and good management are fundamental (albeit insufficient) conditions for better performance of health services. Over the past thirty years the role of managers, economists, and planners in health services has expanded in the industrial countries. For example, in many of these countries professional (nonphysician) hospital managers commonly run hospitals, in contrast to developing countries, where hospitals tend to be run by physicians. As developing countries seek to boost efficiency and as they move toward decentralized management of health facilities, the need for trained managers increases. In most developing countries, however, training programs in these areas are poorly developed.

Distance education can facilitate training in public health, health economics, and management by allowing rapid implantation of what are often new curricula without the time-consuming task of training a new generation of teachers. Distance learning has been used, for example, to build health research capacity in China. The University of Newcastle in Australia, in collaboration with Chinese universities, has set up a postgraduate distance-learning program in clinical epidemiology. The printed materials and academic standards of the distance-learning program are equivalent to those in the Australian program. Chinese professors help the students with applied laboratory and research work.

Reforming the finance of health training

Many of the problems with human resources in the health sector derive from the fundamental flaw of public subsidization of medical training. If physicians paid the full costs of their training, it would be of no concern if they were later employed in nonmedical work. Public subsidies could be specifically targeted to encourage those training and career choices that are in the public interest.

Student loans could replace most of the current public subsidies for training. Repayment of loans might then be forgone if the trainee agreed to work in a priority sector (such as primary care or public health) or in an underserved location. Not only would professionals be better distributed and used, but there would be substantial savings of public resources.

Almost every country today is grappling with problems in the mix and quality of its health professionals. Government financial policies can play a constructive and central role in correcting market failures that lead to distortions in access to training and in the supply of professionals in different fields. (For example, if credit is not widely accessible, only the better-off may be able to go to medical school; if the private rate of return for a certain specialty greatly exceeds the social rate of return, more professionals may choose that field than would be socially optimal.) Government policy can:

• Help meet the need for training primary care providers and other health professionals by improving capital markets—using student loan programs, where feasible—and through national service mechanisms.

• Increase spending on training of, and improve public sector wages and benefits for, health professionals in areas in which social benefits currently exceed private returns. These include, in particular, nonphysician primary care providers, health care managers, and staff in rural areas.

• Limit or eliminate subsidies and financial incentives for specialist training.

Improving the selection, acquisition, and use of drugs

Drugs and vaccines embody much of the power of modern medicine. Governments can enhance their own utilization of drugs and assist the private sector in increasing its efficiency through policies that improve selection, rationalize acquisition and production, and encourage better use. Through drug regulation and the development of a national list of essential drugs of established cost-effectiveness, governments can help providers and consumers make better choices among the approximately 100,000 different drugs—composed of more than 5,000 different active substances—now available worldwide. Governments can encourage health systems to buy drugs of assured quality from the lowest-cost supplier, whether domestic or international. They can eliminate the incentives that in many countries induce physicians to overprescribe drugs because of the profits they earn from directly dispensing them. In China, Japan, and Korea such incentives helped to drive drug spending up to 35 to 50 percent of total health spending.

Selecting essential drugs

The Model List of Essential Drugs developed by WHO suggests a basic list of drugs that WHO considers important and effective for dealing with health problems in developing countries. First drawn up in 1977 by an expert panel, the original list has been revised and updated seven times and now includes about 270 products. It is designed to serve as a template from which countries can develop their own still more specific lists of essential drugs.

Drugs on the national essential list are intended to be available at all times and in the appropriate dosage forms in publicly provided health services. At the health center level about thirty to forty drugs can treat almost all complaints. District hospitals require no more than 120 drugs. If properly purchased, these drugs tend to be relatively inexpensive; almost all have multiple suppliers on international markets. Drugs are listed by international, nonproprietary (generic) names. Although many countries have created these essential drug lists, only a few have used them to guide purchasing and management of public sector (or publicly financed) drug supplies. And occasionally national drug lists have omitted important products, particularly contraceptives.

Bangladesh and Sudan use limited lists not only to select drugs for public financing but also to guide the national drug registration process, thereby affecting the mix of drugs available in the private sector as well. Norway has limited the number of drugs registered by incorporating cost-effectiveness, among other factors, into the review process. Since 1991 Zimbabwe has used its national list to determine which drugs can be imported by the private sector without a permit.

The applicability of the essential drug concept is not limited to developing countries; drug formularies, which are detailed lists of essential drugs, are widely used by institutional health providers (public or private) and insurance companies in industrial countries. The formulary contains the names of drugs that are approved or recommended for health providers and supply systems. It also provides useful information for individual prescribers. In creating formularies, drugs are assessed on the basis of their safety, effectiveness, and cost-effectiveness in comparison with other therapeutic products. Evidence from the United Kingdom and other countries shows that the adoption of formularies can contribute to considerable savings in drug costs if physicians are involved in their development and are educated about the results.

Governments are also responsible for carrying out regulatory functions to ensure that all drugs on the market are of acceptable quality, safety, and efficacy. Building up a national regulatory authority requires the creation of a core group of trained staff, enactment of supporting legislation for administrative drug review, and the establishment of quality assurance laboratories. These are important areas for donor assistance and perhaps for internationally shared efforts.

Acquiring and producing drugs

In 1990 the public and private sectors in developing countries spent an estimated $44 billion, or $10 per capita, on pharmaceuticals. Global expenditures on pharmaceuticals amounted to about $220 billion, or $40 per capita. Total expenditures on human vaccines, excluding those made in developing countries, were between $1.6 billion and $2.0 billion in 1992. Drug expenditures vary widely, from a low of $2 per capita in parts of Sub-Saharan Africa and in Bangladesh to a high of $412 in Japan (Table 6.1).

Table 6.1 Annual drug expenditures per capita, selected countries, 1990

Country	Expenditure (dollars)
Japan	412
Germany	222
United States	191
Canada	124
United Kingdom	97
Norway	89
Costa Rica	37
Chile	30
Mexico	28
Turkey	21
Morocco	17
Brazil	16
Philippines	11
Ghana	10
China	7
Pakistan	7
Indonesia	5
Kenya	4
India	3
Bangladesh	2
Mozambique	2

Source: Ballance, Pogany, and Forstner 1992.

In most established market economies pharmaceuticals and vaccines account for between 5 and 20 percent of health care spending, and, except in Canada and the United States, more than half of all drug expenditures are publicly financed. In developing countries, households' out-of-pocket expenditures make up a much larger proportion of total drug spending. In Côte d'Ivoire and Pakistan, more than 90 percent of household health expenditure is devoted to drugs. In the public sector drugs generally account for between 10 and 30 percent of total recurrent costs, making them the second largest category after salaries. Given this high volume of expenditure, achieving the substantial improvements in efficiency of procurement that are possible becomes a high priority.

PURCHASING DRUGS AND VACCINES EFFICIENTLY. Some countries have achieved savings of 40 to 60 percent in pharmaceutical expenditure by improving selection and by competitive purchasing. For example, for several years the Costa Rican social security agency has been able to purchase drugs at approximately half the price of its counterpart institutions in other Central American countries, partly because of its use of centralized purchasing, more open and transparent purchasing pro-

cedures, and selection of generic drugs on the basis of its national essential drug list. This, of course, is facilitated by Costa Rica's political stability. In 1986 several Caribbean islands joined together to carry out international tenders through the Caribbean Development Bank. In the first year they saved 44 percent over previous prices.

The first step toward efficient procurement is careful quantification of drug and vaccine supply needs over a given period, using essential drug lists or formularies where possible. Large stocks of low-priority drugs have high opportunity costs: they tie up resources and may expire before they can be used. Shortages of high-priority drugs are also costly; emergency purchases from local suppliers are always expensive. Good forecasting permits economical purchasing.

Some governments and many donors purchase drugs through international agencies (see Box 6.3). These agencies use international tendering and, because of the scale of their purchases and their low operating margins, pass on very low prices. (The total amount of drugs procured in this way is, however, small in relation to total drug expenditures in developing countries.) UNICEF purchased about $160 million worth of pharmaceuticals, vaccines, and related supplies for developing countries in 1992. Ethiopia, Sudan, Tanzania, and

---

Box 6.3 Buying right: how international agencies save on purchases of pharmaceuticals

UNICEF and several nonprofit organizations offer purchasing services that enable countries to obtain favorable prices for drugs, vaccines, and some medical equipment. UNICEF, the biggest in the field, has supplied basic drugs and vaccines since the 1960s. In 1983 it issued its first international invitation to tender for the bulk purchase of pharmaceuticals for Tanzania. The prices quoted against the invitation to tender were up to 50 percent lower than previous price quotations. As a result of this experience, UNICEF has continued to use international tendering for the bulk purchase of pharmaceuticals and to pass on these favorable prices to developing countries. UNICEF contracts with the Danish National Board of Health to provide advice on quality assurance for pharmaceutical products. In 1992 UNICEF's purchases of drugs ($61.2 million), vaccines ($63.6 million), and refrigeration equipment, syringes, needles, and sterilizers ($33.4 million) were delivered to more than 120 countries.

The International Dispensary Association (IDA), established in 1972, is a nonprofit supplier of drugs to developing countries. IDA procures drugs and sup-

plies on behalf of governments and nonprofit organizations in more than eighty developing countries. Its current annual turnover amounts to $80 million. IDA also carries out quality assurance, checking that manufacturers produce in accordance with internationally accepted standards. When the drugs are received, IDA tests samples for quality and verifies labels and certificates of analysis.

Price lists from UNICEF and IDA provide valuable market information for countries' own procurement. Competitive tendering in Mali reduced prices by 40 percent. In Kenya bulk purchasing of carefully selected essential drugs was estimated in 1985 to save nearly 40 percent (or $700,000) of the annual drug bill for church health institutions. In 1992 the Chinese government carried out international competitive bidding for drugs for tuberculosis treatment and—perhaps because of the very large scale of procurement involved, the low-cost packaging requirements, and the desire of manufacturers to enter the Chinese market—achieved savings of about 70 percent of UNICEF's published prices.

Zambia have all relied heavily on nonprofit international drug suppliers.

But many other developing countries fail to take advantage of international competition or international agencies. Purchasing methods, as well as import restrictions, tend to restrict competition and thereby raise prices. In addition, price competition is restricted by the industry's extensive drug promotion practices and, in the case of patented products, by monopoly power. Some countries, such as Venezuela and Zimbabwe, protect local pharmaceutical industries from international competition (imported drugs will not be approved for import and sale if there is a local producer), and Belize and other countries impose import tariffs even if there is no local production. This results in great variation in prices for pharmaceuticals and supplies in developing countries. Cross-country data on the retail price of condoms show remarkable variation: condoms cost only $2 to $3 per 100 in China, Egypt, and Tunisia, $15 to $30 per 100 in Costa Rica, Ecuador, and Mexico, and more than $70 per 100 in Brazil, Burundi, Myanmar, and Venezuela. This price variation is attributable to a combination of factors, including import tariffs, import restrictions, and wholesale and retail marketing structures.

Some countries purchase directly from a few local suppliers because of liquidity constraints. International agencies do not extend credit, and they require payment in hard currency. Local suppliers often extend credit in exchange for significantly higher prices. Changing this practice to take advantage of benefits from competitive procurement would require the ministries of both health and finance to make budgetary funds and foreign exchange available when needed for large-scale drug purchases. Governments can also improve drug procurement by passing legislation to facilitate generic drug prescribing. This can increase the affordability of drugs purchased from private outlets.

PHARMACEUTICAL PRODUCTION. The cost of developing a sophisticated pharmaceutical industry with a significant research base is huge. During 1961–90, 90 percent of the approximately 2,000 ''new chemical entities'' (new drugs) brought on the market were discovered in only ten OECD countries. Five countries in the developing world—Argentina, China, India, Korea, and Mexico—discovered, developed, and marketed at least one new chemical entity between 1961 and 1990. Several other developing countries—among them,

Brazil, Indonesia, and Turkey—have primary manufacturing capabilities or the ability to produce both therapeutic ingredients and finished products. But most developing countries either have only the capacity to produce finished products from imported ingredients or have no manufacturing capability whatsoever. (Countries in the latter group are typically very small.)

Except in the largest countries that have primary manufacturing capabilities, local pharmaceutical production in developing countries is likely to make sense only for intravenous fluids, which have relatively high transport costs; for local packaging of bulk imports in finishing plants; and for packaging of oral rehydration salts. Even in these activities local production may be inefficient and waste scarce resources. State-run drug and vaccine companies, from which the public sector purchases preferentially, are common in many countries, including Bangladesh, Brazil, India, and Laos. In some countries the local pharmaceutical industry (public or private) produces drugs that could be purchased less expensively elsewhere. Such industries survive only because of the protection accorded through the prohibition of competing imports, through import tariffs, or through guaranteed agreements for public purchase regardless of price.

The combination of protection and poor regulation can be particularly damaging. A 1990 study of more than 6,000 infants in Bangladesh revealed that the mothers' tetanus toxoid vaccinations did not reduce the risk of tetanus. Subsequent testing in reference laboratories of Bangladesh-produced vaccine indicated no potency in several consecutive batches, raising questions about the efficacy of the more than 40 million doses already administered. Since Bangladesh has no independent national control authority for certifying vaccine safety, all testing had been done by the production facility itself. Evidence suggests that few public sector pharmaceutical and vaccine producers have been able to operate competitively, in terms of price and quality, in the highly competitive and rapidly changing pharmaceuticals market. Improved selection and purchasing practices—rather than protection of drug manufacturing—will usually be the best ways to counter the market power of international suppliers of drugs.

IMPROVING STORAGE AND DISTRIBUTION. Theft, spoilage, and shortages are major problems facing public distribution in many countries. Systems for inventory control, port clearing, storage, and delivery can address many of these problems. In Zimbabwe a standard nationwide system of stock control was fundamental to recent reforms in the drug supply system. Surveys show a gradual improvement in drug availability: in 1991 the facilities surveyed had 78 percent of the representative essential drugs in stock, up from 38 percent in 1987. In hospitals, management information systems help to track periods of drug validity and to analyze rotation rates and drug consumption.

Influencing prescription and self-medication patterns

Significant efficiencies can be achieved by improving prescription and self-medication practices. Widespread overprescription and inappropriate prescription have been documented in most countries. For example, recent surveys found that the average number of drugs prescribed per single consultation in public health centers ranged from 1.3 in Zimbabwe and Ecuador to as high as 3.3 in Indonesia and 3.8 in Nigeria. These surveys also documented that unnecessarily high proportions of drugs were being administered in the form of injections (which carry the risk of abscesses, nerve injuries, and transmission of infectious disease) and that extensive overuse of antibiotics was occurring. A survey of seventy-five pharmacies in three Asian countries found that only sixteen gave appropriate advice regarding oral rehydration for treatment of diarrhea in infants.

Public policies for improving prescription and medication practices include:

• Distribution to health care providers and pharmacists of regularly updated essential drug lists or formularies that include descriptions of use, dose, adverse reactions, and costs; examples include the British National Formulary and the Uganda Drug Formulary

• Strengthening of medical and nursing training regarding pharmacology, appropriate prescribing practices, and problems caused by overprescription and unnecessary use of injections

• Public education on appropriate drug use, the disadvantages of injections when oral doses are available, and the importance of compliance with the full course of therapy

• Removal of financial incentives that encourage physicians to overprescribe.

Unlike facilities, equipment, and human resources, pharmaceuticals and vaccines are an area in which government policies can alter input use relatively quickly. And good policies could make a significant contribution. Because consumers and providers cannot possibly review all the information available on the quality, safety, and efficacy of drugs and vaccines, governmental involvement in regulation and in provision of information is necessary. In addition, the government must manage drug selection, procurement, and distribution for publicly provided health services. To support the rational use of drugs, governments can:

• Develop a national list of essential drugs and direct public finance to those drugs that support the essential package of clinical services and public health interventions.

• Purchase drugs competitively and reduce or eliminate protection of local pharmaceutical production of vaccines and drugs. These policies work to consumers' benefit. Efficient local industry is best created under competitive conditions.

• Provide information to public and private providers and consumers on drug use and cost-effectiveness and establish regulations that discourage overuse or overprescription.

Generating information and strengthening research

In health, as elsewhere, good information facilitates sound decisionmaking. Although some basic health information is generated by the private sector without government involvement, the government has a central role in requiring, standardizing, and financing the collection, analysis, and dissemination of health information, as well as in financing health systems research. Governments are already heavily involved in data collection. Unfortunately, the data are often irrelevant to policy and program design. And too often, the private sector is ignored when statistics are being gathered. Revamping health information systems is an attractive investment, both because it is relatively inexpensive and because poor decisions based on inadequate information can be very costly. But the impact of information systems depends crucially on the decisionmaking environment. Even the best systems may be seen as irrelevant if managers have no incentive or scope for using information to improve efficiency. Information helps guide choices among the existing options, and investments in research and development create new options, both for households and for providers of care. It can be argued that investments in research have been the source of the enormous improvements in health in this century. This section discusses ways of ensuring continued benefits from research, as well as the role of the international community in this task.

Understanding health status and health risks

An essential step toward improving health is to understand the distribution of disease, death, and disability. This requires the systematic collection, analysis, and dissemination of timely and accurate information on mortality, morbidity, and risk factors. Such data are a cornerstone of public health efforts in any country, and the government's role is central in creating them because the private sector has little interest in producing such public goods. Epidemiological data are used to estimate the magnitude of health problems, study risk factors, evaluate health programs and the effectiveness of interventions, detect epidemics, facilitate planning, and monitor changes in health practices. These data could be used to estimate a national burden of disease similar to the global burden of disease estimated for this Report. The national burden of disease would quantify the loss of healthy life from the diseases that are important in the specific country. It could be used to monitor and track over time improvements in both mortality and morbidity.

Some countries have established surveillance systems that rely on sentinel districts selected to be roughly representative of the country. To improve the speed and accuracy of reporting, data collection systems are upgraded in these districts to a greater degree than could be done for the country as a whole. Cause-specific death rates, vaccine coverage, the effectiveness of vaccines, and the impact of specific health interventions are then monitored intensively within the district. National household surveys can also generate a wealth of information on health status, risk factors, and the utilization of health services according to age, sex, region, and racial and ethnic group (see Box 6.4). Unlike government health service statistics, population-based surveys cover nonusers as well as users of public services.

Monitoring health spending and equity

Previous chapters have recommended redirecting public spending to nationally defined essential clinical services, targeted largely to the poor, and to public health interventions, leaving to private

---

Box 6.4 The contribution of standardized survey programs to health information

Three internationally supported standardized household survey programs have contributed immensely to knowledge of health conditions, particularly those of children, in the developing world over the past three decades. The World Fertility Survey (WFS) sponsored forty-three surveys between 1974 and 1982, with funding from the U.S. Agency for International Development (USAID) and the United Nations Population Fund (UNPF) and some country contributions toward the costs of survey fieldwork. The Demographic and Health Surveys (DHS) program, started in 1984, has so far implemented thirty-nine surveys in thirty countries; the third phase of the survey program, with a planned twenty-five surveys, is about to begin. The DHS program has received funding from USAID, with contributions from countries and other donors.

Both the WFS and the DHS program have used a common core questionnaire around which special topics could be explored. The core WFS questionnaire was primarily concerned with fertility and fertility-related behavior; for each eligible woman it included a birth history, recording the date of each birth and, if the child had died, the age at death. This information base has provided much of what is known about child mortality trends and the relationships between child mortality and birth spacing, maternal education, and household characteristics. The DHS questionnaire, in addition to a birth history, includes questions about

immunizations, health care behavior, and other aspects of child health. DHS survey information has been used for purposes as diverse as examining the effects of economic reversals on demographic outcomes and studying small area variations in child mortality risks in urban areas.

Neither survey program has collected detailed economic information on households and communities. The World Bank's Living Standards Measurement Survey (LSMS) was designed to fill this need by studying the determinants and interactions of poverty, health, education, nutrition, and labor activities. The survey collects a wealth of information about incomes, production, and prices. Some LSMS surveys are funded through World Bank–financed projects, but many have received grant support from a variety of bilateral donors, the UNDP, and other agencies.

The experience with these standardized surveys indicates the great value of using comparable survey procedures and instruments across countries and the importance of rigorous supervision at all stages of the survey operation, from sampling to data processing. The LSMS and DHS programs have been particularly successful with respect to turnaround time; preliminary findings from a survey are available within six weeks of the conclusion of fieldwork, and a final report typically becomes available within one year.

finance health services outside the essential package. Private expenditures are always difficult to estimate, but even in the public sector, spending is poorly disaggregated by use. By revamping information systems, estimates can be made of spending on public health interventions and on categories of inputs (essential drugs, nonessential drugs, primary care physicians, other primary care providers, specialists, health centers, district hospitals, and tertiary hospitals). Although still imperfect, such estimates better capture the nature of government spending. In addition, public expenditures need to be regularly consolidated across federal, state, and local levels for analysis. In Brazil, where state and local governments account for about half of all public spending on health, expenditure estimates are available only for federal spending (except for 1984). Much less information is compiled from state and municipal levels, despite their importance. Household surveys can collect appropriate information for monitoring who benefits from public health spending. In part because such data are lacking, analyses of equity in health care have been carried out in only a handful of developing countries, among them Colombia, Costa Rica, Côte d'Ivoire, Indonesia, Malaysia, and Peru.

National research priorities

Governments have a role in supporting the research necessary for understanding specific local health problems and for guiding public policymaking and program design. This "essential national health research," which is also undertaken by the private sector, examines health strategy in more depth than is done with day-to-day budgetary and management information. The international community can help both in gathering data for international comparisons and in assisting local institutions to build up capacity in epidemiology, health economics, health policy, and management. Research priorities in this area include cost-effectiveness analysis of health interventions, evaluations of medical practice and of variations in practice (see Box 6.5), and studies of drug utilization, equity, consumer satisfaction, and women's health.

Where the national burden of disease is high and cost-effective interventions already exist, research can guide program implementation. One such example is the problem of intestinal parasitic worms. How can local programs be best designed to reach children? How can involvement of school officials be fostered? Another area is tuberculosis, where treatment compliance is a chronic problem;

Box 6.5 Evaluating cesarean sections in Brazil

Operations research can examine variations in medical practice with a view to identifying areas in which changes in practice are needed, as well as possible instruments for modifying provider practice. In the early 1980s Brazil was estimated to have the highest overall cesarean section rate in the world—31 percent of all hospital births in 1981. Although cesarean sections are a life-saving procedure in certain circumstances, their unnecessary use raises costs and poses medical risks for the mother and the newborn. The financial cost of unnecessary publicly financed cesareans in Brazil was estimated at about $60 million annually in the late 1980s. Medical risks stem from incorrect estimation of the length of gestation (leading to premature deliveries), infection from surgery, and the use of general anesthesia. Among the many factors responsible for the rising rate of cesareans in Brazil are the financial and administrative incentives for hospitals and doctors to perform cesarean deliveries, the desire to use a cesarean delivery as a vehicle for obtaining a sterilization, and the widespread view that cesarean section is the preferred, "modern" way to deliver.

Brazilian studies of cesarean section rates illustrate systematic variations by region, type of hospital, socioeconomic status of the woman, and reimbursement patterns. Rates in 1981 were higher in the more prosperous Southeast (38 percent) and lowest in the poor Northeast (20 percent). In every region the incidence of cesarean section increased with family income. A 1986 survey showed that rates were highest for women with a university education (61 percent) and for births in private hospitals (57 percent). Other studies showed that rates were lowest among women with no insurance. Women covered under the social security system had higher rates of cesarean section, and women with private insurance had the highest.

The country's social security institute changed its reimbursement policies in the early 1980s to remove some of the financial incentives for cesarean sections, and education campaigns for physicians were initiated. But it is clear that even stronger policies are needed to reverse these trends, as cesarean section rates have continued at high levels. A large sample of births in the state of São Paulo in 1991, for example, indicated a cesarean section rate of 47 percent.

patients often stop taking medication once they feel better, but before the problem has been effectively treated. What program approaches work best in different settings to ensure compliance with directions? In nutrition, how can policies and programs promote dietary change most effectively? Solutions to these problems are not universal. Research must be local, and often public support is needed.

In its 1990 report the Commission on Health Research for Development recommended the formation of international partnerships or networks to focus on ensuring that national health resources are used to maximum effect. The International Network for the Rational Use of Drugs (INRUD), established in 1989, is one such network. Another is the International Clinical Epidemiology Network (INCLEN), which was started in the early 1980s by the Rockefeller Foundation to build up a critical mass of researchers in clinical epidemiology, including epidemiologists, health economists, social scientists, and biostatisticians. INCLEN enrolls midcareer academic physicians who hold positions of influence in the medical systems of developing countries. It provides overseas study opportunities, support for research, and the opportunity to participate in annual scientific meetings. The network concept has permitted units to share experiences and teaching materials and to carry out collaborative research between clinical epidemiology units, training centers, and the international health community. Capacity building is a lengthy process, but INCLEN has already influenced health policy. Research on the effectiveness and efficiency of hepatitis B immunization in the Philippines brought about the addition of hepatitis B vaccine to the national EPI program. Studies on the cost-effectiveness of short-course chemotherapy for tuberculosis have led to a change in national treatment policies in Brazil, the Philippines, and Thailand.

Improving information at the district and facility levels

Health organizations also benefit from improvement of the information needed to make everyday management decisions. In publicly provided district health facilities, simple management information systems for measuring costs, inputs, and production could be helpful for monitoring program efforts over time and for making decisions about how to combine inputs efficiently. Yet many public facilities operate without such information. Without basic data on costs, it is difficult to decide, for example, whether to contract out services such as laundry, food preparation, and laboratory testing. Systems that gather information on vaccine utilization, equipment and vehicle inventories, preventive maintenance for buildings and equipment, personnel management, and the like are also fundamental.

Ministries of health frequently pay little attention to the activities of private providers, instead focusing all data collection efforts on public providers. To remedy this, governments can collect basic information about private providers and the population covered under private insurance plans. They can require standardized reporting from both public and private hospitals through uniform hospital discharge data. The information can then be synthesized to provide consumers, health researchers, and communities with information about the quality of care given by providers, both public and private, and about variations in medical practice. These systems can generate sophisticated information; consumers in California, for example, can obtain risk-adjusted mortality rates by hospital for common procedures. But relatively simple measures can also be useful; an example is cesarean section rates, by hospital, which can help identify overuse of this procedure (see Box 6.5). Such standardized information about hospital performance can help consumers make better choices about health care and can help central authorities identify problems to be corrected.

If there are incentives for using information in decisionmaking, improvements in data gathering can often be inspired simply by giving those who need the information more training in how to collect it and more responsibility for doing so. District medical officers, hospital superintendents, and health care managers are usually not trained to make the best use of data. Whenever possible, tabulation of data should be decentralized so that local decisionmakers can immediately use the information instead of relying on feedback from central levels. In Papua New Guinea, for example, when local-level staff began to see the relevance of management information for their work, they sought to verify data and to eliminate reporting that was irrelevant.

To summarize, governments have a twofold role in health information systems and operational research: generating the information necessary to guide health policies and public spending and providing certain types of information about provider performance that would be too costly for consumers to collect. To this end, governments can:

• Gather and synthesize epidemiological and

Table 6.2 Some priorities for research and product development, ranked by the top six contributors to the global burden of disease

| Disease or injury | Associated DALY loss (millions) | | Priority areas |
	Demographically developing countries	FSE and EME	
Perinatal and maternal causes	125	4	Methods of lowering costs of intervention and improving delivery in rural areas.
Respiratory infections	119	4	Impact of indoor air pollution on pneumonia (to guide interventions designed to reduce pneumonia by use of improved stoves); inexpensive or simplified antibiotic regimens; inexpensive, simple, reliable diagnostics; pneumococcal vaccine
Diarrheal diseases	99	—[a]	Rotavirus and enterotoxigenic *E. coli* vaccines; improved cholera vaccine; ways of improving hygiene; better case management of persistent diarrhea; prevention of diarrhea by the promotion of breastfeeding and improved weaning practices
Ischemic heart and cerebrovascular disease	58	27	Low-cost prevention, diagnosis, and management methods
Childhood cluster: diphtheria, polio, pertussis, measles, and tetanus	67	—[a]	Development of new and improved vaccines to reduce patient contacts, permit immunization at younger ages, and improve heat stability of some vaccines
Tuberculosis	46	1	Methods of ensuring compliance; monitoring tools for drug resistance; simpler diagnostics; new and cheaper drugs
All conditions[b]	1,210	152	

Note: The demographically developing countries are those in the Sub-Saharan Africa, India, China, Other Asia and islands, Latin America and the Caribbean, and Middle Eastern crescent regions. FSE, formerly socialist economies of Europe. EME, established market economies. DALYs, disability-adjusted life years; see Box 1.3.
a. Less than 0.5 million.
b. Total for all conditions presented in Appendix B.
Source: Appendix B.

other information necessary to monitor health status, detect disease outbreaks, and guide public policy and program design
• Support research, where needed, to generate local solutions to local problems
• Facilitate standardization of information about health production and health outcomes by district health systems and other major health providers; where necessary, synthesize and publicize this information to aid consumers in making informed choices about health care.

Expanding the range of choice

A revolution in health care technology has taken place in the course of this century. Significant biomedical breakthroughs that have generated international benefits—for developing countries as well as for the established market economies—include the development of measles, pertussis, polio, and tetanus vaccines; chloroquine for the treatment of

malaria; oral rehydration therapy; antibiotics and other antimicrobials; and synthetic hormonal contraceptives.

Basic research and product development are public goods that require support through government subsidy or intervention (for example, grants of patents). In addition, because the poor in developing countries lack market power, the system of patent protection fails to provide incentives to the commercial sector for developments related to diseases of the poor. Thus, there is a clear argument for government and international assistance to catalyze technological development. In the developing world many serious health problems do not present sufficiently attractive commercial markets to induce the development by private companies of better methods of prevention, diagnosis, and treatment. Developing countries account for almost 90 percent of the global burden of disease, and much of that burden is from conditions such as malaria or tuberculosis that primarily occur in those countries. Only about 5 percent of the $30 billion global investment in health research in 1986 went to health problems unique to developing countries.

Setting priorities

Where is extra research really likely to pay off? Table 6.2 suggests priorities for research on prevention, diagnosis, and case management for the six conditions that make the largest contributions to the global burden of disease. These conditions account for about 40 percent of the DALYs lost in demographically developing countries and for about 25 percent of the losses in industrial countries (where cardiovascular disease accounts for much of the burden). If the global burden caused by a disease is large, if no cost-effective interventions exist, and if experts believe that such interventions might be developed, there is a case for greater investment in research and product development. One example that meets these criteria is inexpensive, simple, and reliable diagnostics for respiratory infections. For problems that create a large burden of disease and for which cost-effective interventions already exist, there is a need to direct efforts more toward program development and operational research to guide implementation. For example, little is known about low-cost methods of managing ischemic heart disease in developing country settings. One low-cost approach that is being adopted in many industrial countries is the use of low daily doses of aspirin to reduce the risk of obstructive blood clots inside the arteries. This approach, developed on the basis of the results of large-scale assessments of the efficacy of the intervention, illustrates the potential benefits of research on low-cost case management.

International agencies and governments can stimulate research on health and product development in several ways. They can provide information on potential markets for new products, including epidemiological data about the disease, the target population, and the technical requirements of desirable innovations. They can subsidize a portion of the development costs. They can facilitate or finance field evaluations in a variety of settings and support introduction of the technology in the field. Finally, they can provide procurement guarantees for new or improved products at an agreed-on price. A few examples illustrate the potential.

NEW AND IMPROVED CHILDHOOD VACCINES. The EPI currently includes vaccines against six dis-

eases: measles, tetanus, pertussis, diphtheria, polio, and tuberculosis. It requires at least seven patient contacts (two for the pregnant mother and five for the infant). Possible improvements in vaccine technology would reduce multidose vaccines to a single dose, improve the heat stability of vaccines, simplify administrative requirements (to permit greater use of oral vaccines as compared with injections, for example), create new combinations of vaccines to reduce patient contacts, integrate new vaccines into the immunization schedule, permit vaccination earlier in life to reduce infant deaths caused by vaccine-preventable diseases, and add to the menu of interventions new vaccines—for example, against diarrhea and pneumonia. These innovations would reduce some of the costs and improve the effectiveness of vaccination programs. An important source of support for this research is the Children's Vaccine Initiative (CVI), which is identifying measures for catalyzing technological development in these areas. The CVI, which has its secretariat at WHO, is an international effort to harness new technologies that can advance the immunization of children.

TROPICAL DISEASES. It is primarily the rural poor who suffer from tropical diseases such as malaria, schistosomiasis, lymphatic filariasis, onchocerciasis (river blindness), trypanosomiasis, and leprosy. These diseases create a high burden, and existing interventions are inadequate against many of them. The UNDP–World Bank–WHO Special Programme for Research and Training in Tropical Diseases (TDR) is developing partnerships with commercial entities, national governments, scientists, and NGOs to support research and drug development for these diseases. One strategy the program has adopted is to look for new applications of drugs already in use in human or veterinary medicine. An example is the use of ivermectin, a drug originally marketed by Merck & Co. for treating worms in animals, in the fight against onchocerciasis in human populations (see Box 1.1). The TDR program facilitated the field testing of this product on a large scale for human use. The results showed that the drug was very safe, that it could be distributed by primary health care workers, and that one oral dose per year could prevent or arrest blindness. As a veterinary product, ivermectin has estimated annual sales of $500 million; Merck & Co. agreed to supply the drug without charge to governments for treatment of human onchocerciasis. The TDR's network of internationally funded research centers in develop-

Box 6.6 An unmet need: inexpensive and simple diagnostics for STDs

This Report recommends that concerted efforts be made to develop or strengthen effective programs for control of STDs. Such efforts will be hampered by the challenges of diagnosing STDs, particularly in women, for whom the vast majority of infections are asymptomatic. Current methods are often unreliable and expensive, and their use requires refrigeration, electricity, and sophisticated equipment and training. In addition, certain tests require patients to return in one or two days, which is not feasible when, as is often the case, the patient must travel a long distance to receive health care. Even if patients return, the period of infectivity is prolonged by this delay in therapy. Syndromic-based approaches to treating STDs are currently being used to bridge this gap and are effective for men. For women, however, these approaches are less accurate.

New diagnostics that are inexpensive, simple, and convenient to use and provide rapid, stable, and accurate results would overcome these problems. An example of such a tool is a new HIV test. The availability of HIV testing has been limited by high cost, complexity, and requirements for reagents that need refrigeration and have a short shelf life. Even when labor costs are excluded, testing and confirmation can cost $25 to $50 (although this cost is declining rapidly). The HIV dip-

stick, developed by the Program for Appropriate Technology for Health with support from Canada's International Development Research Centre (IDRC) and from private funds, uses synthetic peptides and a color change to provide an easily performed test. The test takes twenty minutes, requires only three simple steps, is stable for six months at tropical temperatures, has a pattern of sensitivity and specificity similar to commercially available tests, and costs less than $0.20. Thus, the per patient cost for testing can be brought down to less than $1.00, including a confirmatory second test. This test is now being commercially produced in India and Thailand. The Canadian International Development Agency (CIDA) is funding the establishment of a production facility in Cameroon, and there is interest in production in Brazil, Indonesia, and Zimbabwe.

The STD Diagnostics Initiative, which is funded by multiple donors, was established to facilitate development of appropriate diagnostics for resource-limited settings. The initiative, being carried out in collaboration with industry, clarifies and validates performance criteria for STD diagnostics, organizes and supports field trials, provides seed money for the development of new diagnostics, and brokers bulk purchases to create markets of adequate size.

---

ing countries allowed it to respond quickly and flexibly to the opportunity to test ivermectin.

Women spend up to half of their reproductive lives pregnant or lactating. Many protocols for treating tropical diseases exclude these women and sometimes even large numbers of women who might be pregnant (such as adolescent girls). Blanket exclusion of pregnant or lactating women has been the result not of clear evidence of problems but of reluctance to carry out appropriate drug trials on pregnant women. There is an urgent need to evaluate drug treatments for such women so that health services can offer them better treatment. This is part of a much broader problem of the common omission of women from medical studies and clinical trials in both developing and industrial countries.

MEDICAL EQUIPMENT. Another priority area for research and development is the development of low-cost and efficient diagnostic technologies for use in health centers in developing countries where sophisticated laboratories are unavailable. Examples of potentially important new technologies are visual methods of screening for cervical

cancer, rapid plasma finger-stick diagnostic tools for syphilis, and new diagnostic tests for malaria for use at the local level. (Box 6.6 provides another example.) Rapid diagnostic tests avoid reliance on other levels of the health system because the health center, if supplied with the necessary drugs, can treat the problem on the spot. Innovations in medical equipment to reduce the cost or improve the effectiveness of preventing and treating problems at the health center level are high priorities for research and development.

International aspects

Some types of research and product development are costly; it can cost more than $100 million to bring a new drug to market. But several breakthroughs in medical technology have been inexpensive. (One of them, oral rehydration therapy, is now widely recognized as an effective way of treating acute watery diarrhea, which, untreated, can weaken or kill young children.) The need for public support for certain types of research is widely understood. The international community has played an important role in supporting health research, and most governments support some research as well. Over the short to medium term, developing countries can use their scarce public resources best if:

• Governments reduce or eliminate finance of basic biomedical research that generates international benefits (which is best supported by the international community) and redirect it toward research efforts that generate primarily national benefits

• The international community directs research support toward new and improved technologies where the expected social returns are highest and would benefit many countries.

International financing is needed for important biomedical research when the benefits transcend national borders and the research will not be undertaken by the private sector at socially optimal levels. (Even research that is internationally financed will take place principally in developing countries and will be done increasingly by scientists from developing countries.) The total investment in health technology research relevant to the needs of the developing countries is woefully inadequate in relation to its potential benefits. And the level of international coordination and cooperation falls well short of what is required. An international mechanism with stable funding over the medium to long term could more effectively build research capacity in developing countries. Donors and governments also need to give more support to activities for testing new technologies and incorporating them into health systems.

An agenda for action

The policy conclusions of this Report can be tailored to the widely varying circumstances of developing countries. This chapter highlights the priority policy issues and actions that are likely to be most relevant for three groups of countries: low-income countries in Africa and South Asia, middle-income countries in Latin America and East Asia, and the formerly socialist countries of Europe and Central Asia. It describes the reforms needed in the health sector and assesses their feasibility, examines the principal obstacles to reform, and outlines possible strategies for overcoming these obstacles. Although policy reform must deal with difficult underlying problems, the experience of a number of developing countries with implementing significant policy changes shows that success is possible.

This chapter also examines the role of the international community in supporting improvements in health policies and programs in developing countries. Despite widespread calls for more donor investment in human resources and in poverty reduction programs, aid flows to the health sector declined from 7 percent of total development assistance in the early 1980s to 6 percent in the latter half of the 1980s. Donors need to match their verbal commitments with actions: the share of aid for health should be restored to its previous level immediately and should be increased substantially over the next five years. An additional $2 billion in aid would help to finance the transitional cost of health policy reforms, as well as priority programs, including AIDS prevention. At the same time, donors and developing countries need to focus on measures to improve the effectiveness of external assistance for health. Doing so will re-

quire donor backing for major reforms in the allocation of public spending for health and in health policy more generally.

The effectiveness of donor spending can be improved through increased investment in basic public health measures and essential clinical care, steps to strengthen the policy and regulatory framework for insurance and for delivery of services, and backing for research to expand the range of cost-effective treatments available to the poor in developing countries. Aid for lower-priority items, including tertiary care hospitals and training of medical specialists, needs to be correspondingly reduced or eliminated.

Finally, improved coordination among donors could raise the effectiveness of aid. Despite the many serious obstacles, the recent experience of a number of African and Asian countries shows that such coordination can be achieved.

Health policy reform in developing countries

The policies that this Report suggests should be at the top of the agenda for developing countries and the donor community are summarized in Table 7.1. This section describes those policies and provides examples of successful policy reforms in various developing countries.

Low-income countries

Previous chapters have outlined the main characteristics of health systems in low-income countries. In general, there is little public or private insurance. Out-of-pocket spending for drugs, traditional medicine, and user fees usually accounts

Table 7.1 The relevance of policy changes for three country groups

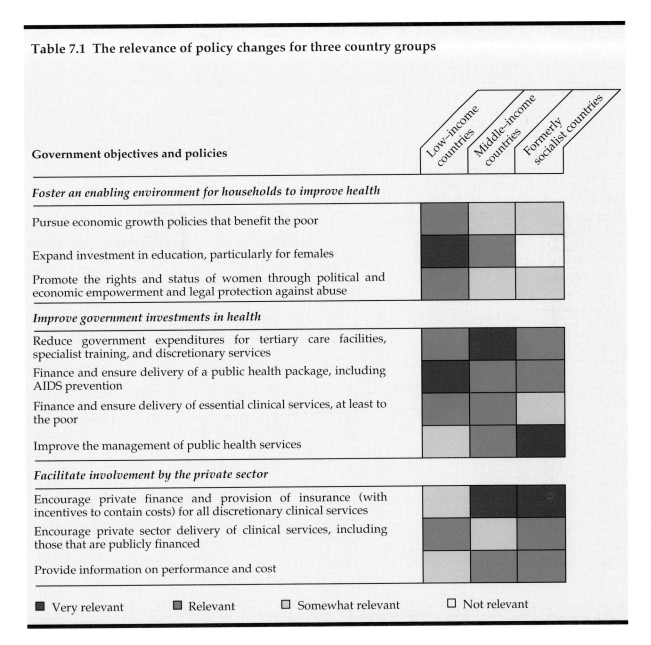

Government objectives and policies — by Low-income countries, Middle-income countries, Formerly socialist countries

Foster an enabling environment for households to improve health

Pursue economic growth policies that benefit the poor

Expand investment in education, particularly for females

Promote the rights and status of women through political and economic empowerment and legal protection against abuse

Improve government investments in health

Reduce government expenditures for tertiary care facilities, specialist training, and discretionary services

Finance and ensure delivery of a public health package, including AIDS prevention

Finance and ensure delivery of essential clinical services, at least to the poor

Improve the management of public health services

Facilitate involvement by the private sector

Encourage private finance and provision of insurance (with incentives to contain costs) for all discretionary clinical services

Encourage private sector delivery of clinical services, including those that are publicly financed

Provide information on performance and cost

■ Very relevant   ■ Relevant   ▢ Somewhat relevant   ☐ Not relevant

for more than half of total spending for health. Government financing from general tax revenues—and sometimes substantial donor contributions—account for the remainder. Government hospitals and clinics provide the bulk of modern medical care, but they suffer from highly centralized decisionmaking, wide fluctuations in annual budget allocations, and poor motivation of both facility managers and health care workers. Ministries of health and other government agencies often have only limited capacity to formulate health policy, implement health plans, and regulate the private sector. Private providers (mainly religious organizations in Africa and private physicians and

unlicensed practitioners in South Asia) account for the remainder of the health facilities and deliver most outpatient care. They offer a service that is perceived to be of higher quality than that provided by the public sector. Large segments of the population, especially the rural poor, do not have access to modern health services. Female literacy and enrollment of girls in primary and secondary school are low.

Five policies for better health are crucial in this environment: providing solid primary schooling for all children, especially girls; investing more resources in highly cost-effective public health activities that can substantially improve the health of the poor; shifting health spending for clinical services from tertiary care facilities to district health infrastructure capable of delivering essential clinical care; reducing waste and inefficiency in government health programs; and encouraging increased community control and financing of essential health care.

INCREASED SCHOOLING. Despite the often formidable obstacles—both in providing access to schools and in eliminating cultural barriers that keep girls out—a number of low-income countries have proved that dramatic change is possible in a short period of time. Between 1970 and 1990 Indonesia and Kenya, for example, achieved rapid and sustained growth of primary school enrollments and raised the proportion of girls to nearly half of all pupils. These gains were brought about by a combination of high-level political commitment to universal primary schooling, information programs that created stronger demand on the part of parents, and support from the international community.

INVESTMENT IN PUBLIC HEALTH ACTIVITIES. The public health activities with the largest payoff will vary from country to country: vitamin A and iodine supplementation in India and Indonesia, antismoking campaigns in China, and policies to reduce traffic injuries in urban areas of Sub-Saharan Africa. Completion of immunization coverage should be a high priority in all low-income countries, especially in India and in much of Sub-Saharan Africa, where coverage remains low. Similarly, a greatly intensified effort to reduce transmission of HIV and other sexually transmitted diseases is warranted. In the parts of Africa in which the AIDS epidemic is already widespread, behavioral change through education and condom distribution should be high on the list of public health actions. And where, as in Bangladesh and Indonesia, the preconditions (widespread commercial sex and high prevalence of other STDs) exist for rapid spread of HIV, governments urgently need to take steps to halt the spread of AIDS from high-risk groups into the population at large.

BETTER ALLOCATION OF SPENDING ON CLINICAL SERVICES. Governments should invest in district health infrastructure by (as described in Chapter 6) expanding training programs for primary care providers, particularly nurses and midwives; targeting construction funds to improve health posts, health centers, and district hospitals; financing ambulances and other vehicles needed for effective emergency transport, together with the necessary radio and telephone networks; and building the capacity to plan and manage health services at the district level and in individual facilities. In many low-income countries, focusing on district health infrastructure will mean limiting new investment in central hospitals and reorienting those facilities toward research and teaching activities that are more relevant to key national health problems. At the same time, there is considerable scope for improving the efficiency of large government hospitals, especially through performance-linked incentives for managers and staff and expanded cost recovery from the wealthy and insured.

To deliver essential clinical services, a greater share of government health budgets needs to be devoted to the operations of lower-level facilities and especially to nonsalary recurrent items. Initial emphasis needs to be placed on building capacity to deliver the services included in the minimum essential package described in Chapter 5. This is now happening in a number of countries. Senegal has set annual targets for increasing its spending for drugs, transport, and maintenance. Ghana is trying to reduce the number of civil servants working for the Ministry of Health. In India, where state governments account for more than three-quarters of total public spending for health, the central government is attempting to act as a catalyst for more cost-effective resource allocation by earmarking its funds for immunization, treatment of leprosy and tuberculosis, and AIDS control.

Some low-income countries will need to increase government outlays for health if they are to finance a package of public health measures and essential clinical services for the poor. In 1990 government spending for health in low-income countries averaged only $6 per capita—1.5 percent of GNP if foreign assistance is excluded and 1.6 percent including aid. The analysis in this Report indicates that provision of a minimum package will cost about $12 per capita in low-income countries, or nearly 3 percent of GNP. Effective targeting of publicly subsidized clinical services to the poor, and corresponding efforts to encourage cost recovery from more affluent groups, would help stretch limited government budgets. Modest fees collected at health centers could also be retained and reinvested locally to improve the quality and reliability of basic services.

But even with these efforts, many governments in low-income countries will have to increase the share of the budget allocated to health. (In Sub-Saharan Africa health spending declined during the 1980s to an average of less than 4 percent of public expenditure and less than 2 percent of

Box 7.1   Community financing of health centers: the Bamako Initiative

The principal aim of the Bamako Initiative, launched in 1988, is to "revitalize the public sector health care delivery system [by] strengthening district management [and] capturing some of the resources the people themselves are spending on health" (UNICEF 1992).

Both revolving funds for drug purchases and community-managed health centers have existed for many years in developing countries, but the Bamako Initiative is attempting to implement these schemes on a much larger scale in Africa and other low-income countries. The initiative is based on two premises: that where public institutions are weak, as they are in many low-income countries, bottom-up action by communities is badly needed to complement top-down health policy reforms, and that even poor households are willing to pay for higher-quality and more reliable health services.

Under the initiative, members of local communities who use a health center or pharmacy agree to pay modest charges for outpatient care, including drugs. The revenues generated from fees are retained by the health centers and managed by local elected committees. The committees reinvest in additional drugs (through a revolving fund), in incentive payments for health workers, and in other improvements. The government and donors assist health centers in purchasing inexpensive generic drugs, thus increasing the cost-effectiveness of services at the health center.

The initiative is only five years old, but its achievements are impressive. Eighteen African countries were participating as of late 1991, and nearly 1,800 health centers located in 221 districts were part of the program. In Benin the first forty-four health centers targeted by the initiative are covering 42 to 46 percent of their operating costs with user charges, and in the first seventeen centers in Guinea's program, user fees cover 38 to 49 percent of expenditures. Utilization of health centers has increased. In Benin average monthly visits to pilot health centers rose from 100 in 1987 to 250 in 1989.

Despite the initiative's promising accomplishments, it is not certain that the reforms can be sustained on a large scale. A number of health centers covered by the initiative have received both financial and technical assistance from UNICEF, WHO, and other donors—more than $36 million has come from UNICEF alone. Problems may emerge when this external assistance ends, particularly in converting local revenues generated through user charges into the foreign exchange needed to purchase imported drugs. In addition, efforts to encourage local private financing of health care by poor urban and rural households may allow governments to avoid tackling basic reforms of their health systems, especially the reallocation of public revenues from tertiary care hospitals to more basic services.

GNP.) Some countries are already moving in this direction. Mozambique, for example, is increasing government outlays for health in 1992 and 1993 as part of a broader program of economic reform, and Mauritania is committed to substantial rises in government health spending during 1992–96. Since shifts in domestic budget resources between sectors take several years to implement, donor funds could play a significant role in increasing government health expenditures, including recurrent spending, in the early years. The budget reforms in both Mozambique and Mauritania are being supported by transitional financing from the donor community.

REDUCTION OF WASTE AND INEFFICIENCY. There is substantial scope for reduction of waste and inefficiency in government health programs, especially in drug management. Pharmaceuticals, which account for 10 to 30 percent of public spending for health in most countries, are the most promising area for efficiency gains in the short run. Very large savings can be achieved by improving the selection and quantification of drug requirements,

in part through the use of essential national drug lists, and by purchasing drugs competitively. Numerous successes have already been recorded. Bulk procurement of drugs enabled a group of church-run African health associations to save 40 percent of their annual drug bill. Similar efforts by several Caribbean states led to an average reduction of 44 percent in the price paid for the twenty-five most frequently used drugs. An essential-drugs revolving fund for several Central American nations yielded savings of 65 percent of the costs of pharmaceuticals.

COMMUNITY CONTROL AND FINANCING. Community financing, in the form of user charges and prepaid insurance schemes, has become a practical necessity in a number of low-income countries. But community financing is also a virtuous necessity: it can help to improve the quality and reliability of services, in part by making health workers more accountable to their clienteles.

This is the approach being taken in the Bamako Initiative, sponsored by WHO and UNICEF (Box 7.1). Recent experience from a number of African countries shows that rural households are prepared to pay modest charges for drugs in government health centers, provided that the quality of services improves, that fees are retained and utilized at the point of service, and that the local population has a strong voice in the operation of the facility. In Guinea, for example, about half of the country's 350 health centers were practicing community financing in 1991. Of these, all the urban-based facilities and a third of the rural clinics were able to cover their operating expenses with income from fees. Governments should act cautiously, however. Experience suggests that fees substantial enough to cover the full cost of clinical services can discourage utilization by the poor. Under these circumstances, the poor should be charged reduced fees or should be exempted from payment.

PROBLEMS AND PROSPECTS. Health policy reforms face formidable obstacles in low-income developing countries. The health ministry often makes only a weak case for a larger share of the (sometimes shrinking) budget. Politicians, doctors, and the urban population exert strong pressures for higher spending on tertiary care facilities in the major metropolitan areas at the expense of the district health infrastructure. Professional associations and trade unions representing doctors and nurses strongly resist both staff cuts designed to increase nonsalary spending and efforts to redeploy health workers to rural areas. Despite these obstacles, some low-income countries are currently carrying out major health policy reforms. Malawi, for example, is implementing sweeping changes as part of a World Bank project. It is increasing the share of the government budget allocated to health from 7.1 percent in 1991 to 9.1 percent by 1995, raising the fraction of health spending for district health services from 15 to 23 percent, and reducing the share devoted to the country's three central hospitals from 35 to 25 percent. To strengthen the district health system, the government is also engaging more than 3,500 new lower-level health workers to serve in rural clinics and communities. Donor funds are being used to help pay for these workers.

Middle-income countries

In middle-income developing countries out-of-pocket payments for health usually account for less than a third of total spending. Some middle-income countries, such as South Africa and Zimbabwe, have private insurance, even though most of the population receives services financed through general tax revenues. Other countries use social insurance, with part of the population covered by mandatory employment-based contributions, usually pooled in a single fund run by a parastatal agency. The share of the population protected by social insurance varies widely, from less than 10 percent in the Dominican Republic, Ecuador, and El Salvador to more than 80 percent in Brazil, Costa Rica, and Cuba. Brazil and Chile employ hybrids of private and public insurance. In Brazil every citizen is legally entitled to services financed from a combination of general revenues and social security contributions, and social insurance is deducted from the wages of every salaried worker. Yet more than one-fifth of the country's population currently opts for some form of private insurance coverage.

Middle-income countries need to focus on at least four key areas of policy reform: phasing out public subsidies to better-off groups; extending insurance coverage more widely; giving consumers a choice of insurer; and encouraging payment methods that control costs.

REDUCTION OF SUBSIDIES TO BETTER-OFF GROUPS. Governments should reduce and eventually eliminate public subsidies to relatively affluent groups. This can be done by charging full-cost fees to insured persons who use government hospitals and clinics for services not included in the national essential clinical package and by cutting tax deductions for insurance contributions. In South Africa and Zimbabwe privately insured individuals have been charged less than the full cost of the services they receive in government health facilities. In addition, they have been allowed to deduct from taxable income part or all of their out-of-pocket payments for health care, as well as their health insurance premiums. Employers can also deduct their insurance contributions. These measures reduce the amounts available for financing essential services. In South Africa individual tax deductions were estimated to be equivalent to 18 percent of total public sector health expenditures in 1990. In a recent effort to reverse a similar situation, Zimbabwe has sharply limited tax deductions for health care and insurance, raised fees, and intensified efforts to collect fees from privately insured patients. Government hospitals have learned that they can often identify insured patients by offering them extra nonmedical amenities, such as private hospital rooms, and can then target them for aggressive cost recovery if they accept.

In countries where social insurance covers only a fraction of the population, governments can increase the extent to which health services are self-financing by eliminating public subsidies to social insurance. These subsidies, which are widespread in Latin America, mostly benefit the middle classes and are therefore regressive. Elimination of the subsidies would free resources for health services for the poor. Eliminating subsidies also imposes more financial discipline on the social insurance agencies, which are often allowed to run deficits that are later covered by transfers from other social security programs or from the general government budget. In Venezuela, for example, the government subsidizes contributions to the medical assistance fund within the parastatal social security agency. Despite this subsidy, in 1990 the fund ran a deficit equivalent to 37 percent of its health expenditures.

EXTENSION OF INSURANCE. Where the bulk of the labor force is already employed, government policies that extend insurance coverage to the rest of the population—including the self-employed, the elderly, and the poor—remove the inequities inherent in multitiered systems of health financing and expand the content of the universally available package of care. When insurance coverage becomes universal, as in Costa Rica and Korea, subsidies actually end up targeting the poor and are thus progressive. But only a few middle-income countries that have adequate financial resources, political resolve, and administrative capacity will be able to achieve such universal insurance coverage. Korea's bold initiative to create a national health insurance system from scratch between 1978 and 1989 and Costa Rica's efforts in the 1980s to universalize a system that had previously covered only the industrial labor force show that this is a difficult but achievable goal. Attaining universal coverage would be more feasible if governments limited the essential package of insured services to those with high cost-effectiveness.

CONSUMER CHOICE. Competition among suppliers of a clearly specified prepaid package of health services would improve quality and encourage efficiency. And even where there is little or no direct competition among insurance funds, as in Japan and Korea, multiple semi-independent insurance institutions may still have advantages over a single large parastatal agency. Local insurance funds managed by boards composed of representatives of workers, employers, and local government, as in Germany, tend to be more accountable to their members. In a number of Latin American countries monolithic social security "institutes" are already heavily discredited because of their past inefficiencies and corruption. Greater competition and accountability are two of the main objectives of current proposals for reforming social insurance in Argentina.

COST CONTAINMENT. Copayment by insured individuals for some services can help to restrain their use of the services but is unlikely to be a very powerful cost-containment method. Copayments amounting to an average 40 percent of expenditures in Korea have done little to slow the rate of increase in health spending, which grew from 3.7 to 6.6 percent of GNP during the 1980s. Similarly, the practice, introduced by private U.S. insurers, of retrospective reviews of utilization of medical care appears to lead to a modest one-time savings in health spending but does not have long-lasting effects on the rate of growth of expenditures.

By contrast, prepayment of health care providers is a promising approach to containing health expenditures. Governments could help to promote such schemes by removing legal barriers that in many countries prevent the same institution from acting as both insurer and provider. In South Africa the government recently decided to allow the creation of health maintenance organizations (HMOs), mainly as a way of containing health costs. More than twenty such organizations have been established in just a few years. They have introduced capitation and negotiated fees, which limit costs more effectively than did the open-ended fee-for-service payment arrangements historically used in South Africa.

Governments can do much to improve the incentives created by social insurance. Where the insured use private providers, fee-for-service payment schemes need to be replaced with an alternative—capitation or annually negotiated uniform fees for doctors and hospitals (based on diagnostic-related groups of procedures, for example) or preset overall budgets for hospitals. Where social insurance covers services by government hospitals, competition with the private sector can improve performance. Other promising approaches are to allow government hospitals to compete with one another as semiautonomous enterprises, as in the United Kingdom in recent years, and to give hospital managers financial and career incentives to meet performance targets, as in Chile.

The example of Chile (Box 7.2) illustrates the

benefits and perils of health sector reform in a middle-income country. Chile has been able to improve efficiency, quality of care, and consumer choice, but the reforms have also created new problems regarding administration, financing, and equity.

Formerly socialist countries

Historically, the government was responsible for both the finance and the delivery of health care in the formerly socialist countries of Eastern Europe and the Soviet Union. Health expenditures were financed from general revenues. In principle, they were provided free of cost to the population at government clinics and hospitals and at facilities run by state enterprises, but in practice, "informal" payments oiled the wheels of bureaucracy. Today the health systems in these countries are in severe crisis. Many doctors and pharmacists are leaving the government health services to practice

---

Box 7.2 Health sector reforms in Chile

Over the past fifteen years Chile has undertaken dramatic reforms of its health sector. Its experience shows that reform is a permanent process, not a one-time effort, and that countries undertaking reform must have both the capacity and the political will to review and revise health policies continuously.

Starting in the late 1970s, Chile (then under a military government) decentralized the government-run health system and created private health insurance institutions. Responsibility for operating primary care services was devolved to the country's 325 municipalities. The Ministry of Health transferred its primary care budget and about half of its personnel to the municipalities, which could also draw for financing on local tax revenues and on resources from the central government's Municipal Common Fund. More important, the government encouraged the establishment of privately owned and operated health insurance funds, known as ISAPREs. The roughly 70 percent of the population covered by social security schemes had the option of using their payroll deduction to buy a prepaid private health plan. The competing plans were regulated by a new oversight unit (*superintendencia*) in the Ministry of Health. By 1990 about 2.5 million people, or 18 percent of the population, were covered by thirty-five ISAPREs.

Both decentralization and the creation of the private insurers brought about some improvements in the health system. The municipalities expanded primary care services. The ISAPREs introduced more competition and consumer choice into the financing and delivery of services and spurred growth in the numbers of private doctors and hospitals.

But the reforms also created new problems. In the early years of the reforms, when local officials were appointed by the military regime, municipal health services were not responsive to the local population. Transfers of Ministry of Health staff to the municipalities created job insecurity and caused a decline in staff morale. Many municipalities lacked the capacity to plan and manage primary health services. The municipalities tended to overrefer patients to hospitals, which were still funded by the ministry. The ministry

had few incentives to help supervise municipal facilities.

Because municipalities were reimbursed for each unit of service delivered, they tended to provide too much high-cost curative care and too few preventive services, which caused costs to explode. The government then moved to cap allocations to local authorities, using as a basis historical budget shares that favored the wealthier municipalities.

The ISAPREs, by targeting the richest segments of Chilean society, impoverished the rest of the social insurance system. Each salaried beneficiary who chose to shift to an ISAPRE cost the public system 2.5 times the contribution of an average salaried worker. Because the ISAPREs are permitted to rate individual health risks, they have "skimmed" the population for good risks, leaving the public sector to care for the sick and the elderly.

The democratically elected government that came to power in 1989 has chosen to maintain the broad thrust of the health reforms while seeking ways to overcome their adverse effects. Municipal elections have been held to ensure that popularly chosen and accountable officials look after primary health services. Training programs have been organized for municipal health officers. Responsibility for hospitals is being decentralized to twenty-seven health service areas that will enter into management contracts with the Ministry of Health. Finally, under a new proposal, central funds would be allocated to the municipalities on a capitation basis, with a further adjustment to favor the poorest localities.

The government is also beginning to look at ways to reduce inequities in the ISAPRE health financing system. The *superintendencia* that regulates ISAPRE is being strengthened. It is considering requiring the private plans to use community risk-rating and to accept all applicants able to pay the community-rated premiums; making it mandatory for all ISAPREs to offer a similar basic medical plan in order to promote direct competition among suppliers (as in the managed care systems being developed in the United States); and eliminating the deduction for employer contributions.

fee-for-service medicine in the private sector. Since real government spending for health has fallen dramatically during the recent transition toward a market economy, the government health system is also experiencing serious shortages of drugs and equipment.

Largely because they know all too well the problems of repressive central government control, policymakers, medical professionals, and consumers in the formerly socialist countries are looking to systems of public and private insurance in industrial countries as possible models for reform. Some countries—for example, the Czech Republic, Hungary, and Poland—have much in common with upper-middle-income countries such as Argentina, Costa Rica, and Korea. They may be also able to adapt some features of the systems of the Nordic countries and the United Kingdom, which are financed from general revenues, or of the universal social insurance approaches of Germany and Japan. Others in this group—including the relatively poor Central Asian republics—face many of the same issues currently confronting lower-middle-income and even low-income countries, such as Pakistan and Yemen.

Despite this diversity, the governments of all the formerly socialist countries need to consider health sector reforms in at least three main areas: improving the efficiency of government health facilities and services, partly by reducing the size of the public system; finding new ways to finance health care; and encouraging private supply of health services while strengthening public regulatory capacity.

EFFICIENCY OF GOVERNMENT SERVICES. Decentralization of government health services is potentially the most important force for improving efficiency and responding to local health conditions and demands. It will be successful only when local government health agencies and hospitals have a sound financial base, solid administrative capacity, and incentives for improving efficiency—and when they are accountable to patients and local citizens. Extreme and hasty decentralization can create inefficiencies. In Poland, for example, the government has decentralized health care to the level of the country's forty-nine provinces. The average provincial population of less than a million is proving too small to make efficient use of the tertiary care hospitals being built in each province, and the available medical personnel are being spread too thin. For these reasons, the government is now experimenting with health regions

covering two to four provinces, but the provinces are reluctant to finance such regions. Moreover, there are political pressures for further decentralization to the level of the district governments, where there is now very little capacity for managing health systems.

At the same time that they decentralize, governments will have to reduce the size of publicly owned health services, which have far too many hospitals, hospital beds, and physicians. In this way, governments can free resources for vital public health services, including immunization, workplace and food safety, environmental regulation, measures such as education and higher taxes to discourage consumption of alcohol and tobacco, and quality control of privately delivered clinical care. The clinical and managerial skills of the remaining government health personnel need to be substantially upgraded and reoriented from the previous system of centralized bureaucratic control toward the emerging system of semi-autonomous health facilities.

NEW MODES OF FINANCING. The examples of other countries could help the formerly socialist countries establish insurance systems that preserve the main virtue of their old system—widespread coverage of the population. It could also help them to recognize the circumstances under which general government revenues can play a positive role, as the dominant source of funding (the pattern in the United Kingdom) or as a complement to insurance (as in Japan). Experience elsewhere offers important lessons on how to create financing systems that are sustainable and that contain costs by, for example, discouraging fee-for-service compensation. The formerly socialist countries will also want to avoid the large and inequitable government subsidies commonly provided to private insurance for the wealthy or to social insurance for the middle class.

Most formerly socialist countries are already on the road to reform. The Czech and Slovak republics and Hungary are experimenting with forms of social insurance. Because the Czech system included a very comprehensive package of health benefits and paid private doctors on a fee-for-service basis, it encountered serious financial difficulties after just a few months of operation. Under the recently revised Hungarian health-financing system, public sector doctors will be salaried employees of the central and local governments, and private general practitioners will be paid on a capitation basis. Russia and Ukraine are also prepar-

Box 7.3 Reform of the Russian health system

Before the political upheavals of 1990–91 that led to the breakup of the Soviet Union, the 3 to 4 percent of GNP that the Russian republic spent on health care for its nearly 150 million inhabitants was financed from general government revenues and delivered through a vast network of public facilities, programs, and employees. This highly centralized and bureaucratic system led to excessive numbers of doctors and hospitals. It gave few incentives for efficiency or for providing quality care, and it neglected the preventive measures needed to combat the country's most serious environmental and behavioral problems: industrial pollution, alcohol and tobacco dependency, and poor nutrition. Consequently, the health status of Russians stagnated during the 1970s and 1980s. In 1990 life expectancy for Russian men was just sixty-four years, a full ten years less than in Western Europe, and the infant mortality rate, at twenty-two per 1,000 live births, was twice the Western European average.

The new Russian government has pursued several fundamental reforms of the old Soviet health system. Health financing and management are being decentralized to eighty-eight regions. Much medical practice is being privatized, and a recent health insurance law provides for the introduction and regulation of new forms of insurance. Under the law and its proposed amendments, each region is to have a social insurance fund, and a national fund will equalize resources across regions. These insurance funds will receive a combination of compulsory payroll deductions and budget transfers from general government revenues.

They will sign contracts for care with public and private providers. Individuals can then voluntarily purchase supplementary private insurance to cover additional health services.

The health insurance legislation has been in effect since late 1991, but progress in implementing it has been slow. Some important issues in the design of the system still need to be resolved. These include the role and extent of competition among public and private insurers; whether risks are to be rated on an individual basis or across larger pools of individuals; and how the insurance funds will pay providers—on a fee-for-service basis, through capitation, or by some other method or combination of methods.

The practical obstacles to the implementation of the new system are formidable, partly because of the unsettled administrative and economic environment. The regional governments lack the capacity to manage and regulate the health system they are inheriting. The economy and the government budget are under severe strain. Real wages have fallen dramatically in the past few years. The costs of drugs and equipment have increased faster than inflation, leading to serious shortages. Payroll taxes to cover employee benefits already absorb 38 percent of wages, making it difficult to finance an affordable package of health services through the social insurance system. To help overcome these problems, a number of international agencies, including the World Bank, are working closely with Russian health officials on designing and carrying out health policy reforms.

---

ing to implement mixed systems of social insurance and general revenue financing. Box 7.3 describes the current efforts in Russia.

COMPETITIVE PROVISION AND PUBLIC REGULATION. Although private medical practice is now permitted in most of the formerly socialist countries, the legal and regulatory environment for private doctors, hospitals, and insurance institutions is often either nonexistent or hostile. With large numbers of private doctors establishing practices and private hospitals and clinics being created, regulation of providers will be critical for reducing the incidence of medical malpractice and financial fraud. It is also essential that regulation encourage the development of efficient institutions, such as health maintenance organizations, for financing and providing clinical care for the bulk of the population. Already there are signs of poorly conceived regulations, such as Romania's recent deci-

sion to issue lifetime licenses to doctors without establishing strict standards of practice or recertification requirements. Since government regulatory capacity is likely to be weak in the next few years, health system reforms should be designed in ways that minimize the need for direct government regulation. Encouraging self-regulation through associations of private medical schools, doctors, and hospitals would be one such approach. In the long run, better regulation will require both training of government inspectors and other regulatory personnel and development of government institutions such as medical licensing boards and national and local medical ethics committees.

Directions and prospects for reform

The world's diversity of health care systems is matched by the diversity of reform movements.

But several common themes are beginning to emerge. First, governments are increasingly recognizing the centrality of their own role in public health—for example, in achieving the enormous global gains in immunization coverage. Second, governments are exploring ways to introduce more competition and foster a diversity of public and private institutions in the delivery of clinical services. Third, governments are examining new approaches to finance and insurance, including selective user fees in the public sector, systems that discourage third-party reimbursement, systems that mix finance from compulsory social insurance and from general tax revenues, and systems that set fixed budgets for each patient or each case.

Everywhere, health sector reform is a continuous and complex struggle. Neither governments nor free markets can by themselves allocate resources for health efficiently. As policymakers try to reach compromises, they must deal with powerful interest groups (private doctors, drug companies, medical equipment manufacturers, and insurers) and strong political constituencies, including urban dwellers and industrial workers.

Strategies for overcoming these obstacles to health sector reform will vary from country to country, but some common approaches are discernible. Political leadership, beginning with the head of state, is an indispensable element in reform programs almost everywhere. The 1990 World Summit for Children proved an effective means for engaging the attention and commitment of heads of state (see Box 2 in the Overview). Senior officials of ministries of health can be strongly influenced by the prevailing views of the international health community, particularly those of WHO and other major donors, and by participation in international meetings and seminars on health policy and management.

Professional associations may be able to bring about some reorientation of health workers, especially physicians. Appeals to the sense of social responsibility of these associations have helped advance agendas for preventive health in the United States and elsewhere. Such groups, however, are often the sources of the strongest resistance to change. Reshaping the training curricula of medical and nursing schools to include a greater emphasis on public health and general practice is likely to be a more effective way to enlist the support of physicians and nurses.

Public opinion can be a powerful force for health reform, not only in industrial countries but also in developing countries such as Brazil, Chile, and South Africa and in Eastern Europe. A free press is important, as are consumer advocacy groups, for conveying a diversity of views on health reform and for stimulating debate.

In many countries, maintaining the support of the middle class and of urban groups for health policy reforms—including the reallocation of public spending from tertiary care to basic public health and clinical care for the poor—will require a gradual shift in resources rather than wholesale changes in just one or two years. For this reason, universal government financing (or government-mandated financing) for a nationally defined essential package of services will often be more successful than a highly targeted approach that may undermine the political base for reform. Similarly, continued government ownership of some hospitals that offer high-quality tertiary care, with a phased reduction in public subsidies to the wealthy for this care, may be more feasible politically than rapid divestiture to the private sector. External financial assistance can help countries handle these politically difficult tradeoffs and can ease the process of policy change.

International assistance for health

After growing rapidly in the 1970s, aid for health stagnated during the 1980s. As a share of official development assistance, aid for health declined from an average of 7 percent for the period 1981–85 to 6 percent during 1986–90. Total aid flows to the health sector in 1990 were $4.8 billion—almost $4 billion in official development assistance and $0.8 billion from NGOs and foundations (Figure 7.1). This amounts to about one dollar per person in developing countries. (The figure for official development assistance is based on reports from donor governments. Only $3.3 billion of the $4 billion can be accounted for as receipts by individual countries; this is the amount that appears in the total health expenditure estimated in Chapter 3 and in Appendix table A.9.) Bilateral agencies accounted for the largest share (40 percent), followed by United Nations agencies (33 percent), NGOs (17 percent), development banks (8 percent), and foundations (2 percent).

The trend is for donors to provide aid for health through multilateral channels. The share of multilateral assistance has grown from 25 percent in 1980 to 40 percent in 1990 and is likely to exceed 50 percent by 1995. As a result of the quadrupling of World Bank lending for health over the past six years, disbursements of Bank funds are expected

External assistance to developing countries for health comes from many sources, public and private.

Figure 7.1 Disbursements of external assistance for the health sector, 1990
(millions of dollars)

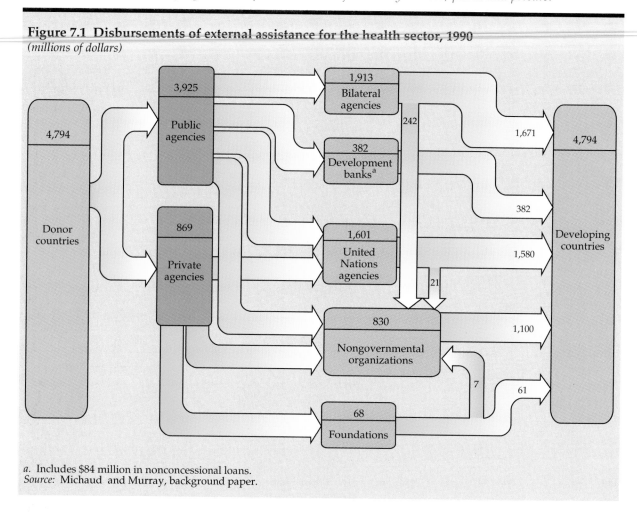

a. Includes $84 million in nonconcessional loans.
Source: Michaud and Murray, background paper.

to grow from about $350 million in 1992 to about $1 billion in 1995, making the World Bank the largest single source of external funding for health. Since the portion of aid going to middle-income countries from the World Bank and other development banks is nonconcessional lending, some of the projected increase in lending for health will involve a hardening of terms. It would be desirable for bilateral grant–funding agencies and concessional arms of the development banks (such as the World Bank's International Development Association) to increase their assistance to health as well.

The amount of health aid has stagnated, and its share in total development assistance has declined, even as donors continue to express concern about health. Over the past ten years the United Nations and other international agencies have called for increased investments in the development of human resources, including health, both by developing countries themselves and by the donor community. The United Nations Development

Programme (UNDP), in its annual *Human Development Report,* has argued for more donor spending on health, and in its recent *World Development Reports* the World Bank has made similar recommendations. *World Development Report 1990* proposed a 3 percent annual increase in aid during the 1990s, to be targeted at poverty-reducing activities, including basic health care. The donor community needs to review these goals and targets in light of the actual trends in aid flows for health.

The share of aid going to health should be restored immediately to its earlier level of 7 percent of total official development assistance and should rise substantially over the next five years. Such an increase would have a significant impact on the health status of the poor, particularly if it is directed toward the transitional costs of reallocating government spending to public health measures and essential clinical care and to seriously underfunded disease control efforts such as those for tuberculosis and AIDS. A rise in donor assistance of $2 billion, for example, could finance a quarter of the estimated additional costs of a basic package in low-income countries and of strengthened efforts to prevent AIDS. Such an increase, which would boost from 6 to 9 percent the share of total official aid going to health, would be feasible if other donors matched the rise in World Bank disbursements for health that is expected to occur in coming years. It would also be consistent with the proposal in the UNDP's *Human Development Report 1993* (also endorsed by UNICEF) that 20 percent of aid be spent on health, education, water and sanitation, and environmental protection for the world's poor.

There are a number of ways, in addition to the traditional annual and multiyear programming of aid by individual donors, for the international community to mobilize more financial resources for health. Coordinated sectorwide pledging at consultative group meetings and donor roundtables has been used successfully in countries such as Tanzania and Zambia. Another approach is program-specific pledging, as illustrated by the dozens of national AIDS-control donor meetings chaired by WHO in recent years. The role of debt-for-development swaps as a means of generating extra resources for both government and NGO-provided health services should be assessed in this context. Ecuador, Sudan, and Zimbabwe have already carried out swaps, and Nigeria is exploring a major swap of its debt currently held by donors in return for increased public spending for essential health services.

Improving the effectiveness of aid for health

It is crucial that the donor community and developing countries focus on ways to improve the effectiveness of existing and future assistance to the health sector, particularly in the low-income countries where donor assistance already accounts for a large share of health expenditure. In Africa aid makes up an average 10 percent of national health spending (Table 7.2), or 20 percent if South Africa is excluded. Aid covers more than half of all health expenditures in countries such as Burkina Faso, Chad, Guinea-Bissau, Mozambique, and Tanzania. In these countries donors finance an important share of recurrent costs, as well as investment items. In Mozambique, for example, aid accounted for more than half of recurrent spending in 1991 and for 90 percent of capital expenditures for health. Even when aid amounts to 2 percent or less of total health spending, as in the other developing regions, improvements in its use would still be an important catalyst for reform.

General lessons on improving aid effectiveness apply equally to the health sector (Box 7.4). Donors need to set their priorities carefully and allocate their resources in accordance with these priorities. The productivity of aid would increase substantially if donors were to direct more of their assistance to public health measures and essential clinical services, especially in low-income countries. They might also usefully focus on capacity building, research, and reform of health policy. Countries that show a willingness to improve access to health services for the poor and to undertake reforms of the health system should be strong candidates for aid.

The World Bank increasingly stresses policy reform in its lending for health, which has grown nearly fourfold in recent years (Box 7.5). For some donors, adjustment of priorities would mean spending less on hospitals, sophisticated medical equipment, and training for medical specialists. During 1988–90 Japan spent more than 33 percent of its bilateral assistance for health on construction of hospitals, France spent 25 percent, and Germany and Italy spent nearly 15 percent each.

Within the domain of public health and essential clinical care, several areas of intervention deserve greater attention from donors, including tuberculosis control, the EPI Plus program, micronutrient supplementation, AIDS prevention and control, and programs to reduce tobacco consumption. These problems impose a large burden of illness, in some cases because rapid growth of the threat has gone unrecognized. Their control offers large externalities or economies of scale. Often, solutions will require a global effort.

The efficiency of aid for health can be greatly enhanced through better coordination of donor projects and policies. Fragmentation of external support in the health sector is a long-standing problem in many countries and imposes a heavy

Table 7.2 Official development assistance for health by demographic region, 1990

Region	Health aid received (millions of dollars)	Health aid per capita (dollars)	Health aid as a percentage of health expenditure
Sub-Saharan Africa	1,251	2.45	10.4
Other Asia and islands	594	0.87	1.4
Latin America and the Caribbean	591	1.33	1.3
Middle Eastern crescent	453	1.31	1.3
India	286	0.34	1.6
China	77	0.07	0.6

Source: Michaud and Murray, background paper.

Recent evaluations of the effectiveness of aid, including a classic 1986 study commissioned by the world donor community, point toward the same conclusion: most aid has been successful, but a considerable share, perhaps a third or more, has been much less so, and a small percentage has failed completely or has even been harmful. These broad-brush averages hide significant regional differences: in Asia and Latin America performance has been better; in Sub-Saharan Africa it has been worse. Aid has been least effective in the poorest countries, where success is most needed.

The reasons for inferior performance lie with both donors and recipients. Poor countries and those experiencing political conflict and instability constitute a difficult environment for aid, as they have little administrative capacity or infrastructure. But these difficulties have in many cases been compounded by unfortunate policies. Aid projects have been poorly designed, both technically and because of inadequate understanding of the human, social, institutional, and political environment. When it comes to coordination, both sides have been at fault. Donors have pursued their own objectives without attempting to ensure that their aid complements that of others. And all too often, aid recipients have played one donor off against another, while ministers and ministries have focused on their own concerns rather than looking to the national good.

Aid for health has generally had a good technical record. It has fit in well with development priorities, especially in recent years, as the concentration on hospitals and high-technology curative medicine has been replaced by an emphasis on primary and preventive care. There have also been major successes—mainly highly focused initiatives such as the program for the eradication of smallpox, the drive against child mortality, and the effort to control river blindness in Africa. What is still lacking is the ability of the aid system to help set in place and sustain locally appropriate public health programs and essential clinical services.

burden on already overextended government officials. In the extreme, fragmentation can lead to conflicting policies being put into effect. Recently in one West African country, for example, three different cost recovery policies, each sponsored by a different donor agency, were being applied in separate regions of the country. The dangers of fragmentation are especially great in poor countries where different donors choose to focus their health sector activities on different provinces or districts and either lose sight of or undermine the formulation of national policies.

Much can be done to improve donor coordination, globally and regionally, but especially at the country level. Donors can agree with countries on overall national health and assistance strategies. This is especially effective when the government takes the lead in planning and in coordinating the donors, as has happened recently in Zimbabwe. Another approach is for donors to form large consortia to fund national programs, as in the case of maternal and child health and family planning in Bangladesh. (The experiences of these two countries are reviewed in Box 7.6.) At a minimum, donors should create informal local groups that meet periodically to review progress and problems in the health sector, as in Mozambique and Senegal.

The efficiency with which aid for health is spent depends critically on building local capacity to plan and manage health systems. This requires strengthening the public institutions that finance and deliver health services, both through broad civil service reform and through changes within the health sector. Donors can play an important role in these areas by supporting decentralization and other organizational reforms and by assisting the groups that formulate national health policies. Additional support is required for initiatives such as the foundation-backed International Health Policy Program and for bilateral projects to train health planners and managers, economists, and sociologists.

International programs for research and development in health

Investments in health research and development have yielded high returns in better health. For example, the programs for tropical disease research and human reproduction funded by donors and executed by WHO have produced a number of new or improved drugs and diagnostic tests and have strengthened research capacity in developing countries. Yet according to the 1990 report of the Commission on Health Research for Development, only 5 percent of global expenditures on health research are directed at the health problems unique to developing countries, and less than 10 percent of donor assistance for health is devoted to research, both biomedical and in the social sciences.

The commission identified several serious deficiencies in the international health research and development system. The expertise of the global pharmaceutical industry is not being adequately applied to the development of drugs and vaccines that could reduce the toll of early childhood diseases. Technology assessment is weak, as is the health policy research needed to determine more equitable and efficient ways to finance and deliver health services. Most important, the commission noted, local research capacity in developing countries is woefully inadequate. A number of promising research efforts, including the Children's Vaccine Initiative and programs to deal with acute respiratory infections, tuberculosis, micronutrient deficiencies and worm infections, suffer from weak and uncertain donor funding. In general, the problems of constrained funding for research are compounded by donors' limited capacity to stay abreast of the latest research proposals and to assess the relative priorities for funding this research.

To help stabilize funding, to improve the setting of priorities, and to boost efficiency, developing countries, donors, and scientists should consider the development of a global mechanism for better coordination of international health research. A number of institutional arrangements are possible, including well-defined networks of research centers, informal consultative bodies, and large global funds that pool donor assistance. Examples of these institutional arrangements in other sectors, such as the Consultative Group for International Agricultural Research and the Global Environment Facility, may provide models for improving the coordination of international health research.

Box 7.5 World Bank support for reform of the health sector

World Bank support for the health sector has grown dramatically over the past six years. The number of new World Bank–financed health, population, and nutrition projects approved each year increased from an average of eight during fiscal 1987–89 to twenty-one during fiscal 1990–92, and the value of credits and loans committed each year rose from $317 million to $1,151 million over the same period. As of June 1992, eighty-one Bank-financed health projects were being implemented. As a share of new World Bank lending, projects for health, population, and nutrition grew from less than 1 percent in 1987 to nearly 7 percent in 1991.

Whereas most of these projects continue the Bank's traditional support for basic health services—including district health infrastructure and personnel, maternal and child health, and control of infectious diseases—World Bank lending for health is increasingly focusing on broad policy reforms in the health sector. For example, in connection with a recent Bank project, the government of *Mauritania* has developed a financing plan to improve the availability of basic health services for its widely dispersed population. The share of the general recurrent budget going to the Ministry of Public Health will increase from 5.5 percent in 1992 to 7.5 percent in 1996. The project is introducing community-based cost recovery in three of the country's thirteen regions as a way of improving the efficiency and quality of services. Revenues are being raised mainly through the sale of drugs, organized and managed by local health communities.

In *Tunisia* the government is carrying out comprehensive reforms, including granting greater management autonomy to health facilities and decentralizing resources to the regional level. Doctors, nurses, and other health personnel are being encouraged to work in better-equipped health centers and other basic facilities. And health-financing mechanisms are being revised, with updated fee schedules, new exemption procedures for the poor, and changes to the health benefits covered by existing insurance schemes. The Hospital Restructuring Project, supported by the World Bank, is assisting the improvement of management systems and the quality of health services in the largest government hospitals, which were recently granted autonomous legal status. The project dovetails with the concurrent World Bank–financed Population and Family Health Project, designed to improve the quality and efficiency of public health services and essential clinical care, especially for mothers and children. It is expected that better basic services at the health center level will reduce the demand for hospital care, thus slowing the expansion of the country's hospitals.

The *Romania* Health Rehabilitation Project supports government efforts to diversify sources of health financing and thus to reduce dependence on the public budget, which is under pressure because of weak and unstable macroeconomic conditions and rising health care costs. The government is pilot testing decentralization of health sector policymaking, planning, management, and evaluation in three subregions. It is also discussing how to create a legal and regulatory environment to support reform of health financing.

Box 7.6 Donor coordination in the health sector in Zimbabwe and Bangladesh

The *Zimbabwe* Second Family Health Project (1992–96) is the culmination of a long period of interaction between the government of Zimbabwe, the World Bank, and other multilateral and bilateral donors. The $120 million project, which supports the government's five-year investment program for population, health, and nutrition, is designed to benefit directly low-income households, especially women and children. Zimbabwe has entered a period of economic adjustment that will necessitate spending cuts. The project will help protect poor and vulnerable households from some adverse effects of adjustment by mobilizing additional resources for human resource development and by improving the equity and efficiency of spending.

Zimbabwean participation was emphasized from the project's beginning. The project preparation committee included representatives from various central government departments, provincial governments, and the Zimbabwe National Family Planning Council. The committee set planning guidelines, including a preliminary outline of project components, costs, and financing. Using these guidelines, proposals were prepared locally and were then reviewed by the committee and by interested donors.

Virtually all the major donors to the health sector in Zimbabwe helped with planning the project by assigning agency officials and technical specialists to the donor team that advised the government on design issues. In the end, the project received financing from Denmark, the European Community, Norway, Sweden, the United Kingdom, and the World Bank. Donors monitor project implementation jointly rather than separately, reducing the time needed for donor review and the administrative burden on the government.

In *Bangladesh* the World Bank and ten bilateral agencies together are contributing $440 million to the Fourth Population and Health Project, and the government is providing $165 million, for a total of $605 million over the five-year project period. The United Nations Population Fund, WHO, and UNICEF are supplying project management, procurement, and technical assistance. All the partners in the project belong to the Bangladesh Population and Health Consortium, which has emerged as an important collective force in the health sector. The Asian Development Bank has joined the consortium with a view to ensuring consistency between the project and its own $60 million investment in population and health in Bangladesh.

During project formulation the government and the donors held several workshops in Dhaka and a special conference in Geneva. These workshops were instrumental in forging a consensus on population and health strategies. The consortium approach enables the government and the donor community to agree on an overall strategy and to work out a consistent financing plan for the sector. The consortium operates on the basis of strict equality of all the partners, independent of the size of their financial contributions.

In addition to strengthening Bangladesh's population program and its delivery system for family planning services, the consortium is attempting to reorient the health care system toward public health, including maternal health. It is also trying to make basic services more easily accessible to the rural and urban poor.

Meeting the challenges of health policy reform

If policymakers are to accelerate the substantial health gains of recent decades, especially for the poor in developing countries, the agenda for reform is clear. It includes increasing overall rates of economic growth and expanding basic schooling, particularly for girls; reallocating government spending for health from tertiary care and specialist training to public health measures and essential clinical services; encouraging more diversity and competition in the provision of clinical care and the development of cost-containing approaches to insurance; increasing the efficiency of government health services; and fostering greater involvement of communities and households in promoting healthier behavior on their own part and in managing their local health services.

Policymakers in developing countries and officials of the international donor community face a number of difficult challenges in pursuing this agenda. The changing demographic profile of the developing world, including the aging of the population, is creating new patterns of disease. Emerging microbial threats, such as AIDS and drug-resistant strains of tuberculosis and malaria, call for changes in personal behavior, new drugs, and new ways of delivering services effectively.

In virtually every country interest groups will resist health policy reforms of the kind suggested in this Report. Health workers will object to changes that threaten their job security, income levels, and degree of professional autonomy. Drug companies, medical equipment manufacturers, and other suppliers will try to block policies that they see as having an adverse effect on their markets, revenues, and profits. Political and economic elites and organized labor groups will seek to preserve existing public subsidies for insurance and health services from which they benefit and to maintain their privileged access to clinical care.

Beyond this, policymakers will have to wrestle with the reality that in the area of health there is no simple paradigm for policy choice. Free markets for public health activities and clinical care often fail, and when governments intervene in financing and delivery, as they frequently do, they can fail just as badly. Effective government regulation of private suppliers of health services and inputs, combined with public financing of cost-effective packages of public health and essential clinical services, is needed to deal with these failures. But this in turn requires strong private and public institutions—and institutional capacity is seriously lacking in many developing countries.

Despite these obstacles, there have been a number of successes in specific intervention programs such as polio eradication and river blindness control and a smaller but still important number of successes in broader health sector reform in such countries as Chile, Tunisia, and Zimbabwe, as well as in many OECD countries. These successes now need to be multiplied, especially in the area of sector reform, if countries are to address the acute weaknesses in existing institutional structures and to lay the foundation for major improvements in future living standards.

Developing country governments need to do more to translate into practice today's rhetoric about reallocating resources, improving access, and increasing efficiency. To do this, higher and sustained rates of macroeconomic growth are required. In many cases countries will also need to enact fundamental political reforms designed to increase participation and to improve the accountability of governments for their health spending, service delivery, and regulatory performance.

The donor community has a major responsibility to back up with concrete actions its verbal commitment to poverty reduction and to investment in health and human resources. In particular, donors should do more to support the formulation of improved health policies and more effective health sector reform programs in developing countries. As suggested in this Report, they can do this by financing some of the transitional costs of reallocating government budgets to public health measures and essential clinical care, by building local planning, management, and research capacity, and by providing sound assessments of the worldwide experience with the cost-effectiveness of interventions and with reform of systems.

If developing country governments and donors accept the challenges and embrace the key health policy reforms outlined above, improvements in human welfare in the coming years will be enormous. A large share of the current burden of disease—perhaps as much as one-quarter—will be prevented. And people around the world, especially the more than 1 billion people now living in poverty, will live longer, healthier, and more productive lives.

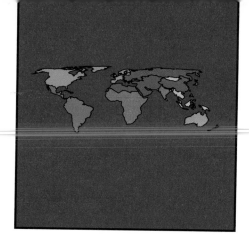

Acknowledgments

This Report benefited greatly from ideas, technical inputs, and critical review from a broad range of individuals and organizations. Contributions to specific chapters are acknowledged in the Bibliographical note. In addition, valuable input was provided through four other mechanisms: a World Health Organization Steering Committee, an Advisory Committee, a series of consultations on specific subjects, and a series of seminars, mostly held at the World Bank. Those from outside the World Bank who contributed to the Report through these mechanisms are listed below.

World Health Organization Steering Committee

This committee provided the focal point for the major contributions from WHO to the *World Development Report*, for WHO's participation in consultations, and for its critical review of various drafts.

Chair: Jean-Paul Jardel

Members: Andrew L. Creese, Michel Jancloes, Yuji Kawaguchi, R. Srinivasan, and Muthu Subramanian

Advisory Committee

The Advisory Committee met on October 7–9, 1992, at the World Bank in Washington, D.C.; in addition, committee members later provided critical review of an early draft of the Report.

Chair: Richard G. A. Feachem

Members: Jane C. Baltazar, José Barzellato, Mayra Buvinić, Lincoln C. Chen, Antoine Degrémont, Nicholas Eberstadt, John Evans, Mahbub ul Haq, Peter Heller, Abraham Horwitz, Jean-Paul Jardel, Richard Jolly, Somkid Kaewsonthi, Pangu Kasa-Asila,

Adolfo Martínez-Palomo, David N. Nabarro, Gen Ohi, Richard Peto, Kenneth I. Shine, Pravin Visaria, and Richard Zeckhauser

Consultations

1. Ministerial Review of Health Transition Issues

June 22–26, 1992, Bellagio Study and Conference Center, Villa Serbelloni, Bellagio, Italy. Partial financial support for the consultation was provided by the Rockefeller Foundation.

Participants: Alfredo R. A. Bengzon, Demissie Habte (provided written comments), Richard G. A. Feachem, Julio Frenk, Mamdouh Gabr, Scott Halstead, Jean-Paul Jardel, Jorge Jiménez de la Jara, Jeffrey R. Koplan, Marthini K. Budi Salyo, Adolfo Martínez-Palomo, Piotr Mierzewski, Rajiv L. Misra, W. Henry Mosley, Samuel Ofosu-Amaah, Raphael Owor, Olikoye Ransome-Kuti, and Leonardo Santos Simão

2. Interventions for Nervous System Disorders

July 6–7, 1992, Pan American Health Organization, Washington, D.C.

Chair: Benedetto Saraceno

Participants: Antonio Campino, Vijay Chandra, Brian Cooper, Bulent Coskun, Marcelo E. Cruz, Mary Jane England, John T. Farrar, Jefferson Fernandes, R. Juan Ramon de la Fuente, Walter Gulbinat, Itzhak Levav, Thomas McGuire, Kay Redfield Jamison, Norman Sartorius, Carole Siegel, Donald H. Silverberg, T. Takayanagi, and Richard Jed Wyatt

3. International Aid Flows to the Health Sector

August 27, 1992, Harvard Center for Population and Development Studies, Cambridge, Massachusetts

Chair: David Bell

Participants: Lincoln C. Chen, Nick Drager, Ramesh Govindaraj, Eva Jespersen, Catherine Michaud, Christopher J. L. Murray, and David Parker

4. Investing in Health Research

September 16, 1992, World Health Organization, Geneva, Switzerland. Financial support was provided by the WHO/UNDP/World Bank Special Programme for Research and Training in Tropical Diseases.

Chair: Carlos Morel

Participants: Eusebe Alihouno, Barry R. Bloom, David J. Bradley, Barbro Carlsson, Gelia T. Castillo, Jacqueline Cattani, Anthony Cerami, Joseph A. Cook, Henry Danielsson, Ronald W. Davis, Peter de Raadt, David Evans, Esmat Ezzat, Tore Godal, Melba Gomes, E. Robert Greenberg, Win E. Gutteridge, Ralph H. Henderson, H. Robert Horvitz, Nathan K. Kere, Veronique Lawson, David N. Nabarro, Richard Peto, Vulimiri Ramalingaswami, Peter Reeve, Hans Remme, Lateef Akinola Salako, Ebrahim M. Samba, Vladimir Petrovich Sergiev, Carol Vlassoff, Gabisiu A. Williams, and Richard Wilson

5. Resource Flows to the Health Sector

September 21, 1992, Harvard Center for Population and Development Studies, Cambridge, Massachusetts

Chair: William Hsiao

Participants: Sudhir Anand, Peter Berman, Mirnal Dutta Choudray, Gnanaraj Chellaraj, Lincoln C. Chen, Michel Cichon, Andrew Creese, Ramesh Govindaraj, Catherine Michaud, Christopher J. L. Murray, Sudhakar Rao, and George Scheiber

6. AIDS Policy

November 5–6, 1992, Rockefeller Foundation, New York. Financial support was provided by the Rockefeller Foundation and the Danish International Development Agency.

Chair: Robert S. Lawrence

Participants: Roy Anderson, José Barzellato, Seth Berkley, Robert Black, Kevin De Cock, Richard G. A. Feachem, Penelope Hitchcock, King Holmes, Robert E. Howells, Jane Hughes, Peter Lamptey, Jonathan Mann, Michael Merson, Daan Mulder, Peter Piot, Peer Sieben, Werasit Sittirai, Judith Wasserheit, Fernando Zacharias, and Richard Zeckhauser

7. Urban Health

November 9–11, 1992, Basel, Switzerland. Financial support was provided by Swiss Development Cooperation and the Swiss Tropical Institute.

Co-chairs: Marcel Tanner and Trudy Harpham

Participants: Antoine Degrémont, Maria Elena Ducci, Lilia Durán Gonzales, Paul Garner, Greg Goldstein, Emile Jeannée, Matthias Kerker, Peter Kilima, Nicolaus Lorenz, Ngudup Paljor, Voahangy Ramahatafandry, Alessandro Rossi-Espagnet, John Seager, Gustavo A. Torres, and Charles Yesudian

8. Human Resources for Health

November 18–19, 1992, McMaster University, Hamilton, Ontario, Canada. Financial support was provided by the Canadian International Development Agency.

Co-chairs: Julio Frenk and Victor Neufeld

Participants: Orvill Adams, Barbara Carpio, Gilles Dussauld, John Evans, Alfonso Mejía, Hiroshi Nakatani, Kenneth Ojo, Una Reid, Charas Suwanwela, and Peter Tugwell

9. Health of the Elderly

November 23–24, 1992, Voksenasen, Norway. The consultation was organized by the London School of Hygiene and Tropical Medicine. Financial support was provided by the Norwegian Ministry of Foreign Affairs.

Chair: Alex Kalache

Participants: Jordi Alonso, Nana Apt, Chris Beer, Felix Bermejo, Ruth Bonita, Carol Brayne, Paul Chen, Yolande Coombes, Xianglin Du, Denise Eldemire, J. Grimley Evans, Richard G. A. Feachem, Joe Hampson, Hana Hermanova, Benedicte Ingstad, Zhang Kaiti, Roberto Kaplan, Luis Ramos, Melba Sánchez-Ayéndez, Bela Shah, Alberto Spagnoli, Knight Steel, and Renato Veras

10. District Health Services

November 24–27, 1992, Institute of Health and Development, University of Dakar, Senegal. Financial support was provided by Swiss Development Cooperation and the Swiss Tropical Institute.

Co-chairs: Antoine Degrémont and Ibrahima Wone

Participants: Abdel Wahed Abassi, Waya Amoula, Anarfi Asamoa-Baah, Hubert Balique, Wolfgang Bichmann, Malang Coly, Christian Darras, Pierre Daveloose, Annemarie Demazy, Issakha Diallo, Isseu Diop-Touré, Gina Etheridge, Georges Fournier, Lucy Gilson, Kathia Janovsky, Emile Jeannée, Pangu Kasa-Asila, Matthias Kerker, Vincent Litt, Mandiaye Loum, Javier Martínez, Sigrun Mogedal, Maty Cissé Samb Ndao, Sène Touré Ngoné, Cornelius Oepen, Bakary Sambou, Lamine Cissé Sarr, Malick Sarr, Peter Schubarth, Michael Singleton, Thierno Mame Aby Sy, Al Hadji Ali Tahirou, James Tumwine, Jean-Pierre Unger, Adamou Yada, and Alfredo Zurita

11. Child Health

November 30–December 2, 1992, Baltimore, Maryland. The consultation was organized by the Johns Hopkins School of Hygiene and Public Health. Financial support was provided by the U.S. Agency for International Development.

Chair: W. Henry Mosley

Participants: Fernando Barros, Al Bartlett, Mark Belsey, Seth Berkley, Robert E. Black, David Boyd, Donald A. P. Bundy, Carlos C. Campbell, Dennis Carroll, Robert Clay, Felicity Cutts, Steve Esrey, Ronald Gray, Jerry Gibson, Bill Hausdorf, Jim Heiby, Donald A. Henderson, Terrel Hill, Sandra L. Huffman, Jessica Jitta, Pamela Johnson, Charlotte Neuman, Alok Perti, Phyllis Piotrow, Kenneth F. Schulz, Jim Shepperd, William A. Smith, Sally Stansfield, Hope Sukin, Nebiat Tafari, Taha el Tahir Taha, Carl E. Taylor, James L. Tulloch, Roxann Van Dusen, Caby C. Verzosa, Kenneth S. Warren, and Vivian Wong

12. Women and Health

December 7–9, 1992, Cumberland Lodge, Windsor, England. The consultation was organized by the London School of Hygiene and Tropical Medicine. Financial support was provided by the U.K. Overseas Development Administration.

Organizers: Oona Campbell, Wendy Graham, and Veronique Filippi

Participants: Uche Amazigo, Carmen Barroso, Loretta Brabin, Mayra Buvinic, Mirai Chatterjee, Ann Coles, Richard G. A. Feachem, Zuzana Feachem, Aleya El Bindari Hammad, Sioban Harlow, Gillian Holmes, Susan Joekes, Marjorie Koblinsky, Joanne Leslie, Claudia García Moreno, Jacky Mundy, Cynthia Myntti, David N. Nabarro, Phoebe Roome, Kasturi Sen, Jacqueline Sherris, Godfrey Walker, and Judith Wasserheit

13. Global Burden of Disease

December 10–11, 1992, World Health Organization, Geneva, Switzerland. The consultation was organized by the World Health Organization. Financial support was provided by the Edna McConnell Clark Foundation.

Chair: Jean-Paul Jardel

Participants: Carla Abou-Zahr, David Barmes, Monika Blössner, Luis López Bravo, Anthony Burton, Yankum Dadzie, Richard G. A. Feachem, Jacques Ferlay, Tore Godal, Ann Goerdt, Sandra Gove, Walter Gulbinat, Habib Rachmat Hapsara, Joachim Hempel, Mark Kane, Hilary King, Jeffrey R. Koplan, Jacob Kumaresan, Marie-Hélène Leclerq, Alan Lopez, Ingrid Martin, Alvaro Moncayo, Christopher J. L. Murray, Jenny Pronczuk, Jean-Marie Robine, Claude Romer, Elizabeth Sherwin, Peter Smith, Jan Stjernswärd, Rand Stoneburner, Muthu Subramanian, Carole Torel, and Godfrey Walker

14. Health Finance

December 14–16, 1992, Montebello, Quebec, Canada. Financial support was provided by the Canadian International Development Agency.

Chair: Stephen Simon

Participants: Nicholas Barr, David Bell, Ricardo Bitran, Åke Blomqvist, Joseph Brunet-Jailly, Claude Castonguay, Andrew L. Creese, Robert G. Evans, Claude Forget, William Hsiao, Naoki Ikegami, Daniel M. Le Touzé, Mario Taguiwalo, Abdelmajid Tibouti, Bokar Touré, and Katarzyna Tymowska

15. Review of WDR Findings

January 26, 1993, Institute of Medicine, Washington, D.C.

Chair: William H. Foege

Participants: Abdelmonem A. Afifi (provided written comments), Carolyn Asbury, David E. Bell, Richard Bissell, Barry R. Bloom, Margaret Catley-Carlson, J. Jarrett Clinton, Joseph A. Cook, Richard G. A. Feachem, Harvey V. Fineberg, Julio Frenk, Susan Gibb, Polly F. Harrison, Donald A. Henderson, Jeffrey R. Koplan, Adetokunbo O. Lucas, Christopher J. L. Murray, June E. Osborn, Adeline Wynante Patterson, David P. Rall, Frederick C. Robbins, Timothy Rothermel, Kenneth I. Shine, Alfred Sommer, Roxann Van Dusen, Noel S. Weiss, Barbara L. Wolfe, and James Wyngaarden

16. Environment and Health

February 4–5, 1993, World Bank, Washington, D.C. Financial support was provided by the Environmental Health Division, World Health Organization.

Chair: Wilfried Kreisel

Participants: Hendrik De Koning, Devra Lee Davis, Richard G. A. Feachem, Jacobo Finkelman, Gregory Goldstein, Tord Kjellstrom, Anthony J. McMichael, Horst Otterstetter, David P. Rall (provided written comments), and Kirk Smith

17. Improving the Effectiveness of International Assistance to Health

February 9–10, 1993, World Bank European Office, Paris, France. Partial financial support was provided by the Danish International Development Agency.

Chair: Anthony R. Measham

Participants: Marja Antilla, Lynn Bailey, José Barzellato, Alfredo R. A. Bengzon, Luciano Carrino, Genevieve Chedville-Murray, Zafrullah Chowdhury,

Immita Cornaz, Göran Dahlgren, François Decaillet, Nicolas de Riviere, Tore Godal, Klaus Gordel, Armelle George-Guiton, Jacques Hallak, Kyo Hanada, Anne Kristin Hermansen, Gillian Holmes, Jean-Paul Jardel, Eva Jespersen, Jorge Jiménez de la Jara, Matthias Kerker, Robert Kestell, Irene Klinger, Rolf Korte, Louise Lassonde, Jean-Marie Laure, Robert S. Lawrence, Rune Andreas Lea, Dominique Maroger, Catherine Michaud, Rajiv L. Misra, Bernard Montaville, W. Muchenje, David N. Nabarro, François Orivel, Tom Ortiz, Aagje Papineau Salm, Liu Peilong, Ines Perin, Martin Pinero, Peter Poore, Vulimiri Ramalingaswami, Olikoye Ransome-Kuti, Brett Ridgeway, Jon Rohde, Yolanda Richardson, Kenneth Ross, Timothy Rothermel, Philippa Saunders, Christopher Shaw, Leonardo Santos Simão, Stephen Simon, Margareta Sköld, Guillermo Soberon, Birgit Storgaard, Muthu Subramanian, Carl Wahren, Ronald Wilson, Robert Wrin, Carlos Yanez-Barneuvo, and Pat Youri

18. Violence against Women

February 12, 1993, Washington, D.C. This follow-up consultation to that on Interventions for Nervous Systems Disorders focused on the health outcomes of violence against women for the global burden of disease exercise.

Chair: Helen Saxenian

Participants: Jacqueline Campbell, Walter Gulbinat, Lori Heise, Dean Kilpatrick, and Christopher J. L. Murray

19. Review of the Global Burden of Disease

March 15, 1993, Centers for Disease Control and Prevention, Atlanta, Georgia

Chair: Jeffrey R. Koplan

Participants: Ruth L. Berkelman, Ruth A. Etzel, Françoise F. Hamers, Jeffrey R. Harris, Nancy C. Lee, Alan Lopez, Christopher J. L. Murray, Mark L. Rosenberg, Richard B. Rothenberg, Frank M. Vinicor, and Ray Yip

Seminars

An important source of ideas for this Report was a series of seminars. Most were held at the World Bank and were cosponsored by the World Bank's Population, Health, and Nutrition Department. The Harvard Center for Population and Development Studies held a series of five seminars to assist in developing *World Development Report* themes; these were organized by Lincoln C. Chen and Julio Frenk. The George Washington University Center for International Health held a seminar, organized by Rosalía Rodrigues-García, to critically review the findings of the *World Development Report*.

The World Bank series included presentations by Henry Aaron, John Akin, Kenneth Arrow, Amie Batson, Jere Behrman, David Bloom, Michael Cichon, Andrew Creese, Anil Deolalikar, Avi Dor and Janet Hunt-McCool, Alain Enthoven, Michelle Fryer, Paul Gertler, Eric Hanushek, Estelle James, Lawrence J. Lau, Beryl Levinger, Joseph Newhouse, Abdel Omran, Joel Nobel, François Orivel, Charles Phelps, Samuel Preston, Barry Popkin, Uwe Reinhardt, George Scheiber, T. Paul Schultz, Donald Shepard, John Strauss, Duncan Thomas, Carol Vlassoff, and Beverly Winikoff.

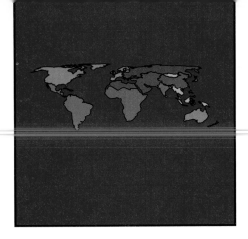

Bibliographical note

The Report has drawn on a wide range of World Bank reports and advice and on numerous outside sources. Special thanks go to the World Health Organization (WHO) for providing extensive expert advice, technical materials, and helpful comments.

The principal sources are noted below and are also listed alphabetically by author or organization in two groups: background papers commissioned for this Report and a selected bibliography.

In addition to the sources listed, many people both inside and outside the World Bank helped with the Report. In particular, helpful comments were received from World Bank staff and consultants, including Alexandre Abrantes, Masood Ahmed, Michael Azefor, Howard Barnum, Alan Berg, Eduard Bos, Patricia Daly, Willy De Geyndt, Janet de Merode, Jean-Jacques de St. Antoine, Dennis de Tray, Alfred Duda, Graham Dukes, Oscar Echeverri, A. Edward Elmendorf, James Green, Charles Griffin, Ann Hamilton, Jeffrey Hammer, Barbara Herz, Janet Hohnen, Ishrat Z. Husain, Estelle James, Emmanuel Jimenez, Elizabeth King, Timothy King, Mubina Kirmani, Kathie Krumm, Joseph Kutzin, Jean-Louis Lamboray, Kye Woo Lee, Danny M. Leipziger, Maureen Lewis, Samuel Lieberman, Bernhart Liese, James Listorti, Marlaine Lockheed, Jack Maas, Jo Martins, Judith McGuire, Mohan Munasinghe, Rieko Niimi, Mead Over, Lisa Pachter, Ok Pannenborg, David Peters, Ian Porter, Juan Prawda, George Psacharopoulos, Sandra Rosenhouse, Anna Sant'Anna, Miguel Schloss, Julian Schweitzer, Iona Sebastian, Paul Shaw, James Socknat, Lyn Squire, Andrew Steer, Susan Stout, Vinod Thomas, Erik Thulstrup, Anne Tinker, Vincent Turbat, Jagadish Upadhyay, Denise Vaillancourt, Armand Van Nimmen, Herman van der Tak, Dominique van de Walle, Claudia Von Monbart, Marie-Odile Waty, Kin Bing Wu, Guillermo Yepes, Mary E. Ming Young, and Shahid Yusuf.

Those outside the World Bank who contributed substantially with comments and material include Aloysio Achutti, Universidade Federal do Rio Grande do Sul, who assisted with the preparation of Figure 3; A. A. Afifi, University of California, Los Angeles; Jere Behrman, University of Pennsylvania; Marit Berggrav, Einar Heldal, Rune Andreas Lea, Johanne Sundby, and Ann-Karin Valle, Norwegian Agency for International Development (NORAD); Barry Bloom, Albert Einstein College of Medicine; Robert H. Cassen, International Development Centre, Oxford University; Immita Cornaz, Swiss Development Cooperation; Göran Dahlgren, Swedish International Development Authority (SIDA); Joe H. Davis, Centers for Disease Control and Prevention; Antoine Degrémont, Swiss Tropical Institute; David Fraser, Aga Khan Institute; Lucy Gilson, London School of Hygiene and Tropical Medicine; Ted Greiner, Uppsala University; Davidson Gwatkin, International Health Policy Program; David J. Halliday, UNICEF; Gillian Holmes and David Nabarro, U.K. Overseas Development Administration (ODA); William C. Hsiao, Harvard School of Public Health; Valerie Hull, Australian International Development Assistance Bureau (AIDAB); Pamela Johnson, Richard Seifman, and Robert Wrin, U.S. Agency for International Development (USAID); Joanne Leslie, UCLA School of Public Health; Adetokunbo O. Lucas, Harvard University; A. J. McMichael, University of Adelaide; Peter Poore, John Seaman, and David Woodward, Save the Children (U.K.); Barry Popkin, University of North Carolina; Vulimiri Ramalingaswami, Task Force on Health Research for Development; Patricia L. Rosenfield, Carnegie Corporation; Timothy S. Rothermel, United Nations Development Programme (UNDP); A. Papineau Salm, Ministry of Foreign Affairs, Netherlands; Philippa Saunders, OXFAM; Alfred Sommer and Carl Taylor, Johns Hopkins School of Hygiene and Public Health; Birgit Storgaard, Ministry of Foreign Affairs, Denmark; Noel S. Weiss, University of Washington; and Hans Emblad, Tore Godal, Marcus Grant, Fritz Kaferstein, Wilfried Kreisel, Alan D. Lopez, and James C. Tulloch, WHO.

Chapter 1

This chapter draws on technical materials from the World Health Organization and the World Bank and on the scientific literature. The smallpox story is adapted from Fenner and others 1988. The discussion of the gains in worker productivity from better health draws on studies by Castro and Mokate 1988, Conly 1975, Max and Shepard 1989, Nur and Mahran 1988, Pitt, Rosenzweig, and Hassan 1990, Sagan and Afifi 1979, Schultz and Tansel 1993, and Hill and others, background paper, as well as on helpful materials provided by John Caldwell, Gavin Jones, and John Anarfi. Anil Deolalikar provided additional material on the economic impact of improved nutrition in India, and John Akin made available unpublished notes on the relationship between health and income. The cost-benefit calculations of malaria eradication in Sri Lanka are derived from Barlow and Grobar 1985. Aehyung Kim and Bruce Benton contributed to Box 1.1.

The discussion of the education benefits of improved health and the related economic benefits of improved education is based on studies by Behrman and others 1991, Boissiere, Knight, and Sabot 1985, Glewwe 1991, Gomes-Neto and Hanushek 1991, Jamison and Leslie 1990, Jamison and Moock 1984, Nokes and others 1992, and Psacharopoulos 1993.

The section on reduced costs of medical care draws on studies by Ainsworth and Over 1992, notes by David Bloom and Ajay Mahal on the implications of reducing the rate of HIV transmission among seropositive individuals (with additional personal communication from the authors) and Musgrove 1988. Martha Ainsworth and Mead Over drafted Box 1.2. Bloom and Lyons 1993 provide analyses pointing to the economic gains associated with AIDS prevention in a number of Asian countries.

The discussion of the impact of health investments on poverty draws on the work of Henry Mosley and on World Bank 1980 and 1990a. The record of success draws heavily on statistical publications of the United Nations (*Demographic Yearbook*, various years) and the World Health Organization (*Statistics Annual*, various years). Ingram 1992 discusses the greater convergence of social (including health) indicators than of income across countries.

Child mortality estimates are derived in part from United Nations 1988 but were mostly calculated from data in United Nations 1992 as part of a joint World Bank–UNICEF exercise to be used in UNICEF forthcoming and described in Hill and Yazbeck, background paper. Eduard Bos and My Vu of the World Bank's Population, Health and Nutrition Department provided invaluable assistance and advice with the base regional population projections underlying much of Chapter 1 and Appendix A. Mortality assumptions were updated and revised in the light of discussions with Larry Heligman of the United Nations Population Division, Gareth Jones of UNICEF, and recent data from the Demographic and Health Surveys program provided by Ties Boerma or extracted from recent reports. Nicholas Eberstadt contributed useful ideas on mortality differentials in adulthood, and the section further benefited from Feachem and others 1992.

The results in the section on the global burden of disease are taken from a joint World Bank–World Health Organization study (Murray and Lopez background paper); many collaborators are listed in Appendix B. Material on measuring the burden of disease for Ghana, to establish health care priorities, came from Ghana Health Assessment Project Team 1981. Feachem 1988 stresses the importance of ''macroepidemiology'' for health planning.

The section on challenges for the future is based on Institute of Medicine 1992, Mackay 1993, and WHO 1992b and 1992c and on information on HIV and AIDS provided by Seth Berkley, Rand Stoneburner, and WHO staff. D. A. Henderson provided information on emerging microbial infections; Tore Godal, Tekle Haimanot, and Hans Remme on malaria; and Alan D. Lopez and Neil Collishaw on smoking. Jacobs and others 1993 report on the development of a test for drug resistance in tuberculosis.

The discussion on demographic and epidemiologic transition draws on studies by Bobadilla and others forthcoming, Frenk and others 1989, and Omran 1971. Country-specific discussions of the implications of epidemiological transition for health policy may be found in World Bank 1984a, World Bank 1990a, and World Bank 1992a. The purchasing power parity per capita incomes used in Figure 1.9 were provided by Angus Maddison. The discussion of the factors explaining mortality declines is based on Ewbank and Preston 1990, McKeown 1976, and Preston and Haines 1991.

The structure and content of the chapter benefited from presentations made by Abdel Omran and Samuel Preston. Valuable comments on earlier drafts were made by Joseph Cook and Richard Morrow.

Chapter 2

This chapter draws on academic sources, presentations by speakers in the seminar series cosponsored by the *World Development Report* and the World Bank Population, Health and Nutrition Department, and on numerous World Bank documents. The discussion on household capacity (income and schooling) was informed by studies that included Anand and Ravallion 1993, Behrman 1990, Benefo and Schultz 1992, Fuchs 1979, Grossman 1975, Hill and Palloni 1992, Jeyaratnam 1985, Lau and others, background paper, Luft 1978, Natale and others 1992, Oganov 1992, Palloni 1981, Pierce 1989, Pritchett and Summers, background paper, Rodgers 1979, Rogot, Sorlie, and Johnson 1992, Strauss and others 1992, United Nations 1985, Wilkinson 1992, and World Bank 1990a.

The discussion on women's schooling and child health drew on the extensive literature, including Bhargava and Yu 1992, Bruce and Lloyd 1992, Caldwell 1986, Cleland 1990, Elo 1992, Engle 1991, Hoddinott and Haddad 1991, Kennedy 1992, King and Hill 1993, Leslie 1989b, Lindenbaum, Chakraborty, and Elias 1985, Louat, Grosh, and van der Gaag 1992, Over and others 1992, Sahn 1990, Summers 1992, Thomas 1990, Thomas, Strauss, and Henriques 1990, and World Bank Water Demand Research Team 1993.

The discussion on economic policy reform and adjustment lending drew on sources that included Behrman 1992, Berg and Hunter 1992, Edwards forthcoming, Kakwani, Makonnen, and van der Gaag 1990, Serageldin, Elmendorf, and El-Tigani forthcoming, Summers and Pritchett 1993, Thomas, Lavy, and Strauss 1992, Woodward 1992, World Bank 1990b, World Bank 1992e, and World Bank 1993c. Duncan Thomas contributed materials on protecting nonsalary spending during economic adjustment.

The presentation on education policies was informed by Alderman and others 1992, Jamison and Leslie 1990, Jarousse and Mingat 1992, Lockheed, Verspoor, and associates 1991, Minhas 1991, Over and Piot forthcoming, Tan and Mingat 1992, and World Bank 1988.

The work on policies for empowering women drew on Akin and others 1985, Birdsall and McGreevey 1983, and Leslie 1989a. The discussion of women and violence benefited from assistance from Jacquelyn Campbell, Rosemary Garner, Lori Heise and Dean Kilpatrick and drew on Archavanitkui and Pramaualrantan 1990, Bradley 1988, CAMVAC 1985, Council on Scientific Affairs 1992, COVAC 1990, Fauveau and Blanchet 1989, Handwerker 1991, Hosken 1988, Koop 1989, Koss, Koss, and Woodruff 1991, Plitcha 1992, Shim 1992, Stark 1984, and Stark and Flitcraft 1991.

Lawrence Lau contributed to the drafting of Box 2.1. Box 2.2 is based on material provided by Michelle Fryer. Carmen Barroso, Lori Heise, and Nahid Toubia contributed to Box 2.3. John Hobcraft and Aloysio Achutti assisted with the preparation of Figures 2.4

and 2.5, respectively. Robert Anda, David Bradley, John Briscoe, Mayra Buvinic, Brigitte Duces, Luis Escobedo, Paul Gertler, A. K. Shiva Kumar, Joanne Leslie, Ruth Levine, Jack Molyneaux, Damianos Odeh, Nick Prescott, Luis Serven, John Strauss, and Molly Tees contributed helpful data and resource materials. Valuable comments on earlier drafts were received from Sue Berryman, Joseph Bredie, Barbara Bruns, Ishac Diwan, Edward Henevald, Eva Jarawan, Himelda Martinez, Kenneth Shine, and David Woodward.

Chapter 3

This chapter draws on a wide range of published and unpublished sources, including documentation and expertise from the World Health Organization and the World Bank and on the academic literature. Discussion of the role of government draws on World Bank 1991. Jamison and others forthcoming summarizes the methods and findings of the cost effectiveness analysis that forms the starting point for the analyses used in this report. The data on health expenditures in the first section were compiled from a background paper by Murray, Govindaraj, and Chellaraj, which used a wide range of government health budgets, World Bank reports, and other country studies of health financing. Heller and Diamond 1990 also treat this issue. Data on equity in health status, access, and expenditure were drawn from the World Bank's Living Standard Measurement Study (LSMS) and were further analyzed by Kalpana Mehra. The analysis of costs and benefits of packages of public health measures and essential clinical services draws on the background paper by Bobadilla and others.

Box 3.1 was drafted by Richard Bumgarner. Box 3.2 is based on unpublished data provided by the Instituto Materno-Infantil de Pernambuco and on UNICEF and IMIP 1992. Box 3.3 is from the chapters on measles and on tuberculosis in Jamison and others forthcoming. The discussion of cost-effective interventions also draws on Halstead, Walsh, and Warren 1985, Walsh 1988, and Walsh and Warren 1979. Basic economic issues and their application are treated in Over 1991. The discussion of market failures in health draws particularly on Arrow 1963. Insurance and regulation are discussed generally in Diamond 1992 and for Brazil in Piola and Vianna 1991. The section on government failures in health policy takes examples from Evans, Barer, and Labelle 1988, Hlady and others 1992, and IDB 1988. Equity examples are drawn from Black and others 1982, Meerman 1980, Musgrove 1986 and 1993, and President's Commission 1983, as well as from the work of Prescott and others on social spending in Indonesia. The discussion of satisfaction with health care uses Bitran and McInnes 1993, Blendon and others 1990, and Gertler and van der Gaag 1990. Leslie 1989a discusses the time cost of health interventions, an issue that is not explicitly addressed in the cost-effectiveness calculations reported here but that deserves further work. Brook and Lohr 1986 provide evidence pointing to huge overuse of medical care in the United States beyond what is of value even at zero cost, resulting in part from third-party financing.

Nicholas Barr, Peter Diamond, Robert Evans, and Fernando Figueira provided valuable ideas and comments.

Chapter 4

This chapter draws on documentation and expertise from the World Health Organization and the World Bank and from the academic literature, as well as on expert consultations and on papers and discussions in the seminar series sponsored by the *World Development Report* and the World Bank Population, Health, and Nutrition Department.

The discussion on immunization and other population-based health services draws on ideas and data discussed at the consultation on Child Health held in Baltimore in 1992. Berkley and Jamison 1991 discuss the cost and effectiveness of school-based programs for mass treatment of worm infections and micronutrient deficiencies. Assistance was also provided by Amie Batson, Donald Bundy, Pamela Johnson, Marjorie Koblinsky, Jim Shepperd, Jacqueline Sherris, and Nebiat Tafari. Other sources were Bourdon, Orivel, and Perrot 1993, Brenzel 1990, Nokes and others 1992, Robertson and others 1992, Shepard and others 1989, and chapters in Jamison and others forthcoming on measles, polio, hepatitis B, tetanus, and helminth infection.

The section on diet and nutrition drew on Levin and others forthcoming, Pinstrup-Anderson and others forthcoming, and a variety of other sources. Valuable summaries of particular topics are given in ACC/SCN 1991, 1992a, and 1992b, Beaton and Ghassemi 1987, Beaton and others 1993, Berg 1987, Drèze and Sen 1989, Elliott 1988, Humphrey, West, and Sommer 1992, Keusch and Scrimshaw 1986, Leslie 1987, Leslie, Jamison, and Musgrove forthcoming, McGuire and Popkin 1990, Monteiro 1988, National Research Council 1989, Pelletier 1991, Pollitt 1990, Popkin 1993, Sen 1981, Tomkins and Watson 1989, and U.S. Centers for Disease Control and Prevention 1992. The section also drew on studies by Adair and others 1993, Bhargava 1992, Black 1991, Bouis 1990, Lutter and others 1992, Mardones and Zamora 1989, Martorell and others 1992, Musgrove 1990, Stamler and others 1989, Thomas, Lavy, and Strauss 1992, Waaler 1984, and Walter, Olivares, and Hertrampf

1990. Joanne Leslie contributed Box 4.1, and Jayshree Balachander contributed Box 4.2. Harold Alderman, George Beaton, Robert Black, Barry Bloom, Leslie Elder, Paul Elliott, Abraham Horwitz, Suraiya Ismail, Francisco Mardones, Reynaldo Martorell, John Mason, Paul McKeigue, Daan Mulder, Philip Payne, David Pelletier, and Peter Piot provided helpful information or comments.

The section on fertility drew on Cochrane and Merrick, background paper, AbouZahr and Royston 1991, Amadeo, Chernichovsky, and Ojeda 1991, Bertrand and Brown 1992, Population Information Program 1992, Population Reference Bureau 1992a and 1992b, Sanderson and Tan forthcoming, Stephenson and others 1992, United Nations forthcoming, World Bank 1984a, 1992c, and 1993a, and Zinanga 1992. Birgitta Bucht, Parker Mauldin, Vincent Miller, Richard Osborn, Warren Sanderson, Beverley Winikoff, and the staff at the Rockefeller Foundation provided helpful materials and advice. John Hobcraft assisted in the preparation of Figure 4.3.

The section on tobacco, alcohol, and drugs benefited from materials and comments from Jerry Husch, Judith Mackay, Richard Peto, and Derek Yack. The discussion drew on background materials from James Cercone and from the U.S. Surgeon-General's 1992 report on smoking in the Americas, as well as on Gutierrez-Fisac, Regidor, and Ronda 1992, Pierce 1991, Walsh and others forthcoming, Wasserman and others 1991, and WHO 1991b and 1992e.

The section on the environment benefited from the contributions of participants in a joint WHO–World Bank consultation (see Acknowledgments) and from additional assistance provided by Carl Bartone, David Bates, Sue Binder, Gloria Davis, Roger Detels, John Dixon, Mohamed T. El-Ashry, Gunnar Eskeland, Ruth Etzel, Philip Graitcer, Peter Kolsky, Tony McMichael, David Rall, Anand Seth, and Anthony Zwi. Data on the health impact of water supply and sanitation were taken from the extensive literature and from recent reviews by Cairncross 1990, Esrey and others 1991, and Huttly 1990. The material on water and sanitation policy drew on Briscoe 1992, World Bank 1992f, and World Bank Water Demand Research Team 1993. Box 4.4 was drafted by Sandy Cairncross. Box 4.5 relies on Blum and others 1990 and on Feachem and others 1978 for time spent collecting water. Michael Garn, Letitia Obeng, and Guillermo Yepes contributed data on water and sanitation costs. Greg Watters collated the data in Figure 4.6. The discussion of indoor air pollution rests on the reviews by Betty Kirkwood and colleagues and on the work of Kirk Smith. Relevant literature included Anderson 1979, Chapman and others 1989, Chen and others 1990, Norboo and others 1991, Pandey and others 1989, Smith forthcoming, Smith and Liu 1993, and Smith and Rodgers 1992. Christopher Curtis prepared Box 4.6, with assistance from Colin Leake, making use of data from Alonso and others 1991, Curtis 1992, and Maxwell and others 1990. Discussion of housing policy was informed by World Bank 1993b.

The discussion of the wider environment drew on Doll 1992 and on the comprehensive accounts contained in WHO 1992d and World Bank 1992f. The discussion on occupational health drew on Andreoni 1986, El Batawi and Husbumrer 1987, and Wegman 1992. The discussion of the ambient environment drew on the extensive literature, including Bellinger and others 1987, Bradley and others 1992, Faiz and others forthcoming, Lancet 1992, MRC 1989, Needleman and others 1990, Romieu 1992, Romieu, Weitzenfeld, and Finkelman 1990, Schwartz and Dockery 1992, WHO 1992a, and WHO/UNEP 1992. The material for Box 4.7 is taken from Bobak 1993, Bobak and Feachem 1992, Bobak and Leon 1992, and World Bank 1992d. Box 4.8 is taken from Study Group for Global Environment and Economics 1991, supplied by Tord Kjellstrom. José Carbajo, Paul Guitink, Zmarak Shalizi, and John Wootton assisted with the section on transport risks, which also drew on Barss and others forthcoming, Downing 1991, Johnston 1992, Smith and Barss 1991, TRRL 1991, WHO 1989a, and Zwi 1992.

The section on AIDS benefited from the contributions made by members of the AIDS consultation (see Acknowledgments) and from additional assistance from Richard Hayes, Daan Mulder, Peter Piot, Wendy Roseberry, Allan Rosenfield, Gary Slutkin, and Peter Smith. Projections of numbers of infections were generated by Tony Burton, Rand Stoneburner, and other staff of the Global Programme on AIDS of the World Health Organization (GPA/WHO). Material on the core groups is drawn from Moses and others 1991 and Over and Piot forthcoming. The account of community intervention in Zimbabwe is drawn from material supplied by David Wilson. Material on HIV and breastfeeding is drawn from Dunn and others 1992 and various WHO materials. Box 4.9 draws on Goodgame 1990, Katabira and Goodgame 1989, and Muller and others 1992. Information on voluntary testing and counseling is drawn from Foster 1990, Muller and others 1992, and WHO Global Programme on AIDS 1993b. Estimations of the cost of worldwide prevention were drawn from WHO Global Programme on AIDS 1993a and WHO forthcoming, and from work by Doris Schopper. The discussion of the cost-effectiveness of treating sexually transmitted diseases is drawn from Moses and others 1992, and Over and Piot forthcoming. Box 4.10 is drawn from Viravaidya, Obremsky, and Myers 1991 and from materials contributed by Werasit Sittitrai.

Material on the success of prevention was drawn from the literature and from a meeting at GPA/WHO in 1992. The costs and benefits of the public health measures in the essential package are presented in Bobadilla and others, background paper.

Chapter 5

The costs and benefits of the clinical services in the essential package are described in Bobadilla and others, background paper. The discussion of the cost of the essential package of clinical services and mechanisms for delivering it drew on the work of the World Bank's Africa Technical Department and World Bank forthcoming. The components of the essential package of clinical services for children drew on analyses from UNICEF 1993 and on priorities proposed in UNICEF, WHO, and UNESCO 1991. The analyses of sources of health financing, provider compensation, and alternative modes of service delivery are based on the work of Arrow 1963, Barr 1992, Griffin 1992, Hsiao 1992, Hurst 1992, Reinhardt 1991, Schneider and others 1992, van Doorslaer, Wagstaff, and Rutten 1993, and World Bank 1992a. It draws on and is closely linked with a series of papers by the World Health Organization: WHO 1991a, on health care reform in Eastern and Central Europe; WHO 1991c, on the public-private mix; and WHO 1993.

The analysis of user charges and community financing draws on the work of Abel-Smith and Dua 1988, Gertler and van der Gaag 1990, Hecht, Overholt, and Holmberg 1993, Korte and others 1992, Lewis and Parker 1991, Litvack and Bodart 1993, McPake, Hanson, and Mills 1992, and others. The discussion of health insurance in developing countries draws on Abel-Smith 1992b, De Geyndt 1991, Ikegami 1992, Kutzin and Barnum 1992, McGreevey 1990, Mesa-Lago 1992, Vogel 1989, Yang 1991, and Yu and Anderson 1992. Analysis of the determinants of health spending in the OECD countries draws on Gerdtham and others 1992. The review of options for improving public and private delivery of clinical services draws on Bennett 1992, Foster 1991, and World Bank 1992g. The discussion of managed competition relies on Enthoven 1988 and Relman 1993. The discussion of decentralization of health services draws on Mills and others 1990 and World Bank 1992b.

Box 5.1 draws on material produced by Marjorie Koblinsky and on Tinker and Koblinsky 1993 and Walsh and others forthcoming. Box 5.2 was prepared with information provided by James C. Tulloch and Sandra Gove of WHO. Box 5.3 draws on material provided by Judith Wasserheit. Box 5.4 was based on Murray, Styblo, and Rouillon forthcoming. Box 5.5 draws on Grosh 1992. Box 5.6 uses material from

Schieber, Poullier, and Greenwald 1992 and the results of analysis by the *WDR* team of the relationship between the public share of health spending and health care costs. Box 5.7 is based on material from Hurst 1992. Werner 1987 discusses approaches to low-cost but effective rehabilitation from disability.

Peter Berman and Louis Vassiliou provided useful material and Alfred Bartlett, Ricardo Bitran, Michael Cichon, Andrew Creese, Jennie Litvack, Kasa Asila Pangu, John Rohde, Abdelmajid Tibouti, Jacques van der Gaag, Ronald Wilson, and Zia Yusuf made valuable comments.

Chapter 6

This chapter draws on technical materials from the World Health Organization and the World Bank and from the scientific literature. Regional estimates of hospital beds, physicians, and nurses are from OECD, WHO, World Bank, and national statistics. The hospital and district health system discussion draws on Barnum and Kutzin 1993 and World Bank forthcoming.

Valuable comments and materials were provided by Orvil Adams, Uche Amazigo, Harvey Bale, Wilbert Bannenberg, Pascal Brudon-Jakobowicz, Robert Cassen, Gilles Dussault, Anibal Faúndes, Enrique Feffer, Michael Free, Julio Frenk, John Gil-Martin, Wendy Graham, Richard Heller, Richard Laing, John Lloyd, Alfonso Mejía, Violaine Mitchell, Hiroshi Nakatani, Vic Neufeld, Joel Nobel, João Batista Oliveira, Diego Palacio, David Porter, Michael Porter, Jim Rankin, Una Reid, and staff of the Aga Khan Development Network and the Aga Khan Foundation.

Box 6.1 was prepared by Tamara Fox and Ruth Levine. Estimates of medical equipment expenditure are from Rozynski and Gallivan 1992.

Estimates on the efficiency of outpatient surgery in Colombia are from Shepard and others 1990. Hospital planning experience in the United States is based on Davis and others 1990. The discussion of regional planning is based in part on Jonsson 1989. The relationship between the volume of surgery and health outcomes is based on Hughes, Hunt, and Luft 1987. Papua New Guinea's experience with containing hospital spending is based on Newbrander 1987. The medical equipment discussion draws on Bloom 1989, Bruley 1991, Garber and Fuchs 1991, Gelijns and Halm 1991, Halbwachs 1992, and WHO various years. Abel-Smith 1992a and Rublee 1989 provided information on medical technology policies in industrial countries.

The human resources for health discussion draws on Abel-Smith 1986, Enthoven and Vorhaus 1992, Evans 1981, Foster 1987, Frenk and others 1991, Fuchs 1978, Institute of Medicine 1988, Javitt forth-

coming, Reyes and Picazo 1990, Richards and Fülöp 1987, Schmidt and others 1991, Schroeder 1984 and 1992, Schwab 1987, Tarlov 1986 as cited in Reinhardt 1991, Welch and others 1993, Whitfield 1987, and unpublished material from Ruth Roemer and WHO. In Box 6.2 the discussion of community health workers in Jamaica draws on Cumper and Vaughan 1985. The discussion of the Pastoral da Criança draws on materials provided by the Coordenação Nacional da Pastoral da Criança and on Victora and Barros 1990.

The drug discussion draws on Andersson 1992, Caplan 1985, Foster 1990, Hlady and others 1992, Holly and Lee 1992, Kanji and others 1992, Laing 1990, Management Sciences for Health 1992, Nazerali 1992, Office of Technology Assessment 1993, Thomas, Lavy, and Strauss 1992, Tomson and Sterky 1986, and WHO 1988a, 1988b, and 1988c. Box 6.5 draws on World Bank material and on Barros and others 1986 and Faúndes and Cecatti 1993. Information on the INCLEN program is from Halstead, Tugwell, and Bennet 1991. The information and research to guide decisionmaking draws on Enthoven 1989. Estimates of global spending on health research are from the Commission on Health Research for Development 1990. The health research discussion also draws on Free 1991, Godal 1993, and WHO 1991d.

Chapter 7

Information on health policy reform was provided by Jonathan Broomberg for South Africa, Louise Fox for Romania, Salim Habayeb for India, Evangeline Javier for Chile, and Mary E. Ming Young for Poland. The section on aid flows is based on the background paper on aid by Michaud and Murray, which used a wide range of data from Organization for Economic Cooperation and Development, United Nations, and bilateral sources. The discussion of international health research draws heavily on Commission on Health Research for Development 1990. John Barton and Selcuk Ozgediz furnished material on the Consultative Group for International Agricultural Research (CGIAR) and its relevance for health research. Valuable comments on the draft chapter were received from John Evans. Box 7.1 is based on UNICEF/Bamako Initiative Management Unit 1990 and 1992 and on the evaluation study by McPake, Hanson, and Mills 1992. Box 7.2 draws on World Bank reports on Chile and on material provided by Thomas Bossert on evaluations of health-financing reforms and decentralization. Box 7.3 uses material provided by Dov Chernichovsky and George Schieber. Box 7.4 encapsulates the findings of Cassen and others 1986 and Riddell 1987 in particular. Guy Ellena and Joseph Kutzin assisted with Box 7.5. Box 7.6 draws heavily on World Bank 1993d.

Appendix A

Appendix A benefited from contributions from many institutions; particularly valuable were the data received from WHO and UNICEF. Richard Bumgarner and Godfrey Walker of WHO provided information for many of the health indicators. Gareth Jones, UNICEF, contributed sources of data for nutritional indicators. Shea Rutstein from the Demographic and Health Surveys project provided data on breastfeeding. Robert Hartford and Francis Notzon made available the database on perinatal and infant mortality from the National Center of Health Statistics. Roy Miller, USAID, commented on an earlier version of the appendix. My Vu of the World Bank's Population, Health, and Nutrition Department was responsible for preparing the statistical appendix for World Bank forthcoming, which was extensively used in the appendix, and processed raw data on several of the selected health indicators. James Cercone helped process data on mortality by broad causes of death.

Appendix B

The global burden of disease study was directed by Christopher Murray and Alan D. Lopez. The results reported here come from Murray and Lopez, background paper; a much expanded discussion will appear in Murray and Lopez forthcoming (a). Contributions from the United Kingdom were coordinated by Jonathan Broomberg.

Substantial contributions and comments on specific diseases and injuries came from the following individuals: Carla AbouZahr, Mike Adams, Paul Arthur, Robert Ashley, Kenneth Bailey, David Barmes, L. Barnes, Robert Beaglehole, Mark Belsey, Stephen Berman, Barry Bloom, M. Blossner, Loretta Brabin, Donald Bundy, A. Burton, P. D. Cattand, Jacqueline Cattani, Chen Chunming, Caroline J. Cook, Edward Cooper, P. M. P. Desjeux, Jacques Ferlay, J. Fomey, Jean-Claude Funck, Michel Garenne, Tore Godal, Anne Goerdt, Johnathan Gorstein, Sandra Gove, Ramesh Govindaraj, Walter Gulbinat, Ivan Gyarfas, Lori Heise, Larry Heligman, Joachim Hempel, Emmanuel Jimenez, Mark Kane, Patrick Kenya, Dean Kilpatrick, Hilary King, Jeffrey Koplan, Marie-Helene Leclerq, Linda Lloyd, Julian Lobb-Levyt, Luis Lopez Bravo, David Mabey, Prasanta Mahapatra, Paul McKeigue, Graham Medley, Edwin Michael, Catherine Michaud, Kenneth Mott, A.-D. Negrel, Magdaline Orzeszyna, Max Parkin, Richard Peto, P. Pisani, Jenny Pronczuk, E. Pupulin, Xinjian Qiao, Ravi Rannan-Eliya, Hans Remme, Jean-Marie Robine, Claude J. Romer, Richard Rothenberg, Peter Sandiford, Elizabeth Sherwin, Alan Silman, Buranaj Smutharaks, Jan Stjernsward, Rand Stoneburner,

Deborah Symmons, B.-I. Thylefors, Ian Timæus, Carol Torel, James C. Tulloch, Ronald Waldman, Godfrey Walker, Jay Wenger, William Whang, Erica Wheeler, Russell Wilkins, G. Yang, R. Yip, and Anthony Zwi.

Others who contributed include M. Adrian, Ann Ashworth-Hill, P. Blake, Uwe Brinkman, C. Broome, Richard Bumgarner, Jacqueline Campbell, P. Carlevaro, Mary Chamie, Lincoln C. Chen, D. P. J. Daumerie, Hans Emblad, R. Etzel, Paul Fine, A. Galazka, Marito Garcia, S. Gillespie, Marcus Grant, R. J. Guidotti, Francoise Hamers, H. R. Hapsara, J. Harris, Peter Heller, Alan Hill, C. J. Hong, H. Jamai, Fritz Kaferstein, Alex Kalache, N. Khaltaeve, Betty Kirkwood, Arata Kochi, Jacob Kumaresan, N. Lee, Anthony Mann, Ingrid Martin, G. Mayberly, Juan Menchaca, Michel Mercier, T. R. Mertens, Alvaro Moncayo, Richard Morrow, Y. Motarjemi, Shaik Nadeen, William Newbrender, M. Noel, Godfrey Oakley, D. Peterson, A. Pio, G. R. Quinke, C. P. Ramachandran, M. Rosenberg, Norman Sartorius, Alan M. Schapira, Gordon Smith, Peter Smith, T. Studwick, M. Thuriaux, Andrew Tomkins, Patrick Vaughan, S. Vidwans, F. Vinicor, and Diana Weil.

The methodology used for this study drew in part on the established literature on quality-adjusted life years (see Torrance 1986). One of the first applications to developing countries was Ghana Health Assessment Project Team 1981.

Background papers

Bobadilla, José-Luis, Peter Cowley, Helen Saxenian, and Philip Musgrove. "The Essential Package of Health Services in Developing Countries."

Cochrane, Susan, and Thomas W. Merrick. "Improving Maternal and Child Health through Family Planning Services."

Hecht, Robert M., and Vito L. Tanzi. "The Role of NGOs in the Delivery of Health Services in Developing Countries."

Hill, Kenneth, and Abdo Yazbeck. "Trends in Child Mortality, 1960–90: Estimates for 84 Developing Countries."

Hill, Kenneth, Dean T. Jamison, Lawrence J. Lau, Jee-Peng Tan, and Abdo Yazbeck. "The Impact of Health Status on Economic Growth."

Lau, Lawrence, Abdo Yazbeck, Kenneth Hill, Dean T. Jamison, and Jee-Peng Tan. "Sources of Child Health Gains since the 1960s: An International Comparison."

Michaud, Catherine, and Christopher Murray. "Aid Flows to the Health Sector in Developing Countries."

Murray, Christopher, and Alan D. Lopez. "The Global Burden of Disease in 1990."

Murray, Christopher, Ramesh Govindaraj, and G. Chellaraj. "Global Domestic Expenditures in Health."

Murray, Christopher, Jay Kreuser, and William Whang. "Cost-Effectiveness Model for Allocating Health Sector Resources."

Pritchett, Lant, and Lawrence H. Summers. "Wealthier Is Healthier."

Yazbeck, Abdo, Jee-Peng Tan, and Vito L. Tanzi. "Public Spending on Health in the 1980s: The Impact of Adjustment Lending Programs."

Selected bibliography

Aaron, Henry J. 1991. *Serious and Unstable Condition: Financing America's Health Care*. Washington, D.C.: Brookings Institution.

Abel-Smith, Brian. 1986. "The World Economic Crisis. Part 2: Health Manpower out of Balance." *Health Policy and Planning* 1(4): 309–16.

———. 1992a. "Cost Containment and New Priorities in the European Community." *Milbank Memorial Fund Quarterly* 70(3): 393–416.

———. 1992b. *Cost Containment and New Priorities in Health Care*. Aldershot, U.K.: Ashgate Publishing.

———. 1992c. "Health Insurance in Developing Countries: Lessons from Experience." *Health Policy and Planning* 7(3): 215–26.

Abel-Smith, Brian, and Ajay Dua. 1988. "Community Financing in Developing Countries: The Potential for the Health Sector." *Health Policy and Planning* 3(2): 95–108.

AbouZahr, Carla, and Erica Royston, comps. 1991. *Maternal Mortality: A Global Factbook*. Geneva: World Health Organization.

ACC/SCN (Administrative Committee on Coordination/ Subcommittee on Nutrition). 1991. *Controlling Iron Deficiency*. Nutrition Policy Discussion Paper 9. Geneva: World Health Organization.

———. 1992a. *Nutrition and Population Links: Breastfeeding, Family Planning and Child Health*. Nutrition Policy Discussion Paper 11. Geneva: World Health Organization.

———. 1992b. *Second Report on the World Nutrition Situation*. Vol. I: *Global and Regional Results*. Geneva: World Health Organization.

Achutti, Aloysio, B. B. Duncan, Luis Ruiz, and M. I. Schmidt. 1988. "Programas de Saúde do Adulto." Paper prepared for the World Bank Study on Adult Health in Brazil. World Bank, Washington, D.C.

Adair, L., Barry M. Popkin, J. VanDerslice, John S. Akin, David K. Guilkey, R. Black, John Briscoe, and W. Flieger. 1993. "Growth Dynamics during the First Two Years of Life: A Prospective Study in the Philippines." *European Journal of Clinical Nutrition* 47: 42–51.

Ainsworth, Martha, and Mead Over. 1992. "The Economic Impact of AIDS: Shocks, Responses, and Outcomes." Technical Working Paper 1. World Bank, Africa Technical Department, Washington, D.C.

Akin, John S., David K. Guilkey, Charles C. Griffin, and Barry M. Popkin. 1985. *The Demand for Primary Health Services in the Third World*. Totowa, N.J.: Roman and Allanheld.

Alderman, Harold, Jere Behrman, Shahrukh Khan, David Ross, and Richard Sabot. 1992. "Public Schooling Expenditures in Rural Pakistan: Efficiently Targeting Girls and a Lagging Region." Paper presented at a World Bank conference on Public Expenditure on the Poor, July 17–19, Washington, D.C.

Alonso, P. L., S. W. Lindsay, J. R. M. Armstrong, M. Conteh, P. H. David, G. Fegan, A. de Francisco, A. J. Hall, F. C. Shenton, K. Cham, and B. M. Greenwood. 1991. "The Effect of Insecticide Treated Bed-Nets on Mortality of Gambian Children." *Lancet* 337: 1499–1515.

Amadeo, Jesus, Dov Chernichovsky, and Gabriel Ojeda. 1991. "The Profamilia Family Planning Program, Colombia." Policy, Research, and External Affairs Working Paper Series 759. World Bank, Population and Human Resources Department, Washington, D.C.

Anand, Sudhir, and Martin Ravallion. 1993. "Human Development in Poor Countries: On the Role of Private Incomes and Public Services." *Journal of Economic Perspectives* 7(1): 133–50.

Anderson, H. R. 1979. "Chronic Lung Disease in the Papua New Guinea Highlands." *Thorax* 34: 647–53.

Andersson, Fredrik. 1992. "Norway's Pivotal Role in Regulatory Health Economics and Pharmaceutical Cost Containment—What Can Other Countries Learn?" *Health Policy* 21: 17–34.

Andreoni, Diego. 1986. "The Cost of Occupational Accidents and Diseases." Occupational Safety and Health Series 54. International Labour Office, Geneva.

Archavanitkui, K., and A. Pramaualrantan. 1990. "Factors Affecting Women's Health in Thailand." Paper presented at the Workshop on Women's Health in Southeast Asia, Population Council, Jakarta, October 29–31.

Arrow, Kenneth. 1963. "Uncertainty and the Welfare Economics of Medical Care." *American Economic Review* 53: 941–73.

Ballance, Robert, Janos Pogany, and Helmut Forstner. 1992. *The World's Pharmaceutical Industries: An International Perspective on Innovation, Competition, and Policy*. Published for the United Nations Industrial Development Organization. Aldershot, U.K.: Edward Elgar Publishing.

Barcellos, Tanya, Carmen Barros, Naia Oliveira, Vera Garcia, Laureane Pastore, and Mercedes Rabelo. 1986. "Segregação Urbana e Mortalidade em Porto Alegre." Fundação de Economia e Estatística, Porto Alegre, Brazil.

Barlow, Robin, and Lisa M. Grobar. 1985. "Costs and Benefits of Controlling Parasitic Diseases." World Bank, Population, Health, and Nutrition Department, Washington, D.C.

Barnum, Howard. 1987. "Evaluating Health Days of Life Gained from Health Projects." *Social Science and Medicine* 24(10): 833–41.

Barnum, Howard, and Joseph Kutzin. 1993. *Public Hospitals in Developing Countries: Resource Use, Cost, Financing*. Baltimore, Md.: Johns Hopkins University Press.

Barr, Nicholas. 1992. "Economic Theory and the Welfare State: A Survey and Interpretation." *Journal of Economic Literature* 30 (June): 741–803.

Barros, F. C., and others. 1986. "Why So Many Cesarean Sections: The Need for Further Policy Change in Brazil." *Health Policy and Planning* 1(19).

Barss, P., G. S. Smith, D. Mohan, and S. P. Baker. Forthcoming. *Injuries in Adults in Developing Countries: Epidemiology and Policy*. New York: Oxford University Press.

Baumol, William J. 1992. "Private Affluence, Public Squalor." C. V. Starr Center for Applied Economics, New York.

Beaton, George H., and Hossein Ghassemi. 1987. "Supplementary Feeding Programs for Young Children in Developing Countries: A Summary of Lessons Learned." In J. Price Gittinger, Joanne Leslie, and Caroline Hoisington, eds., *Food Policy: Integrating Supply, Distribution, and Consumption*. Baltimore, Md.: Johns Hopkins University Press.

183

Beaton, George H., R. Martorell, K. A. L'Abbe, B. Edmonston, G. McCabe, A. C. Ross, and B. Harvey. 1993. "Effectiveness of Vitamin A Supplementation in the Control of Young Child Morbidity and Mortality in Developing Countries." A project of the International Nutrition Program, Department of Nutritional Sciences, University of Toronto.

Behrman, Jere R. 1990. *The Action of Human Resources and Poverty on One Another: What We Have Yet to Learn.* Living Standards Measurement Study Working Paper 74. Washington, D.C.: World Bank.

————. 1992. "The Effect of Structural Adjustment on Food Policy and Nutrition." Paper presented at the International Union for the Scientific Study of Population (IUSSP) seminar on the Demographic Consequences of Structural Adjustment in Latin America, Belo Horizonte, Brazil, September 29–October 2.

Behrman, Jere R., David Ross, Richard Sabot, and Matthew Tropp. 1991. "Improving the Quality versus Increasing the Quantity of Schooling." University of Pennsylvania, Philadelphia, Pa.

Bellinger, D., A. Leviton, C. Waternaux, H. Needleman, and M. Rabinowitz. 1987. "Longitudinal Analyses of Prenatal and Postnatal Lead Exposure and Early Cognitive Development." *New England Journal of Medicine* 316: 1037–43.

Benefo, Kofi, and T. Paul Schultz. 1992. "Fertility and Child Mortality in Côte d'Ivoire and Ghana." World Bank, African Technical Department, Population, Health, and Nutrition Division, Washington, D.C.

Bennett, Sara. 1992. "Promoting the Private Sector: A Review of Developing Country Trends." *Health Policy and Planning* 7(2): 97–110.

Berg, Alan. 1987. *Malnutrition: What Can Be Done? Lessons from World Bank Experience.* Baltimore, Md.: Johns Hopkins University Press.

Berg, Elliot, and Graeme Hunter. 1992. "Social Costs of Adjustment: The Case of Latin America and the Caribbean." Prepared for the U.S. Agency for International Development. Development Alternatives, Inc., Bethesda, Md.

Berkley, Seth, and Dean Jamison. 1991. "Summary Report." Conference on the Health of School-Age Children, sponsored by the United Nations Development Programme and the Rockefeller Foundation, Bellagio, Italy, August 12–16.

Bertrand, Jane T., and Judith Brown. 1992. "Family Planning Success in Two Cities in Zaire." Policy, Research, and External Affairs Working Paper Series 1042. World Bank, Population and Human Resources Department, Washington, D.C.

Bhargava, Alok. 1992. "Malnutrition and the Role of Individual Variation with Evidence from India and the Philippines." *Journal of the Royal Statistical Society* 155.

Bhargava, Alok, and Jiang Yu. 1992. "A Longitudinal Analysis of Infant and Child Mortality Rate in Africa and Non-African Developing Countries." Background paper prepared for the Africa Health Study. World Bank, Africa Technical Department, Washington, D.C.

Birdsall, Nancy. Forthcoming. "Pragmatism, Robin Hood, and Other Themes: Good Government and Social Well-Being in Developing Countries." In Lincoln C. Chen, Arthur Kleinman, and Norma C. P. Ware, eds., *Health and Social Science in International Perspective.* Harvard Series on Population and International Health. Cambridge, Mass.: Harvard University Press.

Birdsall, Nancy, and William McGreevey. 1983. "Women, Poverty and Development." In Mayra Buvinic, Margaret Lycette, and William Paul McGreevey, eds., *Women and Poverty in the Third World.* Baltimore, Md.: Johns Hopkins University Press.

Bitran, Ricardo A., and D. Keith McInnes. 1993. *The Demand for Health Care in Latin America: Lessons from the Dominican Republic and El Salvador.* Economic Development Institute Seminar Paper 46. Washington, D.C.: World Bank.

Black, Douglas, J. N. Morris, Cyril Smith, Peter Townsend, and Nick Davidson, eds. 1982. *The Black Report.* New York: Penguin Books.

Black, Robert E. 1991. "Would Control of Childhood Infectious Diseases Reduce Malnutrition?" *Acta Paediatrica Scandinavica* (Supplement) 374: 133–40.

Blendon, Robert J., R. Leitman, I. Morrison, and K. Donelan. 1990. "Satisfaction with Health Systems in 10 Nations." *Health Affairs* 9(2): 185–92.

Bloom, Barry R., and Christopher J. L. Murray. 1992. "Tuberculosis: Commentary on a Reemergent Killer." *Science* 257(21 August): 1055–64.

Bloom, David E., and Joyce V. Lyons, eds. 1993. *Economic Implications of AIDS in Asia.* UNDP Regional Progamme Division (Regional Bureau for Asia and the Pacific). New Delhi: HIV/AIDS Regional Project.

Bloom, Gerald. 1989. "The Right Equipment . . . in Working Order." *World Health Forum* 10(1): 3–10.

Blum, D., R. N. Emeh, S. R. A. Huttly, O. Dosunmu-Ogunbi, N. Okeke, M. Ajala, J. I. Okoro, C. Akujobi, B. R. Kirkwood, and R. G. Feachem. 1990. "The Imo State Nigeria Drinking Water Supply and Sanitation Project. 1. Description of the Project, Evaluation Methods, and Impact on Intervening Variables." *Transactions of the Royal Society of Tropical Medicine and Hygiene* 84: 309–15.

Bobadilla, José-Luis, Julio Frenk, Tomas Freijka, Rafael Lozano, and Claudio Stern. Forthcoming. "The Epidemiological Transition and Health Priorities." In Dean T. Jamison, W. Henry Mosley, Anthony R. Measham, and José-Luis Bobadilla, eds., *Disease Control Priorities in Developing Countries.* New York: Oxford University Press.

Bobak, M. 1993. "Air Pollution and Health in Central and Eastern Europe: How Bad Is the Problem?" London School of Hygiene and Tropical Medicine.

Bobak, M., and R. G. A. Feachem. 1992. "Health Status in the Czech and Slovak Federal Republic." *Health Policy and Planning* 7: 234–42.

Bobak, M., and D. A. Leon. 1992. "Air Pollution and Infant Mortality in the Czech Republic, 1986–88." *Lancet* 340: 1010–14.

Boissiere, M., J. B. Knight, and R. H. Sabot. 1985. "Earning, Schooling, Ability and Cognitive Skills." *American Economic Review* 75: 1026–30.

Boring, Catherine C., Teresa S. Squires, and Tony Tong. 1993. "Cancer Statistics 1993." *CA—Cancer Journal for Clinicians* 43 (Jan.–Feb.): 7–26.

Bos, Eduard, My T. Vu, Ann Levin, and Rodolfo A. Bulatao. 1992. *World Population Projections 1992–93 Edition: Estimates and Projections with Related Demographic Statistics.* Baltimore, Md.: Johns Hopkins University Press.

Bouis, Howarth E. 1990. "The Determinants of Household-Level Demand for Micronutrients: An Analysis for Philippine Farm Households." International Food Policy Research Institute, Washington, D.C.

Bourdon, Jean, François Orivel, and Jean Perrot. 1993. "Peut-on Apprecier un Lien entre les Acquisitions Scolaires et la Santé: Le Cas de l'Enseignement Primaire au Tchad." Paper presented at meetings of the Association Français de Sciences Economiques, Dijon, May 27–28.

Bradley, Christine. 1988. "How Can We Help Rural Beaten Wives? Some Suggestions from Papua New Guinea." Paper presented at International Women's Aid Conference, Cardiff, Wales.

Bradley, David John, Sandy Cairncross, Trudy Harpham, and Carolyn Stephens. 1992. A Review of Environmental Health Impacts in Developing Country Cities. Urban Management Program Paper 6. Washington, D.C.: World Bank.

Brenzel, Logan. 1990. "The Costs of EPI: Lessons Learned from Cost and Cost-Effectiveness Studies of Immunization Programs." Resources for Child Health (REACH) Project. John Snow, Inc., Arlington, Va.

Briscoe, John. 1992. "Poverty and Water Supply: How to Move Forward." Finance and Development 29: 16–19.

Brook, Robert H., and Kathleen N. Lohr. 1986. "Will We Need to Ration Effective Health Care?" Issues in Science and Technology 3(1): 68–77.

Brotowasisto, Oscar Gish, Ridwan Malik, and Paramita Sudharto. 1988. "Health Care Financing in Indonesia." Health Policy and Planning 3(2): 131–40.

Bruce, Judith, and Cynthia B. Lloyd. 1992. "Finding the Ties That Bind: Beyond Headship and Household." Working Paper 41. Population Council, New York.

Bruley, Mark E. 1991. "Global Trends in Healthcare Technology." Keynote address at Health-Tech 91: Health Technology in Developing Countries: Assessment, Procurement, and Maintenance, Yaoundé, Cameroon, March 11. ECRI, Plymouth Meeting, Pa.

Cairncross, A. M. 1990. "Health Impacts in Developing Countries: New Evidence and New Prospects." Journal of the Institution of Water and Environmental Management 4(6): 571–77.

Cairncross, Sandy. 1992. "Sanitation and Water Supply: Practical Lessons from the Decade." UNDP–World Bank Water and Sanitation Discussion Paper Series 9. World Bank, Washington, D.C.

Caldwell, J. C. 1986. "Routes to Low Mortality in Poor Countries." Population and Development Review 12(2): 171–220.

CAMVAC (Centro de Apoyo a Mujeres Violadas). 1985. "Carpeta de Información Básica para la Atención Solidaria y Feminista a Mujeres Violadas." Mexico City.

Caplan, David. 1985. "Consumption, Production, World Trade and Industry Structure." World Bank, Industry and Energy Department, Washington, D.C.

Cassen, Robert H., and others. 1986. Does Aid Work? New York: Oxford University Press.

Castro, E. B., and K. M. Mokate. 1988. "Malaria and Its Socioeconomic Meaning: The Study of Cunday in Colombia." In A. N. Herrin and P. L. Rosenfield, eds., Economics, Health and Tropical Diseases. Manila: School of Economics, University of the Philippines.

Chapman, R. S., J. L. Mumford, X. He, D. B. Harris, R. Yang, and W. Jiang. 1989. "Assessing Indoor Air Pollution Exposure and Lung Cancer Risk in Xuan Wei, China." Journal of the American College of Toxicology 8(5): 941–48.

Chen, B. H., C. J. Hong, M. R. Pandey, and K. R. Smith. 1990. "Indoor Air Pollution in Developing Countries." World Health Statistics Quarterly 43: 127–38.

Cleland, John. 1990. "Maternal Education and Child Survival: Further Evidence and Explanations." In John Caldwell, Sally Findley, Pat Caldwell, Gigi Santow, Wendy Cosford, Jennifer Braid, and Daphne Broers-Freeman, eds., What We Know about Health Transition: The Cultural, Social, and Behavioural Determinants of Health. Health Transition Series, Vol. I. Canberra: Australian National University.

Coale, Ansley J., and Paul Demeny, with Barbara Vaughan. 1983. Regional Model Life Tables and Stable Populations, 2d ed. New York: Academic Press.

Comanor, William S. 1986. "The Political Economy of the Pharmaceutical Industry." Journal of Economic Literature 24 (September): 1178–1217.

Commission on Health Research for Development. 1990. Health Research: Essential Link to Equity in Development. New York: Oxford University Press.

Conly, G. N. 1975. The Impact of Malaria on Economic Development: A Case Study. Scientific Publication 297. Washington, D.C.: Pan American Health Organization.

Council on Scientific Affairs, American Medical Association. 1992. "Violence against Women: Relevance for Medical Practitioners." JAMA: Journal of the American Medical Association 267(23): 3184–89.

COVAC. 1990. "Evaluación de Proyecto para Educación, Capacitación, y Atención a Mujeres y Menores de Edad en Materia de Violencia Sexual, Enero a Diciembre 1990." Asociación Mexicana Contra la Violencia a las Mujeres, Mexico City.

Cumper, George, and Patrick Vaughan. 1985. "Community Health Aides at the Crossroads," World Health Forum 6: 365–67.

Curtis, C. F. 1992. "Spraying Bed-Nets with Deltamethrin in Sichuan, China." Tropical Diseases Bulletin 89(8): R1–R6.

Davis, Karen, Gerard F. Anderson, Diane Rowland, and Earl P. Steinberg. 1990. Health Care Cost Containment. Johns Hopkins Studies in Health Care Finance and Administration. Baltimore, Md.: Johns Hopkins University Press.

De Geyndt, Willy. 1991. Managing Health Expenditures under National Health Insurance: The Case of Korea. World Bank Technical Paper 156. Washington, D.C.

Diamond, Peter. 1992. "Organizing the Health Insurance Market." Econometrica 60(6): 1233–54.

Doll, Richard. 1992. "Health and the Environment in the 1990s." American Journal of Public Health 82: 933–43.

Downing, A. J. 1991. "Pedestrian Safety in Developing Countries." In Proceedings of the Vulnerable Road User: International Conference on Traffic Safety, New Delhi, January 27–30. New Delhi: Macmillan India.

Drèze, Jean, and Amartya Sen. 1989. Hunger and Public Action. WIDER Studies in Development Economics. Oxford, U.K.: Clarendon Press.

Dunn, D. T., M. L. Newell, A. E. Ades, and C. S. Peckham. 1992. "Risk of Human Immunodeficiency Transmission through Breastfeeding." Lancet 340: 585–88.

Edwards, Sebastian. Forthcoming. "Latin America a Decade after the Debt Crisis." World Bank, Latin America and the Caribbean Regional Office, Office of the Chief Economist, Washington, D.C.

El Batawi, M. A., and C. Husbumrer. 1987. "Epidemiological Approach to Planning and Development of Occupational Health Services at a National Level." International Journal of Epidemiology 16: 288–92.

185

Elliott, Paul. 1988. ''The Intersalt Study: An Addition to the Evidence on Salt and Blood Pressure, and Some Implications.'' *Journal of Human Hypertension* 3: 289–98.

Elo, T. Irma. 1992. ''Utilization of Maternal Health-Care Services in Peru: The Role of Women's Education.'' *Health Transition Review* 2(1): 49–69.

Engle, Patrice L. 1991. ''Mother's Work and Child Care in Peri-Urban Guatemala.'' *Child Development* 62.

Enthoven, Alain C. 1988. *Theory and Practice of Managed Competition in Health Care Finance.* Amsterdam: North-Holland.

———. 1989. ''What Can Europeans Learn from Americans?'' *Health Care Financing Review*, annual supplement (December) 49–63.

Enthoven, Alain, and Carol Vorhaus. 1992. ''Teaching Note: The Physician Personnel Industry.'' Stanford University Graduate School of Business, Palo Alto, Calif.

Esrey, S. A., J. B. Potash, L. Roberts, and C. Shiff. 1991. ''Effects of Improved Water Supply and Sanitation on Ascariasis, Diarrhoea, Dracunculiasis, Hookworm Infection, Schistosomiasis, and Trachoma.'' *Bulletin of the World Health Organization* 69(5): 609–21.

Evans, John R. 1981. *Measurement and Management in Medicine and Health Services: Training Needs and Opportunities.* New York: Rockefeller Foundation.

Evans, John R., Karen Lashman Hall, and Jeremy Warford. 1981. ''Health Care in the Developing World: Problems of Scarcity and Choice.'' Shattuck Lecture. *New England Journal of Medicine* 305 (November): 1117–27.

Evans, Robert G., Morris L. Barer, and Roberta J. Labelle. 1988. ''Fee Controls as Cost Control: Tales from the Frozen North.'' *Milbank Memorial Fund Quarterly* 66(1): 1–64.

Ewbank, Douglas C., and Samuel H. Preston. 1990. ''Personal Health Behaviour and the Decline in Infant and Child Mortality: The United States, 1900–1930.'' In John Caldwell, Sally Findley, Pat Caldwell, Gigi Santow, Wendy Cosford, Jennifer Braid, and Daphne Broers-Freeman, eds., *What We Know about Health Transition: The Cultural, Social, and Behavioural Determinants of Health.* Health Transition Series, Vol. I. Canberra: Australian National University.

Faiz, Asif, Christopher Weaver, Kumares Sinha, Michael Walsh, and Jose Carbajo. Forthcoming. *Air Pollution from Motor Vehicles: Issues and Options for Developing Countries.* Washington, D.C.: World Bank and UNEP.

Faúndes, Anibal, and José Guilherme Cecatti. 1993. ''Which Policy for Caesarian Sections in Brazil? An Analysis of Trends and Consequences.'' *Health Policy and Planning* 8(1): 33–42.

Fauveau, V., and T. Blanchet. 1989. ''Epidemiology and Cause of Deaths among Women in Rural Bangladesh.'' *International Journal of Epidemiology* 18(1): 139–45.

Feachem, R. G. 1988. ''Epidemiology and Tropical Public Health: Current and Future Contributions with Particular Emphasis on the Role of the London School of Hygiene and Tropical Medicine.'' *Transactions of the Royal Society of Tropical Medicine and Hygiene* 82: 790–98.

Feachem, Richard G., and Dean T. Jamison. 1991. *Disease and Mortality in Sub-Saharan Africa.* New York: Oxford University Press.

Feachem, R. G., E. Burns, S. Cairncross, A. Cronin, P. Cross, D. Curtis, M. Khalid Kahn, D. Lamb, and H. Southall. 1978. *Water, Health and Development: An Interdisciplinary Evaluation.* London: Tri-Med Books.

Feachem, Richard G. A., Tord Kjellstrom, Christopher J. L. Murray, Mead Over, and Margaret A. Phillips, eds. 1992. *The Health of Adults in the Developing World.* Washington, D.C.: World Bank.

Fenner, Frank, Donald A. Henderson, Isao Arita, Zdenek Jezek, and Ivan D. Ladnyi. 1988. *Smallpox and Its Eradication.* Geneva: World Health Organization.

Foster, A. 1987. ''Cataract Blindness in Africa.'' *Ophthalmic Surgery* 18: 384–88.

Foster, Stanley O., Deborah McFarland, and Meredith John. Forthcoming. ''Measles.'' In Dean T. Jamison, W. Henry Mosley, Anthony R. Measham, and José-Luis Bobadilla, eds., *Disease Control Priorities in Developing Countries.* New York: Oxford University Press.

Foster, Susan D. 1990. ''Improving the Supply and Use of Essential Drugs in Sub-Saharan Africa.'' Policy, Research, and External Affairs Working Paper Series 456. World Bank, Population and Human Resources Department, Washington, D.C.

———. 1991. ''Supply and Use of Essential Drugs in Sub-Saharan Africa: Some Issues and Possible Solutions.'' *Social Science Medicine* 32(11): 1201–18.

Free, Michael. 1991. ''Health Technologies for the Developing World: Addressing the Unmet Needs.'' Program for Appropriate Technology in Health, Seattle, Washington.

Frenk, Julio, J.-L. Bobadilla, J. Sepúlveda, and M. Lopez Cervantes. 1989. ''Health Transition in Middle-Income Countries: New Challenges for Health Care.'' *Health Policy and Planning* 4:29–39.

Frenk, Julio, Javier Alagon, Gustavo Nigenda, Alejandro Muñoz-del Rio, Cecilia Robledo, Luis A. Vaquez-Segovia, and Catalin Ramirez-Cuadra. 1991. ''Patterns of Medical Employment: A Survey of Imbalances in Urban Mexico.'' *American Journal of Public Health* 81 (January): 123–29.

Fuchs, V. R. 1978. ''The Supply of Surgeons and the Demand for Operations.'' *Journal of Human Resources* 13 (supp.): 35–56.

———. 1979. ''Economics, Health and Post-Industrial Society.'' *Milbank Memorial Fund Quarterly* 57(2): 153–82.

Garber, Alan M., and Victor R. Fuchs. 1991. ''The Expanding Role of Technology Assessment in Health Policy.'' *Stanford Law and Policy Review* (Fall): 203–09.

Gelijns, Annetine C., and Ethan A. Halm, eds. 1991. *Medical Innovation at the Crossroads.* Vol. 2: *The Changing Economics of Medical Technology.* Washington, D.C.: National Academy Press.

Gerdtham, Ulf-G., Jes Søgaard, Fredrik Andersson, and Bengt Jönsson. 1992. ''An Econometric Analysis of Health Care Expenditure: A Cross-Section Study of the OECD Countries.'' *Journal of Health Economics* 11: 63–84.

Gertler, Paul, and Jacques van der Gaag. 1990. *The Willingness to Pay for Medical Care: Evidence from Two Developing Countries.* Baltimore, Md.: Johns Hopkins University Press.

Ghana Health Assessment Project Team. 1981. ''Quantitative Methods of Assessing Health Impact of Different Diseases in Less Developed Countries.'' *International Journal of Epidemiology* 10(1): 73–80.

Glewwe, Paul. 1991. *Are Rates of Return to Schooling Estimated from Wage Data Relevant Guides for Government Investments in Education? Evidence from a Developing Country,* Living Standards Measurement Study Working Paper 76. Washington D.C.: World Bank.

Godal, Tore. 1993. "Introduction." *Tropical Disease Research, Progress 1991–92.* Eleventh Programme Report of the UNDP/World Bank/WHO Special Programme for Research and Training in Tropical Diseases. Geneva: World Health Organization.

Gomes-Neto, J. B., and E. A. Hanushek. 1991. "The Causes and Effects of Grade Repetition: Evidence from Brazil." Working Paper 295. Rochester Center for Economic Research, Rochester, N.Y.

Goodgame, R. W. 1990. "AIDS in Uganda: Clinical and Social Features." *New England Journal of Medicine* 323: 383–89.

Griffin, Charles C. 1992. *Health Care in Asia: A Comparative Study of Cost and Financing.* World Bank Regional and Sectoral Studies. Washington, D.C.

Grosh, Margaret E., ed. 1992. "From Platitudes to Practice: Targeting Social Programs in Latin America." Vol. 1, Synthesis. LAC Regional Studies Program Report 21. World Bank, Washington, D.C.

Grossman, Michael. 1975. "The Correlation between Health and Schooling." In Nestor E. Terleckyj, ed., *Household Production and Consumption.* New York: Columbia University Press.

Gutierrez-Fisac, Juan L., Enrique Regidor, and Elena Ronda. 1992. "Occupational Accidents and Alcohol Consumption in Spain." *International Journal of Epidemiology* 21(6): 1114–19.

Halbwachs, Hans. 1992. "Need for Spares: Excuse or Reality?" Deutsche Gesellschaft für Technische Zusammenarbeit (GTZ), Division of Health, Population, and Nutrition, Eschborn, Germany.

Halstead, Scott, Peter Tugwell, and Kathryn Bennet. 1991. "The International Clinical Epidemiology Network (INCLEN): A Progress Report." *Journal of Clinical Epidemiology* 44: 579–89.

Halstead, Scott B., Julia A. Walsh, and Kenneth S. Warren, eds. 1985. *Good Health at Low Cost.* Proceedings of a conference at Bellagio, Italy, sponsored by the Rockefeller Foundation, April 29–May 3.

Handwerker, W. Penn. 1991. "Gender Power Difference May Be STD Risk Factors for the Next Generation." Paper presented at the 90th Annual Meeting of the American Anthropological Association, Chicago, Ill.

Hecht, Robert, Catherine Overholt, and R. Hopkins Holmberg. 1993. "Improving the Implementation of Cost Recovery for Health: Lessons from Zimbabwe." *Health Policy* 25(1), July.

Heise, Lori. 1993. "Violence Against Women: The Missing Agenda." In Marge Koblinsky, Judith Timyan, and Jill Gay, eds., *The Health of Women: A Global Perspective.* Boulder, Colo.: Westview.

Heller, Peter S., and Jack Diamond. 1990. *International Comparisons of Government Expenditure Revisited: The Developing Countries, 1975–86.* Occasional Paper 69. Washington, D.C.: International Monetary Fund.

Hill, Kenneth, and Alberto Palloni. 1992. "Demographic Responses to Economic Shocks: The Case of Latin America." In *Proceedings of the Peopling of the Americas Conference, Veracruz, Mexico.* Liège: International Union for the Scientific Study of Population.

Hlady, W. Gary, John V. Bennett, Aziz R. Samadi, Jahanara Begum, Abdul Hafez, Aminul I. Tarafdar, and John R. Boring. 1992. "Neonatal Tetanus in Rural Bangladesh: Risk Factors and Toxoid Efficacy." *American Journal of Public Health* 82(10): 1365–69.

Hobcraft, J. N., ed., 1991. *Proceedings of the Demographic and Health Surveys World Conference, Washington, D.C., 1991.* Vol. 2: 1157–82.

———. 1993. "Women's Education, Child Welfare and Child Survival: A Review of the Evidence." *Health Transition Review* 3(2).

Hoddinott, John, and Lawrence Haddad. 1991. "Household Expenditures, Child Anthropometric Status and the Intrahousehold Division of Income: Evidence from the Côte d'Ivoire." Oxford University, Unit for the Study of African Economics, Oxford, U.K.

Holly, John, and David Lee. 1992. "Costa Rica: Proyecto Reforma Salud—Estudio de Financiamiento, Adquisición y Distribución de Farmacéuticos y Materiales Médicos." Management Sciences for Health, Boston, Mass.

Hosken, Fran. 1988. "International Seminar: Female Circumcision—Strategies to Bring About Change." *Women's International Network News* 14(3): 24–37.

Hsiao, William. 1992. "Health Care Finance and Health Insurance Mechanisms in Developing Countries." Paper presented at WHO Workshop on Health Economics, Geneva, June 25.

Hughes, Robert G., Sandra S. Hunt, and Harold S. Luft. 1987. "Effects of Surgeon Volume and Hospital Volume on Quality of Care in Hospitals." *Medical Care* 25(6): 489–503.

Humphrey, J. H., K. P. West, Jr., and Alfred Sommer. 1992. "Vitamin A Deficiency and Attributable Mortality among Under-5-Year-Olds." *Bulletin of the World Health Organization* 70(2): 225–32.

Hurst, Jeremy. 1992. *The Reform of Health Care: A Comparative Analysis of Seven OECD Countries.* Paris: Organization for Economic Cooperation and Development.

Huttly, S. R. A. 1990. "The Impact of Inadequate Sanitary Conditions on Health in Developing Countries." *World Health Statistics Quarterly* 43: 118–26.

IDB (Inter-American Development Bank). 1988. "Summary of the Ex-Post Evaluations of Public Health Programs." IDB, Operations Evaluation Office, Washington, D.C.

Ikegami, Naoki. 1992. "The Economics of Health Care in Japan." *Science* 258 (23 October): 614–18.

Ingram, Gregory. 1992. "Social Indicators and Productivity Convergence in Developing Countries." Policy, Research, and External Affairs Working Paper Series 894. World Bank, Development Economics Research Advisory Staff, Washington, D.C.

Institute of Medicine. 1988. *The Future of Public Health.* Washington, D.C.: National Academy Press.

———. 1992. *Emerging Infections: Microbial Threats to Health in the United States.* Washington, D.C.: National Academy Press.

International Monetary Fund. Various years. *Government Finance Statistics.* Washington, D.C.

Jacobs, William R., Jr., Raúl G. Barletta, Rupa Udani, John Chan, Gary Kalkut, Gabriel Sosne, Tobias Kiese, Gary J. Sarkis, Graham F. Hatfull, and Barry R. Bloom. 1993. "Rapid Assessment of Drug Susceptibilities of *Mycobacterium tuberculosis* by Means of Luciferase Reporter Phages." *Science* 260 (May): 819–22.

Jamison, Dean T. Forthcoming. "Disease Control Priorities in Developing Countries: An Oveview." In Dean T. Jamison, W. Henry Mosley, Anthony R. Measham, and José-Luis Bobadilla, eds., *Disease Control Priorities in Developing Countries.* New York: Oxford University Press.

Jamison, Dean T., and Joanne Leslie. 1990. "Health and Nutrition Considerations in Education Planning: The Cost and Effectiveness of School-Based Interventions." *Food and Nutrition Bulletin (International)* 12(3): 204–14.

Jamison, Dean T., and Peter Moock. 1984. "Farmer Education and Farm Efficiency in Nepal: The Role of Schooling, Extension Services, and Cognitive Skills." *World Development* 12: 67–86.

Jamison, Dean T., W. Henry Mosley, Anthony R. Measham, and José-Luis Bobadilla, eds. Forthcoming. *Disease Control Priorities in Developing Countries.* New York: Oxford University Press.

Jarousse, Jean-Pierre, and Alain Mingat. 1992. "Options for Accelerated Development of Primary Education in the Sahel." World Bank, Sahelian Department, Population and Human Resources Operations Division, Washington, D.C.

Javitt, Jonathan C. Forthcoming. "Cataract." In Dean T. Jamison, W. Henry Mosley, Anthony R. Measham, and José-Luis Bobadilla, eds., *Disease Control Priorities in Developing Countries.* New York: Oxford University Press.

Jeyaratnam, J. 1985. "Health Problems of Pesticide Usage in the Third World." *British Journal of Industrial Medicine* 42: 505–06.

Jimenez, Emmanuel. 1987. *Pricing Policy in the Social Sectors.* Washington, D.C.: World Bank.

Johnston, Ian. 1992. "Action to Reduce Road Casualties." *World Health Forum* 13: 154–62.

Jonsson, Bengt. 1989. "What Can Americans Learn from Europeans?" *Health Care Financing Review*, annual supplement (December) 79–93.

Kakwani, Nanak, Elene Makonnen, and Jacques van der Gaag. 1990. "Structural Adjustment and Living Conditions in Developing Countries." Policy, Research, and External Affairs Working Paper Series 467. World Bank, Population and Human Resources Department, Washington, D.C.

Kanji, Najmi, Anita Hardon, Jan Willem Harnmeijer, Masuma Mamdani, and Gill Walt. 1992. *Drugs Policy in Developing Countries.* London: Zed Books Ltd., in association with the Danish International Development Agency (DANIDA).

Katabira, E., and R. W. Goodgame. 1989. "AIDS Care: Diagnostic and Treatment Strategies for Health Workers." Uganda Ministry of Health, Health Education Printing Unit, Kampala.

Kennedy, Eileen. 1992. "Effects of Gender of Head of Household on Women's and Children's Nutritional Status." Paper presented at workshop on Effects of Policy and Programs on Women, January 16. International Food Policy Research Institute, Washington, D.C.

Keusch, Gerald T., and Nevin Scrimshaw. 1986. "Control of Infection to Reduce Malnutrition." *Reviews of Infectious Diseases* 8(2): 298–312.

King, Elizabeth M., and M. Anne Hill. 1993. "Overview." In Elizabeth M. King and M. Anne Hill, eds., *Women's Education in Developing Countries: Barriers, Benefits, and Policies.* Baltimore, Md.: Johns Hopkins University Press.

Koop, C. Everett. 1989. "Violence against Women: A Global Problem." Address to the Pan American Health Organization, Washington, D.C., May 22.

Korte, R., Heide Richter, F. Merkle, and H. Gorgen. 1992. "Financing Health Services in Sub-Saharan Africa: Options for Decisionmakers during Adjustment." *Social Science and Medicine* 34(1): 1–9.

Koss, Mary, Paul Koss, and Joy Woodruff. 1991. "Deleterious Effects of Criminal Victimization on Women's Health and Medical Utilization." *Archives of Internal Medicine* 151: 342–47.

Kutzin, Joseph, and Howard Barnum. 1992. "Institutional Features of Health Insurance Programs and Their Effects on Developing Country Health Systems." *International Journal of Health Planning and Management* 7: 51-72.

Laing, R. O. 1990. "Rational Drug Use: An Unsolved Problem." *Tropical Doctor* 20 (July): 101–03.

Lancet. 1992. "Environmental Pollution: It Kills Trees, But Does It Kill People?" 340: 821–22.

Leslie, Joanne. 1987. "Interactions of Malnutrition and Diarrhea: A Review of Research." In J. Price Gittinger, Joanne Leslie, and Caroline Hoisington, eds., *Food Policy: Integrating Supply, Distribution, and Consumption.* Baltimore, Md.: Johns Hopkins University Press.

———. 1989a. "Women's Time: A Factor in the Use of Child Survival Technologies." *Health Policy and Planning* 4(1): 1–16.

———. 1989b. "Women's Work and Child Nutrition in the Third World." In Joanne Leslie and Michael Paolisso, eds., *Women, Work, and Child Welfare in the Third World.* Boulder, Colo.: Westview.

Leslie, Joanne, Dean T. Jamison, and Philip Musgrove. Forthcoming. "Protein-Energy Balance in the Diet and Human Growth." World Bank, Washington, D.C.

Levin, Henry M., Ernesto Pollitt, Rae Galloway, and Judith McGuire. Forthcoming. "Micronutrient Deficiency Disorders." In Dean T. Jamison, W. Henry Mosley, Anthony R. Measham, and José-Luis Bobadilla, eds., *Disease Control Priorities in Developing Countries.* New York: Oxford University Press.

Lewis, Maureen A., and Clover Parker. 1991. "Policy and Implementation of User Fees in Jamaican Public Hospitals." *Health Policy* 18: 57–85.

Lindenbaum, S., M. Chakraborty, and M. Elias. 1985. *The Influence of Maternal Education on Infant and Child Mortality in Bangladesh.* Special Publication 23. Dhaka: International Center for Diarrhoeal Disease Research.

Litvack, Jennie, and Claude Bodart. 1993. "User Fees and Improved Quality of Health Care Equals Improved Access: Results of a Field Experiment in Cameroon." *Social Science and Medicine* 37(3).

Lockheed, Marlaine E., Dean T. Jamison, and Lawrence Lau. 1980. "Farmer Education and Farm Efficiency: A Survey." *Economic Development and Cultural Change* 29(1): 37–76.

Lockheed, Marlaine E., Adriaan M. Verspoor, and associates. 1991. *Improving Primary Education in Developing Countries.* New York: Oxford University Press.

Louat, Frederic, Margaret E. Grosh, and Jacques van der Gaag. 1992. *Welfare Implications of Female Headship in Jamaican Households.* Living Standards Measurement Study Working Paper 96. Washington, D.C.: World Bank.

Luft, Harold S. 1978. *Poverty and Health. Economic Causes and Consequences of Health Problems.* Cambridge, Mass.: Ballinger.

Lutter, Chessa K., Jean-Pierre Habicht, Juan A. Rivera, and Reynaldo Martorell. 1992. "The Relationship between Energy Intake and Diarrheal Disease in Their Effects on Child Growth: Biological Model, Evidence, and Implications for Public Health Policy." *Food and Nutrition Bulletin* 14(1): 36–42.

Mackay, Judith. 1993. *The State of Health Atlas*. New York: Simon and Schuster.

Management Sciences for Health. 1992. *International Drug Price Indicator Guide 1991*. Boston, Mass.

Mardones, Francisco, and Rafael Zamora. 1989. "Evaluaciones Socio-económicas del Programa Nacional de Alimentación Complementaria: ¿Que es lo que se ha hecho?" *Revista Chilena de Nutrición* 17(3): 169–74.

Martorell, Reynaldo, Juan Rivera, Haley Kaplowitz, and Ernesto Pollitt. 1992. "Long-Term Consequences of Growth Retardation during Early Childhood." Paper presented at the Sixth International Congress of Auxology, Madrid. Amsterdam: Elsevier Science Publishers.

Max, Emmanuel, and Donald S. Shepard. 1989. "Productivity Loss Due to Deformity from Leprosy in India." *International Journal of Leprosy* 57(2).

Maxwell, C. A., C. F. Curtis, H. Haji, S. Kisumku, A. I. Thalib, and S. A. Yahya. 1990. "Control of Bancroftian Filariasis by Integrating Therapy with Vector Control Using Polystyrene Beads in Wet Pit Latrines." *Transactions of the Royal Society of Tropical Medicine and Hygiene* 84: 709–14.

McGreevey, William. 1990. *Social Security in Latin America: Issues and Options for the World Bank*. World Bank Discussion Paper 110. Washington, D.C.

McGuire, Judith, and Barry M. Popkin. 1990. "Beating the Zero-Sum Game: Women and Nutrition in the Third World: Part 2." *Food and Nutrition Bulletin (International)* 12: 3–11.

McKeown, Thomas. 1976. *The Modern Rise of Population*. London: Edward Arnold.

McPake, Barbara, Kara Hanson, and Anne Mills. 1992. "Experience to Date of Implementing the Bamako Initiative: A Review and Five Country Case Studies." London School of Hygiene and Tropical Medicine, Department of Public Health and Policy.

Meerman, Jacob. 1980. "An Analysis in Development Perspective of Bolivia's Largest Public Enterprises: COMIBOL, YPFB, and ENAF." World Bank, Development Economics Department, Washington, D.C.

Mesa-Lago, Carmelo. 1991. *Social Security and Prospects for Equity in Latin America*. World Bank Discussion Paper 140. Washington, D.C.

———. 1992. "Health Care for the Poor in Latin America and the Caribbean." PAHO Scientific Publication 539. Pan American Health Organization, Washington, D.C.

Mills, Anne, Patrick J. Vaughan, Duane L. Smith, and Iraj Tabizzadeh, eds. 1990. *Health System Decentralization: Concepts, Issues and Country Experience*. Geneva: World Health Organization.

Minhas, B. S. 1991. *Educational Deprivation and Its Role as a Spoiler of Access to Better Life in India*. New Delhi: Indian Statistical Institute.

Monteiro, Carlos Augusto. 1988. *Saúde e Nutrição das Crianças de São Paulo*. São Paulo: Editora Hucitec.

Moses, S., F. A. Plummer, E. N. Ngugi, N. J. Nagelkerke, A. O. Anzala, and J. O. Ndinya-Achola. 1991. "Controlling HIV in Africa: Effectiveness and Cost of an Intervention in a High-Frequency STD Transmitter Core Group." *AIDS* 5: 407–11.

Moses, S., F. Manji, J. E. Bradley, N. J. Nagelkerke, M. A. Malisa, and F. A. Plummer. 1992. "Impact of User Fees on Attendance at a Referral Centre for Sexually Transmitted Diseases in Kenya." *Lancet* 340: 463–66.

Mosley, W. Henry, and Lincoln Chen, eds. 1984. *Child Survival: Strategies for Research*. New York: Population Council.

MRC (Medical Research Council). 1989. "The Neuropsychological Effects of Lead in Children: A Review of the Research 1984–1988." London.

Muller, O., L. Barugahare, B. Schwartlander, E. Byaruhanga, P. Kataaha, D. Kyeyune, W. Heckmann, and M. Ankrah. 1992. "HIV Prevalence, Attitudes and Behaviour in Clients of a Confidential HIV Testing and Counselling Centre in Uganda." *AIDS* 6: 869–74.

Murray, Christopher, and Alan Lopez, eds. Forthcoming (a). "The Global Burden of Disease." Harvard Center for Population and Development Studies, Cambridge, Mass.

———. Forthcoming (b). "Global Causes of Death Pattern in 1990." *Lancet*.

Murray, Christopher, Karel Styblo, and Annik Rouillon. Forthcoming. "Tuberculosis." In Dean T. Jamison, W. Henry Mosley, Anthony R. Measham, and José-Luis Bobadilla, eds., *Disease Control Priorities in Developing Countries*. New York: Oxford University Press.

Musgrove, Philip. 1986. "Measurement of Equity in Health." *World Health Statistics Quarterly* 39: 325–35.

———. 1988. "Is the Eradication of Polio in the Americas Economically Justified?" *Bulletin of the Pan American Sanitary Bureau* 22(1).

———. 1990. *Fighting Malnutrition: An Evaluation of Brazilian Food and Nutrition Programs*. World Bank Discussion Paper 60. Washington, D.C.

———. 1993. "Relaciones entre la Salud y el Desarrollo." *Boletín de la Oficina Sanitaria Panamericana* 114(2): 115–29.

Natale, Joanne E., Jill G. Joseph, Randall Bergen, Ravilla D. Thulasiraj, and Laxmi Rahmathullah. 1992. "Prevalence of Childhood Disability in a Southern Indian City: Independent Effect of Small Differences in Social Status." *International Journal of Epidemiology* 21(2): 367–72.

National Research Council. 1989. *Diet and Health: Implications for Reducing Chronic Disease Risk*. Washington, D.C.: National Academy Press.

Nazerali, Hanif. 1992. "ZEDAP: A Retrospective 1987–1992." *Essential Drugs Monitor* (Newsletter of WHO Action Programme on Essential Drugs and Vaccines) 13: 6–8.

Needleman, H. L., A. Schell, D. Bellinger, A. Leviton, and E. N. Allred. 1990. "The Long-Term Effects of Exposure to Low Doses of Lead in Childhood: An 11-Year Follow-up Report." *New England Journal of Medicine* 322(2): 83–88.

Newbrander, William. 1987. "Papua New Guinea's Expenditure on Hospitals: Policy and Practice since Independence." *Health Policy and Planning* 2(3): 227–35.

Nokes, C., S. M. Grantham-McGregor, A. W. Sawyer, E. S. Cooper, B. A. Robinson, and D. A. P. Bundy. 1992. "Moderate to Heavy Infections of *Trichuris trichiura* Affect Cognitive Function in Jamaican School Children." *Parasitology* 104: 539–47.

Norboo, T., M. Yahya, N. G. Bruce, J. A. Heady, and K. P. Ball. 1991. "Domestic Pollution and Respiratory Illness in a Himalayan Village." *International Journal of Environmental Health* 20: 749–57.

Nur, E. T. M., and H. A. Mahran. 1988. "The Effect of Health on Agricultural Labor Supply: A Theoretical and Empirical Investigation." In A. N. Herrin and P. L. Rosenfield, eds., *Economics, Health and Tropical Diseases*. Manila: School of Economics, University of the Philippines.

Office of Technology Assessment, U.S. Congress. 1993. *Pharmaceutical R & D: Costs, Risks and Rewards*. Report OTA-H-522, February. Washington, D.C.: U.S. Government Printing Office.

Oganov, Raphael G. 1992. "Cardiovascular Diseases in Russia." Paper presented at Institute of Medicine meeting in Washington, D.C., October. National Research for Preventive Medicine, Moscow.

Omran, Abdel R. 1971. "The Epidemiological Transition: A Theory of the Epidemiology of Population Change." *Milbank Memorial Fund Quarterly* 49(4): Part 1, 509–38.

Over, Mead. 1991. *Economics for Health Sector Analysis: Concepts and Cases*. Economic Development Institute Technical Materials. Washington, D.C.: World Bank.

Over, Mead, and Peter Piot. Forthcoming. "HIV Infection and Sexually Transmitted Diseases." In Dean T. Jamison, W. Henry Mosley, Anthony R. Measham, and José-Luis Bobadilla, eds., *Disease Control Priorities in Developing Countries*. New York: Oxford University Press.

Over, Mead, Randal P. Ellis, Joyce Huber, and Orville Solon. 1992. "The Consequences of Adult Ill-Health." In Richard Feachem and others, eds., *The Health of Adults in the Developing World*. New York: Oxford University Press.

Palloni, Alberto. 1981. "Mortality in Latin America: Emerging Patterns." *Population and Development Review* 7(4): 623–51.

Pandey, M. R., J. S. M. Boleij, K. R. Smith, and E. M. Wafula. 1989. "Indoor Air Pollution in Developing Countries and Acute Respiratory Infection in Children." *Lancet* 1: 427–29.

Pauley, Mark V. 1986. "Taxation, Health Insurance, and Market Failure in the Medical Economy." *Journal of Economic Literature* 24 (June): 629–75.

Pelletier, David L. 1991. "Relationships between Child Anthropometry and Mortality in Developing Countries: Implications for Policy, Programs and Future Research." Cornell Food and Nutrition Policy Program Monograph 12. Cornell University, Ithaca, N.Y.

Phelps, Charles E. 1992. *Health Economics*. New York: Harper-Collins.

Pierce, John P. 1989. "International Comparisons of Trends in Cigarette Smoking Prevalence." *American Journal of Public Health* 79(2): 152–57.

————. 1991. "Progress and Problems in International Public Health Efforts to Reduce Tobacco Usage." *Annual Review of Public Health* 12: 383–400.

Pinstrup-Anderson, Per, Susan Burger, Jean-Pierre Habicht, and Karen Peterson. Forthcoming. "Protein Energy Malnutrition." In Dean T. Jamison, W. Henry Mosley, Anthony R. Measham, and José-Luis Bobabdilla, eds., *Disease Control Priorities in Developing Countries*. New York: Oxford University Press.

Piola, Sérgio Francisco, and Solon Magalhães Vianna. 1991. "Políticas e Prioridades do Sistema Único de Saúde—SUS." World Bank, Latin America Country Department 1, Washington, D.C.

Pitt, Mark M., Mark R. Rosenzweig, and Nazmul Hassan. 1990. "Productivity, Health and Inequality in the Intra-houshold Distribution of Food in Low-Income Countries." *American Economic Review* 80: 1139–56.

Plitcha, Stacey. 1992. "The Effects of Woman Abuse on Health Care Utilization and Health Status: A Literature Review." *Women's Health* (Jacobs Institute of Women's Health) 2(3): 154–61.

Pollitt, Ernesto. 1990. *Malnutrition and Infection in the Classroom*. Paris: UNESCO.

Popkin, Barry M. 1993. "Nutritional Patterns and Modes of Change." *Population and Development Review*.

Population Information Program. 1992. *Population Reports* Series M (11): December.

Population Reference Bureau. 1992a. "Adolescent Sexual Activity and Childbearing in Latin America and the Caribbean: Risks and Consequences." Washington, D.C.

————. 1992b. "Adolescent Women in Sub-Saharan Africa: A Chartbook on Marriage and Childbearing." Washington, DC

Potts, Malcolm, Roy Anderson, and Marie-Claude Boily. 1991. "Slowing the Spread of Human Immunodeficiency Virus in Developing Countries." *Lancet* 338 (September 7).

President's Commission for the Study of Ethical Problems in Medicine and Biomedical and Behavioral Research. 1983. "Securing Access to Health Care." Washington, D.C.

Preston, Samuel H., and Michael R. Haines. 1991. *Fatal Years: Child Mortality in Late Nineteenth-Century America*. Princeton, N.J.: Princeton University Press.

Preston, Samuel H., Nathan Keyfitz, and Robert Schoen. 1972. *Causes of Death: Life Tables for National Populations*. New York: Seminar Press.

Psacharopoulos, George. 1993. "Returns to Education: A Global Update." Policy, Research, and External Affairs Working Paper Series 1067. World Bank, Latin America and the Caribbean Technical Department, Washington, D.C.

Reinhardt, Uwe E. 1989. "The U.S. Health Care Financing and Delivery System: Its Experience and Lessons for Other Nations." International Symposium on Health Care Systems, Taiwan, China.

————. 1991. "Health Manpower Forecasting: The Case of Physician Supply." In Eli Ginzberg, ed., *Health Services Research: Key to Health Policy*. Cambridge, Mass.: Harvard University Press.

Relman, Arnold S. 1993. "The Marketplace in Health Care Reform: The Demographic Limitations of Managed Competition." *New England Journal of Medicine* 328 (January): 148–52.

Reyes, Edna A., and Oscar F. Picazo. 1990. "Health Manpower Employment and Productivity in the Philippines." Working Paper Series 90-19. Philippine Institute for Development Studies, Manila.

Richards, R., and T. Fülöp in collaboration with J. Bannerman, G. Greenholm, J.-J. Guilbert, and M. Wunderlich. 1987. *Innovative Schools for Health Personnel: Report on Ten Schools Belonging to the Network of Community-Oriented Educational Institutions for Health Sciences*. Geneva: World Health Organization.

Riddell, Roger C. 1987. *Foreign Aid Reconsidered*. Baltimore, Md.: Johns Hopkins University Press.

Robertson, Robert L., Andrew J. Hall, Paolo E. Crivelli, Yamoundow Lowe, Hazel M. Inskip, and Sharon K. Snow. 1992. "Cost Effectiveness of Immunizations: The Gambia Revisited." *Health Policy and Planning* 7(2): 111–22.

Rodgers, G. B. 1979. "Income and Inequality as Determinants of Mortality: An International Cross-Section Analysis." *Population Studies* 33(2): 343–51.

Roemer, Milton I. 1991. *National Health Systems of the World*. Vol. 1: *The Countries*. New York: Oxford University Press.

Rogot, E., P. D. Sorlie, and N. J. Johnson. 1992. ''Life Expectancy by Employment Status, Income, and Education in the National Longitudinal Mortality Study.'' *Public Health Reports* 107(4): 457–61.

Romieu, Isabell. 1992. ''Air Pollution and Pneumonia in Young Children.'' Centro Panamericano de Ecología Humana y Salud, Mexico City.

Romieu, Isabell, Henyk Weitzenfeld, and Jacobo Finkelman. 1990. ''Urban Air Pollution in Latin America and the Caribbean: Health Perspectives.'' *World Health Statistics Quarterly* 43(3): 153–67.

Rozynski, Edward M., and Matthew S. Gallivan. 1992. ''The Global Medical Device Market Report.'' Health Industry Manufacturers Association, Washington, D.C.

Rublee, Dale A. 1989. ''Medical Technology in Canada, Germany, and the United States.'' *Health Affairs* (Fall):178–81.

Sagan, L. A., and A. A. Afifi. 1979. ''Health and Economic Development Factors Affecting Mortality.'' In G. T. Goodman and W. D. Rowe, eds., *Energy Risk Management*. London: Academic Press.

Sahn, David E. 1990. *Malnutrition in Côte d'Ivoire: Prevalence and Determinants*. Social Dimensions of Adjustment in Sub-Saharan Africa Working Paper 4. Washington, D.C.: World Bank.

Sanderson, Warren C., and Jee-Peng Tan. Forthcoming. ''Population Issues in Asia: Context, Policies, and Prospects.'' World Bank, Asia Technical Department, Washington, D.C.

Schieber, George J., Jean-Pierre Poullier, and Leslie M. Greenwald. 1992. ''U.S. Health Expenditure Performance: An International Comparison and Data Update.'' *Health Care Financing Review* 11(4): 9–15.

Schmidt, Henk G., Victor R. Neufeld, Zohair M. Nooman, and Toye Ogunbode. 1991. ''Network of Community-Oriented Educational Institutions for the Health Services.'' *Academic Medicine* 66: 259–63.

Schneider, Markus, Rudolf K.-H. Dennerlein, Aynur Kose, and Lea Scholtes. 1992. *Health Care in the EC Member States*. Health Policy Monographs, Vol. 1. Amsterdam: Elsevier.

Schroeder, Steven A. 1984. ''Western European Responses to Physician Oversupply—Lessons for the United States.'' *JAMA: Journal of the American Medical Association* 252 (July): 373–84.

———. 1992. ''Physician Supply and the U.S. Medical Marketplace.'' *Health Affairs* (Spring): 234–43.

Schultz, T. Paul, and Aysit Tansel. 1993. ''Estimates of Wage Returns to Adult Health in Côte d'Ivoire and Ghana.'' Yale University, New Haven, Conn.

Schwab, L. 1987. ''Cost Effective Cataract Surgery in Developing Nations.'' *Ophthalmic Surgery* 12: 307–09.

Schwartz, H., and D. W. Dockery. 1992. ''Increased Mortality in Philadelphia Associated with Daily Air Pollution Concentrations.'' *American Reviews of Respiratory Disease* 145: 600–04.

Scrimshaw, Nevin S. 1986. ''Consequences of Hunger for Individuals and Society.'' In Barry R. Bloom, ed., *Proceedings from the Symposium on the Biomedical Aspects of World Famine. Federation Proceedings* (Federation of American Societies for Experimental Biology) 45(10): 2421–26.

Sen, Amartya R. 1981. *Poverty and Famines: An Essay on Entitlement and Deprivation*. Oxford, U.K.: Clarendon Press.

Serageldin, Ismail, A. Edward Elmendorf, and El-Tigani E. El-Tigani. Forthcoming. ''Structural Adjustment and Health in Africa in the 1980s.'' World Bank, Africa Technical Department, Washington, D.C.

Shepard, Donald S., R. L. Robertson, C. S. M. Cameron III, P. Saturno, M. Pollack, J. Manceau, P. Martinez, P. Meissner, and J. Perrone. 1989. ''Cost Effectiveness of Routine and Campaign Vaccination Strategies in Ecuador.'' *Bulletin of the World Health Organization* 67(6): 649–62.

Shepard, Donald, Julia Walsh, Wolfgang Munar, Laura Rose, Rodrigo Guerrero, Luis F. Cruz, Guillermo Reyes, Gail P. Orsolani, and Carlos Solarte. 1990. ''Cost-Effectiveness of Ambulatory Surgery in Cali, Colombia.'' Paper presented at conference on Outpatient Hospitals: Their Role in Health Care Systems in Developing Countries, Harvard School of Public Health, Boston, November.

Shim, Young-Hee. 1992. ''Sexual Violence against Women in Korea: A Victimization Survey of Seoul Women.'' Paper presented at conference on International Perspectives: Crime, Justice and Public Order, St. Petersburg, Russia, June 21–27.

Smith, G. S., and P. Barss. 1991. ''Unintentional Injuries in Developing Countries: The Epidemiology of a Neglected Problem.'' *Epidemiologic Reviews* 13: 228–65.

Smith, Kirk R. Forthcoming. ''Combustion, Air Pollution, and Health in Developing Countries.'' *Annual Review of Energy and Environment* 18(20).

Smith, Kirk R., and Liu Youcheng. 1993. ''Indoor Air Pollution in Developing Countries.'' In Jonathan Samet, ed., *The Epidemiology of Lung Cancer*. New York: Marcel Dekker.

Smith, K. R., and S. Rodgers. 1992. ''Interventions to Reduce Morbidity and Mortality from Pneumonia in Children: Reducing Exposure to Household Biomass Smoke.'' London School of Hygiene and Tropical Medicine.

Solon, Orville, Rhais M. Gamboa, J. Brad Schwartz, and Alejandro N. Herrin. 1992. ''Health Sector Financing in Philippines.'' Health Finance Development Project. HFDP Monograph 2. Government of the Philippines Department of Health, Manila.

Stamler, Jeremiah, Geoffrey Rose, Rose Stamler, Paul Elliot, Alan Dyer, and Michael Marmot. 1989. ''Intersalt Study Findings: Public Health and Medical Care Implications.'' *Hypertension* 14: 570–77.

Stark, Evan. 1984. ''The Battering Syndrome: Social Knowledge, Social Therapy and the Abuse of Women.'' Ph.D. dissertation. State University of New York, Binghamton, Department of Sociology.

Stark, Evan, and Anne Flitcraft. 1991. ''Spouse Abuse.'' In M. Rosenberg and Anne Finley, eds., *Violence in America: A Public Health Approach*. New York: Oxford University Press.

Stephenson, Patricia, Marsden Wagner, Mihaela Badea, and Florina Servanescu. 1992. ''Commentary: The Public Health Consequences of Restricted Induced Abortion—Lessons from Romania.'' *American Journal of Public Health* 82(10): 1328–31.

Strauss, John, Paul Gertler, Omar Rahman, and Kristin Fox. 1992. ''Gender and Life-Cycle Differentials in the Patterns and Determinants of Adult Health.'' Prepared for the Government of Jamaica. RAND, Santa Monica, Calif.

Study Group for Global Environment and Economics. 1991. "Pollution in Japan: Our Tragic Experience." Environment Agency, Office of Policy, Planning and Research, Tokyo.

Summers, Lawrence H. 1989. "What Can Economics Contribute to Social Policy? Some Simple Economics of Mandated Benefits." *AEA Papers and Proceedings* 79(2): 177–83.

————. 1992. "Investing in All the People." Policy, Research, and External Affairs Working Paper 905. World Bank, Washington, D.C.

Summers, Lawrence H., and Lant H. Pritchett. 1993. "The Structural Adjustment Debate." American Economic Review Conference Proceedings, American Economic Association meeting, Anaheim, Calif.

Tan, Jee-Peng, and Alain Mingat. 1992. *Education in Asia: A Comparative Study of Cost and Financing.* World Bank Regional and Sectoral Studies, Washington, D.C.

Tarlov, Alvin R. 1986. "HMO Enrollment Growth and Physicians: The Third Compartment." *Health Affairs* Spring: 23–35.

Thomas, Duncan. 1990. "Intra-Household Resource Allocation: An Inferential Approach." *Journal of Human Resources* 25(4): 635–64.

Thomas, Duncan, Victor Lavy, and John Strauss. 1992. *Public Policy and Anthropometric Outcomes in Côte d'Ivoire.* Living Standards Measurement Study Working Paper 89. Washington, D.C.: World Bank.

Thomas, Duncan, John Strauss, and Maria-Helena Henriques. 1990. "How Does Mother's Education Affect Child Height?" *Journal of Human Resources* 26(2): 183–211.

Tinker, Anne, and Marjorie Koblinsky. 1993. *Making Motherhood Safe.* World Bank Discussion Paper 202. Washington, D.C.

Tomkins, Andrew, and Fiona Watson. 1989. *Malnutrition and Infection.* Administrative Committee on Coordination/Subcommittee on Nutrition. Nutrition Policy Discussion Paper 5. New York: United Nations.

Tomson, Göran, and Göran Sterky. 1986. "Self-Prescribing by Way of Pharmacies in Three Asian Developing Countries." *Lancet* 2 (13 September): 620–21.

Torrance, G. W. 1986. "Measurement of Health State Utilities for Economic Appraisal." *Journal of Health Economics* 5: 1–30.

Toubia, Nahid. 1993. "A Call for Global Action against Female Genital Mutilation." Women, Ink., New York.

TRRL (Transport and Road Research Laboratory). 1991. "Towards Safer Roads in Developing Countries: A Guide for Planners and Engineers." Crowthorne, U.K.

UNDP (United Nations Development Programme). 1993. *Human Development Report 1993.* New York: Oxford University Press.

UNICEF (United Nations Children's Fund). 1993. *The State of the World's Children 1993.* Oxford: Oxford University Press.

————. Forthcoming. *The Progress of Nations 1993.* New York.

UNICEF/Bamako Initiative Management Unit. 1990. *The Bamako Initiative: Reaching Health Goals through Strengthened Services Delivery.* New York.

————. 1992. "Progress Report and Recommendation on the Bamako Initiative," presented to the UNICEF Executive Board, 1992 session. New York.

UNICEF and IMIP (Instituto Materno-Infantil de Pernambuco). 1992. *Cuidados Basicos de Saúde em Comunidades de Baixa Renda.* Recife.

UNICEF, WHO, and UNESCO. 1991. *Facts for Life.* New York.

United Nations. 1985. *Socio-Economic Differentials in Child Mortality in Developing Countries.* Population Study 97. New York.

————. 1988. *Mortality of Children under Age Five.* New York.

————. 1990. *World Population Prospects.* New York.

————. 1991. *Demographic Yearbook.* New York.

————. 1992. *Child Mortality since the 1960s.* New York.

————. Forthcoming. *The Health Rationale for Family Planning: Timing of Births and Child Survival.* New York.

U.S. Centers for Disease Control and Prevention. 1992. "Famine-Affected, Refugee, and Displaced Populations: Recommendations for Public Health Issues." *Morbidity and Mortality Weekly Report* 41 (June 24-RR-13).

Van Doorslaer, Eddy, Adam Wagstaff, and Frans Rutten, eds. 1993. *Equity in the Finance and Delivery of Health Care: An International Perspective.* CEC Health Services Research Series 8. Oxford, U.K.: Oxford University Press.

Victora, Cesar, and Fernando Barros. 1990. "Avaliação Preliminar do Impacto da Pastoral da Criança sobre Alguns Indicadores de Saúde e de Utilização de Serviços." UNICEF, Brasilia.

Viravaidya, M., S. Obremskey, and C. H. Myers. 1991. "The Economic Impact of AIDS on Thailand." Population and Community Development Association, Bangkok.

Vogel, R. J. 1989. "Trends in Health Expenditures and Revenue Sources in Sub-Saharan Africa." Paper prepared in conjunction with the World Bank Sub-Saharan African Health Policy Study, Washington, D.C.

————. 1990. "Health Insurance in Sub-Saharan Africa: A Survey and Analysis." Policy, Research, and External Affairs Working Paper Series 476. World Bank, Africa Technical Department, Washington, D.C.

Waaler, Hans T. 1984. "Height, Weight, and Mortality: The Norwegian Experience." *Acta Medica Scandinavica* 679: 3–56.

Walsh, Julia A. 1988. *Establishing Health Priorities in the Developing World.* UNDP Division for Global and Interregional Programmes. Boston, Mass.: Adams Publishing Group.

Walsh, Julia A., and Kenneth Warren. 1979. "Selective Primary Health Care—An Interim Strategy for Disease Control in Developing Countries." *New England Journal of Medicine* 301 (1 November): 967–74.

Walsh, J. A., C. M. Feifer, A. R. Measham, and P. J. Gertler. Forthcoming. "Maternal and Perinatal Health Problems." In Dean T. Jamison, W. Henry Mosley, Anthony R. Measham, and José-Luis Bobadilla, eds., *Disease Control Priorities in Developing Countries.* New York: Oxford University Press.

Walter, Tomas, Manuel Olivares, and Eva Hertrampf. 1990. "Field Trials of Food Fortification with Iron: The Experience in Chile." In Bo Lonnerdal, ed., *Iron Metabolism in Infants.* Boca Raton, Fla.: CRC Press.

Wasserman, Jeffrey, Willard G. Manning, Joseph P. Newhouse, and John D. Winkler. 1991. "The Effects of Excise Taxes and Regulations on Cigarette Smoking." *Journal of Health Economics* 19: 43–64.

Wegman, David H. 1992. "The Potential Impact of Epidemiology on the Prevention of Occupational Disease." *American Journal of Public Health* 82: 944–54.

Weisbrod, Burton A. 1991. "The Health Care Quadrilemma: An Essay on Technological Change, Insurance, Quality of Care, and Cost Containment." *Journal of Economic Literature* 29 (June): 523–52.

Welch, W. Pete, Mark E. Miller, H. Gilbert Welch, Elliott Fisher, and John E. Wennberg. 1993. "Geographic Variation in Expenditures for Physicians' Services in the United States." *New England Journal of Medicine* 328:9: 621–27.

Werner, David. 1987. *Disabled Village Children: A Guide for Community Health Workers, Rehabilitation Workers, and Families.* Palo Alto, Calif.: Hesperian Foundation.

Whitfield, R., Jr. 1987. "Dealing with Cataract Blindness— Part III: Paramedical Cataract Surgery in Africa." *Ophthalmic Surgery* 18: 765–67.

WHO (World Health Organization). 1977. *International Classification of Diseases.* Ninth Revision. Geneva.

———. 1988a. *Estimating Drug Requirements: A Practical Manual.* Action Programme on Essential Drugs and Vaccines. Geneva.

———. 1988b. *Guidelines for Developing National Drug Policies.* Geneva.

———. 1988c. *The World Drug Situation.* Geneva.

———. 1989a. *New Approaches to Improve Road Safety.* Technical Report Series 781. Geneva.

———. 1989b. *World Health Statistical Annual.* Geneva.

———. 1991a. "Organization and Financing of Health Care Reform in Countries of Central and Eastern Europe." Report by WHO Task Force on Health Development in Countries of Central and Eastern Europe for a meeting at the World Health Organization, April 22–26, Geneva.

———. 1991b. "Programme on Substance Abuse: Inter-Regional Meeting on Alcohol-Related Problems, April 2–8, Tokyo." Division of Health Services, Geneva.

———. 1991c. "The Public/Private Mix in National Health Systems and the Role of Ministries of Health." Interregional Meeting, Hacienda Cocoyoc, State of Morelos, Mexico. Division of Health Services, Geneva.

———. 1991d. *Tropical Diseases: Progress in Research 1989–1990.* Tenth Programme Report of the UNDP/World Bank/ WHO Special Programme for Research and Training in Tropical Diseases (TDR). Geneva.

———. 1991e. *World Health Statistics Annual.* Geneva.

———. 1992a. *Acute Effects on Health of Smog Episodes.* WHO Regional Publications, European Series 43. Copenhagen.

———. 1992b. "Global Health Situation and Projections— Estimates." Division of Epidemiological Surveillance and Health Situation and Trend Assessment, Geneva.

———. 1992c. "Implementation of the Global Strategy for Health for All by the Year 2000, Second Evaluation and Eighth Report on the World Health Situation." March. Geneva.

———. 1992d. *Our Planet, Our Health.* Report of the WHO Commission on Health and Environment. Geneva.

———. 1992e. "Programme on Substance Abuse: Atlas Report." Geneva.

———. 1993. "Evaluation of Recent Changes in the Financing of Health Services." Report of a WHO Study Group. Technical Report Series 829. Geneva.

———. Forthcoming. "Investing in Care for Persons with AIDS." Draft. Geneva.

———. Various years. "Health Equipment Management: A World Health Organization Newsletter." (English only.) Division of Strengthening of Health Services (SHS), Geneva.

WHO Global Programme on AIDS. 1993a. "The Costs of HIV/AIDS Prevention Strategies in Developing Countries." GPA/Dir/93.2. Geneva.

———. 1993b. "Statement from the Consultation on Testing and Counseling for HIV Infection 1992." WHO/GPA/ Inf/93.2. Geneva.

WHO/UNEP (United Nations Environment Programme). 1992. *Urban Air Pollution in Megacities of the World.* Oxford, U.K.: Blackwell Reference.

Wilkinson, R. G. 1992. "Income Distribution and Life Expectancy." *British Medical Journal* 304 (January): 165–68.

Woodward, David. 1992. *Debt, Adjustment and Poverty in Developing Countries.* Vol. 1: *National and International Dimensions of Debt and Adjustment in Developing Countries.* Vol. 2: *The Impact of Debt and Adjustment at the Household Level in Developing Countries.* London: Pinter Publishers in association with Save the Children.

World Bank. 1980. *World Development Report 1980.* New York: Oxford University Press.

———. 1984a. *China: The Health Sector.* A World Bank Country Study. Washington, D.C.

———. 1984b. *World Development Report 1984.* New York: Oxford University Press.

———. 1987. *Financing Health Services in Developing Countries: An Agenda for Reform.* A World Bank Policy Study. Washington, D.C.

———. 1988. *Education in Sub-Saharan Africa: Policies for Adjustment, Revitalization, and Expansion.* A World Bank Policy Study. Washington, D.C.

———. 1990a. *Brazil: The New Challenge of Adult Health.* A World Bank Country Study. Washington, D.C.

———. 1990b. *World Development Report 1990.* New York: Oxford University Press.

———. 1991. *World Development Report 1991.* New York: Oxford University Press.

———. 1992a. *China: Long-Term Issues and Options in the Health Transition.* A World Bank Country Study. Washington, D.C.

———. 1992b. *Poland: Health System Reform.* A World Bank Country Study. Washington, D.C.

———. 1992c. *Romania: Human Resources and the Transition to a Market Economy.* A World Bank Country Study. Washington, D.C.

———. 1992d. "Setting Environmental Priorities in Central and Eastern Europe." World Bank, Washington D.C.

———. 1992e. *Adjustment Lending and Mobilization of Private and Public Resources for Growth.* Policy and Research Series 22. Washington, D.C.

———. 1992f. *World Development Report 1992.* New York: Oxford University Press.

———. 1992g. *Zimbabwe: Financing Health Services.* A World Bank Country Study. Washington, D.C.

———. 1993a. *Effective Family Planning Programs.* Washington, D.C.

———. 1993b. *Housing: Enabling Markets to Work.* A World Bank Policy Paper. Washington, D.C.

———. 1993c. *Implementing the World Bank's Strategy to Reduce Poverty: Progress and Challenges.* Washington, D.C.

———. 1993d. *Poverty Reduction Handbook.* Washington, D.C.

———. Forthcoming. *Better Health in Africa.* Washington, D.C.

World Bank Water Demand Research Team. 1993. "The Demand for Water in Rural Areas: Determinants and Policy Implications." *World Bank Research Observer* 8(1): 47–70.

Yang, Bong-Min. 1991. "Health Insurance in Korea: Opportunities and Challenges." *Health Policy and Planning* 6(2): 119–29.

Yoshikawa, Aki, Norihiko Shirouzu, and Matthew Holt. 1991. "How Does Japan Do It? Doctors and Hospitals in a Universal Health Care System." *Stanford Law and Policy Review* 3 (Fall): 111–37.

Yu, Seung-Hum, and Gerard F. Anderson. 1992. "Achieving Universal Health Insurance in Korea: A Model for Other Developing Countries?" *Health Policy* 20: 289–99.

Zeckhauser, R., and Donald Shepard. 1976. "Where Now for Saving Lives?" *Law and Contemporary Problems* 40: 5–45.

Zinanga, Alex. 1992. "Development of the Zimbabwe Family Planning Program." Policy, Research, and External Affairs Working Paper Series 1053. World Bank, Population and Human Resources Department, Washington, D.C.

Zwi, A. 1992. "Injury in Developing Countries: A Review of the Literature." London School of Hygiene and Tropical Medicine, Department of Public Health and Policy.

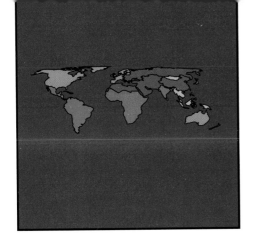

Appendix A. Population and health data

Tables A.1 and A.2 present summary data on population and GNP. Tables A.3 through A.9 provide population and health data as a supplement to the main text and to the data presented in the World Development Indicators. All the tables except A.1 and A.2 are organized by demographic region as presented in Table A.10. Economies are listed in ascending order of GNP per capita as estimated for mid-1991. Regional totals include all the economies listed in Table A.10, but country data are presented only for those economies with estimated populations of 3 million or more in mid-1990. Taiwan (China) is not presented separately in this appendix but is included in the estimates for Other Asia and islands. Countries for which GNP per capita is uncertain are listed at the end of the regional groups and italicized.

Although the data reported here are drawn from the most authoritative sources available, comparability is limited because of variation in data collection, statistical methods, and definitions. Differences in the reliability of the data are indicated by presenting in italics the figures that are deemed to be less precise.

Table A.3 Population structure and dynamics

Population in 1990 by country and the percentages for under age 15 and for age 60 and over were taken from Bos and others 1992. Regional totals were obtained by addition. The regional population totals provide the basis for the regional projections carried out for this Report for the period 1950 to 2050. The basis for the mortality assumptions for these projections varies by region. For the established market economies and the formerly socialist economies of Europe vital registration data from about 1990 were used; future mortality trends were then adapted to agree with Bos and others 1992 for 2050. For the past,

vital registration data and official life tables were used in combination with child mortality estimates averaged across the countries of each region. For China mortality in 1990 was obtained by adjusting upward the deaths by age recorded in the 1990 census, using an adjustment factor of 1.20 for males and 1.25 for females; these adjustment factors were derived from a comparison of the deaths by age and sex with the population distribution in 1982 and 1990. For India the 1988 Sample Registration System life table was taken for 1990 without adjustment. For Latin America and the Caribbean 1990 mortality was based on deaths and population by age as available in the Pan American Health Organization (PAHO) data base for 1990. For Sub-Saharan Africa, Other Asia and islands, and the Middle Eastern crescent mortality estimates were based on country-specific estimates of child mortality, combined with indicators from a small number of accurate life tables of the relationship between child and adult mortality. Fertility estimates by region for the period 1950 to 1990 were determined by the 1990 age distributions and the mortality assumptions. Fertility estimates for the period 1990 to 2050 were taken as weighted averages of the country-specific values used by Bos and others 1992. Estimates of migration were obtained indirectly from United Nations, *World Population Prospects 1990*. Regional summaries for various columns of Table A.3—*total fertility rate, total live births, life expectancy, median age at death, child mortality rate,* and *adult mortality rate* by sex—are taken directly from the regional projections.

Country-specific values for *total fertility rate* and *total live births* in 1990 are taken from projection data bases in Bos and others 1992. Mortality indicators are based on the child mortality estimates for 1960, 1975, and 1990, which, for developing countries, are largely based on the special exercise described below.

Life expectancy at birth, e(0), is the number of years that a person born in a given year could expect to live, given the age-specific mortality rates for that year. *Life expectancy* in 1960 and 1990 and *male and female adult mortality rates* for 1990 were derived from the child mortality estimates for that year, combined with assumptions about the relationship between child and adult mortality based on the country-specific projections in Bos and others 1992. The adult mortality rate for a given sex is the probability of dying between ages 15 and 60, expressed per 1,000. *Median age at death* is the age below which half of all deaths occur in a year.

The *perinatal mortality rate* is the number per 1,000 births of perinatal deaths (late fetal deaths, occurring at twenty-eight weeks of gestation or thereafter, and early neonatal deaths, occurring within the first seven days of life). Estimates of perinatal mortality were derived from various data sources. Vital registration data were used for most of the established market economies and for Argentina, Chile, China, Singapore, and Uruguay. Vital registration data for the republics of the former U.S.S.R. were corrected for underreporting of perinatal deaths by using a regression model of perinatal mortality on postneonatal mortality based on a data series extending over about forty-five years (1945–91) from forty countries with complete vital registration. The remaining estimates drew on community- and hospital-based studies at the district or other subnational level that were expanded to the national level using either percentage of the population living in urban areas in 1990 or percentage of births attended by trained health staff. Vital statistics for the established market economies and the historical data base were obtained from the U.S. National Center for Health Statistics (NCHS).

The *child mortality rate* is defined as the probability of dying by exact age 5. Estimates for the period 1960 to 1990 were obtained from a special exercise carried out jointly for the *World Development Report* and the United Nations Children's Fund (UNICEF), the results of which will be published as UNICEF, *The Progress of Nations 1993.* (The methodology is described in Hill and Yazbeck, background paper.) The sources of information are those given in United Nations, *Child Mortality since the 1960s* (1992), augmented by recently available census and survey data. For each observation of child mortality, there is a corresponding observation of the date to which the measure refers. Point estimates of child mortality were obtained by fitting a line to the observations using weighted least squares, the independent variables being years (to account for trends) and the weights being based on consensus judgment about the relative robustness of estimates derived from different types of data. In order to focus on rates of change, the dependent vari-

able used is the logarithm of the observed child mortality rates. For estimates beyond the range of the observations, extrapolation is used; all estimates based on extrapolation are shown in italics. For countries not included in *Child Mortality since the 1960s,* estimates of child mortality by period have been taken from United Nations, *Mortality of Children under Age Five* (1988). For these countries, point estimates for calendar years have been obtained by averaging estimates for adjacent five-year periods; thus, for example, child mortality for 1960 for Ethiopia is obtained as the average of the estimated values for 1955–60 and 1960–65.

Table A.4 Population and deaths by age group

Population projections for the eight demographic regions were made for the period 1990 to 2030, and reverse projections were made back to 1950. The starting point for these forward and reverse projections is the age and sex distribution of each region's population, as reported in Bos and others 1992. For reverse projections, mortality assumptions are based on child mortality estimates derived for this Report as described above for child mortality rates, with additional information derived from United Nations, *Mortality of Children under Age Five* (1988); migration assumptions were obtained indirectly from United Nations, *World Population Prospects* (1990). For the forward projections, assumptions on fertility, mortality, and migration were chosen to agree with Bos and others 1992, starting from the levels used in the reverse projection for 1985–90. The population projection follows the component projection model used by the World Bank.

Table A.5 Mortality risk and life expectancy across the life cycle

The figures in Table A.5 are derived from the regional population projections described in the note to Table A.4.

Table A.6 Nutrition and health behavior

Stunting is defined as low height-for-age; data are for children ages 24–59 months. *Wasting* is defined as low weight-for-height; data are for children ages 12–23 months. Moderate to severe stunting or wasting means, respectively, height-for-age or weight-for-height more than 2 standard deviations below the median of the NCHS reference population. What matters is the excess over the prevalence in the reference population; the latter includes genetic effects as well as malnutrition. Stunting is interpreted as measuring chronic malnutrition and wasting as measuring acute or short-term malnutrition, whether the cause is inadequate food intake or infectious disease or both. Mild or moderate malnutrition is not considered disease, but all degrees of malnutrition increase the risk of death in children. *Fully breastfed* babies are defined as those given breast milk with or without water, juice, or other liquids but no food or non-breast milk before age 4 months. Women are classified as *anemic* when the blood hemoglobin level is below the WHO norm of 110 grams per liter.

Tobacco consumption per year is an estimate of kilograms of consumption of dry-weight tobacco per adult (age 15 and older). Where consumption in raw-leaf equivalent is not available, data are derived by converting data on consumption or sales of products. In some cases consumption is calculated from production of and net trade in leaf and products. Consumption of tobacco for 1990 and 2000 was projected through a model that used assumptions on the growth of private consumption expenditure to derive per capita demand for tobacco. The demand functions and elasticities were based on analysis of recent national family budget surveys and past time series of consumption. Antismoking campaigns and other preventive activities that have influenced the level of tobacco consumption were considered for some countries through a trend factor, independent of income and price.

Sources for data on child nutrition are World Health Organization (WHO), Demographic and Health Surveys, Institute for Resource Development of Macro Systems (IRD), and UNICEF; for anemia, WHO; and for tobacco consumption, the Commodities and Trade Division of the Food and Agriculture Organization of the United Nations (1990).

Table A.7 Mortality by broad cause, and incidence of tuberculosis

Mortality rates are standardized for age by the direct method, using world population as the standard population. *Infectious diseases and reproductive health problems* include all deaths from infectious diseases listed in the *International Classification of Diseases, Ninth Revision* (1977), plus influenza and pneumonia, nutritional disorders and anemia, maternal causes of death (including abortion), and perinatal causes of death. Injuries include all violent causes, whether intentional, unintentional, or unknown. *Noncommunicable diseases* include all other causes of death. Deaths of which the cause was coded as ill-defined are distributed among the three groups in proportion to the number of deaths in each group. The source is WHO data derived from national vital statistics. Estimates for economies with incomplete death registration (less than 90 percent of deaths), high levels of non-medical certification of causes of death (more than 15 percent), or high proportions of deaths from ill-defined causes (more than 20 percent) are considered unreliable and are shown in italics.

The incidence rate of *tuberculosis* has been estimated using the most recent available information recorded by governments and corrected for many developing countries with additional information from epidemiological studies. The data source is WHO's Tuberculosis Programme.

Table A.8 Health infrastructure and services

Doctor is defined to include only individuals with the professional degree of medical doctor. The definition of *nurse* includes only registered nurses and registered midwives. *Hospital bed* is defined as beds in clinics and hospitals; beds in long-term care facilities and nursing homes are excluded. Data sources are the World Bank, the Organization for Economic Cooperation and Development (OECD), PAHO, and WHO.

Immunization data refer to DPT3—three completed doses of vaccine against diphtheria, pertussis (whooping cough), and tetanus—and to measles. The denominator for estimating coverage is the number of surviving infants age 1 year. The source of data is WHO's Expanded Programme on Immunization.

Table A.9 Health expenditure and total flows from external assistance

Health expenditure includes outlays for prevention, promotion, rehabilitation, and care; population activities; nutrition activities; program food aid; and emergency aid specifically for health. It does not include water and sanitation. Per capita expenditures and per capita aid flows are based on World Bank midyear population estimates.

Total health expenditure is expressed in official exchange rate U.S. dollars. Data on public and private health expenditure for the established market economies and Turkey are from the OECD. For other countries, information on government health expenditures is from national sources, supplemented by *Government Finance Statistics* (published by the International Monetary Fund), World Bank sector studies, and other studies. Data on parastatal expenditures (for health-related social security and social insurance programs) are from the Social Security Division of the International Labour Office (ILO) and the World Bank. Data are drawn from Murray, Govindaraj, and Chellaraj, background paper.

Public sector expenditures include government health expenditures, parastatal expenditures, and foreign aid, making the figures comparable with those for OECD countries. *Private sector* expenditures for countries other than OECD members are based on household surveys carried out by the ILO and other sources, supplemented by information from United Nations National Income Accounts, World Bank studies, and other studies published in the scientific literature.

Estimates for countries with incomplete data were calculated in three steps. First, where data on either private or public expenditures were lacking, the missing figures were imputed from data from countries for which information was available. The imputation followed regressions relating public or private expenditure to GDP per capita. Second, for a country with no health expenditure data, it was assumed that the share of GDP spent on health was the same as the average for the corresponding demographic region. Third, if GDP was also unknown but population was known, it was assumed that per capita health spending was the same as the regional average.

Estimates for *development assistance for health* are expressed in official exchange rate U.S. dollars. *Total aid flows* represent the sum of all health assistance for health to each country by bilateral and multilateral agencies and by international nongovernmental organizations (NGOs). Direct bilateral official development assistance (ODA) comes from the OECD countries. Sources of multilateral development assistance include United Nations agencies, development banks (including the World Bank), the European Community, and the Organization of Petroleum Exporting Countries (OPEC). Major international NGOs include the International Committee for the Red Cross (ICRC) and the International Planned Parenthood Federation (IPPF). National NGOs were not included because the available information was not separated by recipient country.

Information on ODA from bilateral and multilateral organizations was completed by data from the OECD's Development Assistance Committee (DAC) and Creditor Reporting System (CRS) and from the Advisory Committee for the Coordination of Information Systems (ACCIS). DAC has compiled annual aggregate ODA statistics, by sector, since 1960. The OECD's CRS, established in 1970, complements the DAC statistics by identifying contributions allocated by sector. The CRS data base is the most complete source of information for bilateral ODA, but its completeness varies among OECD countries and from year to year. ACCIS has kept, since 1987, a Register of Development Activities of the United Nations that lists sources of funds and executing agencies for all United Nations projects by sector.

The estimates of development assistance in this table were prepared by the Harvard Center for Population and Development Studies as a background paper for this Report.

Table A.1 Population (midyear) and average annual growth

Country group	Population (millions)							Average annual growth (percent)				
	1965	1973	1980	1990	1991	2000[a]	2030[a]	1965–73	1973–80	1980–90	1990–2000[a]	2000–2030[a]
Low- and middle-income economies	2,602	3,166	3,662	4,445	4,528	5,294	7,736	2.5	2.1	2.0	1.8	1.3
Low-income economies	1,776	2,169	2,507	3,066	3,127	3,686	5,459	2.5	2.1	2.0	1.9	1.3
Middle-income economies	826	997	1,155	1,379	1,401	1,608	2,273	2.3	2.2	1.8	1.5	1.2
Severely indebted	274	332	389	477	486	569	841	2.4	2.3	2.1	1.8	1.3
Sub-Saharan Africa[b]	233	288	351	474	489	635	1,313	2.7	2.9	3.1	3.0	2.4
East Asia and the Pacific	1,009	1,240	1,399	1,641	1,667	1,891	2,442	2.6	1.7	1.6	1.4	0.9
South Asia	632	765	903	1,128	1,152	1,368	2,004	2.4	2.4	2.2	1.9	1.3
Europe and Central Asia	. .	. .	448	489	492	517	566	. .	. .	0.9	0.6	0.5
Latin America and the Caribbean	249	305	358	438	455	516	721	2.6	2.4	2.0	1.7	1.1
Middle East and North Africa	114	141	173	236	244	315	600	2.8	3.0	3.2	2.9	2.2
High-income economies	671	725	766	817	822	864	920	1.0	0.8	0.6	0.6	0.2
OECD members	649	698	733	777	783	820	871	0.9	0.7	0.6	0.5	0.2
World	3,281	3,895	4,428	5,262	5,351	6,157	8,664	2.2	1.8	1.7	1.6	1.2

Note: Because of incomplete coverage, discrepancies between summed subgroup figures may occur.
a. Projections. For the assumptions used in the projections, see technical notes for Table 26 in the World Development Indicators.
b. Excludes South Africa.

Table A.2 GNP, population, GNP per capita, and growth of GNP per capita

Country group	1991 GNP (billions of dollars)	1991 population (millions)	1991 GNP per capita (dollars)	Average annual growth of GNP per capita (percent)					
				1965–73	1973–80	1980–90	1989	1990	1991[a]
Low- and middle-income economies	4,571	4,528	1,010	4.3	2.7	1.2	1.1	-0.1	-2.1
Low-income economies	1,097	3,127	350	2.5	2.6	4.0	2.9	2.9	2.1
Middle-income economies	3,474	1,401	2,480	. .	. .	0.5	0.7	-1.0	-3.4
Severely indebted	1,130	486	2,320	5.2	3.4	-0.8	-0.6	-5.4	-2.5
Sub-Saharan Africa[b]	173	489	350	1.7	0.9	-1.3	0.5	-1.4	-0.6
East Asia and the Pacific	1,081	1,667	650	5.0	4.8	6.2	4.5	5.3	5.0
South Asia	372	1,152	320	1.2	1.7	3.2	2.9	3.3	-0.7
Europe	1,314	492	2,670	. .	. .	1.4	1.4	-2.7	-9.8
Latin America and the Caribbean	1,065	445	2,390	4.6	2.2	-0.4	-1.1	-1.4	1.7
Middle East and North Africa	474	244	1,940	6.0	1.7	-2.5	-0.2	-0.2	-1.3
High-income economies	16,920	822	20,570	3.7	2.1	2.3	2.7	1.6	0.3
OECD members	16,463	783	21,020	3.8	2.1	2.3	2.7	1.6	0.1
World	21,464	5,351	4,010	2.8	1.3	1.2	1.6	0.5	-0.1

Note: Because of incomplete coverage, discrepancies between summed subgroup figures may occur.
a. Projections. For the assumptions used in the projections, see technical notes for Table 26 in the World Development Indicators.
b. Excludes South Africa.

Table A.3 Population structure and dynamics

Demographic region and economy	Population and fertility — Population, 1990 (millions)	Under 15 years old, 1990 (percent)	60 years and over, 1990 (percent)	Total fertility rate, 1990	Total live births per year, 1990 (hundreds of thousands)	General mortality — Life expectancy at birth 1960	1990	Median age at death, 1990	Perinatal mortality rate, 1990	Child mortality rate 1960	1975	1990	Adult mortality rate, 1990 (ages 15–59) Male	Female
Sub-Saharan Africa	510 t	46 w	5 w	6.4 w	251.8 t	43 w	52 w	5 w	68 w	251 w	212 w	175 w	381 w	322 w
Mozambique	16	44	5	6.4	7.2	39	43	2	75	280	280	280	490	421
Tanzania	25	47	5	6.6	11.7	42	49	5	71	242	202	165	379	335
Ethiopia	51	47	5	7.5	26.5	37	48	4	87	294	262	197	404	329
Uganda	16	49	5	7.3	8.5	44	47	4	85	224	173	185	424	367
Burundi	5	46	5	6.8	2.7	40	47	11	87	255	209	180	424	367
Chad	6	42	6	6.0	2.5	35	47	7	74	326	271	212	445	358
Madagascar	12	46	5	6.3	5.3	42	51	11	76	250	200	170	389	333
Sierra Leone	4	43	5	6.5	1.9	34	38	2	72	391	375	360	503	436
Malawi	9	47	4	7.6	4.6	35	47	4	83	361	313	201	426	369
Rwanda	7	48	4	8.3	3.9	45	44	3	86	210	223	222	453	395
Mali	8	47	5	7.0	4.3	33	48	4	80	413	321	200	417	361
Burkina Faso	9	46	5	6.5	4.2	35	49	4	85	318	254	159	429	352
Niger	8	47	4	7.1	3.9	35	38	3	79	320	320	320	513	454
Nigeria	96	47	4	6.0	42.5	47	49	7	71	204	198	191	406	354
Kenya	24	50	4	6.6	11.1	46	59	15	77	203	139	83	315	259
Benin	5	48	5	6.4	2.2	35	50	6	69	307	228	170	387	316
Central Africa Rep.	3	42	5	5.8	1.3	35	55	15	64	332	209	132	346	288
Ghana	15	47	5	6.3	6.6	45	52	7	71	213	169	170	344	282
Togo	4	48	5	6.7	1.8	39	54	7	75	264	193	143	325	268
Guinea	6	46	4	6.5	2.7	35	44	2	76	347	297	268	452	395
Zimbabwe	10	45	4	5.0	3.6	52	62	26	55	159	120	58	269	216
Côte d'Ivoire	12	47	4	6.7	5.4	40	57	10	68	260	194	90	332	277
Senegal	7	47	4	6.5	3.4	35	50	15	73	303	265	156	397	340
Cameroon	12	46	6	5.9	4.8	40	57	16	68	265	194	125	316	256
South Africa	36	38	6	4.3	12.1	48	62	41	50	192	141	91	278	209
Somalia	8	46	5	6.8	3.8	36	45	4	70	294	262	214	443	390
Zaire	37	46	4	6.3	17.0	37	49	6	68	286	223	190	387	319
Sudan	25	46	5	6.3	11.2	46	57	13	78	203	152	104	267	234
Zambia	8	49	4	6.7	4.0	45	47	11	63	213	167	190	422	354
Angola	10	45	5	6.5	4.7	35	46	3	75	346	281	214	434	381
India	850	37	7	4.0	258.1	47	58	37	64	235	195	127	272	229
China	1,134	27	9	2.5	251.3	43	69	64	25	210	85	43	201	150
Other Asia and islands	683 t	37 w	6 w	3.3 w	188.7 t	50 w	62 w	42 w	49 w	182 w	135 w	97 w	243 w	177 w
Nepal	19	42	5	5.7	7.6	44	56	12	90	279	202	135	312	243
Cambodia	8	35	5	4.6	3.3	45	50	30	85	218	239	174	347	274
Bangladesh	107	43	5	4.6	37.2	46	56	12	75	251	236	137	295	244
Lao PDR	4	44	5	6.7	2.0	44	50	8	85	232	209	171	345	280
Sri Lanka	17	32	8	2.4	3.5	58	72	73	19	140	69	22	158	92
Indonesia	178	36	6	3.1	45.9	46	59	47	40	214	151	111	278	212
Philippines	61	40	5	3.6	17.8	59	64	49	27	103	75	62	234	172
Papua New Guinea	4	41	5	5.1	1.4	47	52	22	43	204	185	169	374	327
Thailand	56	33	6	2.4	12.0	52	68	71	25	149	85	36	242	163
Malaysia	18	38	6	3.8	5.5	58	71	63	25	106	54	20	177	120
Korea, Rep.	43	26	8	1.8	6.9	53	72	74	10	133	29	10	149	67
Hong Kong	6	21	13	1.5	0.7	64	78	77	8	53	17	7	91	44
Singapore	3	24	8	1.9	0.5	65	74	76	8	48	16	8	135	64
Myanmar	42	37	6	3.9	12.7	43	61	41	50	234	153	101	256	187
Viet Nam	66	40	7	3.9	20.4	57	67	50	40	105	68	46	180	118
Korea, Dem. People's Rep.	22	28	7	2.4	4.7	53	70	71	20	133	55	31	179	84
Latin America and the Caribbean	444 t	36 w	7 w	3.3 w	124.6 t	54 w	70 w	55 w	33 w	161 w	104 w	60 w	228 w	163 w
Nicaragua	4	46	4	5.4	1.5	50	62	13	35	191	149	106	283	264
Haiti	6	40	6	4.8	2.3	47	54	18	43	221	208	156	413	406
Honduras	5	45	5	5.3	2.0	49	67	23	39	203	126	62	220	162
Bolivia	7	43	5	4.9	2.6	43	60	13	37	251	205	125	330	269
Guatemala	9	45	5	5.5	3.6	49	64	23	40	205	152	84	287	227
Dominican Rep.	7	37	6	3.3	2.0	56	68	49	35	149	114	56	212	147
Ecuador	10	39	6	3.8	3.1	53	70	57	37	174	120	42	218	157
Peru	22	38	6	3.8	6.6	45	65	47	40	233	157	73	272	221
El Salvador	5	44	6	4.3	1.7	51	69	32	39	188	146	52	318	217
Colombia	32	35	6	2.7	7.9	58	73	66	33	132	88	21	200	109
Paraguay	4	41	5	4.7	1.5	64	70	42	37	92	70	37	261	210
Chile	13	31	9	2.6	2.9	55	73	69	14	155	68	20	214	112
Venezuela	20	38	6	3.6	5.7	67	72	62	26	78	59	26	196	105
Argentina	32	30	13	2.8	6.5	67	72	72	28	73	56	26	168	90
Uruguay	3	26	16	2.3	0.5	71	74	73	17	55	58	23	194	101
Brazil	150	35	7	3.3	40.4	52	66	57	35	179	110	69	250	182
Mexico	86	37	6	3.3	23.8	56	70	60	30	148	95	38	212	164
Puerto Rico	4	26	14	2.3	0.6	67	76	75	18	70	27	15	155	77
Cuba	11	23	12	1.9	1.9	71	76	77	17	49	34	12	134	95

Demographic region and economy	Population and fertility					General mortality			Age-specific mortality rates						
	Population, 1990 (millions)	Under 15 years old, 1990 (percent)	60 years and over, 1990 (percent)	Total fertility rate, 1990	Total live births per year, 1990 (hundreds of thousands)	Life expectancy at birth		Median age at death, 1990	Perinatal mortality rate, 1990	Child mortality rate			Adult mortality rate, 1990 (ages 15–59)	
						1960	1990			1960	1975	1990	Male	Female
Middle Eastern crescent	503 *t*	41 *w*	6 *w*	5.0 *w*	195.8 *t*	44 *w*	61 *w*	24 *w*	46 *w*	242 *w*	174 *w*	111 *w*	228 *w*	174 *w*
Pakistan	112	44	5	5.9	47.1	49	56	7	65	222	163	139	296	263
Yemen, Rep.	11	49	5	7.7	6.1	33	49	4	60	378	270	183	334	327
Egypt	52	39	6	5.6	16.2	40	64	38	58	256	212	56	214	158
Morocco	25	41	6	4.6	8.7	45	62	41	45	215	174	71	214	183
Tajikistan	5	45	6	5.0	2.0	. .	65	22	37	. .	115	75	190	133
Jordan	3	44	4	5.5	1.3	54	69	35	40	145	85	34	138	93
Syrian Arab Rep.	12	48	4	6.5	5.5	47	66	23	45	199	98	44	157	121
Uzbekistan	21	42	6	4.0	6.6	. .	67	37	33	. .	67	60	225	135
Tunisia	8	38	6	3.7	2.3	41	67	58	40	245	140	45	166	136
Kyrgyzstan	4	38	9	3.7	1.3	. .	68	64	31	. .	63	53	268	131
Georgia	5	24	16	2.1	0.9	. .	72	71	24	. .	39	28	218	94
Azerbaijan	7	33	9	2.7	1.7	. .	69	66	30	. .	69	52	239	106
Turkmenistan	4	41	6	4.1	1.2	. .	64	48	41	. .	101	93	270	155
Turkey	56	35	7	3.5	15.9	47	65	52	45	217	172	94	175	107
Algeria	25	44	5	5.2	9.1	43	65	47	40	242	174	82	135	105
Armenia	3	30	11	2.4	0.6	. .	72	67	25	. .	43	32	195	100
Iran	56	44	5	6.3	25.1	42	63	18	56	234	164	64	174	124
Kazakhstan	17	32	10	2.8	3.7	. .	68	65	27	. .	48	39	291	131
Saudi Arabia	15	46	4	7.0	6.4	38	64	18	40	292	166	81	175	138
Israel	5	31	12	2.9	1.1	72	76	76	11	38	26	10	110	72
Afghanistan	20	45	4	6.9	9.8	34	40	2	75	358	314	307	421	421
Iraq	19	47	4	6.2	8.0	52	63	24	52	163	106	72	194	129
Libya	5	46	4	6.7	2.0	39	62	16	35	269	146	82	191	144
Formerly socialist economies of Europe (FSE)	346 *t*	23 *w*	17 *w*	2.2 *w*	52.9 *t*	66 *w*	72 *w*	72 *w*	19 *w*	68 *w*	36 *w*	22 *w*	281 *w*	112 *w*
Romania	23	24	16	2.2	3.7	63	70	71	12	82	43	31	233	119
Poland	38	25	15	2.2	5.9	65	71	72	15	70	29	20	263	102
Bulgaria	9	20	20	1.9	1.1	67	73	73	11	62	29	21	217	97
Moldova	4	32	11	2.9	0.8	. . .	69	68	24	. .	51	32	271	153
Ukraine	52	21	19	2.1	7.5	. .	72	73	22	. .	25	22	270	107
Czechoslovakia[a]	16	23	17	2.0	2.2	70	72	73	10	32	23	13	243	98
Lithuania	4	30	16	2.0	0.6	. .	72	73	20	. .	23	18	276	108
Hungary	11	20	19	1.8	1.3	68	71	73	15	57	33	20	305	133
Belarus	10	23	18	2.2	1.6	. .	73	73	21	. .	22	18	272	64
Russian Federation	148	24	17	2.3	23.5	. .	71	71	22	. .	33	27	304	110
Albania	3	33	8	3.0	0.8	51	70	67	45	164	71	36	250	110
Yugoslavia[b]	22	23	15	2.1	2.8	59	71	71	16	113	47	28	195	94
Established market economies (EME)	798 *t*	19 *w*	18 *w*	1.7 *w*	104.0 *t*	70 *w*	76 *w*	75 *w*	9 *w*	36 *w*	21 *w*	11 *w*	147 *w*	73 *w*
Portugal	10	21	18	1.6	1.3	60	75	75	13	108	49	13	169	82
Greece	10	19	20	1.5	1.1	68	76	76	13	50	29	13	133	71
Ireland	4	27	15	2.2	0.6	70	74	75	10	35	20	10	186	98
New Zealand	3	23	15	2.0	0.6	71	75	75	7	26	18	11	159	86
Spain	39	20	19	1.5	4.4	68	76	75	10	56	22	10	148	79
United Kingdom	57	19	21	1.9	7.9	71	76	77	8	27	18	9	156	87
Australia	17	22	15	1.9	2.5	71	77	76	10	24	16	9	148	74
Italy	58	16	16	1.3	5.7	68	77	77	12	56	25	11	128	72
Netherlands	15	18	18	1.6	1.9	73	77	77	10	21	12	9	141	72
Belgium	10	18	21	1.7	1.2	70	76	77	10	38	19	11	156	75
Austria	8	18	20	1.5	0.9	69	76	77	8	47	24	10	162	76
France	56	20	19	1.8	7.6	70	77	78	9	33	16	9	159	66
Canada	27	21	16	1.8	3.9	71	77	76	8	33	16	9	146	65
United States	250	22	17	1.9	38.6	70	76	76	10	31	19	11	157	75
Germany	79	16	20	1.6	9.2	69	76	78	7	43	22	9	159	76
Denmark	5	17	20	1.6	0.6	72	75	77	9	25	12	10	162	90
Finland	5	20	18	1.8	0.7	63	75	76	8	27	11	8	168	86
Norway	4	19	21	1.9	0.6	73	77	78	8	22	12	10	140	68
Sweden	9	17	23	2.0	1.2	73	78	78	7	19	10	8	135	71
Japan	124	18	17	1.6	13.5	68	79	78	6	37	11	6	120	63
Switzerland	7	17	20	1.7	0.8	71	78	78	8	25	12	9	136	63
FSE and EME	1,144 *t*	20 *w*	18 *w*	1.9 *w*	156.8 *t*	69 *w*	75 *w*	74 *w*	12 *w*	46 *w*	25 *w*	15 *w*	188 *w*	86 *w*
Demographically developing group	4,123 *t*	36 *w*	7 *w*	3.8 *w*	1,270.3 *t*	46 *w*	63 *w*	39 *w*	45 *w*	226 *w*	152 *w*	106 *w*	250 *w*	199 *w*
World	5,267 *t*	32 *w*	9 *w*	3.4 *w*	1,427.1 *t*	53 *w*	65 *w*	55 *w*	40 *w*	195 *w*	135 *w*	96 *w*	234 *w*	169 *w*

Note: In this appendix the demographically developing group includes the Sub-Saharan Africa, India, China, Other Asia and islands, Latin America and the Caribbean, and Middle Eastern crescent regions. Regional totals and averages include relevant information for less populous countries as listed in Table A.10, except for perinatal mortality.

a. Refers to former Czechoslovakia because disaggregated data are not yet available.

b. Refers to former Socialist Federal Republic of Yugoslavia because disaggregated data are not yet available.

Table A.4 Population and deaths by age group

Demographic region and age group	Population (millions)					Deaths (millions)				
	1950	1980	1990	2000	2030	1950	1980	1990	2000	2030
Sub-Saharan Africa	179	376	510	724	1,628	4.4	6.2	7.9	9.3	11.7
0–4	32	69	95	139	206	2.3	3.3	4.0	4.8	3.4
5–14	46	111	140	205	392	0.4	0.5	0.7	0.7	0.6
15–59	93	179	252	348	945	1.1	1.5	1.9	2.1	3.7
60+	9	17	23	32	85	0.6	0.9	1.3	1.7	4.0
India	358	684	850	1,003	1,357	8.1	9.1	9.3	9.7	11.8
0–4	55	97	117	111	102	4.4	3.9	3.2	2.5	1.0
5–14	84	168	197	223	202	0.6	0.6	0.6	0.6	0.2
15–59	198	378	477	593	870	1.6	1.9	2.3	2.6	2.9
60+	20	42	59	76	182	1.5	2.7	3.3	4.0	7.7
China	547	988	1,134	1,296	1,610	15.2	7.7	8.9	9.1	13.9
0–4	76	97	118	116	105	6.0	1.4	1.1	0.8	0.3
5–14	108	253	187	240	232	1.3	0.3	0.1	0.2	0.1
15–59	322	566	728	808	927	4.5	2.3	2.3	2.3	2.2
60+	41	73	101	132	346	3.4	3.7	5.4	5.8	11.3
Other Asia and islands	281	552	683	808	1,108	5.7	5.7	5.5	6.5	9.2
0–4	42	82	86	87	83	2.5	2.2	1.6	1.5	0.6
5–14	68	141	164	169	165	0.4	0.4	0.4	0.3	0.1
15–59	155	298	390	494	698	1.6	1.5	1.5	1.9	2.3
60+	17	31	43	58	161	1.2	1.6	2.0	2.8	6.2
Latin America and the Caribbean	166	355	444	538	765	2.9	2.7	3.0	3.1	6.0
0–4	27	52	56	59	56	1.3	0.9	0.7	0.6	0.3
5–14	40	89	103	113	114	0.2	0.1	0.1	0.1	0.1
15–59	90	194	254	323	474	0.7	0.9	0.9	0.7	1.5
60+	9	21	31	43	121	0.6	0.9	1.2	1.7	4.1
Middle Eastern crescent	148	382	503	667	1,240	3.9	4.7	4.4	5.6	7.6
0–4	24	62	81	102	130	2.0	2.1	1.8	2.1	1.2
5–14	35	99	127	173	252	0.3	0.3	0.2	0.3	0.2
15–59	79	201	266	353	748	1.0	1.2	0.9	1.4	1.9
60+	10	20	29	39	110	0.7	1.1	1.4	1.8	4.3
Formerly socialist economies of Europe (FSE)	269	324	346	361	395	3.1	3.2	3.8	3.7	4.3
0–4	27	27	27	25	26	0.7	0.3	0.1	0.1	0.0
5–14	50	49	54	51	50	0.1	0.1	0.0	0.0	0.0
15–59	165	204	208	217	225	0.8	0.5	0.9	0.7	0.5
60+	26	45	57	67	94	1.5	2.3	2.7	2.9	3.7
Established market economies (EME)	564	757	798	832	869	6.5	7.5	7.1	8.0	10.1
0–4	58	52	51	50	49	0.6	0.2	0.1	0.1	0.1
5–14	96	117	104	104	99	0.1	0.1	0.0	0.0	0.0
15–59	342	461	497	516	460	1.5	1.0	1.1	1.1	0.7
60+	69	127	145	163	260	4.3	6.2	5.9	6.8	9.3
FSE and EME	832	1,077	1,144	1,194	1,267	9.6	10.7	10.9	11.7	14.3
0–4	85	79	78	75	75	1.3	0.5	0.2	0.2	0.1
5–14	146	166	158	156	149	0.2	0.1	0.0	0.0	0.0
15–59	507	665	705	732	685	2.2	1.5	2.0	1.8	1.2
60+	95	167	203	231	358	5.8	8.5	8.6	9.7	13.0
Demographically developing group	1,678	3,337	4,123	5,034	7,708	40.2	36.2	39.1	43.3	60.2
0–4	255	458	552	613	682	18.5	13.9	12.4	12.3	6.8
5–14	381	851	919	1,123	1,348	3.2	2.2	2.1	2.2	1.3
15–59	937	1,902	2,367	2,918	4,672	10.5	9.2	9.8	11.0	14.5
60+	106	126	286	380	1,005	8.0	10.9	14.6	17.8	37.6
World	2,511	4,414	5,267	6,228	8,975	49.8	46.9	50.0	55.0	74.5
0–4	340	536	631	687	757	19.8	14.4	12.7	12.5	6.9
5–14	527	1,017	1,077	1,279	1,497	3.4	2.3	2.2	2.2	1.3
15–59	1,443	2,489	3,072	3,600	5,358	12.7	10.7	11.8	12.8	15.7
60+	200	371	488	662	1,363	13.8	19.4	23.2	27.5	50.6

Table A.5 Mortality risk and life expectancy across the life cycle

Demographic region and age group	Probability of dying (percent)					Demographic region and age	Life expectancy at different ages (years)				
	1950	1980	1990	2000	2030		1950	1980	1990	2000	2030
Sub-Saharan Africa						**Sub-Saharan Africa**					
0–4	28.6	19.9	17.5	15.2	7.9	0	39	49	52	55	64
5–14	6.2	3.7	3.1	2.7	1.3	5	50	56	58	59	64
15–59	47.9	36.6	34.5	30.6	21.5	15	43	48	50	51	55
60–75	58.0	51.5	49.4	47.7	42.1	60	13	15	15	15	17
India						**India**					
0–4	30.4	17.2	12.4	10.5	4.5	0	42	55	58	61	70
5–14	5.0	3.0	2.7	2.3	1.0	5	54	61	61	63	68
15–59	38.5	26.3	25.0	23.3	15.1	15	47	52	53	54	59
60–75	61.1	51.2	48.9	44.6	33.8	60	14	15	16	16	18
China						**China**					
0–4	31.5	6.7	4.3	3.6	1.6	0	38	63	69	71	77
5–14	6.3	1.2	0.8	0.6	0.3	5	47	64	67	69	73
15–59	53.4	21.6	17.5	15.3	9.7	15	40	55	58	59	63
60–75	65.2	43.5	41.5	34.8	23.0	60	12	17	18	18	20
Other Asia and islands						**Other Asia and islands**					
0–4	23.4	12.0	9.7	8.2	3.8	0	44	58	62	64	72
5–14	4.9	1.9	1.7	1.3	0.6	5	52	61	63	65	70
15–59	45.0	24.5	21.2	19.7	13.9	15	44	51	54	56	60
60–75	59.3	47.8	44.9	41.2	31.4	60	13	15	16	17	19
Latin America and the Caribbean						**Latin America and the Caribbean**					
0–4	19.9	8.6	6.0	5.1	2.3	0	49	65	70	71	76
5–14	3.7	1.5	1.2	0.9	0.3	5	56	66	69	70	73
15–59	36.6	19.1	19.1	13.4	9.6	15	48	57	60	60	63
60–75	51.5	37.9	33.0	30.7	23.4	60	15	17	19	19	20
Middle Eastern crescent						**Middle Eastern crescent**					
0–4	30.1	15.0	11.1	9.4	4.4	0	38	56	61	63	71
5–14	6.8	2.5	1.9	1.5	0.7	5	49	60	63	65	69
15–59	50.1	26.5	20.1	19.3	14.0	15	42	52	55	56	60
60–75	59.2	46.7	42.0	39.4	31.0	60	13	15	17	17	19
Formerly socialist economies of Europe (FSE)						**Formerly socialist economies of Europe (FSE)**					
0–4	12.8	3.0	2.2	1.9	0.9	0	59	71	72	74	78
5–14	2.4	0.5	0.4	0.3	0.1	5	63	68	69	70	74
15–59	22.3	20.2	19.7	13.3	8.9	15	54	58	59	60	64
60–75	54.8	38.9	36.3	32.8	22.1	60	16	18	18	19	21
Established market economies (EME)						**Established market economies (EME)**					
0–4	6.0	1.7	1.1	1.0	0.6	0	65	74	76	77	81
5–14	1.0	0.3	0.3	0.2	0.1	5	65	71	72	73	77
15–59	20.7	11.4	10.7	9.3	6.4	15	55	61	62	63	67
60–75	43.1	31.1	27.6	24.9	16.5	60	17	19	20	20	22
FSE and EME						**FSE and EME**					
0–4	8.4	2.1	1.5	1.3	0.7	0	64	73	75	76	81
5–14	1.5	0.4	0.3	0.2	0.1	5	65	70	71	72	76
15–59	21.2	15.0	13.7	10.6	7.2	15	55	60	61	62	66
60–75	47.0	33.7	30.4	27.5	18.3	60	17	19	19	20	22
Demographically developing group						**Demographically developing group**					
0–4	28.6	13.5	10.6	9.5	4.9	0	40	59	63	65	71
5–14	5.7	2.6	2.2	1.6	0.8	5	50	62	64	66	69
15–59	46.7	26.7	23.5	21.9	15.3	15	43	53	55	56	60
60–75	60.3	46.7	43.8	40.4	32.6	60	13	16	17	17	19
World						**World**					
0–4	24.8	12.0	9.6	8.7	4.5	0	48	62	65	67	73
5–14	4.7	2.1	1.9	1.5	0.8	5	55	64	66	67	70
15–59	40.6	24.7	20.7	19.7	11.7	15	47	55	56	57	61
60–75	56.0	40.1	40.1	38.8	31.0	60	14	17	17	17	19

Table A.6 Nutrition and health behavior

Region and economy	Percentage of children affected by:		Percentage of children fully breastfed, 1985–90 (ages 0–3 months)[a]	Prevalence of anemia in pregnant women, 1970s and 1980s (percentage below the norm for hemoglobin)[a]	Tobacco consumption per year (kilograms per capita in adult population)		
	Stunting, 1980–90 (ages 24–59 months)[a]	Wasting, 1980–90 (ages 12–23 months)[a]			1974–76	1990	2000
Sub-Saharan Africa	39 w	10 w	63 w	41 w	..	..	..
Mozambique	..	..	..	58	0.5	0.4	0.4
Tanzania	46	5	..	80	0.8	0.6	0.6
Ethiopia	43	19	..	6	..	..	..
Uganda	45	2	76	..	..	..	..
Burundi	48	6	98	68	..	..	..
Chad	13	..	..	37	..	..	..
Madagascar	56	17	..	..	..	..	..
Sierra Leone	43	14	..	45	..	..	..
Malawi	61	8	..	49	0.5	0.4	0.4
Rwanda	34	1	..	..	..	..	..
Mali	24	11	82	65	..	..	..
Burkina Faso	28	11	..	24	..	..	..
Niger	38	23	..	47	..	..	..
Nigeria	43	9	61	43	0.4	0.4	0.3
Kenya	32	5	48	57	..	..	..
Benin	..	..	..	55	..	..	..
Central Africa Rep.	..	..	..	67	..	..	..
Ghana	30	8	81	64	..	..	..
Togo	29	6	60	47	..	..	..
Guinea	..	..	..	..	..	..	..
Zimbabwe	31	2	56	..	0.7	0.6	0.6
Côte d'Ivoire	20	17	..	34	1.3	1.0	1.0
Senegal	25	6	77	55	..	..	..
Cameroon	43	2	70	8	..	..	..
South Africa	53	10	..	28	2.3	1.4	1.1
Somalia	30	40	..	73	..	..	..
Zaire	27	3	64	42	0.8	0.5	0.5
Sudan	32	13	84	36	..	..	..
Zambia	59	10	72	34	..	..	..
Angola	..	..	..	29	..	..	..
India	65	27	..	88	0.8	0.8	0.9
China	41	8	..	25	1.6	2.6	2.9
Other Asia and islands	53 w	11 w	..	58 w	1.6 w	1.7 w	1.8 w
Nepal	69	14	..	33	..	..	..
Cambodia	..	..	..	..	..	..	..
Bangladesh	65	16	..	51	1.1	0.9	1.0
Lao PDR	44	20	..	62	..	..	..
Sri Lanka	27	13	79	62	..	..	..
Indonesia	67	9	45	74	1.0	1.4	1.6
Philippines	43	13	..	48	1.5	1.5	1.7
Papua New Guinea	47	10	..	..	..	..	..
Thailand	22	6	33	52	2.4	2.0	2.0
Malaysia	32	6	..	34	1.5	1.8	2.1
Korea, Rep.	18	2	..	..	2.4	2.9	3.5
Hong Kong	..	..	..	..	2.0	1.6	1.8
Singapore	10	7	..	18	6.3	3.4	3.2
Myanmar	50	11	..	58	3.0	3.0	3.1
Viet Nam	49	12	..	..	0.6	1.0	1.1
Korea, Dem. People's Rep.	..	..	..	..	4.3	4.0	3.9
Latin America and the Caribbean	26 w	5 w	41 w	35 w	2.0 w	1.6 w	1.7 w
Nicaragua	22	0	..	..	..	..	..
Haiti	51	17	..	64	..	..	..
Honduras	34	2	..	..	..	..	..
Bolivia	38	2	75	36	..	..	..
Guatemala	57	13	..	..	..	..	..
Dominican Rep.	19	1	42	..	0.8	1.1	1.1
Ecuador	39	4	54	46	..	..	..
Peru	37	2	58	53	..	..	..
El Salvador	36	6	..	14	1.2	0.9	0.9
Colombia	23	1	40	24	1.9	2.0	2.3
Paraguay	17	0	..	63	1.9	0.9	0.9
Chile	10	1	..	20	1.3	0.9	1.0
Venezuela	7	4	..	29	1.8	1.5	1.7
Argentina	..	..	..	..	3.1	1.9	1.9
Uruguay	16	..	..	..	..	..	..
Brazil	29	6	34	34	2.1	1.8	1.9
Mexico	22	6	44	41	1.4	1.0	1.1
Puerto Rico	..	..	..	..	..	..	..
Cuba	..	1	..	..	4.8	4.5	5.0

Region and economy	Percentage of children affected by:		Percentage of children fully breastfed, 1985–90 (ages 0–3 months)[a]	Prevalence of anemia in pregnant women, 1970s and 1980s (percentage below the norm for hemoglobin)[a]	Tobacco consumption per year (kilograms per capita in adult population)		
	Stunting, 1980–90 (ages 24–59 months)[a]	Wasting, 1980–90 (ages 12–23 months)[a]			1974–76	1990	2000
Middle Eastern crescent	..	..	..	..	1.4	1.7	1.9
Pakistan	50	9	25	57	..	..	..
Yemen, Rep.	..	15	15	..	..	..	..
Egypt	31	1	66	47	1.0	1.8	1.8
Morocco	25	4	66	46	1.3	1.7	1.9
Tajikistan	..	..	..	..	..	..	..
Jordan	20	3	32	50	..	..	..
Syrian Arab Rep.	..	..	..	52	3.7	3.2	3.3
Uzbekistan	..	..	..	..	..	..	..
Tunisia	18	3	60	38	..	..	..
Kyrgyzstan	..	..	..	..	..	..	..
Georgia	..	..	..	..	..	..	..
Azerbaijan	..	..	..	..	..	..	..
Turkmenistan	..	..	..	..	..	..	..
Turkey	..	..	..	74	2.5	2.2	2.3
Algeria	13	4	..	42	1.8	1.9	2.1
Armenia	..	..	..	..	..	..	..
Iran	55	23	..	28	1.1	0.9	0.9
Kazakhstan	..	..	..	..	..	..	..
Saudi Arabia	..	..	..	24	1.5	2.0	2.1
Israel	..	..	..	25	2.1	2.4	2.4
Afghanistan	..	..	..	..	1.7	3.0	2.9
Iraq	..	..	..	..	..	..	..
Libya	..	..	..	..	..	..	..
Formerly socialist economies of Europe (FSE)	..	..	..	..	..	..	..
Romania	..	..	..	..	2.0	2.0	2.0
Poland	..	..	..	16	3.4	3.5	3.7
Bulgaria	..	..	..	..	3.6	4.1	4.3
Moldova	..	..	..	..	..	..	..
Ukraine	..	..	..	..	..	..	..
Czechoslovakia[b]	..	..	..	23	2.0	2.5	2.6
Lithuania	..	..	..	..	..	..	..
Hungary	..	..	..	..	2.9	3.3	3.6
Belarus	..	..	..	..	..	..	..
Russian Federation	..	..	..	..	..	..	..
Albania	..	..	..	..	..	..	..
Yugoslavia[c]	4	1	..	..	2.5	2.5	2.8
Established market economies (EME)	..	..	..	15 w	3.2 w	2.4 w	2.0 w
Portugal	..	..	..	..	1.3	1.9	2.0
Greece	..	..	..	24	3.2	3.0	3.3
Ireland	..	..	..	..	3.2	2.4	2.1
New Zealand	3	1	..	22	3.2	2.1	1.9
Spain	..	..	..	9	2.5	2.4	2.6
United Kingdom	2	1	..	19	2.6	1.9	1.6
Australia	..	..	..	8	2.9	2.0	1.7
Italy	2	1	..	10	2.2	1.9	2.0
Netherlands	..	..	..	18	3.8	3.0	2.7
Belgium	..	..	..	6	3.5	2.9	2.7
Austria	..	..	..	..	2.3	2.1	1.9
France	6	0	..	18	2.8	2.3	2.1
Canada	5	1	..	..	3.8	2.6	2.2
United States	2	2	..	17	3.8	2.6	2.2
Germany	..	..	..	12	3.2	2.3	2.1
Denmark	..	..	..	..	3.5	2.6	2.3
Finland	..	..	..	..	2.2	1.6	1.4
Norway	..	..	..	..	2.3	2.0	1.9
Sweden	..	..	..	..	1.9	1.5	1.3
Japan	4	..	..	..	3.5	2.4	1.9
Switzerland	..	..	..	..	3.7	2.9	2.3
FSE and EME	4 w	3 w	..	4 w	2.9 w	2.2 w	1.8 w
Demographically developing group	46 w	13 w	47 w	49 w	1.4 w	1.7 w	1.9 w
World	42 w	12 w	..	42 w	1.7 w	1.9 w	1.9 w

a. Each value refers to one particular but not specified year within the time period denoted.
b. Refers to former Czechoslovakia because disaggregated data are not yet available.
c. Refers to former Socialist Federal Republic of Yugoslavia because disaggregated data are not yet available.

Table A.7 Mortality, by broad cause, and tuberculosis incidence

Demographic region and economy	Mortality rates by major cause of death, 1985–90[a] (deaths per 100,000 population, standardized for age)			Annual incidence rate of tuberculosis, 1990 (per 100,000 population)
	Communicable diseases and maternal and perinatal causes	Noncommunicable diseases	Injuries	
Sub-Saharan Africa	..	..	..	220 w
Mozambique	..	..	..	189
Tanzania	..	..	..	140
Ethiopia	..	..	..	155
Uganda	..	..	..	300
Burundi	..	..	..	367
Chad	..	..	..	167
Madagascar	..	..	..	310
Sierra Leone	..	..	..	167
Malawi	..	..	..	173
Rwanda	..	..	..	260
Mali	..	..	..	289
Burkina Faso	..	..	..	289
Niger	..	..	..	144
Nigeria	..	..	..	222
Kenya	..	..	..	140
Benin	..	..	..	135
Central Africa Rep.	..	..	..	139
Ghana	..	..	..	222
Togo	..	..	..	244
Guinea	..	..	..	166
Zimbabwe	..	..	..	207
Côte d'Ivoire	..	..	..	196
Senegal	..	..	..	166
Cameroon	..	..	..	194
South Africa	..	..	..	250
Somalia	..	..	..	222
Zaire	..	..	..	333
Sudan	..	..	..	211
Zambia	..	..	..	345
Angola	..	..	..	225
India	470	761	97	220
China	117	696	88	166
Other Asia and islands	..	..	..	201 w
Nepal	..	..	..	167
Cambodia	..	..	..	235
Bangladesh	..	..	..	220
Lao PDR	..	..	..	235
Sri Lanka	232	459	194	167
Indonesia	..	..	..	220
Philippines	..	..	..	280
Papua New Guinea	..	..	..	275
Thailand	..	..	..	173
Malaysia	..	..	..	67
Korea, Rep.	113	454	194	162
Hong Kong	71	354	28	140
Singapore	114	498	39	82
Myanmar	..	..	..	189
Viet Nam	..	..	..	166
Korea, Dem. People's Rep.	..	..	..	162
Latin America and the Caribbean	193 w	494 w	95 w	92 w
Nicaragua	..	..	..	110
Haiti	..	..	..	333
Honduras	..	..	..	133
Bolivia	..	..	..	335
Guatemala	595	523	113	110
Dominican Rep.	206	443	88	110
Ecuador	210	448	119	166
Peru	327	392	53	250
El Salvador	202	385	201	110
Colombia	..	..	..	67
Paraguay	..	..	..	166
Chile	131	444	88	67
Venezuela	151	449	110	44
Argentina	107	530	59	50
Uruguay	98	519	67	15
Brazil	..	..	..	56
Mexico	168	490	102	110
Puerto Rico	78	447	59	8
Cuba	73	472	82	10

Demographic region and economy	Mortality rates by major cause of death, 1985–90[a] (deaths per 100,000 population, standardized for age)			Annual incidence rate of tuberculosis, 1990 (per 100,000 population)
	Communicable diseases and maternal and perinatal causes	Noncommunicable diseases	Injuries	
Middle Eastern crescent	116 w	619 w	72 w	99 w
Pakistan	..	..	..	150
Yemen, Rep.	..	..	..	96
Egypt	..	..	..	78
Morocco	..	..	..	125
Tajikistan	182	558	53	133
Jordan	..	..	..	14
Syrian Arab Rep.	..	..	..	58
Uzbekistan	137	601	65	55
Tunisia	..	..	..	55
Kyrgyzstan	124	651	95	68
Georgia	69	591	56	36
Azerbaijan	110	595	46	47
Turkmenistan	216	737	68	72
Turkey	..	..	..	57
Algeria	..	..	..	53
Armenia	60	580	66	127
Iran	..	..	..	83
Kazakhstan	86	700	103	77
Saudi Arabia	..	..	..	22
Israel	64	444	53	12
Afghanistan	..	..	..	278
Iraq	..	..	..	111
Libya	..	..	..	12
Formerly socialist economies of Europe (FSE)	52 w	658 w	94 w	52 w
Romania	93	685	65	70
Poland	73	603	80	43
Bulgaria	73	619	64	30
Moldova	54	704	104	54
Ukraine	32	673	93	50
Czechoslovakia[b]	51	646	62	22
Lithuania	25	598	107	82
Hungary	55	690	90	38
Belarus	28	625	90	50
Russian Federation	47	704	115	56
Albania	..	..	..	40
Yugoslavia[c]	87	559	68	30
Established market economies (EME)	47 w	416 w	49 w	20 w
Portugal	70	429	78	57
Greece	51	393	48	12
Ireland	57	526	39	18
New Zealand	50	487	58	10
Spain	45	410	42	49
United Kingdom	49	478	31	10
Australia	31	424	48	6
Italy	38	425	39	25
Netherlands	40	416	36	9
Belgium	52	459	68	16
Austria	30	437	55	20
France	40	362	70	16
Canada	39	395	48	8
United States	54	447	58	10
Germany	35	468	45	18
Denmark	..	..	..	7
Finland	43	450	76	15
Norway	52	399	53	8
Sweden	41	397	46	7
Japan	51	306	41	42
Switzerland	..	..	..	18
FSE and EME	49 w	488 w	63 w	29 w
Demographically developing group	253 w	692 w	94 w	173 w
World	187 w	626 w	84 w	142 w

a. Each value refers to one particular but not specified year within the time period denoted.
b. Refers to former Czechoslovakia because disaggregated data are not yet available.
c. Refers to former Socialist Federal Republic of Yugoslavia because disaggregated data are not yet available.

Table A.8 Health infrastructure and services

Demographic region and economy	Doctors per 1,000 population 1988-92[a]	Nurse-to-doctor ratio, 1988-92[a]	Hospital beds per 1,000 population, 1985-90[a]	Percentage of children immunized, age less than 1 year	
				Third dose of DPT, 1990-91[a]	Measles 1990-91[a]
Sub-Saharan Africa	0.12 w	5.1 w	1.4 w	52 w	52 w
Mozambique	0.02	13.1	0.9	19	23
Tanzania	0.03	7.3	1.1	79	75
Ethiopia	0.03	2.4	0.3	44	37
Uganda	0.04	8.4	0.8	77	74
Burundi	0.06	4.3	1.3	83	75
Chad	0.03	0.9	. .	18	28
Madagascar	0.12	3.5	0.9	46	33
Sierra Leone	0.07	5.0	1.0	75	74
Malawi	0.02	2.8	1.6	81	78
Rwanda	0.02	1.7	1.7	89	89
Mali	0.05	2.5	. .	35	40
Burkina Faso	0.03	8.2	0.3	37	42
Niger	0.03	11.3	. .	18	24
Nigeria	0.15	6.0	1.4	65	70
Kenya	0.14	3.2	1.7	36	36
Benin	0.07	5.8	. .	67	70
Central Africa Rep.	0.04	4.5	0.9	82	82
Ghana	0.04	9.1	1.5	39	39
Togo	0.08	6.2	1.6	73	61
Guinea	0.02	4.3	0.6	41	39
Zimbabwe	0.16	6.1	2.1	89	87
Côte d'Ivoire	0.06	4.8	0.8	48	42
Senegal	0.05	2.6	0.8	60	59
Cameroon	0.08	6.4	2.7	56	56
South Africa	0.61	4.5	4.1	67	63
Somalia	0.07	7.1	0.8	18	30
Zaire	0.07	2.1	1.6	32	31
Sudan	0.09	2.7	0.9	63	58
Zambia	0.09	6.0	. .	79	76
Angola	0.07	16.4	1.2	26	39
India	0.41	1.1	0.7	83	77
China	1.37	0.5	2.6	95	96
Other Asia and islands	0.31 w	3.0 w	1.8 w	81 w	78 w
Nepal	0.06	2.7	0.3	74	63
Cambodia	0.04	8.0	2.2	38	38
Bangladesh	0.15	0.8	0.3	87	83
Lao PDR	0.23	5.9	2.5	22	47
Sri Lanka	0.14	5.1	2.8	86	79
Indonesia	0.14	2.8	0.7	86	80
Philippines	0.12	3.1	1.3	88	85
Papua New Guinea	0.08	8.1	3.4	64	63
Thailand	0.20	5.5	1.6	69	60
Malaysia	0.37	3.9	2.4	90	79
Korea, Rep.	0.73	1.0	3.0	74	93
Hong Kong	0.93	4.5	4.2	83	42
Singapore	1.09	3.8	3.3	91	92
Myanmar	0.08	4.0	0.6	69	73
Viet Nam	0.35	4.9	3.3	85	85
Korea, Dem. People's Rep.	2.72	. .	13.5	90	96
Latin America and the Caribbean	1.25 w	0.5 w	2.7 w	71 w	75 w
Nicaragua	0.60	0.5	1.8	71	54
Haiti	0.14	0.8	0.8	41	31
Honduras	0.32	1.0	1.1	94	86
Bolivia	0.48	0.7	1.3	58	73
Guatemala	0.44	2.5	1.7	63	48
Dominican Rep.	1.08	0.7	2.0	47	69
Ecuador	1.04	0.3	1.7	89	54
Peru	1.03	0.9	1.5	71	59
El Salvador	0.64	1.5	1.5	60	53
Colombia	0.87	0.6	1.5	84	75
Paraguay	0.62	1.7	1.0	79	74
Chile	0.46	0.8	3.3	91	93
Venezuela	1.55	0.5	2.9	54	54
Argentina	2.99	0.2	4.8	84	99
Uruguay	2.90	0.2	4.6	88	82
Brazil	1.46	0.1	3.5	75	83
Mexico	0.54	0.8	1.3	64	78
Puerto Rico	2.55	. .	4.0	. .	. .
Cuba	3.75	1.7	5.0	99	99

Demographic region and economy	Doctors per 1,000 population 1988–92[a]	Nurse-to-doctor ratio, 1988–92[a]	Hospital beds per 1,000 population, 1985–90[a]	Percentage of children immunized, age less than 1 year	
				Third dose of DPT, 1990–91[a]	Measles 1990–91[a]
Middle Eastern crescent	1.04 w	1.5 w	2.9 w	75 w	74 w
Pakistan	0.34	0.8	0.6	81	77
Yemen, Rep.	0.18	2.9	0.9	62	57
Egypt	0.77	1.2	1.9	86	89
Morocco	0.21	4.5	1.2	79	76
Tajikistan	2.71	2.8	10.6	89	89
Jordan	1.54	0.3	1.9	92	85
Syrian Arab Rep.	0.85	1.2	1.1	89	84
Uzbekistan	3.58	2.9	12.4	57	81
Tunisia	0.53	2.7	2.0	90	80
Kyrgyzstan	3.67	2.8	12.0	78	94
Georgia	5.92	2.2	11.1	65	74
Azerbaijan	3.93	2.4	10.2	89	91
Turkmenistan	3.57	2.8	11.3	78	68
Turkey	0.74	1.5	2.1	72	66
Algeria	0.26	4.7	2.6	89	83
Armenia	4.28	2.5	9.0	88	92
Iran	0.32	1.1	1.5	88	84
Kazakhstan	4.12	3.0	13.6	84	94
Saudi Arabia	1.52	1.5	2.7	94	90
Israel	2.90	2.3	6.3	88	88
Afghanistan	0.11	0.8	0.3	. .	. .
Iraq	0.58	1.2	1.6	69	73
Libya	1.04	2.9	4.1	62	59
Formerly socialist economies of Europe (FSE)	4.07 w	2.2 w	11.4 w	77 w	86 w
Romania	1.79	. .	8.9	97	92
Poland	2.06	. .	6.6	98	94
Bulgaria	3.19	2.1	9.8	99	97
Moldova	4.00	3.0	7.8	87	95
Ukraine	4.40	2.7	13.6	78	88
Czechoslovakia[b]	3.23	2.4	7.9	99	98
Lithuania	. .	. .	. .	80	92
Hungary	2.98	1.1	10.1	100	100
Belarus	4.05	. .	13.2	90	97
Russian Federation	4.69	. .	13.8	65	83
Albania	1.39	2.5	4.1	94	87
Yugoslavia[c]	2.63	1.9	6.0	79	75
Established market economies (EME)	2.52 w	2.1 w	8.3 w	80 w	77 w
Portugal	2.57	0.8	4.2	95	96
Greece	1.73	1.6	5.1	54	76
Ireland	1.58	4.7	3.9	65	78
New Zealand	1.74	0.1	6.6	81	82
Spain	3.60	1.1	4.8	73	84
United Kingdom	1.40	2.0	6.3	85	89
Australia	2.29	3.8	5.6	90	68
Italy	4.69	0.6	7.5	95	50
Netherlands	2.43	3.4	5.9	97	94
Belgium	3.21	0.1	8.3	94	75
Austria	4.34	2.4	10.8	90	60
France	2.89	1.6	9.3	95	69
Canada	2.22	4.7	16.1	85	85
United States	2.38	2.8	5.3	67	80
Germany	2.73	1.7	8.7	80	90
Denmark	2.56	5.6	5.7	95	86
Finland	2.47	4.3	10.8	95	97
Norway	2.43	4.4	4.8	89	90
Sweden	2.73	3.4	6.2	99	95
Japan	1.64	1.8	15.9	87	66
Switzerland	1.59	2.6	11.0	90	90
FSE and EME	3.09 w	2.1 w	9.3 w	79 w	80 w
Demographically developing group	0.78 w	0.9 w	2.0 w	80 w	79 w
World	1.34 w	1.4 w	3.6 w	80 w	79 w

Note: Regional totals and averages include relevant information for less populous countries, as listed in Table A.10, except for the indicator "percentage of children immunized."
a. Each value refers to one particular but not specified year within the time period denoted.
b. Refers to former Czechoslovakia because disaggregated data are not yet available.
c. Refers to former Socialist Federal Republic of Yugoslavia because disaggregated data are not yet available.

Table A.9 Health expenditure and total flows from external assistance

Demographic region and economy	Total health expenditure (official exchange rate dollars)		Health expenditures as a percentage of GDP			Development assistance for health		Aid flows as a percentage of total health expenditure, 1990
	Millions, 1990	Per capita, 1990	Total, 1990	Public sector, 1990	Private sector, 1990	Total aid flows in dollars, 1990 (millions)[a]	Aid flows per capita, 1990	
Sub-Saharan Africa	12,080 t	24 w	4.5 w	2.5 w	2.0 w	1,251 t	2.5 w	10.4 w
Mozambique	85	5	5.9	4.4	1.5	45	2.9	52.9
Tanzania	109	4	4.7	3.2	1.5	53	2.1	48.3
Ethiopia	229	4	3.8	2.3	1.5	43	0.8	18.8
Uganda	95	6	3.4	1.6	1.8	46	2.8	48.4
Burundi	36	7	3.3	1.7	1.6	15	2.8	42.7
Chad	76	13	6.3	4.7	1.6	33	5.8	43.0
Madagascar	79	7	2.6	1.3	1.3	17	1.5	21.5
Sierra Leone	22	5	2.4	1.7	0.8	7	1.7	33.0
Malawi	93	11	5.0	2.9	2.1	22	2.5	23.3
Rwanda	74	10	3.5	1.9	1.6	29	4.1	39.5
Mali	130	15	5.2	2.8	2.4	36	4.3	27.7
Burkina Faso	219	24	8.5	7.0	1.5	42	4.7	19.4
Niger	126	16	5.0	3.4	1.6	43	5.6	34.0
Nigeria	906	9	2.7	1.2	1.6	58	0.6	6.4
Kenya	375	16	4.3	2.7	1.6	84	3.5	22.3
Benin	79	17	4.3	2.8	1.6	33	7.0	41.8
Central Africa Rep.	55	18	4.2	2.6	1.6	20	6.5	35.8
Ghana	204	14	3.5	1.7	1.8	29	1.9	14.2
Togo	67	18	4.1	2.5	1.6	14	3.9	21.0
Guinea	106	19	3.9	2.3	1.6	20	3.5	23.8
Zimbabwe	416	42	6.2	3.2	3.0	42	4.2	10.0
Côte d'Ivoire	332	28	3.3	1.7	1.6	11	0.9	3.4
Senegal	214	29	3.7	2.3	1.4	36	4.9	16.9
Cameroon	286	24	2.6	1.0	1.6	38	3.3	13.4
South Africa	5,671	158	5.6	3.2	2.4	2	. .	. .
Somalia	60	8	1.5	0.9	0.6	27	3.5	45.6
Zaire	179	5	2.4	0.8	1.5	48	1.3	26.7
Sudan	300	12	3.3	0.5	2.8	39	1.5	13.0
Zambia	117	14	3.2	2.2	1.0	6	0.7	4.9
Angola	. .	. .	. .	. .	. .	28	2.8	. .
India	17,740	21	6.0	1.3	4.7	286	0.3	1.6
China	12,969	11	3.5	2.1	1.4	77	0.1	0.6
Other Asia and islands	41,752 t	61 w	4.5 w	1.8 w	2.7 w	594 t	0.9 w	1.4 w
Nepal	141	7	4.5	2.2	2.3	33	1.8	23.6
Cambodia	. .	. .	. .	. .	. .	. .	. .	. .
Bangladesh	715	7	3.2	1.4	1.8	128	1.2	17.9
Lao PDR	22	5	2.5	1.0	1.5	5	1.2	22.7
Sri Lanka	305	18	3.7	1.8	1.9	26	1.5	7.4
Indonesia	2,148	12	2.0	0.7	1.3	159	0.9	7.4
Philippines	883	14	2.0	1.0	1.0	69	1.1	7.8
Papua New Guinea	142	36	4.4	2.8	1.6	7	1.8	4.9
Thailand	4,061	73	5.0	1.1	3.9	36	0.7	0.9
Malaysia	1,259	67	3.0	1.3	1.7	3	0.1	0.2
Korea, Rep.	16,130	377	6.6	2.7	3.9	32	. .	0.2
Hong Kong	4,060	699	5.7	1.1	4.6	. .	. .	. .
Singapore	658	219	1.9	1.1	0.8	1	0.2	0.1
Myanmar	. .	. .	. .	. .	. .	12	0.3	. .
Viet Nam	157	2	2.1	1.1	1.0	25	0.4	15.9
Korea, Dem. People's Rep	. .	. .	. .	. .	. .	. .	. .	. .
Latin America and the Caribbean	46,660 t	105 w	4.0 w	2.4 w	1.6 w	591 t	1.3 w	1.3 w
Nicaragua	133	35	8.6	6.7	1.9	27	6.6	20.0
Haiti	193	30	7.0	3.2	3.8	33	5.1	17.0
Honduras	134	26	4.5	2.9	1.6	20	4.0	15.1
Bolivia	181	25	4.0	2.4	1.6	37	5.1	20.3
Guatemala	283	31	3.7	2.1	1.6	32	3.4	11.1
Dominican Rep.	263	37	3.7	2.1	1.6	11	1.5	4.1
Ecuador	441	43	4.1	2.6	1.6	31	3.0	7.0
Peru	1,065	49	3.2	1.9	1.3	29	1.4	2.7
El Salvador	317	61	5.9	2.6	3.3	44	8.5	13.9
Colombia	1,604	50	4.0	1.8	2.2	26	0.8	1.6
Paraguay	160	37	2.8	1.2	1.6	10	2.4	6.4
Chile	1,315	100	4.7	3.4	1.4	10	0.7	0.7
Venezuela	1,747	89	3.6	2.0	1.6	2	0.1	0.1
Argentina	4,441	138	4.2	2.5	1.7	11	0.3	0.2
Uruguay	383	124	4.6	2.5	2.1	5	1.7	1.4
Brazil	19,871	132	4.2	2.8	1.4	84	0.6	0.4
Mexico	7,648	89	3.2	1.6	1.6	65	0.8	0.9
Puerto Rico	. .	. .	. .	. .	. .	. .	. .	. .
Cuba	. .	. .	. .	. .	. .	3	0.3	. .

Demographic region and economy	Total health expenditure (official exchange rate dollars)		Health expenditures as a percentage of GDP			Development assistance for health		
	Millions, 1990	Per capita, 1990	Total, 1990	Public sector, 1990	Private sector, 1990	Total aid flows in dollars, 1990 (millions)[a]	Aid flows per capita, 1990	Aid flows as a percentage of total health expenditure, 1990
Middle Eastern crescent	38,961 t	77 w	4.1 w	2.4 w	1.7 w	453 t	0.9 w	1.2 w
Pakistan	1,394	12	3.4	1.8	1.6	76	0.7	5.4
Yemen, Rep.	217	19	3.2	1.5	1.7	25	2.2	11.6
Egypt	921	18	2.6	1.0	1.6	111	2.1	12.1
Morocco	661	26	2.6	0.9	1.6	20	0.8	3.0
Tajikistan	532	100	6.0	4.4	1.6	. .	. .	. .
Jordan	149	48	3.8	1.8	2.0	18	5.9	12.4
Syrian Arab Rep.	283	23	2.1	0.4	1.6	20	1.6	7.1
Uzbekistan	2,388	116	5.9	4.3	1.6	. .	. .	. .
Tunisia	614	76	4.9	3.3	1.6	18	2.3	3.0
Kyrgyzstan	517	118	5.0	3.3	1.6	. .	. .	. .
Georgia	830	152	4.5	2.8	1.7	. .	. .	. .
Azerbaijan	785	98	4.3	2.6	1.7	. .	. .	. .
Turkmenistan	459	125	5.0	3.3	1.7	2	0.5	0.4
Turkey	4,281	76	4.0	1.5	2.5	23	0.4	0.5
Algeria	4,159	166	7.0	5.4	1.6	2	0.1	0.1
Armenia	506	152	4.2	2.5	1.7	. .	. .	. .
Iran	3,024	54	2.6	1.5	1.1	2	. .	. .
Kazakhstan	2,572	154	4.4	2.8	1.7	. .	. .	. .
Saudi Arabia	4,784	322	4.8	3.1	1.7	1	0.1	. .
Israel	2,301	494	4.2	2.1	2.1	3	0.6	0.1
Afghanistan	. .	. .	. .	. .	. .	53	2.6	. .
Iraq	. .	. .	. .	. .	. .	4	0.2	. .
Libya	. .	. .	. .	. .	. .	. .	. .	. .
Formerly socialist economies of Europe (FSE)	49,143 t	142 w	3.6 w	2.5 w	1.0 w	. .	. .	. .
Romania	1,455	63	3.9	2.4	1.5	. .	. .	. .
Poland	3,157	83	5.1	4.1	1.0	. .	. .	. .
Bulgaria	1,154	131	5.4	4.4	1.0	. .	. .	. .
Moldova	623	143	3.9	2.9	1.0	. .	. .	. .
Ukraine	6,803	131	3.3	2.3	1.0	. .	. .	. .
Czechoslovakia[b]	2,711	173	5.9	5.0	0.9	. .	. .	. .
Lithuania	594	159	3.6	2.6	1.0	. .	. .	. .
Hungary	1,958	185	6.0	5.0	0.9	. .	. .	. .
Belarus	1,613	157	3.2	2.2	1.0	. .	. .	. .
Russian Federation	23,527	157	3.0	2.0	1.0	. .	. .	. .
Albania	84	26	4.0	3.4	0.6	. .	. .	. .
Yugoslavia[c]	4,512	205	3.0	4.0	1.0	. .	. .	. .
Established market economies (EME)	1,483,196 t	1,860 w	9.2 w	5.6 w	3.5 w	. .	. .	. .
Portugal	3,970	383	7.0	4.3	2.7	. .	. .	. .
Greece	3,609	358	5.5	4.2	1.3	. .	. .	. .
Ireland	3,068	876	7.1	5.8	1.4	. .	. .	. .
New Zealand	3,150	925	7.2	5.9	1.3	. .	. .	. .
Spain	32,375	831	6.6	5.2	1.4	. .	. .	. .
United Kingdom	59,623	1,039	6.1	5.2	0.9	. .	. .	. .
Australia	22,736	1,331	7.7	5.4	2.3	. .	. .	. .
Italy	82,214	1,426	7.5	5.8	1.7	. .	. .	. .
Netherlands	22,423	1,500	7.9	5.7	2.2	. .	. .	. .
Belgium	14,428	1,449	7.5	6.2	1.3	. .	. .	. .
Austria	13,193	1,711	8.3	5.5	2.8	. .	. .	. .
France	105,467	1,869	8.9	6.6	2.3	. .	. .	. .
Canada	51,594	1,945	9.1	6.8	2.4	. .	. .	. .
United States	690,667	2,763	12.7	5.6	7.0	. .	. .	. .
Germany	120,072	1,511	8.0	5.8	2.2	. .	. .	. .
Denmark	8,160	1,588	6.3	5.3	1.0	. .	. .	. .
Finland	10,200	2,046	7.4	6.2	1.2	. .	. .	. .
Norway	7,782	1,835	7.4	7.0	0.3	. .	. .	. .
Sweden	20,055	2,343	8.8	7.9	0.9	. .	. .	. .
Japan	189,930	1,538	6.5	4.8	1.6	. .	. .	. .
Switzerland	16,916	2,520	7.5	5.1	2.4	. .	. .	. .
FSE and EME	1,532,340 t	1,340 w	8.7 w	5.4 w	3.4 w	. .	. .	. .
Demographically developing group	170,115 t	41 w	4.7 w	2.3 w	2.5 w	3,252 t	0.8 w	1.9 w
World	1,702,455 t	323 w	8.0 w	4.9 w	3.2 w	. .	. .	. .

Note: Regional totals and averages include relevant information for less populous countries, as listed in Table A.10.
a. Aid flows are official development assistance and include only a small portion of private flows, that is NGO assistance.
b. Refers to former Czechoslovakia because disaggregated data are not yet available.
c. Refers to former Socialist Federal Republic of Yugoslavia because disaggregated data are not yet available.

Table A.10 Economies and populations by demographic region, mid-1990
(population in thousands)

Sub-Saharan Africa (49 economies)			510,271
Nigeria	96,203	Burkina Faso	9,016
Ethiopia	51,180	Malawi	8,507
Zaire	37,320	Mali	8,460
South Africa	35,919	Zambia	8,111
Sudan	25,188	Somalia	7,805
Tanzania	24,517	Niger	7,666
Kenya	24,160	Senegal	7,404
Uganda	16,330	Rwanda	7,118
Mozambique	15,707	Guinea	5,717
Ghana	14,870	Chad	5,680
Côte d'Ivoire	11,902	Burundi	5,427
Cameroon	11,739	Benin	4,740
Madagascar	11,673	Sierra Leone	4,136
Angola	10,012	Togo	3,638
Zimbabwe	9,805	Central Africa Republic	3,035

Less than 3 million population

Liberia	2,561	Comoros	475
Congo	2,276	Djibouti	427
Mauritania	1,969	Equatorial Guinea	417
Namibia	1,780	Cape Verde	371
Lesotho	1,768	São Tomé and Principe	117
Botswana	1,254	Mayotte	73
Gabon	1,136	St. Helena	6
Guinea-Bissau	980	Ascencion	1
Gambia, The	875	Tristan da Cunha	0.3
Swaziland	797		

India			849,515

China			1,133,698

Other Asia and islands (49 economies)			682,533
Indonesia	178,232	Nepal	18,916
Bangladesh	106,656	Malaysia	17,857
Viet Nam	66,312	Sri Lanka	17,002
Philippines	61,480	Cambodia	8,469
Thailand	55,853	Hong Kong	5,806
Korea, Rep.	42,797	Lao PDR	4,186
Myanmar	41,609	Papua New Guinea	3,915
Korea, Dem. People's Rep.	21,576	Singapore	3,003
Taiwan, China	20,313		

Less than 3 million population

Mongolia	2,124	Kiribati	70
Bhutan	1,433	Seychelles	68
Mauritius	1,074	Marshall Islands	41
Fiji	744	American Samoa	39
Reunion	593	Northern Mariana Islands	23
Macao	459	Cook Islands	19
Solomon Islands	316	Trust Territory of the Pacific	18
Brunei	256	Wallis and Futuna Islands	14
Maldives	214	Nauru	9
French Polynesia	197	Tuvalu	9
New Caledonia	165	Niue	3
Western Samoa	165	Midway Island	2
Vanuatu	151	Tokelau Island	2
Guam	137	Wake Island	2
Fed. States of Micronesia	103	Johnston Island	1
Tonga	99	Pitcairn Island	0.1

Latin America and the Caribbean (46 economies)			444,297
Brazil	150,368	Bolivia	7,171
Mexico	86,154	Dominican Rep.	7,074
Colombia	32,345	Haiti	6,472
Argentina	32,293	El Salvador	5,213
Peru	21,663	Honduras	5,105
Venezuela	19,738	Paraguay	4,314
Chile	13,173	Nicaragua	3,853
Cuba	10,617	Puerto Rico	3,530
Ecuador	10,284	Uruguay	3,094
Guatemala	9,197	(Continued in next column)	

Latin America and the Caribbean (continued)			

Less than 3 million population

Costa Rica	2,807	St. Vincent	107
Jamaica	2,420	French Guiana	92
Panama	2,418	Grenada	91
Trinidad and Tobago	1,236	Antigua and Barbuda	79
Guyana	798	Dominica	72
Suriname	447	Aruba	66
Guadeloupe	387	St. Kitts and Nevis	40
Martinique	360	Cayman Islands	24
Barbados	257	British Virgin Islands	13
Bahamas, The	255	Montserrat	12
Netherlands Antilles	189	Turks and Caicos Islands	9
Belize	188	Anguilla	8
St. Lucia	150	Falkland/Malvinas Islands	2
Virgin Islands (U. S.)	110		

Middle Eastern crescent (34 economies)			503,075
Pakistan	112,351	Yemen, Rep.	11,282
Turkey	56,098	Tunisia	8,060
Iran	55,779	Azerbaijan	7,149
Egypt	52,061	Georgia	5,462
Morocco	25,091	Tajikistan	5,302
Algeria	25,056	Israel	4,659
Uzbekistan	20,532	Libya	4,546
Afghanistan	20,445	Kyrgyzstan	4,395
Iraq	18,914	Turkmenistan	3,669
Kazakhstan	16,746	Armenia	3,325
Saudi Arabia	14,870	Jordan	3,098
Syrian Arab Rep.	12,360		

Less than 3 million population

Lebanon	2,681	Gaza Strip	588
Kuwait	2,143	Bahrain	503
United Arab Emirates	1,592	Qatar	439
Oman	1,554	Malta	354
West Bank	1,088	Western Sahara	179
Cyprus	702		

Demographically developing group (180 economies)			4,123,389

Formerly socialist economies of Europe (14 economies)			346,237
Russian Federation	148,255	Hungary	10,553
Ukraine	51,860	Belarus	10,278
Poland	38,180	Bulgaria	8,823
Romania	23,199	Moldova	4,367
Yugoslaviaa	23,808	Lithuania	3,731
Czechoslovakiab	15,662	Albania	3,250

Less than 3 million population

Latvia	2,686	Estonia	1,583

Established market economies (35 economies)			797,788
United States	249,975	Greece	10,067
Japan	123,519	Belgium	9,956
Germany	79,484	Sweden	8,559
Italy	57,663	Austria	7,712
United Kingdom	57,395	Switzerland	6,712
France	56,440	Denmark	5,140
Spain	38,959	Finland	4,986
Canada	26,522	Norway	4,242
Australia	17,085	Ireland	3,503
Netherlands	14,943	New Zealand	3,405
Portugal	10,354		

Less than 3 million population

Luxembourg	378	Andorra	47
Iceland	255	Gibraltar	30
Channel Islands	144	Liechtenstein	28
Isle of Man	66	Monaco	28
Bermuda	59	San Marino	23
Greenland	56	St. Pierre and Miquelon	6
Faeroe Islands	48	Holy See	1

FSE and EME (49 economies)			1,144,025

World (229 economies)			5,267,414

a. Refers to former Socialist Federal Republic of Yugoslavia because disaggregated data are not yet available.
b. Refers to former Czechoslovakia because disaggregated data are not yet available.

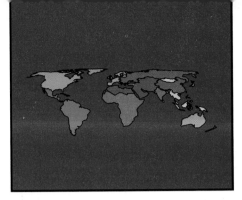

Appendix B. The global burden of disease, 1990

The World Bank and the World Health Organization have undertaken a joint exercise for this Report that quantifies the impact in loss of healthy life from about 100 diseases and injuries in 1990 (Murray and Lopez, background paper). The global burden of disease (GBD) combines the loss of life from premature death in 1990 with the loss of healthy life from disability. The GBD is measured in units of disability-adjusted life years (DALYs) except in Table B.8, which presents only deaths. Disease and injury categories are based on the *International Classification of Diseases, Ninth Revision* (1977). The criterion for selecting the diseases and injuries studied was the expected magnitude of the burden within a specific age group. The selected diseases and injuries account for more than 90 percent of premature deaths and probably for a similar proportion of the burden attributable to disability. The tables presented in this appendix include subtotals for different disease groups; the numbers presented in the subtotals include DALYs lost as a result of the specified diseases and, in some cases, several residual conditions.

Calculation of the disease burden is based on several assumptions, some of which involve decisions about ethical values or social preferences. The key choices are the potential years of life lost as a result of a death at a given age; the relative value of a year of healthy life lived at different ages; the discount rate, or extent of time preference for human life and health; and the disability weights used to convert life lived with a disability to a common measure with premature death. The choices are described below. A full presentation of the methodology will appear in Murray and Lopez (forthcoming).

Duration of life lost due to a death at each age. The number of years of life lost as a result of a death at each age is obtained from a standard schedule of expectations of life at that age. A Coale and Demeny (1983) "West" family model life table (level 26 with an expectation of life of 82.5 years) has been used as the standard for females. A comparable model with an expectation of life of 80 years has been used as the standard for males. For example, a female death at

age 40 is assumed to represent a stream of lost life that is equal to the female expectation of life at age 40, or 43 years. Longer streams of life lost as a result of a female death as compared with a male death at any given age seem to be justified by data for high-income groups in low-mortality populations. These data show that women's expectations of life at birth are still two to three years higher than males'.

Value of a healthy year of life lived at each age. Most societies attach more importance to a year of life lived by a young or middle-aged adult than to a year of life lived by a child or an elderly person. The relative value of a year of life at each age has been modeled for this exercise as an exponential function of the form $ka \exp(-Ba)$, where a is age and B is equal to 0.04. This function rises quickly from zero at birth to a peak at age 25 and then declines asymptotically toward zero. The constant k is chosen so that the total number of DALYs is the same as though uniform age weights had been used (see Box figure 1.3). It is important to note that while the first year of life receives a very low weight, the life of a newborn is valued according to the weights of all the years he or she is expected to live, that is, according to the sum of the function over future years. In the absence of discounting, therefore, the greatest loss of DALYs from premature death occurs from infant deaths. The introduction of discounting means that the greatest loss from premature death occurs in early adulthood, but that loss is only slightly greater than the loss from an infant death. Largely because loss of life is valued according to the future stream of age-specific age weights and not just the weight for one year, the results of the analysis are not very sensitive to the introduction of nonuniform age weights.

Time preference. Since the stream of damage to health from current illness and injury can extend years or even decades into the future, it must be decided how to value the future relative to the present. This is a controversial and unresolved issue because there are two different arguments concerning how to regard the future. First, societies typically prefer to have a given amount of consumption today rather than tomorrow. This "pure social rate of time preference" is usually assumed to be quite low, of the order of 0-3 percent per year, meaning that the future is valued exactly or almost as much as the present. Second, there is a reason for discounting the future much more, if resources are not consumed today but are invested so as to generate higher consumption tomorrow. The expected rate of growth of consumption times the elasticity of utility with respect to consumption yields a term typically assumed to be about 8-10 percent, comparable to the rate of return on investments involving risk and taxation. In evaluating the global burden of disease, it is assumed that this argument does not apply to human lives, which are incommensurable with consumption; adding to healthy years does not necessarily raise consumption per person. This Report therefore uses a discount rate of 3 percent per year, which could be entirely attributed to pure time preference.

Higher discount rates would reduce the total burden of disease because future health damage from health losses in 1990 would count for less. More important, higher discount rates would also alter the relative importance of different diseases. Because the stream of life lost as a result of mortality is, on average, longer than that caused by disability, higher discount rates raise the importance of disability compared with that of premature mortality. For the same reason, higher discount rates reduce the importance of premature deaths at young ages in relation to those at older ages.

Disability weights. Disabilities were assigned severity weights ranging from zero, representing perfect health, to one, representing death. These disability weights were determined at a meeting of experts in international health who had not participated in the study. In order to reduce the number of weights to be assigned and to emphasize large differences in the severity of disability, each disability condition was assigned to one of six classes of severity. The disabilities in a particular class differ in kind (for example, blindness versus paralysis) but were considered to be of equal severity. Each participant then voted on the weight to be assigned to the entire class, not to individual disabilities, and the class was weighted according to the average vote. It is important to note that many disabling conditions lead to two or more distinct disabilities, which may be classified in more than one class of severity.

The burden of disease could be computed using a prevalence perspective (the extent of burden during a given year, no matter when a disease condition began) or an incidence perspective (the future burden of that year's new cases or incident diseases). An incidence perspective was chosen: the burden of disease is the future stream of disability caused by incident cases in 1990. This is the more logical way of dealing

with mortality, and it is easy to apply to nonfatal disabilities. Disability-adjusted life years attributable to premature mortality are calculated on the basis of 1990 deaths by cause, as presented in Table B.8.

Estimates of mortality by cause were based on three types of source: vital registration data, model-based estimates, and epidemiological estimates for particular diseases. Vital registration data for all countries with good registration systems that attribute a cause of death were used with only minor modifications; such countries include most of the established market economies, the formerly socialist economies of Europe, and a large proportion of the countries of Latin America and the Caribbean. For China high-quality sample registration data from the Disease Surveillance Points System were used with some modifications. Vital registration data were also used for some countries in the Middle Eastern crescent and Other Asia and islands regions.

A variety of models relating cause-specific mortality to total mortality by age have been developed on the basis of the patterns of causes of death recorded in nations with good registration systems. For the large groups of causes—communicable plus maternal and perinatal, noncommunicable, and injuries—these models have been used to allocate deaths to cause groups. Whenever possible, these estimates have been validated by examining the results of small-scale longitudinal population surveillance systems. Estimates for more detailed causes were built up from assessments by disease experts of incidence, remission, and case-fatality rates. These epidemiological estimates by cause have been constructed so as to add up to total mortality.

A different approach was used to estimate the DALYs lost through life lived with a disability. A group of experts estimated the incidence, age of onset, and duration of disability for each specific disease on the basis of community-based epidemiological data, routine health facilities information, and, where necessary, expert judgment. Separate estimates were made for the five age groups, two sexes, and eight regions in the study. When prevalence was used to estimate incidence, the GBD incidence prevalence model was used to check for consistency between the estimated incidence, remission rate, case-fatality rate, and general background mortality rate. The same model was also used to check estimated duration for each disability. A completed first-round set of estimates was reviewed at a conference hosted by the World Health Organization, and comments were taken into account. A second round of estimates was undertaken and was subjected to the same review. The third round of estimates is presented here. A fourth and final round of revisions will appear in Murray and Lopez (forthcoming).

Table B.1 Burden of disease by age and sex, 1990

Demographic region and age group	Millions of disability-adjusted life years (DALYs) lost			Percentage of DALYs lost	DALYs per 1,000 population			
	Male	Female	Total		Male	Female	Total	Male/female ratio
Sub-Saharan Africa	152.8	139.9	292.7	100.0	606	542	574	1.12
0–5	83.8	73.3	157.1	53.7	1,765	1,559	1,662	1.13
5–14	19.7	17.5	37.2	12.7	280	251	266	1.12
15–44	36.2	35.6	71.9	24.6	349	335	342	1.04
45–59	7.9	7.1	15.1	5.1	391	323	355	1.21
60+	5.2	6.2	11.4	3.9	494	491	492	1.01
India	145.3	147.1	292.4	100.0	331	359	344	0.92
0–5	67.3	70.0	137.2	46.9	1,125	1,234	1,178	0.91
5–14	15.8	16.5	32.3	11.1	155	173	164	0.90
15–44	30.8	35.0	65.8	22.5	154	191	172	0.81
45–59	16.5	12.3	28.9	9.9	348	268	308	1.30
60+	14.9	13.3	28.2	9.6	500	460	480	1.09
China	103.5	97.8	201.3	100.0	177	178	178	0.99
0–5	23.7	26.2	49.9	24.8	394	452	422	0.87
5–14	8.8	7.4	16.3	8.1	91	82	87	1.11
15–44	31.0	31.4	62.4	31.0	101	111	106	0.91
45–59	17.3	12.2	29.6	14.7	239	190	216	1.26
60+	22.6	20.5	43.1	21.4	462	397	429	1.16
Other Asia and islands	95.1	81.6	176.7	100.0	277	240	259	1.15
0–5	36.8	30.4	67.1	38.0	840	724	783	1.16
5–14	15.0	11.7	26.7	15.1	179	146	163	1.22
15–44	24.3	22.4	46.8	26.5	151	140	146	1.08
45–59	10.1	8.1	18.2	10.3	296	230	263	1.29
60+	8.9	9.0	17.9	10.1	441	397	418	1.11
Latin America and the Caribbean	57.2	45.7	102.9	100.0	258	205	232	1.26
0–5	18.1	14.4	32.5	31.5	629	520	575	1.21
5–14	6.5	5.5	12.0	11.6	125	108	116	1.16
15–44	20.8	15.6	36.4	35.4	199	150	175	1.33
45–59	6.4	4.9	11.3	10.9	287	209	247	1.37
60+	5.5	5.3	10.8	10.5	383	316	347	1.21
Middle Eastern crescent	73.9	70.3	144.2	100.0	288	285	287	1.01
0–5	38.1	36.2	74.3	51.5	925	912	919	1.01
5–14	9.3	8.2	17.5	12.1	142	133	137	1.07
15–44	14.4	15.4	29.8	20.6	127	143	135	0.88
45–59	6.3	4.7	11.1	7.7	284	211	248	1.35
60+	5.8	5.8	11.6	8.0	427	372	398	1.15
Formerly socialist economies of Europe (FSE)	33.2	25.0	58.2	100.0	201	138	168	1.45
0–5	3.0	2.4	5.4	9.2	216	181	199	1.19
5–14	1.0	1.0	2.0	3.4	37	37	37	1.00
15–44	11.3	6.3	17.6	30.2	148	84	116	1.77
45–59	9.1	5.0	14.1	24.3	337	168	248	2.00
60+	8.8	10.3	19.1	32.9	420	284	334	1.48
Established market economies (EME)	52.0	41.6	93.6	100.0	133	102	117	1.30
0–5	3.5	2.9	6.4	6.8	132	115	124	1.15
5–14	1.3	0.9	2.2	2.4	24	19	21	1.30
15–44	16.1	11.4	27.4	29.3	87	64	76	1.37
45–59	11.6	7.2	18.7	20.0	175	106	140	1.65
60+	19.6	19.2	38.8	41.5	324	227	267	1.43
FSE and EME	85.2	66.6	151.8	100.0	153	113	133	1.35
0–5	6.5	5.3	11.7	7.7	161	138	150	1.17
5–14	2.3	1.9	4.2	2.8	29	25	27	1.15
15–44	27.3	17.7	45.0	29.7	105	70	87	1.51
45–59	20.6	12.2	32.8	21.6	222	125	172	1.77
60+	28.4	29.5	58.0	38.2	349	244	286	1.43
Demographically developing group	628.0	582.3	1,210.3	100.0	299	288	294	1.04
0–5	267.7	250.5	518.1	42.8	952	924	938	1.03
5–14	75.1	66.9	142.0	11.7	160	149	155	1.07
15–44	157.6	155.5	313.1	25.9	159	165	162	0.97
45–59	64.6	49.4	114.0	9.4	295	231	264	1.27
60+	62.9	60.2	123.0	10.2	458	406	431	1.13
World	713.1	648.9	1,362.1	100.0	269	248	259	1.08
0–5	274.1	255.7	529.9	38.9	853	822	840	1.03
5–14	77.4	68.8	146.2	10.7	140	131	136	1.07
15–44	185.0	173.1	358.1	26.3	148	144	146	1.02
45–59	85.3	61.6	146.9	10.8	273	198	236	1.38
60+	91.3	89.7	181.0	13.3	417	333	371	1.25

Note: In this appendix the demographically developing group includes the Sub-Saharan Africa, India, China, Other Asia and islands, Latin America and the Caribbean, and Middle Eastern crescent regions.

Table B.2 Burden of disease in females by cause, 1990

(hundreds of thousands of DALYs lost)

Disease or injury	Sub-Saharan Africa	India	China	Other Asia and islands	Latin America and the Caribbean	Middle Eastern crescent	Formerly socialist economies of Europe (FSE)	Established market economies (EME)	FSE and EME	Demographically developing group	World
Communicable, maternal, and perinatal	1,038.7	772.9	281.4	419.8	207.6	387.8	25.7	48.8	74.5	3,108.2	3,182.7
Infectious and parasitic	716.7	409.9	133.0	228.8	120.6	189.6	8.5	22.8	31.4	1,769.6	1,830.0
Tuberculosis	62.1	45.2	24.4	37.7	10.6	18.8	0.5	0.5	1.0	198.8	199.8
STDs excluding HIV	45.8	32.0	33.3	12.6	21.6	6.3	5.0	15.4	20.5	151.7	172.2
Syphilis	23.9	3.4	0.0	0.1	1.6	0.0	0.0	0.0	0.0	29.0	29.1
Chlamydia	1.5	2.7	3.1	2.3	1.5	0.6	0.3	0.8	1.1	11.7	12.8
Gonorrhea	1.6	0.1	0.2	0.2	0.1	0.1	0.0	0.0	0.1	2.2	2.3
Pelvic inflammatory disease	18.7	25.8	30.0	10.1	18.3	5.7	4.8	14.5	19.3	108.7	128.0
Human immunodeficiency virus	89.9	13.6	0.0	4.9	10.2	0.6	0.2	3.4	3.6	119.1	122.8
Diarrheal diseases	146.2	143.9	21.7	68.8	27.6	78.9	1.1	1.2	2.2	487.2	489.4
Acute watery	78.8	78.9	14.1	37.6	15.9	41.7	1.0	1.0	1.9	267.1	269.0
Persistent	44.6	42.6	3.6	20.5	7.1	24.6	0.0	0.1	0.1	142.9	143.0
Dysentery	22.8	22.4	4.0	10.8	4.6	12.6	0.1	0.1	0.2	77.2	77.4
Childhood cluster	132.8	98.7	8.1	36.5	7.5	43.4	0.2	0.4	0.6	327.1	327.7
Pertussis	22.0	15.2	2.7	5.6	3.4	7.9	0.2	0.3	0.5	56.8	57.3
Polio	6.0	7.5	0.9	1.7	1.0	2.8	0.0	0.0	0.0	19.9	19.9
Diphtheria	0.2	0.6	0.0	0.2	0.1	0.1	0.0	0.0	0.0	1.2	1.2
Measles	77.5	48.5	1.5	19.3	1.9	19.9	0.0	0.0	0.1	168.5	168.5
Tetanus	27.2	27.0	3.0	9.8	1.1	12.7	0.0	0.0	0.0	80.7	80.7
Meningitis	6.4	8.2	2.8	4.1	3.3	5.3	0.6	0.5	1.0	30.1	31.1
Hepatitis	1.3	1.7	2.2	1.4	0.9	1.0	0.2	0.3	0.4	8.4	8.9
Malaria	154.1	4.7	0.0	12.5	2.2	1.5	0.0	0.0	0.0	175.0	175.0
Tropical cluster	25.8	7.5	2.3	1.0	13.4	1.0	0.0	0.0	0.0	51.0	51.0
Trypanosomiasis	8.8	0.0	0.0	0.0	0.0	0.0	0.0	0.0	0.0	8.8	8.8
Chagas' disease	0.0	0.0	0.0	0.0	12.6	0.0	0.0	0.0	0.0	12.6	12.6
Schistosomiasis	11.8	0.9	1.5	0.3	0.6	0.3	0.0	0.0	0.0	15.4	15.4
Leishmaniasis	2.0	5.0	0.4	0.4	0.1	0.6	0.0	0.0	0.0	8.6	8.6
Lymphatic filariasis	0.5	1.6	0.4	0.3	0.0	0.1	0.0	0.0	0.0	2.9	2.9
Onchocerciasis	2.7	0.0	0.0	0.0	0.0	0.0	0.0	0.0	0.0	2.7	2.7
Leprosy	1.1	2.6	0.0	0.8	0.3	0.2	0.0	0.0	0.0	5.1	5.1
Trachoma	6.9	2.0	3.6	7.0	0.7	3.6	0.0	0.0	0.0	23.7	23.7
Intestinal helminths	4.3	10.0	30.6	28.5	11.9	2.6	0.0	0.0	0.0	87.9	87.9
Ascaris	2.2	5.7	18.7	15.7	6.7	2.4	0.0	0.0	0.0	51.4	51.4
Trichuris	1.5	2.4	10.9	11.6	4.5	0.0	0.0	0.0	0.0	30.9	30.9
Hookworm	0.5	1.9	0.9	1.2	0.7	0.2	0.0	0.0	0.0	5.6	5.6
Respiratory infections	153.9	161.9	69.0	93.0	29.9	84.9	6.6	11.7	18.3	592.5	610.8
Lower respiratory infections	148.5	154.0	61.0	87.3	26.5	80.9	4.8	8.0	12.8	558.3	571.1
Upper respiratory infections	1.7	2.8	2.7	2.3	1.3	0.4	1.0	2.3	3.3	11.1	14.4
Otitis media	3.7	5.1	5.3	3.3	2.2	3.5	0.8	1.4	2.2	23.1	25.3
Maternal	79.9	78.2	25.0	43.6	18.0	42.1	4.8	5.5	10.4	286.8	297.2
Hemorrhage	14.3	13.7	6.4	7.5	2.5	4.7	0.5	0.9	1.4	49.1	50.4
Sepsis	27.5	27.5	6.3	15.8	4.1	17.5	1.5	2.0	3.5	98.7	102.2
Eclampsia	4.2	3.9	0.7	2.0	1.6	1.3	0.0	0.1	0.1	13.7	13.8
Hypertension	2.0	1.9	0.3	2.5	0.7	1.8	0.1	0.0	0.1	9.3	9.4
Obstructed labor	19.0	19.4	7.9	10.2	5.7	13.3	2.0	2.3	4.3	75.4	79.8
Abortion	7.9	9.5	0.9	2.6	2.2	2.0	0.4	0.1	0.6	25.1	25.6
Perinatal	88.2	122.9	54.4	54.5	39.1	71.2	5.7	8.8	14.5	430.3	444.7
Noncommunicable	280.5	578.9	558.1	349.8	212.0	255.2	203.5	334.8	538.3	2,234.5	2,772.8
Malignant neoplasms	22.3	53.6	72.0	36.7	27.8	22.3	36.0	79.5	115.5	234.7	350.1
Mouth and oropharynx	1.0	6.3	1.8	2.5	0.4	1.1	0.4	0.9	1.3	13.2	14.5
Esophagus	0.7	3.5	5.3	0.7	0.2	0.7	0.3	0.7	1.0	11.2	12.2
Stomach	1.6	2.4	11.1	2.1	1.4	1.5	3.9	4.3	8.2	20.0	28.2
Colon and rectum	0.8	1.9	4.4	1.9	1.3	1.1	3.5	9.4	12.9	11.5	24.4
Liver	2.1	0.6	9.0	1.8	0.2	0.6	0.3	0.8	1.1	14.3	15.4
Pancreas	0.4	0.5	1.1	0.3	0.3	0.3	0.4	2.6	3.0	2.8	5.8
Trachea, bronchus, and lung	0.5	0.9	6.0	2.0	0.7	1.0	2.2	8.3	10.5	11.1	21.6
Melanoma	0.5	0.1	0.1	0.1	0.3	0.1	0.5	1.2	1.6	1.2	2.8
Breast	2.5	6.1	4.0	4.0	4.7	3.1	5.2	15.7	20.8	24.3	45.1
Cervix	4.6	9.6	3.1	4.7	4.3	1.9	2.0	2.3	4.4	28.1	32.5
Uterus	0.4	0.5	0.9	0.4	0.8	0.4	0.6	2.3	2.8	3.4	6.2
Ovary	1.0	2.0	1.6	1.5	0.7	0.8	1.4	4.0	5.4	7.6	13.0

Disease or injury	Sub-Saharan Africa	India	China	Other Asia and islands	Latin America and the Caribbean	Middle Eastern crescent	Formerly socialist economies of Europe (FSE)	Established market economies (EME)	FSE and EME	Demographically developing group	World
Noncommunicable diseases, malignant neoplasms (continued)											
Prostate	0.0	0.0	0.0	0.0	0.0	0.0	0.0	0.0	0.0	0.0	0.0
Bladder	0.6	0.2	0.4	0.3	0.2	0.4	0.6	1.1	1.7	2.0	3.7
Lymphoma	1.3	1.4	1.2	1.1	1.1	0.7	1.0	3.5	4.6	6.8	11.4
Leukemia	0.6	2.3	7.1	1.6	1.1	1.3	1.3	2.6	3.9	14.0	18.0
Diabetes mellitus	2.1	10.3	4.1	6.9	5.8	6.3	2.3	7.1	9.5	35.5	45.0
Nutritional and endocrine	39.9	90.6	38.6	41.6	23.9	27.4	5.1	8.6	13.7	262.1	275.8
Protein-energy malnutrition	10.4	29.2	10.1	4.4	4.6	5.1	1.1	1.2	2.4	63.9	66.3
Iodine deficiency	8.5	6.9	4.9	6.4	2.6	6.7	0.0	0.0	0.0	35.8	35.9
Vitamin A deficiency	10.7	20.2	4.9	12.2	6.9	2.6	0.0	0.0	0.0	57.7	57.7
Anemia	6.0	25.0	16.6	13.9	5.9	8.9	3.0	3.9	6.9	76.2	83.0
Neuropsychiatric	41.3	83.6	78.5	57.4	35.7	38.9	29.3	62.0	91.3	335.3	426.6
Depressive disorders	11.2	20.2	31.9	17.7	11.8	11.9	7.9	14.3	22.1	104.8	127.0
Bipolar affective disorders	0.6	1.0	1.6	0.9	0.6	0.6	0.4	0.6	1.0	5.2	6.2
Psychoses	2.7	11.4	7.8	4.2	2.7	2.8	1.2	2.9	4.1	31.6	35.7
Epilepsy	5.5	9.5	6.9	7.0	3.5	5.1	2.6	2.8	5.4	37.4	42.9
Alcohol dependence	2.2	2.4	2.4	1.4	2.0	0.5	2.4	3.7	6.1	10.9	17.0
Alzheimer's and other dementias	4.3	9.7	13.6	7.3	4.7	4.9	8.7	23.2	31.9	44.5	76.4
Parkinson's disease	0.3	0.7	1.0	0.6	0.6	0.3	0.8	1.9	2.7	3.4	6.2
Multiple sclerosis	0.7	1.3	1.7	1.1	0.5	0.7	0.6	1.1	1.7	5.9	7.6
Drug dependence	0.9	1.7	0.7	2.3	2.1	0.9	0.6	3.9	4.5	8.7	13.3
Posttraumatic stress disorder	3.2	5.1	7.0	4.4	2.8	3.1	2.7	4.5	7.2	25.5	32.7
Sense organ	7.9	11.4	9.0	7.5	3.3	3.1	0.3	0.6	0.9	42.2	43.1
Glaucoma	1.7	1.7	3.4	2.9	0.4	0.1	0.1	0.4	0.5	10.2	10.7
Cataract	5.8	8.8	3.6	4.2	2.6	2.7	0.2	0.1	0.3	27.7	28.0
Cardiovascular	66.3	138.0	133.4	86.5	45.9	62.8	82.2	98.1	180.3	532.9	713.2
Rheumatic	6.1	12.7	12.2	3.9	1.8	3.1	1.8	0.9	2.7	39.8	42.6
Ischemic heart disease	5.4	31.9	17.6	26.7	11.3	10.6	34.3	37.2	71.5	103.4	175.0
Cerebrovascular	25.3	35.0	58.1	21.8	14.0	18.5	29.7	26.6	56.3	172.6	229.0
Peri-, endo-, and myocarditis and cardiomyopathy	16.0	31.7	4.4	9.4	7.2	8.9	1.3	2.5	3.8	77.5	81.3
Respiratory	21.2	39.5	85.4	18.4	15.0	16.8	7.6	14.9	22.6	196.3	218.9
Chronic obstructive pulmonary disease	3.0	7.3	50.9	3.7	2.9	3.0	3.1	5.7	8.7	70.7	79.4
Asthma	10.0	8.7	17.1	7.0	5.6	4.9	2.7	5.8	8.4	53.2	61.7
Digestive	25.4	55.3	37.8	24.6	12.8	21.9	8.5	14.7	23.2	177.8	201.0
Peptic ulcer disease	1.5	3.6	3.9	1.9	0.7	1.2	0.8	1.8	2.6	12.8	15.4
Cirrhosis	4.8	8.4	10.0	5.3	3.0	2.7	1.4	5.1	6.5	34.3	40.8
Genitourinary	10.1	20.3	12.8	11.4	6.6	8.2	3.8	6.2	10.0	69.5	79.5
Nephritis and nephrosis	5.6	10.6	11.1	6.9	4.5	4.5	1.9	4.3	6.2	43.2	49.4
Benign prostatic hypertrophy	0.0	0.0	0.0	0.0	0.0	0.0	0.0	0.0	0.0	0.0	0.0
Musculoskeletal	4.6	8.4	40.0	17.0	13.0	7.2	11.3	24.5	35.8	90.2	126.1
Rheumatoid arthritis	1.1	1.1	5.2	1.6	4.6	3.6	4.1	11.3	15.4	17.3	32.7
Osteoarthritis	1.7	3.1	31.1	12.9	6.6	1.9	6.4	11.3	17.7	57.2	74.9
Congenital abnormalities	29.6	45.9	35.4	25.5	14.9	27.1	7.3	11.2	18.6	178.4	197.0
Oral health	5.2	14.1	8.9	11.7	5.9	10.2	9.0	5.7	14.6	56.0	70.6
Dental caries	0.7	1.6	1.1	1.3	2.2	1.6	0.8	0.4	1.2	8.5	9.6
Periodontal disease	4.2	10.6	4.9	5.2	2.9	2.9	0.4	0.5	0.9	30.8	31.7
Edentulism	0.2	1.9	2.9	5.2	0.8	5.6	7.8	4.8	12.6	16.7	29.3
Injuries	79.6	119.4	138.5	46.2	37.2	59.9	21.1	32.1	53.1	480.8	533.9
Unintentional	42.6	104.8	84.7	34.7	31.1	37.0	15.3	22.9	38.2	335.1	373.3
Motor vehicle	8.1	9.4	12.3	8.5	17.9	16.4	4.5	9.2	13.7	72.6	86.3
Poisoning	1.4	0.8	6.6	1.3	0.3	1.0	1.8	0.7	2.5	11.4	13.9
Falls	9.5	21.1	19.2	7.3	2.7	4.6	2.8	7.4	10.2	64.4	74.6
Fires	4.2	8.5	5.6	2.9	1.9	2.6	1.1	1.9	3.1	25.7	28.8
Drowning	4.2	8.3	16.6	3.0	1.1	2.6	0.8	0.5	1.4	35.7	37.1
Occupational	0.5	3.9	1.1	0.7	0.5	0.4	0.4	0.3	0.7	7.0	7.7
Intentional	36.9	14.6	53.8	11.5	6.1	22.8	5.8	9.2	14.9	145.7	160.6
Self-inflicted	3.0	10.8	40.0	4.4	1.0	2.7	2.6	4.9	7.4	61.9	69.3
Homicide and violence	4.7	2.8	13.8	5.8	3.2	3.6	3.2	4.3	7.5	34.0	41.4
War	29.2	0.9	0.0	1.3	1.9	16.5	0.0	0.0	0.0	49.8	49.8
Total	1,398.8	1,471.1	978.0	815.7	456.9	702.9	250.2	415.7	665.9	5,823.4	6,489.4

Table B.3 Burden of disease in males by cause, 1990
(hundreds of thousands of DALYs lost)

Disease or injury	Sub-Saharan Africa	India	China	Other Asia and islands	Latin America and the Caribbean	Middle Eastern crescent	Formerly socialist economies of Europe (FSE)	Established market economies (EME)	FSE and EME	Demographically developing group	World
Communicable, maternal, and perinatal	1,046.8	704.4	228.0	438.0	226.3	347.2	24.5	42.3	66.8	2,990.9	3,057.7
Infectious and parasitic	763.7	404.9	117.6	258.4	137.7	180.2	8.0	18.2	26.3	1,862.5	1,888.8
Tuberculosis	74.6	62.8	34.7	51.6	15.1	21.6	3.1	1.1	4.1	260.5	264.7
STDs excluding HIV	28.9	5.3	0.8	0.6	2.4	0.3	0.1	0.2	0.3	38.3	38.6
Syphilis	27.2	4.7	0.1	0.1	2.1	0.0	0.0	0.0	0.0	34.1	34.1
Chlamydia	0.3	0.6	0.6	0.5	0.3	0.3	0.1	0.1	0.2	2.5	2.7
Gonorrhea	1.4	0.0	0.1	0.1	0.1	0.0	0.0	0.0	0.0	1.8	1.8
Pelvic inflammatory disease	0.0	0.0	0.0	0.0	0.0	0.0	0.0	0.0	0.0	0.0	0.0
Human immunodeficiency virus	93.7	27.1	0.0	8.0	34.1	2.6	1.4	12.4	13.7	165.5	179.3
Diarrheal diseases	157.3	136.4	20.7	78.5	31.3	75.1	1.1	1.2	2.3	499.4	501.7
Acute watery	84.1	75.0	14.1	42.6	17.5	39.5	1.0	1.0	2.0	272.8	274.8
Persistent	48.8	40.2	2.7	23.7	8.7	23.7	0.1	0.1	0.1	147.7	147.8
Dysentery	24.4	21.3	4.0	12.2	5.1	12.0	0.1	0.1	0.2	79.0	79.1
Childhood cluster	148.1	95.8	9.3	43.3	8.6	42.5	0.2	0.4	0.7	347.7	348.4
Pertussis	26.1	14.3	2.8	7.1	3.9	7.5	0.2	0.4	0.6	61.7	62.2
Polio	8.3	10.9	1.4	2.4	1.3	3.9	0.0	0.0	0.0	28.1	28.2
Diphtheria	0.1	0.5	0.0	0.2	0.1	0.1	0.0	0.0	0.0	1.1	1.1
Measles	83.0	44.9	1.5	22.3	1.9	18.8	0.0	0.1	0.1	172.5	172.6
Tetanus	30.6	25.3	3.6	11.3	1.3	12.2	0.0	0.0	0.0	84.2	84.2
Meningitis	11.5	11.9	4.0	9.7	3.8	7.4	0.8	0.6	1.4	48.4	49.8
Hepatitis	1.1	1.4	4.5	1.4	0.7	0.8	0.2	0.4	0.6	9.8	10.4
Malaria	161.0	4.8	0.1	12.9	2.2	1.3	0.0	0.0	0.0	182.3	182.3
Tropical cluster	39.0	11.3	3.8	3.1	16.3	1.5	0.0	0.0	0.0	75.0	75.0
Trypanosomiasis	9.0	0.0	0.0	0.0	0.0	0.0	0.0	0.0	0.0	9.0	9.0
Chagas' disease	0.0	0.0	0.0	0.0	14.8	0.0	0.0	0.0	0.0	14.8	14.8
Schistosomiasis	23.1	1.7	2.8	0.7	1.2	0.5	0.0	0.0	0.0	29.9	29.9
Leishmaniasis	1.9	6.8	0.6	1.5	0.3	0.9	0.0	0.0	0.0	12.0	12.0
Lymphatic filariasis	1.3	2.8	0.5	0.9	0.0	0.1	0.0	0.0	0.0	5.6	5.6
Onchocerciasis	3.7	0.0	0.0	0.0	0.0	0.0	0.0	0.0	0.0	3.7	3.7
Leprosy	1.2	2.6	0.0	0.8	0.3	0.2	0.0	0.0	0.0	5.1	5.1
Trachoma	2.1	1.1	1.1	2.4	0.4	2.2	0.0	0.0	0.0	9.3	9.3
Intestinal helminths	4.2	10.6	32.6	29.6	12.0	2.8	0.0	0.0	0.0	91.8	91.8
Ascaris	2.2	6.0	19.9	16.3	6.8	2.6	0.0	0.0	0.0	53.8	53.8
Trichuris	1.5	2.5	11.6	12.0	4.5	0.0	0.0	0.0	0.0	32.2	32.2
Hookworm	0.5	2.1	1.0	1.2	0.7	0.2	0.0	0.0	0.0	5.8	5.8
Respiratory infections	162.5	155.7	60.0	103.4	33.9	80.8	8.2	12.5	20.7	596.3	617.1
Lower respiratory infections	157.1	147.3	52.1	97.4	30.2	76.9	6.5	8.9	15.4	560.9	576.4
Upper respiratory infections	1.6	3.2	2.8	2.5	1.3	0.5	0.9	2.1	2.9	11.9	14.8
Otitis media	3.8	5.1	5.0	3.6	2.4	3.5	0.9	1.5	2.3	23.6	25.9
Maternal	0.0	0.0	0.0	0.0	0.0	0.0	0.0	0.0	0.0	0.0	0.0
Hemorrhage	0.0	0.0	0.0	0.0	0.0	0.0	0.0	0.0	0.0	0.0	0.0
Sepsis	0.0	0.0	0.0	0.0	0.0	0.0	0.0	0.0	0.0	0.0	0.0
Eclampsia	0.0	0.0	0.0	0.0	0.0	0.0	0.0	0.0	0.0	0.0	0.0
Hypertension	0.0	0.0	0.0	0.0	0.0	0.0	0.0	0.0	0.0	0.0	0.0
Obstructed labor	0.0	0.0	0.0	0.0	0.0	0.0	0.0	0.0	0.0	0.0	0.0
Abortion	0.0	0.0	0.0	0.0	0.0	0.0	0.0	0.0	0.0	0.0	0.0
Perinatal	120.6	143.8	50.4	76.2	54.8	86.2	8.3	11.6	19.8	532.0	551.8
Noncommunicable	287.9	601.3	609.6	359.7	228.6	264.0	231.6	399.0	630.6	2,351.0	2,981.6
Malignant neoplasms	22.5	65.7	113.1	41.4	25.3	26.5	49.9	99.5	149.4	294.6	444.0
Mouth and oropharynx	1.2	12.8	3.8	3.8	1.3	1.9	2.1	3.3	5.4	24.7	30.0
Esophagus	1.5	5.0	11.7	1.3	0.7	1.0	1.3	2.8	4.1	21.2	25.3
Stomach	1.6	4.7	19.9	3.3	2.4	2.1	6.4	7.0	13.4	34.0	47.4
Colon and rectum	0.6	2.5	5.3	1.9	1.2	1.1	3.4	10.2	13.7	12.7	26.4
Liver	3.9	1.6	27.4	4.8	0.3	0.9	0.4	2.5	2.9	38.8	41.7
Pancreas	0.3	0.8	1.8	0.5	0.3	0.5	0.6	3.3	3.9	4.3	8.2
Trachea, bronchus, and lung	1.3	4.7	13.6	5.5	2.2	4.0	13.2	22.4	35.6	31.3	66.9
Melanoma	0.3	0.1	0.1	0.1	0.2	0.1	0.5	1.5	2.0	1.0	2.9
Breast	0.0	0.0	0.0	0.0	0.0	0.0	0.0	0.0	0.0	0.0	0.0
Cervix	0.0	0.0	0.0	0.0	0.0	0.0	0.0	0.0	0.0	0.0	0.0
Uterus	0.0	0.0	0.0	0.0	0.0	0.0	0.0	0.0	0.0	0.0	0.0
Ovary	0.0	0.0	0.0	0.0	0.0	0.0	0.0	0.0	0.0	0.0	0.0

Disease or injury	Sub-Saharan Africa	India	China	Other Asia and islands	Latin America and the Caribbean	Middle Eastern crescent	Formerly socialist economies of Europe (FSE)	Established market economies (EME)	FSE and EME	Demographically developing group	World
Noncommunicable diseases, malignant neoplasms (continued)											
Prostate	2.2	1.9	0.3	0.9	1.6	0.7	1.1	6.7	7.8	7.7	15.6
Bladder	0.8	0.8	1.4	0.7	0.7	1.3	1.8	3.3	5.1	5.7	10.9
Lymphoma	3.2	3.1	2.6	1.8	1.7	1.6	1.6	4.8	6.4	13.9	20.3
Leukemia	0.7	3.2	8.1	2.7	1.5	1.9	1.7	3.5	5.2	18.1	23.3
Diabetes mellitus	1.2	8.4	3.6	4.6	4.3	4.8	1.7	6.2	7.9	26.8	34.7
Nutritional and endocrine	42.5	91.4	27.7	40.5	23.0	25.4	2.9	6.9	9.8	250.6	260.3
Protein-energy malnutrition	11.2	26.3	6.5	4.9	5.2	5.2	0.6	1.2	1.8	59.3	61.1
Iodine deficiency	8.2	7.1	5.0	6.5	2.6	6.9	0.0	0.0	0.0	36.3	36.3
Vitamin A deficiency	11.1	20.9	4.9	12.9	7.2	2.9	0.0	0.0	0.0	59.9	59.9
Anemia	4.1	19.7	10.2	9.5	3.9	6.3	1.3	2.2	3.5	53.6	57.2
Neuropsychiatric	55.8	93.7	81.7	66.7	46.8	41.7	35.1	78.2	113.3	386.4	499.8
Depressive disorders	5.3	10.7	16.6	8.6	5.7	6.0	3.5	6.8	10.3	52.8	63.1
Bipolar affective disorders	0.5	1.1	1.6	0.9	0.6	0.6	0.3	0.6	0.9	5.3	6.1
Psychoses	3.1	10.0	10.3	4.7	3.1	3.3	1.4	3.3	4.8	34.5	39.2
Epilepsy	8.0	13.3	10.2	9.9	4.7	7.3	2.3	4.1	6.4	53.4	59.8
Alcohol dependence	14.9	16.6	16.6	9.4	14.1	3.7	16.4	24.5	40.9	75.3	116.2
Alzheimer's and other dementias	4.1	9.8	12.6	6.8	4.0	4.6	5.1	16.7	21.8	41.9	63.7
Parkinson's disease	0.3	0.8	0.9	0.6	0.6	0.3	0.5	1.6	2.1	3.6	5.7
Multiple sclerosis	0.6	1.4	1.5	1.0	0.4	0.6	0.5	1.0	1.5	5.5	7.0
Drug dependence	2.8	4.8	2.2	6.8	6.3	2.7	1.8	11.8	13.6	25.7	39.3
Posttraumatic stress disorder	1.9	3.3	4.4	2.6	1.7	1.9	1.2	2.7	3.9	15.8	19.6
Sense organ	6.0	12.4	7.5	5.8	3.1	3.9	0.2	0.3	0.5	38.6	39.1
Glaucoma	0.0	2.3	1.5	1.3	0.2	0.3	0.1	0.1	0.2	5.6	5.7
Cataract	5.5	9.3	4.0	4.2	2.5	3.3	0.1	0.1	0.2	28.8	29.1
Cardiovascular	55.6	146.7	148.4	85.0	48.9	64.0	89.8	120.9	210.7	548.6	759.3
Rheumatic	2.4	6.0	9.1	2.0	1.4	1.6	1.6	0.5	2.1	22.5	24.6
Ischemic heart disease	6.7	49.5	24.8	35.4	16.0	15.5	45.2	56.4	101.7	147.9	249.6
Cerebrovascular	17.4	27.5	68.4	16.1	13.2	15.5	21.8	23.1	44.9	158.2	203.1
Peri-, endo-, and myocarditis and cardiomyopathy	17.1	36.3	5.2	9.6	8.7	9.5	2.3	4.1	6.4	86.2	92.6
Respiratory	22.6	38.5	96.0	21.5	17.3	21.1	13.0	21.2	34.2	217.1	251.3
Chronic obstructive pulmonary disease	3.5	9.7	60.8	4.8	4.1	4.2	6.4	10.3	16.7	87.1	103.8
Asthma	7.8	8.5	18.2	7.5	5.4	6.6	2.7	5.6	8.3	54.0	62.3
Digestive	28.8	55.3	49.9	30.3	20.5	23.0	14.3	23.7	37.9	207.8	245.7
Peptic ulcer disease	2.0	6.4	7.3	2.9	1.2	1.7	1.8	2.7	4.5	21.4	26.0
Cirrhosis	8.7	18.5	22.0	10.9	8.7	4.5	3.3	11.7	15.1	73.4	88.5
Genitourinary	10.9	18.7	21.8	12.3	7.7	10.4	5.3	8.5	13.8	81.8	95.6
Nephritis and nephrosis	6.2	10.4	14.8	7.3	4.2	4.6	2.4	4.5	6.9	47.6	54.5
Benign prostatic hypertrophy	2.3	3.7	5.5	2.7	2.2	2.3	1.3	2.5	3.9	18.6	22.5
Musculoskeletal	1.9	4.0	13.3	10.9	8.8	2.0	2.9	14.4	17.3	40.9	58.2
Rheumatoid arthritis	0.5	1.0	2.3	1.0	2.5	0.5	1.6	2.4	4.0	7.9	11.9
Osteoarthritis	0.6	1.2	8.5	8.9	5.6	0.7	0.8	11.1	11.9	25.4	37.3
Congenital abnormalities	33.8	48.4	34.8	27.8	16.2	29.7	8.4	12.3	20.7	190.7	211.4
Oral health	5.0	15.1	9.2	11.3	5.6	10.4	7.5	5.0	12.5	56.5	69.0
Dental caries	0.7	1.7	1.2	1.3	2.2	1.7	0.7	0.4	1.0	8.7	9.8
Periodontal disease	4.1	11.5	5.3	5.2	2.8	3.1	0.4	0.5	0.9	32.0	32.8
Edentulism	0.2	1.9	2.7	4.8	0.7	5.5	6.4	4.1	10.5	15.8	26.4
Injuries	193.6	147.6	197.6	153.8	117.2	127.9	75.5	78.8	154.3	937.8	1,092.1
Unintentional	107.9	126.3	148.3	109.2	79.4	76.2	53.6	50.8	104.4	647.3	751.7
Motor vehicle	29.0	23.1	33.0	32.6	41.2	31.2	17.2	24.0	41.2	190.1	231.3
Poisoning	3.9	2.1	8.0	3.9	0.5	2.3	6.7	2.0	8.7	20.7	29.5
Falls	20.3	28.9	23.5	21.0	7.2	9.7	5.7	7.9	13.6	110.6	124.2
Fires	5.9	7.1	8.1	5.1	2.7	3.9	2.6	3.2	5.8	32.7	38.6
Drowning	11.3	9.0	27.6	10.5	4.8	7.0	4.8	2.2	7.0	70.2	77.3
Occupational	3.6	5.1	5.0	3.9	2.8	1.9	2.7	1.7	4.4	22.3	26.7
Intentional	85.7	21.4	49.3	44.6	37.8	51.7	21.9	28.0	49.9	290.5	340.4
Self-inflicted	13.9	11.1	29.8	14.9	2.9	7.2	11.6	14.6	26.3	79.7	106.0
Homicide and violence	21.2	8.2	19.5	27.1	30.8	11.5	10.2	13.4	23.7	118.3	142.0
War	50.6	2.0	0.0	2.6	4.1	33.1	0.0	0.0	0.0	92.5	92.5
Total	1,528.3	1,453.3	1,035.2	951.4	572.1	739.2	331.6	520.1	851.7	6,279.7	7,131.4

Table B.4 Burden of disease by age and the three main groups of causes, 1990

Demographic region and age group	Communicable diseases and maternal and perinatal causes DALYs lost (millions)	Percentage	Rate (per 1,000 population)	Noncommunicable diseases DALYs lost (millions)	Percentage	Rate (per 1,000 population)	Injuries DALYs lost (millions)	Percentage	Rate (per 1,000 population)
Sub-Saharan Africa	208.6	100.0	408.7	56.8	100.0	111.4	27.3	100.0	53.5
0–4	132.5	63.5	1,401.5	18.2	32.1	193.0	6.4	23.4	67.7
5–14	25.5	12.2	181.8	7.2	12.7	51.5	4.6	16.7	32.5
15–44	44.8	21.5	213.2	12.3	21.6	58.4	14.8	54.3	70.6
45–59	3.7	1.8	87.7	10.2	18.0	240.5	1.1	4.2	27.1
60+	2.1	1.0	92.4	8.9	15.7	383.0	0.4	1.4	16.7
India	147.7	100.0	173.9	118.0	100.0	138.9	26.7	100.0	31.4
0–4	97.9	66.3	840.7	33.4	28.3	286.6	5.9	22.2	50.9
5–14	15.4	10.4	78.3	9.8	8.3	49.6	7.1	26.7	36.1
15–44	27.1	18.3	70.5	27.3	23.1	71.1	11.5	43.1	30.0
45–59	4.7	3.2	50.2	22.6	19.2	242.0	1.5	5.7	16.3
60+	2.6	1.8	44.8	25.0	21.1	425.2	0.6	2.3	10.4
China	50.9	100.0	44.9	116.8	100.0	103.0	33.6	100.0	29.7
0–4	25.5	50.0	215.5	16.4	14.0	138.4	8.1	24.0	68.3
5–14	7.9	15.5	42.1	4.7	4.1	25.3	3.6	10.8	19.4
15–44	12.3	24.2	20.9	33.0	28.2	55.8	17.1	50.9	29.0
45–59	2.7	5.4	20.0	24.3	20.8	177.1	2.6	7.6	18.6
60+	2.5	4.9	24.6	38.4	32.9	381.7	2.2	6.7	22.2
Other Asia and islands	85.8	100.0	125.7	70.9	100.0	103.9	20.0	100.0	29.3
0–4	49.7	58.0	580.1	14.4	20.3	167.8	3.0	15.0	35.0
5–14	15.2	17.8	92.7	8.0	11.2	48.5	3.5	17.6	21.5
15–44	16.0	18.7	50.1	19.2	27.1	59.9	11.5	57.6	36.0
45–59	2.7	3.1	38.5	14.2	20.0	204.8	1.3	6.7	19.3
60+	2.1	2.4	48.5	15.2	21.5	355.0	0.6	3.1	14.4
Latin America and the Caribbean	43.4	100.0	97.7	44.1	100.0	99.2	15.4	100.0	34.8
0–4	22.3	51.5	396.1	8.6	19.5	152.7	1.5	9.7	26.7
5–14	6.2	14.4	60.7	3.6	8.1	34.5	2.2	14.1	21.2
15–44	13.0	29.9	62.2	13.2	30.0	63.5	10.2	66.3	49.2
45–59	1.2	2.8	26.7	9.0	20.5	198.2	1.0	6.6	22.2
60+	0.6	1.5	20.8	9.6	21.8	310.0	0.5	3.2	16.1
Middle Eastern crescent	73.5	100.0	146.1	51.9	100.0	103.2	18.8	100.0	37.3
0–4	55.1	75.0	681.5	15.2	29.3	188.3	4.0	21.1	48.9
5–14	7.0	9.5	54.9	6.2	12.0	48.7	4.3	22.8	33.6
15–44	9.1	12.4	41.1	11.5	22.1	51.8	9.2	49.1	41.7
45–59	1.2	1.7	27.2	8.9	17.2	200.1	0.9	4.8	20.4
60+	1.1	1.5	36.7	10.1	19.5	347.2	0.4	2.2	14.0
Formerly socialist economies of Europe (FSE)	5.0	100.0	14.5	43.5	100.0	125.7	9.7	100.0	27.9
0–4	2.5	50.0	93.4	2.3	5.2	84.9	0.6	5.8	20.9
5–14	0.1	2.7	2.6	1.2	2.7	22.1	0.7	7.0	12.5
15–44	1.8	35.0	11.6	9.7	22.4	64.5	6.1	62.8	40.1
45–59	0.3	6.8	6.0	12.2	28.0	213.7	1.6	16.6	28.0
60+	0.3	5.4	4.7	18.1	41.6	315.9	0.8	7.9	13.3
Established market economies (EME)	9.1	100.0	11.4	73.4	100.0	92.0	11.1	100.0	13.9
0–4	2.7	29.3	51.8	3.2	4.3	61.5	0.5	4.9	10.6
5–14	0.2	2.1	1.9	1.4	2.0	13.8	0.6	5.4	5.8
15–44	4.4	48.8	12.2	16.0	21.8	44.1	7.0	62.8	19.2
45–59	0.5	5.8	3.9	16.9	23.0	126.2	1.3	11.8	9.7
60+	1.3	14.0	8.8	35.9	48.9	247.1	1.7	15.1	11.5
FSE and EME	14.1	100.0	12.4	116.9	100.0	102.2	20.7	100.0	18.1
0–4	5.2	36.6	66.1	5.4	4.7	69.5	1.1	5.3	14.1
5–14	0.3	2.4	2.1	2.6	2.2	16.6	1.3	6.1	8.1
15–44	6.2	43.9	12.1	25.8	22.1	50.1	13.0	62.8	25.3
45–59	0.9	6.2	4.6	29.1	24.9	152.3	2.9	14.0	15.2
60+	1.5	10.9	7.6	54.0	46.2	266.6	2.4	11.7	12.0
Demographically developing group	609.9	100.0	147.9	458.5	100.0	111.2	141.9	100.0	34.4
0–4	383.1	62.8	693.7	106.2	23.2	192.3	28.9	20.3	52.3
5–14	77.3	12.7	84.1	39.5	8.6	42.9	25.3	17.8	27.5
15–44	122.3	20.0	63.2	116.4	25.4	60.2	74.5	52.5	38.5
45–59	16.3	2.7	37.6	89.3	19.5	206.4	8.5	6.0	19.6
60+	11.0	1.8	38.7	107.2	23.4	375.4	4.8	3.4	16.7
World	624.0	100.0	118.5	575.4	100.0	109.2	162.6	100.0	30.9
0–4	388.2	62.2	615.7	111.7	19.4	177.1	30.0	18.4	47.5
5–14	77.6	12.4	72.1	42.1	7.3	39.1	26.6	16.3	24.7
15–44	128.5	20.6	52.5	142.2	24.7	58.1	87.5	53.8	35.7
45–59	17.1	2.7	27.5	118.3	20.6	189.8	11.4	7.0	18.3
60+	12.6	2.0	25.8	161.2	28.0	330.3	7.2	4.4	14.8

Table B.5 Burden of disease by consequence, sex, and age, 1990
(millions of DALYs lost)

Demographic region and age group	As result of premature death			As result of disability		
	Males	Females	Total	Males	Females	Total
Sub-Saharan Africa	119.5	105.7	225.2	33.3	34.2	67.5
0–4	71.6	61.8	133.4	12.2	11.6	23.7
5–14	13.4	12.7	26.1	6.3	4.8	11.1
15–44	26.1	22.7	48.8	10.1	12.9	23.1
45–59	4.9	4.4	9.3	3.0	2.8	5.8
60+	3.5	4.1	7.6	1.7	2.1	3.8
India	100.8	99.7	200.6	44.5	47.4	91.9
0–4	53.0	55.1	108.1	14.2	14.9	29.1
5–14	9.4	10.8	20.2	6.4	5.7	12.1
15–44	18.9	17.7	36.6	12.0	17.2	29.2
45–59	9.8	7.3	17.2	6.7	5.0	11.7
60+	9.7	8.7	18.4	5.2	4.6	9.8
China	62.2	53.3	115.5	41.3	44.5	85.8
0–4	16.6	18.7	35.3	7.1	7.5	14.6
5–14	3.2	2.3	5.5	5.7	5.1	10.8
15–44	17.4	13.2	30.6	13.7	18.2	31.9
45–59	10.8	7.0	17.8	6.6	5.2	11.8
60+	14.3	12.1	26.4	8.3	8.5	16.7
Other Asia and islands	62.9	50.1	113.0	32.2	31.5	63.7
0–4	29.7	23.9	53.6	7.0	6.5	13.5
5–14	8.4	6.3	14.7	6.6	5.4	12.0
15–44	13.3	10.1	23.4	11.1	12.3	23.4
45–59	5.8	4.3	10.1	4.3	3.8	8.1
60+	5.7	5.5	11.2	3.3	3.5	6.7
Latin America and the Caribbean	33.8	24.3	58.0	23.5	21.4	44.9
0–4	13.2	10.1	23.3	4.8	4.3	9.1
5–14	2.6	2.0	4.6	3.9	3.5	7.3
15–44	11.4	6.6	18.0	9.4	9.0	18.5
45–59	3.4	2.6	6.0	3.0	2.3	5.3
60+	3.1	3.0	6.1	2.3	2.3	4.7
Middle Eastern crescent	51.5	46.9	98.4	22.4	23.4	45.8
0–4	31.1	29.6	60.7	7.0	6.6	13.6
5–14	5.4	4.9	10.4	3.8	3.3	7.1
15–44	7.7	6.2	13.9	6.8	9.1	15.9
45–59	3.6	2.6	6.2	2.7	2.1	4.9
60+	3.7	3.6	7.3	2.1	2.2	4.3
Formerly socialist economies of Europe (FSE)	21.5	13.0	34.5	11.7	12.1	23.7
0–4	2.1	1.5	3.5	0.9	0.9	1.8
5–14	0.5	0.3	0.9	0.5	0.7	1.1
15–44	6.9	2.1	9.0	4.4	4.2	8.6
45–59	6.1	2.7	8.8	3.0	2.3	5.3
60+	5.9	6.4	12.3	2.9	3.9	6.9
Established market economies (EME)	29.5	19.6	49.2	22.5	22.0	44.4
0–4	2.0	1.5	3.5	1.5	1.4	2.9
5–14	0.5	0.3	0.8	0.8	0.6	1.4
15–44	8.5	3.5	12.0	7.6	7.9	15.4
45–59	6.7	3.7	10.3	4.9	3.5	8.4
60+	11.9	10.6	22.6	7.7	8.5	16.2
FSE and EME	51.0	32.6	83.6	34.1	34.0	68.2
0–4	4.0	3.0	7.0	2.4	2.3	4.7
5–14	1.1	0.6	1.7	1.3	1.3	2.6
15–44	15.4	5.6	21.0	11.9	12.1	24.0
45–59	12.7	6.4	19.1	7.9	5.9	13.8
60+	17.8	17.0	34.9	10.6	12.5	23.1
Demographically developing group	430.7	380.0	810.7	197.2	202.4	399.6
0–4	215.3	199.1	414.4	52.4	51.3	103.7
5–14	42.4	39.1	81.5	32.7	27.8	60.5
15–44	94.6	76.6	171.3	63.0	78.8	141.9
45–59	38.3	28.2	66.5	26.3	21.2	47.5
60+	40.1	37.0	77.0	22.8	23.2	46.0
World	481.8	412.6	894.3	231.4	236.4	467.8
0–4	219.3	202.1	421.4	54.8	53.6	108.5
5–14	43.5	39.7	83.2	33.9	29.1	63.0
15–44	110.0	82.2	192.3	74.9	90.9	165.9
45–59	51.1	34.5	85.6	34.2	27.1	61.3
60+	57.9	54.0	111.9	33.4	35.7	69.1

Table B.6 Distribution of the disease burden in children in demographically developing economies, showing the ten main causes, 1990

	Children under 5				Children ages 5–14			
	Female		Male		Female		Male	
Total DALYs lost (millions)	250		268		67		75	
Diseases and injuries	Rank	Percent	Rank	Percent	Rank	Percent	Rank	Percent
Communicable and perinatal		73.2		74.6		57.1		52.0
Infectious and parasitic		37.5		37.2		48.5		45.2
Tuberculosis		0.5		0.5	5	5.7	7	4.1
STDs and HIV		1.0	10	1.0	10	2.4		1.9
Syphilis		0.5		0.5		0.0		0.0
Human immunodeficiency virus		0.5		0.5		0.3		0.1
Diarrheal diseases	3	16.2	3	15.7	4	7.1	4	6.1
Childhood cluster	4	10.7	4	10.6	2	8.6	2	8.1
Pertussis		1.8		1.9		1.6		1.5
Polio		0.3		0.4		2.0		2.5
Measles		5.6		5.5		4.1		3.4
Tetanus		2.9		2.9		0.8		0.7
Malaria	6	4.7	6	4.7	6	4.9	6	4.3
Intestinal helminths		0.0		0.0	1	12.3	1	11.4
Ascaris		0.0		0.0		7.6		7.1
Trichuris		0.0		0.0		4.6		4.2
Respiratory infections	1	18.5	2	17.6	3	7.9	3	6.9
Perinatal	2	17.2	1	19.9		0.0		0.0
Noncommunicable		21.1		19.9		28.4		27.2
Nutritional and endocrine		6.4		6.1		3.7		2.4
Protein-energy malnutrition	7	2.4	8	2.1		0.3		0.3
Iodine deficiency	9	1.3	9	1.2		0.2		0.2
Vitamin A deficiency	8	2.3	7	2.2		0.0		0.0
Anemias		0.3		0.3	8	3.0		1.9
Neuropsychiatric		1.1		1.0		7.5		9.1
Epilepsy		0.2		0.3	9	2.6	8	3.5
Respiratory		2.0		1.8		3.2		4.0
Asthma		0.2		0.2		2.3		2.6
Congenital	5	6.5	5	6.6		1.2		1.0
Injuries		5.7		5.5		14.5		20.7
Unintentional		4.6		4.6		12.6		18.1
Motor vehicle		0.4		0.4	7	3.7	5	4.4
Falls	10	1.2		1.0		1.9	10	3.1
Drowning		0.6		0.7		1.7	9	3.2
Intentional		1.0		0.8		2.0		2.6

Note: The rankings refer to health intervention priorities; disease groups are ranked only when there is a single intervention or accepted cluster of interventions for controlling the diseases included in the group.

☐ Can be substantially controlled with cost-effective intervention; less than $100 per DALY saved.

☐ Can be partially controlled with moderately cost-effective interventions; $250 to $999 per DALY saved. (There are few or no interventions in the range of $100 to $250 per DALY saved.)

▨ Cannot be controlled in a cost-effective manner; $1,000 or more per DALY saved.

▩ Preventive and therapeutic interventions have not been evaluated for cost-effectiveness.

Table B.7 Distribution of the disease burden in the adult and elderly populations in demographically developing economies, showing the ten main causes, 1990

Diseases and injuries	Young adults (ages 15–44) Female Rank	Percent	Male Rank	Percent	Mature adults (ages 45–59) Female Rank	Percent	Male Rank	Percent	Elderly (60+ years old) Female Rank	Percent	Male Rank	Percent
Total DALYs lost (millions)		155		158		49		65		60		63
Communicable and maternal		50.0		28.2		13.2		15.1		8.4		9.5
Infectious and parasitic		29.5		25.8		10.6		13.6		3.8		5.5
Tuberculosis	3	7.0	2	8.4	2	5.6	1	9.3	8	1.9	5	4.0
Sexually transmitted diseases	2	8.9		1.5		0.3		0.2		0.0		0.0
Human immunodeficiency virus	4	6.6	1	9.3		0.3		0.6		0.0		0.0
Respiratory infections	7	2.5	10	2.4		2.0		1.5	5	4.6	6	4.0
Maternal	1	18.0				0.5				0.0		
Noncommunicable		37.6		36.8		81.6		75.8		87.8		86.5
Malignant neoplasms		4.5		4.3		16.7		15.9		10.4		14.5
Stomach		0.3		0.3		1.4		2.2		1.3	8	2.3
Liver		0.3		0.8		1.1	10	2.5		0.7		1.4
Trachea, bronchus, and lung		0.1		0.2		0.9		2.0		0.8	9	2.3
Cervix		0.6			10	2.6				1.0		
Diabetes mellitus		0.4		0.4	8	2.8		1.6	7	2.4		1.5
Nutritional and endocrine		3.6		3.5		2.4		1.4		1.4		0.9
Anemia	8	2.5		1.5		1.3		0.9		0.7		0.5
Neuropsychiatric		11.9		12.1		6.9		8.5		6.7		7.1
Depressive disorders	5	5.8	7	2.9		2.2		0.9		0.5		0.2
Alcohol dependence syndrome		0.4	9	2.7		0.7	5	3.6		0.2		1.6
Alzheimer's disease and other dementias		0.1		0.1		2.2		1.7	4	4.8	4	4.1
Sense organ		0.2		0.2		4.6		3.0		2.1		2.1
Cataracts		0.2		0.1	6	3.1		2.3	10	1.6		1.7
Cardiovascular		6.0		6.5		25.2		23.7		44.3		39.3
Ischemic heart disease		0.6		1.5	3	4.7	2	7.6	2	11.6	2	11.7
Cerebrovascular		1.5		1.4	1	8.7	3	6.7	1	16.5	1	13.8
Peri-, endo-, and myocarditis		1.1		1.6	4	3.2	6	3.4	6	3.6	7	3.6
Respiratory		2.3		2.3		5.4		4.5		10.5		11.7
Chronic obstructive pulmonary		0.3		0.3	7	2.8	7	2.7	3	8.1	3	9.6
Digestive		2.7		4.0		5.8		7.2		3.8		4.8
Cirrhosis		0.8		1.9		2.4	4	4.2		1.2	10	2.1
Genitourinary system		1.4		1.1		3.1		4.2		2.5		2.4
Benign prostatic hypertrophy				0.0			8	2.5				0.4
Musculoskeletal		3.2		1.1		3.9		2.1		2.3		1.2
Osteoarthritis	9	2.2		0.7	9	2.7		1.5		1.5		0.6
Oral health		0.6		0.6		4.4		3.4		1.1		0.9
Periodontal disease		0.1		0.1	5	3.1	9	2.5		0.0		0.0
Injuries		12.4		35.0		5.2		9.1		3.8		4.0
Unintentional		6.4		20.7		3.4		6.4		3.0		3.1
Motor vehicle injuries	10	2.1	3	8.2		0.9		1.8		0.3		0.6
Falls		0.4	8	2.8		0.8		1.5	9	1.8		1.2
Intentional		6.0		14.3		1.9		2.7		0.8		0.9
Self-inflicted	6	3.2	6	4.0		1.1		1.3		0.5		0.6
Homicide and violence		1.0	4	6.1		0.3		1.0		0.1		0.2
War		1.8	5	4.2		0.4		0.5		0.1		0.1

Note: The rankings refer to health intervention priorities; disease groups are ranked only when there is a single intervention or accepted cluster of interventions for controlling the diseases included in the group.

☐ Can be substantially controlled with cost-effective intervention; less than $100 per DALY saved.

☐ Can be partially controlled with moderately cost-effective interventions; $250 to $999 per DALY saved. (There are few or no interventions in the range of $100 to $250 per DALY saved.)

☐ Cannot be controlled in a cost-effective manner; $1,000 or more per DALY saved.

■ Preventive and therapeutic interventions have not been evaluated for cost-effectiveness.

Table B.8 Deaths by cause and demographic group, 1990

(thousands of deaths)

Disease or injury	Demographically developing group Males Ages 0–4	Males Age 5 and older	Females Ages 0–4	Females Age 5 and older	Total	FSE and EME Males Ages 0–4	Males Age 5 and older	Females Ages 0–4	Females Age 5 and older	Total	World
Communicable, maternal and perinatal	5,539	2,801	5,038	2,738	16,115	73	243	52	207	575	16,690
Infectious and parasitic	2,814	2,179	2,651	1,658	9,301	9	92	7	46	153	9,454
Tuberculosis	34	1,187	37	720	1,978	0	29	0	9	38	2,016
STDs excluding HIV	41	62	37	53	192	0	0	0	1	1	193
Syphilis	39	62	35	50	186	0	0	0	0	0	186
Chlamydia	0	1	0	1	1	0	0	0	0	0	1
Gonorrhea	2	0	1	0	3	0	0	0	0	0	3
Pelvic inflammatory disease	0	0	0	2	2	0	0	0	0	0	2
Human immunodeficiency virus	29	101	27	92	248	1	35	1	6	43	291
Diarrheal diseases	1,263	191	1,211	201	2,866	2	1	2	2	7	2,873
Acute watery	635	148	609	155	1,547	2	1	2	2	7	1,553
Persistent	439	5	421	6	871	0	0	0	0	0	872
Dysentery	189	38	181	40	448	0	0	0	0	0	448
Childhood cluster	824	129	774	133	1,860	0	0	0	0	1	1,861
Pertussis	146	22	131	22	321	0	0	0	0	0	321
Polio	4	9	3	7	24	0	0	0	0	0	24
Diphtheria	1	1	1	2	4	0	0	0	0	0	4
Measles	442	69	421	74	1,006	0	0	0	0	0	1,006
Tetanus	232	27	219	28	505	0	0	0	0	0	505
Meningitis	71	73	50	39	232	3	3	2	3	10	242
Hepatitis	6	33	6	27	72	0	3	0	2	6	77
Malaria	332	143	301	151	926	0	0	0	0	0	926
Tropical cluster	6	105	6	82	199	0	0	0	0	0	199
Trypanosomiasis	2	27	3	24	55	0	0	0	0	0	55
Chagas' disease	0	11	0	12	23	0	0	0	0	0	23
Schistosomiasis	1	23	0	14	38	0	0	0	0	0	38
Leishmaniasis	4	26	3	20	54	0	0	0	0	0	54
Lymphatic filariasis	0	0	0	0	0	0	0	0	0	0	0
Onchocerciasis	0	17	0	12	30	0	0	0	0	0	30
Leprosy	0	1	0	1	3	0	0	0	0	0	3
Trachoma	0	0	0	0	0	0	0	0	0	0	0
Intestinal helminths	0	15	0	14	29	0	0	0	0	0	29
Acaris	0	7	0	6	13	0	0	0	0	0	13
Trichuris	0	5	0	5	9	0	0	0	0	0	9
Hookworm	0	3	0	3	6	0	0	0	0	0	6
Respiratory infections	1,371	622	1,339	652	3,984	12	151	9	158	330	4,314
Lower respiratory infections	1,343	620	1,311	650	3,924	12	150	9	157	328	4,251
Upper respiratory infections	3	3	3	2	10	0	1	0	1	2	12
Otitis media	25	0	25	0	51	1	0	0	0	1	52
Maternal	0	0	0	428	428	0	0	0	3	3	431
Hemorrhage	0	0	0	130	130	0	0	0	0	0	130
Sepsis	0	0	0	79	79	0	0	0	0	0	79
Eclampsia	0	0	0	45	45	0	0	0	0	0	45
Hypertension	0	0	0	31	31	0	0	0	0	0	32
Obstructed labor	0	0	0	40	40	0	0	0	0	0	40
Abortion	0	0	0	60	60	0	0	0	1	1	61
Perinatal	1,353	0	1,048	0	2,402	52	0	36	0	89	2,491
Noncommunicable	693	9,562	687	8,612	19,553	37	4,626	30	4,808	9,502	29,055
Malignant neoplasms	16	2,150	27	1,504	3,698	2	1,352	2	1,075	2,431	6,129
Mouth and oropharynx	0	211	1	103	315	0	39	0	11	51	366
Esophagus	0	220	0	112	332	0	43	0	14	58	389
Stomach	0	337	0	185	522	0	143	0	101	244	766
Colon and rectum	0	116	0	99	215	0	136	0	144	280	496
Liver	0	299	1	119	420	0	30	0	13	44	463
Pancreas	0	44	0	29	73	0	49	0	47	96	169
Trachea, bronchus, and lung	0	329	0	111	441	0	402	0	124	526	967
Melanoma	0	8	0	9	17	0	17	0	14	31	48
Breast	0	0	0	158	158	0	0	0	175	175	332
Cervix	0	0	0	183	183	0	0	0	32	32	215
Uterus	0	0	0	27	27	0	0	0	29	29	56
Ovary	0	0	1	50	51	0	0	0	56	56	106

Disease or injury	Demographically developing group					FSE and EME					World
	Males		Females			Males		Females			
	Ages 0–4	Age 5 and older	Ages 0–4	Age 5 and older	Total	Ages 0–4	Age 5 and older	Ages 0–4	Age 5 and older	Total	

Noncommunicable diseases, malignant neoplasms (*continued*)

Disease or injury	Ages 0–4 (M)	Age 5 and older (M)	Ages 0–4 (F)	Age 5 and older (F)	Total	Ages 0–4 (M)	Age 5 and older (M)	Ages 0–4 (F)	Age 5 and older (F)	Total	World
Prostate	0	105	0	0	105	0	108	0	0	108	213
Bladder	0	61	0	18	80	0	51	0	20	71	151
Lymphoma	3	74	3	42	121	0	51	0	45	96	218
Leukemia	6	72	10	55	143	1	41	1	34	77	219
Diabetes mellitus	0	198	0	284	483	0	69	0	108	177	660
Nutritional and endocrine	119	148	127	185	578	1	30	1	41	74	651
Protein-energy malnutrition	66	26	82	33	207	0	2	0	4	6	213
Iodine deficiency	4	7	3	6	19	0	0	0	0	0	19
Vitamin A deficiency	19	0	16	0	35	0	0	0	0	0	35
Anemia	20	31	16	79	147	0	7	0	10	17	163
Neuropsychiatric	36	309	38	218	600	2	111	2	117	232	832
Depressive disorders	0	0	0	0	0	0	0	0	0	0	0
Bipolar affective disorders	0	1	0	1	1	0	0	0	2	2	3
Psychoses	0	26	0	17	42	0	7	0	9	16	58
Epilepsy	4	56	4	39	103	0	8	0	5	13	115
Alcohol dependence	0	27	0	4	31	0	18	0	4	22	53
Alzheimer's and other dementias	5	45	7	43	100	1	36	1	58	95	195
Parkinson's disease	0	19	0	12	32	0	16	0	15	30	62
Multiple sclerosis	0	11	0	13	25	0	3	0	5	8	33
Drug dependence	0	10	0	4	14	0	3	0	1	3	18
Posttraumatic stress disorder	0	0	0	0	0	0	0	0	0	0	0
Sense organ	3	10	3	9	25	0	0	0	0	1	26
Glaucoma	0	1	0	1	2	0	0	0	0	0	2
Cataract	0	1	0	1	1	0	0	0	0	0	1
Cardiovascular	64	4,436	59	4,459	9,017	2	2,399	2	2,925	5,328	14,345
Rheumatic	1	146	2	292	440	0	17	0	29	46	486
Ischemic heart disease	2	1,348	1	1,118	2,469	0	1,283	0	1,395	2,678	5,147
Cerebrovascular	8	1,516	6	1,652	3,181	0	565	0	882	1,448	4,629
Peri-, endo-, and myocarditis and cardiomyopathy	32	621	36	540	1,229	0	70	1	64	136	1,364
Respiratory	78	1,172	79	1,008	2,336	1	308	1	199	509	2,845
Chronic obstructive pulmonary disease	11	938	9	756	1,714	0	228	0	130	358	2,072
Asthma	5	61	5	77	147	0	17	0	18	34	181
Digestive	87	738	106	484	1,416	2	231	1	194	427	1,843
Peptic ulcer disease	1	121	1	71	194	0	26	0	20	46	241
Cirrhosis	4	380	3	176	563	0	97	0	49	146	709
Genitourinary	12	264	8	251	535	0	83	0	85	169	704
Nephritis and nephrosis	6	171	4	146	327	0	49	0	50	100	427
Benign prostatic hypertrophy	0	30	0	0	31	0	10	0	0	10	41
Musculoskeletal	0	41	1	63	106	0	10	0	27	37	143
Rheumatoid arthritis	0	2	0	2	4	0	2	0	8	10	14
Osteoarthritis	0	0	0	0	0	0	0	0	0	0	0
Congenital abnormalities	271	40	232	52	595	25	8	21	7	61	656
Oral health	0	0	0	0	0	0	0	0	0	0	0
Injuries	254	2,010	233	923	3,420	13	559	8	227	807	4,227
Unintentional	217	1,297	192	531	2,237	12	375	8	163	558	2,794
Motor vehicle	28	457	22	130	637	2	160	2	55	219	856
Poisoning	13	75	7	38	132	1	41	1	13	56	188
Falls	10	87	12	59	168	1	45	0	51	97	265
Fires	18	29	12	23	83	1	10	1	6	18	100
Drowning	59	172	48	71	349	2	27	1	6	36	384
Occupational	0	88	0	28	115	0	19	0	3	22	137
Intentional	37	712	41	393	1,183	1	184	1	64	249	1,432
Self-inflicted	0	359	0	269	629	0	140	0	49	190	818
Homicide and violence	11	171	15	37	233	1	43	1	15	59	292
War	27	182	27	86	322	0	0	0	0	0	322
Total	6,485	14,372	5,958	12,273	39,088	123	5,428	91	5,242	10,883	49,971

Note: FSE, Formerly socialist economies of Europe; EME, established market economies.

World Development Indicators

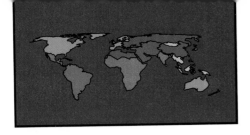

Contents

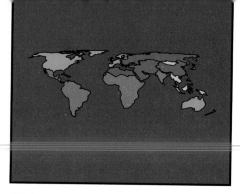

Key

In each table, economies are listed within their groups in ascending order of GNP per capita except those for which no GNP per capita can be calculated. These are italicized, in alphabetical order, at the end of their group. The ranking below refers to the order in the tables. Note that two economies, Zimbabwe and Botswana, with recently revised population data, have not been moved in the list to reflect their new ranking.

The key shows the years of the most recent census and the years of the latest demographic survey or vital registration-based estimates. This information is included to show the currentness of the sources of demographic indicators, which can be a reflection of the overall quality of a country's indicators. Beyond these years, demographic estimates may be generated by projection models, extrapolation routines, or other methods. Other demographic indicators, such as life expectancy, birth and death rates, and under-5 mortality rates,

are usually derived from the same sources. Explanations of how World Bank estimates and projections are derived from the sources, as well as more information on the sources, are given in *World Population Projections, 1992–93 Edition.*

Figures in colored bands in the tables are summary measures for groups of economies.

The letter *w* means weighted average; *m*, median value; *t*, total.

All growth rates are in real terms.

Data cutoff date is April 30, 1993.

The symbol . . means not available

The figures 0 and 0.0 mean zero or less than half the unit shown.

A blank means not applicable.

Figures in italics indicate data that are for years or periods other than those specified.

The symbol † indicates economies classified by the United Nations or otherwise regarded by their authorities as developing.

Economy	Country ranking in tables	Population census	Infant mortality	Total fertility
Algeria	73	1987	1985	1984
Argentina	89	1991	1988	1990
Armenia	75	1989	1991	1991
Australia	113	1991	1990	1990
Austria	117	1981	1991	1991
Azerbaijan	67	1989	1991	1991
Bangladesh	12	1991	1989	1989
Belarus	93	1989	1991	1991
Belgium	116	1991	1991	1991
Benin	24	1979	1981–82	1981–82
Bhutan	5	1969	. .	1984
Bolivia	41	*1992	1989	1989
Botswana	84	1991	1988	1988
Brazil	91	1991	1986	1986
Bulgaria	71	1985	1991	1991
Burkina Faso	17	1985	1976	1961
Burundi	8	1979	1987	1987
Cameroon	46	1987	1991	1991
Canada	119	1991	1990	1991
Central African Rep.	25	1975	1975	1959

Economy	Country ranking in tables	Population census	Infant mortality	Total fertility
Chad	9	1964	1964	1964
Chile	76	1982	1990	1990
China	22	1990	1990	1987
Colombia	57	1985	1990	1990
Congo	55	1984	1974	1974
Costa Rica	72	1984	1990	1990
Côte d'Ivoire	42	1988	1979	1988
Czechoslovakia[a]	81	1991	1991	1991
Denmark	122	1981	1991	1991
Dominican Rep.	48	1990	1991	1991
Ecuador	49	1990	1989	1989
Egypt, Arab Rep.	37	1986	1988	1988
El Salvador	54	1971	1988	1988
Estonia	98	1989	1990	1990
Ethiopia	3	1984	. .	1988
Finland	123	1990	1991	1991
France	118	1990	1991	1991
Gabon	97	1981	1960–61	1960–61
Georgia	66	1989	1991	1991
Germany[b]	121	1987	1991	1991
Ghana	26	1984	1988	1988
Greece	103	1991	1991	1991
Guatemala	47	1981	1987	1987
Guinea	29	1983	1954–55	1954–55
Guinea-Bissau	6	1989	1991	1991
Haiti	23	1982	1987	1987
Honduras	34	1988	1987–88	1987–88
†Hong Kong	110	1991	1990	1990
Hungary	87	1990	1991	1991
India	19	1991	1986	1985
Indonesia	36	1990	1991	1991
Iran, Islamic Rep.	77	1986	1986	1975
Ireland	106	1986	1990	1991
†Israel	107	1983	1990	1990
Italy	114	1991	1991	1991
Jamaica	60	1991	1989	1990
Japan	126	1990	1991	1991
Jordan	51	1979	1990–91	1990–91
Kazakhstan	82	1989	1991	1991
Kenya	20	1989	1989	1989
Korea, Rep.	102	1990	1985	1985
Kyrgyzstan	64	1989	1991	1991
Lao PDR	8	1985	1988	1988
Latvia	95	1989	1990	1990
Lesotho	35	1986	1977	1986
Lithuania	86	1989	1991	1991
Madagascar	10	1974–75	1992	1992
Malawi	14	1987	1982	1977
Malaysia	83	1991	1988	1984
Mali	16	1987	1987	1987
Mauritania	32	1988	1975	1987–88
Mauritius	80	1990	1991	1987
Mexico	92	1990	1987	1987
Moldova	78	1989	1991	1991
Morocco	50	1982	1992	1992
Mozambique	1	1980	1980	1980

Economy	Country ranking in tables	Population census	Infant mortality	Total fertility
Namibia	62	1991	. .	1992
Nepal	7	1991	1987	1987
Netherlands	115	1991	1991	1991
New Zealand	108	1991	1991	1991
Nicaragua	30	1971	1985	1985
Niger	18	1988	1992	1992
Nigeria	21	*1991	1990	1990
Norway	124	1980	1991	1991
Oman	100	. .	1986	1986
Pakistan	27	1981	1990–91	1990–91
Panama	74	1990	1985–87	1990
Papua New Guinea	45	1990	1980	1980
Paraguay	58	1982	1990	1990
Peru	53	1981	1991–92	1991–92
Philippines	44	1990	1986	1988
Poland	70	1988	1991	1991
Portugal	99	1991	1991	1991
Puerto Rico	101	. .	. .	. .
Romania	61	1992	1990	1990
Russian Federation	94	1989	1991	1991
Rwanda	15	1991	1983	1992
†Saudi Arabia	104	*1992	. .	. .
Senegal	43	1988	1986	1986
Sierra Leone	11	1985	1971	1975
†Singapore	111	1990	1991	1991
South Africa	85	1985	1980	1981
Spain	109	1992	1990	1990
Sri Lanka	31	1981	1988	1989
Sudan	39	1983	1989–90	1989–90
Sweden	125	1990	1991	1991
Switzerland	127	1980	1991	1991
Syrian Arab Rep.	56	1981	1981	1981
Tajikistan	52	1989	1991	1991
Tanzania	2	1988	1991–92	1991–92
Thailand	65	1990	1989	1987
Togo	28	1981	1988	1988
Trinidad and Tobago	96	1990	1989	1989
Tunisia	63	1984	1988	1990
Turkey	69	1990	1988	1988
Turkmenistan	68	1989	1991	1991
Uganda	4	1991	1988–89	1988–89
Ukraine	79	1989	1991	1991
United Kingdom	112	1992	1991	1991
United States	120	1990	1991	1991
Uruguay	90	1985	1990	1990
Uzbekistan	59	1989	1991	1991
Venezuela	88	1990	1989	1989
Yemen Rep.	33	1986/1988	1991–92	1991–92
Yugoslaviac	105	1991	1990	1990
Zambia	40	1990	1992	1992
Zimbabwe	38	1982	1988–89	1988–89

* Census data are not yet incorporated in the population estimates.
Note: Economies with sparse data or with populations of more than 30,000 and fewer than 1 million are included only as part of the country groups in the main tables but are shown in greater detail in Table 1a. For data comparability and coverage throughout the tables, see the technical notes.
a. In all tables data refer to the former Czechoslovakia; disaggragated data are not yet available. b. In all tables, data refer to the unified Germany, unless otherwise stated. c. In all tables, data refer to the former Socialist Federal Republic of Yugoslavia; disaggregated data are not yet available.

Introduction

This sixteenth edition of the World Development Indicators provides economic, social, and natural resource indicators for selected periods or years for 200 economies and various analytical and geographic groups of economies. Although most of the data collected by the World Bank are on low- and middle-income economies, comparable data for high-income economies, where readily available, are also included in the tables. Additional information may be found in the *World Bank Atlas*, *World Tables*, *World Debt Tables*, and *Social Indicators of Development*. These data are now also available on diskette, in the World Bank's ★STARS★ retrieval system.

Changes in this edition

With the independence of several new economies during the past year, coupled with space limitations in the main tables, a new criterion—data availability—has been introduced. To be included in the main tables, an economy must have reasonable coverage of key socio-economic indicators. Basic indicators for economies excluded for lack of data are presented, along with countries with fewer than 1 million population, in Table 1a, following Table 33.

To preserve a 20-year interval between the two years shown for most indicators, the earliest year presented has been changed from 1965 to 1970 or 1975. Readers wanting data for earlier periods can refer to previous editions or to the publications noted above, which present data in time series.

The following changes have also been made. (They are described more fully in the technical notes.)

Estimates of fish products as a percentage of daily protein supply have been added to Table 4, *Agriculture and food*, because fish is an important source of protein for some countries and is not included in the food production per capita estimates in the table.

Table 21, *Total external debt*, includes two new indicators: total arrears on long-term debt outstanding and disbursed, and ratio of present value to nominal value of debt. Total arrears denotes principal and interest due but not paid, and the present value to nominal value of debt is a measure of the degree of concessionality of a country's external obligations.

Table 24, *Total external debt ratios*, includes two new indicators: concessional debt as a percentage of total external debt, and multilateral debt as a percentage of total external debt. These two sources of external financing are shown separately to reflect their importance for many developing economies.

In Table 28, *Health and nutrition*, the prevalence of malnutrition in children under 5 is used; it is considered a better measure of nutritional status than the previously used indicator, daily calorie supply.

Table 30, on income estimates, has been refined to make use of the purchasing power of currencies (PPCs). It contains country-specific observations as well as data derived from a regression equation.

Classification of economies

The main criterion used to classify economies and broadly distinguish different stages of economic development is GNP per capita. This year the per capita income groups are low-income, $635 or less in 1991 (40 economies); middle-income, $636 to $7,909 (65 economies); and high-income, $7,910 or more (22 economies). Economies with populations of fewer than 1 million and those with sparse data are not shown separately in the main tables but are included in the aggregates. Basic indicators for these economies may also be found in Table 1a.

Further classification of economies is by geographic location. "Europe and Central Asia" now includes the newly independent economies of the former Soviet Union. Economies formerly grouped in "Other economies" are now included in the appropriate income and geographic groupings. Other classifications include severely indebted middle-income economies and fuel exporters. (See Definitions and data notes, and the tables on classification of economies at the back of this book.)

Methodology

The Bank continually reviews methodology in an effort to improve the international comparability and analytical significance of the indicators. Differences between data in this year's and last year's edition reflect not only updates but also revisions to historical series and changes in methodology.

All dollar figures are U.S. dollars unless otherwise stated. The various methods used for converting from national currency figures are described in the technical notes.

Summary measures

The summary measures in the colored bands are totals (indicated by t), weighted averages (w), or median values (m) calculated for groups of economies. Countries for which individual estimates are not shown, because of size, nonreporting, or insufficient history, have been implicitly included by assuming that they follow the trend of reporting countries during such periods. This gives a more consistent aggregate measure by standardizing country coverage for each period shown. Group aggregates include countries for which country-specific data do not appear in the tables. Where missing information accounts for a

third or more of the overall estimate, however, the group measure is reported as not available. The weightings used for computing the summary measures are stated in each technical note.

Terminology and data coverage

In these notes the term ''country'' does not imply political independence but may refer to any territory whose authorities present for it separate social or economic statistics.

The unified Germany does not yet have a fully merged statistical system. Throughout the tables, data for Germany are footnoted to explain coverage; most economic data refer to the former Federal Republic, but demographic and social data generally refer to the unified Germany. The data for China do not include Taiwan, China, but footnotes to Tables 14, 15, 16, and 18 provide estimates of the international transactions for Taiwan, China. In all tables, Czechoslovakia refers to the former Czechoslovakia and Yugoslavia to the former Socialist Federal Repub-

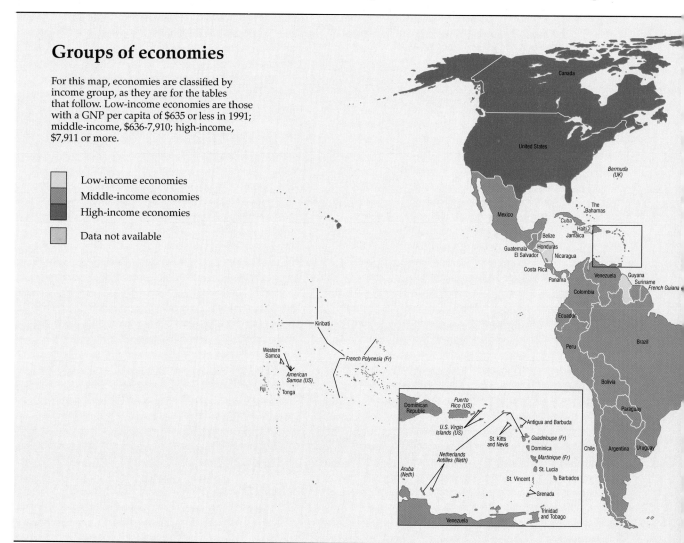

Groups of economies

For this map, economies are classified by income group, as they are for the tables that follow. Low-income economies are those with a GNP per capita of $635 or less in 1991; middle-income, $636-7,910; high-income, $7,911 or more.

- Low-income economies
- Middle-income economies
- High-income economies

- Data not available

lic of Yugoslavia because disaggregated data are not yet available.

Table content

The indicators in Table 1 give a summary profile of economies. Data in the other tables fall into six broad areas: production, domestic absorption, fiscal and monetary accounts, core international transactions, external finance, and human and natural resources. The table format of this edition follows that of previous years. In each group, economies are listed in ascending order of GNP per capita, except those for which no such figure can be calculated. These are italicized and in alphabetical order at the end of the group deemed appropriate. This order is used in all tables except Table 19, which covers only high-income OPEC and OECD countries. The alphabetical list in the key shows the reference number for each economy; here, too, italics indicate economies with no current estimates of GNP per capita. Economies in the high-income group marked by the symbol † are those classified by the United Nations or otherwise regarded by their authorities as developing.

Technical notes

The technical notes and the footnotes should be referred to in any use of the data. The notes outline the methods, concepts, definitions, and data sources used in compiling the tables. A bibliography at the end of the notes lists the data sources, which contain comprehensive definitions and descriptions of concepts used. Country notes to the *World Tables* provide additional explanations of sources used, breaks in comparability, and other exceptions to standard statistical practices that Bank staff have identified in national accounts and international transactions.

Comments and questions relating to the World Development Indicators should be addressed to Socio-Economic Data Division, International Economics Department, The World Bank, 1818 H Street, N.W., Washington, D.C. 20433.

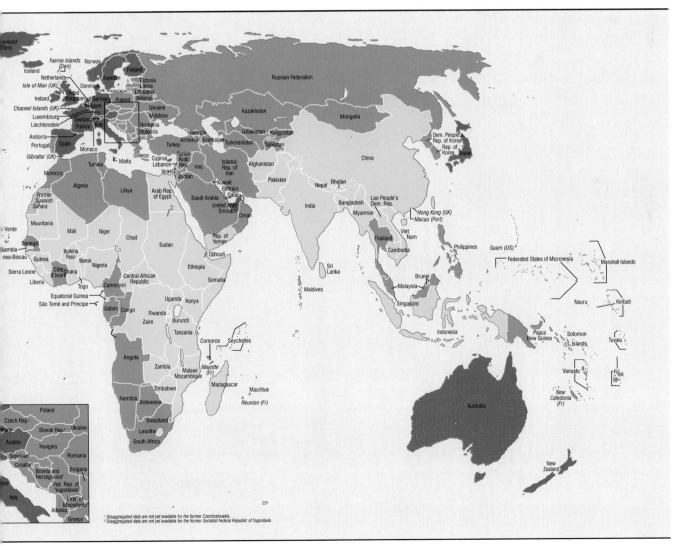

¹ Disaggregated data are not yet available for the former Czechoslovakia.
² Disaggregated data are not yet available for the former Socialist Federal Republic of Yugoslavia.

Population density

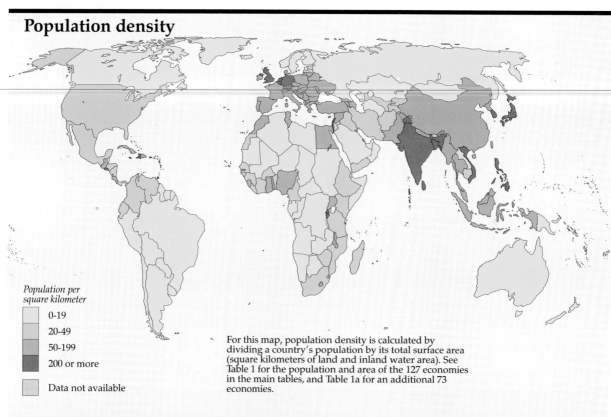

Population per
square kilometer

- 0-19
- 20-49
- 50-199
- 200 or more

Data not available

For this map, population density is calculated by
dividing a country's population by its total surface area
(square kilometers of land and inland water area). See
Table 1 for the population and area of the 127 economies
in the main tables, and Table 1a for an additional 73
economies.

Fertility and mortality

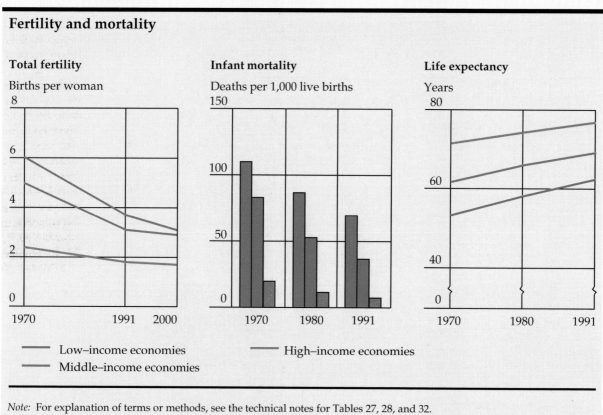

Total fertility

Births per woman

Infant mortality

Deaths per 1,000 live births

Life expectancy

Years

Low–income economies

Middle–income economies

High–income economies

Note: For explanation of terms or methods, see the technical notes for Tables 27, 28, and 32.

Share of agriculture in GDP

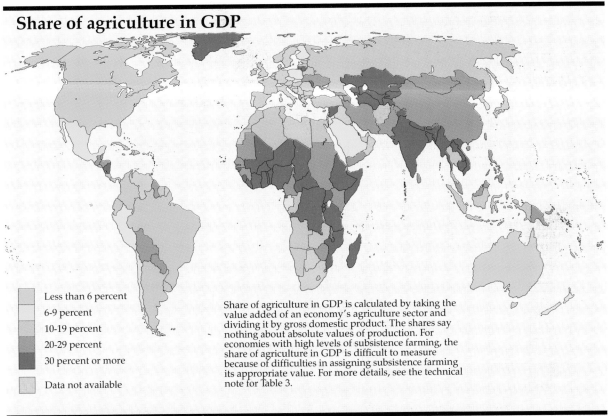

Less than 6 percent

6-9 percent

10-19 percent

20-29 percent

30 percent or more

Data not available

Share of agriculture in GDP is calculated by taking the value added of an economy's agriculture sector and dividing it by gross domestic product. The shares say nothing about absolute values of production. For economies with high levels of subsistence farming, the share of agriculture in GDP is difficult to measure because of difficulties in assigning subsistence farming its appropriate value. For more details, see the technical note for Table 3.

Median age at death, 1990

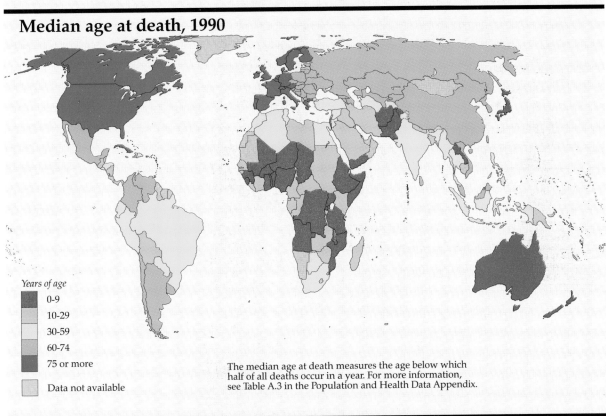

Years of age

0-9

10-29

30-59

60-74

75 or more

Data not available

The median age at death measures the age below which half of all deaths occur in a year. For more information, see Table A.3 in the Population and Health Data Appendix.

Table 1. Basic indicators

		Population (millions) mid-1991	Area (thousands of square kilometers)	GNP per capita[a] Dollars 1991	GNP per capita[a] Average annual growth rate (percent) 1980-91	Average annual rate of inflation[a] (percent) 1970-80	Average annual rate of inflation[a] (percent) 1980-91	Life expectancy at birth (years) 1991	Adult illiteracy (percent) Female 1990	Adult illiteracy (percent) Total 1990
	Low-income economies	**3,127.3** t	**38,828** t	**350** w	**3.9** w	**8.2** w	**12.6** w	**62** w	**52** w	**40** w
	China and India	2,016.0 t	12,849 t	350 w	5.6 w	4.3 w	6.9 w	66 w	50 w	37 w
	Other low-income	1,111.2 t	25,980 t	350 w	1.0 w	15.7 w	23.4 w	55 w	56 w	45 w
1	Mozambique	16.1	802	80	-1.1	. .	37.6	47	79	67
2	Tanzania[b]	25.2	945	100	-0.8	14.1	25.7	51	. .	. .
3	Ethiopia	52.8	1,222	120	-1.6	4.3	2.4	48	. .	. .
4	Uganda	16.9	236	170	. .	. .	. .	46	65	52
5	Bhutan	1.5	47	180	. .	. .	8.4	48	75	62
6	Guinea-Bissau	1.0	36	180	1.1	5.7	56.2	39	76	64
7	Nepal	19.4	141	180	2.1	8.5	9.1	53	87	74
8	Burundi	5.7	28	210	1.3	10.7	4.3	48	60	50
9	Chad	5.8	1,284	210	3.8	7.7	1.1	47	82	70
10	Madagascar	12.0	587	210	-2.5	9.9	16.8	51	27	20
11	Sierra Leone	4.2	72	210	-1.6	12.5	59.3	42	89	79
12	Bangladesh	110.6	144	220	1.9	20.8	9.3	51	78	65
13	Lao PDR	4.3	237	220	. .	. .	. .	50	. .	. .
14	Malawi	8.8	118	230	0.1	8.8	14.9	45	. .	. .
15	Rwanda	7.1	26	270	-2.4	15.1	4.1	46	63	50
16	Mali	8.7	1,240	280	-0.1	9.7	4.4	48	76	68
17	Burkina Faso	9.3	274	290	1.2	8.6	3.8	48	91	82
18	Niger	7.9	1,267	300	-4.1	9.7	2.3	46	83	72
19	India	866.5	3,288	330	3.2	8.4	8.2	60	66	52
20	Kenya	25.0	580	340	0.3	10.1	9.2	59	42	31
21	Nigeria	99.0	924	340	-2.3	15.2	18.1	52	61	49
22	China	1,149.5	9,561	370	7.8	0.9	5.8	69	38	27
23	Haiti	6.6	28	370	-2.4	9.3	7.1	55	53	47
24	Benin	4.9	113	380	-0.9	10.3	1.6	51	84	77
25	Central African Rep.	3.1	623	390	-1.4	12.1	5.1	47	75	62
26	Ghana	15.3	239	400	-0.3	35.2	40.0	55	49	40
27	Pakistan	115.8	796	400	3.2	13.4	7.0	59	79	65
28	Togo	3.8	57	410	-1.3	8.9	4.4	54	69	57
29	Guinea	5.9	246	460	. .	. .	. .	44	87	76
30	Nicaragua	3.8	130	460	-4.4	12.8	583.7	66	. .	. .
31	Sri Lanka	17.2	66	500	2.5	12.3	11.2	71	17	12
32	Mauritania	2.0	1,026	510	-1.8	9.9	8.7	47	79	66
33	Yemen, Rep.	12.5	528	520	. .	. .	. .	52	74	62
34	Honduras	5.3	112	580	-0.5	8.1	6.8	65	29	27
35	Lesotho	1.8	30	580	-0.5	9.7	13.6	56	. .	. .
36	Indonesia	181.3	1,905	610	3.9	21.5	8.5	60	32	23
37	Egypt, Arab Rep.	53.6	1,001	610	1.9	9.6	12.5	61	66	52
38	Zimbabwe	10.1	391	650[a]	-0.2	9.4	12.5	60	40	33
39	Sudan	25.8	2,506	. .	. .	14.5	. .	51	88	73
40	Zambia	8.3	753	. .	. .	7.6	. .	49	35	27
	Middle-income economies	**1,401.0** t	**40,796** t	**2,480** w	**0.3** w	**28.4** w	**67.1** w	**68** w	**26** w	**21** w
	Lower-middle-income	773.8 t	19,309 t	1,590 w	-0.1 w	22.8 w	23.1 w	67 w	32 w	26 w
41	Bolivia	7.3	1,099	650	-2.0	21.0	263.4	59	29	23
42	Côte d'Ivoire	12.4	322	690	-4.6	13.0	3.8	52	60	46
43	Senegal	7.6	197	720	0.1	8.5	6.0	48	75	62
44	Philippines	62.9	300	730	-1.2	13.3	14.6	65	11	10
45	Papua New Guinea	4.0	463	830	-0.6	9.1	5.2	56	62	48
46	Cameroon	11.9	475	850	-1.0	9.8	4.5	55	57	46
47	Guatemala	9.5	109	930	-1.8	10.5	15.9	64	53	45
48	Dominican Rep.	7.2	49	940	-0.2	9.1	24.5	67	18	17
49	Ecuador	10.8	284	1,000	-0.6	13.8	38.0	66	16	14
50	Morocco	25.7	447	1,030	1.6	8.3	7.1	63	62	51
51	Jordan[c]	3.7	89	1,050	-1.7	. .	1.6	69	30	20
52	Tajikistan[d]	5.5	143	1,050	. .	. .	. .	69	. .	. .
53	Peru	21.9	1,285	1,070	2.4	30.1	287.3	64	21	15
54	El Salvador	5.3	21	1,080	-0.3	10.7	17.4	66	30	27
55	Congo	2.4	342	1,120	-0.2	8.4	0.4	52	56	43
56	Syrian Arab Rep.	12.5	185	1,160	-1.4	11.8	14.3	67	49	36
57	Colombia	32.8	1,139	1,260	1.2	22.3	25.0	69	14	13
58	Paraguay	4.4	407	1,270	-0.8	12.7	25.1	67	12	10
59	Uzbekistan[d]	20.9	447	1,350	. .	. .	. .	69	. .	. .
60	Jamaica	2.4	11	1,380	0.0	17.3	19.6	73	1	2
61	Romania	23.0	238	1,390	0.0	. .	6.2	70	. .	. .
62	Namibia	1.5	824	1,460	-1.2	. .	12.6	58	. .	. .
63	Tunisia	8.2	164	1,500	1.1	8.7	7.3	67	44	35
64	Kyrgyzstan[d]	4.5	199	1,550	. .	. .	. .	66	. .	. .
65	Thailand	57.2	513	1,570	5.9	9.2	3.7	69	10	7
66	Georgia[d]	5.5	70	1,640	. .	. .	. .	73	. .	. .

Note: For other economies see Table 1a.   For data comparability and coverage, see the technical notes.   Figures in italics are for years other than those specified.

		Population (millions) mid-1991	Area (thousands of square kilometers)	GNP per capita[a] Dollars 1991	GNP per capita[a] Average annual growth rate (percent) 1980-91	Average annual rate of inflation[a] (percent) 1970-80	Average annual rate of inflation[a] (percent) 1980-91	Life expectancy at birth (years) 1991	Adult illiteracy (percent) Female 1990	Adult illiteracy (percent) Total 1990
67	Azerbaijan[d]	7.1	87	1,670	. .	. .	. .	71	. .	. .
68	Turkmenistan[d]	3.8	488	1,700	. .	. .	. .	66		
69	Turkey	57.3	779	1,780	2.9	29.4	44.7	67	29	19
70	Poland	38.2	313	1,790	0.6	. .	63.1	71	. .	. .
71	Bulgaria	9.0	111	1,840	1.7	. .	7.8	72	. .	. .
72	Costa Rica	3.1	51	1,850	0.7	15.3	22.9	76	7	7
73	Algeria	25.7	2,382	1,980	-0.7	14.5	10.1	66	55	43
74	Panama	2.5	77	2,130	-1.8	7.5	2.4	73	12	12
75	Armenia[d]	3.4	30	2,150	. .	. .	. .	72	. .	. .
76	Chile	13.4	757	2,160	1.6	188.1	20.5	72	7	7
77	Iran, Islamic Rep.	57.7	1,648	2,170	-1.3	22.4	13.8	65	57	46
78	Moldova[d]	4.4	34	2,170	. .	. .	. .	69	. .	. .
79	Ukraine[d]	52.0	604	2,340	. .	. .	. .	70	. .	. .
80	Mauritius	1.1	2	2,410	6.1	15.3	8.1	70	. .	. .
81	Czechoslovakia[e]	15.7	128	2,470	0.5	. .	3.5	72	. .	. .
82	Kazakhstan[d]	16.8	2,717	2,470	. .	. .	. .	69	. .	. .
83	Malaysia	18.2	330	2,520	2.9	7.3	1.7	71	30	22
	Upper-middle-income	**627.0** t	**21,486** t	**3,530** w	**0.6** w	**31.7** w	**95.4** w	**69** w	**17** w	**14** w
84	Botswana	1.3	582	2,530[a]	5.6	11.6	13.2	68	35	26
85	South Africa	38.9	1,221	2,560	0.7	13.0	14.4	63	. .	. .
86	Lithuania[d]	3.7	65	2,710	. .	. .	. .	71	. .	. .
87	Hungary	10.3	93	2,720	0.7	2.8	10.3	70	. .	. .
88	Venezuela	19.8	912	2,730	-1.3	14.0	21.2	70	10	12
89	Argentina	32.7	2,767	2,790	-1.5	133.9	416.9	71	5	5
90	Uruguay	3.1	177	2,840	-0.4	65.1	64.4	73	4	4
91	Brazil	151.4	8,512	2,940	0.5	38.6	327.6	66	20	19
92	Mexico	83.3	1,958	3,030	-0.5	18.1	66.5	70	15	13
93	Belarus[d]	10.3	208	3,110	. .	. .	. .	71	. .	. .
94	Russian Federation[d]	148.7	17,075	3,220	. .	. .	. .	69	. .	. .
95	Latvia[d]	2.6	65	3,410	. .	. .	. .	69	. .	. .
96	Trinidad and Tobago	1.3	5	3,670	-5.2	18.5	6.5	71	. .	. .
97	Gabon	1.2	268	3,780	-4.2	17.5	1.5	54	52	39
98	Estonia[d]	1.6	45	3,830	. .	. .	. .	70	. .	. .
99	Portugal	9.9	92	5,930	3.1	16.7	17.4	74	19	15
100	Oman	1.6	212	6,120	4.4	28.0	-3.1	69	. .	. .
101	Puerto Rico	3.6	9	6,320	0.9	6.5	3.4	76	. .	. .
102	Korea, Rep.	43.3	99	6,330	8.7	20.1	5.6	70	7	4
103	Greece	10.3	132	6,340	1.1	14.5	17.7	77	11	7
104	Saudi Arabia	15.4	2,150	7,820	-3.4	24.9	-2.4	69	52	38
105	Yugoslavia[e]	23.9	256	. .	. .	18.4	123.0	73	12	7
	Low- and middle-income	**4,528.0** t	**79,624** t	**1,010** w	**1.0** w	**21.8** w	**53.9** w	**64** w	**46** w	**35** w
	Sub-Saharan Africa	**488.9** t	**23,066** t	**350** w	**-1.2** w	**13.9** w	**18.4** w	**51** w	**62** w	**50** w
	East Asia & Pacific	**1,666.5** t	**16,369** t	**650** w	**6.1** w	**9.1** w	**6.3** w	**68** w	**34** w	**24** w
	South Asia	**1,152.2** t	**5,133** t	**320** w	**3.1** w	**9.7** w	**8.3** w	**59** w	**69** w	**54** w
	Europe and Central Asia	**492.0** t	**2,314** t	**2,670** w	**0.9** w	**18.7** w	**18.2** w	**70** w	**22** w	**16** w
	Middle East & N. Africa	**244.1** t	**11,015** t	**1,940** w	**-2.4** w	**18.8** w	**8.6** w	**64** w	**57** w	**45** w
	Latin America & Caribbean	**445.3** t	**20,507** t	**2,390** w	**-0.3** w	**43.1** w	**208.2** w	**68** w	**17** w	**16** w
	Severely indebted	**486.2** t	**23,574** t	**2,350** w	**-1.0** w	**39.1** w	**189.6** w	**67** w	**27** w	**22** w
	High-income economies	**822.3** t	**31,682** t	**21,050** w	**2.3** w	**9.1** w	**4.5** w	**77** w	**5** w	**4** w
	OECD members	**783.1** t	**31,135** t	**21,530** w	**2.3** w	**9.0** w	**4.3** w	**77** w	**5** w	**4** w
106	Ireland	3.5	70	11,120	3.3	14.2	5.8	75	. .	. .
107	†Israel	4.9	21	11,950	1.7	39.5	89.0	76	. .	. .
108	New Zealand	3.4	271	12,350	0.7	12.5	10.3	76	f	f
109	Spain	39.0	505	12,450	2.8	16.1	8.9	77	7	5
110	†Hong Kong	5.8	1	13,430[g]	5.6	9.2	7.5	78	. .	. .
111	†Singapore	2.8	1	14,210	5.3	5.9	1.9	74	. .	. .
112	United Kingdom	57.6	245	16,550	2.6	14.5	5.8	75	f	f
113	Australia	17.3	7,687	17,050	1.6	11.8	7.0	77	f	f
114	Italy	57.8	301	18,520	2.2	15.6	9.5	77	f	f
115	Netherlands	15.1	37	18,780	1.6	7.9	1.8	77	f	f
116	Belgium	10.0	31	18,950	2.0	7.8	4.2	76	f	f
117	Austria	7.8	84	20,140	2.1	6.5	3.6	76	f	f
118	France	57.0	552	20,380	1.8	10.2	5.7	77	f	f
119	Canada	27.3	9,976	20,440	2.0	8.7	4.3	77	f	f
120	United States	252.7	9,373	22,240	1.7	7.5	4.2	76	f	f
121	Germany[e]	80.1	357	23,650[h]	2.2[h]	5.1[h]	2.8[h]	76[h]	f	f
122	Denmark	5.2	43	23,700	2.2	10.1	5.2	75	f	f
123	Finland	5.0	338	23,980	2.5	12.3	6.6	76	f	f
124	Norway	4.3	324	24,220	2.3	8.4	5.2	77	f	f
125	Sweden	8.6	450	25,110	1.7	10.0	7.4	78	f	f
126	Japan	123.9	378	26,930	3.6	8.5	1.5	79	f	f
127	Switzerland	6.8	41	33,610	1.6	5.0	3.8	78	f	f
	World	**5,351.0** t	**111,306** t	**4,010** w	**1.2** w	**11.2** w	**15.4** w	**66** w	**45** w	**35** w
	Fuel exporters	**262.8** t	**12,387** t	**1,990** w	**-3.1** w	**19.6** w	**9.6** w	**60** w	**54** w	**44** w

† Economies classified by the United Nations or otherwise regarded by their authorities as developing. a. See the technical notes. b. In all tables GDP and GNP data cover mainland Tanzania only. c. In all tables, data for Jordan cover the East Bank only. d. Estimates for economies of the former Soviet Union are subject to more than the usual range of uncertainty and should be regarded as very preliminary. e. See the footnotes to the Key for data coverage. f. According to UNESCO, illiteracy is less than 5 percent. g. Data refer to GDP. h. Data refer to the Federal Republic of Germany before unification.

Table 2. Growth of production

		\multicolumn{10}{c}{Average annual growth rate (percent)}									
		GDP		Agriculture		Industry		Manufacturing[a]		Services, etc.[b]	
		1970–80	1980–91	1970–80	1980–91	1970–80	1980–91	1970–80	1980–91	1970–80	1980–91
	Low-income economies	**4.5** *w*	**6.0** *w*	**2.1** *w*	**3.7** *w*	**6.3** *w*	**7.5** *w*	**7.2** *w*	**9.3** *w*	**5.7** *w*	**7.0** *w*
	China and India	**4.3** *w*	**7.5** *w*	**2.2** *w*	**4.4** *w*	**6.3** *w*	**9.3** *w*	**7.6** *w*	**9.9** *w*	**5.2** *w*	**8.8** *w*
	Other low-income	**4.8** *w*	**3.7** *w*	**2.1** *w*	**2.5** *w*	**6.4** *w*	**4.0** *w*	**5.7** *w*	**6.8** *w*	**6.5** *w*	**4.8** *w*
1	Mozambique	. .	–0.1	. .	1.6	. .	–3.6	. .	. .	. .	–1.7
2	Tanzania	3.0	2.9	0.7	4.4	2.6	–2.4	3.7	–0.8	8.4	2.0
3	Ethiopia	1.9	1.6	0.7	0.3	1.6	1.8	2.5	1.9	3.9	3.1
4	Uganda	. .	. .	. .	. .	. .	. .	. .	. .	. .	. .
5	Bhutan	. .	7.6	. .	4.8	. .	14.8	. .	15.2	. .	7.3
6	Guinea-Bissau	2.4	3.7	–1.2	5.0	2.1	2.6	. .	. .	11.0	2.8
7	Nepal	. .	. .	0.5	4.9	. .	. .	. .	. .	. .	. .
8	Burundi	4.2	4.0	3.2	3.1	11.6	4.6	3.8	5.8	3.5	5.4
9	Chad[c]	0.1	5.5	–0.4	3.4	–2.1	7.1	. .	. .	2.2	7.3
10	Madagascar	0.5	1.1	0.4	2.4	0.6	0.9	. .	. .	0.6	0.2
11	Sierra Leone	1.6	1.1	6.0	2.7	–3.2	–0.8	–2.1	–1.4	2.3	0.9
12	Bangladesh[c]	2.3	4.3	0.6	2.7	5.2	4.9	5.1	2.9	3.8	5.6
13	Lao PDR[c]	. .	. .	. .	. .	. .	. .	. .	. .	. .	. .
14	Malawi	5.8	3.1	4.4	2.4	6.3	3.3	. .	3.9	7.0	3.7
15	Rwanda[c]	4.7	0.6	7.1	–1.5	. .	0.5	4.9	0.5	. .	3.1
16	Mali[c]	4.9	2.5	4.2	2.4	2.0	4.0	. .	. .	6.9	2.4
17	Burkina Faso	4.4	4.0	1.0	3.2	2.5	3.8	4.1	2.6	19.9	5.4
18	Niger	1.7	–1.0	–3.7	. .	11.3	. .	. .	. .	2.9	. .
19	India	3.4	5.4	1.8	3.2	4.5	6.3	4.6	6.7	4.6	6.7
20	Kenya	6.4	4.2	4.8	3.2	8.6	4.0	9.9	4.9	6.8	4.9
21	Nigeria	4.6	1.9	–0.1	3.5	7.3	–0.4	5.2	. .	9.6	3.1
22	China[c]	5.2	9.4	2.6	5.7	7.8[d]	11.0[d]	9.5	11.1	6.1	11.2
23	Haiti	3.7	–0.7	. .	. .	. .	. .	. .	. .	. .	. .
24	Benin[c]	2.2	2.4	1.8	4.9	1.4	3.6	. .	4.8	2.7	0.5
25	Central African Rep.	2.4	1.4	1.9	2.4	4.1	3.2	. .	. .	2.3	–0.2
26	Ghana	–0.1	3.2	–0.3	1.2	–1.0	3.7	–0.5	4.1	1.1	6.6
27	Pakistan	4.9	6.1	2.3	4.2	6.1	7.5	5.4	7.8	6.3	6.6
28	Togo	4.0	1.8	1.9	5.3	7.7	1.5	. .	2.5	3.6	–0.2
29	Guinea[c]	. .	. .	. .	. .	. .	. .	. .	. .	. .	. .
30	Nicaragua[c]	1.1	–1.9	1.9	–2.2	1.1	–1.7	2.8	–3.1	0.4	–1.7
31	Sri Lanka	4.1	4.0	2.8	2.3	3.4	4.7	1.9	6.3	5.7	4.6
32	Mauritania	1.3	1.4	–1.0	0.7	0.5	4.9	. .	. .	3.7	0.5
33	Yemen, Rep.[c]	. .	. .	. .	. .	. .	. .	. .	. .	. .	. .
34	Honduras	5.8	2.7	2.2	2.9	6.7	3.3	6.9	3.7	7.1	2.5
35	Lesotho	8.6	5.5	0.2	1.8	27.8	8.2	18.0	12.8	13.6	5.3
36	Indonesia[c]	7.2	5.6	4.1	3.1	9.6	5.9	14.0	12.3	7.7	6.8
37	Egypt, Arab Rep.	9.5	4.8	2.8	2.4	9.4	4.2	. .	. .	17.5	6.2
38	Zimbabwe	1.6	3.1	0.6	2.2	1.1	2.1	2.8	3.1	2.4	4.0
39	Sudan	5.6	. .	3.3	. .	4.5	. .	3.9	. .	8.1	. .
40	Zambia[c]	1.4	0.8	2.1	3.3	1.5	0.9	2.4	3.7	1.2	0.0
	Middle-income economies	. .	**2.3** *w*	. .	. .	. .	. .	. .	. .	. .	. .
	Lower-middle-income	. .	**2.7** *w*	. .	. .	. .	. .	. .	. .	. .	. .
41	Bolivia[c]	4.5	0.3	3.9	1.8	2.6	–0.8	6.0	–0.1	6.8	–0.1
42	Côte d'Ivoire	6.6	–0.5	2.7	–1.2	9.1	–1.6	. .	. .	10.9	0.8
43	Senegal[c]	2.3	3.1	1.3	2.7	5.3	3.8	2.4	5.1	2.0	3.0
44	Philippines[c]	6.0	1.1	4.0	1.1	8.2	–0.5	6.1	0.4	5.1	2.8
45	Papua New Guinea[c]	2.2	2.0	2.8	1.6	. .	2.4	. .	0.3	. .	1.8
46	Cameroon[c]	7.2	1.4	4.0	1.1	10.9	2.2	7.0	. .	7.8	1.1
47	Guatemala[c]	5.8	1.1	4.6	1.2	7.7	–0.2	6.2	–7.0	5.6	1.0
48	Dominican Rep.[c]	6.5	1.7	3.1	0.3	8.3	1.6	6.5	0.6	7.2	2.3
49	Ecuador[c]	9.6	2.1	2.8	4.4	13.9	1.1	10.5	–0.1	9.5	2.1
50	Morocco[c]	5.6	4.2	1.1	6.8	6.5	3.0	. .	4.2	7.0	4.2
51	Jordan	. .	–1.5	. .	8.1	. .	–0.2	. .	1.4	. .	–2.7
52	Tajikistan	. .	. .	. .	. .	. .	. .	. .	. .	. .	. .
53	Peru[c]	3.5	–0.4	0.0	2.2	4.4	–1.1	3.1	–0.7	4.6	–0.9
54	El Salvador[c]	4.2	1.0	3.4	–0.4	5.2	1.6	4.1	1.4	4.0	1.1
55	Congo[c]	5.8	3.3	2.5	3.3	10.3	4.7	. .	6.3	4.5	2.4
56	Syrian Arab Rep.[c]	9.9	2.6	8.6	–0.6	9.0	6.8	. .	. .	11.1	1.6
57	Colombia	5.4	3.7	4.6	3.2	5.1	4.8	5.8	3.4	5.9	3.1
58	Paraguay[c]	8.5	2.7	6.2	3.6	11.2	0.2	7.9	2.2	8.6	3.5
59	Uzbekistan	. .	. .	. .	. .	. .	. .	. .	. .	. .	. .
60	Jamaica[c]	–1.2	1.6	0.3	1.0	–3.4	2.6	–2.1	2.5	0.0	1.1
61	Romania	. .	0.1	. .	0.1	. .	–0.8	. .	. .	. .	1.9
62	Namibia	. .	1.0	. .	0.3	. .	–2.0	. .	1.7	. .	3.1
63	Tunisia	6.3	3.7	4.1	3.1	6.8	2.9	10.3	6.2	6.7	4.3
64	Kyrgyzstan[c]	. .	. .	. .	. .	. .	. .	. .	. .	. .	. .
65	Thailand[c]	7.1	7.9	4.4	3.8	9.5	9.6	10.5	9.4	7.2	8.0
66	Georgia	. .	. .	. .	. .	. .	. .	. .	. .	. .	. .

Note: For data comparability and coverage, see the technical notes.   Figures in italics are for years other than those specified.

		Average annual growth rate (percent)									
		GDP		Agriculture		Industry		Manufacturing[a]		Services, etc.[b]	
		1970–80	1980–91	1970–80	1980–91	1970–80	1980–91	1970–80	1980–91	1970–80	1980–91
67	Azerbaijan	..	..	..	..	..	..	..	..	..	..
68	Turkmenistan	..	5.0	..	..	..	..	..	..	..	..
69	Turkey	5.9	5.0	3.4	3.0	6.6	6.0	6.1	7.2	6.5	5.0
70	Poland[c]	..	1.1	..	..	..	..	..	..	..	..
71	Bulgaria	..	1.9	..	–2.5	..	3.2	..	..	..	1.4
72	Costa Rica[c]	5.7	3.1	2.5	3.3	8.2	2.9	..	3.1	5.9	3.2
73	Algeria	4.6	3.0	7.5	5.0	3.8	1.8	7.6	3.3	5.0	3.6
74	Panama[c]	4.4	0.5	2.0	2.1	3.9	–5.7	2.8	–0.4	5.0	1.6
75	Armenia[c]	..	..	..	..	..	..	..	..	..	..
76	Chile[c]	1.4	3.6	3.1	4.1	–0.1	3.6	–0.8	3.6	2.3	3.4
77	Iran, Islamic Rep.	2.2	2.2	3.9	2.5	–4.8	3.9	6.4	–0.1	5.6	1.6
78	Moldova	..	..	..	..	..	..	..	..	..	..
79	Ukraine	..	..	..	..	..	..	..	..	..	..
80	Mauritius	6.8	6.7	–3.3	3.2	10.4	10.1	7.1	11.2	10.9	5.8
81	Czechoslovakia[c]	..	0.6	..	–0.4	..	0.3	..	..	..	1.2
82	Kazakhstan	..	..	..	3.7	..	7.7	..	9.6	..	4.7
83	Malaysia[c]	7.9	5.7	..	3.7	..	7.7	..	9.6	..	4.7
	Upper-middle-income	**6.1 w**	**2.1 w**	..	..	..	..	..	..	..	..
84	Botswana[c]	14.5	9.8	8.3	3.0	17.6	10.7	22.9	7.5	14.5	10.3
85	South Africa	3.0	1.3	3.2	2.6	2.3	0.0	4.7	–0.1	3.8	2.5
86	Lithuania	..	..	..	..	..	..	..	..	..	..
87	Hungary[c]	5.2	0.6	2.8	0.9	6.3	–1.6	5.7	1.3	5.2	2.4
88	Venezuela[c]	3.5	1.5	3.4	2.8	0.5	2.1	..	..	6.3	0.9
89	Argentina	2.5	–0.4	2.5	1.5	2.1	–1.4	..	..	2.9	0.1
90	Uruguay[c]	3.0	0.6	0.8	0.2	4.1	0.0	..	0.4	2.9	1.2
91	Brazil	8.1	2.5	4.2	2.6	9.4	1.7	9.0	1.7	7.8	3.2
92	Mexico[c]	6.3	1.2	3.2	0.5	7.2	1.3	7.0	1.8	6.3	1.3
93	Belarus	..	..	..	..	..	..	..	..	..	..
94	Russian Federation	..	..	..	..	..	..	..	..	..	..
95	Latvia	..	..	..	..	..	..	..	..	..	..
96	Trinidad and Tobago	5.9	–4.4	–1.4	–6.8	5.6	–6.6	1.7	–8.7	7.4	–2.3
97	Gabon[c]	9.0	0.2	..	0.9	..	1.1	..	–1.5	..	–0.8
98	Estonia	..	..	..	..	..	..	..	..	..	..
99	Portugal[c]	4.3	2.9	..	..	..	9.6	..	18.3	..	6.0
100	Oman[c]	6.2	7.9	..	7.1	..	..	..	..	..	..
101	Puerto Rico[c]	3.9	4.1	2.3	2.2	5.0	3.6	7.9	1.0	3.2	4.6
102	Korea, Rep.[c]	9.6	9.6	2.7	2.1	15.2	12.1	17.0	12.4	8.8	9.3
103	Greece	4.7	1.8	1.9	0.2	5.0	1.2	6.0	0.4	5.6	2.5
104	Saudi Arabia[c]	10.1	–0.2	5.3	14.0	10.2	–2.9	6.4	8.1	10.3	–0.2
105	Yugoslavia	6.0	0.8	3.1	0.6	8.0	0.8	..	..	4.9	1.0
	Low- and middle-income	**5.3 w**	**3.3 w**	**2.7 w**	**2.8 w**	..	**3.3 w**	..	..	**6.2 w**	**3.5 w**
	Sub-Saharan Africa	**4.0 w**	**2.1 w**	**1.5 w**	**1.8 w**	**5.3 w**	**2.0 w**	**3.5 w**	..	**5.5 w**	**2.5 w**
	East Asia & Pacific	**6.6 w**	**7.7 w**	**3.1 w**	**4.3 w**	**9.4 w**	**9.4 w**	**10.5 w**	**10.6 w**	**7.1 w**	**8.6 w**
	South Asia	**3.5 w**	**5.4 w**	**1.8 w**	**3.3 w**	**4.6 w**	**6.4 w**	**4.6 w**	**6.7 w**	**4.7 w**	**6.6 w**
	Europe and Central Asia	..	**1.5 w**	..	..	..	..	..	**3.5 w**	..	**2.1 w**
	Middle East & N. Africa	**5.2 w**	**2.1 w**	**4.2 w**	**3.6 w**	**3.2 w**	**0.9 w**	**8.0 w**	**1.3 w**	**6.1 w**	**2.0 w**
	Latin America & Caribbean	**5.5 w**	**1.7 w**	**3.5 w**	**1.9 w**	**6.1 w**	**1.4 w**	**8.2 w**	**2.0 w**	**6.4 w**	**2.2 w**
	Severely indebted	**6.1 w**	**1.7 w**	**3.8 w**	**1.5 w**	**6.7 w**	**1.4 w**	**8.2 w**	**2.0 w**	**6.4 w**	**2.2 w**
	High-income economies	**3.2 w**	**2.9 w**	**0.8 w**	..	**2.7 w**	..	**3.4 w**	..	**3.8 w**	..
	OECD members	**3.1 w**	**2.9 w**	**0.8 w**	..	**2.7 w**	..	**3.3 w**	..	**3.8 w**	..
106	Ireland	4.9	3.5	..	..	..	..	..	..	..	..
107	†Israel[c]	4.8	3.7	..	..	..	..	..	..	..	..
108	New Zealand[c]	1.9	1.5	..	3.8	..	1.3	..	0.7	..	1.6
109	Spain[c]	3.5	3.2	..	..	..	..	..	..	..	..
110	†Hong Kong	9.2	6.9	..	..	..	..	..	..	..	..
111	†Singapore[c]	8.3	6.6	1.4	–6.6	8.6	5.8	9.7	7.0	8.3	7.3
112	United Kingdom	2.0	2.9	..	..	..	3.0	..	2.1	..	3.6
113	Australia[c]	3.0	3.1	..	2.9	..	..	..	..	..	..
114	Italy[c]	3.8	2.4	0.9	0.5	3.6	2.1	5.8	2.9	4.0	2.7
115	Netherlands[c]	2.9	2.1	3.9	3.7	2.3	..	..	..	3.8	1.8
116	Belgium[c]	3.0	2.1	..	1.5	..	2.2	..	3.0	..	1.9
117	Austria[c]	3.4	2.3	2.6	1.0	3.1	2.0	3.2	2.6	3.7	2.2
118	France[c]	3.2	2.3	..	1.9	..	0.9	..	0.6	..	2.9
119	Canada	4.6	3.1	1.2	1.6	3.2	3.0	3.5	3.1	6.6	3.3
120	United States[c]	2.8	2.6	0.6	..	2.1	..	3.0	..	3.3	..
121	Germany[c,e]	2.6	2.3	1.1	1.8	1.7	0.9	2.0	1.4	3.5	2.6
122	Denmark	2.2	2.3	2.3	3.2	1.1	2.9	2.6	1.4	2.7	2.1
123	Finland	3.1	3.0	0.2	–0.2	3.0	3.0	3.3	3.1	3.9	3.4
124	Norway	4.8	2.7	1.3	0.8	7.1	5.2	1.2	0.6	3.9	1.1
125	Sweden	1.9	2.0	..	1.6	..	2.8	..	2.5	..	1.3
126	Japan[c]	4.3	4.2	–0.2	1.2	4.0	4.9	4.7	5.6	4.9	3.7
127	Switzerland[c]	0.5	2.2	..	..	..	..	..	..	..	..
	World	**3.5 w**	**3.0 w**	**1.9 w**	**2.6 w**	**3.2 w**	..	**3.9 w**	..	**4.1 w**	..
	Fuel exporters	**5.0 w**	**1.3 w**	**3.2 w**	**3.6 w**	**3.3 w**	**–0.5 w**	**6.5 w**	**2.3 w**	**6.9 w**	**1.5 w**

a. Because manufacturing is generally the most dynamic part of the industrial sector, its growth rate is shown separately.   b. Services, etc. includes unallocated items.
c. GDP and its components are at purchaser values.   d. World Bank estimate.   e. Data refer to the Federal Republic of Germany before unification.

Table 3. Structure of production

		GDP (millions of dollars)		Distribution of gross domestic product (percent)							
				Agriculture		Industry		Manufacturing [a]		Services, etc. [b]	
		1970	1991	1970	1991	1970	1991	1970	1991	1970	1991
	Low-income economies	**225,563** *t*	**920,160** *t*	**38** *w*	**29** *w*	**29** *w*	**34** *w*	**20** *w*	**26** *w*	**33** *w*	**38** *w*
	China and India	**146,193** *t*	**591,577** *t*	**38** *w*	**29** *w*	**32** *w*	**36** *w*	**24** *w*	**30** *w*	**29** *w*	**35** *w*
	Other low-income	**79,034** *t*	**338,471** *t*	**39** *w*	**29** *w*	**21** *w*	**29** *w*	**10** *w*	..	**40** *w*	**42** *w*
1	Mozambique	..	1,219	..	*64*	..	*15*	..	..	..	*21*
2	Tanzania	1,174	2,223	41	61	17	5	10	4	42	34
3	Ethiopia	1,669	5,982	56	47	14	13	9	9	30	40
4	Uganda	1,286	2,527	..	51	..	12	..	4	..	37
5	Bhutan	..	240	..	43	..	27	..	10	..	29
6	Guinea-Bissau	79	211	47	46	21	12	21	*8*	31	42
7	Nepal	861	3,063	67	59	12	14	4	*5*	21	27
8	Burundi	225	1,035	71	55	10	16	7	12	19	29
9	Chad[c]	302	1,236	47	43	18	18	17	16	35	39
10	Madagascar	995	2,488	24	33	16	14	..	..	59	53
11	Sierra Leone	383	743	28	43	30	14	6	3	42	43
12	Bangladesh[c]	6,664	23,394	55	36	9	16	6	9	37	48
13	Lao PDR[c]	..	1,027	..	..	..	..	..	..	..	..
14	Malawi	271	1,986	44	35	17	20	..	13	39	45
15	Rwanda[c]	220	1,579	62	*38*	9	22	4	*20*	30	*40*
16	Mali[c]	338	2,451	61	44	11	12	7	11	28	43
17	Burkina Faso	335	2,629	42	*44*	21	*20*	14	*12*	37	*37*
18	Niger	647	2,284	65	38	7	19	5	8	28	42
19	India	52,949	221,925	45	31	22	27	15	18	33	41
20	Kenya	1,453	7,125	33	27	20	22	12	12	47	51
21	Nigeria	12,546	34,124	41	37	14	38	4	..	45	26
22	China[c]	93,244	369,651	34	27	38	42	30[d]	38[d]	28	32
23	Haiti	394	2,641	..	..	..	..	..	..	..	..
24	Benin[c]	332	1,886	36	37	12	14	..	9	52	49
25	Central African Rep.	169	1,202	35	41	26	16	7	..	38	42
26	Ghana	2,214	6,413	47	53	18	17	11	10	35	29
27	Pakistan	9,102	40,244	37	26	22	26	16	17	41	49
28	Togo	253	1,633	34	33	21	23	10	10	45	44
29	Guinea[c]	..	2,937	..	29	..	35	..	5	..	36
30	Nicaragua[c]	785	6,950	25	30	26	23	20	19	49	47
31	Sri Lanka	2,215	8,195	28	27	24	25	17	14	48	48
32	Mauritania	197	1,030	29	22	38	31	5	..	32	47
33	Yemen, Rep.[c]	..	7,524	..	22	..	26	..	9	..	52
34	Honduras	654	2,661	32	22	22	27	14	*16*	45	51
35	Lesotho	67	578	35	14	9	38	4	13	56	48
36	Indonesia[c]	9,657	116,476	45	19	19	41	10	21	36	39
37	Egypt, Arab Rep.	6,598	30,265	29	18	28	30	..	..	42	52
38	Zimbabwe	1,415	5,543	15	20	36	32	21	26	49	49
39	*Sudan*	*1,901*	..	*44*	..	*14*	..	*8*	..	*42*	..
40	*Zambia*[c]	1,789	3,831	11	16	55	47	10	36	35	37
	Middle-income economies	..	..	..	..	..	..	..	..	..	..
	Lower-middle-income	..	**1,167,639** *t*	..	..	..	..	..	..	..	..
41	Bolivia[c]	1,020	5,019	20	..	32	..	13	..	48	..
42	Côte d'Ivoire	1,147	7,283	40	38	23	22	13	21	36	40
43	Senegal[c]	865	5,774	24	20	20	19	16	13	56	62
44	Philippines[c]	6,691	44,908	30	21	32	34	25	26	39	44
45	Papua New Guinea[c]	646	3,734	37	26	22	35	5	10	41	38
46	Cameroon[c]	1,160	11,666	31	27	19	22	10	12	50	51
47	Guatemala[c]	1,904	9,353	..	26	..	20	..	..	..	55
48	Dominican Rep.[c]	1,485	7,172	23	18	26	25	19	13	51	57
49	Ecuador[c]	1,673	11,595	24	15	25	35	18	21	51	50
50	Morocco[c]	3,956	27,652	20	19	27	31	16	18	53	50
51	Jordan	..	3,524	..	7	..	26	..	13	..	67
52	Tajikistan	..	..	..	..	..	..	..	..	..	..
53	Peru[c]	7,234	48,366	19	..	32	..	20	..	50	..
54	El Salvador[c]	1,029	5,915	28	10	23	24	19	19	48	66
55	Congo[c]	274	2,909	18	12	24	37	..	8	58	50
56	Syrian Arab Rep.[c]	2,140	17,236	20	*30*	25	23	..	..	55	*47*
57	Colombia	7,199	41,692	25	17	28	35	21	20	47	48
58	Paraguay[c]	595	6,254	32	22	21	24	17	18	47	54
59	Uzbekistan	..	..	..	..	..	..	..	..	..	..
60	Jamaica[c]	1,405	3,497	7	5	43	40	16	17	51	56
61	Romania	..	27,619	..	19	..	49	..	..	..	33
62	Namibia	..	1,961	..	10	..	28	..	4	..	62
63	Tunisia	1,244	11,594	20	18	24	32	10	17	56	50
64	Kyrgyzstan[c]	..	..	..	..	..	..	..	..	..	..
65	Thailand[c]	7,087	93,310	26	12	25	39	16	27	49	49
66	Georgia	..	..	..	..	..	..	..	..	..	..

Note: For data comparability and coverage, see the technical notes. Figures in italics are for years other than those specified.

		GDP (millions of dollars)		Distribution of gross domestic product (percent)								
				Agriculture		Industry		Manufacturing[a]		Services, etc.[b]	
		1970	1991	1970	1991	1970	1991	1970	1991	1970	1991
67	Azerbaijan	..	..	..	..	..	..	..	..	..	..
68	Turkmenistan	..	..	..	..	..	..	..	..	..	..
69	Turkey	11,400	95,763	30	18	27	34	17	24	43	49
70	Poland[c]	..	78,031	..	7	..	50	..	..	..	43
71	Bulgaria	..	7,909	..	13	..	50	..	..	..	37
72	Costa Rica[c]	985	5,560	23	18	24	25	..	19	53	56
73	Algeria	4,541	32,678	11	14	41	50	15	10	48	36
74	Panama[c]	1,021	5,544	15	10	21	11	12	..	64	79
75	Armenia[c]	..	..	..	..	..	..	..	..	..	..
76	Chile[c]	8,186	31,311	7	..	41	..	26	..	52	..
77	Iran, Islamic Rep.	10,914	96,989	19	21	43	21	14	9	38	58
78	Moldova	..	..	..	..	..	..	..	..	..	..
79	Ukraine	..	..	..	..	..	..	..	..	..	..
80	Mauritius	184	2,253	16	11	22	33	14	23	62	56
81	Czechoslovakia[c]	..	33,172	..	8	..	56	..	..	..	36
82	Kazakhstan	..	..	..	..	..	..	..	..	..	..
83	Malaysia[c]	4,200	46,980	29	..	25	..	12	..	46	..
	Upper-middle-income	265,930 t	..	12 w	..	37 w	..	..	..	50 w	..
84	Botswana[c]	84	3,644	33	5	28	54	6	4	39	41
85	South Africa	16,293	91,167	8	5	40	44	24	25	52	51
86	Lithuania	..	..	..	20	..	45	..	..	..	35
87	Hungary[c]	5,543	30,795	18	10	45	34	..	29	37	55
88	Venezuela[c]	13,432	53,440	6	5	39	47	16	17	54	48
89	Argentina	20,526	114,344	13	15	38	40	27	..	49	46
90	Uruguay	1,940	9,479	19	10	37	32	..	25	44	58
91	Brazil	35,546	414,061	12	10	38	39	29	26	49	51
92	Mexico[c]	38,318	282,526	12	9	29	30	22	22	59	61
93	Belarus	..	..	..	..	..	..	..	..	..	..
94	Russian Federation	..	..	..	13	..	48	..	..	..	39
95	Latvia	..	..	..	20	..	48	..	41	..	32
96	Trinidad and Tobago	775	4,920	5	3	44	39	26	9	51	58
97	Gabon[c]	322	4,863	19	9	48	45	7	6	34	46
98	Estonia	..	..	..	..	..	..	..	..	..	..
99	Portugal[c]	6,184	65,103	..	..	..	..	..	..	..	..
100	Oman[c]	256	10,236	16	4	77	52	0	4	7	44
101	Puerto Rico[c]	5,035	32,469	3	1	34	41	24	39	62	57
102	Korea, Rep.[c]	8,887	282,970	26	8	29	45	21	28	45	47
103	Greece	8,600	57,900	18	17	31	27	19	14	50	56
104	Saudi Arabia[c]	3,866	108,640	6	7	63	52	10	7	31	41
105	*Yugoslavia*	12,566	82,317	18	12	41	48	..	..	41	40
	Low- and middle-income	..	..	25 w	..	33 w	..	..	..	42 w	..
	Sub-Saharan Africa	40,073 t	164,339 t	35 w	31 w	23 w	29 w	8 w	..	41 w	40 w
	East Asia & Pacific	143,054 t	961,754 t	34 w	19 w	34 w	41 w	26 w	33 w	32 w	40 w
	South Asia	73,546 t	302,014 t	44 w	31 w	21 w	26 w	14 w	17 w	34 w	43 w
	Europe and Central Asia	..	..	..	..	..	..	..	..	..	..
	Middle East & N. Africa	43,980 t	413,241 t	16 w	14 w	42 w	..	11 w	..	42 w	..
	Latin America & Caribbean	154,857 t	1,203,873 t	13 w	..	34 w	..	24 w	..	53 w	..
	Severely indebted	147,806 t	..	14 w	..	35 w	..	24 w	..	52 w	..
	High-income economies	2,106,085 t	17,053,744 t	4 w	..	39 w	..	29 w	..	58 w	..
	OECD members	2,078,060 t	16,626,259 t	4 w	..	39 w	..	29 w	..	58 w	..
106	Ireland	3,323	39,028	17	11	37	9	24	3	46	80
107	†Israel[c]	5,603	62,687	..	..	..	..	..	..	55	65
108	New Zealand[c]	6,415	42,861	12	9	33	27	24	18	55	65
109	Spain[c]	37,909	527,131	..	..	..	..	..	..	..	..
110	†Hong Kong	3,463	67,555	2	0	36	25	29	17	62	75
111	†Singapore[c]	1,896	39,984	2	0	30	38	20	29	68	62
112	United Kingdom	106,502	876,758	3	..	44	..	33	..	53	..
113	Australia[c]	39,330	299,800	6	3	39	31	24	15	55	65
114	Italy[c]	107,485	1,150,516	8	3	41	33	27	21	51	64
115	Netherlands[c]	34,285	290,725	6	4	37	32	26	20	57	64
116	Belgium[c]	25,242	196,873	..	2	..	30	..	22	..	68
117	Austria[c]	14,457	163,992	7	3	45	36	34	25	48	61
118	France[c]	142,869	1,199,286	..	3	..	29	..	21	..	68
119	Canada	73,847	510,835	4	..	36	..	23	..	59	..
120	United States[c]	1,011,563	5,610,800	3	..	35	..	25	..	63	..
121	Germany[c,e]	184,508	1,574,316	3	2	49	39	38	23	47	59
122	Denmark	13,511	112,084	7	5	35	28	22	19	59	67
123	Finland	9,762	110,033	12	6	40	34	27	24	48	60
124	Norway	11,183	105,929	6	3	32	36	22	14	62	62
125	Sweden	29,835	206,411	..	3	..	34	..	22	..	63
126	Japan[c]	203,736	3,362,282	6	3	47	42	36	25	47	56
127	Switzerland[c]	20,733	232,000	..	..	..	..	..	..	..	..
	World	2,792,782 t	21,639,120 t	8 w	..	38 w	..	27 w	..	55 w	..
	Fuel exporters	57,618 t	458,283 t	17 w	12 w	39 w	..	11 w	..	43 w	..

a. Because manufacturing is generally the most dynamic part of the industrial sector, its share of GDP is shown separately. b. Services, etc. includes unallocated items. c. GDP and its components are at purchaser values. d. World Bank estimate. e. Data refer to the Federal Republic of Germany before unification.

243

Table 4. Agriculture and food

		Value added in agriculture (millions of current dollars)		Cereal imports (thousands of metric tons)		Food aid in cereals (thousands of metric tons)		Fertilizer consumption (hundreds of grams of plant nutrient per hectare of arable land)		Food production per capita (average growth rate; 1979-81=100)	Fish products (percentage of daily protein supply)	
		1970	1991	1980	1991	1979/80	1990/91	1979/80	1990/91	1979-91	1970	1990
	Low-income economies	**85,549** *t*	**276,360** *t*	**35,359** *t*	**36,510** *t*	**6,913** *t*	**7,373** *t*	**474** *w*	**993** *w*	..	**5.8** *w*	**6.3** *w*
	China and India	**55,737** *t*	**170,532** *t*	**13,376** *t*	**13,489** *t*	**355** *t*	**351** *t*	**669** *w*	**1,478** *w*	..	**2.3** *w*	**2.9** *w*
	Other low-income	**29,615** *t*	**109,326** *t*	**21,983** *t*	**23,021** *t*	**6,557** *t*	**7,022** *t*	**204** *w*	**394** *w*	..	**5.9** *w*	**6.4** *w*
1	Mozambique	..	854	368	479	151	454	78	8	-3.1	4.6	3.0
2	Tanzania	483	1,352	399	130	89	24	90	144	-1.4	8.1	7.7
3	Ethiopia	931	2,822	397	802	111	894	27	80	-1.4	0.2	0.0
4	Uganda	..	1,425	52	26	17	61	..	0	-0.6	7.5	7.2
5	Bhutan	..	104	5	26	1	4	8	8	-0.6	..	..
6	Guinea-Bissau	37	96	21	64	18	7	5	17	0.3	3.1	2.1
7	Nepal	579	1,807	56	6	21	1	90	274	2.2	0	0.3
8	Burundi	159	565	18	31	8	3	7	16	-0.6	1.6	1.3
9	Chad [a]	142	528	16	73	16	30	..	18	-0.4	7	9.9
10	Madagascar	243	822	110	114	14	38	25	26	-1.4	3.6	4.4
11	Sierra Leone	108	319	83	183	36	17	46	20	-1.1	10.9	10.8
12	Bangladesh[a]	3,636	8,428	2,194	1,631	1,480	1,356	445	1,022	-0.6	7.4	4.8
13	Lao PDR	..	..	121	44	3	0	1	16	0.8	3.8	2.1
14	Malawi	119	701	36	120	5	181	110	198	-2.7	5.9	5.1
15	Rwanda[a]	135	812	16	19	14	9	3	26	-1.8	0.2	0.2
16	Mali[a]	207	1,082	87	226	22	37	69	73	-0.7	4.6	3.5
17	Burkina Faso	139	1,074	77	177	37	56	26	39	2.4	0.7	0.9
18	Niger	420	877	90	143	9	79	5	3	-3.4	0.2	0.2
19	India	23,916	71,103	424	58	344	217	313	743	1.6	1.6	1.6
20	Kenya	484	1,895	387	330	86	63	169	477	0.5	1.5	2.9
21	Nigeria	4,787	12,271	1,828	763	..	..	36	124	1.5	2.7	3.5
22	China[a]	31,821	99,429	12,952	13,431	12	134	1,273	2,777	3.0	3.1	3.9
23	Haiti	..	..	195	348	53	37	44	11	-1.2	0.7	2.8
24	Benin[a]	121	692	61	216	5	8	7	38	1.5	10	4.8
25	Central African Rep.	60	497	12	27	3	3	1	4	-1.0	4.2	3.0
26	Ghana	1,030	3,404	247	344	110	72	65	48	0.2	19.9	18.7
27	Pakistan	3,352	10,318	613	972	146	343	488	912	0.2	0.6	0.8
28	Togo	85	531	41	238	7	16	49	172	-1.0	5.7	8.4
29	Guinea[a]	..	850	171	296	24	12	31	7	-0.5	1.5	4.5
30	Nicaragua[a]	199	2,024	149	176	70	117	185	314	-5.1	1.1	0.4
31	Sri Lanka	627	2,203	884	918	170	200	776	901	-1.3	10	9.9
32	Mauritania	58	226	166	342	26	101	108	93	-1.5	9.2	3.3
33	Yemen, Rep.[a]	..	1,657	..	..	..	149	98	..	..	..	..
34	Honduras	212	592	139	284	27	84	111	273	-1.6	0.9	1.8
35	Lesotho	23	82	107	100	29	31	144	144	-1.7	0	0.8
36	Indonesia[a]	4,340	22,465	3,534	2,795	831	45	440	1,141	2.2	7.9	8.7
37	Egypt, Arab Rep.	1,942	5,491	6,028	7,807	1,758	1,525	2,469	3,722	1.1	1.2	2.4
38	Zimbabwe	214	1,082	156	131	..	8	443	606	-1.0	0.8	1.1
39	*Sudan*	..	2,625	236	1,188	212	453	27	63	-2.8	0.8	0.5
40	*Zambia*[a]	191	603	498	104	167	4	114	113	-0.7	8.3	4.3
	Middle-income economies	..	..	**73,200** *t*	**77,351** *t*	**1,777** *t*	**4,394** *t*	**715** *w*	**697** *w*	..	**6.5** *w*	**6.8** *w*
	Lower-middle-income	..	..	**40,137** *t*	**40,279** *t*	**1,292** *t*	**4,119** *t*	**721** *w*	**744** *w*	..	**6.2** *w*	**6.4** *w*
41	Bolivia[a]	202	..	263	219	150	229	16	58	0.7	0.6	0.6
42	Côte d'Ivoire	462	2,754	469	644	2	59	165	97	-0.1	10.3	8.7
43	Senegal[a]	208	1,129	452	784	61	39	123	50	0.4	8	9.8
44	Philippines[a]	1,975	9,489	1,053	1,848	95	81	444	738	-1.9	26.3	20.9
45	Papua New Guinea[a]	240	980	152	287	..	..	151	311	-0.1	11	11.8
46	Cameroon[a]	364	3,172	140	532	4	9	47	31	-1.8	5.5	6.7
47	Guatemala[a]	..	2,410	204	410	10	170	582	700	-0.7	0.2	0.4
48	Dominican Rep.[a]	345	1,289	365	712	120	6	517	614	-2.6	5.7	2.8
49	Ecuador[a]	402	1,749	387	481	8	98	319	232	0.0	3.8	6.8
50	Morocco[a]	789	5,228	1,821	1,957	119	201	240	332	2.3	1.3	2.8
51	Jordan	..	263	505	1,539	72	481	433	475	-1.2	0.6	1.2
52	Tajikistan	..	..	..	..	..	..	..	..	..	..	..
53	Peru[a]	1,351	..	1,309	1,432	109	371	338	336	-0.6	5.4	10.6
54	El Salvador[a]	292	604	144	324	3	84	1,030	1,027	0.3	1.1	0.7
55	Congo[a]	49	356	88	96	4	15	6	119	-0.1	17.2	22.8
56	Syrian Arab Rep.[a]	435	4,091	726	1,741	74	30	224	539	-2.9	0.5	0.1
57	Colombia	1,806	7,258	1,068	780	3	1	603	1,112	0.6	1.7	1.4
58	Paraguay[a]	191	1,358	75	24	11	0	36	65	1.1	0.3	1.0
59	Uzbekistan	..	..	..	..	..	..	..	..	..	..	..
60	Jamaica[a]	93	177	469	413	117	163	503	710	-0.5	12.2	8.9
61	Romania	..	5,121	2,369	1,834	..	480	1,365	1,099	-2.3	1.8	3.3
62	Namibia	..	194	..	18	..	..	..	..	-2.9	2.8	3.5
63	Tunisia	245	2,084	817	920	165	348	122	181	0.5	1.9	3.7
64	Kyrgyzstan	..	..	..	..	..	..	..	..	..	..	..
65	Thailand[a]	1,837	11,063	213	521	3	104	160	471	0.5	14.4	12.0
66	Georgia	..	..	..	..	..	..	..	..	..	..	..

Note: For data comparability and coverage, see the technical notes. Figures in italics are for years other than those specified.

		Value added in agriculture (millions of current dollars)		Cereal imports (thousands of metric tons)		Food aid in cereals (thousands of metric tons)		Fertilizer consumption (hundreds of grams of plant nutrient per hectare of arable land)		Food production per capita (average growth rate; 1979-81=100)	Fish products (percentage of daily protein supply)	
		1970	1991	1980	1991	1979/80	1990/91	1979/80	1990/91	1979-91	1970	1990
67	Azerbaijan	..	..	..	..	..	..	..	..	..	..	..
68	Turkmenistan	..	..	..	..	..	..	..	..	..	..	..
69	Turkey	3,383	17,090	6	638	16	4	451	676	-0.2	1.9	2.3
70	Poland[a]	..	5,342	7,811	166	..	742	2,425	1,046	1.1	4.2	4.8
71	Bulgaria	..	1,021	693	633	..	100	1,928	1,728	-0.9	2.4	1.7
72	Costa Rica[a]	222	1,013	180	320	1	31	1,573	2,091	-0.7	2.9	2.2
73	Algeria	492	4,608	3,414	5,436	19	26	227	167	0.6	1.3	2.1
74	Panama[a]	149	530	87	101	2	1	540	588	-2.0	5.7	7.4
75	Armenia	..	..	..	..	..	..	..	..	..	..	..
76	Chile[a]	557	..	1,264	588	22	11	333	653	1.5	4.2	7.8
77	Iran, Islamic Rep.	2,120	21,186	2,779	5,025	..	70	297	771	1.3	0.3	1.6
78	Moldova	..	..	..	..	..	..	..	..	..	..	..
79	Ukraine	..	..	181	183	22	7	2,564	2,616	-0.6	6.9	8.5
80	Mauritius	30	248	181	183	22	7	2,564	2,616	-0.6	6.9	8.5
81	Czechoslovakia	..	..	2,102	136	..	..	3,347	2,558	1.5	2.3	2.4
82	Kazakhstan	..	..	..	..	..	4	912	1,950	4.1	13.7	13.8
83	Malaysia[a]	1,198	..	1,336	3,014	..	4	912	1,950	4.1	13.7	13.8
	Upper-middle-income	..	..	33,063 *t*	37,072 *t*	485 *t*	275 *t*	707 *w*	639 *w*	..	6.9 *w*	7.4 *w*
84	Botswana[a]	28	190	68	99	20	0	8	7	-3.7	0.5	1.3
85	South Africa	1,292	4,594	159	1,345	..	..	726	592	-1.1	4.6	3.8
86	Lithuania	..	..	..	..	..	..	..	..	..	..	..
87	Hungary[a]	1,010	3,181	155	128	..	..	2,805	1,269	1.2	1.1	1.3
88	Venezuela[a]	835	2,662	2,484	1,468	..	..	599	1,137	0.0	5.2	6.7
89	Argentina[a]	2,693	16,588	8	31	..	..	48	61	-0.6	1.1	1.7
90	Uruguay	378	926	45	83	7	20	633	551	0.8	0.8	1.1
91	Brazil	4,388	42,288	6,740	6,332	3	16	755	525	1.7	3.6	2.6
92	Mexico[a]	4,462	25,221	7,226	5,433	..	239	465	631	0.2	1.8	3.3
93	Belarus	..	..	..	..	..	..	..	..	..	..	..
94	Russian Federation	..	..	..	..	..	..	..	..	..	..	..
95	Latvia	..	..	..	..	..	..	..	..	..	..	..
96	Trinidad and Tobago	40	144	252	201	..	..	670	650	-1.7	6.2	3.6
97	Gabon[a]	60	425	27	70	..	..	3	25	-1.4	15.6	12.9
98	Estonia	..	..	..	..	..	..	..	..	..	..	..
99	Portugal	..	..	3,372	1,369	267	..	877	877	1.5	15.7	15.0
100	Oman[a]	40	374	120	345	..	..	306	1,554	..	..	..
101	Puerto Rico[a]	161	470	..	..	..	..	..	..	-1.4	..	..
102	Korea, Rep.[a]	2,311	22,793	5,143	10,411	184	..	3,857	4,601	-0.1	6.7	15.8
103	Greece	1,569	..	1,199	753	..	..	1,480	1,741	0.3	5	4.8
104	Saudi Arabia[a]	219	6,713	3,061	5,891	..	..	115	2,068	9.4	2.5	2.3
105	Yugoslavia	2,212	9,641	1,420	217	..	..	1,102	991	-0.7	1.1	1.1
	Low- and middle-income	..	..	108,569 *t*	113,875 *t*	8,690 *t*	11,767 *t*	576 *w*	867 *w*	..	6.2 *w*	6.6 *w*
	Sub-Saharan Africa	13,394 *t*	52,122 *t*	8,434 *t*	10,626 *t*	1,602 *t*	3,221 *t*	59 *w*	90 *w*	..	6.1 *w*	6.2 *w*
	East Asia & Pacific	47,923 *t*	188,371 *t*	26,833 *t*	34,264 *t*	1,525 *t*	486 *t*	953 *w*	1,902 *w*	..	10.2 *w*	11.4 *w*
	South Asia	32,720 *t*	95,645 *t*	4,211 *t*	3,787 *t*	2,339 *t*	2,161 *t*	328 *w*	740 *w*	..	11.7 *w*	14.4 *w*
	Europe and Central Asia	..	..	19,269 *t*	6,265 *t*	284 *t*	1,326 *t*	1,446 *w*	1,094 *w*	..	3.6 *w*	4.0 *w*
	Middle East & N. Africa	7,243 *t*	57,177 *t*	23,881 *t*	34,911 *t*	2,220 *t*	2,857 *t*	337 *w*	681 *w*	..	1.4 *w*	1.7 *w*
	Latin America & Caribbean	19,755 *t*	..	25,782 *t*	22,677 *t*	721 *t*	1,716 *t*	495 *w*	508 *w*	..	6.5 *w*	6.7 *w*
	Severely indebted	20,522 *t*	..	37,723 *t*	30,886 *t*	691 *t*	2,901 *t*	651 *w*	501 *w*	..	3.8 *w*	4.5 *w*
	High-income economies	85,407 *t*	..	79,798 *t*	75,096 *t*	36 *t*	2 *t*	1,321 *w*	1,158 *w*	..	8.2 *w*	8.6 *w*
	OECD members	83,985 *t*	..	70,764 *t*	63,536 *t*	..	..	1,312 *w*	1,145 *w*	..	7.5 *w*	8.4 *w*
106	Ireland	559	..	553	341	..	..	5,219	7,323	1.5	2.7	3.9
107	†Israel[a]	295	..	1,601	1,635	31	2	1,885	2,343	-0.5	3.8	5.0
108	New Zealand[a]	914	..	63	223	..	..	12,060	8,796	0.1	3.1	8.5
109	Spain[a]	..	22,189	6,073	4,016	..	..	821	979	1.3	9.2	9.8
110	†Hong Kong	62	185	812	785	..	..	..	..	0.7	19	16.9
111	†Singapore[a]	44	96	1,324	780	..	..	5,375	56,000	-5.1	16.5	9.2
112	United Kingdom	2,975	..	5,498	2,799	..	..	3,235	3,680	0.4	5.6	5.1
113	Australia[a]	2,277	9,718	5	36	..	..	275	238	-0.4	3.3	4.1
114	Italy[a]	8,387	34,456	7,629	8,466	..	..	1,892	1,480	-0.5	3.9	5.6
115	Netherlands[a]	1,894	11,988	5,246	4,925	..	..	8,472	6,160	0.8	4.6	2.9
116	Belgium	..	3,461	5,599[b]	6,041[b]	..	..	5,282	4,902	1.4	5.1	5.0
117	Austria[a]	992	4,968	131	88	..	..	2,484	1,997	0.7	2	2.7
118	France[a]	..	40,012	1,570	1,206	..	..	3,120	2,953	0.3	5.1	5.8
119	Canada	3,238	..	1,383	448	..	..	398	451	1.2	3.4	6.6
120	United States[a]	27,937	..	199	2,834	..	..	1,099	970	-0.6	3.3	4.3
121	Germany[a]	5,951[c]	23,867[c]	9,500	3,545	..	..	4,227	2,637	1.6	4.1	4.0
122	Denmark	882	5,082	355	207	..	..	2,627	2,463	2.6	9.1	10.5
123	Finland	1,205	7,485	367	58	..	..	1,892	1,819	0.1	7.2	8.7
124	Norway	624	3,084	725	196	..	..	3,220	2,355	0.5	14.5	15.2
125	Sweden	..	5,825	124	117	..	..	1,699	1,162	-0.6	10.2	9.3
126	Japan[a]	12,467	73,671	24,473	27,474	..	..	4,777	4,001	-0.1	24.4	28.0
127	Switzerland[a]	..	..	1,247	493	..	..	4,654	4,075	-0.1	2.7	3.7
	World	238,777 *t*	..	188,971 *t*	188,958 *t*	8,726 *t*	11,769 *t*	813 *w*	957 *w*	..	6.7 *w*	7.1 *w*
	Fuel exporters	9,929 *t*	55,828 *t*	18,772 *t*	24,024 *t*	34 *t*	210 *t*	167 *w*	404 *w*	..	6.4 *w*	6.1 *w*

a. Value added in agriculture data are at purchaser values.   b. Includes Luxembourg.   c. Data refer to the Federal Republic of Germany before unification.

245

Table 5. Commercial energy

		Average annual growth rate (percent)				Energy consumption per capita (kilograms of oil equivalent)		Energy imports as a percentage of merchandise exports	
		Energy production		Energy consumption					
		1970–80	1980–91	1970–80	1980–91	1970	1991	1970	1991
	Low-income economies	**7.3** w	**4.8** w	**7.0** w	**5.6** w	**166** w	**376** w	**6.0** w	**10.0** w
	China and India	**7.7** w	**5.5** w	**7.3** w	**5.8** w	**200** w	**488** w	**4.0** w	**7.0** w
	Other low-income	**6.7** w	**3.2** w	**6.0** w	**4.7** w	**94** w	**173** w	**7.0** w	**13.0** w
1	Mozambique	32.3	−39.3	−1.6	1.0	113	59	. .	. .
2	Tanzania	7.3	3.2	−0.2	2.0	49	37	10.0	65.0
3	Ethiopia	5.5	5.2	0.9	3.4	20	20	11.0	37.0
4	Uganda	−3.2	2.8	−6.4	4.1	58	25	. .	. .
5	Bhutan	. .	. .	. .	. .	. .	15	. .	. .
6	Guinea-Bissau			4.0	2.2	38	38	. .	. .
7	Nepal	12.7	10.9	6.0	8.0	10	22	19.0	38.0
8	Burundi	. .	6.6	6.9	7.4	7	24	6.0	20.0
9	Chad	. .	. .	4.0	0.4	17	17	35.0	31.0
10	Madagascar	0.4	6.8	−2.5	1.8	60	39	9.0	36.0
11	Sierra Leone	. .	. .	−1.7	0.1	158	75	8.0	32.0
12	Bangladesh	. .	11.3	8.8	7.7	. .	57	. .	26.0
13	Lao PDR	41.3	−0.4	−4.0	2.3	73	42		
14	Malawi	11.8	4.2	7.8	1.3	35	41	10.0	24.0
15	Rwanda	4.6	4.0	12.3	1.8	11	29	. .	. .
16	Mali	8.3	6.1	7.8	2.1	15	23	11.0	. .
17	Burkina Faso	. .	. .	12.0	1.1	8	17	21.0	35.0
18	Niger	. .	13.5	11.8	2.3	16	41	7.0	22.0
19	India	6.8	6.6	6.4	7.2	113	337	8.0	26.0
20	Kenya	15.0	6.4	3.0	1.6	138	104	20.0	25.0
21	Nigeria	4.8	1.0	16.0	4.4	43	154	3.0	1.0
22	China	7.9	5.3	7.5	5.3	258	602	1.0	3.0
23	Haiti	14.0	5.7	9.8	1.7	27	49	7.0	43.0
24	Benin	. .	7.4	2.8	3.7	41	46	7.0	29.0
25	Central African Rep.	4.3	2.6	−1.6	3.3	44	29	1.0	10.0
26	Ghana	5.8	−0.1	2.3	0.4	180	130	6.0	44.0
27	Pakistan	8.1	6.5	5.3	6.5	139	243	11.0	23.0
28	Togo	9.2	. .	9.4	0.8	43	47	5.0	14.0
29	Guinea	15.8	4.1	2.3	1.4	68	68	. .	. .
30	Nicaragua	1.7	2.6	4.1	2.7	253	254	7.0	36.0
31	Sri Lanka	8.0	8.5	1.2	4.9	139	177	3.0	17.0
32	Mauritania	. .	. .	4.7	0.3	115	111	5.0	7.0
33	Yemen, Rep.	. .	. .	23.3	7.9	9	96	. .	. .
34	Honduras	13.9	4.1	6.1	2.0	191	181	9.0	20.0
35	Lesotho	. .	. .	. .	. .	. .	. .	. .	. .
36	Indonesia	7.9	1.6	9.9	4.8	99	279	2.0	8.0
37	Egypt, Arab Rep.	10.7	4.6	10.9	4.6	213	594	10.0	5.0
38	Zimbabwe	−1.9	3.0	1.0	3.0	580	517	21.0	28.0
39	*Sudan*	21.0	2.2	−4.3	0.6	113	54	9.0	. .
40	*Zambia*	16.0	1.8	7.7	1.3	299	369	5.0	21.0
	Middle-income economies	**3.1** w	**2.3** w	**5.4** w	**3.4** w	**918** w	**1,351** w	**10.0** w	**11.0** w
	Lower-middle-income	**2.0** w	**4.3** w	**5.0** w	**2.9** w	**865** w	**1,102** w	**9.0** w	**11.0** w
41	Bolivia	6.8	0.8	9.5	−0.1	183	251	1.0	1.0
42	Côte d'Ivoire	20.5	4.5	6.5	2.7	154	170	4.0	12.0
43	Senegal	. .	. .	−2.9	−1.6	180	105	6.0	28.0
44	Philippines	13.6	6.3	4.0	1.9	235	218	14.0	20.0
45	Papua New Guinea	11.4	5.6	8.4	2.4	114	231	39.0	11.0
46	Cameroon	24.4	11.5	6.2	4.4	84	147	6.0	1.0
47	Guatemala	8.5	4.5	6.5	0.6	170	155	2.0	26.0
48	Dominican Rep.	17.0	4.2	6.7	0.9	216	341	14.0	. .
49	Ecuador	36.3	2.9	13.5	3.7	216	598	9.0	1.0
50	Morocco	2.4	1.5	6.8	2.9	170	252	8.0	25.0
51	Jordan	. .	. .	13.1	5.3	322	856	40.0	41.0
52	Tajikistan	. .	. .	. .	. .	. .	. .	. .	. .
53	Peru	10.6	−1.6	4.4	1.4	468	451	1.0	9.0
54	El Salvador	14.5	3.7	7.7	2.4	157	230	2.0	31.0
55	Congo	41.0	6.9	6.2	3.3	138	214	4.0	1.0
56	Syrian Arab Rep.	9.3	8.0	14.4	3.9	313	955	17.0	10.0
57	Colombia	0.3	10.6	5.9	3.1	490	778	1.0	4.0
58	Paraguay	13.5	12.9	9.7	4.9	114	231	17.0	24.0
59	Uzbekistan	. .	. .	. .	. .	. .	. .	. .	. .
60	Jamaica	−0.9	4.3	3.6	−1.4	968	858	25.0	35.0
61	Romania	3.3	−0.4	5.9	0.6	2,136	3,048	. .	. .
62	Namibia[a]	. .	. .	. .	. .	. .	. .	. .	. .
63	Tunisia	4.0	−0.2	8.7	4.5	230	556	8.0	13.0
64	Kyrgyzstan	. .	. .	. .	. .	. .	. .	. .	. .
65	Thailand	5.5	24.1	7.9	7.4	150	438	17.0	12.0
66	Georgia	. .	. .	. .	. .	. .	. .	. .	. .

Note: For data comparability and coverage, see the technical notes. Figures in italics are for years other than those specified.

| | | Average annual growth rate (percent) | | | | Energy consumption per capita (kilograms of oil equivalent) | | Energy imports as a percentage of merchandise exports | |
| | | Energy production | | Energy consumption | | | | | |
		1970–80	1980–91	1970–80	1980–91	1970	1991	1970	1991
67	Azerbaijan	..	..	..	..	..	..	..	..
68	Turkmenistan	..	..	..	..	362	809	11.0	32.0
69	Turkey	3.5	7.7	7.4	6.5	2,512	3,165	20.0	23.0
70	Poland	3.6	0.9	4.6	1.1	2,657	3,540	..	..
71	Bulgaria	2.0	2.3	5.1	0.8	..	..	..	..
72	Costa Rica	6.9	6.3	6.6	3.7	378	570	5.0	21.0
73	Algeria	5.1	4.9	16.9	15.1	219	1,956	3.0	2.0
74	Panama	10.8	9.5	-6.6	0.2	2,524	1,661	..	..
75	Armenia	..	..	..	..	..	..	..	..
76	Chile	-0.1	3.1	0.1	3.1	867	892	5.0	13.0
77	Iran, Islamic Rep.	-5.6	6.2	5.2	4.5	938	1,078	0.0	0.0
78	Moldova	..	..	..	..	..	..	..	..
79	Ukraine	..	..	..	..	..	..	..	..
80	Mauritius	1.9	8.1	4.9	3.4	266	389	8.0	24.0
81	Czechoslovakia	0.8	0.0	2.8	0.6	3,893	4,681	10.0	5.0
82	Kazakhstan	..	..	..	..	..	..	..	..
83	Malaysia	22.5	13.5	5.4	7.9	452	1,066	10.0	5.0
	Upper-middle-income	**3.9 w**	**0.9 w**	**5.8 w**	**3.8 w**	**989 w**	**1,701 w**	**10.0 w**	**11.0 w**
84	Botswana[a]	9.1	1.2	10.5	3.0	232	408	..	..
85	South Africa[a]	6.6	4.0	3.7	2.9	1,909	2,262	1.0	0.0
86	Lithuania	..	..	..	..	..	..	..	..
87	Hungary	1.1	0.2	3.9	0.7	2,053	2,830	10.0	17.0
88	Venezuela	-4.7	0.7	4.4	2.3	2,206	2,521	1.0	1.0
89	Argentina	3.3	3.2	3.3	3.6	1,208	1,764	5.0	6.0
90	Uruguay	5.6	7.2	1.0	0.8	797	816	15.0	15.0
91	Brazil	8.7	7.3	8.8	4.7	410	908	13.0	19.0
92	Mexico	13.7	1.2	8.7	1.4	786	1,383	6.0	5.0
93	Belarus	..	..	..	..	..	..	..	..
94	Russian Federation	..	..	..	..	..	..	..	..
95	Latvia	..	..	..	..	..	..	..	..
96	Trinidad and Tobago	6.2	-2.5	4.5	1.7	4,795	4,907	1.0	0.0
97	Gabon	7.0	4.6	11.3	2.5	805	1,154	..	..
98	Estonia	..	..	..	..	..	..	..	..
99	Portugal	4.5	3.2	5.1	2.9	747	1,584	15.0	15.0
100	Oman	0.3	8.6	5.9	10.1	660	2,859	..	..
101	Puerto Rico	-5.0	2.3	-1.5	0.5	3,497	2,015	..	..
102	Korea, Rep.	4.3	9.5	10.1	7.9	495	1,936	16.0	18.0
103	Greece	8.7	5.9	6.6	2.8	976	2,110	21.0	24.0
104	Saudi Arabia	8.7	-1.7	4.5	9.3	3,137	4,866	0.0	0.0
105	*Yugoslavia*	3.2	3.2	5.3	3.6	1,140	2,296	8.0	19.0
	Low- and middle-income	**4.2 w**	**3.1 w**	**6.0 w**	**4.3 w**	**362 w**	**631 w**	**9.0 w**	**11.0 w**
	Sub-Saharan Africa	**5.4 w**	**4.7 w**	**4.4 w**	**3.5 w**	**96 w**	**135 w**	**6.0 w**	**12.0 w**
	East Asia & Pacific	**7.8 w**	**5.0 w**	**7.1 w**	**5.3 w**	**255 w**	**571 w**	**9.0 w**	**10.0 w**
	South Asia	**6.7 w**	**6.5 w**	**6.4 w**	**7.2 w**	**102 w**	**289 w**	**8.0 w**	**25.0 w**
	Europe and Central Asia	**2.9 w**	**1.2 w**	**4.8 w**	**1.7 w**	**1,714 w**	**2,387 w**	**13.0 w**	**18.0 w**
	Middle East & N. Africa	**3.3 w**	**1.7 w**	**7.5 w**	**7.3 w**	**545 w**	**1,185 w**	**2.0 w**	**4.0 w**
	Latin America & Caribbean	**2.1 w**	**2.5 w**	**5.6 w**	**2.7 w**	**722 w**	**1,051 w**	**11.0 w**	**13.0 w**
	Severely indebted	**6.9 w**	**3.4 w**	**6.3 w**	**3.1 w**	**818 w**	**1,252 w**	**10.0 w**	**11.0 w**
	High-income economies	**1.4 w**	**1.7 w**	**1.8 w**	**1.5 w**	**4,463 w**	**5,106 w**	**11.0 w**	**11.0 w**
	OECD members	**1.5 w**	**1.7 w**	**1.7 w**	**1.5 w**	**4,572 w**	**5,122 w**	**11.0 w**	**11.0 w**
106	Ireland	2.1	2.7	3.1	0.8	2,008	2,754	13.0	5.0
107	†Israel	-42.6	-7.4	3.0	2.3	1,876	1,931	9.0	11.0
108	New Zealand	4.5	6.1	2.6	5.0	2,834	4,893	7.0	7.0
109	Spain	3.7	2.6	5.1	1.7	1,276	2,229	26.0	17.0
110	†Hong Kong	..	..	5.4	3.1	973	1,438	4.0	7.0
111	†Singapore	..	..	2.8	5.6	3,863	6,178	21.0	16.0
112	United Kingdom	7.2	0.4	-0.2	0.7	3,847	3,688	12.0	7.0
113	Australia	6.2	5.7	3.8	2.2	4,032	5,211	5.0	6.0
114	Italy	0.9	1.0	1.6	0.9	2,334	2,756	16.0	10.0
115	Netherlands	8.7	-2.4	2.6	1.4	4,531	5,147	12.0	9.0
116	Belgium	..	..	..	..	..	2,793	..	..
117	Austria	1.1	-0.2	2.0	1.4	2,773	3,500	10.0	7.0
118	France	0.8	6.3	2.3	1.2	3,182	3,854	13.0	10.0
119	Canada	3.2	3.3	3.5	2.0	7,467	9,390	5.0	5.0
120	United States	0.0	0.7	1.3	1.4	7,665	7,681	7.0	15.0
121	Germany[b]	-0.2[b]	0.0[b]	1.8[b]	0.4[b]	3,077[b]	3,463[b]	8.0[b]	8.0[b]
122	Denmark	25.0	34.0	0.6	0.0	4,176	3,747	14.0	5.0
123	Finland	6.4	4.3	3.0	2.8	3,418	5,602	13.0	13.0
124	Norway	17.6	7.8	3.3	1.8	6,029	9,130	12.0	3.0
125	Sweden	6.7	4.2	1.2	1.3	5,398	5,901	11.0	8.0
126	Japan	1.6	3.9	2.2	2.2	2,654	3,552	20.0	17.0
127	Switzerland	4.5	1.0	1.2	1.4	3,186	3,943	7.0	5.0
	World	**2.7 w**	**2.4 w**	**2.9 w**	**2.5 w**	**1,195 w**	**1,343 w**	**10.0 w**	**11.0 w**
	Fuel exporters	**2.5 w**	**1.6 w**	**7.0 w**	**6.8 w**	**658 w**	**1,261 w**	**3.0 w**	**1.0 w**

a. Figures for the South African Customs Union comprising South Africa, Namibia, Lesotho, Botswana, and Swaziland are included in South African data; trade among the component territories is excluded.   b. Data refer to the Federal Republic of Germany before unification.

Table 6. Structure of manufacturing

		Value added in manufacturing (millions of current dollars)		Distribution of manufacturing value added (percent; current prices)									
				Food, beverages, and tobacco		Textiles and clothing		Machinery and transport equipment		Chemicals		Other[a]	
		1970	1990	1970	1990	1970	1990	1970	1990	1970	1990	1970	1990
	Low-income economies	**44,177** t	**240,456** t										
	China and India	**35,483** t	**181,072** t										
	Other low-income	**8,256** t	..										
1	Mozambique			51	..	13	..	5	..	3	..	28	..
2	Tanzania	118	86	36	30	28	18	5	7	4	16	26	29
3	Ethiopia	149	614	46	48	31	19	0	2	2	4	21	28
4	Uganda	..	107	40	..	20	..	2	..	4	..	34	..
5	Bhutan	..	27	..	..	..	..	..	..	..	..	..	..
6	Guinea-Bissau	17	18	..	..	..	..	..	..	..	..	..	..
7	Nepal	32	152	..	35	..	25	..	2	..	8	..	30
8	Burundi	16	99	53	..	25	..	0	..	6	..	16	..
9	Chad[b]	51	250	..	..	..	..	..	..	..	..	..	..
10	Madagascar	..	..	36	39	28	36	6	3	7	7	23	14
11	Sierra Leone	22	52	..	..	..	..	..	..	..	..	..	..
12	Bangladesh[b]	387	1,959	30	24	47	35	3	5	11	17	10	18
13	Lao PDR	..	..	..	..	..	..	..	..	..	..	..	..
14	Malawi	..	227	51	..	17	..	3	..	10	..	20	..
15	Rwanda[b]	8	316	86	..	0	..	3	..	2	..	8	..
16	Mali[b]	25	286	36	..	40	..	4	..	5	..	14	..
17	Burkina Faso	47	325	69	..	9	..	2	..	1	..	19	..
18	Niger[b]	30	219	..	..	..	..	..	..	..	..	..	..
19	India	7,928	48,930	13	12	21	12	20	26	14	17	32	33
20	Kenya	174	862	33	38	9	10	16	10	9	9	33	33
21	Nigeria	426	..	36	..	26	..	1	..	6	..	31	..
22	China[b]	27,555	132,142	..	15	..	15	..	24	..	13	..	34
23	Haiti	..	..	..	..	..	..	..	..	..	..	..	..
24	Benin[b]	38	162	..	..	..	..	..	..	..	..	..	..
25	Central African Rep.	12	..	..	..	..	..	..	..	..	..	..	..
26	Ghana[b]	252	575	34	..	16	..	4	..	4	..	41	..
27	Pakistan	1,462	6,184	24	29	38	19	6	7	9	15	23	30
28	Togo[b]	25	162	..	..	..	..	..	..	..	..	..	..
29	Guinea[b]	..	123	..	..	..	..	..	..	..	..	..	..
30	Nicaragua[b]	159	260	53	..	14	..	2	..	8	..	23	..
31	Sri Lanka	369	1,077	26	51	19	23	10	4	11	3	33	20
32	Mauritania	10		..	..	..	..	..	..	..	..	..	..
33	Yemen, Rep.[b]	..	549	20	..	50	..	..	..	1	..	28	..
34	Honduras	91	428	58	51	10	9	1	2	4	5	28	33
35	Lesotho	3	64	..	..	..	..	..	..	..	..	..	..
36	Indonesia[b]	994	21,722	65	24	14	14	2	10	6	10	13	42
37	Egypt, Arab Rep.	..	..	17	31	35	16	9	9	12	8	27	36
38	Zimbabwe	293	1,508	24	30	16	17	9	8	11	10	40	34
39	Sudan	..	772	39	..	34	..	3	..	5	..	19	..
40	Zambia	181	1,180	49	37	9	12	5	9	10	11	27	31
	Middle-income economies	..	..										
	Lower-middle-income	..	..										
41	Bolivia[b]	135	585	33	37	34	8	1	1	6	6	26	47
42	Côte d'Ivoire	149	..	27	..	16	..	10	..	5	..	42	..
43	Senegal[b]	141	775	51	..	19	..	2	..	6	..	22	..
44	Philippines[b]	1,665	11,160	39	36	8	10	8	8	13	12	32	34
45	Papua New Guinea[b]	35	320	23	..	1	..	35	..	4	..	37	..
46	Cameroon[b]	119	1,363	50	61	15	-13	4	5	3	5	27	42
47	Guatemala[b]	..	..	42	43	14	9	4	3	12	16	27	28
48	Dominican Rep.[b]	275	955	74	..	5	..	1	..	6	..	14	..
49	Ecuador[b]	306	2,091	43	31	14	13	3	7	8	11	32	39
50	Morocco[b]	641	4,886	..	31	..	25	..	6	..	16	..	22
51	Jordan	..	441	21	26	14	7	7	4	6	15	52	49
52	Tajikistan	..	..	..	..	..	..	..	..	..	..	..	..
53	Peru[b]	1,430	..	25	23	14	14	7	10	7	10	47	43
54	El Salvador[b]	194	1,008	40	..	30	..	3	..	8	..	18	..
55	Congo[b]	..	220	65	58	4	4	1	3	8	10	22	24
56	Syrian Arab Rep.[b]	..	..	37	24	40	31	3	6	2	5	20	34
57	Colombia	1,487	8,192	31	30	20	15	8	10	11	14	29	31
58	Paraguay[b]	99	994	56	..	16	..	1	..	5	..	21	..
59	Uzbekistan	..	..	..	..	..	..	..	..	..	..	..	..
60	Jamaica[b]	221	793	46	..	7	..	11	..	5	..	30	..
61	Romania	..	..	..	13	..	19	..	25	..	5	..	38
62	Namibia	..	77	..	..	..	..	..	..	..	..	..	..
63	Tunisia	121	1,869	29	17	18	19	4	6	13	9	36	49
64	Kyrgyzstan	..	..	..	..	..	..	..	..	..	..	..	..
65	Thailand[b]	1,130	20,926	43	29	13	25	9	12	6	3	29	31
66	Georgia	..	..	..	..	..	..	..	..	..	..	..	..

Note: For data comparability and coverage, see the technical notes.   Figures in italics are for years other than those specified.

No.	Country	Value added in manufacturing (millions of current dollars) 1970	1990	Food, beverages, and tobacco 1970	1990	Textiles and clothing 1970	1990	Machinery and transport equipment 1970	1990	Chemicals 1970	1990	Other[a] 1970	1990
67	Azerbaijan	..	..	..	..	..	..	..	..	..	..	..	..
68	Turkmenistan	..	..	..	..	..	..	..	..	..	..	..	..
69	Turkey	1,930	22,685	26	16	15	14	8	17	7	11	45	43
70	Poland[b]	..	..	20	21	19	9	24	26	8	7	28	37
71	Bulgaria	..	..	..	..	..	..	..	..	..	..	..	..
72	Costa Rica[b]	203	1,071	48	47	12	8	6	6	7	9	28	30
73	Algeria	682	4,816	32	..	20	..	9	..	4	..	35	..
74	Panama[b]	127	..	41	52	9	6	1	3	5	8	44	31
75	Armenia	..	..	..	..	..	..	..	..	..	..	..	..
76	Chile	2,088	..	17	24	12	7	11	5	5	9	55	56
77	Iran, Islamic Rep.	1,501	8,819	30	..	20	..	18	..	6	..	26	..
78	Moldova	..	..	..	..	..	..	..	..	..	..	..	..
79	Ukraine	..	..	..	..	..	..	..	..	..	..	..	..
80	Mauritius	26	496	75	23	6	50	5	3	3	5	12	19
81	Czechoslovakia[b]	..	..	9	10	12	11	34	35	6	7	39	37
82	Kazakhstan	..	..	..	..	..	..	..	..	..	..	..	..
83	Malaysia[b]	500	..	26	13	3	6	8	31	9	11	54	39
	Upper-middle-income	..	..										
84	Botswana[b]	5	128	..	52	..	8	..	..	..	9	..	31
85	South Africa	3,892	23,197	15	14	13	8	17	18	10	11	45	50
86	Lithuania	..	..	12	10	13	9	28	27	8	13	39	41
87	Hungary[b]	..	8,831	30	17	13	5	9	5	8	9	39	64
88	Venezuela[b]	2,163	8,109	18	20	17	10	17	13	8	12	40	44
89	Argentina	5,523	..	34	32	21	18	7	9	6	10	32	31
90	Uruguay	619	2,173	16	13	13	12	22	23	10	12	39	40
91	Brazil	10,421	108,789	28	22	15	9	13	15	11	14	34	40
92	Mexico[b]	8,449	55,621	..	..	..	..	..	..	..	..	..	..
93	Belarus	..	..	..	..	..	..	..	..	..	..	..	..
94	Russian Federation	..	..	..	..	..	..	..	..	..	..	..	..
95	Latvia	..	3,825	18	..	3	..	7	..	2	..	70	..
96	Trinidad and Tobago	198	435	37	..	7	..	6	..	6	..	44	..
97	Gabon[b]	22	264	..	..	..	..	..	..	..	..	..	..
98	Estonia	..	..	..	..	..	..	..	..	..	..	..	..
99	Portugal[b]	..	396	18	18	19	20	13	14	10	10	39	39
100	Oman[c]	0	..	..	15	..	5	..	18	..	45	..	17
101	Puerto Rico	1,190	12,181	..	..	..	..	..	..	..	..	..	..
102	Korea, Rep.[b]	1,880	70,497	26	11	17	13	11	32	11	9	36	35
103	Greece	1,642	8,291	20	22	20	21	13	12	7	8	40	38
104	Saudi Arabia[b]	372	7,962	..	7	..	1	..	4	..	39	..	50
105	*Yugoslavia*	..	..	10	16	15	19	23	24	7	8	45	31
	Low- and middle-income	..	..										
	Sub-Saharan Africa	3,046 *t*	..										
	East Asia & Pacific	36,524 *t*	287,606 *t*										
	South Asia	10,362 *t*	59,372 *t*										
	Europe and Central Asia	..	..										
	Middle East & N. Africa	4,797 *t*	40,563 *t*										
	Latin America & Caribbean	36,590 *t*	254,873 *t*										
	Severely indebted	35,985 *t*	277,462 *t*										
	High-income economies	605,102 *t*	..										
	OECD members	599,875 *t*	..										
106	Ireland	786	1,535	31	26	19	4	13	32	7	15	30	23
107	†Israel[b]	..	..	15	13	14	9	23	32	7	10	41	37
108	New Zealand[b]	1,811	7,572	24	26	13	9	15	14	4	6	43	46
109	Spain[b]	..	124,454	13	18	15	8	16	25	11	10	45	38
110	†Hong Kong	1,013	11,403	4	7	41	38	16	20	2	2	36	33
111	†Singapore[b]	379	10,351	12	4	5	3	28	53	4	10	51	29
112	United Kingdom	35,415	..	13	13	9	5	31	32	10	11	37	38
113	Australia[b]	9,551	44,589	16	18	9	7	24	19	7	8	43	48
114	Italy[b]	29,093	242,899	10	8	13	*13*	24	*33*	13	*10*	40	*36*
115	Netherlands[b]	8,861	58,147	17	16	8	3	27	25	13	18	36	39
116	Belgium[b]	..	43,260	17	17	13	8	25	23	9	11	37	41
117	Austria[b]	4,873	41,526	17	15	12	6	19	28	6	7	45	44
118	France[b]	..	251,143	12	13	10	6	26	31	8	9	44	41
119	Canada	16,782	..	16	14	8	6	23	26	7	10	46	44
120	United States[b]	254,858	..	12	12	8	5	31	31	10	12	39	40
121	Germany[b,d]	70,888	460,983	13	9	8	4	32	42	9	12	38	32
122	Denmark	2,929	21,376	20	21	8	4	24	23	8	11	40	40
123	Finland	2,588	26,170	13	13	10	4	20	25	6	8	51	51
124	Norway	2,416	14,472	15	21	7	2	23	24	7	9	49	44
125	Sweden	..	45,021	10	10	6	2	30	32	5	9	49	47
126	Japan[b]	73,342	849,308	8	9	8	5	34	39	11	10	40	37
127	Switzerland[b]	..	..	10	..	7	..	31	..	9	..	42	..
	World	754,620 *t*	..										
	Fuel exporters	6,221 *t*	41,957 *t*										

a. Includes unallocated data; see the technical notes. b. Value added in manufacturing data are at purchaser values. c. World Bank estimates. d. Data refer to the Federal Republic of Germany before unification.

Table 7. Manufacturing earnings and output

		Earnings per employee					Total earnings as a percentage of value added				Gross output per employee (1980=100)			
		Growth rate		Index (1980=100)										
		1970–80	1980–90	1988	1989	1990	1970	1988	1989	1990	1970	1988	1989	1990
Low-income economies														
China and India														
Other low-income														
1	Mozambique	..					29	..						
2	Tanzania	..	–13.5				42	25			122	97	..	..
3	Ethiopia	–4.6	0.5	102	94	86	24	20	19	19	61	110	112	103
4	Uganda	..	..	..	..	..	..	..			..	..	..	..
5	Bhutan	..	..	..	..	..	..	..			..	..	..	..
6	Guinea-Bissau	..	..	..	..	..	..	..			..	..	..	..
7	Nepal	..	..	..	..	..	..	26	..	..	..	..	..	..
8	Burundi	–7.5	..	..	..	..	..	..			..	..	..	..
9	Chad	..	..	..	..	..	..	..			..	..	..	..
10	Madagascar	–0.8	6.6	56	..	..	36	37	..	..	106	60	..	..
11	Sierra Leone	..	..	..	..	..	..	..			..	..	..	..
12	Bangladesh	–3.0	0.6	99	98	95	26	34	34	33	206	110	111	113
13	Lao PDR	..	..	..	..	..	..	..			..	..	..	..
14	Malawi	..	–0.8	..	..	..	37	..	..	..	126	..	..	..
15	Rwanda	..	..	..	..	..	22	..	..	..	..	..	..	..
16	Mali	..	..	..	..	..	46	..	..	..	139	..	..	..
17	Burkina Faso	11.7	..	..	..	..	..	..	..	..	..	..	..	..
18	Niger	..	..	..	..	..	..	6	..	..	..	..	..	..
19	India	0.4	3.4	127	134	..	47	48	47	..	83	175	179	..
20	Kenya	–3.4	–0.7	101	97	92	50	44	43	42	43	202	218	235
21	Nigeria	–0.8	..	..	..	..	18	..	..	..	182	..	..	..
22	China	..	3.5	..	..	..	..	..	..	..	220	244	251	..
23	Haiti	–3.3	4.6	157	..	..	..	..	..	..	..	..	..	..
24	Benin	..	..	..	..	..	..	..			..	..	..	..
25	Central African Rep.	..	..	..	..	..	..	..	..	..	..	124	160	..
26	Ghana	–14.8	7.8	..	..	..	23	..	..	..	193	..	..	..
27	Pakistan	3.4	6.6	159	..	..	21	22	..	..	51	164	..	..
28	Togo	..	..	..	..	..	..	..			..	..	..	..
29	Guinea	..	..	..	..	..	..	..			..	..	..	..
30	Nicaragua	–2.0	..	..	..	..	16	..	..	..	210	..	..	..
31	Sri Lanka	..	1.8	106	100	..	..	18	18	..	70	137	134	..
32	Mauritania	..	..	..	..	..	..	..			..	..	..	..
33	Yemen, Rep.	..	..	..	..	..	..	..			..	..	..	..
34	Honduras	..	0.9	..	..	..	..	40	38	36	..	..	..	..
35	Lesotho	..	..	..	..	..	..	..			..	..	..	..
36	Indonesia	5.2	5.1	149	155	186	26	23	20	21	42	180	204	211
37	Egypt, Arab Rep.	4.1	–2.1	94	91	..	54	37	35	..	89	206	220	..
38	Zimbabwe	1.6	0.5	107	115	112	43	35	35	34	98	124	128	135
39	Sudan	..	..	..	..	..	31	..	..	..	..	..	..	..
40	Zambia	–3.2	3.1	168	125	98	34	27	27	27	109	128	93	90
Middle-income economies														
Lower-middle-income														
41	Bolivia	0.0	–6.4	64	55	49	43	27	27	27	65	41	..	..
42	Côte d'Ivoire	–0.9	..	..	..	..	27	..	..	..	52	..	..	..
43	Senegal	–4.9	0.5	..	..	..	..	..			..	..	..	..
44	Philippines	–3.7	5.6	154	160	174	21	24	23	23	104	100	112	119
45	Papua New Guinea	2.9	–1.5	..	..	..	40	..	..	..	..	..	..	..
46	Cameroon	3.2	..	..	72	..	30	..	47	45	81	..	153	184
47	Guatemala	–3.2	–1.9	89	100	..	..	19	20	..	..	..	..	..
48	Dominican Rep.	–1.1	..	..	..	..	35	..	..	..	63	..	..	..
49	Ecuador	3.3	–1.5	95	80	96	27	33	33	41	83	114	101	112
50	Morocco	..	–3.5	..	..	..	..	..	..	..	..	89	..	..
51	Jordan	8.6	–3.9	101	74	63	37	23	25	24	..	..	..	..
52	Tajikistan	..	..	..	..	..	..	..			..	..	..	..
53	Peru	..	–3.5	71	..	..	..	14	..	..	80	..	..	..
54	El Salvador	2.4	..	..	..	..	28	..	..	..	71	..	..	..
55	Congo	..	–2.6	..	..	..	34	43	..	..	..	..	..	..
56	Syrian Arab Rep.	2.6	–5.4	64	66	65	33	27	28	..	70	..	..	..
57	Colombia	–0.2	1.6	114	117	116	25	15	15	..	86	148	158	164
58	Paraguay	..	..	..	..	..	..	..			..	..	..	..
59	Uzbekistan	..	..	..	..	..	..	..			..	..	..	..
60	Romania	..	..	..	..	..	..	..	..	39	..	..	..	..
61	Namibia	..	..	..	..	..	..	..			..	..	..	..
62	Tunisia	4.2	..	..	..	..	44	..	..	..	95	..	..	..
63	Jamaica	–0.2	–0.8	101	..	..	43	..	..	..	99	78	..	..
64	Kyrgyzstan	..	..	..	..	..	..	..			..	..	..	..
65	Thailand	0.3	5.9	160	160	158	25	28	28	28	77	109	112	113
66	Georgia	..	..	..	..	..	..	..	..	..	..	..	..	..

Note: For data comparability and coverage, see the technical notes.   Figures in italics are for years other than those specified.

250

		Earnings per employee					Total earnings as a percentage of value added				Gross output per employee (1980=100)			
		Growth rate		Index (1980=100)										
		1970–80	1980–90	1988	1989	1990	1970	1988	1989	1990	1970	1988	1989	1990
67	Azerbaijan	..	..	..	..	..	..	..	..	..	..	..	..	..
68	Turkmenistan	..	..	80	100	98	26	15	19	19	108	166	181	195
69	Turkey	6.1	-1.2	..	..	..	24	23	19	17	..	..	..	..
70	Poland	5.5	0.1	103	114	78	..	..	..	..	..	..	..	..
71	Bulgaria	..	..	..	..	..	..	..	..	..	..	..	..	..
72	Costa Rica	..	-2.2	..	..	..	41	38	39	39	120	..	..	..
73	Algeria	-1.0	..	123	126	134	45	..	..	..	67	73	74	81
74	Panama	0.2	2.2	..	..	..	32	37	37	37	..	..	..	..
75	Armenia	..	..	..	..	..	19	16	15	15	60	..	..	..
76	Chile	8.1	-1.0	103	106	106	25	..	..	..	84	..	..	..
77	Iran, Islamic Rep.	7.9	-8.2	..	..	..	..	..	..	..	..	..	..	..
78	Moldova	..	..	..	..	..	..	..	..	..	..	..	..	..
79	Ukraine	..	..	..	..	..	34	45	45	46	139	69	75	84
80	Mauritius	1.8	-0.1	98	97	101	49	39	42	43	..	131	129	..
81	Czechoslovakia	2.3	0.4	106	107	100	..	..	..	..	..	..	..	..
82	Kazakhstan	..	..	..	..	..	29	27	26	27	96	..	..	..
83	Malaysia	2.0	2.6	126	128	128	..	..	..	..	..	..	..	..
Upper-middle-income														
84	Botswana	2.6	-5.5	66	..	..	..	35	..	..	..	67	..	..
85	South Africa	2.7	0.2	104	106	106	46	47	47	..	64	88	88	..
86	Lithuania	..	..	..	..	..	..	..	..	..	..	..	..	..
87	Hungary	3.6	2.3	125	127	120	28	39	36	40	41	105	103	100
88	Venezuela	4.9	-5.2	80	63	58	31	28	21	16	103	111	103	107
89	Argentina	-2.1	-0.8	94	75	..	28	20	16	..	75	74	73	..
90	Uruguay	..	0.8	116	107	..	26	26	..	..	111	112	..	..
91	Brazil	4.0	4.8	161	163	121	22	20	21	20	71	123	124	120
92	Mexico	1.2	-3.9	67	72	75	44	18	19	20	77	119	132	138
93	Belarus	..	..	..	..	..	..	..	..	..	..	..	..	..
94	Russian Federation	..	..	..	..	..	..	..	..	..	..	..	..	..
95	Latvia	..	..	..	..	..	..	..	..	..	..	..	..	..
96	Trinidad and Tobago	..	-0.7	..	..	..	..	..	..	..	..	..	..	..
97	Gabon	..	..	..	..	..	..	..	..	..	..	..	..	..
98	Estonia	..	..	..	..	..	..	..	..	..	..	..	..	..
99	Portugal	2.5	0.7	103	103	106	34	36	36	36	..	..	..	..
100	Oman	..	..	..	..	..	..	21	22	..	..	..	..	..
101	Puerto Rico	..	..	..	..	..	25	28	31	31	..	..	..	..
102	Korea, Rep.	10.0	7.4	161	191	189	32	39	40	40	40	177	193	204
103	Greece	4.9	0.6	104	112	110	..	..	..	..	56	109	115	..
104	Saudi Arabia	..	..	..	..	..	..	..	26	..	59	97	75	..
105	*Yugoslavia*	1.3	-0.7	88	102	..	39	26	26	..	..	..	..	..
Low- and middle-income														
Sub-Saharan Africa														
East Asia & Pacific														
South Asia														
Europe and Central Asia														
Middle East & N. Africa														
Latin America & Caribbean														
Severely indebted														
High-income economies														
OECD members														
106	Ireland	4.1	1.9	111	112	114	49	29	27	26	..	..	..	..
107	†Israel	8.8	-3.6	95	71	72	36	62	37	36	..	141	140	..
108	New Zealand	1.2	-0.7	94	90	95	62	55	53	55	..	..	..	..
109	Spain	4.4	0.9	106	109	109	52	38	39	39	..	..	..	..
110	†Hong Kong	6.4	4.9	143	150	147	..	55	55	55	..	..	..	..
111	†Singapore	2.9	5.0	149	165	175	36	28	30	32	73	122	129	135
112	United Kingdom	1.7	2.6	123	124	125	52	40	41	40	..	128	139	136
113	Australia	2.9	-0.3	103	101	96	53	47	45	45	..	..	..	..
114	Italy	4.1	1.0	109	110	..	41	41	41	..	50	136	141	..
115	Netherlands	2.5	1.1	107	108	109	52	49	48	48	..	..	..	..
116	Belgium	4.7	0.1	99	101	104	46	41	40	41	..	141	146	142
117	Austria	3.4	1.8	114	116	121	47	54	53	54	65	119	127	134
118	France	..	2.2	117	121	123	63	63	63	..	116	123	..	..
119	Canada	1.8	0.0	101	101	99	53	43	44	44	68	112	..	..
120	United States	0.1	0.7	107	106	104	47	36	35	36	64	..	..	..
121	Germany[a]	3.5	1.8	113	114	116	46	42	41	42	60	109	114	115
122	Denmark	2.5	0.6	105	104	..	56	52	51	..	64	103	107	..
123	Finland	2.6	2.8	122	126	130	47	44	43	47	73	132	140	148
124	Norway	2.6	1.6	110	110	112	50	56	54	57	74	118	127	135
125	Sweden	0.4	0.9	103	107	106	52	34	34	35	..	126	131	132
126	Japan	3.1	2.0	117	120	121	32	34	33	33	48	120	131	137
127	Switzerland	..	..	..	..	..	..	..	..	..	..	..	..	..
World														
Fuel exporters														

a. Data refer to the Federal Republic of Germany before unification.

Table 8. Growth of consumption and investment

		Average annual growth rate (percent)					
		General government consumption		Private consumption, etc.		Gross domestic investment	
		1970–80	1980–91	1970–80	1980–91	1970–80	1980–91
	Low-income economies	**5.4** w	**6.5** w	**4.1** w	**4.8** w	**7.0** w	**7.0** w
	China and India	**4.8** w	**8.6** w	**3.7** w	**6.2** w	**6.2** w	**9.4** w
	Other low-income	**6.2** w	**3.5** w	**4.9** w	**2.7** w	**8.5** w	**1.7** w
1	Mozambique	..	-2.1	..	1.4	..	3.0
2	Tanzania	a	..	4.4	..	3.1	..
3	Ethiopia	2.4	2.1	8.3	5.2	-0.8	2.0
4	Uganda	..	0.9	..	3.3	..	11.9
5	Bhutan	..	..	..	..	..	..
6	Guinea-Bissau	1.3	3.1	-1.8	4.0	-1.7	4.3
7	Nepal	..	..	..	..	..	..
8	Burundi	3.5	4.5	4.5	4.2	16.3	2.7
9	Chad	..	..	..	..	..	..
10	Madagascar	1.5	0.2	-0.2	-0.8	0.4	2.6
11	Sierra Leone	a	-0.4	7.0	-1.3	-1.2	-5.3
12	Bangladesh	a	a	2.3	3.6	4.8	-1.0
13	Lao PDR	..	..	..	..	..	..
14	Malawi	7.9	5.8	3.5	2.7	4.2	-0.8
15	Rwanda	7.5	6.8	4.3	-0.4	10.4	-1.0
16	Mali	1.9	4.1	6.2	1.7	3.3	6.9
17	Burkina Faso	6.6	6.0	4.7	2.8	4.4	9.3
18	Niger	3.0	1.8	0.4	-0.9	7.6	-4.6
19	India	4.1	7.5	2.9	5.3	4.5	5.1
20	Kenya	9.2	3.4	6.4	5.1	2.4	0.6
21	Nigeria	11.4	-2.1	7.8	-1.9	11.4	-8.1
22	China	5.7	10.0	4.9	7.3	7.9	12.4
23	Haiti	1.6	-1.4	3.4	0.3	13.7	-3.4
24	Benin	-1.9	0.3	3.2	0.9	11.4	-4.8
25	Central African Rep.	-2.4	-0.9	5.2	1.9	-9.7	3.6
26	Ghana	5.1	0.5	1.7	2.6	-2.5	9.0
27	Pakistan	4.1	9.1	4.2	4.7	3.7	5.6
28	Togo	10.2	1.0	2.0	5.3	11.9	-0.7
29	Guinea	..	..	..	..	..	..
30	Nicaragua	10.7	0.3	0.9	-1.8	..	-5.3
31	Sri Lanka	0.3	6.9	4.9	3.6	13.8	1.2
32	Mauritania	10.8	-4.7	0.2	3.7	19.8	-5.6
33	Yemen, Rep.	..	..	..	..	..	..
34	Honduras	6.5	2.0	5.9	2.8	9.1	3.4
35	Lesotho	17.8	2.9	10.6	-0.6	23.4	9.1
36	Indonesia	13.1	4.7	6.5	4.7	14.1	6.9
37	Egypt, Arab Rep.	a	3.3	7.4	3.3	18.7	-0.1
38	Zimbabwe	12.1	10.1	3.8	2.8	-4.2	0.3
39	*Sudan*	..	-1.5	6.9	0.8	8.2	-1.2
40	*Zambia*	1.4	-3.2	0.2	3.7	-10.9	0.2
	Middle-income economies	..	..	..	..	..	..
	Lower-middle-income	..	**1.1** w	..	**3.6** w	..	**-0.7** w
41	Bolivia	7.9	-1.2	4.5	2.2	2.3	-8.0
42	Côte d'Ivoire	12.1	-4.0	6.9	-1.7	12.6	-11.5
43	Senegal	5.9	2.5	3.0	2.6	0.3	3.7
44	Philippines	6.8	0.9	4.3	2.4	11.3	-1.8
45	Papua New Guinea	-1.3	0.1	4.5	0.6	-5.4	-0.9
46	Cameroon	5.2	6.2	6.2	1.7	11.2	-5.4
47	Guatemala	6.5	2.2	5.3	1.2	7.9	-0.7
48	Dominican Rep.	2.7	0.2	5.8	1.7	9.4	4.5
49	Ecuador	14.5	-1.1	8.2	2.0	11.0	-2.4
50	Morocco	14.0	5.1	5.5	4.0	9.9	2.5
51	Jordan	..	*1.7*	..	*1.9*	..	-6.9
52	Tajikistan	..	..	..	..	..	..
53	Peru	4.0	-0.7	2.2	0.5	6.5	-3.4
54	El Salvador	6.8	2.8	4.2	0.6	7.3	2.3
55	Congo	4.1	3.3	1.5	3.1	1.5	-11.7
56	Syrian Arab Rep.	..	-2.2	..	*3.9*	..	-6.8
57	Colombia	5.4	4.5	5.3	3.1	5.0	-0.2
58	Paraguay	4.8	1.6	8.6	1.7	18.6	0.3
59	Uzbekistan	..	..	..	..	..	..
60	Jamaica	6.5	-0.2	1.4	1.8	-9.6	3.6
61	Romania	..	..	..	..	..	-2.1
62	Namibia	..	3.2	..	1.1	..	-5.0
63	Tunisia	7.8	3.7	8.6	3.3	6.8	-1.1
64	Kyrgyzstan	..	..	..	..	..	..
65	Thailand	9.8	4.1	6.3	6.7	7.2	9.8
66	Georgia	..	..	..	..	..	..

Note: For data comparability and coverage, see the technical notes.   Figures in italics are for years other than those specified.

		Average annual growth rate (percent)					
		General government consumption		Private consumption, etc.		Gross domestic investment	
		1970–80	1980–91	1970–80	1980–91	1970–80	1980–91
67	Azerbaijan	..	..	..	..	..	..
68	Turkmenistan	..	..	..	..	..	..
69	Turkey	6.3	3.5	4.8	6.1	6.9	2.8
70	Poland	..	0.2	..	1.1	..	–0.2
71	Bulgaria	..	0.8	..	6.5	..	–2.1
72	Costa Rica	6.6	1.2	4.8	3.4	9.2	4.4
73	Algeria	10.8	4.7	4.1	2.3	13.6	–3.2
74	Panama	5.8	0.7	4.4	1.3	0.3	–7.5
75	Armenia	..	..	..	..	..	..
76	Chile	2.4	0.2	–0.5	2.2	1.0	5.1
77	Iran, Islamic Rep.	10.8	–3.8	2.3	5.5	10.4	–5.4
78	Moldova	..	..	..	..	..	..
79	Ukraine	..	..	..	..	..	..
80	Mauritius	9.8	3.2	9.2	6.4	10.0	11.2
81	Czechoslovakia	..	2.6	..	1.7	..	0.2
82	Kazakhstan	..	..	..	..	..	..
83	Malaysia	9.3	3.2	7.5	5.1	10.8	4.4
	Upper-middle-income	..	..	..	..	..	..
84	Botswana	15.4	12.5	10.7	5.6	6.9	0.4
85	South Africa	5.5	3.4	2.3	1.8	2.5	–3.9
86	Lithuania	..	..	..	..	..	..
87	Hungary	2.5	2.2	3.6	0.2	7.5	–1.6
88	Venezuela	..	2.5	..	1.7	7.1	–3.9
89	Argentina	3.8	–9.3	2.4	0.0	3.1	–6.9
90	Uruguay	4.0	2.1	–1.9	1.0	..	–5.9
91	Brazil	6.0	8.7	8.0	1.6	8.9	–0.1
92	Mexico	8.3	1.8	5.9	1.8	8.3	–1.9
93	Belarus	..	..	..	..	..	..
94	Russian Federation	..	..	..	..	..	..
95	Latvia	..	..	..	..	..	..
96	Trinidad and Tobago	9.0	1.5	6.3	–7.4	14.2	–7.1
97	Gabon	10.2	–1.1	7.3	–2.6	13.6	–6.2
98	Estonia	..	..	..	..	..	..
99	Portugal	8.6	2.5	4.5	5.0	3.1	–2.6
100	Oman	..	..	..	2.7	..	7.0
101	Puerto Rico	..	5.1	..	..	..	..
102	Korea, Rep.	7.4	6.6	7.4	8.3	14.2	13.0
103	Greece	6.9	2.3	4.0	2.5	2.1	1.6
104	Saudi Arabia	..	..	..	..	7.2	–3.3
105	*Yugoslavia*	4.5	0.3	5.6	–0.1	..	..
	Low- and middle-income	..	4.0 w	..	3.4 w	..	1.4 w
	Sub-Saharan Africa	6.3 w	0.9 w	5.1 w	0.7 w	7.3 w	–3.3 w
	East Asia & Pacific	7.5 w	6.6 w	5.8 w	6.5 w	9.7 w	10.1 w
	South Asia	4.0 w	8.1 w	3.0 w	5.1 w	4.6 w	4.9 w
	Europe and Central Asia	..	..	..	..	..	..
	Middle East & N. Africa	..	..	..	..	..	..
	Latin America & Caribbean	6.0 w	4.3 w	5.5 w	1.4 w	7.0 w	–1.3 w
	Severely indebted	7.3 w	3.9 w	5.7 w	1.7 w	8.2 w	–1.8 w
	High-income economies	2.6 w	2.5 w	3.5 w	2.8 w	2.0 w	4.0 w
	OECD members	2.6 w	2.5 w	3.5 w	2.8 w	1.9 w	4.0 w
106	Ireland	6.0	–0.1	4.3	2.2	5.2	0.0
107	†Israel	3.9	0.6	5.8	5.2	0.6	3.6
108	New Zealand	3.6	1.1	1.7	1.9	–1.0	2.9
109	Spain	5.8	5.2	3.8	3.2	1.5	6.0
110	†Hong Kong	8.3	5.4	9.0	6.9	12.1	4.4
111	†Singapore	6.2	6.5	5.8	6.0	7.8	4.3
112	United Kingdom	2.4	1.2	1.8	3.8	0.2	5.3
113	Australia	5.1	3.4	3.2	3.2	1.9	2.2
114	Italy	3.0	2.6	4.0	3.1	1.6	2.1
115	Netherlands	2.9	1.4	3.9	1.8	0.1	2.4
116	Belgium	4.1	0.5	3.8	1.9	2.1	3.8
117	Austria	3.8	1.3	3.8	2.6	2.7	3.0
118	France	3.4	2.2	3.3	2.4	1.4	2.9
119	Canada	3.8	2.4	5.3	3.4	5.6	4.5
120	United States	1.0	3.2	3.3	2.4	2.4	3.3
121	Germany[b]	3.3	1.3	3.3	2.2	0.6	2.6
122	Denmark	4.1	0.9	2.0	1.7	–0.8	3.2
123	Finland	5.3	3.6	2.8	4.3	0.5	2.0
124	Norway	5.4	2.9	3.8	1.2	3.3	–0.2
125	Sweden	3.3	1.5	1.9	2.0	–0.7	3.5
126	Japan	4.9	2.4	4.7	3.7	2.5	6.0
127	Switzerland	1.8	3.0	1.1	1.7	–1.8	4.5
	World	3.0 w	2.7 w	3.7 w	3.0 w	2.8 w	3.4 w
	Fuel exporters	..	..	..	..	..	..

a. General government consumption figures are not available separately; they are included in private consumption, etc.   b. Data refer to the Federal Republic of Germany before unification.

Table 9. Structure of demand

	Distribution of gross domestic product (percent)											
	General government consumption		*Private consumption, etc.*		*Gross domestic investment*		*Gross domestic savings*		*Exports of goods and nonfactor services*		*Resource balance*	
	1970	*1991*	*1970*	*1991*	*1970*	*1991*	*1970*	*1991*	*1970*	*1991*	*1970*	*1991*
Low-income economies	**10** *w*	**10** *w*	**71** *w*	**64** *w*	**21** *w*	**27** *w*	**20** *w*	**27** *w*	**7** *w*	**19** *w*	**−1** *w*	**−1** *w*
China and India	**8** *w*	**10** *w*	**68** *w*	**59** *w*	**24** *w*	**29** *w*	**24** *w*	**31** *w*	**3** *w*	**16** *w*	**0** *w*	**1** *w*
Other low-income	**13** *w*	**12** *w*	**76** *w*	**71** *w*	**15** *w*	**22** *w*	**12** *w*	**17** *w*	**14** *w*	**26** *w*	**−4** *w*	**−6** *w*
1 Mozambique	. .	20	. .	90	. .	42	. .	−10	. .	23	. .	−52
2 Tanzania	11	16	69	96	23	22	20	−11	26	20	−2	−33
3 Ethiopia	10	21	79	78	11	10	11	0	11	8	0	−10
4 Uganda	a	8	84	93	13	12	164	−1	22	7	3	−13
5 Bhutan	. .	. .	. .	. .	. .	. .	. .	. .	. .	29	. .	−12
6 Guinea-Bissau	20	17	77	85	30	30	3	−3	4	13	−26	−33
7 Nepal	a	10	97	85	6	19	3	5	5	14	−3	−14
8 Burundi	10	16	87	85	5	17	4	−1	11	10	−1	−18
9 Chad	27	20	64	97	18	8	10	−17	23	19	−8	−25
10 Madagascar	13	9	79	92	10	8	7	−1	19	17	−2	−9
11 Sierra Leone	12	11	74	85	17	11	15	4	30	19	−2	−6
12 Bangladesh	13	11	79	86	11	10	7	3	8	9	−4	−7
13 Lao PDR	. .	11	. .	. .	. .	. .	. .	. .	. .	15	. .	−14
14 Malawi	16	14	73	77	26	20	11	9	24	24	−15	−11
15 Rwanda	9	20	88	78	7	13	3	1	12	12	−4	−11
16 Mali	10	12	80	82	16	23	10	6	13	17	−6	−16
17 Burkina Faso	9	17	92	79	12	23	−1	4	7	12	−12	−19
18 Niger	9	8	89	86	10	9	3	7	11	16	−7	−3
19 India	9	12	75	69	17	20	16	19	4	9	−1	−1
20 Kenya	16	17	60	63	24	21	24	19	30	27	−1	−1
21 Nigeria	8	13	80	65	15	16	12	23	8	36	−3	6
22 China	8	9	64	52	28	36	29	39	3	20	0	3
23 Haiti	10	. .	83	. .	11	. .	7	. .	14	. .	−4	. .
24 Benin	10	12	85	85	12	12	5	3	22	24	−6	−9
25 Central African Rep.	21	15	75	86	19	11	4	−1	28	15	−15	−12
26 Ghana	13	9	74	83	14	16	13	8	21	17	−1	−8
27 Pakistan	10	13	81	75	16	19	9	12	8	16	−7	−7
28 Togo	16	15	58	74	15	19	26	10	50	42	11	−9
29 Guinea	. .	10	. .	76	. .	18	. .	14	. .	26	. .	−4
30 Nicaragua	9	21	75	89	18	21	16	−10	26	22	−2	−31
31 Sri Lanka	12	10	72	77	19	23	16	13	25	28	−3	−10
32 Mauritania	14	9	56	81	22	16	30	10	41	50	8	−6
33 Yemen, Rep.	. .	28	. .	70	. .	13	. .	2	. .	29	. .	−11
34 Honduras	11	10	74	70	21	24	15	20	28	31	−6	−4
35 Lesotho	12	18	120	95	12	93	−32	−13	11	13	−44	−106
36 Indonesia	8	9	78	55	16	35	14	36	13	27	−2	1
37 Egypt, Arab Rep.	25	10	66	83	14	20	9	7	14	30	−5	−13
38 Zimbabwe	12	21	67	61	20	22	21	18	. .	33	. .	−4
39 *Sudan*	21	. .	64	. .	14	. .	15	. .	16	. .	2	. .
40 *Zambia*	16	10	39	78	28	13	45	12	54	29	17	−1
Middle-income economies	. .	. .	. .	. .	. .	. .	. .	. .	. .	. .	. .	. .
Lower-middle-income	. .	. .	. .	. .	. .	. .	. .	. .	. .	. .	. .	. .
41 Bolivia	10	15	66	77	24	14	24	9	25	18	0	−5
42 Côte d'Ivoire	14	18	57	67	22	10	29	15	36	37	7	5
43 Senegal	15	13	74	78	16	14	11	9	27	25	−5	−5
44 Philippines	9	9	69	72	21	20	22	19	22	30	1	−1
45 Papua New Guinea	30	24	64	63	42	29	6	13	18	39	−35	−16
46 Cameroon	12	14	70	71	16	15	18	15	26	18	2	0
47 Guatemala	8	6	78	84	13	14	14	10	19	18	1	−4
48 Dominican Rep.	12	9	77	77	19	17	12	14	17	27	−7	−3
49 Ecuador	11	8	75	70	18	22	14	22	14	31	−5	0
50 Morocco	12	15	73	68	18	22	15	17	18	22	−4	−6
51 Jordan	. .	23	. .	78	. .	21	. .	−1	. .	57	. .	−22
52 Tajikistan	. .	. .	. .	. .	. .	. .	. .	. .	. .	. .	. .	. .
53 Peru	12	5	70	82	16	16	17	13	18	9	2	−3
54 El Salvador	11	11	76	88	13	14	13	1	25	15	0	−12
55 Congo	17	22	82	58	24	11	1	20	35	42	−23	9
56 Syrian Arab Rep.	17	. .	72	. .	14	. .	10	. .	18	. .	−4	. .
57 Colombia	9	11	72	66	20	15	18	23	14	21	−2	8
58 Paraguay	9	8	77	75	15	25	14	17	15	26	−1	−8
59 Uzbekistan	. .	. .	. .	. .	. .	. .	. .	. .	. .	. .	. .	. .
60 Jamaica	12	12	61	68	32	20	27	20	33	64	−4	0
61 Romania	. .	14	. .	57	. .	34	. .	29	. .	17	. .	−5
62 Namibia	. .	27	. .	64	. .	14	. .	9	. .	58	. .	−5
63 Tunisia	17	16	66	66	21	23	17	18	22	39	−4	−5
64 Kyrgyzstan	. .	16	. .	50	. .	34	. .	34	. .	. .	. .	−1
65 Thailand	11	10	68	58	26	39	21	32	15	38	−4	−7
66 Georgia	. .	. .	. .	. .	. .	. .	. .	. .	. .	. .	. .	. .

Note: For data comparability and coverage, see the technical notes. Figures in italics are for years other than those specified.

		General government consumption		Private consumption, etc.		Gross domestic investment		Gross domestic savings		Exports of goods and nonfactor services		Resource balance	
		Distribution of gross domestic product (percent)											
		1970	1991	1970	1991	1970	1991	1970	1991	1970	1991	1970	1991
67	Azerbaijan	..	..	..	..	..	..	..	..	..	..	..	..
68	Turkmenistan	..	..	..	..	..	..	..	..	..	..	..	..
69	Turkey	13	17	70	66	20	20	17	17	6	20	-2	-3
70	Poland	..	20	..	58	..	21	..	22	..	20	..	0
71	Bulgaria	..	13	..	73	..	13	..	15	..	63	..	2
72	Costa Rica	13	16	74	61	21	23	14	22	28	39	-7	-1
73	Algeria	15	16	56	48	36	30	29	36	22	31	-7	6
74	Panama	15	21	61	72	28	15	24	7	38	29	-3	-8
75	Armenia	..	..	..	..	..	..	..	..	..	..	..	..
76	Chile	13	10	70	66	16	19	17	24	15	36	1	5
77	Iran, Islamic Rep.	16	13	59	77	19	20	25	10	24	20	6	-11
78	Moldova	..	..	..	..	..	..	..	..	..	..	..	..
79	Ukraine	..	..	..	..	..	..	..	..	..	..	..	..
80	Mauritius	14	12	75	65	10	28	11	23	43	64	1	-5
81	Czechoslovakia	..	a	..	67	..	31	..	..	..	42	..	2
82	Kazakhstan	..	..	..	..	..	..	..	..	..	..	..	..
83	Malaysia	16	14	58	56	22	36	27	30	42	81	4	-5
	Upper-middle-income	**11 w**	..	**66 w**	..	**24 w**	..	**23 w**	..	**16 w**	..	**-1 w**	..
84	Botswana	20	..	78	..	42	..	2	..	23	..	-41	..
85	South Africa	12	21	63	58	28	16	24	21	22	25	-4	5
86	Lithuania	..	16	..	63	..	21	..	21	..	..	..	..
87	Hungary	10	13	58	67	34	19	31	19	30	34	-2	0
88	Venezuela	11	9	52	67	33	19	37	23	21	31	4	5
89	Argentina	10	4	68	81	22	12	22	15	9	11	a	2
90	Uruguay	19	13	83	70	a	13	-1	17	15	24	-1	4
91	Brazil	11	9	69	70	21	20	20	30	7	10	0	0
92	Mexico	7	8	75	72	21	23	19	20	6	16	-3	-3
93	Belarus	..	a	..	71	..	30	..	..	..	50	..	-1
94	Russian Federation	..	20	..	41	..	39	..	40	..	35	..	0
95	Latvia	..	10	..	46	..	34	..	43	..	35	..	10
96	Trinidad and Tobago	13	15	60	59	26	18	27	26	43	41	1	8
97	Gabon	20	17	37	41	32	26	44	42	50	50	12	16
98	Estonia	..	10	..	65	..	29	..	25	..	..	..	-4
99	Portugal	14	..	67	..	26	..	20	..	24	..	-7	..
100	Oman	13	35	19	38	14	17	68	26	74	..	54	10
101	Puerto Rico	15	15	74	64	29	16	10	22	44	76	-18	6
102	Korea, Rep.	10	11	75	53	25	39	15	36	14	29	-10	-3
103	Greece	13	20	68	72	28	17	20	8	10	23	-8	-9
104	Saudi Arabia	20	..	34	..	16	..	47	..	59	..	31	..
105	*Yugoslavia*	18	7	55	72	32	21	27	21	18	24	-5	-1
	Low- and middle-income	**11 w**	..	**68 w**	..	**23 w**	**24 w**	**21 w**	..	**13 w**	..	**-1 w**	..
	Sub-Saharan Africa	**12 w**	**15 w**	**73 w**	**71 w**	**17 w**	**16 w**	**16 w**	**14 w**	**21 w**	**28 w**	**-1 w**	**-3 w**
	East Asia & Pacific	**9 w**	**10 w**	**66 w**	**55 w**	**26 w**	**35 w**	**25 w**	**36 w**	**7 w**	**30 w**	**-1 w**	**-1 w**
	South Asia	**10 w**	**12 w**	**76 w**	**72 w**	**16 w**	**19 w**	**14 w**	**17 w**	**5 w**	**10 w**	**-2 w**	**-3 w**
	Europe and Central Asia	..	..	..	..	..	..	..	..	..	..	..	..
	Middle East & N. Africa	**18 w**	..	**57 w**	..	**19 w**	..	**25 w**	..	**29 w**	..	**5 w**	..
	Latin America & Caribbean	**10 w**	**13 w**	**70 w**	..	**21 w**	**19 w**	**20 w**	..	**13 w**	**18 w**	**-2 w**	**-1 w**
	Severely indebted	**10 w**	..	**72 w**	..	**22 w**	**20 w**	**21 w**	..	..	**16 w**	..	..
	High-income economies	**16 w**	**17 w**	**60 w**	**61 w**	**23 w**	**21 w**	**24 w**	**22 w**	**14 w**	**20 w**	**1 w**	**1 w**
	OECD members	**16 w**	**17 w**	**60 w**	**61 w**	**23 w**	**21 w**	**24 w**	**22 w**	**13 w**	**19 w**	**1 w**	**1 w**
106	Ireland	15	16	69	56	24	19	16	28	37	62	-8	9
107	†Israel	34	28	58	58	27	23	8	14	25	28	-20	-9
108	New Zealand	13	17	65	63	25	18	22	20	23	28	-3	2
109	Spain	10	16	64	62	27	25	26	22	13	17	-1	-3
110	†Hong Kong	7	8	68	60	21	29	25	32	92	141	4	3
111	†Singapore	12	11	70	43	39	37	18	47	102	185	-20	9
112	United Kingdom	18	21	62	64	20	16	21	15	23	24	1	-1
113	Australia	14	19	59	62	27	19	27	19	14	18	0	0
114	Italy	13	17	60	62	27	20	28	20	16	20	0	0
115	Netherlands	15	14	57	59	30	21	28	26	42	54	-2	5
116	Belgium	13	15	60	63	24	20	27	23	52	73	2	3
117	Austria	15	18	55	55	30	26	31	26	31	41	1	1
118	France	15	18	58	60	27	21	27	21	16	23	1	0
119	Canada	19	21	57	60	22	20	24	19	23	25	3	-1
120	United States	19	18	63	67	18	15	18	15	6	11	0	-1
121	Germany b	16	18	55	54	28	21	30	28	21	34	2	6
122	Denmark	20	25	57	52	26	17	23	23	28	36	-3	6
123	Finland	14	24	57	56	30	21	29	20	26	22	-1	-1
124	Norway	17	21	54	51	30	19	29	28	42	45	-1	9
125	Sweden	22	27	54	54	25	17	24	19	24	28	-1	2
126	Japan	7	9	52	57	39	32	40	34	11	10	1	2
127	Switzerland	10	14	59	57	32	27	31	29	33	35	-2	1
	World	**15 w**	**16 w**	**61 w**	**62 w**	**23 w**	**22 w**	**24 w**	**23 w**	**14 w**	**21 w**	**0 w**	**1 w**
	Fuel exporters	**14 w**	..	**55 w**	**51 w**	**23 w**	..	**31 w**	..	**29 w**	..	**8 w**	..

a. General government consumption figures are not available separately; they are included in private consumption, etc.   b. Data refer to the Federal Republic of Germany before unification.

Table 10. Structure of consumption

		Food		Clothing and footwear	Gross rents, fuel and power		Medical care	Education	Transport and communication		Other consumption	
		Total	Cereals and tubers		Total	Fuel and power			Total	Automobiles	Total	Other consumer durables

Percentage share of total household consumption[a]

		Total	Cereals and tubers	Clothing and footwear	Total	Fuel and power	Medical care	Education	Total	Automobiles	Total	Other consumer durables
	Low-income economies											
	China and India											
	Other low-income											
1	Mozambique	..	..	..	..	..	..	..	..	..	..	..
2	Tanzania	64	32	10	8	3	3	3	2	0	10	3
3	Ethiopia	49	24	6	14	7	3	4	8	1	17	2
4	Uganda	..	..	..	..	..	..	..	..	..	..	..
5	Bhutan	..	..	..	..	..	..	..	..	..	..	..
6	Guinea-Bissau	..	..	..	..	..	..	..	..	..	..	..
7	Nepal	57	38	12	14	6	3	1	1	0	13	2
8	Burundi	..	..	..	..	..	..	..	..	..	..	..
9	Chad	..	..	..	..	..	..	..	..	..	..	..
10	Madagascar	59	26	6	12	6	2	4	4	1	14	1
11	Sierra Leone	56	22	4	15	6	2	3	12	..	8	1
12	Bangladesh	59	36	8	17	7	2	1	3	0	10	3
13	Lao PDR	..	..	..	..	..	..	..	..	..	..	..
14	Malawi	30	9	9	9	5	4	10	10	3	27	3
15	Rwanda	29	10	11	15	6	3	6	9	..	27	9
16	Mali	57	22	6	8	6	2	4	10	1	12	1
17	Burkina Faso	..	..	..	..	..	..	..	..	..	..	..
18	Niger	..	..	..	..	..	..	..	..	..	..	..
19	India	52	18	11	10	3	3	4	7	0	13	3
20	Kenya	38	16	7	12	2	3	10	8	1	22	6
21	Nigeria	48[b]	18	5	4	1	3	4	3	1	35	6
22	China	*61*[b]	..	*13*	8	*3*	*1*	*1*	*1*	..	*15*	..
23	Haiti	..	..	..	..	..	..	..	..	..	..	..
24	Benin	37	12	14	12	2	5	4	14	2	15	5
25	Central African Rep.	..	..	..	..	..	..	..	..	..	..	..
26	Ghana	*50*	..	*13*	*11*	..	*3*	*5*[c]	*3*	..	*15*	..
27	Pakistan	37	12	6	16	5	1	1	13	..	26	5
28	Togo	..	..	..	..	..	..	..	..	..	..	..
29	Guinea	..	..	..	..	..	..	..	..	..	..	..
30	Nicaragua	..	..	..	..	..	..	..	..	..	..	..
31	Sri Lanka	43	18	7	6	3	2	3	15	1	24	5
32	Mauritania	..	..	..	..	..	..	..	..	..	..	..
33	Yemen, Rep.	..	..	..	..	..	..	..	..	..	..	..
34	Honduras	39	..	9	21	..	8	5[c]	3	..	15	..
35	Lesotho	..	..	..	..	..	..	..	..	..	..	..
36	Indonesia	48	21	7	13	7	2	4	4	0	22	5
37	Egypt, Arab Rep.	49	10	11	9	3	3	6	4	1	18	3
38	Zimbabwe	40	9	11	12	5	4	7	6	1	20	3
39	*Sudan*	*60*	..	*5*	*15*	*4*	*5*	*3*	*2*	..	*11*	..
40	*Zambia*	36	8	10	11	4	8	14	5	1	16	1
	Middle-income economies											
	Lower-middle-income											
41	*Bolivia*	*33*	..	*9*	*12*	*1*	*5*	*7*	*12*	..	*22*	..
42	Côte d'Ivoire	39	13	9	5	1	9	6	10	..	22	3
43	Senegal	49	15	11	11	4	2	6	5	0	14	2
44	Philippines	51	21	4	19	5	2	4	4	2	16	2
45	Papua New Guinea	..	..	..	..	..	..	..	..	..	..	..
46	Cameroon	24	7	7	16	3	12	9	12	1	20	3
47	Guatemala	36	10	10	14	5	13	4	3	0	20	5
48	Dominican Rep.	46	13	3	15	5	8	3	4	0	21	8
49	Ecuador	30	..	10	7[d]	1[d]	5	6[c]	12[e]	..	30	..
50	Morocco	38	12	11	9	2	5	8	8	1	21	5
51	Jordan	35	..	5	6	..	5	8	6	..	35	..
52	Tajikistan	..	..	..	..	..	..	..	..	..	..	..
53	Peru	35	8	7	15	3	4	6	10	0	24	7
54	El Salvador	33	12	9	7	2	8	5	10	1	28	7
55	Congo	37	16	6	9	3	6	8	15	1	19	4
56	Syrian Arab Rep.	..	..	..	..	..	..	..	..	..	..	..
57	Colombia	29	..	6	12	2	7	6	13	..	27	..
58	Paraguay	30	6	12	21	4	2	3	10	1	22	3
59	Uzbekistan	..	..	..	..	..	..	..	..	..	..	..
60	Jamaica	36	14	5	15	5	5	5	16	1	18	..
61	Romania	..	..	..	..	..	..	..	..	..	..	..
62	Namibia	..	..	..	..	..	..	..	..	..	..	..
63	Tunisia	37	7	10	13	4	7	10	7	1	18	5
64	Kyrgyzstan	..	..	..	..	..	..	..	..	..	..	..
65	Thailand	30	7	16	7	3	5	5	13	0	24	5
66	Georgia	..	..	..	..	..	..	..	..	..	..	..

Note: For data comparability and coverage, see the technical notes. Figures in italics are for years other than those specified.

		Food		Clothing and footwear	Gross rents, fuel and power		Medical care	Education	Transport and communication		Other consumption	
		Total	*Cereals and tubers*		*Total*	*Fuel and power*			*Total*	*Automobiles*	*Total*	*Other consumer durables*

Percentage share of total household consumption[a]

		Food Total	Cereals and tubers	Clothing and footwear	Rents Total	Fuel and power	Medical care	Education	Transport Total	Automobiles	Other Total	Other consumer durables
67	Azerbaijan	..	..	..	..	..	..	..	..	..	..	..
68	Turkmenistan	..	..	..	..	..	..	..	..	..	..	..
69	Turkey	40	9	15	13	7	4	1	5	0	23	..
70	Poland	29	4	9	6	2	6	7	8	2	35	9
71	Bulgaria	..	..	..	..	..	..	..	..	..	..	..
72	Costa Rica	33	8	8	9	1	7	8	8	0	28	9
73	Algeria	..	..	..	..	..	..	..	..	..	..	..
74	Panama	38	7	3	11	3	8	9	7	0	24	6
75	Armenia	..	..	..	..	..	..	..	..	..	..	..
76	Chile	29	7	8	13	2	5	6	11	0	29	5
77	Iran, Islamic Rep.	37	10	9	23	2	6	5	6	1	14	5
78	Moldova	..	..	..	..	..	..	..	..	..	..	..
79	Ukraine	..	..	..	..	..	..	..	..	..	..	..
80	Mauritius	24	7	5	19	3	5	8	11	1	28	4
81	Czechoslovakia	..	..	..	..	..	..	..	..	..	..	..
82	Kazakhstan	..	..	..	..	..	..	..	..	..	..	..
83	Malaysia	*23*	..	*4*	*9*	..	*5*	*7*	*19*	..	*33*	..
	Upper-middle-income											
84	Botswana	25	12	8	8	2	8	18	8	2	26	7
85	South Africa	34	..	7	12	..	5[f]	..	17	..	26	..
86	Lithuania	..	..	..	..	..	..	..	..	..	..	..
87	Hungary	25	3	9	9	5	5	7	9	2	36	8
88	Venezuela	23	..	7	10	..	8	5[c]	11	..	36	..
89	Argentina	35	4	6	9	2	4	6	13	0	26	6
90	Uruguay	31	7	7	12	2	6	4	13	0	27	5
91	Brazil	35	9	10	11	2	6	5	8	1	27	8
92	Mexico	35[b]	..	*10*	8	..	5	5	*12*	..	25	..
93	Belarus	..	..	..	..	..	..	..	..	..	..	..
94	Russian Federation	..	..	..	..	..	..	..	..	..	..	..
95	Latvia	..	..	..	..	..	..	..	..	..	..	..
96	Trinidad and Tobago	19	3	14	18	1	8	8	12	4	21	..
97	Gabon	..	..	..	..	..	..	..	..	..	..	..
98	Estonia	..	..	..	..	..	..	..	..	..	..	..
99	Portugal	34	8	10	9	3	6	5	13	3	24	7
100	Oman	..	..	..	..	..	..	..	..	..	..	..
101	Puerto Rico	..	..	..	..	..	..	..	..	..	25	5
102	Korea, Rep.	35	14	6	11	5	5	9	9	..	25	5
103	Greece	30	3	8	12	3	6	5	13	2	26	5
104	Saudi Arabia	..	..	..	..	..	..	..	..	..	..	..
105	*Yugoslavia*	27	4	10	9	4	6	5	11	2	32	9

Low- and middle-income
   Sub-Saharan Africa
   East Asia & Pacific
   South Asia
   Europe and Central Asia
   Middle East & N. Africa
   Latin America & Caribbean
Severely indebted
High-income economies
   OECD members

		Food Total	Cereals and tubers	Clothing and footwear	Rents Total	Fuel and power	Medical care	Education	Transport Total	Automobiles	Other Total	Other consumer durables
106	Ireland	22	4	5	11	5	10	7	11	3	34	5
107	†Israel	21	..	5	20	2	9	12	10	..	23	..
108	New Zealand	12	2	6	14	2	9	6	19	6	35	9
109	Spain	24	3	7	16	3	7	5	14	3	27	6
110	†Hong Kong	12	1	9	15	2	6	5	9	1	44	15
111	†Singapore	19	..	8	11	..	7	12	13	..	30	..
112	United Kingdom	12	2	6	17	4	8	6	14	4	36	7
113	Australia	13	2	5	21	2	10	7	13	4	31	7
114	Italy	19	2	8	14	4	10	7	11	3	30	7
115	Netherlands	13	2	6	18	6	11	8	10	3	34	8
116	Belgium	15	2	6	17	7	10	9	11	3	31	7
117	Austria	16	2	9	17	5	10	8	15	3	26	7
118	France	16	2	6	17	5	13	7	13	3	30	7
119	Canada	11	2	6	21	4	5	12	14	5	32	8
120	United States	10	2	6	18	4	14	8	14	5	30	7
121	Germany[g]	12	2	7	18	5	13	6	13	4	31	9
122	Denmark	13	2	5	19	5	9	9	13	5	33	7
123	Finland	16	3	4	15	4	9	8	14	4	35	6
124	Norway	15	2	6	14	5	11	8	14	6	32	7
125	Sweden	13	2	5	19	4	11	8	11	2	32	7
126	Japan	17	4	6	17	3	10	7	9	1	34	6
127	Switzerland	*17*	..	*4*	*17*	*6*	*15*	..	*9*	..	*38*	..

World
   Fuel exporters

a. Data refer to either 1980 or 1985.   b. Includes beverages and tobacco.   c. Refers to government expenditure.   d. Excludes fuel.   e. Includes fuel.   f. Excludes government expenditure.   g. Data refer to the Federal Republic of Germany before unification.

Table 11. Central government expenditure

	Defense 1980	Defense 1991	Education 1980	Education 1991	Health 1980	Health 1991	Housing, amenities; social security and welfare 1980	... 1991	Economic services 1980	Economic services 1991	Other[a] 1980	Other[a] 1991	Total expenditure (percentage of GNP) 1980	... 1991	Overall surplus/deficit (percentage of GNP) 1980	... 1991
Low-income economies																
China and India																
Other low-income																
1 Mozambique	..	..	..	..	..	..	..	..	..	..	..	..	..	..	..	..
2 Tanzania	9.2	..	13.3	..	6.0	..	2.5	..	42.9	..	26.1	..	28.8	..	-8.4	..
3 Ethiopia	..	..	10.1	..	3.7	..	5.4	..	23.8	..	57.0	..	23.4	..	-4.5	..
4 Uganda	25.2	..	14.9	..	5.1	..	4.2	..	11.1	..	39.5	..	6.1	..	-3.1	..
5 Bhutan	0.0	0.0	12.8	10.7	5.0	4.8	4.9	8.2	56.8	48.2	20.5	28.2	40.6	43.3	0.9	-2.6
6 Guinea-Bissau	..	4.2	..	2.7	..	1.4	..	..	..	..	..	91.7	..	63.0	..	-17.7
7 Nepal	6.7	5.9	9.9	10.9	3.9	4.7	1.7	6.8	58.8	43.0	19.1	28.8	14.2	18.4	-3.0	-6.2
8 Burundi	..	..	..	..	..	..	..	..	..	..	..	..	21.7	..	-3.9	..
9 Chad	..	..	..	..	..	..	..	..	..	..	..	..	..	31.2	..	-7.3
10 Madagascar	..	7.5	..	17.2	..	6.6	..	1.5	..	35.9	..	31.2	..	16.1	..	-5.9
11 Sierra Leone[b]	4.1	9.9	14.9	13.3	9.1	9.6	3.6	3.1	..	29.0	68.3	35.2	29.8	9.8	-13.2	-2.9
12 Bangladesh[b]	9.4	10.1	11.5	11.2	6.4	4.8	5.3	8.0	46.9	34.4	20.4	31.5	10.0	15.0	2.5	-0.4
13 Lao PDR	..	..	..	..	..	..	..	..	..	..	..	..	..	..	..	..
14 Malawi[b]	12.8	5.4	9.0	8.8	5.5	7.4	1.6	3.2	43.7	35.0	27.3	40.2	37.6	29.2	-17.3	-1.9
15 Rwanda	13.1	..	18.8	..	4.5	..	4.1	..	41.4	..	18.0	..	14.3	..	-1.7	..
16 Mali	11.0	..	15.7	..	3.1	..	3.0	..	11.2	..	56.0	..	21.6	..	-4.7	..
17 Burkina Faso	17.0	..	15.5	..	5.8	..	7.6	..	19.3	..	34.8	..	14.1	..	0.3	..
18 Niger	3.8	..	18.0	..	4.1	..	3.8	..	32.4	..	38.0	..	18.7	..	-4.8	..
19 India	19.8	17.0	1.9	2.5	1.6	1.6	4.3	6.9	24.2	20.8	48.3	51.2	13.2	17.5	-6.5	-7.0
20 Kenya[b]	16.4	10.0	19.6	19.9	7.8	5.4	5.1	3.9	22.7	20.7	28.2	40.1	26.1	28.3	-4.6	-5.8
21 Nigeria[b]	..	..	..	..	..	..	..	..	..	..	..	..	..	..	..	..
22 China	..	..	..	..	..	..	..	..	..	..	..	..	..	..	..	..
23 Haiti	9.6	..	6.6	..	4.5	..	5.0	..	28.0	..	46.3	..	17.5	..	-4.7	..
24 Benin	..	..	..	..	..	..	..	..	..	..	..	..	..	..	..	..
25 Central African Rep.	9.7	..	17.6	..	5.1	..	6.3	..	19.6	..	41.7	..	21.9	..	-3.5	..
26 Ghana[b]	3.7	..	22.0	..	7.0	..	6.8	..	20.7	..	39.8	..	10.9	..	-4.2	..
27 Pakistan	30.6	27.9	2.7	1.6	1.5	1.0	4.1	3.4	37.2	11.6	23.9	54.6	17.7	21.9	-5.8	-6.2
28 Togo	7.2	..	16.7	..	5.3	..	12.0	..	25.2	..	33.7	..	31.9	..	-2.0	..
29 Guinea	..	..	..	..	..	..	..	..	..	..	..	..	..	24.9	..	-4.2
30 Nicaragua	11.0	..	11.6	..	14.6	..	7.4	..	20.6	..	34.9	..	32.6	33.8	-7.3	-15.2
31 Sri Lanka	1.7	9.4	6.7	8.3	4.9	4.8	12.7	18.4	15.9	24.6	58.2	34.5	41.6	29.4	-18.4	-9.5
32 Mauritania	..	..	..	..	..	..	..	..	..	..	..	..	..	..	..	..
33 Yemen, Rep.	..	..	..	..	..	..	..	..	..	..	..	..	..	..	..	..
34 Honduras	..	..	..	..	..	..	..	..	..	..	..	..	..	..	..	..
35 Lesotho	0.0	6.5	15.3	21.9	6.2	11.5	1.3	5.5	35.9	31.6	41.2	23.1	22.7	31.8	-3.7	-0.3
36 Indonesia	13.5	8.2	8.3	9.1	2.5	2.4	1.8	1.8	40.2	27.1	33.7	51.5	23.1	20.7	-2.3	0.4
37 Egypt, Arab Rep.	11.4	12.7	8.1	13.4	2.4	2.8	13.1	17.8	7.2	8.2	57.7	45.3	53.7	39.6	-12.5	-6.8
38 Zimbabwe	25.0	16.5	15.5	23.4	5.4	7.6	7.8	3.9	18.1	22.4	28.2	26.2	35.3	35.9	-11.1	-6.9
39 Sudan[b]	13.2	..	9.8	..	1.4	..	0.9	..	19.8	..	54.9	..	19.8	..	-3.3	..
40 Zambia[b]	0.0	..	11.4	..	6.1	..	3.4	..	32.6	..	46.6	..	40.0	21.9	-20.0	-5.0
Middle-income economies																
Lower-middle-income																
41 Bolivia	..	13.1	..	18.7	..	3.3	..	18.8	..	16.9	..	29.3	29.0	18.8	0	-0.1
42 Côte d'Ivoire	3.9	..	16.3	..	3.9	..	4.3	..	13.4	..	58.1	..	32.4	30.1	-11.1	-3.6
43 Senegal	16.8	..	23.0	..	4.7	..	9.5	..	14.4	..	31.6	..	23.9	..	0.9	..
44 Philippines[b]	15.7	10.9	13.0	16.1	4.5	4.2	6.6	3.7	56.9	24.7	3.4	40.3	13.4	19.1	-1.4	-2.1
45 Papua New Guinea[b]	4.4	..	16.5	..	8.6	..	2.6	..	22.7	..	45.1	..	35.2	..	-2.0	..
46 Cameroon	9.1	6.7	12.4	12.0	5.1	3.4	8.0	8.7	24.0	48.1	41.4	21.2	15.5	22.3	0.5	-3.5
47 Guatemala	..	13.3	..	19.5	..	9.9	..	7.8	..	21.7	..	27.8	14.4	12.0	-3.9	-1.8
48 Dominican Rep.	7.8	4.8	12.6	10.2	9.3	14.0	13.8	20.2	37.1	36.5	19.3	14.2	17.5	12.3	-2.7	0.6
49 Ecuador[b]	12.5	12.9	34.7	18.2	7.8	11.0	1.3	2.5	21.1	11.8	22.6	43.6	15.0	16.0	-1.5	2.1
50 Morocco	17.9	..	17.3	..	3.4	..	6.5	..	27.8	..	27.1	..	34.2	..	-10	..
51 Jordan	25.3	21.3	7.6	14.8	3.7	5.0	14.5	17.7	28.3	10.4	20.6	30.9	..	41.4	..	-4.0
52 Tajikistan	..	..	..	..	..	..	..	..	..	..	..	..	..	..	..	..
53 Peru[b]	21.0	16.4	15.6	21.1	5.6	5.6	0.0	0.5	22.1	..	35.7	56.4	20.4	8.8	-2.5	-0.5
54 El Salvador[b]	8.8	20.6	19.8	14.4	9.0	7.7	2.1	1.4	21.0	19.1	39.3	36.7	17.6	10.4	-5.9	-2.1
55 Congo	9.7	..	11.0	..	5.1	..	7.0	..	34.2	..	33.0	..	54.6	..	-5.8	..
56 Syrian Arab Rep.	35.8	31.5	5.5	7.4	0.8	1.9	11.3	3.3	41.1	30.7	5.4	25.2	48.1	24.3	-9.7	0.4
57 Colombia	6.7	..	19.1	..	3.9	..	21.2	..	27.1	..	22.0	..	13.5	15.1	-1.8	2.0
58 Paraguay	12.4	13.3	12.9	12.7	3.6	4.3	19.2	14.8	18.9	12.8	33.0	42.1	9.8	9.4	0.3	3.0
59 Uzbekistan	..	..	..	..	..	..	..	..	..	..	..	..	..	..	..	..
60 Jamaica	..	..	..	..	..	..	..	..	..	..	..	..	45.7	..	-17.1	..
61 Romania	..	10.3	..	10.0	..	9.2	..	26.6	..	33.0	..	10.9	..	37.0	..	2.0
62 Namibia	..	6.5	..	22.2	..	9.7	..	14.8	..	17.3	..	29.5	..	48.2	..	-7.6
63 Tunisia	12.2	5.6	17.0	17.5	7.2	6.3	13.4	18.3	27.8	24.4	22.4	27.9	32.5	34.6	-2.9	-4.3
64 Kyrgyzstan	..	..	..	..	..	..	..	..	..	..	..	..	..	..	..	..
65 Thailand	21.7	17.1	19.8	20.2	4.1	7.4	5.1	5.9	24.2	24.3	25.1	25.1	19.1	15.5	-4.9	5.0
66 Georgia	..	..	..	..	..	..	..	..	..	..	..	..	..	..	..	..

Note: For data comparability and coverage, see the technical notes. Figures in italics are for years other than those specified.

		Percentage of total expenditure												Total expenditure (percentage of GNP)		Overall surplus/deficit (percentage of GNP)	
		Defense		Education		Health		Housing, amenities; social security and welfare		Economic services		Other [a]					
		1980	1991	1980	1991	1980	1991	1980	1991	1980	1991	1980	1991	1980	1991	1980	1991
67	Azerbaijan	..	..	..	..	..	..	..	..	..	..	..	..	..	..	..	..
68	Turkmenistan	..	..	..	..	..	..	..	..	..	..	..	..	..	..	..	..
69	Turkey	15.2	10.4	14.2	17.6	3.6	3.0	6.1	3.3	34.0	25.2	26.9	40.5	26.3	30.4	-3.8	-7.6
70	Poland	..	..	..	..	..	..	..	..	..	..	..	..	..	..	..	..
71	Bulgaria	..	5.6	..	6.2	..	4.8	..	23.9	..	46.6	..	12.8	..	77.3	..	-9.9
72	Costa Rica	2.6	..	24.6	19.1	28.7	32.0	9.5	13.3	18.2	8.6	16.4	27.0	26.3	25.9	-7.8	-1.4
73	Algeria	..	..	..	..	..	..	..	..	..	..	..	..	..	..	..	..
74	Panama	0.0	5.3	13.4	17.1	12.7	20.5	13.5	23.8	21.9	6.1	38.4	27.2	34.2	30.3	-5.8	3.5
75	Armenia	..	..	..	..	..	..	..	..	..	..	..	..	..	..	..	..
76	Chile	12.4	..	14.5	..	7.4	..	37.1	..	13.8	..	14.8	..	29.1	..	5.6	..
77	Iran, Islamic Rep.	15.9	9.6	21.3	20.9	6.4	7.9	8.7	15.5	24.0	16.1	23.7	29.9	35.7	22.8	-13.8	-2.8
78	Moldova	..	..	..	..	..	..	..	..	..	..	..	..	..	..	..	..
79	Ukraine	..	..	..	..	..	..	..	..	..	..	..	..	..	..	..	..
80	Mauritius	0.8	1.5	17.6	14.6	7.5	8.7	21.4	17.8	11.7	15.0	41.0	42.3	27.4	23.8	-10.4	0.0
81	Czechoslovakia	..	7.1	..	1.9	..	0.4	..	27.0	..	40.2	..	23.4	..	55.6	..	-6.9
82	Kazakhstan	..	..	..	..	..	..	..	..	..	..	..	..	..	..	..	..
83	Malaysia	..	..	..	..	..	..	..	..	..	..	..	..	29.6	30.6	-6.2	-2.3

Upper-middle-income

84	Botswana[b]	9.8	13.3	22.2	20.5	5.4	5.1	7.9	16.2	26.9	16.8	27.9	28.2	36.5	41.9	-0.2	14.0
85	South Africa	..	..	..	..	..	..	..	..	..	..	..	..	23.5	33.6	-2.5	-0.3
86	Lithuania	..	..	..	..	..	..	..	..	..	..	..	..	..	..	..	..
87	Hungary	4.4	3.6	1.8	3.3	2.7	7.9	22.3	35.3	44.0	22.0	24.7	27.9	58.3	54.7	-2.9	0.8
88	Venezuela	5.8	..	19.9	..	8.8	..	9.5	..	20.2	..	35.7	..	18.7	23.9	0	4.5
89	Argentina	..	9.9	..	9.9	..	3.0	..	39.4	..	16.0	..	21.7	19.2	13.1	-3.6	-0.5
90	Uruguay	13.4	9.2	8.8	7.4	4.9	4.5	48.5	50.3	11.4	8.7	13.0	20.0	22.7	27.2	0	0.4
91	Brazil	4.0	3.5	0.0	3.1	8.0	6.7	32.0	25.5	24.0	3.2	32.0	57.9	20.9	35.1	-2.5	-5.9
92	Mexico	2.3	2.4	18.0	13.9	2.4	1.9	18.5	13.0	31.2	13.4	27.6	55.5	17.4	18.1	-3.1	0.8
93	Belarus	..	..	..	..	..	..	..	..	..	..	..	..	..	..	..	..
94	Russian Federation	..	..	..	..	..	..	..	..	..	..	..	..	..	..	..	..
95	Latvia	..	..	..	..	..	..	..	..	..	..	..	..	..	..	..	..
96	Trinidad and Tobago	1.7	..	11.6	..	5.8	..	15.9	..	43.5	..	21.5	..	32.5	..	7.8	..
97	Gabon[b]	..	..	..	..	..	..	..	..	..	..	..	..	40.5	37.8	6.8	-2.0
98	Estonia	..	..	..	..	..	..	..	..	..	..	..	..	..	..	..	..
99	Portugal	7.4	..	11.2	..	10.3	..	27.0	..	19.9	..	24.2	..	39.6	43.3	-10.1	-5
100	Oman	51.2	35.4	4.8	11.4	2.9	5.4	2.0	13.1	18.4	10.3	20.8	24.4	43.1	44.6	0.5	-8.1
101	Puerto Rico	..	..	..	..	..	..	..	..	..	..	..	..	..	..	..	..
102	Korea, Rep.	34.3	22.2	17.1	15.8	1.2	2.0	7.5	11.3	15.6	19.2	24.3	29.5	17.9	17.3	-2.3	-1.7
103	Greece	12.6	6.7	10.0	6.0	10.3	8.7	31.3	0.8	16.6	8.8	19.2	68.9	34.4	60.0	-4.8	-26.2
104	Saudi Arabia	..	..	..	..	..	..	..	..	..	..	..	..	..	..	..	..
105	*Yugoslavia*	50.0	53.4	0.0	0.0	0.0	0.0	6.3	6.0	18.8	19.6	25.0	21.0	9.0	5.2	-1.1	0.3

Low- and middle-income
Sub-Saharan Africa
East Asia & Pacific
South Asia
Europe and Central Asia
Middle East & N. Africa
Latin America & Caribbean

Severely indebted

High-income economies
OECD members

106	Ireland	3.4	3.3	11.4	12.2	13.7	13.0	27.7	29.1	18.4	12.8	25.4	29.4	48.9	47.5	-13.6	-2.4
107	†Israel	39.8	22.4	9.9	10.4	3.6	3.7	14.4	30.5	13.4	10.1	19.0	22.9	72.4	36.2	-16.1	-5.7
108	New Zealand[b]	5.1	4.1	14.7	12.4	15.2	12.0	31.1	37.4	15.0	10.6	18.9	23.7	39.0	43.7	-6.8	1.5
109	Spain	4.3	5.4	8.0	5.6	0.7	13.7	60.3	37.7	11.9	11.0	14.8	26.6	26.6	34.0	-4.2	-2.3
110	†Hong Kong	..	..	..	..	..	..	..	..	..	..	..	..	..	..	..	..
111	†Singapore	25.2	24.0	14.6	19.9	7.0	4.6	7.6	8.2	17.7	16.8	27.9	26.5	20.8	22.1	2.2	11.2
112	United Kingdom	13.8	11.1	2.4	3.2	13.5	13.3	30.0	31.8	7.5	8.5	32.9	32.0	38.2	38.2	-4.6	0.8
113	Australia	9.4	8.6	8.2	7.0	10.0	12.7	28.5	31.2	8.1	8.3	35.8	32.2	23.1	27.7	-1.5	0.6
114	Italy	3.4	..	8.4	..	12.6	..	29.6	..	7.2	..	38.7	..	41.0	49.6	-10.7	-10.0
115	Netherlands	5.6	4.8	13.1	10.5	11.7	12.4	39.5	42.5	10.9	6.4	19.2	23.4	52.5	52.5	-4.5	-2.8
116	Belgium	5.7	..	15.0	..	1.6	..	44.7	..	16.0	..	17.0	..	51.3	49.2	-8.2	-5.4
117	Austria	3.0	2.4	9.7	9.4	13.3	12.9	48.7	47.9	11.7	9.1	13.5	18.3	37.7	39.8	-3.4	-4.8
118	France	7.4	6.3	8.6	6.9	14.8	15.3	46.8	46.4	6.8	5.1	15.6	20.0	39.3	43.7	-0.1	-1.4
119	Canada	7.7	7.4	3.8	2.9	6.7	5.2	35.1	36.4	19.4	11.2	27.3	36.8	21.8	23.9	-3.6	-2.7
120	United States	21.2	21.6	2.6	1.7	10.4	13.8	37.8	28.7	9.7	10.1	18.2	25.3	21.7	25.3	-2.8	-4.8
121	Germany[c]	9.1	8.3	0.9	0.6	19.0	18.1	49.6	48.9	8.7	8.7	12.6	15.4	30.3	32.5	-1.8	-2.5
122	Denmark	6.5	5.1	10.4	9.5	1.8	1.1	44.7	39.9	6.5	7.6	30.0	36.8	40.4	41.7	-2.7	-0.3
123	Finland	5.6	4.7	14.7	14.9	10.5	11.2	28.2	36.7	27.0	18.8	14.0	13.7	28.4	31.0	-2.2	0.1
124	Norway	7.7	8.0	8.7	9.4	10.6	10.3	34.7	39.3	22.7	17.5	15.6	15.5	39.2	46.3	-2	0.7
125	Sweden	7.7	6.3	10.4	9.7	2.2	0.8	51.5	56.4	10.9	8.0	17.3	18.8	39.8	44.2	-8.2	0.7
126	Japan[b]	..	..	..	..	..	..	..	..	..	..	..	..	18.4	15.8	-7	-1.6
127	Switzerland	10.2	..	3.4	..	11.7	..	49.3	..	14.2	..	11.2	..	19.5	..	-0.2	..

World
Fuel exporters

a. See the technical notes.   b. Data are for budgetary accounts only.   c. Data refer to the Federal Republic of Germany before unification.

Table 12. Central government current revenue

		Percentage of total current revenue												
		Tax revenue												
		Income, profit, and capital gains		Social security		Goods and services (domestic taxes)		International trade and transactions		Other[a]		Nontax revenue		Total current revenue (percentage of GNP)	
		1980	1991	1980	1991	1980	1991	1980	1991	1980	1991	1980	1991	1980	1991
Low-income economies															
China and India															
Other low-income															
1	Mozambique	..	..	..	..	..	..	..	..	..	..	..	..	..	..
2	Tanzania	32.5	..	0.0	..	40.8	..	17.3	..	1.6	..	7.8	..	17.6	..
3	Ethiopia	20.9	..	0.0	..	24.3	..	35.7	..	3.7	..	15.4	..	18.7	..
4	Uganda	11.5	..	0.0	..	41.0	..	44.3	..	0.2	..	3.1	..	3.1	..
5	Bhutan	13.8	7.5	0.0	0.0	39.1	16.6	0.4	0.4	2.3	0.6	44.3	75.0	11.4	19.6
6	Guinea-Bissau	..	..	..	..	..	..	..	..	..	..	..	..	..	14.1
7	Nepal	5.5	9.9	0.0	0.0	36.8	36.7	33.2	30.8	8.2	5.5	16.2	17.1	7.8	9.5
8	Burundi	19.3	..	1.0	..	25.3	..	40.4	..	8.4	..	5.6	..	14.0	..
9	Chad	..	22.6	..	0.0	..	33.7	..	15.3	..	6.6	..	21.8	..	8.9
10	Madagascar	16.6	15.3	11.3	0.0	39.3	19.5	27.6	44.5	2.7	1.1	2.4	19.5	13.4	9.1
11	Sierra Leone[b]	22.4	31.5	0.0	0.0	16.3	23.4	49.6	40.4	1.5	0.2	10.1	4.6	16.9	6.6
12	Bangladesh[b]	10.1	8.6	0.0	0.0	25.5	25.8	28.6	27.3	3.9	15.2	31.9	23.0	11.3	11.4
13	Lao PDR	..	..	..	..	..	..	..	..	..	..	..	..	..	..
14	Malawi[b]	33.9	35.0	0.0	0.0	30.9	33.2	22.0	17.7	0.3	1.2	12.9	12.9	20.7	23.7
15	Rwanda	17.8	..	4.1	..	19.3	..	42.4	..	2.4	..	14.0	..	12.8	..
16	Mali	17.9	..	0.0	..	36.8	..	17.9	..	19.5	..	8.0	..	11.0	..
17	Burkina Faso	17.8	..	7.8	..	15.9	..	43.7	..	4.3	..	10.5	..	13.6	..
18	Niger	23.8	..	4.0	..	18.0	..	36.4	..	2.6	..	15.3	..	14.7	..
19	India	18.3	15.4	0.0	0.0	42.5	35.5	22.0	28.8	0.6	0.4	16.6	19.9	11.7	14.3
20	Kenya[b]	29.1	29.8	0.0	0.0	38.8	43.2	18.5	15.0	1.0	1.5	12.6	10.5	22.6	21.2
21	Nigeria[b]	..	..	..	..	..	..	..	..	..	..	..	..	..	..
22	China	..	..	..	..	..	..	..	..	..	..	..	..	..	..
23	Haiti	13.9	..	0.0	..	15.5	..	48.4	..	9.6	..	12.6	..	10.7	..
24	Benin	..	..	..	..	..	..	..	..	..	..	..	..	..	..
25	Central African Rep.	16.1	..	6.4	..	20.8	..	39.8	..	7.8	..	9.1	..	16.4	..
26	Ghana[b]	20.5	..	0.0	..	28.2	..	44.2	..	0.2	..	6.9	..	6.9	..
27	Pakistan	13.8	10.0	0.0	0.0	33.6	32.2	34.4	30.2	0.2	0.3	17.9	27.2	16.4	16.9
28	Togo	34.4	..	5.8	..	15.3	..	32.0	..	-1.7	..	14.2	..	31.4	..
29	Guinea	28.1	..	1.0	..	6.4	17.1	27.9	74.4	0.7	2.4	35.8	6.1	..	14.6
30	Nicaragua	7.8	16.9	8.9	11.8	37.3	37.5	25.2	17.6	10.7	10.5	10.1	5.8	24.9	16.8
31	Sri Lanka	15.5	12.8	0.0	0.0	26.8	46.1	50.5	25.9	1.9	4.7	5.3	10.5	20.3	20.4
32	Mauritania	..	..	..	..	..	..	..	..	..	..	..	..	..	..
33	Yemen, Rep.	..	..	..	..	..	..	..	..	..	..	..	..	..	..
34	Honduras	30.8	..	0.0	..	23.8	..	37.2	..	1.8	..	6.5	..	15.4	..
35	Lesotho	13.4	16.9	0.0	0.0	10.2	16.7	61.3	51.8	1.2	0.1	13.9	14.5	17.1	26.8
36	Indonesia	78.0	61.8	0.0	0.0	8.6	23.7	7.2	6.4	1.2	2.7	4.9	5.4	22.2	21.1
37	Egypt, Arab Rep.	16.2	15.9	9.1	14.2	15.1	11.9	17.3	14.0	7.7	8.2	34.6	35.8	47.1	35.4
38	Zimbabwe	46.2	44.4	0.0	0.0	27.9	26.3	4.4	19.0	1.2	1.0	20.2	9.3	24.4	31.5
39	Sudan[b]	14.4	..	0.0	..	26.0	..	42.6	..	0.7	..	16.3	..	14.0	..
40	Zambia[b]	38.1	..	0.0	..	43.1	..	8.3	..	3.1	95.8	7.3	4.2	27.0	11.9
Middle-income economies															
Lower-middle-income															
41	Bolivia	..	5.1	..	8.6	..	34.0	..	6.0	..	8.4	..	37.9	..	16.6
42	Côte d'Ivoire	13.0	16.7	5.8	6.8	24.8	27.8	42.8	27.8	6.1	11.3	7.5	9.6	23.4	26.5
43	Senegal	18.4	..	3.7	..	26.0	..	34.2	..	11.4	..	6.3	..	24.9	..
44	Philippines[b]	21.1	28.5	0.0	0.0	41.9	25.8	24.2	28.5	2.2	2.7	10.6	14.6	14.0	17.0
45	Papua New Guinea[b]	60.5	..	0.0	..	12.1	..	16.4	..	0.6	..	10.5	..	23.5	..
46	Cameroon	21.7	45.2	8.0	6.4	18.0	20.2	38.4	14.0	5.9	9.1	7.9	5.1	16.2	19.0
47	Guatemala	11.2	18.1	11.2	0.0	26.4	23.2	30.2	33.8	11.1	7.2	9.9	17.7	11.3	9.7
48	Dominican Rep.	19.3	21.4	3.9	4.5	21.6	22.5	31.2	40.3	1.7	1.3	22.4	10.0	14.7	12.7
49	Ecuador[b]	44.6	56.9	0.0	0.0	17.4	21.5	30.8	14.3	3.0	5.5	4.3	1.7	13.5	18.1
50	Morocco	19.2	..	5.4	..	34.7	..	20.8	..	7.4	..	12.5	..	24.0	..
51	Jordan	13.2	16.1	0.0	1.6	7.3	20.5	47.8	26.4	9.5	7.2	22.2	28.3	..	30.5
52	Tajikistan	..	..	..	..	..	..	..	..	..	..	..	..	..	..
53	Peru[b]	25.9	9.0	0.0	0.0	37.2	74.0	27.1	10.8	2.2	3.5	7.7	2.7	17.9	8.3
54	El Salvador[b]	23.2	23.1	0.0	0.0	29.8	45.5	37.0	20.6	5.6	5.2	4.5	5.5	11.7	9.1
55	Congo	48.8	..	4.4	..	7.6	..	13.0	..	2.7	..	23.5	..	39.1	..
56	Syrian Arab Rep.	9.7	30.7	0.0	0.0	5.3	3.2	14.3	7.4	10.1	35.1	60.7	23.5	26.8	24.4
57	Colombia	24.9	27.8	11.2	12.6	22.6	27.7	20.6	17.8	6.8	6.7	13.9	7.4	12.1	13.4
58	Paraguay	15.2	9.3	13.1	0.0	17.7	19.5	24.8	20.1	20.5	24.8	8.8	26.2	10.6	12.3
59	Uzbekistan	..	..	..	..	..	..	..	..	..	..	..	..	..	..
60	Jamaica	33.7	..	3.7	..	49.3	..	3.1	..	6.3	..	4.0	..	31.9	..
61	Romania	..	35.2	..	28.9	..	23.2	..	3.1	..	1.5	..	8.1	..	37.3
62	Namibia	..	23.4	..	0.0	..	25.1	..	37.5	..	0.5	..	13.5	..	39.1
63	Tunisia	14.6	14.5	9.3	12.3	23.9	22.6	24.7	28.4	5.6	4.9	22.0	17.4	32.3	30.0
64	Kyrgyzstan	..	..	..	..	..	..	..	..	..	..	..	..	..	..
65	Thailand	17.7	25.8	0.2	0.7	46.0	43.6	26.2	19.1	1.8	3.1	8.1	7.7	14.5	20.5
66	Georgia	..	..	..	..	..	..	..	..	..	..	..	..	..	..

Note: For data comparability and coverage, see the technical notes.   Figures in italics are for years other than those specified.

		Income, profit, and capital gains		Social security		Goods and services (domestic taxes)		International trade and transactions		Other[a]		Nontax revenue		Total current revenue (percentage of GNP)	
		1980	1991	1980	1991	1980	1991	1980	1991	1980	1991	1980	1991	1980	1991
67	Azerbaijan	..	..	..	..	..	..	..	..	..	..	..	..	..	..
68	Turkmenistan	..	..	..	..	..	..	..	..	..	..	..	..	..	..
69	Turkey	49.1	44.9	0.0	0.0	19.7	34.6	6.0	5.1	4.6	2.9	20.7	12.6	22.3	20.7
70	Poland	..	..	..	..	..	..	..	..	..	..	..	..	..	..
71	Bulgaria	..	31.7	..	13.5	..	12.7	..	1.2	..	0.4	..	40.4	..	74.3
72	Costa Rica	13.7	8.9	28.9	28.6	30.4	27.7	18.9	19.7	2.3	1.1	5.8	14.0	18.7	24.6
73	Algeria	..	..	..	..	..	..	..	..	..	..	..	..	..	..
74	Panama	21.2	15.6	21.2	21.3	16.7	15.8	10.3	11.1	3.8	3.1	26.7	33.1	28.4	32.5
75	Armenia	..	..	..	..	..	..	..	..	..	..	..	..	..	..
76	Chile	17.6	..	17.4	..	35.8	..	4.3	..	4.9	..	19.9	..	33.2	..
77	Iran, Islamic Rep.	3.9	11.5	7.4	5.3	3.6	6.7	11.7	45.5	5.3	4.9	68.2	26.1	21.6	19.9
78	Moldova	..	..	..	..	..	..	..	..	..	..	..	..	..	..
79	Ukraine	..	..	..	..	..	..	..	..	..	..	..	..	..	..
80	Mauritius	15.3	13.7	0.0	4.2	17.2	22.6	51.6	46.7	4.3	6.8	11.6	5.9	21.0	24.2
81	Czechoslovakia	..	23.4	..	0.0	..	36.9	..	6.4	..	23.0	..	10.2	..	49.2
82	Kazakhstan	..	..	..	..	..	..	..	..	..	..	..	..	..	..
83	Malaysia	37.5	33.1	0.4	0.0	16.8	20.9	33.0	18.0	1.8	2.4	10.5	25.6	27.3	28.1
	Upper-middle-income														
84	Botswana[b]	33.3	38.8	0.0	0.0	0.7	1.9	39.1	13.4	0.1	0.1	26.7	45.9	36.6	63.4
85	South Africa	55.8	46.8	1.1	1.9	23.8	32.7	3.3	8.8	3.2	2.7	12.7	7.1	25.0	32.3
86	Lithuania	..	..	..	..	..	..	..	..	..	..	..	..	..	..
87	Hungary	18.5	17.9	15.3	29.2	38.3	31.3	6.9	5.8	4.8	0.2	16.1	15.5	55.5	55.6
88	Venezuela	67.4	61.4	4.6	5.3	4.2	3.4	6.8	8.2	1.8	1.0	15.2	20.8	22.2	24.3
89	Argentina	0.0	5.6	16.7	33.6	16.7	15.6	0.0	25.9	33.3	10.5	33.3	8.9	17.4	13.7
90	Uruguay	10.9	6.7	23.4	27.0	43.3	35.9	14.2	9.8	2.7	15.5	5.5	5.1	23.1	27.8
91	Brazil	14.3	6.9	28.6	10.4	28.6	8.2	7.1	0.7	3.6	2.0	17.9	71.8	23.4	67.9
92	Mexico	36.7	36.5	14.1	13.6	28.9	56.0	27.6	4.6	-12.6	-18.3	5.3	7.7	15.6	14.7
93	Belarus	..	..	..	..	..	..	..	..	..	..	..	..	..	..
94	Russian Federation	..	..	..	..	..	..	..	..	..	..	..	..	..	..
95	Latvia	..	..	..	..	..	..	..	..	..	..	..	..	..	..
96	Trinidad and Tobago	69.8	..	1.0	..	4.0	..	7.0	..	0.7	..	17.5	..	42.8	..
97	Gabon[b]	39.9	27.6	0.0	0.8	4.8	23.7	19.7	17.4	2.0	1.2	33.7	29.3	39.4	35.8
98	Estonia	..	..	..	..	..	..	..	..	..	..	..	..	..	..
99	Portugal	19.4	23.8	26.0	25.9	33.7	36.9	5.1	2.5	8.7	3.2	7.1	7.7	31.1	36.6
100	Oman	26.0	21.3	0.0	0.0	0.5	1.0	1.4	3.1	0.3	0.7	71.8	73.9	42.9	35.6
101	Puerto Rico	..	..	..	..	..	..	..	..	..	..	..	..	..	..
102	Korea, Rep.	22.3	31.3	1.1	5.0	45.9	33.3	15.0	9.2	3.2	10.9	12.5	10.4	18.3	17.4
103	Greece	17.4	19.8	25.8	32.1	31.6	40.4	5.0	0.1	9.6	-2.3	10.6	9.9	29.7	32.2
104	Saudi Arabia	..	..	..	..	..	..	..	..	..	..	..	..	..	..
105	*Yugoslavia*	0.0	0.0	0.0	0.0	64.3	66.4	35.7	31.3	0.0	0.0	0.0	2.3	7.9	5.5
	Low- and middle-income														
	Sub-Saharan Africa														
	East Asia & Pacific														
	South Asia														
	Europe and Central Asia														
	Middle East & N. Africa														
	Latin America & Caribbean														
	Severely indebted														
	High-income economies														
	OECD members														
106	Ireland	34.3	36.3	13.4	14.4	30.1	31.3	9.2	8.1	1.9	3.4	11.1	6.5	37.7	42.9
107	†Israel	40.7	32.9	10.1	7.4	24.5	36.1	3.6	1.8	7.0	5.0	14.1	16.8	52.0	29.1
108	New Zealand[b]	67.3	57.3	0.0	0.0	18.0	26.1	3.2	1.9	1.3	3.0	10.3	11.8	34.9	39.1
109	Spain	23.2	32.1	48.0	36.9	12.6	22.6	3.8	2.1	4.4	0.8	8.0	5.6	24.0	32.0
110	†Hong Kong	..	..	..	..	..	..	..	..	..	..	..	..	..	..
111	†Singapore	32.5	25.6	0.0	0.0	15.8	16.0	6.9	2.0	13.9	13.8	30.9	42.6	26.3	27.7
112	United Kingdom	37.7	39.0	15.6	16.3	27.8	29.0	0.1	0.1	5.7	6.9	13.1	8.8	35.2	37.4
113	Australia	60.8	64.8	0.0	0.0	23.3	20.6	5.4	3.3	0.3	1.5	10.1	9.9	22.1	27.8
114	Italy	30.0	35.1	34.7	28.7	24.7	30.7	0.1	0.0	2.5	2.4	8.1	3.1	31.2	39.9
115	Netherlands	29.6	31.7	36.3	35.9	20.8	21.1	0.0	0.0	2.7	2.8	10.6	8.6	49.1	49.7
116	Belgium	38.5	34.9	30.6	35.3	24.2	23.4	0.0	0.0	2.5	3.2	4.3	3.2	44.0	44.3
117	Austria	21.1	19.6	35.0	36.4	25.6	24.7	1.6	1.5	9.1	8.7	7.7	8.9	34.9	35.6
118	France	17.7	18.2	41.2	43.8	30.9	27.2	0.1	0.0	2.7	3.8	7.4	7.0	39.4	40.9
119	Canada	52.6	52.4	10.4	13.5	16.6	18.8	7.0	3.5	-0.2	0.1	13.6	11.6	19.2	21.3
120	United States	56.6	50.7	28.2	35.1	4.4	3.7	1.4	1.5	1.2	1.0	8.2	8.0	19.9	19.8
121	Germany[c]	18.7	16.0	54.2	51.0	23.1	27.5	0.0	0.0	0.1	-0.4	3.9	6.0	28.7	30.6
122	Denmark	35.9	37.5	2.3	3.8	46.9	40.8	0.1	0.1	3.3	3.3	11.6	14.6	36.4	40.7
123	Finland	26.7	28.4	11.5	11.6	49.1	45.5	2.0	0.9	3.0	3.4	7.7	10.1	27.5	31.3
124	Norway	27.4	16.6	22.3	24.2	39.6	34.4	0.6	0.5	1.1	1.3	8.9	23.0	42.4	47.4
125	Sweden	18.2	12.3	33.2	32.4	29.1	30.4	1.2	0.5	4.3	9.4	14.1	15.1	35.4	44.4
126	Japan[b]	70.8	69.2	0.0	0.0	20.8	16.9	2.4	1.3	0.8	7.4	5.2	5.2	11.6	14.5
127	Switzerland	14.0	..	48.0	..	19.3	..	9.5	..	2.0	..	7.3	..	18.9	..
	World														
	Fuel exporters														

a. See the technical notes.   b. Data are for budgetary accounts only.   c. Data refer to the Federal Republic of Germany before unification.

Table 13. Money and interest rates

| | | Monetary holdings, broadly defined | | | | | Average annual inflation (GDP deflator) | Nominal interest rates of banks (average annual percentage) | | | |
| | | Average annual nominal growth rate (percent) | | Average outstanding as a percentage of GDP | | | | Deposit rate | | Lending rate | |
		1970–80	1980–91	1970	1980	1991	1980–91	1980	1991	1980	1991
	Low-income economies										
	China and India										
	Other low-income										
1	Mozambique	..	..	..	..	..	37.6	..	..	..	..
2	Tanzania	22.6	..	22.9	37.2	..	25.7	4.0	*17.0*	11.5	*31.0*
3	Ethiopia	14.4	12.5	14.0	25.3	56.9	2.4	..	1.0	..	6.0
4	Uganda	28.1	..	16.3	12.7	..	..	6.8	31.2	10.8	34.4
5	Bhutan	..	32.3	..	..	22.0	8.3	..	6.5	..	15.0
6	Guinea-Bissau	..	..	..	..	..	56.3	..	..	..	..
7	Nepal	19.9	19.9	10.6	21.9	36.1	9.1	4.0	*8.5*	14.0	*14.4*
8	Burundi	20.1	9.9	9.1	13.5	..	4.3	2.5	..	12.0	..
9	Chad	15.2	9.0	9.4	20.0	19.4	1.1	5.5	7.5	11.0	..
10	Madagascar	13.8	16.0	17.3	22.3	19.0	16.8	5.6	..	9.5	..
11	Sierra Leone	19.9	57.7	12.6	20.6	15.3	59.0	9.2	40.5	11.0	52.5
12	Bangladesh	..	21.0	..	16.7	30.0	9.3	8.3	12.1	11.3	15.9
13	Lao PDR	..	..	..	..	..	..	7.2	*14.0*	4.8	*15.0*
14	Malawi	14.7	..	21.6	20.5	..	14.9	7.9	12.5	16.7	20.0
15	Rwanda	21.5	8.5	10.7	13.6	16.6	4.1	6.3	8.8	13.5	19.0
16	Mali	18.5	8.7	13.8	17.9	20.8	4.3	6.2	7.0	*9.4*	16.0
17	Burkina Faso	21.5	10.9	9.3	15.9	20.2	4.0	6.2	7.0	*9.4*	16.0
18	Niger	23.9	5.2	5.2	13.3	19.8	2.5	6.2	7.0	9.4	16.0
19	India	17.3	16.8	23.9	36.2	44.1	8.2	..	..	16.5	17.9
20	Kenya	19.8	15.1	31.2	36.8	40.7	9.3	5.8	*13.7*	10.6	*18.8*
21	Nigeria	33.7	15.7	9.2	23.8	20.2	18.2	5.3	14.9	8.4	20.0
22	China	..	25.4	..	33.6	84.6	5.8	5.4	..	5.0	*11.2*
23	Haiti	24.5	8.6	12.0	26.1	..	7.1	10.0	..	..	..
24	Benin	19.0	5.4	10.1	17.1	26.5	1.6	6.2	7.0	..	16.0
25	Central African Rep.	16.0	4.4	16.0	18.9	17.1	5.2	5.5	7.5	10.5	16.2
26	Ghana	36.4	42.9	18.0	16.2	12.5	40.2	11.5	21.3	19.0	..
27	Pakistan	17.1	13.3	41.2	38.7	35.9	7.0	..	..	..	..
28	Togo	22.2	5.9	17.2	29.0	35.2	4.4	6.2	7.0	..	16.0
29	Guinea	..	..	..	..	..	..	..	..	..	..
30	Nicaragua	18.2	..	0.0	0.0	..	583.4	7.5	..	..	..
31	Sri Lanka	23.1	15.2	22.0	35.3	33.1	11.2	14.5	18.5	19.0	13.8
32	Mauritania	21.5	11.6	9.5	21.3	26.5	8.6	5.5	5.0	12.0	10.0
33	Yemen, Rep.	..	18.7	..	..	..	..	9.3	..	..	..
34	Honduras	16.0	13.1	19.5	22.6	29.0	6.8	7.0	11.5	18.5	21.9
35	Lesotho	..	17.1	..	..	34.6	13.8	..	13.0	11.0	20.0
36	Indonesia	35.4	26.2	8.0	13.2	40.5	8.5	6.0	23.3	..	*20.6*
37	Egypt, Arab Rep.	26.0	21.8	33.5	52.2	91.7	12.6	8.3	*12.0*	13.3	*19.0*
38	Zimbabwe	..	..	..	..	45.1	13.5	3.5	8.8	17.5	15.5
39	Sudan	28.3	*28.0*	17.5	32.5	..	..	6.0	..	..	..
40	Zambia	10.7	..	29.9	32.6	..	..	7.0	..	9.5	..
	Middle-income economies										
	Lower-middle-income										
41	Bolivia	29.4	*444.2*	14.8	16.2	*318.4*	263.8	18.0	23.8	28.0	41.2
42	Côte d'Ivoire	22.6	3.7	24.7	25.8	31.5	3.9	6.2	7.0	*9.4*	16.0
43	Senegal	19.6	5.9	14.0	26.6	22.2	5.9	6.2	7.0	*9.4*	16.0
44	Philippines	19.2	16.8	29.9	26.4	32.2	14.6	12.3	18.8	14.0	23.1
45	Papua New Guinea	..	8.1	..	32.9	33.1	5.2	6.9	9.1	11.2	14.1
46	Cameroon	22.5	7.0	13.5	18.3	24.4	4.5	7.5	8.0	13.0	..
47	Guatemala	18.6	17.2	17.1	20.5	19.3	15.9	9.0	24.4	11.0	34.1
48	Dominican Rep.	18.1	28.0	17.9	21.8	20.1	24.5	..	..	..	..
49	Ecuador	24.2	35.5	20.0	20.2	*13.4*	38.1	..	41.5	9.0	46.7
50	Morocco	18.7	14.5	31.1	42.4	58.3	7.1	4.9	8.5	7.0	9.0
51	Jordan	24.3	13.0	..	..	134.8	*1.6*	..	..	..	..
52	Tajikistan	..	..	..	..	..	..	..	..	..	..
53	Peru	33.6	*224.0*	17.8	16.4	..	287.4	..	172.9	..	793.2
54	El Salvador	17.3	17.2	22.5	28.1	27.8	17.4	..	16.1	..	19.7
55	Congo	15.7	6.7	16.5	14.7	20.0	0.6	6.5	7.8	11.0	12.5
56	Syrian Arab Rep.	26.5	*19.2*	34.8	40.9	..	*14.4*	5.0	..	..	..
57	Colombia	32.7	..	20.5	23.7	26.1	25.0	..	37.2	*19.0*	47.1
58	Paraguay	25.9	..	16.9	19.8	..	25.1	..	..	..	..
59	Uzbekistan	..	..	..	..	..	..	..	..	..	..
60	Jamaica	15.7	24.4	31.4	35.4	40.3	19.6	10.3	27.4	13.0	35.6
61	Romania	..	10.3	..	33.4	36.6	6.2	..	..	..	..
62	Namibia	..	..	..	..	..	12.5	..	..	..	..
63	Tunisia	20.3	*15.5*	33.0	42.1	..	7.3	2.5	*7.4*	7.3	9.9
64	Kyrgyzstan	..	..	..	..	..	..	..	..	..	..
65	Thailand	*17.9*	18.9	23.6	37.3	*71.5*	3.7	12.0	*12.3*	18.0	25.0
66	Georgia	..	..	..	..	..	..	..	..	..	..

Note: For data comparability and coverage, see the technical notes.   Figures in italics are for years other than those specified.

262

| | | Monetary holdings, broadly defined | | | | | Average annual inflation (GDP deflator) | Nominal interest rates of banks (average annual percentage) | | | |
| | | Average annual nominal growth rate (percent) | | Average outstanding as a percentage of GDP | | | | Deposit rate | | Lending rate | |
		1970–80	1980–91	1970	1980	1991	1980–91	1980	1991	1980	1991
67	Azerbaijan	..	..	..	..	..	..	..	..	..	..
68	Turkmenistan										
69	Turkey	32.9	52.7	27.9	17.2	21.6	44.7	8.0	62.9	25.7	..
70	Poland	..	58.6	..	58.4	29.4	63.1	3.0	27.8	8.0	101.4
71	Bulgaria	..	..	..	..	..	7.9	..	1.6	..	5.1
72	Costa Rica	30.6	25.7	18.9	38.8	38.3	22.9	..	27.3	..	38.9
73	Algeria	24.1	14.3	53.6	58.5	..	10.2	..	..	..	..
74	Panama	..	..	..	36.9	..	2.4	..	..	..	..
75	Armenia	..	..	..	..	..	..	..	..	..	..
76	Chile	194.2	29.8	12.5	21.0	38.5	20.5	37.5	22.3	47.1	28.6
77	Iran, Islamic Rep.	33.2	16.7	26.1	54.5	..	14.1	..	..	..	..
78	Moldova	..	..	..	..	..	..	..	..	..	..
79	Ukraine	..	..	..	..	..	..	..	..	..	..
80	Mauritius	24.3	22.0	37.5	41.1	65.4	8.1	..	12.3	..	17.8
81	Czechoslovakia	..	6.6	..	..	63.8	3.5	2.7	8.1	..	..
82	Kazakhstan	..	..	..	..	..	..	..	..	..	..
83	Malaysia	25.2	12.6	34.4	69.8	..	1.7	6.2	7.2	7.8	8.1
Upper-middle-income											
84	Botswana	..	25.8	..	28.2	27.0	13.3	5.0	11.4	8.5	11.8
85	South Africa	15.6	16.6	59.9	50.9	56.2	14.4	5.5	17.3	9.5	20.3
86	Lithuania	..	..	..	..	..	10.3	3.0	23.0	9.0	28.0
87	Hungary	..	..	..	..	..	21.2	..	31.1	..	29.8
88	Venezuela	26.4	20.2	24.1	43.0	37.3	416.8	79.4	60.3	..	112.9
89	Argentina	140.8	368.5	27.5	22.2	7.6	64.4	50.3	75.2	66.6	152.9
90	Uruguay	78.4	69.1	24.5	32.1	43.8	327.7	115.0	913.2	..	..
91	Brazil	9.7	..	..	18.4	..	66.5	20.6	17.1	28.1	..
92	Mexico	–47.0	62.0	26.1	26.2	24.1	..	..	..	..	..
93	Belarus	..	..	..	..	..	..	..	..	..	..
94	Russian Federation	..	..	..	..	..	..	..	..	..	..
95	Latvia	..	..	..	..	..	6.4	..	5.8	10.0	13.2
96	Trinidad and Tobago	27.9	5.9	28.2	32.0	53.6	1.3	7.5	8.8	12.5	16.0
97	Gabon	31.3	5.2	14.5	15.2	21.7	..	..	..	..	..
98	Estonia	..	..	..	..	..	17.4	19.0	14.6	18.8	22.9
99	Portugal	20.2	18.6	87.6	80.8	74.7	–3.0	..	7.1	..	9.5
100	Oman	29.4	11.0	..	13.8	30.6	3.4	..	..	..	..
101	Puerto Rico	..	..	..	..	..	5.7	19.5	10.0	18.0	10.0
102	Korea, Rep.	30.4	21.3	32.1	31.7	52.3	17.7	14.5	20.7	21.3	29.5
103	Greece	23.9	22.3	42.9	61.6	79.3	–3.1	..	..	..	..
104	Saudi Arabia	43.7	7.8	17.6	18.6	..	122.9	5.9	..	11.5	..
105	*Yugoslavia*	28.4	119.0	54.8	59.1	..					
Low- and middle-income											
Sub-Saharan Africa											
East Asia & Pacific											
South Asia											
Europe and Central Asia											
Middle East & N. Africa											
Latin America & Caribbean											
Severely indebted											
High-income economies											
OECD members											
106	Ireland	19.1	6.7	64.0	58.1	46.8	5.8	12.0	5.2	16.0	10.6
107	†Israel	54.5	99.2	15.0	14.7	56.6	89.0	..	13.9	176.9	26.6
108	New Zealand	15.1	..	51.4	50.9	..	10.3	..	9.0	12.6	12.1
109	Spain	20.1	10.8	68.8	74.4	68.8	8.9	13.1	10.5	16.9	14.4
110	†Hong Kong	..	..	..	69.5	..	7.5	..	..	..	..
111	†Singapore	17.1	13.5	66.2	74.4	126.1	1.9	9.4	4.6	11.7	7.6
112	United Kingdom	15.2	..	49.2	46.0	..	5.8	14.1	5.3	16.2	11.5
113	Australia	20.4	12.2	43.6	57.9	74.5	7.0	8.6	10.4	10.6	16.4
114	Italy	20.1	12.0	79.3	81.9	78.9	9.5	12.7	6.6	19.0	13.9
115	Netherlands	14.6	..	53.9	77.2	..	1.8	6.0	3.2	13.5	12.4
116	Belgium	10.8	7.0	56.7	57.0	..	4.2	7.7	6.3	..	12.9
117	Austria	13.7	7.4	54.0	72.6	87.3	3.6	5.0	3.8	..	..
118	France	15.6	9.9	57.8	69.7	..	5.7	6.3	6.7	18.7	16.0
119	Canada	17.5	8.4	48.4	65.0	75.7	4.3	12.9	8.6	14.3	9.9
120	United States	10.0	8.0	60.4	58.3	67.0	4.2	..	..	15.3	8.5
121	Germany [a]	9.4	6.4	52.8	60.7	68.2	2.8	8.0	7.6	12.0	12.5
122	Denmark	12.4	11.1	44.8	42.6	59.6	5.2	10.8	7.2	17.2	11.4
123	Finland	15.4	12.9	39.8	39.5	56.2	6.6	..	7.5	9.8	11.8
124	Norway	12.8	10.6	54.6	51.6	63.9	5.2	5.0	9.6	12.6	14.2
125	Sweden	11.4	9.2	48.1	46.5	45.5	7.4	11.3	8.0	15.1	16.1
126	Japan	16.0	8.9	94.7	134.0	183.1	1.5	5.5	3.3	8.4	7.5
127	Switzerland	5.4	6.8	109.8	107.4	112.0	3.8	..	7.6	..	7.8
World											
Fuel exporters											

a. Data refer to the Federal Republic of Germany before unification.

Table 14. Growth of merchandise trade

		Merchandise trade (millions of dollars)		Average annual growth rate[a] (percent)				Terms of trade (1987 = 100)	
		Exports 1991	Imports 1991	Exports 1970–80	Exports 1980–91	Imports 1970–80	Imports 1980–91	1985	1991
	Low-income economies	**161,496** t	**167,270** t	**3.5** w	**6.6** w	**6.0** w	**2.7** w	**106** m	**94** m
	China and India	**90,539** t	**84,209** t	**6.9** w	**10.4** w	**7.3** w	**7.8** w	**103** m	**106** m
	Other low-income	**70,957** t	**83,062** t	**2.0** w	**3.3** w	**5.4** w	**–1.3** w	**106** m	**93** m
1	Mozambique	. .	. .	. .	. .	. .	. .	. .	. .
2	Tanzania	394	1,381	–7.5	–1.9	–0.6	2.8	101	84
3	Ethiopia	276	1,031	–2.3	1.9	–0.6	3.3	117	60
4	Uganda	200	550	–8.4	2.3	–1.5	3.6	143	48
5	Bhutan	. .	. .	. .	. .	. .	. .	. .	. .
6	Guinea-Bissau	28	78	15.9	–2.5	–5.2	3.6	91	138
7	Nepal	238	740	10.9	8.1	8.8	4.9	98	85
8	Burundi	91	254	0.2	8.6	5.0	–0.1	133	43
9	Chad	194	408	. .	. .	. .	. .	. .	. .
10	Madagascar	344	523	–3.0	0.3	–0.8	0.5	98	85
11	Sierra Leone	145	163	–5.7	–3.0	–2.0	–7.2	106	116
12	Bangladesh	1,718	3,470	3.8	7.2	–2.4	4.3	122	105
13	Lao PDR	97	228	. .	. .	. .	. .	. .	. .
14	Malawi	470	719	5.4	5.6	1.0	2.2	104	87
15	Rwanda	. .	. .	. .	. .	. .	. .	. .	. .
16	Mali	354	638	8.3	6.7	5.2	3.5	95	99
17	Burkina Faso	116	602	7.3	6.5	6.4	3.3	108	89
18	Niger	385	431	21.0	1.8	10.9	–3.0	126	82
19	India	17,664	20,418	4.3	7.4	3.0	4.2	96	100
20	Kenya	1,203	2,034	2.9	2.9	1.9	1.0	114	87
21	Nigeria	12,071	6,525	0.4	1.2	19.4	–14.3	167	82
22	China*	72,875	63,791	8.7	11.5	11.3	9.5	109	111
23	Haiti	103	374	5.6	–4.5	6.3	–2.1	89	77
24	Benin	103	398	–11.6	11.3	4.0	–0.2	103	85
25	Central African Rep.	133	196	–0.6	1.3	–2.9	6.1	107	111
26	Ghana	992	1,418	–6.3	5.2	–2.2	1.8	106	62
27	Pakistan	6,528	8,439	0.7	9.9	4.2	2.6	90	80
28	Togo	292	548	4.9	6.5	11.2	2.5	118	80
29	Guinea	. .	. .	. .	. .	. .	. .	. .	. .
30	Nicaragua	268	751	0.8	–4.2	0.1	–1.2	108	107
31	Sri Lanka	2,629	3,861	2.0	6.3	4.5	2.1	103	87
32	Mauritania	438	470	–2.0	5.6	1.4	3.1	113	109
33	Yemen, Rep.	. .	. .	. .	. .	. .	. .	. .	. .
34	Honduras	679	880	3.8	–0.7	2.1	–1.2	111	113
35	Lesotho[b]	. .	. .	. .	. .	. .	. .	. .	. .
36	Indonesia	28,997	25,869	7.2	4.5	13.0	2.6	134	101
37	Egypt, Arab Rep.	3,887	7,862	–2.6	2.8	7.8	–2.3	131	93
38	Zimbabwe	1,779	2,110	2.3	0.4	–3.5	–1.0	100	101
39	Sudan	329	1,433	–3.5	–1.2	–0.6	–4.0	106	94
40	Zambia	1,082	1,255	–0.2	–3.2	–9.2	–1.8	90	116
	Middle-income economies	**524,948** t	**552,257** t	**4.1** w	**3.4** w	**6.1** w	**1.1** w	**109** m	**103** m
	Lower-middle-income	**214,977** t	**243,207** t	**6.7** w	**5.3** w	**5.9** w	**1.8** w	**108** m	**103** m
41	Bolivia	760	992	–0.8	4.5	7.3	0.2	167	73
42	Côte d'Ivoire	3,011	1,671	4.8	4.5	9.1	–2.3	110	67
43	Senegal	977	1,407	1.8	5.6	3.7	3.4	106	93
44	Philippines	8,754	12,145	6.0	3.3	3.3	3.0	93	91
45	Papua New Guinea	1,361	1,614	10.6	6.8	1.8	1.6	111	80
46	Cameroon	2,022	1,448	4.2	11.5	5.4	–1.5	139	81
47	Guatemala	1,202	1,850	5.7	–0.7	5.8	–0.8	108	103
48	Dominican Rep.	658	1,729	–2.7	–1.5	2.0	1.4	109	112
49	Ecuador	2,957	2,328	12.5	4.8	6.7	–2.1	153	90
50	Morocco	4,278	6,872	3.9	5.9	6.6	3.8	88	98
51	Jordan	879	2,507	19.3	6.9	15.3	–0.8	95	116
52	Tajikistan	. .	. .	. .	. .	. .	. .	. .	. .
53	Peru	3,307	2,813	3.3	1.1	–1.7	–4.7	111	67
54	El Salvador	367	885	1.3	–2.7	4.6	–3.7	126	103
55	Congo	1,455	524	16.8	6.6	5.3	–1.9	145	84
56	Syrian Arab Rep.	5,594	3,002	7.0	20.6	12.4	3.9	125	182
57	Colombia	7,269	4,967	1.9	12.0	6.0	–1.7	140	84
58	Paraguay	737	1,460	8.3	12.2	5.3	5.8	108	117
59	Uzbekistan	. .	. .	. .	. .	. .	. .	. .	. .
60	Jamaica	1,081	1,843	–1.7	0.8	–6.8	2.0	95	91
61	Romania	. .	. .	. .	. .	. .	. .	. .	. .
62	Namibia[b]	. .	. .	. .	. .	. .	. .	. .	. .
63	Tunisia	3,709	5,180	7.5	5.6	12.5	1.5	105	95
64	Kyrgyzstan	. .	. .	. .	. .	. .	. .	. .	. .
65	Thailand	28,324	37,408	10.3	14.4	5.0	11.1	91	91
66	Georgia	. .	. .	. .	. .	. .	. .	. .	. .
*	Data for Taiwan, China, are:	76,090	61,723	15.6	11.0	12.2	10.1	100	106

Note: For data comparability and coverage, see the technical notes. Figures in italics are for years other than those specified.

		Merchandise trade (millions of dollars)		Average annual growth rate[a] (percent)				Terms of trade (1987 = 100)	
				Exports		Imports			
		Exports 1991	Imports 1991	1970–80	1980–91	1970–80	1980–91	1985	1991
67	Azerbaijan	..	..	..	..	..	..	..	..
68	Turkmenistan	..	..	..	..	..	..	..	..
69	Turkey	13,594	21,038	4.3	7.2	5.7	7.4	82	108
70	Poland	14,903	15,757	5.4	3.3	5.8	2.0	94	104
71	Bulgaria	..	..	..	..	..	..	..	..
72	Costa Rica	1,490	1,864	5.2	4.6	4.2	3.4	111	109
73	Algeria	11,790	7,683	–0.5	2.4	12.1	–5.6	174	95
74	Panama	333	1,681	–7.3	0.0	–5.1	–3.4	130	112
75	Armenia	..	..	..	..	..	..	..	..
76	Chile	8,552	7,453	10.4	5.2	2.2	1.9	102	122
77	Iran, Islamic Rep.	15,916	21,688	–6.8	14.7	10.3	7.9	160	88
78	Moldova	..	..	..	..	..	..	..	..
79	Ukraine	..	..	..	..	..	..	..	..
80	Mauritius	1,193	1,575	3.8	9.9	8.2	10.8	83	104
81	Czechoslovakia	16,317	7,947	6.4	0.1	5.7	–6.0	98	137
82	Kazakhstan	..	..	..	..	..	..	..	..
83	Malaysia	34,300	35,183	4.8	10.9	3.7	7.2	117	93
	Upper-middle-income	**309,972** *t*	**309,050** *t*	**2.3** *w*	**2.3** *w*	**6.2** *w*	**0.6** *w*	**117** *m*	**105** *m*
84	Botswana[b]	..	..	..	..	..	..	..	..
85	South Africa[b]	24,164	17,503	13.4	0.9	–2.0	–4.4	105	86
86	Lithuania	..	..	..	..	..	..	..	..
87	Hungary	10,180	11,370	3.8	2.2	2.0	1.0	104	102
88	Venezuela	15,127	10,181	–11.6	0.1	10.9	–6.6	174	101
89	Argentina	11,975	8,100	7.1	2.1	2.3	–5.5	110	113
90	Uruguay	1,574	1,552	6.5	3.1	3.1	0.2	89	105
91	Brazil	31,610	22,959	8.5	4.3	4.0	0.8	92	119
92	Mexico	27,120	38,184	13.5	3.5	5.5	2.2	133	100
93	Belarus	..	..	..	..	..	..	..	..
94	Russian Federation	..	..	..	..	..	..	..	..
95	Latvia	..	..	..	..	..	..	..	..
96	Trinidad and Tobago	1,985	1,667	–7.3	–2.6	–9.6	–10.8	156	97
97	Gabon	3,183	806	5.7	5.1	11.6	–3.0	140	79
98	Estonia	..	..	..	..	..	..	..	..
99	Portugal	16,326	26,329	1.2	11.1	1.0	10.0	85	112
100	Oman	..	..	..	..	..	..	..	..
101	Puerto Rico	..	..	..	..	..	..	..	..
102	Korea, Rep.	71,672	81,251	23.5	12.2	11.6	11.1	103	108
103	Greece	8,647	21,552	10.9	3.9	3.2	5.4	94	107
104	Saudi Arabia	54,736	25,540	5.7	–4.2	35.9	–9.0	176	79
105	*Yugoslavia*	13,953	14,737	5.3	–1.2	3.4	–1.2	95	107
	Low- and middle-income	**686,445** *t*	**719,528** *t*	**3.9** *w*	**4.1** *w*	**6.0** *w*	**1.5** *w*	**107** *m*	**100** *m*
	Sub-Saharan Africa	**38,085** *t*	**35,207** *t*	**0.2** *w*	**2.7** *w*	**5.2** *w*	**–4.0** *w*	**107** *m*	**87** *m*
	East Asia & Pacific	**251,448** *t*	**265,796** *t*	**9.5** *w*	**10.2** *w*	**7.6** *w*	**8.4** *w*	**96** *m*	**108** *m*
	South Asia	**29,012** *t*	**37,928** *t*	**3.6** *w*	**7.4** *w*	**2.5** *w*	**3.6** *w*	**97** *m*	**86** *m*
	Europe and Central Asia	**95,153** *t*	**120,861** *t*	..	..	..	..	**94** *m*	**108** *m*
	Middle East & N. Africa	**126,136** *t*	**119,025** *t*	**3.9** *w*	**–0.5** *w*	**15.6** *w*	**–3.2** *w*	**129** *m*	**95** *m*
	Latin America & Caribbean	**122,446** *t*	**123,207** *t*	**–0.1** *w*	**2.9** *w*	**3.6** *w*	**–1.1** *w*	**111** *m*	**105** *m*
	Severely indebted	**138,113** *t*	**140,829** *t*	**9.7** *w*	**2.8** *w*	**5.9** *w*	**–0.6** *w*	**111** *m*	**98** *m*
	High-income economies	**2,650,106** *t*	**2,788,686** *t*	**5.3** *w*	**4.1** *w*	**2.3** *w*	**5.1** *w*	**97** *m*	**101** *m*
	OECD members	**2,441,157** *t*	**2,520,853** *t*	**5.6** *w*	**4.1** *w*	**2.0** *w*	**5.1** *w*	**94** *m*	**101** *m*
106	Ireland	24,240	20,754	11.7	7.1	4.7	3.7	97	92
107	†Israel	11,891	16,753	10.0	6.7	3.5	5.1	105	104
108	New Zealand	9,269	8,494	3.4	3.6	–0.3	3.2	88	94
109	Spain	60,134	93,062	9.1	7.5	1.9	9.4	91	108
110	†Hong Kong	29,738	100,255	9.7	4.4	7.8	11.3	97	101
111	†Singapore	58,871	65,982	4.2	8.9	5.0	7.2	99	101
112	United Kingdom	185,095	209,982	4.4	2.6	0.3	4.4	103	104
113	Australia	37,724	39,460	3.8	4.6	1.8	5.0	111	107
114	Italy	169,365	178,240	6.0	3.4	0.7	4.2	84	101
115	Netherlands	133,527	125,838	3.3	4.4	1.1	3.5	101	100
116	Belgium[c]	118,222	121,038	5.6	4.6	2.9	3.3	94	95
117	Austria	41,082	50,697	6.2	6.2	4.0	5.3	87	89
118	France	212,868	230,257	6.6	3.5	2.4	3.3	96	102
119	Canada	124,797	117,633	2.0	5.7	0.4	7.8	110	105
120	United States	397,705	506,242	6.5	4.0	4.3	7.0	100	102
121	Germany[d]	401,848	387,882	5.0	4.1	2.8	4.5	82	95
122	Denmark	35,687	32,158	4.3	5.0	–0.4	4.0	93	104
123	Finland	23,081	21,708	5.3	2.6	0.1	4.0	85	99
124	Norway	34,037	25,523	7.9	7.4	0.7	2.2	130	90
125	Sweden	55,042	49,760	2.5	3.8	–0.2	3.1	94	103
126	Japan	314,395	234,103	9.0	3.9	0.4	5.6	71	99
127	Switzerland	61,468	66,285	4.9	3.3	2.6	3.4	86	96
	World	**3,336,550** *t*	**3,508,214** *t*	**5.0** *w*	**4.1** *w*	**3.1** *w*	**4.3** *w*	**106** *m*	**100** *m*
	Fuel exporters	**171,293** *t*	**123,270** *t*	**1.4** *w*	**–0.1** *w*	**14.9** *w*	**–5.5** *w*	**167** *m*	**85** *m*

a. See the technical notes.   b. Data are for the South African Customs Union comprising South Africa, Namibia, Lesotho, Botswana, and Swaziland; trade among the component territories is excluded.   c. Includes Luxembourg.   d. Data refer to the Federal Republic of Germany before unification.

Table 15. Structure of merchandise imports

	Food		Fuels		Other primary commodities		Machinery and transport equipment		Other manufactures	
Percentage share of merchandise imports										
	1970	1991	1970	1991	1970	1991	1970	1991	1970	1991
Low-income economies	**15** w	**10** w	**6** w	**9** w	**8** w	**8** w	**31** w	**34** w	**40** w	**38** w
China and India	**14** w	**6** w	**4** w	**8** w	**14** w	**10** w	**32** w	**35** w	**36** w	**41** w
Other low-income	**16** w	**14** w	**7** w	**11** w	**5** w	**7** w	**30** w	**32** w	**42** w	**36** w
1 Mozambique	..	..	..	..	..	..	..	..	..	..
2 Tanzania	7	11	9	19	2	4	40	33	42	33
3 Ethiopia	9	14	8	10	4	3	35	45	45	28
4 Uganda	6	8	2	30	3	2	34	27	55	34
5 Bhutan	..	..	..	..	..	..	..	..	..	..
6 Guinea-Bissau	28	32	7	7	4	3	16	15	45	43
7 Nepal	5	9	11	12	0	14	25	24	60	41
8 Burundi	18	17	7	7	8	7	23	28	45	40
9 Chad	19	17	15	15	4	3	23	27	38	38
10 Madagascar	12	13	7	24	3	3	30	32	48	28
11 Sierra Leone	23	24	7	28	4	3	22	19	44	26
12 Bangladesh	*23*	26	*13*	13	*11*	6	*22*	17	*32*	38
13 Lao PDR	..	..	..	..	..	..	..	..	..	..
14 Malawi	15	7	5	16	6	4	30	26	44	47
15 Rwanda	..	..	..	..	..	..	..	..	..	..
16 Mali	29	18	9	28	6	2	21	25	36	28
17 Burkina Faso	19	23	8	16	8	5	27	24	37	31
18 Niger	13	15	4	20	6	6	26	28	51	31
19 India	21	5	8	23	19	12	23	18	29	42
20 Kenya	6	6	10	15	4	4	34	38	46	37
21 Nigeria	8	18	3	1	3	5	37	36	48	41
22 China*	7	6	1	3	10	9	39	41	43	41
23 Haiti	19	24	6	12	4	5	21	20	51	39
24 Benin	12	16	4	7	8	11	21	21	55	45
25 Central African Rep.	17	17	1	7	2	5	36	33	44	38
26 Ghana	20	9	6	31	4	3	26	26	44	31
27 Pakistan	21	17	6	18	7	8	31	28	35	29
28 Togo	16	20	4	7	11	6	22	24	47	43
29 Guinea	..	..	..	..	..	..	..	..	..	..
30 Nicaragua	10	16	6	13	3	2	28	33	54	36
31 Sri Lanka	47	17	3	11	4	4	18	19	29	49
32 Mauritania	23	23	8	7	2	1	38	40	29	29
33 Yemen, Rep.	..	..	..	..	..	..	..	..	..	..
34 Honduras	11	13	7	16	2	3	29	25	51	44
35 Lesotho[a]	..	..	..	..	..	..	..	..	..	..
36 Indonesia	11	5	2	9	4	9	35	45	47	32
37 Egypt, Arab Rep.	21	29	9	3	14	10	27	24	29	34
38 Zimbabwe	5	5	24	24	6	6	29	29	37	37
39 Sudan	20	22	8	16	4	3	27	25	41	34
40 Zambia	11	8	10	18	2	2	39	35	38	37
Middle-income economies	**12** w	**10** w	**9** w	**11** w	**10** w	**8** w	**35** w	**36** w	**34** w	**36** w
Lower-middle-income	**14** w	**10** w	**9** w	**10** w	**9** w	**7** w	**33** w	**38** w	**34** w	**35** w
41 Bolivia	20	14	1	1	3	3	37	43	40	39
42 Côte d'Ivoire	15	18	5	21	3	3	33	23	44	34
43 Senegal	28	26	5	20	5	5	25	21	38	29
44 Philippines	11	7	12	15	9	7	35	26	33	46
45 Papua New Guinea	23	17	10	9	2	2	30	38	36	34
46 Cameroon	12	14	5	1	2	3	32	35	49	47
47 Guatemala	11	12	2	17	3	3	27	26	57	42
48 Dominican Rep.	17	17	14	26	5	4	27	21	38	32
49 Ecuador	7	8	6	1	3	5	35	41	49	46
50 Morocco	20	11	5	15	11	14	32	28	32	33
51 Jordan	30	26	6	14	5	4	17	18	42	37
52 Tajikistan	..	..	..	..	..	..	..	..	..	..
53 Peru	20	20	2	11	5	3	35	35	38	31
54 El Salvador	13	16	2	13	5	6	23	24	56	41
55 Congo	19	18	2	3	2	2	33	35	44	41
56 Syrian Arab Rep.	15	17	10	18	7	7	33	26	36	32
57 Colombia	7	7	1	6	9	8	46	33	37	47
58 Paraguay	13	8	15	12	7	5	32	36	33	39
59 Uzbekistan	..	..	..	..	..	..	..	..	..	..
60 Jamaica	22	20	15	21	5	4	21	18	37	38
61 Romania	..	..	..	..	..	..	..	..	..	..
62 Namibia[a]	..	..	..	..	..	..	..	..	..	..
63 Tunisia	27	15	5	9	9	11	26	24	32	41
64 Kyrgyzstan	..	..	..	..	..	..	..	..	..	..
65 Thailand	4	5	9	9	8	8	36	39	43	38
66 Georgia	..	..	..	..	..	..	..	..	..	..
* Data for Taiwan, China, are:	15	6	5	10	18	12	35	36	28	36

Note: For data comparability and coverage, see the technical notes. Figures in italics are for years other than those specified.

		Food		Fuels		Other primary commodities		Machinery and transport equipment		Other manufactures	
	Percentage share of merchandise imports										
		1970	1991	1970	1991	1970	1991	1970	1991	1970	1991
67	Azerbaijan	..	..	..	..	..	..	..	..	..	..
68	Turkmenistan	..	..	..	..	..	..	..	..	..	..
69	Turkey	8	7	8	21	8	12	41	29	36	31
70	Poland	14	7	18	22	11	8	27	34	24	28
71	Bulgaria	..	..	..	..	..	..	..	..	..	..
72	Costa Rica	11	9	4	17	3	4	29	20	53	50
73	Algeria	13	26	2	3	6	6	37	32	42	34
74	Panama	10	10	19	15	2	2	27	26	42	47
75	Armenia	..	..	..	..	..	..	..	..	..	..
76	Chile	14	6	6	15	7	4	43	38	30	38
77	Iran, Islamic Rep.	7	13	0	0	8	5	41	44	45	38
78	Moldova	..	..	..	..	..	..	..	..	..	..
79	Ukraine	..	..	..	..	..	..	..	..	..	..
80	Mauritius	36	27	7	18	3	5	13	12	41	37
81	Czechoslovakia	12	8	11	9	19	14	36	39	23	29
82	Kazakhstan	..	..	..	..	..	..	..	..	..	..
83	Malaysia	20	6	12	4	9	5	28	55	31	30
	Upper-middle-income	**11 w**	**10 w**	**9 w**	**11 w**	**11 w**	**8 w**	**37 w**	**34 w**	**33 w**	**36 w**
84	Botswana[a]	..	..	..	..	..	..	..	..	..	..
85	South Africa[a]	4	3	0	0	6	4	53	43	36	50
86	Lithuania	..	..	..	..	..	..	..	..	..	..
87	Hungary	10	5	9	15	19	8	31	30	31	42
88	Venezuela	10	12	1	2	5	9	45	44	38	33
89	Argentina	6	4	5	9	16	11	31	33	42	44
90	Uruguay	11	7	15	16	14	6	31	30	29	41
91	Brazil	11	10	12	26	8	8	35	27	34	29
92	Mexico	7	14	3	3	9	8	50	41	31	33
93	Belarus	..	..	..	..	..	..	..	..	..	..
94	Russian Federation	..	..	..	..	..	..	..	..	..	..
95	Latvia	..	..	..	..	..	..	..	..	..	..
96	Trinidad and Tobago	11	15	53	15	2	6	13	26	22	38
97	Gabon	14	17	1	1	1	2	39	40	44	39
98	Estonia	..	..	..	..	..	..	..	..	..	..
99	Portugal	13	13	9	9	14	5	30	36	34	37
100	Oman	..	..	..	..	..	..	..	..	..	..
101	Puerto Rico	..	..	..	..	..	..	..	..	..	..
102	Korea, Rep.	17	6	7	16	21	13	30	34	25	31
103	Greece	11	13	7	10	10	6	48	33	25	38
104	Saudi Arabia	26	15	1	0	5	4	33	35	35	47
105	*Yugoslavia*	8	10	5	18	18	10	33	26	37	36
	Low- and middle-income	**13 w**	**10 w**	**8 w**	**10 w**	**10 w**	**8 w**	**34 w**	**35 w**	**35 w**	**36 w**
	Sub-Saharan Africa	**14 w**	**16 w**	**7 w**	**12 w**	**4 w**	**4 w**	**32 w**	**31 w**	**44 w**	**37 w**
	East Asia & Pacific	**13 w**	**6 w**	**7 w**	**9 w**	**10 w**	**10 w**	**33 w**	**39 w**	**37 w**	**36 w**
	South Asia	**24 w**	**11 w**	**7 w**	**19 w**	**13 w**	**10 w**	**24 w**	**20 w**	**31 w**	**40 w**
	Europe and Central Asia	..	..	..	..	..	..	..	..	..	..
	Middle East & N. Africa	**18 w**	**17 w**	**3 w**	**4 w**	**8 w**	**6 w**	**32 w**	**35 w**	**39 w**	**38 w**
	Latin America & Caribbean	**11 w**	**12 w**	**11 w**	**13 w**	**7 w**	**7 w**	**35 w**	**34 w**	**36 w**	**35 w**
	Severely indebted	**13 w**	**13 w**	**9 w**	**11 w**	**9 w**	**7 w**	**34 w**	**35 w**	**34 w**	**34 w**
	High-income economies	**15 w**	**9 w**	**10 w**	**10 w**	**16 w**	**7 w**	**25 w**	**34 w**	**33 w**	**40 w**
	OECD members	**15 w**	**9 w**	**10 w**	**10 w**	**17 w**	**7 w**	**25 w**	**34 w**	**33 w**	**39 w**
106	Ireland	13	11	8	6	9	4	27	35	43	44
107	†Israel	14	7	5	8	9	5	30	32	42	49
108	New Zealand	6	8	7	8	11	4	34	37	43	44
109	Spain	14	11	13	11	18	7	26	37	28	34
110	†Hong Kong	19	6	3	2	10	5	16	27	52	60
111	†Singapore	15	6	13	14	13	4	23	44	35	32
112	United Kingdom	23	10	10	6	21	6	17	36	29	41
113	Australia	5	5	5	6	7	3	41	42	42	45
114	Italy	19	13	14	10	21	10	20	32	26	36
115	Netherlands	14	13	11	9	11	5	25	31	39	42
116	Belgium[b]	13	10	9	8	19	7	26	26	33	48
117	Austria	9	5	8	6	13	7	31	39	39	44
118	France	14	10	12	10	15	6	25	34	33	40
119	Canada	9	6	6	5	6	4	49	51	31	34
120	United States	16	6	8	11	13	5	28	41	36	37
121	Germany[c]	18	10	9	8	18	7	19	35	36	41
122	Denmark	10	12	10	5	9	5	28	31	42	46
123	Finland	9	6	11	13	9	7	33	34	37	39
124	Norway	8	6	8	4	13	7	35	38	36	44
125	Sweden	10	7	11	9	11	5	30	37	39	42
126	Japan	17	15	21	23	37	15	11	16	14	30
127	Switzerland	12	6	5	5	10	5	27	32	46	52
	World	**15 w**	**9 w**	**10 w**	**10 w**	**15 w**	**7 w**	**27 w**	**35 w**	**34 w**	**39 w**
	Fuel exporters	**13 w**	**15 w**	**5 w**	**2 w**	**5 w**	**5 w**	**36 w**	**40 w**	**41 w**	**39 w**

a. Data are for the South African Customs Union comprising South Africa, Namibia, Lesotho, Botswana, and Swaziland; trade among the component territories is excluded.   b. Includes Luxembourg.   c. Data refer to the Federal Republic of Germnay before unification.

Table 16. Structure of merchandise exports

Percentage share of merchandise exports

	Fuels, minerals, and metals		Other primary commodities		Machinery and transport equipment		Other manufactures		Textiles and clothing [a]	
	1970	1991	1970	1991	1970	1991	1970	1991	1970	1991
Low- income economies	**28 w**	**23 w**	**44 w**	**20 w**	**3 w**	**10 w**	**24 w**	**46 w**	**13 w**	**23 w**
China and India	12 w	9 w	27 w	16 w	10 w	17 w	51 w	58 w	27 w	28 w
Other low-income	36 w	42 w	52 w	26 w	0 w	2 w	12 w	31 w	7 w	17 w
1 Mozambique	..	..	..	..	..	..	..	..	..	..
2 Tanzania	7	5	80	84	0	1	13	10	2	3
3 Ethiopia	2	3	97	94	0	0	2	3	0	1
4 Uganda	9	4	90	95	0	0	0	0	0	0
5 Bhutan	..	..	..	..	..	..	..	..	..	..
6 Guinea-Bissau	0	0	98	97	1	..	1	0	0	..
7 Nepal	0	0	65	11	0	..	35	88	25	76
8 Burundi	1	1	97	97	0	0	2	2	0	0
9 Chad	0	3	95	93	1	1	4	3	0	1
10 Madagascar	9	8	84	85	2	2	5	6	1	3
11 Sierra Leone	15	34	22	33	..	..	63	32	0	..
12 Bangladesh	*1*	1	*35*	29	*1*	0	*64*	70	*49*	62
13 Lao PDR	..	..	..	..	..	..	..	..	..	..
14 Malawi	0	0	96	96	0	0	3	4	1	3
15 Rwanda	..	..	..	..	..	..	..	..	..	..
16 Mali	1	0	89	93	0	0	10	7	8	6
17 Burkina Faso	0	0	95	88	1	4	3	8	0	2
18 Niger	0	86	96	12	1	0	2	1	0	1
19 India	13	8	35	19	5	7	47	66	25	25
20 Kenya	12	16	75	64	0	5	12	15	1	2
21 Nigeria	62	96	36	3	..	0	1	1	0	0
22 China*	11	9	19	15	15	19	55	57	29	28
23 Haiti	17	12	57	46	..	5	26	37	4	8
24 Benin	0	3	89	67	3	3	8	28	6	1
25 Central African Rep.	0	1	55	55	1	0	44	43	1	0
26 Ghana	13	15	86	84	0	0	1	1	0	0
27 Pakistan	2	1	41	26	0	0	57	72	47	60
28 Togo	25	49	69	42	2	1	4	9	1	2
29 Guinea	..	..	..	..	..	..	..	..	..	..
30 Nicaragua	3	2	81	86	0	0	16	12	3	1
31 Sri Lanka	1	1	98	34	0	2	1	62	0	43
32 Mauritania	88	86	11	9	0	4	0	1	0	0
33 Yemen, Rep.	..	..	..	..	..	..	..	..	..	..
34 Honduras	9	5	82	89	0	0	8	6	2	1
35 Lesotho[b]	..	..	..	..	..	..	..	..	..	..
36 Indonesia	44	43	54	16	0	2	1	39	0	14
37 Egypt, Arab Rep.	5	40	68	20	1	1	26	40	19	27
38 Zimbabwe	18	17	47	51	2	4	33	28	4	6
39 *Sudan*	1	3	99	96	0	0	0	1	0	0
40 Zambia	99	98	1	1	0	0	0	1	0	0
Middle-income economies	**40 w**	**34 w**	..	..	**14 w**		..	..	..	..
Lower-middle-income	31 w	29 w	41 w	27 w	14 w	17 w	16 w	29 w	3 w	9 w
41 Bolivia	93	74	4	21	..	0	3	4	0	1
42 Côte d'Ivoire	2	11	92	79	1	2	5	9	1	2
43 Senegal	12	22	69	56	4	3	15	20	6	2
44 Philippines	23	9	70	20	0	14	8	57	1	9
45 Papua New Guinea	42	62	55	35	0	2	3	1	0	0
46 Cameroon	..	..	..	..	..	..	..	..	..	..
47 Guatemala	0	2	72	70	2	1	26	26	8	5
48 Dominican Rep.	4	1	77	79	0	3	20	17	0	0
49 Ecuador	1	43	97	55	0	0	2	2	1	0
50 Morocco	33	20	57	29	0	3	9	48	4	20
51 Jordan	24	38	59	16	3	1	13	44	3	4
52 Tajikistan	..	..	..	..	..	..	..	..	..	..
53 Peru	49	52	49	30	0	2	1	17	0	9
54 El Salvador	2	3	70	56	3	3	26	37	11	15
55 Congo	1	92	70	5	1	0	28	3	0	0
56 Syrian Arab Rep.	62	62	29	15	3	1	7	23	4	15
57 Colombia	11	29	81	38	1	3	7	31	2	11
58 Paraguay	0	0	91	89	..	0	9	11	0	1
59 Uzbekistan	..	..	..	..	..	..	..	..	..	..
60 Jamaica	25	17	22	27	0	1	53	56	2	14
61 Romania	..	..	..	..	..	..	..	..	..	..
62 Namibia[b]	..	..	..	..	..	..	..	..	..	..
63 Tunisia	46	21	35	11	0	7	19	61	2	33
64 Kyrgyzstan	..	..	..	..	..	..	..	..	..	..
65 Thailand	15	2	77	32	0	22	8	45	1	17
66 Georgia	..	..	..	..	..	..	..	..	..	..
* Data for Taiwan, China, are:	2	2	22	6	17	38	59	55	29	16

Note: For data comparability and coverage, see the technical notes.   Figures in italics are for years other than those specified.

Percentage share of merchandise exports

		Fuels, minerals, and metals		Other primary commodities		Machinery and transport equipment		Other manufactures		Textiles and clothing[a]	
		1970	*1991*	*1970*	*1991*	*1970*	*1991*	*1970*	*1991*	*1970*	*1991*
67	Azerbaijan	..	..	..	..	..	..	..	..	..	..
68	Turkmenistan	..	..	..	..	..	..	..	..	..	..
69	Turkey	8	7	83	26	0	6	9	61	5	36
70	Poland	20	20	9	16	36	26	25	38	6	5
71	Bulgaria	..	..	..	..	..	..	..	..	..	..
72	Costa Rica	0	2	80	72	3	3	17	23	4	5
73	Algeria	73	97	20	0	2	1	5	2	1	0
74	Panama	21	2	75	77	2	1	2	21	0	7
75	Armenia	..	..	..	..	..	..	..	..	..	..
76	Chile	88	50	7	35	1	1	4	14	0	1
77	Iran, Islamic Rep.	90	90	6	7	0	0	4	4	3	3
78	Moldova	..	..	..	..	..	..	..	..	..	..
79	Ukraine	..	..	..	..	..	..	..	..	..	..
80	Mauritius	0	0	98	70	0	0	2	30	1	24
81	Czechoslovakia	7	4	6	6	50	54	37	36	7	6
82	Kazakhstan	..	..	..	..	..	..	..	..	..	..
83	Malaysia	30	17	63	22	2	38	6	23	1	6
	Upper-middle-income	..	..	..	..	..	..	..	..	..	..
84	Botswana[b]	..	..	..	..	..	..	..	..	..	..
85	South Africa[b]	..	..	..	..	..	..	..	..	..	..
86	Lithuania	..	..	..	..	..	..	..	..	..	..
87	Hungary	7	8	26	28	32	22	35	42	8	9
88	Venezuela	97	86	2	2	0	1	1	11	0	1
89	Argentina	1	8	85	64	4	7	10	21	1	2
90	Uruguay	1	1	79	59	1	2	20	38	14	16
91	Brazil	11	16	75	28	4	18	11	38	1	4
92	Mexico	19	41	49	14	11	24	22	20	3	2
93	Belarus	..	..	..	..	..	..	..	..	..	..
94	Russian Federation	..	..	..	..	..	..	..	..	..	..
95	Latvia	..	..	..	..	..	..	..	..	..	..
96	Trinidad and Tobago	78	65	9	6	1	1	12	28	1	0
97	Gabon	56	89	35	7	1	0	8	4	0	0
98	Estonia	..	..	..	..	..	..	..	..	..	..
99	Portugal	5	5	31	13	8	19	56	63	25	30
100	Oman	..	..	..	..	..	..	..	..	..	..
101	Puerto Rico	..	..	..	..	..	..	..	..	..	..
102	Korea, Rep.	7	3	17	4	7	38	69	55	36	21
103	Greece	14	15	51	33	1	4	33	48	7	26
104	Saudi Arabia	100	99	0	0	0	1	0	0	0	0
105	*Yugoslavia*	15	9	26	12	23	29	37	50	10	7
	Low- and middle-income	37 *w*	32 *w*	39 *w*	20 *w*	10 *w*	16 *w*	19 *w*	35 *w*	7 *w*	13 *w*
	Sub-Saharan Africa	41 *w*	58 *w*	51 *w*	34 *w*	0 *w*	1 *w*	7 *w*	7 *w*	1 *w*	2 *w*
	East Asia & Pacific	22 *w*	12 *w*	46 *w*	16 *w*	6 *w*	25 *w*	27 *w*	47 *w*	13 *w*	19 *w*
	South Asia	9 *w*	5 *w*	44 *w*	23 *w*	3 *w*	5 *w*	45 *w*	67 *w*	28 *w*	37 *w*
	Europe and Central Asia	..	..	..	..	..	..	..	..	..	..
	Middle East & N. Africa	73 *w*	81 *w*	20 *w*	9 *w*	4 *w*	1 *w*	7 *w*	10 *w*	3 *w*	4 *w*
	Latin America & Caribbean	40 *w*	34 *w*	51 *w*	32 *w*	2 *w*	12 *w*	9 *w*	24 *w*	1 *w*	3 *w*
	Severely indebted	21 *w*	34 *w*	56 *w*	30 *w*	11 *w*	13 *w*	15 *w*	25 *w*	3 *w*	4 *w*
	High-income economies	11 *w*	8 *w*	16 *w*	11 *w*	35 *w*	42 *w*	38 *w*	39 *w*	6 *w*	5 *w*
	OECD members	9 *w*	7 *w*	16 *w*	11 *w*	36 *w*	43 *w*	38 *w*	39 *w*	6 *w*	6 *w*
106	Ireland	8	2	52	24	7	30	34	44	10	4
107	†Israel	4	2	26	10	5	24	66	64	12	7
108	New Zealand	1	8	88	65	2	5	9	22	1	2
109	Spain	10	7	37	17	20	41	34	35	6	4
110	†Hong Kong	1	2	3	3	12	24	84	72	44	40
111	†Singapore	25	18	45	8	11	48	20	26	5	5
112	United Kingdom	8	10	9	8	41	41	42	41	6	4
113	Australia	28	35	53	28	6	7	13	29	1	1
114	Italy	7	3	10	8	37	38	46	52	13	12
115	Netherlands	14	12	29	25	20	22	37	41	8	4
116	Belgium[c]	13	8	11	12	21	27	55	54	10	7
117	Austria	6	4	14	7	24	38	56	51	11	8
118	France	6	5	19	17	33	39	42	39	8	5
119	Canada	26	19	22	17	32	38	19	26	1	1
120	United States	9	6	21	14	42	48	28	32	2	2
121	Germany[d]	6	4	5	6	47	49	43	41	6	5
122	Denmark	4	5	42	31	27	25	27	39	6	5
123	Finland	4	7	29	11	16	28	50	55	2	1
124	Norway	25	58	20	9	23	15	32	18	3	2
125	Sweden	8	6	18	9	40	43	35	42	2	2
126	Japan	2	1	5	1	41	66	53	31	11	2
127	Switzerland	3	3	8	4	32	32	58	62	8	5
	World	16 *w*	13 *w*	21 *w*	13 *w*	30 *w*	37 *w*	34 *w*	38 *w*	6 *w*	6 *w*
	Fuel exporters	83 *w*	89 *w*	13 *w*	6 *w*	1 *w*	1 *w*	4 *w*	4 *w*	1 *w*	1 *w*

a. See the technical notes. b. Data are for the South African Customs Union comprising South Africa, Namibia, Lesotho, Botswana, and Swaziland; trade among the component territories is excluded. c. Includes Luxembourg. d. Data refer to the Federal Republic of Germany before unification.

Table 17. OECD imports of manufactured goods: origin and composition

		Value of imports of manufactures, by origin (millions of dollars)		Composition of 1991 imports of manufactures (percent)				
		1970	1991	Textiles and clothing	Chemicals	Electrical machinery and electronics	Transport equipment	Others
Low-income economies		**1,266** *t*	**73,602** *t*	**40** *w*	**4** *w*	**7** *w*	**2** *w*	**46** *w*
China and India		**777** *t*	**55,576** *t*	**37** *w*	**5** *w*	**9** *w*	**1** *w*	**48** *w*
Other low-income		**489** *t*	**18,026** *t*	**51** *w*	**3** *w*	**2** *w*	**4** *w*	**41** *w*
1	Mozambique	7	10	60	0	0	0	40
2	Tanzania	9	48	56	4	0	2	38
3	Ethiopia	4	59	12	9	2	5	73
4	Uganda	1	2	0	0	50	0	50
5	Bhutan	0	1	0	0	0	0	100
6	Guinea-Bissau	0	0	0	0	0	0	0
7	Nepal	1	240	93	0	0	0	6
8	Burundi	0	2	50	0	0	0	50
9	Chad	0	2	0	0	0	0	100
10	Madagascar	7	49	69	8	0	2	20
11	Sierra Leone	2	135	1	0	1	0	99
12	Bangladesh	0	1,372	93	0	0	0	7
13	Lao PDR	0	26	92	0	0	0	8
14	Malawi	1	18	67	0	0	0	33
15	Rwanda	0	2	0	0	0	50	50
16	Mali	2	51	0	0	20	0	80
17	Burkina Faso	0	3	0	0	0	0	100
18	Niger	0	175	0	96	0	2	2
19	India	534	9,428	45	6	1	1	47
20	Kenya	16	108	15	5	3	6	72
21	Nigeria	13	238	6	16	2	2	74
22	China	243	46,148	35	5	11	2	48
23	Haiti	17	301	60	1	10	1	29
24	Benin	0	4	50	0	0	25	25
25	Central African Rep.	12	80	0	0	0	0	100
26	Ghana	8	98	0	1	1	0	98
27	Pakistan	207	3,234	85	0	0	0	15
28	Togo	0	9	11	0	0	0	89
29	Guinea	38	147	0	34	1	0	65
30	Nicaragua	6	7	14	14	14	0	57
31	Sri Lanka	9	1,346	73	1	2	0	24
32	Mauritania	0	4	25	0	25	0	50
33	Yemen, Rep.	0	0	0	0	0	0	0
34	Honduras	3	261	82	1	0	0	17
35	Lesotho[b]	. .	. .	. .	. .	. .	. .	. .
36	Indonesia	15	7,302	36	2	3	1	58
37	Egypt, Arab Rep.	33	793	61	5	1	15	18
38	Zimbabwe	0	261	22	0	2	1	74
39	*Sudan*	1	7	0	0	0	14	86
40	*Zambia*	4	40	23	0	0	5	73
Middle-income economies		**5,016** *t*	**185,948** *t*	**25** *w*	**7** *w*	**18** *w*	**7** *w*	**44** *w*
Lower-middle-income		**1,778** *t*	**66,559** *t*	**33** *w*	**6** *w*	**18** *w*	**3** *w*	**41** *w*
41	Bolivia	1	54	20	6	0	0	74
42	Côte d'Ivoire	7	239	21	2	1	2	75
43	Senegal	4	34	3	12	15	3	68
44	Philippines	108	5,637	33	2	31	1	33
45	Papua New Guinea	4	35	6	0	0	3	91
46	Cameroon	4	47	21	2	2	2	72
47	Guatemala	5	426	89	2	0	0	9
48	Dominican Rep.	10	1,807	55	1	7	0	38
49	Ecuador	3	83	17	4	5	6	69
50	Morocco	32	2,364	69	12	8	1	10
51	Jordan	1	67	5	27	6	27	36
52	Tajikistan	. .	. .	. .				. .
53	Peru	12	453	58	7	2	1	33
54	El Salvador	2	184	65	1	22	0	13
55	Congo	4	205	0	0	0	0	100
56	Syrian Arab Rep.	2	53	68	0	2	8	23
57	Colombia	52	1,070	33	6	0	0	61
58	Paraguay	5	82	9	27	0	0	65
59	Uzbekistan	. .	. .	. .		. .	. .	. .
60	Jamaica	117	799	38	58	0	0	4
61	Romania	188	1,648	32	6	4	3	56
62	Namibia[a]	. .	. .	. .		. .	. .	. .
63	Tunisia	19	2,135	70	7	9	2	12
64	Kyrgyzstan	. .	. .	. .			. .	. .
65	Thailand	32	12,851	21	2	17	2	59
66	Georgia	. .	. .	. .			. .	. .

Note: For data comparability and coverage, see the technical notes. Figures in italics are for years other than those specified.

		Value of imports of manufactures, by origin (millions of dollars)		Composition of 1991 imports of manufactures (percent)				
		1970	1991	Textiles and clothing	Chemicals	Electrical machinery and electronics	Transport equipment	Others
67	Azerbaijan	..	..	..	..	..	..	..
68	Turkmenistan	..	..	..	..	..	..	..
69	Turkey	47	6,770	71	3	6	2	18
70	Poland	287	5,515	23	16	7	4	51
71	Bulgaria	68	553	29	18	6	1	47
72	Costa Rica	5	700	69	2	9	0	19
73	Algeria	39	1,686	0	4	0	0	96
74	Panamab	18	462	15	4	1	46	36
75	Armenia	..	..	..	..	..	..	..
76	Chile	15	697	9	26	0	2	63
77	Iran, Islamic Rep.	133	676	92	1	0	0	7
78	Moldova	..	..	..	..	..	..	..
79	Ukraine	..	..	..	..	..	..	..
80	Mauritius	1	750	86	1	0	0	13
81	Czechoslovakia	467	4,930	16	14	5	9	56
82	Kazakhstan	..	..	..	..	..	..	..
83	Malaysia	39	12,857	14	3	48	2	34
	Upper-middle-income	**3,238** *t*	**119,389** *t*	**21** *w*	**7** *w*	**17** *w*	**10** *w*	**45** *w*
84	Botswanaa	..	..	..	..	..	..	..
85	South Africaa	325	2,989	7	14	2	3	75
86	Lithuania	..	..	..	..	..	..	..
87	Hungary	210	4,128	23	16	12	5	45
88	Venezuela	24	724	4	16	2	8	70
89	Argentina	104	1,375	8	23	2	4	64
90	Uruguay	23	300	51	3	0	1	45
91	Brazil	197	10,295	8	10	5	9	68
92	Mexico	508	26,519	5	4	32	21	38
93	Belarus	..	..	..	..	..	..	..
94	Russian Federation	..	..	..	..	..	..	..
95	Latvia	..	..	..	..	..	..	..
96	Trinidad and Tobago	39	334	1	68	1	0	31
97	Gabon	8	66	0	46	2	15	38
98	Estonia	..	..	..	..	..	..	..
99	Portugal	396	13,171	39	5	10	8	39
100	Oman	0	188	28	1	13	23	35
101	Puerto Rico	..	..	..	..	..	..	..
102	Korea, Rep.	524	41,091	23	3	20	7	47
103	Greece	185	4,006	60	5	3	1	31
104	Saudi Arabia	16	1,749	0	47	8	6	39
105	*Yugoslavia*	443	8,791	29	7	9	12	43
	Low- and middle-income	**6,282** *t*	**259,562** *t*	**29** *w*	**6** *w*	**15** *w*	**6** *w*	**44** *w*
	Sub-Saharan Africa	**193** *t*	**4,223** *t*	**21** *w*	**8** *w*	**1** *w*	**11** *w*	**58** *w*
	East Asia & Pacific	**1,087** *t*	**128,170** *t*	**28** *w*	**3** *w*	**19** *w*	**3** *w*	**47** *w*
	South Asia	**760** *t*	**15,695** *t*	**61** *w*	**4** *w*	**1** *w*	**1** *w*	**34** *w*
	Europe and Central Asia	**2,316** *t*	**50,571** *t*	**37** *w*	**8** *w*	**9** *w*	**6** *w*	**40** *w*
	Middle East & N. Africa	**306** *t*	**10,385** *t*	**42** *w*	**17** *w*	**6** *w*	**4** *w*	**32** *w*
	Latin America & Caribbean	**1,295** *t*	**47,529** *t*	**13** *w*	**8** *w*	**20** *w*	**14** *w*	**45** *w*
	Severely indebted	**1,420** *t*	**50,899** *t*	**12** *w*	**9** *w*	**19** *w*	**14** *w*	**47** *w*
	High-income economies	**120,492** *t*	**1,578,136** *t*	**6** *w*	**13** *w*	**12** *w*	**19** *w*	**50** *w*
	OECD members	**117,366** *t*	**1,472,714** *t*	**5** *w*	**13** *w*	**11** *w*	**20** *w*	**50** *w*
106	Ireland	439	15,906	7	29	11	2	51
107	†Israel	308	7,878	10	14	10	4	62
108	New Zealand	121	1,967	9	23	7	4	57
109	Spain	773	33,133	4	9	8	36	43
110	†Hong Kong	1,861	24,794	43	1	13	1	43
111	†Singapore	112	20,668	5	6	29	2	58
112	United Kingdom	10,457	108,160	5	17	10	14	53
113	Australia	471	6,676	4	32	5	11	49
114	Italy	7,726	113,636	16	8	8	11	57
115	Netherlands	5,678	74,299	7	27	9	10	47
116	Belgiumc	7,660	80,272	9	20	6	22	44
117	Austria	1,637	29,461	9	9	13	7	62
118	France	9,240	137,947	6	16	9	26	44
119	Canada	8,088	73,986	1	8	8	39	43
120	United States	21,215	213,854	2	12	13	22	51
121	Germany	23,641	266,516	5	15	11	20	50
122	Denmark	1,413	18,766	8	14	10	5	63
123	Finland	1,170	16,343	3	8	9	7	73
124	Norway	1,059	9,007	2	21	8	11	59
125	Sweden	4,143	39,320	2	11	9	19	60
126	Japan	8,851	184,917	1	4	20	31	45
127	Switzerland	3,568	48,409	5	22	10	3	60
	World	**126,774** *t*	**1,837,698** *t*	**9** *w*	**12** *w*	**12** *w*	**17** *w*	**50** *w*
	Fuel exporters	**290** *t*	**7,401** *t*	**15** *w*	**23** *w*	**3** *w*	**3** *w*	**56** *w*

Note: Data cover high-income OECD countries only.   a. Data are for the South African Customs Union comprising South Africa, Namibia, Lesotho, Botswana, and Swaziland; trade among the component territories is excluded.   b. Excludes the Canal Zone.   c. Includes Luxembourg.

Table 18. Balance of payments and reserves

		Current account balance (millions of dollars)				Net workers' remittances (millions of dollars)		Gross international reserves		
		After official transfers		Before official transfers				Millions of dollars		Months of import coverage
		1970	1991	1970	1991	1970	1991	1970	1991	1991
	Low-income economies							3,907 *t*	86,647 *t*	5.1 *w*
	China and India							1,023 *t*	55,781 *t*	7.9 *w*
	Other low-income							2,884 *t*	30,866 *t*	3.1 *w*
1	Mozambique	..	−245[a]	..	−783	..	−30[a]	..	240	2.3
2	Tanzania	−36	−284[a]	−37	−832[a]	..	..	65	204	1.4
3	Ethiopia	−32	−222[a]	−43	−585[a]	..	201	72	106	1.0
4	Uganda	20	−182[a]	19	−393[a]	−5	..	57	59	1.0
5	Bhutan	..	17[a]	..	−36[a]	..	0	..	99	9.3
6	Guinea-Bissau	..	−19	..	−86	..	−2	..	..	..
7	Nepal	−1[a]	−320[a]	−25[a]	−380[a]	..	0[a]	94	451	5.9
8	Burundi	2[a]	−31[a]	−2[a]	−214[a]	..	..	15	147	5.0
9	Chad	2	−80	−33	−347	−6	−39	2	124	2.6
10	Madagascar	10	−192	−42	−318	−26	1	37	89	1.2
11	Sierra Leone	−16	−95	−20	−136	..	..	39	10	0.2
12	Bangladesh	−114[a]	−210[a]	−234[a]	−932[a]	0[a]	764[a]	..	1,308	4.0
13	Lao PDR	..	−52	..	−121	..	..	6	61	3.3
14	Malawi	−35	−184[a]	−46	−244[a]	−4	0	29	158	2.5
15	Rwanda	7	−34	−12	−194	−4	−11	8	110	3.7
16	Mali	−2	−37	−22	−344	−1	76	1	326	4.5
17	Burkina Faso	9	−90	−21	−426	16	79	36	350	4.8
18	Niger	0	−4	−32	−164	−3	−38	19	207	5.3
19	India	−385[a]	−3,026[a]	−591[a]	−3,477[a]	80	2,540[a]	1,023	7,616	3.3
20	Kenya	−49	−231	−86	−435	..	−2	220	145	0.6
21	Nigeria	−368	1,203	−412	470	..	12	223	4,678	4.4
22	China*	−81[a]	13,272	−81[a]	12,885	0[a]	189	..	48,165	10.1
23	Haiti	11	−11	4	−176	13	86	4	24	0.6
24	Benin	−3	−89	−23	−174	0	70	16	196	3.6
25	Central African Rep.	−12	−80[a]	−24	−219[a]	−4	−36	1	107	4.4
26	Ghana	−68	−220[a]	−76	−442[a]	−9	0	43	644	4.4
27	Pakistan	−667	−1,558	−705	−2,171	86	1,848	195	1,220	1.2
28	Togo	3	−83	−14	−170	−3	5	35	369	5.0
29	Guinea	..	−236[a]	..	−329[a]	..	0	..	..	..
30	Nicaragua	−40	−5	−43	−849	..	10	49	..	..
31	Sri Lanka	−59	−268	−71	−472	3	442	43	724	2.5
32	Mauritania	−5	−125	−13	−209	−6	0	3	72	1.2
33	Yemen, Rep.	..	22[a]	..	−106[a]	..	800[a]	..	..	..
34	Honduras	−64	−220	−68	−368	..	0	20	112	1.0
35	Lesotho	18[a]	63	−1[a]	−443	29[a]	0	..	115	1.3
36	Indonesia	−310	−4,080	−376	−4,212	..	130	160	10,358	3.3
37	Egypt, Arab Rep.	−148	2,404[a]	−452	−2,438[a]	29	3,755[a]	165	6,185	4.4
38	Zimbabwe	−14[a]	−552[a]	−26[a]	−693[a]	..	0	59	295	1.4
39	*Sudan*	−42	−1,652[a]	−43	−1,857[a]	..	62[a]	22	8	0.0
40	*Zambia*	108	1[a]	107	−487[a]	−48	0	515	186	1.4
	Middle-income economies							23,267 *t*	241,422 *t*	3.6 *w*
	Lower-middle-income							13,049 *t*	103,643 *t*	3.6 *w*
41	Bolivia	4	−262	2	−422	..	−1	46	422	3.7
42	Côte d'Ivoire	−38	−1,451	−73	−1,614	−56	−491	119	29	0.1
43	Senegal	−16	−133	−66	−503	−16	32	22	23	0.1
44	Philippines	−48	−1,034	−138	−1,388	..	329	255	4,436	3.3
45	Papua New Guinea	−89[a]	−838[a]	−239[a]	−1,053[a]	..	57[a]	..	345	1.6
46	Cameroon	−30	−658[a]	−47	−658[a]	−11	3[a]	81	43	0.2
47	Guatemala	−8	−184	−8	−186	..	123	79	881	4.8
48	Dominican Rep.	−102	−58	−103	−115	25	330	32	448	2.2
49	Ecuador	−113	−467	−122	−577	..	0	76	1,081	3.2
50	Morocco	−124	−396	−161	−676	27	1,973	142	3,349	4.5
51	Jordan	−20	−712[a]	−130	−876[a]	..	450[a]	258	1,105	3.4
52	Tajikistan	..	..	..	..	..	..	..	..	..
53	Peru	202	−1,478	146	−1,794	..	..	339	3,090	6.1
54	El Salvador	9	−168	7	−369	..	468	64	453	3.1
55	Congo	−45[a]	−169	−53[a]	−231	−3[a]	−53[a]	9	9	0.1
56	Syrian Arab Rep.	−69	*1,827*	−72	*1,747*	7	375	57	..	..
57	Colombia	−293	2,349	−333	2,363	6	866	207	6,335	8.6
58	Paraguay	−16	−476[a]	−19	−476[a]	..	0	18	974	5.2
59	Uzbekistan	..	..	..	..	..	..	..	..	..
60	Jamaica	−153	−198	−149	−303	29	144	139	106	0.5
61	Romania	*−23*	−1,184	*−23*	−1,306	..	..	..	1,219	2.4
62	Namibia	..	82[a]	..	−257[a]	..	..	..	..	..
63	Tunisia	−53	−191	−88	−322	20	562	60	866	1.6
64	Kyrgyzstan	..	..	..	..	..	..	..	..	..
65	Thailand	−250	−7,564	−296	−7,609	..	0	911	18,393	4.8
66	Georgia	..	..	..	..	..	..	..	..	..
*	Data for Taiwan, China, are:	1	12,015	2	12,036	..	..	627	74,548	11.2

Note: For data comparability and coverage, see the technical notes.   Figures in italics are for years other than those specified.

		Current account balance (millions of dollars)				Net workers' remittances (millions of dollars)		Gross international reserves		
		After official transfers		Before official transfers				Millions of dollars		Months of import coverage
		1970	1991	1970	1991	1970	1991	1970	1991	1991
67	Azerbaijan	..	..	..	..	..	..	..	..	..
68	Turkmenistan	..	..	..	..	..	..	..	..	..
69	Turkey	−44	272	−57	−1,973	273	2,819	440	6,616	2.9
70	Poland	..	−1,282	..	−2,191	..	0	..	3,800	2.1
71	Bulgaria	..	−718[a]	..	−718[a]			..	..	..
72	Costa Rica	−74	−82	−77	−165	..	0	16	931	4.5
73	Algeria	−125	2,555[a]	−163	2,555[a]	178	274	352	3,460	3.5
74	Panama	−64	135	−79	−105	..	..	16	499	0.9
75	Armenia	..	..	..	..	..	0	..	..	
76	Chile	−91	142	−95	−158	..	..	392	7,700	7.8
77	Iran, Islamic Rep.	−507	−7,806[a]	−511	−7,806[a]	..	..	217	..	..
78	Moldova	..	..	..	..	..	..	..	..	..
79	Ukraine	..	..	..	..	..	..	46	915	5.5
80	Mauritius	8	−37	5	−39	..	0	..	..	
81	Czechoslovakia	146	947[a]	156	961[a]	..	0	..	4,176	3.8
82	Kazakhstan	..	..	..	..	..	0	..	..	
83	Malaysia	8	−4,530	2	−4,617	..	0	667	11,717	3.2
								10,219 t	137,779 t	3.6 w
Upper-middle-income										
84	Botswana	−30	47	−35	−251	−9	0	..	3,772	17.6
85	South Africa	−1,215	2,664	−1,253	2,696	..	..	1,057	3,187	1.5
86	Lithuania	..	..	..	370[a]	..	..	..	4,028	3.7
87	Hungary	..	403[a]	..	370[a]	..	..	1,047	14,719	10.8
88	Venezuela	−104	1,663	−98	1,696	−87	−661	682	8,073	5.5
89	Argentina	−163	−2,832	−160	−2,832	..	..	186	1,146	5.9
90	Uruguay	−45	105	−55	65	..	..	1,190	8,749	2.7
91	Brazil	−837	−3,071[a]	−861	−3,071[a]	..	0	756	18,052	3.7
92	Mexico	−1,068	−13,282	−1,098	−13,468	..	1,853	..	..	..
93	Belarus	..	..	..	..	..	..	..	..	..
94	Russian Federation	..	..	..	..	..	..	..	..	..
95	Latvia	..	..	..	..	..	..	..	..	..
96	Trinidad and Tobago	−109	−17	−104	−20	3	5	43	358	1.9
97	Gabon	−3	−160	−15	−185	−8	−125	15	332	1.6
98	Estonia	..	..	..	..	..	..	..	..	..
99	Portugal	−158[a]	−716	−158[a]	−2,098	504[a]	4,517	1,565	26,239	10.5
100	Oman	..	1,095	..	1,153	..	−845	13	1,765	5.5
101	Puerto Rico	..	..	..	..	..	..	..	..	..
102	Korea, Rep.	−623	−8,726	−706	−8,553	..	..	610	13,815	1.8
103	Greece	−422	−1,521	−424	−5,555	333	2,115	318	6,400	3.5
104	Saudi Arabia	71	−25,738	152	−19,250	−183	−13,746	670	13,298	2.4
105	*Yugoslavia*	−372	−1,161	−378	−1,159	441	2,024	143	3,360	2.0
Low- and middle-income								27,175 t	328,069 t	4.0 w
Sub-Saharan Africa								2,028 t	14,735 t	3.0 w
East Asia & Pacific								2,983 t	108,057 t	4.3 w
South Asia								1,404 t	12,018 t	2.8 w
Europe and Central Asia								9,699 t	71,987 t	4.3 w
Middle East & N. Africa								4,477 t	43,101 t	3.0 w
Latin America & Caribbean								5,527 t	74,986 t	4.6 w
Severely indebted								11,726 t	66,599 t	3.3 w
High-income economies								71,762 t	851,061 t	2.7 w
OECD members								69,820 t	797,852 t	2.6 w
106	Ireland	−198	921	−228	−1,761	..	..	698	5,867	2.1
107	†Israel	−562	−822	−766	−5,257	..	..	452	6,428	3.0
108	New Zealand	−232	−20	−222	30	16	245	258	2,950	2.6
109	Spain	79	−15,954	79	−19,810	469	1,603	1,851	71,345	7.1
110	†Hong Kong	225	2,487	225	2,487	..	..	..	..	..
111	†Singapore	−572	4,208	−585	4,350	..	..	1,012	34,133	5.4
112	United Kingdom	1,970	−11,438	2,376	−9,575	..	..	2,764	48,373	1.5
113	Australia	−785	−9,853	−691	−9,655	..	..	1,709	19,339	3.4
114	Italy	798	−21,454	1,094	−16,670	446	779	5,547	72,254	3.3
115	Netherlands	−489	8,760	−513	11,950	−51	−315	3,362	33,335	2.4
116	Belgium[b]	717	4,731	904	6,201	38	−274	1,806	17,415	2.7
117	Austria	−75	−252	−73	−144	−7	367	5,199	60,227	2.0
118	France	−204	−6,148	18	−1,194	−641	−1,786	4,733	20,836	1.4
119	Canada	1,008	−25,529	960	−24,600	..	..	15,237	159,273	2.6
120	United States	2,330	−3,690	4,680	−24,670	−650	−7,600	13,879	96,657	2.3
121	Germany[c]	837	−19,497	1,839	9,978	−1,366	−4,213	488	7,990	1.7
122	Denmark	−544	2,167	−510	2,513	..	..	455	8,317	2.8
123	Finland	−240	−6,695	−233	−5,998	..	−140	813	13,651	3.7
124	Norway	−242	4,939	−200	6,125	..	20	775	20,477	3.0
125	Sweden	−265	−3,243	−160	−1,636	..	..	..	..	..
126	Japan	1,990	72,905	2,170	84,740	..	..	4,876	80,626	2.4
127	Switzerland	161	9,847	203	10,307	−313	−2,062	5,317	58,451	6.5
World								98,937 t	1,179,130 t	3.0 w
Fuel exporters								4,693 t	52,194 t	3.9 w

a. World Bank estimate.   b. Includes Luxembourg.   c. Data prior to July 1990 refer to the Federal Republic of Germany before unification.

Table 19. Official development assistance from OECD and OPEC members

OECD: Total net flows[a]	1965	1970	1975	1980	1985	1988	1989	1990	1991
				Millions of US dollars					
106 Ireland	0	0	8	30	39	57	49	57	72
108 New Zealand	..	14	66	72	54	104	87	95	100
112 United Kingdom	472	500	904	1,854	1,530	2,645	2,587	2,638	3,348
113 Australia	119	212	552	667	749	1,101	1,020	955	1,050
114 Italy	60	147	182	683	1,098	3,193	3,613	3,395	3,352
115 Netherlands	70	196	608	1,630	1,136	2,331	2,094	2,592	2,517
116 Belgium	102	120	378	595	440	601	703	889	831
117 Austria	10	11	79	178	248	301	283	394	548
118 France	752	971	2,093	4,162	3,995	6,865	7,450	9,380	7,484
119 Canada	96	337	880	1,075	1,631	2,347	2,320	2,470	2,604
120 United States	4,023	3,153	4,161	7,138	9,403	10,141	7,676	11,394	11,362
121 Germany[b]	456	599	1,689	3,567	2,942	4,731	4,949	6,320	6,890
122 Denmark	13	59	205	481	440	922	937	1,171	1,300
123 Finland	2	7	48	110	211	608	706	846	930
124 Norway	11	37	184	486	574	985	917	1,305	1,178
125 Sweden	38	117	566	962	840	1,534	1,799	2,012	2,116
126 Japan	244	458	1,148	3,353	3,797	9,134	8,965	9,069	10,952
127 Switzerland	12	30	104	253	302	617	558	750	863
Total	6,480	6,968	13,855	27,396	29,429	48,114	46,713	55,632	55,519
				As a percentage of donor GNP					
106 Ireland	0.00	0.00	0.09	0.16	0.24	0.20	0.17	0.16	0.19
108 New Zealand	..	0.23	0.52	0.33	0.25	0.27	0.22	0.23	0.25
112 United Kingdom	0.47	0.41	0.39	0.35	0.33	0.32	0.31	0.27	0.32
113 Australia	0.53	0.59	0.65	0.48	0.48	0.46	0.38	0.34	0.38
114 Italy	0.10	0.16	0.11	0.15	0.26	0.39	0.42	0.32	0.30
115 Netherlands	0.36	0.61	0.75	0.97	0.91	0.98	0.94	0.94	0.88
116 Belgium	0.60	0.46	0.59	0.50	0.55	0.39	0.46	0.45	0.42
117 Austria	0.11	0.07	0.21	0.23	0.38	0.24	0.23	0.25	0.34
118 France	0.76	0.66	0.62	0.63	0.78	0.72	0.78	0.79	0.62
119 Canada	0.19	0.41	0.54	0.43	0.49	0.50	0.44	0.44	0.45
120 United States	0.58	0.32	0.27	0.27	0.24	0.21	0.15	0.21	0.20
121 Germany[b]	0.40	0.32	0.40	0.44	0.47	0.39	0.41	0.42	0.41
122 Denmark	0.13	0.38	0.58	0.74	0.80	0.89	0.93	0.93	0.96
123 Finland	0.02	0.06	0.18	0.22	0.40	0.59	0.63	0.64	0.76
124 Norway	0.16	0.32	0.66	0.87	1.01	1.13	1.05	1.17	1.14
125 Sweden	0.19	0.38	0.82	0.78	0.86	0.86	0.96	0.90	0.92
126 Japan	0.27	0.23	0.23	0.32	0.29	0.32	0.31	0.31	0.32
127 Switzerland	0.09	0.15	0.19	0.24	0.31	0.32	0.30	0.31	0.36
				National currencies					
106 Ireland (millions of pounds)	0	0	4	15	37	37	34	35	41
108 New Zealand (millions of dollars)	..	13	55	74	109	158	146	160	185
112 United Kingdom (millions of pounds)	169	208	409	798	1,180	1,485	1,577	1,478	1,736
113 Australia (millions of dollars)	106	189	402	591	966	1,404	1,386	1,323	1,382
114 Italy (billions of lire)	38	92	119	585	2,097	4,156	4,958	4,068	3,859
115 Netherlands (millions of guilders)	253	710	1,538	3,341	3,773	4,410	4,440	4,720	4,306
116 Belgium (millions of francs)	5,100	6,000	13,902	17,399	26,145	22,088	27,714	29,720	26,050
117 Austria (millions of schillings)	260	286	1,376	2,303	5,132	3,722	3,737	4,477	5,861
118 France (millions of francs)	3,713	5,393	8,971	17,589	35,894	40,897	47,529	51,076	38,777
119 Canada (millions of dollars)	104	353	895	1,357	2,327	2,888	2,747	2,882	3,009
120 United States (millions of dollars)	4,023	3,153	4,161	7,138	9,403	10,141	7,676	11,394	11,362
121 Germany (millions of deutsche marks)[b]	1,824	2,192	4,155	6,484	8,661	8,319	9,302	10,311	10,446
122 Denmark (millions of kroner)	90	443	1,178	2,711	4,657	6,304	6,850	7,347	7,096
123 Finland (millions of markkaa)	6	29	177	414	1,308	2,542	3,031	3,336	3,845
124 Norway (millions of kroner)	79	264	962	2,400	4,946	6,418	6,335	7,542	7,037
125 Sweden (millions of kronor)	197	605	2,350	4,069	7,326	9,396	11,600	11,909	11,704
126 Japan (billions of yen)	88	165	341	760	749	1,171	1,336	1,313	1,371
127 Switzerland (millions of francs)	52	131	268	424	743	903	912	1,041	1,170

Summary

	1965	1970	1975	1980	1985	1988	1989	1990	1991
				Billions of US dollars					
ODA (current prices)	6.5	7.0	13.9	27.3	29.4	48.1	46.7	55.6	55.5
ODA (1987 prices)	28.2	25.3	29.8	36.8	39.4	44.9	43.6	47.6	45.7
GNP (current prices)	1,374.0	2,079.0	4,001.0	7,488.0	8,550.0	13,547.0	13,968.0	15,498.0	16,818.6
				Percent					
ODA as a percentage of GNP	0.47	0.34	0.35	0.35	0.34	0.34	0.32	0.33	0.33
				Index (1987 = 100)					
GDP deflator[c]	23.0	27.6	46.5	74.1	74.6	107.1	107.5	116.8	121.4

OECD: Total net bilateral flows to low-income economies[a]	1965	1970	1975	1980	1985	1986	1988	1989	1990	1991
	As a percentage of donor GNP									
106 Ireland	..	..	..	0.01	0.03	0.02	0.02	0.01	0.01	..
108 New Zealand	..	..	0.14	0.01	0.00	0.01	0.01	0.01	0.00	..
112 United Kingdom	0.23	0.09	0.11	0.10	0.07	0.07	0.06	0.07	0.05	..
113 Australia	0.08	0.00	0.10	0.07	0.04	0.04	0.04	0.06	0.05	..
114 Italy	0.04	0.06	0.01	0.00	0.06	0.12	0.17	0.12	0.09	..
115 Netherlands	0.08	0.24	0.24	0.32	0.23	0.28	0.27	0.23	0.25	..
116 Belgium	0.56	0.30	0.31	0.13	0.13	0.12	0.09	0.05	0.09	..
117 Austria	0.06	0.05	0.02	0.11	0.05	0.03	0.03	0.07	0.10	..
118 France	0.12	0.09	0.10	0.06	0.11	0.10	0.12	0.14	0.13	..
119 Canada	0.10	0.22	0.24	0.13	0.14	0.13	0.13	0.09	0.10	..
120 United States	0.26	0.14	0.08	0.06	0.06	0.04	0.03	0.02	0.05	..
121 Germany [b]	0.14	0.10	0.12	0.07	0.13	0.10	0.08	0.08	0.10	..
122 Denmark	0.02	0.10	0.20	0.17	0.26	0.23	0.25	0.26	0.24	..
123 Finland	..	..	0.06	0.03	0.09	0.10	0.24	0.22	0.17	..
124 Norway	0.04	0.12	0.25	0.28	0.34	0.43	0.37	0.32	0.37	..
125 Sweden	0.07	0.12	0.41	0.26	0.24	0.30	0.21	0.23	0.25	..
126 Japan	0.13	0.11	0.08	0.12	0.10	0.10	0.13	0.13	0.10	..
127 Switzerland	0.02	0.05	0.10	0.07	0.11	0.10	0.10	0.12	0.11	..
Total	0.20	0.13	0.11	0.08	0.08	0.08	0.09	0.08	0.09	..

OPEC: Total net flows[d]	1976	1980	1984	1985	1986	1987	1988	1989	1990	1991
	Millions of US dollars									
21 Nigeria	80	35	51	45	52	30	14	70	13	..
Qatar	180	277	10	8	18	0	4	-2	1	1
73 Algeria	11	81	52	54	114	39	13	40	7	5
77 Iran, Islamic Rep.	751	-72	52	-72	69	-10	39	-94	2	..
88 Venezuela	109	135	90	32	85	24	55	52	15	..
Iraq	123	864	-22	-32	-21	-35	-22	21	55	0
Libya	98	376	24	57	68	66	129	86	4	25
104 Saudi Arabia	2,791	5,682	3,194	2,630	3,517	2,888	2,048	1,171	3,692	1,704
United Arab Emirates	1,028	1,118	88	122	87	15	-17	2	888	558
Kuwait	706	1,140	1,020	771	715	316	108	169	1,666	387
Total OPEC [d]	5,877	9,636	4,559	3,615	4,704	3,333	2,369	1,514	6,341	..
Total OAPEC [e]	4,937	9,538	4,366	3,610	4,498	3,389	2,361	..	..	..
	As a percentage of donor GNP									
21 Nigeria	0.19	0.04	0.06	0.06	0.13	0.12	0.05	0.28	0.06	..
Qatar	7.35	4.16	0.18	0.12	0.36	0.00	0.08	-0.04	0.02	0.01
73 Algeria	0.07	0.20	0.10	0.10	0.19	0.07	0.03	0.11	0.03	0.01
77 Iran, Islamic Rep.	1.16	-0.08	0.03	-0.04	0.03	0.00	0.01	-0.02	..	..
88 Venezuela	0.35	0.23	0.16	0.06	0.14	0.06	0.09	0.13	0.03	..
Iraq	0.76	2.36	-0.05	-0.06	-0.05	-0.08	-0.04	0.04	..	..
Libya	0.66	1.16	0.10	0.24	0.30	0.30	0.63	0.41	0.01	0.09
104 Saudi Arabia	5.95	4.87	3.20	2.92	3.99	3.70	2.53	1.37	3.90	1.44
United Arab Emirates	8.95	4.06	0.32	0.45	0.41	0.07	-0.07	0.02	2.65	1.66
Kuwait	4.82	3.52	3.95	2.96	2.84	1.15	0.40	0.54	..	..
Total OPEC [d]	2.32	1.85	0.76	0.60	0.78	0.52	0.34	0.21	..	..
Total OAPEC [e]	4.23	3.22	1.60	1.39	1.80	1.10	0.86	..	..	..

a. Organization of Economic Cooperation and Development.   b. Data refer to the Federal Republic of Germany before unification.   c. See the technical notes.
d. Organization of Petroleum Exporting Countries.   e. Organization of Arab Petroleum Exporting Countries.

Table 20. Official development assistance: receipts

Net disbursement of ODA from all sources

	Millions of dollars							Per capita (dollars) 1991	As percentage of GNP 1991
	1985	1986	1987	1988	1989	1990	1991		
Low-income economies	17,432 t	19,484 t	21,412 t	24,513 t	24,763 t	30,653 t	31,921 t	10.2 w	3.0 w
China and India	2,532 t	3,254 t	3,300 t	4,086 t	4,048 t	3,605 t	4,701 t	2.3 w	0.8 w
Other low-income	14,900 t	16,230 t	18,112 t	20,427 t	20,715 t	27,047 t	27,220 t	24.5 w	6.6 w
1 Mozambique	300	422	651	893	772	935	920	57.0	69.2
2 Tanzania	484	681	882	982	920	1,141	1,076	42.7	39.2
3 Ethiopia	710	636	634	970	752	1,014	1,091	20.7	16.5
4 Uganda	180	198	280	363	443	551	525	31.1	19.5
5 Bhutan	24	40	42	42	42	48	64	43.8	25.9
6 Guinea-Bissau	58	71	111	99	101	117	101	101.3	48.2
7 Nepal	234	301	347	399	493	430	453	23.4	13.8
8 Burundi	139	187	202	189	199	265	253	44.7	21.8
9 Chad	181	165	198	264	241	303	262	44.9	20.2
10 Madagascar	185	316	321	304	321	386	437	36.3	16.4
11 Sierra Leone	65	87	68	102	100	65	105	24.7	12.9
12 Bangladesh	1,131	1,455	1,635	1,592	1,800	2,048	1,636	14.8	7.0
13 Lao PDR	37	48	58	77	140	152	131	30.8	12.8
14 Malawi	113	198	280	366	412	481	495	56.2	22.6
15 Rwanda	180	211	245	252	232	293	351	49.2	22.2
16 Mali	376	372	366	427	454	467	455	52.2	18.5
17 Burkina Faso	195	284	281	298	272	336	409	44.1	14.8
18 Niger	303	307	353	371	296	391	376	47.5	16.5
19 India	1,592	2,120	1,839	2,097	1,895	1,524	2,747	3.2	1.1
20 Kenya	430	455	572	808	967	1,053	873	34.9	10.6
21 Nigeria	1,032	59	69	120	346	250	262	2.6	0.8
22 China	940	1,134	1,462	1,989	2,153	2,081	1,954	1.7	0.5
23 Haiti	150	175	218	147	200	172	182	27.5	6.9
24 Benin	94	138	138	162	263	271	256	52.4	13.6
25 Central African Rep.	104	139	176	196	192	244	174	56.5	13.8
26 Ghana	196	371	373	474	550	498	724	47.2	11.3
27 Pakistan	769	970	879	1,408	1,129	1,149	1,226	10.6	2.7
28 Togo	111	174	126	199	183	241	204	54.0	12.5
29 Guinea	115	175	213	262	346	296	371	63.1	12.6
30 Nicaragua	102	150	141	213	225	320	826	217.8	12.0
31 Sri Lanka	468	570	502	598	547	674	814	47.4	8.8
32 Mauritania	207	225	185	184	242	202	208	102.9	18.4
33 Yemen, Rep.	392	328	422	304	370	405	313	25.0	3.9
34 Honduras	270	283	258	321	242	450	275	52.2	9.1
35 Lesotho	93	88	107	108	127	139	123	67.9	18.9
36 Indonesia	603	711	1,246	1,632	1,839	1,724	1,854	10.2	1.6
37 Egypt, Arab Rep.	1,760	1,716	1,773	1,537	1,568	5,444	4,988	93.1	15.2
38 Zimbabwe	237	225	294	273	265	340	393	39.0	6.2
39 *Sudan*	1,128	945	898	937	772	825	887	34.3	. .
40 *Zambia*	322	464	430	478	392	486	884	106.3	. .
Middle-income economies	9,037 t	9,439 t	10,430 t	9,621 t	10,013 t	15,412 t	15,500 t	16.2 w	0.7 w
Lower-middle-income	7,049 t	8,087 t	9,027 t	8,257 t	8,533 t	13,629 t	13,639 t	24.3 w	1.8 w
41 Bolivia	197	322	318	394	440	506	473	64.4	9.4
42 Côte d'Ivoire	117	186	254	439	403	693	633	51.2	6.6
43 Senegal	289	567	641	569	650	788	577	75.7	10.0
44 Philippines	460	956	770	854	844	1,279	1,051	16.7	2.3
45 Papua New Guinea	257	263	322	380	339	416	397	100.1	10.6
46 Cameroon	153	224	213	284	458	431	501	42.2	4.3
47 Guatemala	83	135	241	235	261	203	197	20.8	2.1
48 Dominican Rep.	207	93	130	118	142	100	66	9.1	0.9
49 Ecuador	136	147	203	137	160	155	220	20.4	1.9
50 Morocco	766	403	447	480	450	1,026	1,075	41.9	3.9
51 Jordan	538	564	577	417	273	884	905	247.1	22.0
52 Tajikistan	. .	. .	. .	. .	. .	. .	. .		
53 Peru	316	272	292	272	305	395	590	26.9	1.2
54 El Salvador	345	341	426	420	443	349	290	54.9	4.9
55 Congo	69	110	152	89	91	214	133	56.8	4.6
56 Syrian Arab Rep.	610	728	684	191	127	684	373	29.8	2.2
57 Colombia	62	63	78	61	67	88	123	3.8	0.3
58 Paraguay	50	66	81	76	92	56	144	32.6	2.3
59 Uzbekistan	. .	. .	. .	. .	. .	. .	. .		
60 Jamaica	169	178	168	193	262	273	166	69.7	4.7
61 Romania	. .	. .	. .	. .	. .	. .	. .		
62 Namibia	6	15	17	22	59	123	184	124.0	8.1
63 Tunisia	163	222	274	316	283	393	322	39.1	2.5
64 Kyrgyzstan	. .	. .	. .	. .	. .	. .	. .		
65 Thailand	459	496	504	563	739	802	722	12.6	0.8
66 Georgia	. .	. .	. .	. .	. .	. .	. .		

Note: For data comparability and coverage, see the technical notes. Figures in italics are for years other than those specified.

		Net disbursement of ODA from all sources							Per capita (dollars)	As percentage of GNP
		Millions of dollars							1991	1991
		1985	1986	1987	1988	1989	1990	1991		
67	Azerbaijan	..	..	..	..	..	..	..	..	..
68	Turkmenistan	..	..	..	..	..	..	..	..	..
69	Turkey	179	339	376	267	140	1,219	1,675	29.2	1.6
70	Poland	..	..	..	..	..	..	..	..	..
71	Bulgaria	..	..	..	..	..	..	..	..	..
72	Costa Rica	280	196	228	187	226	227	173	56.4	3.1
73	Algeria	173	165	214	171	152	217	310	12.1	0.7
74	Panama	69	52	40	22	18	93	101	40.9	1.8
75	Armenia	..	..	..	..	61	102	120	9.0	0.4
76	Chile	40	−5	21	44	61	102	120	9.0	0.4
77	Iran, Islamic Rep.	16	27	71	82	96	105	194	3.4	0.2
78	Moldova	..	..	..	..	..	..	..	..	..
79	Ukraine	..	..	..	..	..	..	..	..	..
80	Mauritius	27	56	65	59	58	89	67	61.8	2.5
81	Czechoslovakia	..	..	..	..	..	..	..	..	..
82	Kazakhstan	..	..	..	..	..	..	..	..	..
83	Malaysia	229	192	363	104	140	469	289	15.9	0.6
Upper-middle-income		**1,988 _t_**	**1,353 _t_**	**1,403 _t_**	**1,365 _t_**	**1,480 _t_**	**1,783 _t_**	**1,862 _t_**	**4.7 _w_**	**0.1 _w_**
84	Botswana	96	102	156	151	160	149	135	102.5	3.7
85	South Africa	..	..	..	..	..	..	..	..	..
86	Lithuania	..	..	..	..	..	..	..	..	..
87	Hungary	..	..	..	..	..	79	33	1.7	0.1
88	Venezuela	11	16	19	18	21	79	33	1.7	0.1
89	Argentina	39	88	99	152	211	171	253	7.7	0.2
90	Uruguay	5	27	18	41	38	47	51	16.3	0.5
91	Brazil	123	178	289	210	206	167	182	1.2	0.0
92	Mexico	144	252	155	173	86	141	185	2.2	0.1
93	Belarus	..	..	..	..	..	..	..	..	..
94	Russian Federation	..	..	..	..	..	..	..	..	..
95	Latvia	..	..	..	..	..	..	..	..	..
96	Trinidad and Tobago	7	19	34	9	6	18	−2	−1.3	0.0
97	Gabon	61	79	82	106	133	132	142	121.4	2.9
98	Estonia	..	..	..	..	..	..	..	..	..
99	Portugal	..	..	..	..	..	..	..	..	..
100	Oman	78	84	16	1	18	66	14	8.8	0.1
101	Puerto Rico	..	..	..	..	..	..	..	..	..
102	Korea, Rep.	−9	−18	11	10	52	52	54	1.3	0.0
103	Greece	11	19	35	35	30	37	39	3.8	0.1
104	Saudi Arabia	29	31	22	19	36	44	45	2.9	0.0
105	_Yugoslavia_	11	19	35	44	43	47	159	6.6	..
Low- and middle-income		**26,469 _t_**	**29,155 _t_**	**32,027 _t_**	**34,286 _t_**	**34,934 _t_**	**46,127 _t_**	**47,453 _t_**	**11.6 _w_**	**1.5 _w_**
Sub-Saharan Africa		**9,522 _t_**	**10,587 _t_**	**11,926 _t_**	**13,470 _t_**	**13,848 _t_**	**16,538 _t_**	**16,158 _t_**	**33.1 _w_**	**10.0 _w_**
East Asia & Pacific		**4,881 _t_**	**4,955 _t_**	**5,935 _t_**	**6,869 _t_**	**7,251 _t_**	**8,007 _t_**	**7,594 _t_**	**4.5 _w_**	**0.7 _w_**
South Asia		**4,244 _t_**	**5,474 _t_**	**5,307 _t_**	**6,236 _t_**	**6,101 _t_**	**6,030 _t_**	**7,488 _t_**	**6.5 _w_**	**2.1 _w_**
Europe and Central Asia		**247 _t_**	**403 _t_**	**458 _t_**	**359 _t_**	**207 _t_**	**1,307 _t_**	**1,896 _t_**	**20.6 _w_**	**1.0 _w_**
Middle East & N. Africa		**4,710 _t_**	**4,474 _t_**	**4,700 _t_**	**3,670 _t_**	**3,517 _t_**	**9,747 _t_**	**9,300 _t_**	**38.1 _w_**	**2.3 _w_**
Latin America & Caribbean		**3,024 _t_**	**3,262 _t_**	**3,701 _t_**	**3,682 _t_**	**4,010 _t_**	**4,498 _t_**	**5,017 _t_**	**11.4 _w_**	**0.5 _w_**
Severely indebted		**3,633 _t_**	**3,851 _t_**	**4,166 _t_**	**3,544 _t_**	**3,373 _t_**	**5,976 _t_**	**6,488 _t_**	**14.9 _w_**	**0.6 _w_**
High-income economies		**2,232 _t_**	**2,306 _t_**	**1,746 _t_**	**1,655 _t_**	**1,667 _t_**	**1,804 _t_**	**2,150 _t_**	**55.3 _w_**	**0.4 _w_**
OECD members		..	..	..	..	..	..	..	..	..
106	Ireland	..	..	..	..	..	..	..	..	..
107	†Israel	1,978	1,937	1,251	1,241	1,192	1,372	1,749	353.6	2.8
108	New Zealand	..	..	..	..	..	..	..	..	..
109	Spain	..	..	..	..	..	..	..	..	..
110	†Hong Kong	20	18	19	22	40	38	36	6.3	0.0
111	†Singapore	24	29	23	22	95	−3	8	2.8	0.0
112	United Kingdom	..	..	..	..	..	..	..	..	..
113	Australia	..	..	..	..	..	..	..	..	..
114	Italy	..	..	..	..	..	..	..	..	..
115	Netherlands	..	..	..	..	..	..	..	..	..
116	Belgium	..	..	..	..	..	..	..	..	..
117	Austria	..	..	..	..	..	..	..	..	..
118	France	..	..	..	..	..	..	..	..	..
119	Canada	..	..	..	..	..	..	..	..	..
120	United States	..	..	..	..	..	..	..	..	..
121	Germany	..	..	..	..	..	..	..	..	..
122	Denmark	..	..	..	..	..	..	..	..	..
123	Finland	..	..	..	..	..	..	..	..	..
124	Norway	..	..	..	..	..	..	..	..	..
125	Sweden	..	..	..	..	..	..	..	..	..
126	Japan	..	..	..	..	..	..	..	..	..
127	Switzerland	..	..	..	..	..	..	..	..	..
World		**28,701 _t_**	**31,461 _t_**	**33,773 _t_**	**35,491 _t_**	**36,601 _t_**	**47,931 _t_**	**49,603 _t_**	**12.0 _w_**	**1.4 _w_**
Fuel exporters		**1,606 _t_**	**805 _t_**	**1,033 _t_**	**781 _t_**	**1,076 _t_**	**1,468 _t_**	**1,948 _t_**	**7.5 _w_**	**0.3 _w_**

Table 21. Total external debt

		Long-term debt (millions of dollars)		Use of IMF credit (millions of dollars)		Short-term debt (millions of dollars)		Total external debt (millions of dollars)		Total arrears on LDOD (millions of dollars)		Ratio of present value to nominal value of debt
		1980	1991	1980	1991	1980	1991	1980	1991	1980	1991	1991
Low-income economies **China and India** **Other low-income**												
1	Mozambique	0	4,055	0	118	0	527	0	4,700	0	1,442	82.7
2	Tanzania	1,999	5,798	171	143	306	519	2,476	6,460	3	1,257	74.7
3	Ethiopia	669	3,301	79	0	57	174	804	3,475	1	388	68.9
4	Uganda	542	2,325	89	330	64	175	695	2,830	20	470	63.2
5	Bhutan	0	86	0	0	0	1	0	87	0	0	58.4
6	Guinea-Bissau	128	574	1	5	5	74	134	653	1	89	69.6
7	Nepal	156	1,705	42	39	7	26	205	1,769	0	12	46.8
8	Burundi	118	899	36	49	12	13	166	961	0	0	47.7
9	Chad	204	547	14	31	11	29	229	606	6	18	48.0
10	Madagascar	892	3,381	87	127	244	208	1,223	3,715	6	366	71.6
11	Sierra Leone	323	642	59	101	53	547	435	1,291	7	396	84.8
12	Bangladesh	3,417	12,103	424	727	212	221	4,053	13,051	0	18	49.1
13	Lao PDR	277	1,096	16	21	1	4	295	1,121	1	1	26.8
14	Malawi	625	1,530	80	115	116	31	821	1,676	3	7	49.8
15	Rwanda	150	780	14	13	26	52	190	845	0	19	49.5
16	Mali	669	2,392	39	60	24	79	732	2,531	1	164	58.3
17	Burkina Faso	281	871	15	9	35	76	330	956	0	37	59.9
18	Niger	687	1,503	16	73	159	77	863	1,653	0	77	65.5
19	India	18,709	64,315	977	3,451	926	3,791	20,611	71,557	0	0	78.9
20	Kenya	2,557	5,776	254	493	638	744	3,449	7,014	0	108	77.3
21	Nigeria	5,381	33,588	0	0	3,553	909	8,934	34,497	0	1,353	97.1
22	China	4,504	50,502	0	0	0	10,300	4,504	60,802	0	0	92.6
23	Haiti	242	610	46	33	14	105	303	747	0	57	56.5
24	Benin	334	1,221	16	22	73	57	424	1,300	5	38	53.6
25	Central African Rep.	147	803	24	33	25	48	195	884	11	53	55.6
26	Ghana	1,171	2,992	105	834	131	384	1,407	4,209	5	77	63.9
27	Pakistan	8,525	17,745	674	1,068	737	4,157	9,936	22,969	0	0	74.8
28	Togo	899	1,143	33	79	113	134	1,045	1,356	8	25	66.8
29	Guinea	1,004	2,401	35	55	71	170	1,110	2,626	20	306	70.4
30	Nicaragua	1,661	8,703	49	24	466	1,718	2,176	10,446	6	3,743	89.3
31	Sri Lanka	1,231	5,758	391	401	220	394	1,841	6,553	0	0	60.8
32	Mauritania	718	1,912	62	57	65	330	844	2,299	10	335	77.1
33	Yemen, Rep.	1,453	5,207	48	0	183	1,264	1,684	6,471	1	1,597	83.5
34	Honduras	1,165	2,940	33	34	272	203	1,470	3,177	0	270	83.8
35	Lesotho	57	406	6	18	8	4	71	428	0	7	55.6
36	Indonesia	18,169	59,960	0	166	2,775	13,503	20,944	73,629	0	1	92.3
37	Egypt, Arab Rep.	16,477	36,978	411	127	4,027	3,466	20,915	40,571	383	1,739	52.8
38	Zimbabwe	696	2,868	0	0	90	561	786	3,429	0	0	88.1
39	*Sudan*	4,147	9,717	431	961	585	5,229	5,163	15,907	49	9,620	90.4
40	Zambia	2,227	4,958	447	918	586	1,403	3,261	7,279	6	1,268	86.0
Middle-income economies **Lower-middle-income**												
41	Bolivia	2,274	3,675	126	245	300	155	2,700	4,075	0	36	75.8
42	Côte d'Ivoire	4,724	15,167	65	372	1,059	3,308	5,848	18,847	0	3,426	92.9
43	Senegal	1,114	2,890	140	327	219	305	1,473	3,522	0	29	69.2
44	Philippines	8,817	25,893	1,044	1,086	7,556	4,919	17,417	31,897	0	101	96.7
45	Papua New Guinea	624	2,566	31	61	64	128	719	2,755	0	21	90.6
46	Cameroon	2,183	5,254	59	121	271	903	2,513	6,278	2	657	89.3
47	Guatemala	831	2,230	0	64	335	411	1,166	2,704	0	565	90.6
48	Dominican Rep.	1,473	3,554	49	89	480	849	2,002	4,492	7	1,314	92.1
49	Ecuador	4,422	10,094	0	182	1,575	2,192	5,997	12,469	0	3,654	97.6
50	Morocco	8,475	20,332	457	574	778	312	9,710	21,219	3	739	92.0
51	Jordan	1,486	7,570	0	95	486	977	1,972	8,641	6	1,134	91.5
52	Tajikistan	. .	. .	. .	. .	. .	. .	. .	. .	. .	. .	. .
53	Peru	6,828	15,298	474	706	2,084	4,705	9,386	20,709	0	7,852	92.6
54	El Salvador	659	2,070	32	0	220	102	911	2,172	0	16	74.8
55	Congo	1,257	3,989	22	6	246	749	1,526	4,744	3	1,010	86.1
56	Syrian Arab Rep.	2,918	14,932	0	0	631	1,882	3,549	16,815	0	1,426	72.1
57	Colombia	4,604	15,617	0	0	2,337	1,752	6,941	17,369	0	167	100.4
58	Paraguay	780	1,799	0	0	174	377	954	2,177	0	532	90.8
59	Uzbekistan	. .	. .	. .	. .	. .	. .	. .	. .	. .	. .	. .
60	Jamaica	1,496	3,779	309	391	98	286	1,904	4,456	0	353	91.2
61	Romania	7,131	334	328	809	2,303	770	9,762	1,913	0	0	99.7
62	Namibia	. .	. .	. .	. .	. .	. .	. .	. .	. .	. .	. .
63	Tunisia	3,390	7,369	0	258	136	670	3,526	8,296	0	78	90.1
64	Kyrgyzstan	. .	. .	. .	. .	. .	. .	. .	. .	. .	. .	. .
65	Thailand	5,646	23,336	348	0	2,303	12,492	8,297	35,828	0	0	95.2
66	Georgia	. .	. .	. .	. .	. .	. .	. .	. .	. .	. .	. .

Note: For data comparability and coverage, see the technical notes.   Figures in italics are for years other than those specified.

		Long-term debt (millions of dollars)		Use of IMF credit (millions of dollars)		Short-term debt (millions of dollars)		Total external debt (millions of dollars)		Total arrears on LDOD (millions of dollars)		Ratio of present value to nominal value of debt
		1980	1991	1980	1991	1980	1991	1980	1991	1980	1991	1991
67	Azerbaijan	..	..	..	..	..	..	..	..	..	..	..
68	Turkmenistan	..	..	..	..	..	..	..	..	0	0	95.4
69	Turkey	15,575	41,135	1,054	0	2,490	9,117	19,120	50,252	0	0	101.6
70	Poland	6,594	44,057	0	853	2,300	7,571	8,894	52,481	300	11,296	97.1
71	Bulgaria	272	11,023	0	414	0	487	272	11,923	0	2,673	
72	Costa Rica	2,112	3,620	57	83	575	340	2,744	4,043	0	219	91.7
73	Algeria	17,034	26,557	0	995	2,325	1,084	19,359	28,636	0	0	98.1
74	Panama	2,271	3,939	23	216	680	2,637	2,974	6,791	0	3,265	98.2
75	Armenia	..	..	..	..	..	..	..	..	0	1	99.9
76	Chile	9,399	14,744	123	958	2,560	2,200	12,081	17,902			
77	Iran, Islamic Rep.	4,508	2,736	0	0	0	8,775	4,508	11,511	0	1,944	100.2
78	Moldova	..	..	..	..	..	..	..	..	..	..	..
79	Ukraine	..	..	..	..	..	..	..	..			
80	Mauritius	318	961	102	0	47	31	467	991	0	17	87.2
81	Czechoslovakia	0	5,845	0	1,313	3,989	2,635	3,989	9,793	0	4	99.3
82	Kazakhstan	..	..	..	..	..	..	..	..	..	..	97.5
83	Malaysia	5,256	18,753	0	0	1,355	2,692	6,611	21,445	0	0	
	Upper-middle-income											
84	Botswana	129	536	0	0	4	7	133	543	0	9	83.8
85	South Africa	..	..	..	..	..	..	..	..	..	..	..
86	Lithuania	..	..	..	..	..	..	..	..	0	0	100.3
87	Hungary	6,416	19,221	0	1,259	3,347	2,177	9,764	22,658	0	0	99.0
88	Venezuela	13,795	28,839	0	3,249	15,550	2,284	29,345	34,372	15	0	
89	Argentina	16,774	47,188	0	2,483	10,383	14,036	27,157	63,707	0	13,818	103.9
90	Uruguay	1,338	3,128	0	58	322	1,003	1,660	4,189	0	0	99.4
91	Brazil	57,500	95,130	0	1,238	13,546	20,147	71,046	116,514	20	10,832	99.9
92	Mexico	41,215	83,891	0	6,766	16,163	11,080	57,378	101,737	0	0	96.9
93	Belarus	..	..	..	..	..	..	..	..	..	..	..
94	Russian Federation	..	..	..	..	..	..	..	..	..	..	..
95	Latvia	..	..	..	..	..	..	..	..	0	33	97.8
96	Trinidad and Tobago	713	1,817	0	385	116	130	829	2,332	0	466	95.7
97	Gabon	1,271	2,935	15	121	228	787	1,513	3,842			
98	Estonia	..	..	..	..	..	..	..	..	..	..	..
99	Portugal	7,215	20,170	119	0	2,395	8,398	9,729	28,568	0	0	97.0
100	Oman	436	2,270	0	0	163	427	599	2,697	0	0	96.7
101	Puerto Rico	..	..	..	..	..	..	..	..			
102	Korea, Rep.	18,236	29,318	683	0	10,561	11,200	29,480	40,518	0	0	97.6
103	Greece	..	..	..	..	..	..	..	..	..	..	..
104	Saudi Arabia	..	..	..	..	..	..	..	..	0	636	102.5
105	*Yugoslavia*	15,586	15,872	760	307	2,140	293	18,486	16,471			
	Low- and middle-income											
	Sub-Saharan Africa											
	East Asia & Pacific											
	South Asia											
	Europe and Central Asia											
	Middle East & N. Africa											
	Latin America & Caribbean											
	Severely indebted											
	High-income economies											
	OECD members											
106	Ireland											
107	†Israel											
108	New Zealand											
109	Spain											
110	†Hong Kong											
111	†Singapore											
112	United Kingdom											
113	Australia											
114	Italy											
115	Netherlands											
116	Belgium											
117	Austria											
118	France											
119	Canada											
120	United States											
121	Germany											
122	Denmark											
123	Finland											
124	Norway											
125	Sweden											
126	Japan											
127	Switzerland											
	World											
	Fuel exporters											

Table 22. Flow of public and private external capital

		Disbursements (millions of dollars)				Repayment of principal (millions of dollars)				Interest payments (millions of dollars)			
		Long-term public and publicly guaranteed		Private nonguaranteed		Long-term public and publicly guaranteed		Private nonguaranteed		Long-term public and publicly guaranteed		Private nonguaranteed	
		1980	1991	1980	1991	1980	1991	1980	1991	1980	1991	1980	1991
Low-income economies													
China and India													
Other low-income													
1	Mozambique	0	141	0	0	0	23	0	3	0	10	0	0
2	Tanzania	373	257	31	0	26	64	16	0	38	33	7	0
3	Ethiopia	102	260	0	0	17	90	0	0	17	36	0	0
4	Uganda	92	179	0	0	32	68	0	0	4	24	0	0
5	Bhutan	0	10	0	0	0	4	0	0	0	2	0	0
6	Guinea-Bissau	69	29	0	0	3	2	0	0	1	2	0	0
7	Nepal	50	155	0	0	2	30	0	0	2	27	0	0
8	Burundi	39	85	0	0	4	26	0	0	2	12	0	0
9	Chad	6	97	0	0	3	4	0	0	0	5	0	0
10	Madagascar	350	198	0	0	30	48	0	0	26	67	0	0
11	Sierra Leone	86	47	0	0	32	1	0	0	8	1	0	0
12	Bangladesh	657	873	0	0	63	259	0	0	47	153	0	0
13	Lao PDR	38	50	0	0	1	5	0	0	1	3	0	0
14	Malawi	153	170	0	0	33	61	0	0	35	41	0	0
15	Rwanda	27	100	0	0	3	13	0	0	2	7	0	0
16	Mali	95	95	0	0	6	5	0	0	3	6	0	0
17	Burkina Faso	65	146	0	0	11	25	0	0	6	15	0	0
18	Niger	167	67	113	0	23	98	35	36	16	11	49	10
19	India	1,895	7,147	285	317	664	3,403	91	278	502	2,585	30	116
20	Kenya	550	424	87	60	117	320	88	40	130	202	39	45
21	Nigeria	1,187	844	565	0	65	1,069	177	47	440	2,218	91	13
22	China	2,539	9,992	0	0	613	4,323	0	0	318	2,946	0	0
23	Haiti	47	34	0	0	15	6	0	0	5	6	0	0
24	Benin	62	99	0	0	6	16	0	0	3	12	0	0
25	Central African Rep.	25	114	0	0	1	4	0	0	0	5	0	0
26	Ghana	220	440	0	9	77	101	0	8	31	60	0	3
27	Pakistan	1,052	1,737	9	19	346	907	7	41	247	565	2	11
28	Togo	100	65	0	0	19	19	0	0	19	18	0	0
29	Guinea	121	237	0	0	75	82	0	0	23	39	0	0
30	Nicaragua	266	134	0	0	45	168	0	0	42	218	0	0
31	Sri Lanka	269	755	2	0	51	162	0	3	33	127	0	2
32	Mauritania	130	57	0	0	17	40	0	0	13	20	0	0
33	Yemen, Rep.	566	163	0	0	25	83	0	0	10	28	0	0
34	Honduras	264	209	81	23	39	126	48	15	58	135	25	4
35	Lesotho	13	50	0	0	3	17	0	0	1	10	0	0
36	Indonesia	2,551	5,606	695	3,467	940	4,172	693	1,948	824	2,645	358	844
37	Egypt, Arab Rep.	2,803	1,799	126	120	368	1,247	46	170	378	580	23	72
38	Zimbabwe	132	379	0	112	40	227	0	33	10	237	0	15
39	*Sudan*	711	130	0	0	53	13	0	0	49	10	0	0
40	*Zambia*	597	336	6	2	181	248	31	0	106	236	10	0
Middle-income economies													
Lower-middle-income													
41	Bolivia	441	287	16	0	126	114	19	25	164	107	9	12
42	Côte d'Ivoire	1,413	401	262	900	517	226	38	529	353	273	31	228
43	Senegal	327	131	0	9	152	133	4	8	67	89	0	3
44	Philippines	1,382	1,682	472	261	221	1,392	320	112	375	1,395	204	66
45	Papua New Guinea	120	213	15	228	32	159	40	203	30	78	22	55
46	Cameroon	562	425	50	76	82	149	32	86	104	157	15	18
47	Guatemala	138	80	32	3	15	157	62	3	30	97	30	10
48	Dominican Rep.	415	108	67	0	62	103	74	16	92	77	29	7
49	Ecuador	968	521	315	1	272	474	263	22	288	453	78	4
50	Morocco	1,703	1,276	75	8	565	940	25	8	607	1,083	11	5
51	Jordan	369	611	0	0	103	279	0	0	79	304	0	0
52	Tajikistan	. .	. .	. .	. .	. .	. .	. .	. .	. .	. .	. .	. .
53	Peru	1,248	500	60	0	959	454	60	112	547	340	124	19
54	El Salvador	110	275	0	0	17	155	18	5	25	69	11	2
55	Congo	520	32	0	0	34	178	0	0	37	38	0	0
56	Syrian Arab Rep.	1,148	531	0	0	225	496	0	0	77	131	0	0
57	Colombia	1,016	1,643	55	298	250	1,906	13	307	279	1,183	31	99
58	Paraguay	158	130	48	8	44	109	36	7	35	76	9	0
59	Uzbekistan	. .	. .	. .	. .	. .	. .	. .	. .	. .	. .	. .	. .
60	Jamaica	328	432	25	0	91	377	10	6	114	189	7	3
61	Romania	2,797	304	0	0	824	23	0	0	332	6	0	0
62	Namibia	. .	. .	. .	. .	. .	. .	. .	. .	. .	. .	. .	. .
63	Tunisia	558	1,142	53	30	216	764	43	35	212	372	16	12
64	Kyrgyzstan	. .	. .	. .	. .	. .	. .	. .	. .	. .	. .	. .	. .
65	Thailand	1,315	1,453	1,288	3,846	172	1,147	610	1,140	269	709	204	1,069
66	Georgia	. .	. .	. .	. .	. .	. .	. .	. .	. .	. .	. .	. .

Note: For data comparability and coverage, see the technical notes.   Figures in italics are for years other than those specified.

		Disbursements (millions of dollars)				Repayment of principal (millions of dollars)				Interest payments (millions of dollars)			
		Long-term public and publicly guaranteed		Private nonguaranteed		Long-term public and publicly guaranteed		Private nonguaranteed		Long-term public and publicly guaranteed		Private nonguaranteed	
		1980	1991	1980	1991	1980	1991	1980	1991	1980	1991	1980	1991
67	Azerbaijan	..	..	..	..	..	..	..	..	..	..	..	..
68	Turkmenistan	..	..	..	..	..	..	..	..	..	..	..	..
69	Turkey	2,400	4,740	75	310	566	3,946	29	630	487	2,659	20	146
70	Poland	5,058	859	0	0	2,054	383	0	0	704	451	0	0
71	Bulgaria	222	674	0	0	5	802	0	0	23	274	0	0
72	Costa Rica	435	329	102	8	76	168	88	9	130	173	41	26
73	Algeria	3,398	6,391	0	0	2,529	7,712	0	0	1,439	1,952	0	0
74	Panama	404	1	0	0	215	73	0	0	252	108	0	0
75	Armenia	..	..	..	..	..	..	..	..	..	..	..	..
76	Chile	857	703	2,694	943	891	594	571	327	483	2,199	435	292
77	Iran, Islamic Rep.	264	1,086	0	0	531	174	0	0	432	25	0	0
78	Moldova	..	..	..	..	..	..	..	..	..	..	..	..
79	Ukraine	..	..	..	..	..	..	..	..	..	..	..	..
80	Mauritius	93	103	4	50	15	55	4	31	20	45	3	5
81	Czechoslovakia	0	1,358	0	0	0	984	0	0	0	329	0	0
82	Kazakhstan	..	..	..	..	..	..	..	..	..	..	..	..
83	Malaysia	1,015	1,646	441	747	127	1,606	218	296	250	1,119	88	112
	Upper-middle-income												
84	Botswana	27	68	0	0	6	47	0	0	7	32	0	0
85	South Africa	..	..	..	..	..	..	..	..	..	..	..	..
86	Lithuania	..	..	..	..	..	..	..	..	..	..	..	..
87	Hungary	1,552	3,114	0	0	824	2,333	0	0	636	1,439	0	0
88	Venezuela	2,870	1,527	1,891	173	1,737	607	1,235	173	1,218	1,706	257	400
89	Argentina	2,839	1,641	1,869	0	1,146	2,432	707	0	841	3,017	496	133
90	Uruguay	293	507	63	299	93	468	37	124	105	170	17	16
91	Brazil	8,335	3,674	3,192	628	3,864	3,911	2,970	752	4,202	3,693	2,132	338
92	Mexico	9,131	5,819	2,450	1,771	4,010	3,602	750	1,491	3,880	5,776	700	595
93	Belarus	..	..	..	..	..	..	..	..	..	..	..	..
94	Russian Federation	..	..	..	..	..	..	..	..	..	..	..	..
95	Latvia	..	..	..	..	..	..	..	..	..	..	..	..
96	Trinidad and Tobago	363	93	0	0	176	173	0	0	50	143	0	0
97	Gabon	171	70	0	0	279	38	0	0	119	41	0	0
98	Estonia	..	..	..	..	..	..	..	..	..	..	..	..
99	Portugal	1,950	5,546	149	195	538	3,781	126	109	486	1,296	43	39
100	Oman	98	434	0	0	179	385	0	0	44	156	0	0
101	Puerto Rico	..	..	..	..	..	..	..	..	..	..	..	..
102	Korea, Rep.	3,429	4,752	551	2,994	1,490	2,009	64	1,360	1,293	1,195	343	503
103	Greece	..	..	..	..	..	..	..	..	..	..	..	..
104	Saudi Arabia	..	..	..	..	..	..	..	..	..	..	..	..
105	*Yugoslavia*	1,366	105	3,223	666	368	1,351	2,012	1,039	249	988	829	235

Low- and middle-income
  Sub-Saharan Africa
  East Asia & Pacific
  South Asia
  Europe and Central Asia
  Middle East & N. Africa
  Latin America & Caribbean

Severely indebted

High-income economies
  OECD members

106	Ireland
107	†Israel
108	New Zealand
109	Spain
110	†Hong Kong
111	†Singapore
112	United Kingdom
113	Australia
114	Italy
115	Netherlands
116	Belgium
117	Austria
118	France
119	Canada
120	United States
121	Germany
122	Denmark
123	Finland
124	Norway
125	Sweden
126	Japan
127	Switzerland

World
  Fuel exporters

Table 23. Aggregate net resource flows and net transfers

| | Net flows on long-term debt (millions of dollars) | | | | Official grants (millions of dollars) | | Foreign direct investment in the reporting economy (millions of dollars) | | Aggregate net resource flows (millions of dollars) | | Aggregate net transfers (millions of dollars) | |
| | Public and publicly guaranteed | | Private nonguaranteed | | | | | | | | | |
	1980	1991	1980	1991	1980	1991	1980	1991	1980	1991	1980	1991
Low-income economies												
China and India												
Other low-income												
1 Mozambique	0	118	0	−3	76	752	0	23	76	889	76	879
2 Tanzania	348	193	15	0	485	688	0	0	848	880	804	847
3 Ethiopia	84	171	0	0	125	460	0	0	209	631	192	595
4 Uganda	60	111	0	0	62	253	0	1	122	365	118	341
5 Bhutan	0	5	0	0	2	28	0	0	2	33	2	31
6 Guinea-Bissau	66	28	0	0	37	60	0	0	103	88	102	85
7 Nepal	48	125	0	0	79	160	0	0	127	285	125	259
8 Burundi	35	59	0	0	39	126	0	1	74	186	72	171
9 Chad	3	93	0	0	22	106	0	0	25	199	25	194
10 Madagascar	319	150	0	0	30	352	0	14	349	516	322	447
11 Sierra Leone	54	46	0	0	24	33	−19	0	59	79	46	78
12 Bangladesh	594	614	0	0	1,001	1,070	0	1	1,595	1,685	1,548	1,532
13 Lao PDR	37	45	0	0	16	54	0	0	53	99	52	96
14 Malawi	120	109	0	0	49	219	10	0	178	328	135	287
15 Rwanda	25	87	0	0	68	181	16	5	109	273	98	261
16 Mali	89	89	0	0	104	209	2	4	195	302	192	278
17 Burkina Faso	55	121	0	0	88	200	0	0	142	321	128	306
18 Niger	144	−32	79	−36	51	249	49	0	324	181	248	160
19 India	1,231	3,744	194	39	649	562	0	0	2,073	4,345	1,541	1,643
20 Kenya	433	104	−1	20	121	836	79	43	632	1,003	312	696
21 Nigeria	1,122	−225	388	−47	3	141	−740	712	773	581	−1,357	−1,836
22 China	1,927	5,669	0	0	7	262	0	4,366	1,934	10,298	1,616	7,342
23 Haiti	32	28	0	0	30	142	13	14	75	183	59	169
24 Benin	56	83	0	0	41	147	4	0	101	231	96	218
25 Central African Rep.	24	110	0	0	56	61	5	−5	85	166	85	161
26 Ghana	143	340	0	1	23	581	16	0	181	922	135	859
27 Pakistan	706	830	2	−22	482	429	63	257	1,254	1,494	1,000	876
28 Togo	82	46	0	0	15	92	42	0	139	139	119	99
29 Guinea	47	155	0	0	25	138	0	0	72	293	49	254
30 Nicaragua	221	−33	0	0	48	730	0	0	269	696	207	478
31 Sri Lanka	219	593	2	−3	161	200	43	98	425	887	377	737
32 Mauritania	113	17	0	0	61	97	27	0	201	113	165	93
33 Yemen, Rep.	542	80	0	0	335	87	34	0	910	167	900	139
34 Honduras	225	83	33	9	20	475	6	45	283	611	123	401
35 Lesotho	10	33	0	0	52	48	5	8	66	88	59	−72
36 Indonesia	1,611	1,434	2	1,519	109	300	180	1,482	1,902	4,735	−2,514	−1,056
37 Egypt, Arab Rep.	2,435	552	80	−50	165	3,355	548	253	3,229	4,110	2,813	3,451
38 Zimbabwe	93	152	0	80	127	231	2	0	221	462	133	210
39 *Sudan*	658	117	0	0	388	416	0	0	1,046	533	997	523
40 *Zambia*	416	89	−25	2	71	697	62	0	524	788	324	552
Middle-income economies												
Lower-middle-income												
41 Bolivia	315	173	−3	−25	48	599	47	52	407	800	214	663
42 Côte d'Ivoire	896	175	224	371	27	264	95	46	1,241	856	670	309
43 Senegal	175	−2	−4	1	78	532	15	0	263	531	161	404
44 Philippines	1,161	290	152	149	59	400	−106	544	1,266	1,383	488	−381
45 Papua New Guinea	89	54	−25	25	279	280	76	0	418	359	163	227
46 Cameroon	480	277	18	−10	29	269	130	0	656	536	422	361
47 Guatemala	123	−77	−30	0	14	51	111	91	217	66	114	−85
48 Dominican Rep.	353	5	−7	−16	14	40	93	145	454	174	267	89
49 Ecuador	696	46	52	−21	7	56	70	85	825	166	349	−419
50 Morocco	1,138	336	50	0	75	553	89	320	1,353	1,209	685	26
51 Jordan	266	332	0	0	1,127	407	34	−12	1,427	727	1,348	422
52 Tajikistan	. .	. .	. .	. .	. .	. .	. .	. .	. .	. .	. .	. .
53 Peru	289	46	0	−112	31	197	27	−7	347	124	−580	−269
54 El Salvador	92	120	−18	−5	31	114	6	25	111	255	34	147
55 Congo	486	−147	0	0	20	38	40	0	546	−109	503	−147
56 Syrian Arab Rep.	924	35	0	0	1,651	109	0	0	2,574	144	2,497	13
57 Colombia	766	−263	42	−9	8	51	157	420	974	199	553	−2,030
58 Paraguay	114	21	13	1	10	22	32	80	168	124	70	47
59 Uzbekistan	. .	. .	. .	. .	. .	. .	. .	. .	. .	. .	. .	. .
60 Jamaica	236	55	15	−6	13	248	28	127	292	424	57	59
61 Romania	1,973	281	0	0	. .	. .	0	40	1,973	321	1,641	315
62 Namibia												
63 Tunisia	342	378	10	−5	26	143	235	150	612	667	232	16
64 Kyrgyzstan	. .	. .	. .	. .	. .	. .	. .	. .	. .	. .	. .	. .
65 Thailand	1,143	306	678	2,706	75	220	190	2,014	2,087	5,245	1,576	3,412
66 Georgia	. .	. .	. .	. .	. .	. .	. .	. .	. .	. .	. .	. .

Note: For data comparability and coverage, see the technical notes. Figures in italics are for years other than those specified.

| | | Net flows on long-term debt (millions of dollars) | | | | Official grants (millions of dollars) | | Foreign direct investment in the reporting economy (millions of dollars) | | Aggregate net resource flows (millions of dollars) | | Aggregate net transfers (millions of dollars) | |
| | | Public and publicly guaranteed | | Private nonguaranteed | | | | | | | | | |
		1980	1991	1980	1991	1980	1991	1980	1991	1980	1991	1980	1991
67	Azerbaijan	..	..	..	..	..	..	..	..	..	..	..	..
68	Turkmenistan	..	..	..	..	..	..	..	..	..	..	..	..
69	Turkey	1,834	794	46	−319	185	1,147	18	810	2,083	2,432	1,545	−541
70	Poland	3,005	476	0	0	..	..	10	291	3,015	767	2,311	266
71	Bulgaria	217	−128	0	0	..	..	0	0	217	−128	193	−402
72	Costa Rica	359	160	14	0	0	83	53	142	425	385	235	140
73	Algeria	869	−1,321	0	0	77	79	349	0	1,295	−1,242	−830	−3,194
74	Panama	189	−73	0	0	6	89	−47	−62	149	−45	−174	−193
75	Armenia	..	..	..	..	..	..	..	..	..	..	..	..
76	Chile	−34	109	2,123	616	9	97	213	576	2,312	1,398	1,307	−1,738
77	Iran, Islamic Rep.	−267	912	0	0	1	70	0	0	−265	982	−1,095	958
78	Moldova	..	..	..	..	..	..	..	..	..	..	..	..
79	Ukraine	..	..	..	..	..	..	..	..	..	..	..	..
80	Mauritius	78	48	0	19	13	16	1	19	93	101	69	29
81	Czechoslovakia	0	374	0	0	..	..	0	600	0	974	0	643
82	Kazakhstan	..	..	..	..	..	..	..	..	..	..	..	..
83	Malaysia	889	41	223	451	6	57	934	3,455	2,052	4,003	524	837
Upper-middle-income													
84	Botswana	21	21	0	0	51	62	112	0	184	83	69	51
85	South Africa	..	..	..	..	..	..	..	..	..	..	..	..
86	Lithuania	..	..	..	..	..	..	..	..	..	..	..	..
87	Hungary	728	781	0	0	..	..	0	1,462	728	2,243	92	760
88	Venezuela	1,133	920	656	0	0	5	55	1,914	1,844	2,839	47	505
89	Argentina	1,693	−791	1,162	0	2	40	678	2,439	3,535	1,688	1,593	−2,269
90	Uruguay	200	39	26	175	1	10	290	0	516	224	395	38
91	Brazil	4,472	−237	222	−124	14	46	1,911	1,600	6,618	1,286	−670	−4,545
92	Mexico	5,121	2,217	1,700	280	14	62	2,156	4,762	8,991	7,321	3,043	−556
93	Belarus	..	..	..	..	..	..	..	..	..	..	..	..
94	Russian Federation	..	..	..	..	..	..	..	..	..	..	..	..
95	Latvia	..	..	..	..	..	..	..	..	..	..	..	..
96	Trinidad and Tobago	187	−80	0	0	1	4	185	169	372	93	−157	−286
97	Gabon	−109	32	0	0	4	35	32	125	−73	192	−465	−32
98	Estonia	..	..	..	..	..	..	..	..	..	..	..	..
99	Portugal	1,411	1,765	23	86	28	15	157	2,021	1,620	3,887	1,074	2,488
100	Oman	−81	49	0	0	157	3	98	0	174	51	−156	−105
101	Puerto Rico	..	..	..	..	..	..	..	..	..	..	..	..
102	Korea, Rep.	1,940	2,743	487	1,633	8	6	6	1,116	2,440	5,498	740	3,504
103	Greece	..	..	..	..	..	..	..	..	..	..	..	..
104	Saudi Arabia	..	..	..	..	..	..	..	..	..	..	..	..
105	*Yugoslavia*	998	−1,247	1,211	−373	..	..	0	0	2,208	−1,620	1,131	−2,843
Low- and middle-income													
Sub-Saharan Africa													
East Asia & Pacific													
South Asia													
Europe and Central Asia													
Middle East & N. Africa													
Latin America & Caribbean													
Severely indebted													
High-income economies													
OECD members													
106	Ireland												
107	†Israel												
108	New Zealand												
109	Spain												
110	†Hong Kong												
111	†Singapore												
112	United Kingdom												
113	Australia												
114	Italy												
115	Netherlands												
116	Belgium												
117	Austria												
118	France												
119	Canada												
120	United States												
121	Germany												
122	Denmark												
123	Finland												
124	Norway												
125	Sweden												
126	Japan												
127	Switzerland												
World													
Fuel exporters													

Table 24. Total external debt ratios

| | | Total external debt as a percentage of | | | | Total debt service as a percentage of exports of goods and services | | Interest payments as a percentage of exports of goods and services | | Concessional debt as a percentage of total external debt | | Multilateral debt as a percentage of total external debt | |
| | | Exports of goods and services | | GNP | | | | | | | | | |
		1980	1991	1980	1991	1980	1991	1980	1991	1980	1991	1980	1991
	Low-income economies	**105.5** w	**225.7** w	**16.6** w	**44.6** w	**10.1** w	**21.0** w	**5.0** w	**9.4** w	**45.9** w	**38.2** w	**15.9** w	**24.1** w
	China and India	**69.1** w	**140.7** w	**5.3** w	**21.5** w	**6.4** w	**16.9** w	**2.6** w	**7.4** w	**61.7** w	**30.6** w	**24.2** w	**23.8** w
	Other low-income	**120.2** w	**307.7** w	**33.5** w	**85.7** w	**11.6** w	**25.0** w	**6.0** w	**11.3** w	**42.2** w	**41.4** w	**14.0** w	**24.2** w
1	Mozambique	0.0	1,117.1	0.0	426.0		10.6	0.0	4.3	0.0	59.7	0.0	12.0
2	Tanzania	321.7	1,207.8	48.3	250.8	19.6	24.6	10.0	7.6	55.3	60.0	21.4	30.5
3	Ethiopia	131.4	464.7	19.5	53.4	7.3	18.6	4.5	5.8	70.6	81.5	42.2	39.1
4	Uganda	210.3	1,429.4	55.1	109.2	17.4	70.0	3.7	18.8	26.9	58.7	12.4	51.2
5	Bhutan	. .	95.4	0.0	38.8	. .	7.2	. .	2.4	0.0	80.1	0.0	57.3
6	Guinea-Bissau	. .	. .	128.0	323.7	. .	. .	. .	. .	64.3	67.9	21.3	42.9
7	Nepal	85.5	370.0	10.4	53.5	3.2	13.6	2.1	6.2	75.7	90.4	62.0	78.7
8	Burundi	180.1	758.8	18.2	83.8	9.5	31.5	4.8	10.9	62.6	88.2	35.7	74.9
9	Chad	320.2	251.1	31.6	47.0	8.3	4.5	0.7	2.7	50.9	80.1	32.6	63.9
10	Madagascar	235.7	744.6	30.6	148.3	17.1	32.0	10.9	15.6	39.3	57.6	14.9	37.4
11	Sierra Leone	157.7	. .	40.7	167.5	23.2	. .	5.7	. .	32.8	31.0	14.2	14.4
12	Bangladesh	345.3	443.7	31.3	56.0	23.2	19.9	6.4	6.4	82.4	91.0	30.3	53.6
13	Lao PDR	. .	996.2	. .	109.8	. .	7.6	. .	2.9	92.1	97.3	7.1	28.6
14	Malawi	260.8	318.8	72.1	78.5	27.7	25.0	16.7	9.4	33.8	76.8	26.7	71.5
15	Rwanda	103.4	591.8	16.3	53.7	4.2	17.6	2.8	8.6	74.4	91.9	47.8	73.9
16	Mali	227.3	442.7	45.4	104.8	5.1	4.6	2.3	2.1	84.5	91.9	23.7	38.0
17	Burkina Faso	88.0	188.8	22.3	34.9	5.9	9.1	3.1	4.2	66.9	77.5	42.9	67.0
18	Niger	132.8	466.8	34.5	72.9	21.7	50.4	12.9	9.3	18.0	49.9	16.5	43.7
19	India	136.2	295.3	11.9	29.3	9.3	30.7	4.2	13.6	75.1	41.6	29.5	33.5
20	Kenya	167.3	318.4	49.0	89.6	21.8	32.7	11.4	14.5	20.8	40.6	18.3	38.2
21	Nigeria	32.2	257.1	10.1	108.8	4.2	25.2	3.3	16.8	6.1	3.1	6.4	11.6
22	China	21.2	87.1	1.5	16.4	4.4	12.1	1.5	5.3	0.5	17.6	0.0	12.4
23	Haiti	72.9	186.5	20.9	28.8	6.2	6.6	1.8	4.0	70.7	75.1	43.8	67.5
24	Benin	133.1	262.2	30.2	70.1	6.3	6.2	4.5	3.0	39.2	78.2	24.5	45.7
25	Central African Rep.	94.7	671.9	24.3	71.5	4.9	11.4	1.6	5.9	30.1	78.1	27.4	57.8
26	Ghana	116.0	384.5	31.8	66.9	13.1	26.9	4.4	9.9	57.9	56.9	19.8	49.2
27	Pakistan	208.8	244.9	42.4	50.1	17.9	21.1	7.6	10.0	73.1	54.9	15.4	35.0
28	Togo	180.1	187.2	95.3	85.0	9.0	7.3	5.8	3.5	24.4	57.5	11.4	44.9
29	Guinea	200.5	351.0	. .	94.8	19.8	17.9	6.0	5.8	59.7	70.3	11.7	31.5
30	Nicaragua	423.4	2,917.8	108.5	153.5	22.3	109.3	13.4	62.4	21.5	28.7	19.4	9.2
31	Sri Lanka	123.4	211.0	46.1	72.6	12.0	13.9	5.7	5.7	56.2	73.3	11.7	31.8
32	Mauritania	306.6	458.2	125.7	214.7	17.3	16.8	7.9	6.2	60.5	68.1	14.9	26.9
33	Yemen, Rep.	104.7	292.5	. .	88.1	4.5	7.3	2.3	3.5	83.9	73.8	14.9	16.4
34	Honduras	152.0	330.8	60.5	113.8	21.4	30.6	12.4	15.8	23.4	37.2	31.1	50.9
35	Lesotho	19.5	73.2	11.2	39.2	1.5	4.6	0.6	1.8	61.0	77.0	55.3	72.9
36	Indonesia	94.2	223.2	28.0	66.4	13.9	32.7	6.5	13.2	36.4	28.3	8.8	21.7
37	Egypt, Arab Rep.	227.0	280.0	97.5	133.1	14.7	16.7	9.1	6.3	46.1	37.6	12.6	8.2
38	Zimbabwe	45.4	164.9	14.9	57.0	3.8	27.2	1.5	14.4	2.3	29.1	0.4	21.2
39	*Sudan*	499.4	3,465.6	77.2	. .	25.5	. .	12.8	. .	34.4	29.0	12.3	11.7
40	*Zambia*	200.7	624.8	90.7	. .	25.3	50.3	8.7	26.1	25.4	35.9	12.2	20.9
	Middle-income economies	**132.5** w	**159.8** w	**31.9** w	**41.2** w	**23.9** w	**20.3** w	**12.2** w	**9.3** w	**8.1** w	**9.9** w	**6.4** w	**13.0** w
	Lower-middle-income	**100.2** w	**157.6** w	**28.7** w	**53.2** w	**16.7** w	**19.5** w	**8.0** w	**8.3** w	**14.8** w	**16.5** w	**8.6** w	**14.9** w
41	Bolivia	258.2	432.4	93.3	85.3	35.0	34.0	21.1	14.7	24.7	42.1	16.6	42.2
42	Côte d'Ivoire	160.7	566.1	58.8	222.6	28.3	43.4	13.0	17.6	7.6	12.5	9.0	15.6
43	Senegal	162.7	224.6	50.5	63.1	28.7	19.9	10.5	7.9	55.0	55.0	17.8	40.1
44	Philippines	212.3	215.6	53.8	70.2	26.6	23.2	18.2	11.0	6.7	25.9	7.5	20.9
45	Papua New Guinea	66.0	160.7	28.9	84.6	13.8	29.6	6.6	8.5	12.2	25.5	21.2	31.6
46	Cameroon	136.7	252.7	36.8	57.5	15.2	18.7	8.1	8.8	31.4	23.9	16.8	22.6
47	Guatemala	63.6	142.9	14.9	29.5	7.9	15.3	3.7	6.7	21.6	25.4	30.0	35.2
48	Dominican Rep.	133.8	193.1	31.2	65.7	25.3	11.6	12.0	4.6	20.5	27.5	10.2	19.6
49	Ecuador	201.6	362.7	53.8	114.5	33.9	32.2	15.9	14.7	5.0	8.1	5.4	17.9
50	Morocco	224.5	257.5	53.3	80.0	32.7	27.8	17.0	14.2	37.6	25.9	7.4	23.9
51	Jordan	79.0	283.4	. .	226.9	8.4	20.9	4.3	11.8	41.5	34.1	8.0	10.8
52	Tajikistan	. .	. .	. .	. .	. .	. .	. .	. .	. .	. .	. .	. .
53	Peru	194.2	483.6	47.6	44.3	44.5	27.7	19.9	13.4	15.1	11.5	5.5	9.2
54	El Salvador	71.1	155.4	26.2	37.4	7.5	17.2	4.7	5.8	25.9	59.3	28.3	38.7
55	Congo	148.1	386.3	99.0	181.7	10.6	21.3	6.6	6.4	26.4	36.4	7.7	12.1
56	Syrian Arab Rep.	106.2	. .	27.1	103.8	11.4	. .	4.7	. .	63.5	78.4	8.8	6.2
57	Colombia	117.1	167.7	20.9	43.5	16.0	35.2	11.6	13.8	16.3	5.6	19.5	35.5
58	Paraguay	121.9	125.7	20.7	35.0	18.6	11.9	8.5	5.3	31.9	30.7	20.2	33.2
59	Uzbekistan	. .	. .	. .	. .	. .	. .	. .	. .	. .	. .	. .	. .
60	Jamaica	129.3	186.3	78.3	134.9	19.0	29.4	10.8	9.7	20.9	27.4	15.0	26.8
61	Romania	80.3	39.3	. .	6.9	12.6	2.0	4.9	1.5	0.0	1.0	8.3	1.4
62	Namibia	. .	. .	. .	. .	. .	. .	. .	. .	. .	. .	. .	. .
63	Tunisia	96.0	137.2	41.6	66.2	14.8	22.7	6.9	7.3	39.9	35.3	12.3	32.7
64	Kyrgyzstan	. .	. .	. .	. .	. .	. .	. .	. .	. .	. .	. .	. .
65	Thailand	96.8	94.9	26.0	39.0	18.9	13.1	9.5	7.0	10.9	13.2	12.0	9.9
66	Georgia	. .	. .	. .	. .	. .	. .	. .	. .	. .	. .	. .	. .

Note: For data comparability and coverage, see the technical notes.   Figures in italics are for years other than those specified.

| | | Total external debt as a percentage of | | | | Total debt service as a percentage of exports of goods and services | | Interest payments as a percentage of exports of goods and services | | Concessional debt as a percentage of total external debt | | Multilateral debt as a percentage of total external debt | |
| | | Exports of goods and services | | GNP | | | | | | | | | |
		1980	1991	1980	1991	1980	1991	1980	1991	1980	1991	1980	1991
67	Azerbaijan	..	..	..	..	..	..	..	..	..	..	..	..
68	Turkmenistan	..	..	..	..	..	..	..	..	..	..	..	..
69	Turkey	332.9	194.7	34.3	48.1	28.0	30.5	14.9	12.8	23.0	15.6	11.2	20.2
70	Poland	54.9	281.4	16.3	68.5	17.9	5.4	5.2	3.3	9.1	2.9	0.0	1.7
71	Bulgaria	2.9	237.9	1.4	151.7	0.3	22.1	0.2	6.1	0.0	0.0	0.0	4.6
72	Costa Rica	225.2	177.8	59.7	74.9	29.1	18.4	14.6	10.3	9.5	22.8	16.4	29.4
73	Algeria	129.9	214.8	47.0	70.4	27.4	73.7	10.4	15.8	6.5	3.4	1.5	9.5
74	Panama	38.4	106.4	87.5	130.1	6.3	3.9	3.3	1.9	9.0	6.7	11.0	14.1
75	Armenia	..	..	..	..	..	..	..	..	..	..	2.9	24.1
76	Chile	192.5	153.5	45.5	60.7	43.1	33.9	19.0	24.3	6.2	2.1		
77	Iran, Islamic Rep.	32.0	57.3	4.9	11.5	6.8	3.9	3.1	3.0	7.4	0.8	13.8	0.7
78	Moldova	..	..	..	..	..	..	..	..	..	..	..	..
79	Ukraine	..	..	..	..	..	..	..	..	..	..	..	..
80	Mauritius	80.7	53.2	41.6	37.0	9.1	8.8	5.9	3.0	15.6	39.3	16.6	29.7
81	Czechoslovakia	28.0	68.9	9.8	29.5	3.9	11.6	3.9	4.7	0.0	0.0	0.0	4.8
82	Kazakhstan	..	..	..	..	..	..	..	..	..	..	..	..
83	Malaysia	44.6	53.7	28.0	47.6	6.3	8.3	4.0	3.6	10.1	12.1	11.3	9.1
	Upper-middle-income	**173.1** *w*	**162.2** *w*	**34.4** *w*	**33.2** *w*	**33.0** *w*	**21.1** *w*	**17.5** *w*	**10.4** *w*	**3.5** *w*	**2.9** *w*	**4.8** *w*	**11.1** *w*
84	Botswana	17.8	23.0	14.8	15.7	1.9	3.4	1.1	1.4	46.6	40.3	63.3	71.4
85	South Africa	..	..	..	..	..	..	..	..	..	..	..	..
86	Lithuania	..	..	..	..	..	..	..	..	..	..	..	..
87	Hungary	..	180.8	44.8	77.0	..	32.5	..	13.2	5.6	0.4	0.0	14.8
88	Venezuela	132.0	187.0	42.1	65.3	27.2	18.7	13.8	13.9	0.4	0.2	0.7	6.4
89	Argentina	242.4	433.0	48.4	49.2	37.3	48.4	20.8	25.1	1.8	0.9	4.0	8.5
90	Uruguay	104.1	175.3	17.0	45.3	18.8	38.2	10.6	11.7	5.2	1.7	11.0	20.5
91	Brazil	305.2	324.9	31.3	28.8	63.1	30.0	33.8	15.4	2.5	2.5	4.4	9.5
92	Mexico	259.2	224.1	30.5	36.9	49.5	30.9	27.4	17.3	0.9	1.0	5.6	15.2
93	Belarus	..	..	..	..	..	..	..	..	..	..	..	..
94	Russian Federation	..	..	..	..	..	..	..	..	..	..	..	..
95	Latvia	..	..	..	..	..	..	..	..	..	..	..	..
96	Trinidad and Tobago	24.6	105.4	14.0	48.2	6.8	16.2	1.6	8.4	4.7	2.4	8.6	6.7
97	Gabon	62.2	152.5	39.2	88.1	17.7	6.5	6.3	4.0	8.2	21.4	2.6	9.1
98	Estonia	..	..	..	..	..	..	..	..	..	..	..	..
99	Portugal	99.5	103.2	40.5	43.9	18.3	21.1	10.5	7.1	4.4	3.3	5.5	9.8
100	Oman	15.4	..	11.2	29.4	6.4	..	1.8	..	43.6	10.3	5.8	4.9
101	Puerto Rico	..	..	..	..	..	..	..	..	..	..	..	..
102	Korea, Rep.	130.6	47.6	48.7	14.4	19.7	7.1	12.7	3.1	9.7	11.6	8.0	8.9
103	Greece	..	..	..	..	..	..	..	..	..	..	..	..
104	Saudi Arabia	..	..	..	..	..	..	..	..	..	..	..	..
105	*Yugoslavia*	103.1	87.8	25.6	..	20.8	20.4	7.2	6.9	7.9	4.3	7.6	16.9
	Low- and middle-income	**124.9** *w*	**176.9** *w*	**26.2** *w*	**42.3** *w*	**20.0** *w*	**20.5** *w*	**10.2** *w*	**9.3** *w*	**16.9** *w*	**19.3** *w*	**8.6** *w*	**16.7** *w*
	Sub-Saharan Africa	**96.6** *w*	**329.4** *w*	**28.6** *w*	**107.9** *w*	**10.9** *w*	**20.8** *w*	**5.7** *w*	**10.5** *w*	**26.9** *w*	**33.8** *w*	**13.4** *w*	**22.7** *w*
	East Asia & Pacific	**89.8** *w*	**96.2** *w*	**16.9** *w*	**28.2** *w*	**13.5** *w*	**13.3** *w*	**7.7** *w*	**5.9** *w*	**16.4** *w*	**21.2** *w*	**8.7** *w*	**15.4** *w*
	South Asia	**160.4** *w*	**287.1** *w*	**17.0** *w*	**35.6** *w*	**11.9** *w*	**26.0** *w*	**5.1** *w*	**11.5** *w*	**74.4** *w*	**52.4** *w*	**25.0** *w*	**36.7** *w*
	Europe and Central Asia	**81.2** *w*	**152.2** *w*	**24.3** *w*	**51.4** *w*	**14.0** *w*	**20.0** *w*	**6.0** *w*	**7.7** *w*	**9.6** *w*	**5.8** *w*	**6.1** *w*	**10.8** *w*
	Middle East & N. Africa	**114.4** *w*	**185.8** *w*	**31.0** *w*	**58.8** *w*	**16.1** *w*	**25.9** *w*	**7.3** *w*	**8.4** *w*	**31.8** *w*	**31.4** *w*	**8.3** *w*	**11.7** *w*
	Latin America & Caribbean	**195.5** *w*	**256.0** *w*	**35.1** *w*	**41.3** *w*	**37.1** *w*	**29.2** *w*	**19.6** *w*	**15.8** *w*	**4.5** *w*	**5.4** *w*	**5.8** *w*	**14.2** *w*
	Severely indebted	**176.6** *w*	**285.9** *w*	**34.0** *w*	**46.4** *w*	**34.0** *w*	**30.8** *w*	**17.1** *w*	**14.1** *w*	**6.7** *w*	**8.3** *w*	**5.0** *w*	**10.9** *w*
	High-income economies												
	OECD members												
106	Ireland												
107	†Israel												
108	New Zealand												
109	Spain												
110	†Hong Kong												
111	†Singapore												
112	United Kingdom												
113	Australia												
114	Italy												
115	Netherlands												
116	Belgium												
117	Austria												
118	France												
119	Canada												
120	United States												
121	Germany												
122	Denmark												
123	Finland												
124	Norway												
125	Sweden												
126	Japan												
127	Switzerland												
	World												
	Fuel exporters												

Table 25. Terms of external public borrowing

		Commitments (millions of dollars)		Average interest rate (percent)		Average maturity (years)		Average grace period (years)		Public loans with variable interest rates, as a percentage of public debt	
		1980	1991	1980	1991	1980	1991	1980	1991	1980	1991
	Low-income economies	**30,186** *t*	**37,643** *t*	**6.3** *w*	**5.3** *w*	**23** *w*	**22** *w*	**6** *w*	**6** *w*	**16.6** *w*	**22.0** *w*
	China and India	**8,728** *t*	**17,985** *t*	**7.6** *w*	**6.1** *w*	**24** *w*	**18** *w*	**6** *w*	**5** *w*	**14.8** *w*	**26.3** *w*
	Other low-income	**21,457** *t*	**19,657** *t*	**5.8** *w*	**4.6** *w*	**23** *w*	**25** *w*	**6** *w*	**7** *w*	**17.0** *w*	**20.2** *w*
1	Mozambique	479	80	5.2	1.4	15	34	4	9	0.0	3.7
2	Tanzania	710	246	4.1	1.9	23	42	8	12	4.4	5.5
3	Ethiopia	175	100	3.7	3.5	18	20	4	7	1.5	2.9
4	Uganda	209	437	4.6	2.2	25	37	6	9	1.3	1.3
5	Bhutan	7	7	1.0	1.0	50	39	10	10	0.0	0.0
6	Guinea-Bissau	38	16	2.4	0.7	18	39	4	10	1.6	0.2
7	Nepal	92	68	0.8	1.0	46	38	10	10	0.0	0.0
8	Burundi	102	102	1.3	1.2	42	40	9	10	0.0	0.0
9	Chad	0	73	0.0	0.7	0	50	0	10	0.2	0.0
10	Madagascar	445	53	5.6	0.7	18	40	5	10	8.3	6.1
11	Sierra Leone	70	46	5.2	0.7	26	48	7	10	0.0	1.1
12	Bangladesh	1,034	952	1.7	1.0	36	38	9	10	0.1	0.0
13	Lao PDR	94	147	0.2	0.8	40	40	31	10	0.0	0.0
14	Malawi	130	187	6.0	0.7	24	41	6	10	23.2	3.4
15	Rwanda	48	181	1.5	0.8	39	42	9	11	0.0	0.0
16	Mali	145	152	2.2	0.8	23	42	5	10	0.0	0.3
17	Burkina Faso	115	167	4.3	1.0	21	37	6	10	4.3	0.0
18	Niger	341	48	7.4	2.7	18	30	5	10	56.4	16.5
19	India	4,902	8,538	5.4	5.8	34	20	7	6	4.2	21.0
20	Kenya	560	476	3.9	2.4	30	35	8	9	27.0	20.2
21	Nigeria	1,904	1,362	10.5	6.1	11	22	4	6	74.4	31.8
22	China	3,826	9,447	10.4	6.4	11	16	3	4	58.8	33.1
23	Haiti	51	52	5.5	1.3	20	39	6	10	3.1	0.6
24	Benin	448	145	8.3	1.1	12	36	4	9	0.4	2.1
25	Central African Rep.	38	118	0.6	2.9	13	32	4	8	1.9	0.1
26	Ghana	170	333	1.4	2.6	44	33	10	8	0.9	2.6
27	Pakistan	1,115	1,558	4.4	6.6	30	19	7	5	1.5	14.4
28	Togo	97	14	4.0	0.8	24	40	7	10	12.0	3.3
29	Guinea	269	100	4.6	2.6	19	24	6	5	0.3	7.2
30	Nicaragua	424	244	3.9	1.8	25	39	7	10	47.9	25.9
31	Sri Lanka	752	948	3.9	2.2	30	34	8	9	6.9	5.6
32	Mauritania	215	0	3.6	0.0	21	0	8	0	2.4	5.6
33	Yemen, Rep.	553	128	2.7	0.9	27	39	6	10	0.0	1.5
34	Honduras	495	254	6.8	3.1	24	27	7	8	34.3	21.7
35	Lesotho	59	176	5.9	5.6	24	25	6	7	3.5	0.0
36	Indonesia	4,277	7,840	8.1	6.1	19	20	6	6	30.7	43.1
37	Egypt, Arab Rep.	2,558	1,375	5.0	5.2	28	23	9	7	4.5	11.5
38	Zimbabwe	171	953	7.1	6.0	15	14	6	4	0.4	26.8
39	*Sudan*	905	16	6.1	0.7	18	40	5	10	10.6	19.6
40	*Zambia*	645	324	6.7	1.1	19	39	4	10	12.6	12.0
	Middle-income economies	**67,406** *t*	**65,111** *t*	**10.7** *w*	**7.2** *w*	**12** *w*	**14** *w*	**4** *w*	**4** *w*	**54.9** *w*	**50.6** *w*
	Lower-middle-income	**33,634** *t*	**34,445** *t*	**9.5** *w*	**6.8** *w*	**14** *w*	**15** *w*	**5** *w*	**5** *w*	**38.8** *w*	**45.3** *w*
41	Bolivia	370	408	8.4	5.1	15	25	5	6	31.6	24.2
42	Côte d'Ivoire	1,685	362	11.4	6.0	10	23	4	6	42.4	65.7
43	Senegal	470	295	5.9	3.7	20	29	6	7	12.7	4.4
44	Philippines	2,143	2,751	9.9	4.9	17	24	5	7	49.9	41.7
45	Papua New Guinea	184	261	11.2	4.5	18	24	5	7	43.5	52.7
46	Cameroon	164	353	6.9	6.2	24	18	6	5	22.9	18.6
47	Guatemala	247	35	7.9	2.3	15	32	4	3	35.6	16.8
48	Dominican Rep.	519	166	8.9	4.7	12	20	4	7	47.2	31.5
49	Ecuador	1,148	547	10.7	7.6	14	16	4	4	62.5	61.0
50	Morocco	1,686	1,834	8.0	6.5	15	19	5	6	31.0	52.5
51	Jordan	768	505	7.3	1.7	15	29	4	9	13.4	28.2
52	Tajikistan	. .	. .	. .	. .	. .	. .	. .	. .	. .	. .
53	Peru	1,614	328	9.4	3.1	12	30	3	10	31.2	27.8
54	El Salvador	225	379	4.2	7.4	28	17	8	5	27.4	14.1
55	Congo	966	0	7.7	0.0	11	0	3	0	6.6	27.3
56	Syrian Arab Rep.	1,168	401	1.3	6.0	24	27	5	5	0.0	0.0
57	Colombia	1,566	2,323	12.9	7.3	15	12	4	6	40.8	50.7
58	Paraguay	99	0	7.0	0.0	24	0	7	0	27.3	16.8
59	Uzbekistan	. .	. .	. .	. .	. .	. .	. .	. .	. .	. .
60	Jamaica	225	444	7.6	7.2	14	19	5	4	23.0	25.7
61	Romania	1,886	1,435	14.1	6.2	8	10	4	5	59.2	5.0
62	Namibia	. .	. .	. .	. .	. .	. .	. .	. .	. .	. .
63	Tunisia	777	1,366	6.7	6.7	18	16	5	5	20.0	23.4
64	Kyrgyzstan	. .	. .	. .	. .	. .	. .	. .	. .	. .	. .
65	Thailand	1,877	1,156	9.5	5.0	17	19	5	5	51.4	56.6
66	Georgia	. .	. .	. .	. .	. .	. .	. .	. .	. .	. .

Note: For data comparability and coverage, see the technical notes. Figures in italics are for years other than those specified.

		Commitments (millions of dollars)		Average interest rate (percent)		Average maturity (years)		Average grace period (years)		Public loans with variable interest rates, as a percentage of public debt	
		1980	1991	1980	1991	1980	1991	1980	1991	1980	1991
67	Azerbaijan	..	..	..	..	..	..	..	..	..	..
68	Turkmenistan	..	..	..	..	..	..	..	..	..	..
69	Turkey	2,925	3,880	8.3	7.9	16	13	5	6	26.5	35.5
70	Poland	1,715	1,637	9.3	7.9	11	14	4	4	37.8	67.7
71	Bulgaria	1,578	269	13.9	7.7	9	17	6	5	76.7	73.0
72	Costa Rica	621	179	11.2	7.1	13	6	5	3	57.0	32.1
73	Algeria	3,538	8,429	8.1	7.4	12	8	4	2	25.0	41.6
74	Panama	534	0	11.3	0.0	11	0	5	0	52.7	61.3
75	Armenia	..	..	..	..	..	..	..	..	..	..
76	Chile	835	1,223	13.9	7.0	8	15	4	4	75.6	76.6
77	Iran, Islamic Rep.	0	759	0.0	6.1	0	21	0	2	37.8	84.7
78	Moldova	..	..	..	..	..	..	..	..	..	..
79	Ukraine	..	..	..	..	..	..	..	..	..	..
80	Mauritius	121	107	10.4	6.1	14	17	4	7	47.0	32.8
81	Czechoslovakia	8	1,423	8.2	8.3	12	8	4	4	0.0	33.3
82	Kazakhstan	..	..	..	..	..	..	..	..	..	..
83	Malaysia	1,423	868	11.2	7.4	14	13	5	7	50.7	52.2
	Upper-middle-income	**33,772** t	**30,666** t	**11.9** w	**7.7** w	**11** w	**14** w	**4** w	**4** w	**67.0** w	**56.3** w
84	Botswana	69	28	6.0	0.5	18	48	4	10	0.0	14.5
85	South Africa	..	..	..	..	..	..	..	..	..	..
86	Lithuania	..	..	..	..	..	..	..	..	..	..
87	Hungary[a]	1,225	2,627	9.8	8.5	13	9	3	6	39.8	56.4
88	Venezuela	2,769	1,055	12.1	8.4	8	15	3	5	81.4	62.7
89	Argentina	3,023	2,374	13.8	8.0	9	20	4	5	74.0	58.3
90	Uruguay	347	447	10.1	7.9	14	14	6	3	35.4	60.1
91	Brazil	9,638	3,975	12.5	7.6	10	11	4	4	72.2	71.8
92	Mexico	7,632	7,279	11.3	8.2	10	13	4	4	75.9	45.9
93	Belarus	..	..	..	..	..	..	..	..	..	..
94	Russian Federation	..	..	..	..	..	..	..	..	..	..
95	Latvia	..	..	..	..	..	..	..	..	..	..
96	Trinidad and Tobago	211	283	10.4	7.7	9	20	4	5	31.9	51.7
97	Gabon	196	169	11.2	5.4	11	16	3	5	39.3	10.2
98	Estonia	..	..	..	..	..	..	..	..	..	..
99	Portugal	2,015	6,531	10.9	7.0	10	19	3	2	30.6	27.0
100	Oman	454	362	7.9	5.8	9	7	3	5	0.0	59.7
101	Puerto Rico	..	..	..	..	..	..	..	..	..	..
102	Korea, Rep.	4,928	4,910	11.3	7.7	15	11	4	4	36.4	41.8
103	Greece	..	..	..	..	..	..	..	..	..	..
104	Saudi Arabia	..	..	..	..	..	..	..	..	..	..
105	*Yugoslavia*	1,187	595	15.1	8.0	9	14	3	5	77.6	75.1
	Low- and middle-income	**97,592** t	**102,753** t	**9.4** w	**6.5** w	**16** w	**17** w	**5** w	**5** w	**45.0** w	**40.7** w
	Sub-Saharan Africa	**13,271** t	**7,548** t	**7.1** w	**3.8** w	**17** w	**28** w	**5** w	**7** w	**23.7** w	**21.2** w
	East Asia & Pacific	**19,468** t	**27,414** t	**9.8** w	**6.3** w	**16** w	**17** w	**5** w	**5** w	**40.0** w	**41.6** w
	South Asia	**7,925** t	**12,074** t	**4.6** w	**5.2** w	**33** w	**22** w	**7** w	**7** w	**3.1** w	**16.1** w
	Europe and Central Asia	**12,542** t	**18,397** t	**11.2** w	**7.6** w	**11** w	**14** w	**4** w	**4** w	**47.4** w	**52.4** w
	Middle East & N. Africa	**11,616** t	**15,229** t	**6.3** w	**6.7** w	**19** w	**14** w	**5** w	**4** w	**18.2** w	**27.0** w
	Latin America & Caribbean	**32,770** t	**22,092** t	**11.6** w	**7.5** w	**11** w	**15** w	**4** w	**5** w	**68.0** w	**55.1** w
	Severely indebted	**37,501** t	**28,948** t	**10.7** w	**7.4** w	**11** w	**13** w	**4** w	**4** w	**59.4** w	**53.7** w

High-income economies
  OECD members

106	Ireland										
107	†Israel										
108	New Zealand										
109	Spain										
110	†Hong Kong										
111	†Singapore										
112	United Kingdom										
113	Australia										
114	Italy										
115	Netherlands										
116	Belgium										
117	Austria										
118	France										
119	Canada										
120	United States										
121	Germany										
122	Denmark										
123	Finland										
124	Norway										
125	Sweden										
126	Japan										
127	Switzerland										

World
  Fuel exporters

a. Includes debt in convertible currencies only.

Table 26. Population growth and projections

		Average annual growth of population (percent)			Population (millions)			Hypothetical size of stationary population (millions)	Age structure of population (percent)			
									0–14 years		15–64 years	
		1970–80	1980–91	1991–2000[a]	1991	2000[a]	2025[a]		1991	2025[a]	1991	2025[a]
	Low-income economies	**2.2** w	**2.0** w	**1.8** w	**3,127** t	**3,686** t	**5,184** t		**35.4** w	**26.8** w	**60.6** w	**65.6** w
	China and India	**2.0** w	**1.7** w	**1.5** w	**2,016** t	**2,307** t	**2,934** t		**31.1** w	**22.4** w	**63.6** w	**67.6** w
	Other low-income	**2.6** w	**2.6** w	**2.4** w	**1,111** t	**1,379** t	**2,250** t		**43.1** w	**32.4** w	**55.2** w	**63.0** w
1	Mozambique	2.6	2.6	2.9	16	21	43	113	44.5	42.2	52.1	55.0
2	Tanzania	3.0	3.0	3.0	25	33	59	116	46.7	36.4	50.5	60.9
3	Ethiopia	2.7	3.1	2.7	53	67	130	303	45.9	41.2	51.1	56.3
4	Uganda	2.7	2.5	3.3	17	23	48	137	48.7	45.1	48.6	53.4
5	Bhutan	1.8	2.1	2.4	1	2	3	6	40.6	34.3	55.8	61.7
6	Guinea-Bissau	4.7	1.9	2.0	1	1	2	4	43.2	38.6	53.5	59.2
7	Nepal	2.6	2.6	2.5	19	24	38	65	43.4	30.8	53.7	64.7
8	Burundi	1.6	2.9	2.9	6	7	14	33	45.6	40.8	50.7	56.6
9	Chad	2.1	2.4	2.6	6	7	14	29	42.2	39.0	53.4	57.4
10	Madagascar	2.6	3.0	2.8	12	15	26	49	45.1	33.9	52.5	62.5
11	Sierra Leone	2.1	2.4	2.6	4	5	10	23	43.5	40.5	52.6	56.4
12	Bangladesh	2.7	2.2	1.9	111	131	180	268	42.3	26.2	56.8	69.0
13	Lao PDR	1.6	2.7	2.9	4	6	10	20	44.5	37.1	51.7	59.3
14	Malawi	3.1	3.3	3.1	9	12	24	73	46.9	45.0	49.7	52.8
15	Rwanda	3.4	3.0	2.3	7	9	17	37	48.9	40.8	50.6	57.2
16	Mali	2.1	2.6	3.1	9	11	24	59	46.8	41.0	49.8	56.5
17	Burkina Faso	2.1	2.6	3.0	9	12	23	50	45.7	38.6	50.9	58.8
18	Niger	2.9	3.3	3.5	8	11	24	76	47.8	45.6	49.1	52.2
19	India	2.3	2.1	1.8	866	1,017	1,365	1,886	35.8	23.9	60.2	68.1
20	Kenya	3.8	3.8	3.5	25	34	73	192	48.8	41.0	49.4	56.3
21	Nigeria	2.9	3.0	2.8	99	128	217	382	46.5	31.9	52.3	63.9
22	China	1.8	1.5	1.3	1,150	1,290	1,569	1,890	27.0	21.2	66.4	67.1
23	Haiti	1.7	1.9	1.7	7	8	10	17	39.8	29.1	56.8	65.8
24	Benin	2.7	3.2	2.9	5	6	11	20	47.5	34.9	50.8	62.0
25	Central African Rep.	2.2	2.7	2.5	3	4	7	18	42.3	41.4	53.5	56.3
26	Ghana	2.2	3.2	3.2	15	20	36	69	46.8	34.6	50.5	62.0
27	Pakistan	3.1	3.1	2.8	116	148	244	402	44.0	29.6	53.5	65.5
28	Togo	2.6	3.4	3.1	4	5	9	19	45.4	36.6	51.1	60.0
29	Guinea	1.4	2.6	2.9	6	8	14	33	46.7	40.6	50.7	56.8
30	Nicaragua	3.1	2.7	3.1	4	5	8	14	47.7	28.7	50.6	66.4
31	Sri Lanka	1.7	1.4	1.1	17	19	24	29	31.7	21.3	64.2	66.1
32	Mauritania	2.4	2.4	2.9	2	3	5	14	44.8	42.6	50.8	54.9
33	Yemen, Rep.	2.7	3.8	3.7	13	17	37	86	49.3	40.2	49.7	57.5
34	Honduras	3.4	3.3	2.9	5	7	11	18	39.8	28.1	56.8	66.9
35	Lesotho	2.3	2.8	2.4	2	2	3	6	41.9	29.0	55.0	65.7
36	Indonesia	2.4	1.8	1.4	181	206	265	354	35.8	23.6	60.2	68.4
37	Egypt, Arab Rep.	2.1	2.5	2.1	54	65	92	134	39.1	25.5	57.5	66.8
38	Zimbabwe	2.9	3.4	2.3	10	12	18	28	44.5	28.5	53.7	67.5
39	*Sudan*	3.0	2.7	3.0	26	34	60	117	45.2	35.5	52.4	60.9
40	*Zambia*	3.0	3.6	3.0	8	11	21	49	48.3	41.6	49.7	56.6
	Middle-income economies	**2.2** w	**1.8** w	**1.5** w	**1,401** t	**1,561** t	**2,140** t		**35.4** w	**25.3** w	**60.1** w	**65.0** w
	Lower-middle-income	**2.2** w	**2.0** w	**1.8** w	**774** t	**894** t	**1,302** t		**36.8** w	**27.0** w	**58.7** w	**64.8** w
41	Bolivia	2.6	2.5	2.4	7	9	14	22	41.2	28.1	55.9	66.3
42	Côte d'Ivoire	4.1	3.8	3.3	12	17	32	67	48.2	38.2	49.7	59.0
43	Senegal	2.9	3.0	2.8	8	10	18	38	45.5	38.1	51.6	59.3
44	Philippines	2.5	2.4	1.9	63	74	102	140	39.2	24.0	59.1	68.5
45	Papua New Guinea	2.4	2.3	2.3	4	5	7	12	40.3	29.0	57.2	66.5
46	Cameroon	3.0	2.8	3.1	12	16	29	56	44.7	35.7	51.6	61.0
47	Guatemala	2.8	2.9	2.9	9	12	21	36	45.2	30.3	52.3	65.0
48	Dominican Rep.	2.6	2.2	1.6	7	8	11	14	37.4	23.0	60.6	67.7
49	Ecuador	3.0	2.6	2.1	11	13	18	25	38.9	23.9	58.9	68.5
50	Morocco	2.4	2.6	2.2	26	31	45	65	40.7	24.6	57.5	68.7
51	Jordan	3.7	4.7	4.0	4	5	9	14	43.6	27.4	56.7	67.3
52	Tajikistan	. .	3.0	3.1	5	7	13	21	44.9	30.3	50.2	64.2
53	Peru	2.8	2.2	1.9	22	26	36	48	37.1	23.4	60.8	68.4
54	El Salvador	2.4	1.4	2.0	5	6	9	14	43.0	25.2	55.2	69.1
55	Congo	3.0	3.4	3.4	2	3	6	15	45.5	40.8	49.5	56.9
56	Syrian Arab Rep.	3.3	3.3	3.4	13	17	34	69	48.1	35.5	49.3	61.0
57	Colombia	2.2	2.0	1.5	33	38	50	63	34.8	22.2	62.9	67.8
58	Paraguay	3.0	3.1	2.6	4	6	9	13	40.3	27.1	56.7	66.2
59	Uzbekistan	. .	2.4	2.4	21	26	42	65	41.6	27.5	53.9	65.5
60	Jamaica	1.3	1.0	0.5	2	2	3	4	33.0	21.7	61.8	67.3
61	Romania	0.9	0.4	0.2	23	23	25	26	23.1	18.5	66.8	64.3
62	Namibia	2.8	3.1	3.2	1	2	3	7	44.8	34.2	51.5	61.9
63	Tunisia	2.2	2.4	1.9	8	10	13	18	37.0	23.3	60.2	68.5
64	Kyrgyzstan	. .	1.9	1.4	4	5	7	11	38.2	25.8	55.6	66.3
65	Thailand	2.7	1.9	1.4	57	65	82	104	32.4	21.8	65.9	68.5
66	Georgia	. .	0.7	0.4	5	6	6	7	23.9	19.6	64.5	62.1

Note: For data comparability and coverage, see the technical notes.   Figures in italics are for years other than those specified.

		Average annual growth of population (percent)			Population (millions)			Hypothetical size of stationary population (millions)	Age structure of population (percent)			
									0–14 years		15–64 years	
		1970–80	1980–91	1991–2000[a]	1991	2000[a]	2025[a]		1991	2025[a]	1991	2025[a]
67	Azerbaijan	. .	1.4	1.4	7	8	11	13	33.1	22.6	60.1	65.3
68	Turkmenistan	. .	2.5	2.5	4	5	8	13	41.3	29.5	54.2	64.1
69	Turkey	2.3	2.3	1.9	57	68	91	121	35.2	23.1	61.8	68.0
70	Poland	0.9	0.7	0.3	38	39	43	49	24.8	19.9	65.7	62.9
71	Bulgaria	0.4	0.1	−0.2	9	9	8	9	20.1	17.5	66.8	62.8
72	Costa Rica	2.8	2.7	2.0	3	4	5	6	48.2	22.5	49.7	66.2
73	Algeria	3.1	3.0	2.7	26	33	53	82	43.1	27.0	53.5	67.4
74	Panama	2.5	2.1	1.7	2	3	4	5	34.6	22.4	61.9	67.4
75	Armenia	. .	0.9	1.5	3	4	5	6	30.1	21.8	62.3	64.1
76	Chile	1.6	1.7	1.3	13	15	19	23	30.6	21.8	63.3	65.9
77	Iran, Islamic Rep.	3.3	3.6	3.4	58	78	160	354	45.8	37.3	51.0	58.6
78	Moldova	. .	0.9	0.1	4	4	5	7	31.6	23.0	60.0	63.4
79	Ukraine	. .	0.4	0.0	52	52	52	55	21.2	18.4	65.6	62.2
80	Mauritius	1.5	1.0	1.1	1	1	1	2	29.0	20.4	67.5	66.7
81	Czechoslovakia	0.7	0.3	. .	16	. .	. .	. .	21.2		67.5	
82	Kazakhstan	. .	1.2	0.7	17	18	22	28	31.6	22.3	62.4	64.6
83	Malaysia	2.4	2.6	2.2	18	22	31	43	38.6	23.9	58.5	67.6
	Upper-middle-income	**2.2** *w*	**1.5** *w*	**1.1** *w*	**627** *t*	**667** *t*	**839** *t*		**33.5** *w*	**22.6** *w*	**62.1** *w*	**65.5** *w*
84	Botswana	3.8	3.5	2.8	1	2	3	4	45.7	26.9	52.2	68.0
85	South Africa	2.8	2.5	2.2	39	47	69	103	38.6	25.6	58.3	67.4
86	Lithuania	. .	0.8	0.2	4	4	4	5	22.5	19.6	65.6	62.5
87	Hungary	0.4	−0.2	−0.4	10	10	10	10	20.0	17.8	67.7	61.8
88	Venezuela	3.5	2.6	1.9	20	23	32	41	36.7	23.0	61.3	67.5
89	Argentina	1.7	1.3	1.0	33	36	43	53	29.4	21.7	62.2	65.2
90	Uruguay	0.4	0.6	0.6	3	3	4	4	25.4	20.2	63.3	63.8
91	Brazil	2.4	2.0	1.4	151	172	224	285	34.2	22.6	62.8	67.5
92	Mexico	2.9	2.0	1.9	83	99	136	182	37.6	23.3	60.0	68.3
93	Belarus	. .	0.6	0.2	10	11	11	12	22.9	19.0	64.8	62.1
94	Russian Federation	. .	0.6	0.0	149	149	153	162	23.2	18.7	65.6	61.9
95	Latvia	. .	0.3	−0.1	3	3	3	3	21.7	19.6	65.1	61.7
96	Trinidad and Tobago	1.1	1.3	0.9	1	1	2	2	34.2	22.6	60.9	66.4
97	Gabon	4.7	3.5	2.9	1	2	3	7	39.7	39.8	53.4	56.2
98	Estonia	0.8	0.6	0.0	2	2	2	2	22.3	18.5	65.8	62.7
99	Portugal	1.3	0.1	0.0	10	10	10	9	20.2	16.0	67.9	65.0
100	Oman	4.2	4.3	3.9	2	2	5	10	46.6	37.1	51.1	58.3
101	Puerto Rico	1.7	0.9	0.9	4	4	5	5	27.5	19.7	64.6	64.0
102	Korea, Rep.	1.8	1.1	0.8	43	47	53	56	25.1	18.2	71.0	66.6
103	Greece	1.0	0.5	0.1	10	10	10	9	18.6	15.1	67.2	61.4
104	Saudi Arabia	5.0	4.6	3.5	15	21	41	82	43.0	34.8	54.7	59.6
105	*Yugoslavia*	0.9	0.6	. .	24	. .	. .	. .	22.5	. .	67.7	. .
	Low- and middle-income	**2.2** *w*	**2.0** *w*	**1.7** *w*	**4,528** *t*	**5,247** *t*	**7,325** *t*		**35.4** *w*	**26.3** *w*	**60.5** *w*	**65.4** *w*
	Sub-Saharan Africa	**2.8** *w*	**3.1** *w*	**3.0** *w*	**489** *t*	**635** *t*	**1,192** *t*		**48.5** *w*	**38.0** *w*	**53.1** *w*	**59.0** *w*
	East Asia & Pacific	**1.9** *w*	**1.6** *w*	**1.4** *w*	**1,667** *t*	**1,891** *t*	**2,367** *t*		**29.5** *w*	**22.0** *w*	**65.1** *w*	**67.5** *w*
	South Asia	**2.4** *w*	**2.2** *w*	**1.9** *w*	**1,152** *t*	**1,368** *t*	**1,908** *t*		**38.0** *w*	**25.4** *w*	**57.7** *w*	**67.4** *w*
	Europe and Central Asia	. .	**0.9** *w*	**0.6** *w*	**492** *t*	**475** *t*	**546** *t*		**26.1** *w*	**20.9** *w*	**64.8** *w*	**63.9** *w*
	Middle East & N. Africa	**2.9** *w*	**3.2** *w*	**2.9** *w*	**244** *t*	**315** *t*	**552** *t*		**42.9** *w*	**32.1** *w*	**53.4** *w*	**62.7** *w*
	Latin America & Caribbean	**2.4** *w*	**2.0** *w*	**1.6** *w*	**445** *t*	**515** *t*	**691** *t*		**36.0** *w*	**23.3** *w*	**60.8** *w*	**67.3** *w*
	Severely indebted	**2.3** *w*	**2.1** *w*	**1.8** *w*	**486** *t*	**569** *t*	**800** *t*		**36.7** *w*	**25.5** *w*	**59.9** *w*	**66.0** *w*
	High-income economies	**0.8** *w*	**0.6** *w*	**0.5** *w*	**822** *t*	**864** *t*	**922** *t*		**19.7** *w*	**17.2** *w*	**67.1** *w*	**61.2** *w*
	OECD members	**0.7** *w*	**0.6** *w*	**0.5** *w*	**783** *t*	**820** *t*	**869** *t*		**19.3** *w*	**17.2** *w*	**67.0** *w*	**61.2** *w*
106	Ireland	1.5	0.2	0.3	4	4	4	5	26.0	19.1	65.0	65.2
107	†Israel	2.7	2.2	2.8	5	6	8	10	30.9	21.0	65.8	65.6
108	New Zealand	1.1	0.7	0.8	3	4	4	5	22.8	19.4	65.8	63.1
109	Spain	1.0	0.4	0.1	39	39	39	33	19.3	14.5	68.6	63.3
110	†Hong Kong	2.4	1.2	0.8	6	6	7	6	20.6	15.4	70.3	61.4
111	†Singapore	2.0	1.7	1.5	3	3	4	4	22.9	18.3	70.7	63.5
112	United Kingdom	0.1	0.2	0.2	58	58	60	61	19.0	17.8	64.7	62.0
113	Australia	1.5	1.5	1.3	17	19	23	25	22.1	18.8	67.0	63.5
114	Italy	0.5	0.2	0.1	58	58	55	45	16.2	14.0	68.6	60.9
115	Netherlands	0.8	0.6	0.8	15	16	16	15	18.3	16.4	67.3	58.5
116	Belgium	0.2	0.1	0.2	10	10	10	10	17.7	16.7	66.0	60.6
117	Austria	0.1	0.2	0.4	8	8	8	7	17.3	15.7	66.8	61.5
118	France	0.6	0.5	0.4	57	59	63	63	19.9	17.3	65.6	60.9
119	Canada	1.2	1.2	0.8	27	29	34	35	20.9	18.0	67.1	61.2
120	United States	1.0	0.9	0.9	253	274	319	348	21.5	19.1	65.6	61.8
121	Germany	0.0	0.1	0.0	80	80	75	65	16.2	15.1	67.9	60.5
122	Denmark	0.4	0.1	0.2	5	5	5	5	17.0	16.2	67.7	60.8
123	Finland	0.4	0.4	0.3	5	5	5	5	19.2	17.2	66.7	59.2
124	Norway	0.5	0.4	0.4	4	4	5	5	18.9	17.7	64.5	61.5
125	Sweden	0.3	0.3	0.6	9	9	10	10	18.1	18.1	63.8	59.8
126	Japan	1.2	0.5	0.3	124	127	126	111	18.1	15.1	69.6	59.2
127	Switzerland	0.0	0.6	0.7	7	7	7	7	16.9	16.0	67.5	59.0
	World	**1.9** *w*	**1.7** *w*	**1.6** *w*	**5,350** *t*	**6,111** *t*	**8,247** *t*		**32.8** *w*	**25.3** *w*	**61.5** *w*	**65.0** *w*
	Fuel exporters	**3.2** *w*	**3.3** *w*	**3.0** *w*	**263** *t*	**342** *t*	**613** *t*		**48.6** *w*	**33.2** *w*	**57.0** *w*	**62.1** *w*

a. For the assumptions used in the projections, see the technical notes.

Table 27. Demography and fertility

		Crude birth rate (per 1,000 population)		Crude death rate (per 1,000 population)		Women of childbearing age as a percentage of all women		Total fertility rate			Assumed year of reaching net reproduction rate of 1	Married women of childbearing age using contraception (percent)[b]
		1970	1991	1970	1991	1965	1991	1970	1991	2000[a]		1989
	Low-income economies	**39** *w*	**30** *w*	**14** *w*	**10** *w*	**46** *w*	**51** *w*	**6.0** *w*	**3.8** *w*	**3.2** *w*		
	China and India	**37** *w*	**26** *w*	**12** *w*	**9** *w*	**46** *w*	**53** *w*	**5.8** *w*	**3.1** *w*	**2.5** *w*		
	Other low-income	**45** *w*	**38** *w*	**19** *w*	**13** *w*	**45** *w*	**47** *w*	**6.3** *w*	**5.2** *w*	**4.5** *w*		
1	Mozambique	48	45	24	19	47	45	6.7	6.5	6.7	2050	..
2	Tanzania	49	46	22	18	45	45	6.4	6.3	6.6	2035	..
3	Ethiopia	43	50	20	21	46	44	5.8	7.5	7.3	2045	..
4	Uganda	50	52	17	19	44	43	7.1	7.3	6.6	2050	11
5	Bhutan	41	39	22	17	48	47	5.9	5.9	5.4	2035	..
6	Guinea-Bissau	41	45	27	25	50	47	5.9	6.0	6.0	2040	..
7	Nepal	46	38	22	13	50	46	6.4	5.5	4.6	2030	..
8	Burundi	46	46	24	17	44	45	6.8	6.8	6.6	2045	9
9	Chad	45	44	26	18	47	46	6.0	5.9	6.1	2040	..
10	Madagascar	46	43	20	14	47	45	6.6	6.2	5.2	2035	..
11	Sierra Leone	49	48	30	22	47	45	6.5	6.5	6.5	2045	..
12	Bangladesh	48	34	21	13	44	48	7.0	4.4	3.3	2015	31
13	Lao PDR	44	44	23	16	47	45	6.1	6.7	6.0	2040	..
14	Malawi	56	53	24	21	46	45	7.8	7.6	7.4	2055	..
15	Rwanda	52	42	18	17	45	43	7.8	6.4	7.6	2040	..
16	Mali	51	50	26	19	46	45	6.5	7.0	7.0	2050	5
17	Burkina Faso	48	47	25	18	47	45	6.4	6.5	6.3	2045	..
18	Niger	50	52	28	19	45	44	7.2	7.4	7.3	2055	..
19	India	41	30	18	10	48	50	5.8	3.9	3.0	2015	45
20	Kenya	53	45	18	11	41	43	8.0	6.5	5.5	2050	27
21	Nigeria	51	44	21	14	45	45	6.9	5.9	5.0	2035	6
22	China	33	22	8	7	45	56	5.8	2.4	2.1	1995	72
23	Haiti	39	35	19	13	45	48	5.9	4.7	4.2	2025	11
24	Benin	50	45	22	15	44	44	6.9	6.3	5.2	2035	..
25	Central African Rep.	37	42	22	17	47	46	4.9	5.8	5.3	2045	..
26	Ghana	46	45	16	13	45	44	6.7	6.2	5.1	2035	13
27	Pakistan	48	41	19	11	43	46	7.0	5.7	4.6	2030	12
28	Togo	50	48	20	14	46	45	6.5	6.6	5.5	2040	33
29	Guinea	52	49	27	21	45	44	6.0	6.5	6.5	2045	..
30	Nicaragua	48	40	14	7	43	46	6.9	5.1	4.2	2025	..
31	Sri Lanka	29	21	8	6	47	54	4.3	2.5	2.1	2000	62
32	Mauritania	47	49	25	19	47	44	6.5	6.8	6.8	2050	..
33	Yemen, Rep.	53	52	23	14	47	44	7.8	7.5	7.5	2045	..
34	Honduras	49	38	15	7	44	46	7.2	5.0	4.1	2025	41
35	Lesotho	43	35	20	11	47	46	5.7	5.1	4.5	2025	..
36	Indonesia	42	25	18	9	47	52	5.5	3.0	2.4	2005	50
37	Egypt, Arab Rep.	40	32	17	9	43	48	5.9	4.2	3.1	2020	38
38	Zimbabwe	53	36	16	8	42	47	7.7	4.7	3.4	2020	43
39	*Sudan*	47	44	22	15	46	45	6.7	6.3	5.4	2035	9
40	*Zambia*	49	47	19	15	46	45	6.7	6.5	6.1	2045	..
	Middle-income economies	**35** *w*	**25** *w*	**11** *w*	**8** *w*	**45** *w*	**49** *w*	**5.0** *w*	**3.2** *w*	**3.1** *w*		
	Lower-middle-income	**36** *w*	**28** *w*	**12** *w*	**8** *w*	**45** *w*	**49** *w*	**5.3** *w*	**3.6** *w*	**3.4** *w*		
41	Bolivia	46	36	19	10	46	48	6.5	4.8	3.7	2025	30
42	Côte d'Ivoire	51	46	20	14	44	42	7.4	6.6	5.8	2040	..
43	Senegal	47	43	22	16	45	45	6.5	6.1	6.3	2040	..
44	Philippines	38	28	11	7	44	50	6.4	3.6	2.7	2010	..
45	Papua New Guinea	42	34	18	11	47	49	6.1	4.9	4.0	2025	..
46	Cameroon	43	42	18	12	47	44	5.8	5.8	5.3	2035	16
47	Guatemala	45	39	14	8	44	45	6.5	5.4	4.3	2030	23
48	Dominican Rep.	41	27	11	6	43	51	6.3	3.1	2.4	2005	56
49	Ecuador	43	30	12	7	43	50	6.3	3.7	2.8	2010	53
50	Morocco	47	32	16	8	45	49	7.0	4.3	3.4	2015	36
51	Jordan	..	37	..	5	45	46	..	5.3	5.6	2025	35
52	Tajikistan	..	39	..	6	..	44	5.9	5.3	..	2030	..
53	Peru	41	27	14	8	44	51	6.0	3.4	2.8	2010	..
54	El Salvador	44	34	12	7	44	47	6.3	4.1	3.2	2015	47
55	Congo	43	49	16	16	45	43	5.9	6.6	6.3	2045	..
56	Syrian Arab Rep.	47	44	13	6	..	43	7.7	6.3	5.4	2040	..
57	Colombia	36	24	9	6	43	54	5.3	2.7	2.2	2000	66
58	Paraguay	38	33	7	6	41	49	6.0	4.4	4.0	2025	48
59	Uzbekistan	..	35	..	6	..	47	5.7	4.3	..	2025	..
60	Jamaica	34	24	8	7	42	52	5.3	2.7	2.1	2000	55
61	Romania	21	14	10	11	50	48	2.9	1.9	2.1	2030	..
62	Namibia	44	43	18	11	46	45	6.0	5.7	4.8	2035	..
63	Tunisia	39	27	14	6	43	50	6.4	3.5	2.7	2010	50
64	Kyrgyzstan	..	29	..	8	..	46	4.9	3.9	..	2020	..
65	Thailand	39	21	9	6	44	55	5.5	2.3	2.1	1995	66
66	Georgia	..	15	..	8	..	48	2.6	2.1	..	1995	..

Note: For data comparability, see the technical notes.   Figures in italics are for years other than those specified.

		Crude birth rate (per 1,000 population)		Crude death rate (per 1,000 population)		Women of childbearing age as a percentage of all women		Total fertility rate			Assumed year of reaching net reproduction rate of 1	Married women of childbearing age using contraception (percent)[b]
		1970	1991	1970	1991	1965	1991	1970	1991	2000[a]		1989
67	Azerbaijan	..	27	..	6	..	50	4.7	2.8	..	2010	..
68	Turkmenistan	..	34	..	7	..	47	6.0	4.5	..	2030	..
69	Turkey	36	28	12	7	45	50	4.9	3.4	2.7	2010	63
70	Poland	17	14	8	11	47	48	2.2	2.1	2.1	2030	..
71	Bulgaria	16	11	9	12	51	47	2.2	1.8	1.9	2030	..
72	Costa Rica	33	27	7	4	42	51	4.9	3.2	2.3	2005	..
73	Algeria	49	34	16	7	44	46	7.4	5.0	3.7	2025	36
74	Panama	37	25	8	5	44	52	5.2	2.9	2.2	2005	..
75	Armenia	..	23	..	7	..	50	3.2	2.7	..	2005	..
76	Chile	29	23	10	6	45	53	4.0	2.7	2.1	2000	..
77	Iran, Islamic Rep.	45	44	16	9	42	44	6.7	6.2	5.6	2045	..
78	Moldova	..	17	..	11	..	43	2.6	2.5	..	2000	..
79	Ukraine	..	12	..	13	..	45	2.1	1.8	..	2030	..
80	Mauritius	29	17	7	6	45	56	3.6	2.0	1.8	2030	..
81	Czechoslovakia	16	14	12	12	46	..	2.1	1.9	2.0	..	..
82	Kazakhstan	..	21	..	8	..	49	3.4	2.8	..	2000	..
83	Malaysia	36	29	10	5	44	50	5.5	3.7	3.0	2015	..
	Upper-middle-income	**32** w	**21** w	**10** w	**8** w	**46** w	**50** w	**4.6** w	**2.7** w	**2.6** w		
84	Botswana	53	36	17	6	45	46	6.9	4.8	3.1	2020	33
85	South Africa	39	31	14	9	46	49	5.7	4.1	3.4	2020	..
86	Lithuania	..	15	..	11	..	48	2.4	2.0	..	2030	..
87	Hungary	15	12	12	14	48	47	2.0	1.8	1.8	2030	..
88	Venezuela	38	29	7	5	44	52	5.3	3.7	2.7	2005	..
89	Argentina	23	21	9	9	50	47	3.1	2.8	2.3	2000	..
90	Uruguay	21	17	10	10	49	47	2.9	2.4	2.1	1995	..
91	Brazil	35	24	10	7	45	52	4.9	2.8	2.4	2000	65
92	Mexico	43	28	10	5	43	51	6.5	3.2	2.4	2010	53
93	Belarus	..	13	..	11	..	46	2.4	1.9	..	2030	..
94	Russian Federation	..	12	..	11	..	46	2.0	1.7	..	2030	..
95	Latvia	..	14	..	13	..	45	1.9	2.0	..	2030	..
96	Trinidad and Tobago	28	24	8	6	46	51	3.6	2.8	2.3	2000	53
97	Gabon	31	42	21	15	48	46	4.2	5.8	6.1	2045	..
98	Estonia	15	14	11	12	..	46	2.1	2.1	..	2030	..
99	Portugal	20	12	10	11	48	49	2.8	1.4	1.6	2030	..
100	Oman	50	41	21	5	47	42	7.2	6.8	5.9	2040	..
101	Puerto Rico	25	18	7	7	48	52	3.2	2.3	2.1	1995	..
102	Korea, Rep.	30	16	9	6	46	57	4.3	1.8	1.8	2030	77
103	Greece	17	10	8	9	51	47	2.3	1.4	1.6	2030	..
104	Saudi Arabia	48	37	18	5	45	43	7.3	6.5	5.9	2040	..
105	*Yugoslavia*	18	14	9	9	50	..	2.3	2.0	2.0	..	..
	Low- and middle-income	**38** w	**28** w	**13** w	**10** w	**46** w	**50** w	**5.7** w	**3.6** w	**3.2** w		
	Sub-Saharan Africa	**48** w	**46** w	**21** w	**16** w	**45** w	**44** w	**6.6** w	**6.4** w	**5.9** w		
	East Asia & Pacific	**35** w	**24** w	**9** w	**7** w	**45** w	**55** w	**5.7** w	**2.7** w	**2.2** w		
	South Asia	**42** w	**32** w	**18** w	**11** w	**47** w	**49** w	**6.0** w	**4.2** w	**3.3** w		
	Europe and Central Asia	**22** w	**17** w	**10** w	**10** w	**48** w	**47** w	**2.9** w	**2.3** w	**2.3** w		
	Middle East & N. Africa	**45** w	**38** w	**16** w	**8** w	**44** w	**46** w	**6.8** w	**5.3** w	**4.6** w		
	Latin America & Caribbean	**36** w	**26** w	**10** w	**7** w	**45** w	**51** w	**5.2** w	**3.1** w	**2.6** w		
	Severely indebted	**36** w	**27** w	**11** w	**8** w	**46** w	**50** w	**5.2** w	**3.5** w	**3.0** w		
	High-income economies	**18** w	**13** w	**10** w	**9** w	**47** w	**50** w	**2.4** w	**1.8** w	**1.7** w		
	OECD members	**17** w	**13** w	**10** w	**9** w	**47** w	**50** w	**2.4** w	**1.8** w	**1.7** w		
106	Ireland	22	15	11	9	42	49	3.9	2.1	2.1	2030	60
107	†Israel	26	21	7	6	46	50	3.8	2.8	2.3	2000	..
108	New Zealand	22	17	9	8	45	52	3.2	2.1	2.0	1995	..
109	Spain	20	10	8	9	49	50	2.8	1.3	1.5	2030	..
110	†Hong Kong	21	13	5	6	45	56	3.3	1.4	1.5	2030	81
111	†Singapore	23	18	5	5	45	60	3.1	1.8	1.9	2030	..
112	United Kingdom	16	14	12	11	45	48	2.4	1.8	1.8	2030	..
113	Australia	21	15	9	7	47	53	2.9	1.9	1.9	2030	..
114	Italy	17	10	10	9	48	49	2.4	1.3	1.4	2030	..
115	Netherlands	18	13	8	9	47	51	2.6	1.6	1.6	2030	76
116	Belgium	15	13	12	11	44	48	2.2	1.7	1.6	2030	..
117	Austria	15	12	13	11	43	49	2.3	1.6	1.6	2030	..
118	France	17	13	11	9	43	49	2.5	1.8	1.8	2030	80
119	Canada	17	15	7	7	47	53	2.3	1.9	1.7	2030	..
120	United States	18	16	10	9	46	51	2.5	2.1	1.9	1995	74
121	Germany	14	10	13	11	45	47	2.1	1.4	1.6	2030	..
122	Denmark	14	13	10	12	47	50	1.9	1.7	1.6	2030	..
123	Finland	14	13	10	10	48	49	1.8	1.9	1.8	2030	84
124	Norway	17	14	10	11	45	49	2.5	1.9	1.8	2030	..
125	Sweden	14	14	10	11	47	47	1.9	2.1	1.9	1995	..
126	Japan	19	10	7	7	56	50	2.1	1.5	1.6	2030	56
127	Switzerland	16	13	9	9	48	50	2.1	1.6	1.7	2030	..
	World	**34** w	**26** w	**13** w	**9** w	**46** w	**50** w	**5.0** w	**3.3** w	**3.0** w		
	Fuel exporters	**47** w	**41** w	**18** w	**11** w	**44** w	**45** w	**6.8** w	**5.7** w	**5.0** w		

a. For assumptions used in the projections, see the technical notes to Table 26.   b. Data include women whose husbands practice contraception; see the technical notes.

Table 28. Health and nutrition

		Population per			Births attended by health staff (percent)	Babies with low birth weight (percent)	Infant mortality rate (per 1,000 live births)		Years of life lost per 1,000 population	Prevalence of malnutrition (under 5)
		Physician		Nursing person						
		1970	1990	1970	1990	1985	1985	1970	1991	1990	1990
	Low-income economies	**14,080** w	**6,760** w	**5,580** w	..			**109** w	**71** w		
	China and India	**4,890** w	**2,460** w	**2,990** w	..			**96** w	**60** w		
	Other low-income	**22,380** w	**11,730** w	**11,580** w	..			**136** w	**91** w		
1	Mozambique	18,860	..	4,280	..	28	15	171	149	141	..
2	Tanzania	22,600	24,880	3,310	5,470	74	14	132	115	112	20
3	Ethiopia	86,120	32,650	..	..	58	..	158	130	107	..
4	Uganda	9,210	..	..	..	..	10	109	118	107	45
5	Bhutan	..	13,110	..	..	3	..	182	132	..	..
6	Guinea-Bissau	17,500	..	2,820	..	16	20	185	148	..	..
7	Nepal	51,360	16,830	17,700	2,760	10	..	157	101	67	..
8	Burundi	58,570	..	6,870	..	12	14	138	107	81	38
9	Chad	61,900	30,030	8,010	..	..	11	171	124	106	35
10	Madagascar	10,120	8,130	240	..	62	10	181	114	63	53
11	Sierra Leone	17,830	..	2,700	..	25	14	197	145	188	..
12	Bangladesh	8,450	..	65,780	..	..	31	140	103	69	60
13	Lao PDR	15,160	4,380	1,390	490	..	39	146	100	93	..
14	Malawi	76,580	45,740	5,330	1,800	59	10	193	143	110	60
15	Rwanda	59,600	72,990	5,610	4,190	..	17	142	111	124	33
16	Mali	44,090	19,450	2,590	1,890	27	17	204	161	108	31
17	Burkina Faso	97,120	57,320	..	1,680	..	18	178	133	114	46
18	Niger	60,000	34,850	5,610	650	47	20	170	126	121	49
19	India	4,890	2,460	3,710	..	33	30	137	90	..	..
20	Kenya	8,000	10,130	2,520	..	..	13	102	67	45	..
21	Nigeria	19,830	..	4,240	..	..	25	139	85	98	..
22	China	..	..	2,500	..	..	6	69	38	..	..
23	Haiti	12,520	..	7,410	..	20	17	141	94	69	..
24	Benin	28,570	..	2,600	..	34	10	155	111	89	35
25	Central African Rep.	44,740	25,930	2,460	..	..	15	139	106	74	..
26	Ghana	12,910	22,970	690	1,670	73	17	111	83	55	36
27	Pakistan	4,310	2,940	6,600	5,040	24	25	142	97	61	57
28	Togo	28,860	..	1,590	..	..	20	134	87	79	14
29	Guinea	50,010	..	3,720	..	..	18	181	136	125	..
30	Nicaragua	2,150	1,450	..	..	..	15	106	56	45	..
31	Sri Lanka	5,900	..	1,280	..	87	28	53	18	14	45
32	Mauritania	17,960	..	3,740	..	23	10	165	119	..	30
33	Yemen, Rep.	34,790	..	..	..	..	..	175	109	104	..
34	Honduras	3,770	3,090	1,470	..	50	20	110	49	27	21
35	Lesotho	30,400	..	3,860	..	28	10	134	81	..	27
36	Indonesia	26,820	7,030	4,810	..	43	14	118	74	36	14
37	Egypt, Arab Rep.	1,900	1,320	2,320	490	24	7	158	59	33	13
38	Zimbabwe	6,300	7,180	640	1,000	69	15	96	48	37	12
39	Sudan	14,520	..	990	..	20	15	149	101	84	55
40	Zambia	13,640	11,290	1,730	600	..	14	106	106	86	..
	Middle-income economies	**3,640** w	**2,060** w	**1,640** w	..			**80** w	**38** w		
	Lower-middle-income	**5,000** w	**2,850** w	**1,300** w	..			**87** w	**42** w		
41	Bolivia	2,020	..	3,070	..	36	15	153	83	59	18
42	Côte d'Ivoire	15,520	..	1,930	..	20	14	135	95	50	12
43	Senegal	15,810	17,650	1,670	..	..	10	135	81	99	22
44	Philippines	9,270	8,120	2,690	..	..	18	66	41	27	19
45	Papua New Guinea	11,640	12,870	1,710	1,180	34	25	112	55	79	..
46	Cameroon	28,920	12,190	2,560	1,690	..	13	126	64	67	..
47	Guatemala	3,660	..	..	..	19	10	100	60	41	34
48	Dominican Rep.	..	..	1,400	..	57	16	90	54	24	13
49	Ecuador	2,910	980	2,680	620	27	10	100	47	21	38
50	Morocco	13,090	4,840	..	1,050	..	9	128	57	43	12
51	Jordan	2,480	770	870	500	75	7	..	29	18	..
52	Tajikistan	..	350	..	..	..	..	..	50	24	..
53	Peru	1,920	..	..	..	55	9	108	53	32	13
54	El Salvador	4,100	..	890	..	35	15	103	42	28	..
55	Congo	9,510	..	780	..	..	12	126	115	..	24
56	Syrian Arab Rep.	3,860	1,160	1,790	870	37	9	96	37	25	..
57	Colombia	2,260	..	..	..	51	15	77	23	11	12
58	Paraguay	2,300	..	2,210	..	22	6	57	35	22	4
59	Uzbekistan	..	280	..	..	..	..	..	44	20	..
60	Jamaica	2,630	..	530	..	89	8	43	15	..	8
61	Romania	840	560	430	..	99	6	49	27	19	..
62	Namibia	..	4,620	..	..	..	..	118	72	..	..
63	Tunisia	5,930	1,870	940	300	60	7	127	38	21	10
64	Kyrgyzstan	..	280	..	..	..	..	..	40	20	..
65	Thailand	8,290	5,000	1,170	550	33	12	73	27	22	26
66	Georgia	..	170	..	..	..	..	..	16	15	..

Note: For data comparability and coverage, see the technical notes. Figures in italics are for years other than those specified.

292

		Population per				Births attended by health staff (percent)	Babies with low birth weight (percent)	Infant mortality rate (per 1,000 live births)		Years of life lost per 1,000 population	Prevalence of malnutrition (under 5)
		Physician		Nursing person							
		1970	1990	1970	1990	1985	1985	1970	1991	1990	1990
67	Azerbaijan	..	250	..	..	..	..	..	33	16	..
68	Turkmenistan	..	290	..	..	..	..	..	56	29	..
69	Turkey	2,230	1,260	1,010	..	78	7	147	58	31	..
70	Poland	700	490	250	..	..	8	33	15	16	..
71	Bulgaria	540	320	240	..	100	..	27	17	15	..
72	Costa Rica	1,620	1,030	460	..	93	9	62	14	..	..
73	Algeria	8,100	2,330	..	330	..	9	139	64	27	25
74	Panama	1,660	840	1,560	..	83	8	47	21	..	..
75	Armenia	..	250	..	..	..	..	..	22	14	..
76	Chile	2,160	2,150	460	340	97	7	78	17	13	2
77	Iran, Islamic Rep.	3,270	3,140	1,780	1,150	..	9	131	68	32	..
78	Moldova	..	250	..	..	..	..	..	23	19	..
79	Ukraine	..	230	..	..	..	..	..	18	16	..
80	Mauritius	4,190	1,180	610	..	90	9	60	19	..	24
81	Czechoslovakia	470	310	170	..	100	6	22	11	16	..
82	Kazakhstan	..	250	..	..	..	..	..	32	19	..
83	Malaysia	4,310	2,700	1,270	380	82	9	45	15	15	24
	Upper-middle-income	**1,740** *w*	**640** *w*	**2,010** *w*	..			**72** *w*	**34** *w*		
84	Botswana	15,220	5,150	1,900	..	52	8	101	36	..	15
85	South Africa	..	1,750	300	..	..	12	79	54	40	..
86	Lithuania	..	220	..	..	..	..	..	14	19	..
87	Hungary	510	340	210	..	99	10	36	16	15	..
88	Venezuela	1,120	630	440	330	82	9	53	34	13	5
89	Argentina	530	..	960	..	..	6	52	25	12	..
90	Uruguay	910	..	..	..	..	8	46	21	15	9
91	Brazil	2,030	..	4,140	..	73	8	95	58	26	13
92	Mexico	1,480	..	1,610	..	..	15	72	36	17	14
93	Belarus	..	250	..	..	..	..	..	15	14	..
94	Russian Federation	..	210	..	..	..	..	..	20	17	..
95	Latvia	..	200	..	..	..	..	23	16	..	..
96	Trinidad and Tobago	2,250	..	190	..	90	..	44	19	..	9
97	Gabon	5,250	..	570	..	92	16	138	95	..	25
98	Estonia	..	210	..	..	..	..	20	14	..	..
99	Portugal	1,110	490	820	..	..	8	56	11	12	..
100	Oman	8,380	1,060	3,420	400	60	14	159	31	..	..
101	Puerto Rico	..	..	..	..	..	..	29	14	10	..
102	Korea, Rep.	2,220	1,370	1,190	..	65	9	51	16	10	..
103	Greece	620	580	990	..	..	6	30	10	10	..
104	Saudi Arabia	7,460	660	2,070	420	78	6	119	32	37	..
105	*Yugoslavia*	1,000	530	420	110	..	7	56	21	16	..
	Low- and middle-income	**10,260** *w*	**4,970** *w*	**4,640** *w*	..			**102** *w*	**61** *w*		
	Sub-Saharan Africa	**31,730** *w*	**23,540** *w*	**3,460** *w*	..			**144** *w*	**104** *w*		
	East Asia & Pacific	**15,760** *w*	**6,170** *w*	**2,720** *w*	..			**76** *w*	**42** *w*		
	South Asia	**6,120** *w*	**2,930** *w*	**10,150** *w*	..			**138** *w*	**92** *w*		
	Europe and Central Asia	**1,070** *w*	**420** *w*	**520** *w*	..			**63** *w*	**26** *w*		
	Middle East & N. Africa	**6,410** *w*	**2,240** *w*	**1,940** *w*	..			**135** *w*	**60** *w*		
	Latin America & Caribbean	**2,020** *w*	**1,180** *w*	**2,640** *w*	..			**82** *w*	**44** *w*		
	Severely indebted	**2,910** *w*	**1,680** *w*	**2,330** *w*	..			**85** *w*	**48** *w*		
	High-income economies	**710** *w*	**420** *w*	**220** *w*	..			**20** *w*	**8** *w*		
	OECD members	**700** *w*	**420** *w*	**220** *w*	..			**20** *w*	**8** *w*		
106	Ireland	980	630	160	..	..	4	20	8	11	..
107	†Israel	410	..	..	..	99	7	25	9	9	..
108	New Zealand	870	..	150	..	99	5	17	9	11	..
109	Spain	750	280	..	..	96	..	28	8	10	..
110	†Hong Kong	1,510	..	560	..	..	4	19	7	7	..
111	†Singapore	1,370	820	250	..	100	7	20	6	9	..
112	United Kingdom	810	..	240	..	98	7	19	7	12	..
113	Australia	830	..	..	..	99	6	18	8	9	..
114	Italy	550	210	..	..	..	7	30	8	10	..
115	Netherlands	800	410	300	..	..	4	13	7	10	..
116	Belgium	650	310	..	..	100	5	21	8	11	..
117	Austria	540	230	300	70	..	6	26	8	11	..
118	France	750	350	270	..	..	5	18	7	10	..
119	Canada	680	450	140	..	99	6	19	7	9	..
120	United States	630	420	160	..	100	7	20	9	11	..
121	Germany	580[a]	370[a]	..	..	..	5[a]	23	7	12	..
122	Denmark	690	390	..	..	..	6	14	8	12	..
123	Finland	960	410	130	..	..	4	13	6	11	..
124	Norway	720	..	160	..	100	4	13	8	10	..
125	Sweden	730	370	140	..	100	4	11	6	11	..
126	Japan	890	610	310	..	100	5	13	5	8	..
127	Switzerland	700	630	..	..	..	5	15	7	10	..
	World	**7,640** *w*	**3,980** *w*	**3,940** *w*	..			**85** *w*	**53** *w*		
	Fuel exporters	**10,730** *w*	**2,030** *w*	**2,770** *w*	..			**128** *w*	**70** *w*		

a. Data refer to the Federal Republic of Germany before unification.

Table 29. Education

		Percentage of age group enrolled in education										Primary net enrollment (percent)		Primary pupil/ teacher ratio	
		Primary				Secondary				Tertiary (total)					
		Total		Female		Total		Female							
		1970	1990	1970	1990	1970	1990	1970	1990	1970	1990	1975	1990	1970	1990
	Low-income economies	**74** w	**105** w	..	**98** w	**21** w	**41** w	..	**34** w	**2** w	..	..	..	**36** w	**38** w
	China and India	**83** w	**119** w	..	**109** w	**25** w	**46** w	..	**38** w	**1** w	..	..	..	**34** w	**38** w
	Other low-income	**55** w	**79** w	**44** w	**73** w	**13** w	**28** w	**8** w	**24** w	**3** w	**4** w	..	**72** w	**39** w	**39** w
1	Mozambique	47	58	..	48	5	7	..	5	0	..	..	41	69	58
2	Tanzania	34	63	27	63	3	4	2	4	..	0	..	47	47	35
3	Ethiopia	16	38	10	30	4	15	2	12	0	1	..	28	48	36
4	Uganda	38	76	30	..	4	13	2	..	1	1	..	..	34	35
5	Bhutan	6	26	1	20	1	5	0	2	0	..	..	..	21	37
6	Guinea-Bissau	39	59	23	42	8	7	6	4	0	0	59	..	45	..
7	Nepal	26	86	8	57	10	30	3	17	3	6	..	64	22	37
8	Burundi	30	72	20	64	2	5	1	4	1	1	..	..	37	67
9	Chad	35	57	17	35	2	7	0	3	..	1	..	..	65	67
10	Madagascar	90	92	82	90	12	19	9	18	..	3	..	64	65	40
11	Sierra Leone	34	48	27	39	8	16	5	12	1	1	..	..	32	34
12	Bangladesh	54	73	35	68	..	17	..	11	3	3	..	65	46	63
13	Lao PDR	53	104	40	91	3	26	2	21	1	1	..	69	36	28
14	Malawi	..	71	..	64	..	4	..	3	1	1	..	54	43	64
15	Rwanda	68	69	60	68	2	7	1	6	0	1	..	65	60	57
16	Mali	22	24	15	17	5	6	2	4	..	..	..	19	40	42
17	Burkina Faso	13	36	10	28	1	7	1	5	0	1	..	29	44	57
18	Niger	14	29	10	21	1	7	1	4	0	1	..	25	39	42
19	India	73	97	56	83	26	44	15	33	6	..	..	..	41	61
20	Kenya	58	94	48	92	9	23	5	19	1	2	88	..	34	31
21	Nigeria	37	72	27	63	4	20	3	17	2	3	..	..	34	41
22	China	89	135	..	129	24	48	..	41	1	2	..	100	29	22
23	Haiti	53	..	..	..	6	..	4	..	..	..	..	..	47	21
24	Benin	36	61	22	44	5	11	3	6	2	3	..	52	41	35
25	Central African Rep.	64	67	41	51	4	11	2	6	1	2	..	55	64	90
26	Ghana	64	75	54	67	14	39	8	31	2	2	..	..	30	29
27	Pakistan	40	37	22	26	13	22	5	13	..	3	..	..	41	41
28	Togo	71	103	44	80	7	22	3	10	2	3	..	72	58	59
29	Guinea	33	37	21	24	13	10	5	5	5	1	..	26	44	40
30	Nicaragua	80	98	81	101	18	38	17	44	14	..	65	75	37	33
31	Sri Lanka	99	107	94	105	47	74	48	77	3	4	..	..	..	..
32	Mauritania	14	51	8	42	2	16	0	10	..	4	..	..	24	49
33	Yemen, Rep.	22	..	7	..	3	..	..	..	..	..	..	..	..	..
34	Honduras	87	108	87	109	14	..	13	..	8	9	..	..	35	..
35	Lesotho	87	107	101	115	7	26	7	31	2	5	..	70	46	55
36	Indonesia	80	117	73	114	16	45	11	41	..	..	72	98	29	23
37	Egypt, Arab Rep.	72	98	57	90	35	82	23	71	18	19	..	..	38	25
38	Zimbabwe	74	117	66	116	7	50	6	46	1	5	..	..	..	36
39	Sudan	38	49	29	..	7	20	4	..	2	3	..	..	47	34
40	Zambia	90	93	80	91	13	20	8	14	2	2	..	80	47	44
	Middle-income economies	**94** w	**103** w	**88** w	**99** w	**33** w	**126** w	**28** w	**59** w	**14** w	**16** w	..	**89** w	**33** w	**25** w
	Lower-middle-income	**93** w	**100** w	**83** w	**97** w	**31** w	**172** w	**24** w	**57** w	**12** w	**16** w	..	**87** w	**33** w	**25** w
41	Bolivia	76	82	62	78	24	34	20	31	17	23	73	82	27	25
42	Côte d'Ivoire	58	..	45	..	9	..	4	..	3	..	..	..	45	36
43	Senegal	41	58	32	49	10	16	6	11	3	3	..	48	45	58
44	Philippines	108	111	..	110	46	73	..	75	3	27	95	99	29	33
45	Papua New Guinea	52	71	39	65	8	12	4	10	2	..	..	73	30	32
46	Cameroon	89	101	75	93	7	26	4	21	2	4	69	75	48	51
47	Guatemala	57	79	51	..	8	..	8	..	8	..	53	..	36	..
48	Dominican Rep.	100	95	100	96	21	..	..	..	..	..	..	..	55	47
49	Ecuador	97	..	95	..	22	..	23	..	37	20	78	..	38	..
50	Morocco	52	68	36	55	13	36	7	30	6	10	47	55	34	27
51	Jordan	..	..	..	..	..	..	..	..	..	..	..	..	39	17
52	Tajikistan	..	..	..	..	..	..	..	..	..	..	..	..	..	..
53	Peru	107	126	99	..	31	70	27	..	19	36	..	95	35	28
54	El Salvador	85	78	83	78	22	26	21	26	4	17	..	70	36	40
55	Congo	..	..	..	..	..	..	..	..	..	6	..	..	62	66
56	Syrian Arab Rep.	78	109	59	102	38	52	21	43	18	20	87	98	37	25
57	Colombia	108	110	110	111	25	52	24	57	10	14	..	73	38	30
58	Paraguay	109	107	103	106	17	30	17	30	9	8	83	95	32	25
59	Uzbekistan	..	..	..	..	..	..	..	..	..	..	..	..	..	..
60	Jamaica	119	105	119	105	46	60	45	63	7	5	90	99	47	37
61	Romania	112	91	113	96	44	92	38	90	11	9	..	..	..	..
62	Namibia	..	94	..	99	..	34	..	38	..	..	..	64	47	28
63	Tunisia	100	116	79	109	23	45	13	40	5	9	..	95	..	..
64	Kyrgyzstan	..	..	..	..	..	..	..	..	..	..	..	..	..	..
65	Thailand	83	85	79	85	17	32	15	32	13	16	..	..	35	18
66	Georgia	..	..	..	..	..	..	..	..	..	..	..	..	..	..

Note: For data comparability and coverage, see the technical notes. Figures in italics are for years other than those specified.

		Percentage of age group enrolled in education										Primary net enrollment (percent)		Primary pupil/ teacher ratio	
		Primary				Secondary				Tertiary (total)					
		Total		Female		Total		Female							
		1970	1990	1970	1990	1970	1990	1970	1990	1970	1990	1975	1990	1970	1990
67	Azerbaijan	..	..	..	..	..	..	..	..	..	..	..	..	..	..
68	Turkmenistan	..	..	..	..	..	..	..	..	..	..	..	99	38	30
69	Turkey	110	110	94	105	27	54	15	42	6	14	96	97	23	16
70	Poland	101	98	99	98	62	82	65	84	18	22	96	85	22	15
71	Bulgaria	101	96	100	95	79	74	..	75	16	31	..	..	..	..
72	Costa Rica	110	102	109	101	28	42	29	43	23	26	92	87	30	32
73	Algeria	76	95	58	88	11	60	6	53	6	12	77	88	40	28
74	Panama	99	107	97	105	38	59	40	62	22	21	87	92	27	20
75	Armenia	..	..	..	..	..	..	..	..	13	19	94	86	50	29
76	Chile	107	98	107	97	39	74	42	77	..	..	..	94	32	28
77	Iran, Islamic Rep.	72	112	52	106	27	56	18	47	..	6	..	..	32	28
78	Moldova	..	..	..	..	..	..	..	..	..	..	..	..	15	8
79	Ukraine	..	..	..	..	..	..	..	..	..	..	..	..	..	..
80	Mauritius	94	106	93	104	30	52	25	53	1	2	82	92	32	21
81	Czechoslovakia	98	93	98	93	31	84	39	87	17	18	..	..	20	19
82	Kazakhstan	..	..	..	..	..	..	..	..	..	..	..	..	31	20
83	Malaysia	87	93	84	93	34	56	28	58	4	7	..	..	31	20
	Upper-middle-income	**95 w**	**106 w**	**93 w**	**105 w**	**35 w**	**54 w**	**31 w**	**..**	**15 w**	**17 w**	**80 w**	**91 w**	**34 w**	**25 w**
84	Botswana	65	110	67	112	7	46	6	47	1	3	58	91	36	32
85	South Africa	99	..	99	..	18	..	17	..	..	..	..	..	34	..
86	Lithuania	..	..	..	..	..	..	..	..	..	..	..	90	18	12
87	Hungary	97	94	97	94	63	79	55	79	13	15	..	..	35	23
88	Venezuela	94	92	94	94	33	35	34	41	21	29	81	61	19	19
89	Argentina	105	111	106	114	44	..	47	..	22	50	96	..	29	23
90	Uruguay	112	106	109	106	59	77	64	..	18	50	..	..	28	23
91	Brazil	82	108	82	..	26	39	26	..	12	12	71	88	..	..
92	Mexico	104	112	101	110	22	53	17	53	14	14	..	98	46	31
93	Belarus	..	..	..	..	..	..	..	..	..	..	..	..	..	..
94	Russian Federation	..	..	..	..	..	..	..	..	..	..	..	..	..	..
95	Latvia	..	..	..	..	..	..	..	..	..	..	..	..	..	..
96	Trinidad and Tobago	106	95	107	96	42	80	44	82	5	6	87	90	34	26
97	Gabon	85	..	81	..	8	..	5	..	..	4	..	..	46	..
98	Estonia	..	..	..	..	..	..	..	..	..	..	..	..	..	..
99	Portugal	98	119	96	117	57	59	51	59	11	18	91	99	18	28
100	Oman	3	103	1	99	..	54	..	48	..	5	32	84	30	..
101	Puerto Rico	117	..	115	..	71	..	..	..	..	..	..	..	..	..
102	Korea, Rep.	103	108	103	110	42	87	32	85	16	39	99	100	57	36
103	Greece	107	100	106	101	63	99	55	97	17	29	97	96	31	21
104	Saudi Arabia	45	78	29	72	12	48	5	41	7	14	42	62	24	16
105	*Yugoslavia*	106	95	103	95	63	79	58	79	22	18	..	..	27	23
	Low- and middle-income	**79 w**	**104 w**	**64 w**	**98 w**	**24 w**	**61 w**	**18 w**	**39 w**	**6 w**	**7 w**	**..**	**91 w**	**35 w**	**35 w**
	Sub-Saharan Africa	**46 w**	**68 w**	**36 w**	**61 w**	**6 w**	**17 w**	**4 w**	**16 w**	**1 w**	**2 w**	**..**	**46 w**	**43 w**	**41 w**
	East Asia & Pacific	**88 w**	**127 w**	**77 w**	**123 w**	**24 w**	**49 w**	**16 w**	**44 w**	**4 w**	**5 w**	**..**	**100 w**	**30 w**	**23 w**
	South Asia	**67 w**	**88 w**	**50 w**	**75 w**	**25 w**	**39 w**	**14 w**	**29 w**	**3 w**	**..**	**..**	**67 w**	**42 w**	**58 w**
	Europe and Central Asia	**105 w**	**101 w**	**100 w**	**100 w**	**50 w**	**71 w**	**44 w**	**70 w**	**14 w**	**16 w**	**..**	**89 w**	**27 w**	**19 w**
	Middle East & N. Africa	**68 w**	**97 w**	**50 w**	**90 w**	**24 w**	**56 w**	**15 w**	**50 w**	**10 w**	**12 w**	**..**	**85 w**	**35 w**	**26 w**
	Latin America & Caribbean	**95 w**	**107 w**	**94 w**	**106 w**	**28 w**	**49 w**	**26 w**	**57 w**	**15 w**	**16 w**	**..**	**88 w**	**34 w**	**26 w**
	Severely indebted	**90 w**	**104 w**	**85 w**	**98 w**	**31 w**	**59 w**	**27 w**	**56 w**	**14 w**	**15 w**	**78 w**	**88 w**	**32 w**	**25 w**
	High-income economies	**106 w**	**104 w**	**106 w**	**104 w**	**73 w**	**92 w**	**71 w**	**96 w**	**36 w**	**33 w**	**88 w**	**97 w**	**26 w**	**17 w**
	OECD members	**106 w**	**104 w**	**106 w**	**104 w**	**74 w**	**93 w**	**73 w**	**96 w**	**36 w**	**33 w**	**88 w**	**97 w**	**26 w**	**17 w**
106	Ireland	106	100	106	101	74	98	77	102	20	26	91	88	24	27
107	†Israel	96	93	95	95	57	83	60	86	29	33	..	..	17	18
108	New Zealand	110	106	109	105	77	89	76	91	29	41	100	100	21	19
109	Spain	123	109	125	108	56	107	48	112	24	34	100	100	34	21
110	†Hong Kong	117	106	115	..	36	..	31	..	11	..	92	..	33	..
111	†Singapore	105	110	101	109	46	69	45	71	..	8	100	100	30	26
112	United Kingdom	104	107	104	107	73	84	73	85	20	25	97	100	23	20
113	Australia	115	105	115	105	82	83	80	85	25	35	98	97	28	17
114	Italy	110	97	109	96	61	79	55	78	28	31	97	..	22	12
115	Netherlands	102	117	102	118	75	103	69	101	30	34	92	100	30	13
116	Belgium	103	102	104	103	81	104	80	104	26	37	..	99	20	10
117	Austria	104	103	103	102	72	83	73	85	23	33	89	93	21	11
118	France	117	111	117	110	74	99	77	100	26	40	98	100	26	12
119	Canada	101	105	100	104	65	106	65	107	42	70	..	96	23	15
120	United States	..	105	..	104	..	92	..	91	56	75	72	99	27	..
121	Germany	..	105	..	105	..	97	..	103	..	32	..	87	9	18
122	Denmark	96	98	97	98	78	109	75	110	29	32	..	100	22	11
123	Finland	82	99	79	99	102	114	106	124	32	47	100	98	20	6
124	Norway	89	99	94	99	83	100	83	102	26	43	100	100	20	6
125	Sweden	94	107	95	107	86	91	85	93	31	33	100	100	20	6
126	Japan	99	101	99	101	86	96	86	97	31	31	99	100	26	21
127	Switzerland	..	..	..	..	..	..	..	..	18	26	..	..	..	..
	World	**83 w**	**104 w**	**71 w**	**99 w**	**31 w**	**65 w**	**28 w**	**46 w**	**13 w**	**11 w**	**..**	**92 w**	**33 w**	**33 w**
	Fuel exporters	**59 w**	**89 w**	**44 w**	**83 w**	**15 w**	**39 w**	**11 w**	**35 w**	**5 w**	**11 w**	**..**	**90 w**	**34 w**	**32 w**

Table 30. Income distribution and PPC estimates of GDP

			Percentage share of income or consumption						PPC estimates of GDP per capita [a]			
									United States = 100		Current international dollars	
		Year	Lowest 20 percent	Second quintile	Third quintile	Fourth quintile	Highest 20 percent	Highest 10 percent	1987	1991	Observed [a]	Regression [b]
Low-income economies												
China and India												
Other low-income												
1	Mozambique								2.7c	2.7c	. .	600
2	Tanzania	1991 d.e	2.4	5.7	10.4	18.7	62.7	46.5	2.5	2.6	570f	640
3	Ethiopia	1981–82 d.g	8.6	12.7	16.4	21.1	41.3	27.5	1.9	1.7	370f	620
4	Uganda	1989–90 d.e	8.5	12.1	16.0	21.5	41.9	27.2	4.7c	5.1c	. .	1,120
5	Bhutan								2.8c	2.8c	. .	620
6	Guinea-Bissau								3.1c	3.1c	. .	690
7	Nepal	1984–85 h.i	9.1	12.9	16.7	21.8	39.5	25.0	4.8c	5.1c	. .	1,130
8	Burundi								3.2c	3.3c	. .	720
9	Chad								2.9c	3.3c	. .	730
10	Madagascar								3.6	3.2	710f	1,120
11	Sierra Leone								3.5	3.6	800f	1,190
12	Bangladesh	1988–89 d.e	9.5	13.4	17.0	21.6	38.6	24.6	5.0	5.2	1,160f	990
13	Lao PDR								8.3c	8.7c	. .	1,930
14	Malawi								3.5	3.6	800f	570
15	Rwanda	1983–85 d.e	9.7	13.1	16.7	21.6	38.9	24.6	3.9	3.1	680f	750
16	Mali								2.3	2.2	480f	730
17	Burkina Faso								3.4c	3.4c	. .	750
18	Niger								3.9c	3.6c	. .	790
19	India	1989–90 d.e	8.8	12.5	16.2	21.3	41.3	27.1	4.6	5.2	1,150f	1,900
20	Kenya	1981–83 j.k	2.7	6.4	11.1	18.9	60.9	45.4	6.1	6.1	1,350f	1,490
21	Nigeria								5.5	6.1	1,360f	1,900
22	China	1990 h.i	6.4	11.0	16.4	24.4	41.8	24.6	6.5	7.6	1,680l	2,040
23	Haiti								6.7c	5.5c	. .	1,220
24	Benin								7.3	6.8	1,500f	1,180
25	Central African Rep.								5.5c	4.9c	. .	1,090
26	Ghana	1988–89 d.e	7.0	11.3	15.8	21.8	44.1	29.0	8.9c	9.0c	. .	2,000
27	Pakistan	1991 d.e	8.4	12.9	16.9	22.2	39.7	25.2	8.3	8.9	1,970f	1,570
28	Togo								6.4c	5.9c	. .	1,310
29	Guinea											
30	Nicaragua								15.5c	11.5c	. .	2,550
31	Sri Lanka	1985–86 h.i	4.9	8.4	12.4	18.2	56.2	43.0	11.0	12.0	2,650f	2,580
32	Mauritania								6.9c	6.3c	. .	1,390
33	Yemen, Rep.											
34	Honduras	1989 h.i	2.7	6.0	10.2	17.6	63.5	47.9	8.5	8.2	1,820m	2,670
35	Lesotho	1986–87 h.i	4.5	6.5	10.0	17.6	61.3	45.0	7.2c	8.5c	. .	1,890
36	Indonesia	1990 d.e	8.7	12.1	15.9	21.1	42.3	27.9	10.5	12.3	2,730m	2,720
37	Egypt, Arab Rep.								16.3	16.3	3,600f	3,140
38	Zimbabwe								9.2	9.8	2,160f	2,580
39	Sudan											
40	Zambia								5.3	4.6	1,010f	1,010
Middle-income economic												
Lower-middle-income												
41	Bolivia								9.6	9.8	2,170m	2,260
42	Côte d'Ivoire	1988 d.e	7.3	11.9	16.3	22.3	42.2	26.9	9.1	6.8	1,510f	1,680
43	Senegal								7.9	7.6	1,680f	1,600
44	Philippines	1988 d.e	6.5	10.1	14.4	21.2	47.8	32.1	10.8	11.0	2,440f	2,900
45	Papua New Guinea								8.8c	8.3c	. .	1,830
46	Cameroon								15.1	10.8	2,400f	1,970
47	Guatemala	1989 h.i	2.1	5.8	10.5	18.6	63.0	46.6	14.4	14.4	3,180m	2,600
48	Dominican Rep.	1989 h.i	4.2	7.9	12.5	19.7	55.6	39.6	15.5	13.9	3,080m	3,040
49	Ecuador								17.8	18.7	4,140m	3,950
50	Morocco	1990–91 d.e	6.6	10.5	15.0	21.7	46.3	30.5	13.8	15.1	3,340f	2,800
51	Jordan								29.3c	22.0c	. .	4,870
52	Tajikistan								11.9	9.9	2,180l	. .
53	Peru	1985–86 d.e	4.9	9.2	13.7	21.0	51.4	35.4	19.7	14.1	3,110m	2,930
54	El Salvador								9.5	9.5	2,110m	2,750
55	Congo								13.1	12.7	2,800f	
56	Syrian Arab Rep.								20.9	23.6	5,220n	4,630
57	Colombia	1988 h.i	4.0	8.7	13.5	20.8	53.0	37.1	23.7	24.7	5,460m	4,080
58	Paraguay								14.9	15.5	3,420m	2,900
59	Uzbekistan								12.1	12.6	2,790l	
60	Jamaica	1990 d.e	6.0	9.9	14.5	21.3	48.4	32.6	15.1	16.6	3,670l	4,050
61	Romania								42.3	31.2	6,900n	
62	Namibia											
63	Tunisia	1990 d.e	5.9	10.4	15.3	22.1	46.3	30.7	20.2	21.2	4,690f	3,780
64	Kyrgyzstan								14.2	14.8	3,280l	
65	Thailand	1988 d.i	6.1	9.4	13.5	20.3	50.7	35.3	17.1	23.8	5,270l	3,740
66	Georgia								24.7	16.6	3,670l	. .

Note: For data comparability and coverage, see the technical notes.   Figures in italics are for years other than specified.

			Percentage share of income or consumption						PPC estimates of GDP per capita [a]			
									United States = 100		Current international dollars	
		Year	Lowest 20 percent	Second quintile	Third quintile	Fourth quintile	Highest 20 percent	Highest 10 percent	1987	1991	Observed [a]	Regression [b]
67	Azerbaijan		..	..	..	..	..	..	20.2	16.6	3,670 [l]	..
68	Turkmenistan		..	..	..	..	..	..	17.3	16.0	3,540 [l]	
69	Turkey		..	..	..	..	..	..	21.0	21.9	4,840	3,950
70	Poland	1989 [h,i]	9.2	13.8	17.9	23.0	36.1	21.6	24.8	20.3	4,500 [f]	4,720
71	Bulgaria		..	..	..	..	..	..	31.1 [c]	22.5 [c]		4,980
72	Costa Rica	1989 [h,i]	4.0	9.1	14.3	21.9	50.8	34.1	22.5	23.0	5,100 [m]	4,320
73	Algeria								28.6 [c]	25.5 [c]		5,640
74	Panama	1989 [h,i]	2.0	6.3	11.6	20.3	59.8	42.1	25.6	22.2	4,910 [m]	5,030
75	Armenia		..	..	..	..	..	..	24.3	20.8	4,610 [l]	
76	Chile	1989 [h,i]	3.7	6.8	10.3	16.2	62.9	48.9	27.3	31.9	7,060 [m]	5,380
77	Iran, Islamic Rep.		..	..	..	..	..	..	22.1	21.1	4,670 [f]	6,760
78	Moldova		..	..	..	..	..	..	23.1	21.0	4,640 [l]	..
79	Ukraine		..	..	..	..	..	..	25.7	23.4	5,180 [l]	
80	Mauritius		..	..	..	..	..	..	40.8	50.5	11,180 [f]	5,480
81	Czechoslovakia		..	..	..	..	..	..	35.0 [c]	28.4 [c]		6,280
82	Kazakhstan		..	..	..	..	..	..	23.0	20.3	4,490 [l]	..
83	Malaysia	1989 [h,i]	4.6	8.3	13.0	20.4	53.7	37.9	26.5	33.4	7,400 [n]	6,530
	Upper-middle-income											
84	Botswana	1985–86 [d,g]	1.4	4.6	9.4	18.2	66.4	49.6	16.7	21.2	4,690 [f]	4,080
85	South Africa		..	..	..	..	..	..				
86	Lithuania								29.4	24.4	5,410 [l]	
87	Hungary	1989 [h,i]	10.9	14.8	18.0	22.0	34.4	20.8	31.9	27.5	6,080 [f]	5,260
88	Venezuela	1989 [h,i]	4.8	9.5	14.4	21.9	49.5	33.2	36.3	36.7	8,120 [m]	6,990
89	Argentina		..	..	..	..	..	..	25.6	23.1	5,120 [m]	5,840
90	Uruguay								30.4	30.1	6,670 [m]	5,690
91	Brazil	1989 [h,i]	2.1	4.9	8.9	16.8	67.5	51.3	26.0	23.7	5,240 [m]	4,180
92	Mexico	1984 [h,i]	4.1	7.8	12.3	19.9	55.9	39.5	31.4	32.4	7,170 [n]	5,190
93	Belarus		..	..	..	..	..	..	29.7	31.0	6,850 [l]	
94	Russian Federation		..	..	..	..	..	..	35.2	31.3	6,930 [l]	..
95	Latvia		..	..	..	..	..	..	37.2	34.1	7,540 [l]	
96	Trinidad and Tobago		..	..	..	..	..	..	42.5 [c]	37.9 [c]		8,380
97	Gabon		..	..	..	..	..	..	..	..		..
98	Estonia		..	..	..	..	..	..	45.8	36.6	8,000 [l]	
99	Portugal		..	..	..	..	..	..	35.9	42.7	9,450	7,730
100	Oman		..	..	..	..	..	..	38.5 [c]	40.6 [c]		8,990
101	Puerto Rico		..	..	..	..	..	..	44.7 [c]	49.3 [c]		10,920
102	Korea, Rep.		..	..	..	..	..	..	28.6	37.6	8,320 [f]	10,070
103	Greece		..	..	..	..	..	..	33.8	34.7	7,680	9,700
104	Saudi Arabia								45.1 [c]	49.0 [c]		10,850
105	*Yugoslavia*	1989 [h,i]	5.3	10.7	16.2	23.7	44.2	27.4	28.4 [c]	..	..	..

Low- and middle-income
Sub-Saharan Africa
East Asia & Pacific
South Asia
Europe and Central Asia
Middle East & N. Africa
Latin America & Caribbean
Severely indebted

High-income economies
OECD members

106	Ireland		..	..	..	..	..	..	42.3	51.6	11,430	15,060
107	†Israel	1979 [j,k]	6.0	12.1	17.8	24.5	39.6	23.5	60.2	60.8	13,460 [m]	12,980
108	New Zealand	1981–82 [j,k]	5.1	10.8	16.2	23.2	44.7	28.7	68.0	63.1	13,970	12,660
109	Spain	1980–81 [j,k]	6.9	12.5	17.3	23.2	40.0	24.5	50.5	57.3	12,670	13,760
110	†Hong Kong	1980 [j,k]	5.4	10.8	15.2	21.6	47.0	31.3	74.0	83.7	18,520 [f]	14,470
111	†Singapore	1982–83 [j,k]	5.1	9.9	14.6	21.4	48.9	33.5	57.1 [c]	71.2 [c]		15,760
112	United Kingdom	1979 [j,k]	5.8	11.5	18.2	25.0	39.5	23.3	73.0	73.8	16,340	15,470
113	Australia	1985 [j,k]	4.4	11.1	17.5	24.8	42.2	25.8	76.7	75.4	16,680	15,820
114	Italy	1986 [j,k]	6.8	12.0	16.7	23.5	41.0	25.3	71.4	77.0	17,040	15,960
115	Netherlands	1983 [j,k]	6.9	13.2	17.9	23.7	38.3	23.0	70.0	76.0	16,820	19,110
116	Belgium	1978–79 [j,k]	7.9	13.7	18.6	23.8	36.0	21.5	71.5	79.1	17,510	18,470
117	Austria		..	..	..	..	..	..	72.6	79.9	17,690	17,850
118	France	1979 [j,k]	6.3	12.1	17.2	23.5	40.8	25.5	78.1	83.3	18,430	18,990
119	Canada	1987 [j,k]	5.7	11.8	17.7	24.6	40.2	24.1	90.7	87.3	19,320	19,370
120	United States	1985 [j,k]	4.7	11.0	17.4	25.0	41.9	25.0	100.0	100.0	22,130	22,130
121	Germany	1984 [j,k]	6.8	12.7	17.8	24.1	38.7	23.4	80.5	89.3	19,770	21,130
122	Denmark	1981 [j,k]	5.4	12.0	18.4	25.6	38.6	22.3	79.1	80.8	17,880	20,780
123	Finland	1981 [j,k]	6.3	12.1	18.4	25.5	37.6	21.7	73.0	72.9	16,130	19,850
124	Norway	1979 [j,k]	6.2	12.8	18.9	25.3	36.7	21.2	79.8	77.6	17,170	20,290
125	Sweden	1981 [j,k]	8.0	13.2	17.4	24.5	36.9	20.8	80.3	79.0	17,490	19,510
126	Japan	1979 [j,k]	8.7	13.2	17.5	23.1	37.5	22.4	74.4	87.6	19,390	23,830
127	Switzerland	1982 [j,k]	5.2	11.7	16.4	22.1	44.6	29.8	95.6	98.4	21,780	..

World
Fuel exporters

a. Extrapolated from 1990 ICP estimates unless noted otherwise; b. See technical notes; c. Obtained from the regression estimates; d. Data refer to expenditure shares by fractiles of persons; e. Data ranked by per capita expenditure; f. Extrapolated from 1985 ICP estimates; g. Data ranked by household expenditure; h. Data refer to income shares by fractiles of persons; i. Data ranked by per capita income; j. Data refer to income shares by fractiles of households; k. Data ranked by household income; l. These values are subject to more than the usual margin of error (see technical notes); m and n are extrapolated, respectively, from 1980 and 1975 ICP estimates and scaled up by the corresponding US deflator.

Table 31. Urbanization

	Urban population				Population in capital city as a percentage of		Population in cities of 1 million or more in 1990, as a percentage of			
	As a percentage of total population		Average annual growth rate (percent)		Urban	Total	Urban		Total	
	1970	1991	1970-80	1980-91	1990	1990	1965	1990	1965	1990
Low-income economies	**18** w	**39** w	**3.7** w	..	**11** w	**3** w	**41** w	**31** w	**7** w	**9** w
China and India	**18** w	**46** w	**3.2** w	..	**3** w	**1** w	**42** w	**29** w	**8** w	**9** w
Other low-income	**18** w	**28** w	**4.7** w	**5.0** w	**27** w	**7** w	**38** w	**35** w	**6** w	**10** w
1 Mozambique	6	28	11.5	10.1	38	10	68	38	3	10
2 Tanzania	7	34	12.7	10.1	21	7	38	18	2	6
3 Ethiopia	9	13	4.8	5.3	29	4	27	30	2	4
4 Uganda	8	11	3.6	4.5	41	4	..	..	..	..
5 Bhutan	3	6	4.1	5.7	22	1	..	..	..	..
6 Guinea-Bissau	15	20	5.8	3.7	36	7	..	..	..	..
7 Nepal	4	10	7.3	7.3	20	2	..	..	..	..
8 Burundi	2	6	7.7	5.7	81	4	..	..	..	..
9 Chad	11	30	8.1	6.3	43	13	..	..	..	..
10 Madagascar	14	25	5.3	6.2	23	6	..	..	..	..
11 Sierra Leone	18	33	5.2	5.3	52	17	..	..	..	..
12 Bangladesh	8	17	6.8	6.1	37	6	50	47	3	8
13 Lao PDR	10	19	5.1	6.0	53	10	..	..	..	..
14 Malawi	6	12	7.5	6.0	31	4	..	..	..	..
15 Rwanda	3	8	8.1	7.6	56	4	..	..	..	..
16 Mali	14	20	4.1	3.8	41	8	..	..	..	..
17 Burkina Faso	6	9	4.3	5.2	51	5	..	..	..	..
18 Niger	9	20	7.5	7.4	39	8	..	..	..	..
19 India	20	27	3.9	3.7	4	1	32	32	6	9
20 Kenya	10	24	8.5	7.8	26	6	41	27	4	6
21 Nigeria	20	36	6.1	5.8	23	8	23	24	4	8
22 China	18	60	2.6	..	2	1	49	27	9	9
23 Haiti	20	29	3.5	3.8	56	16	47	56	8	16
24 Benin	18	38	8.4	5.1	12	4	..	..	..	..
25 Central African Rep.	30	48	4.5	4.8	52	24	..	..	..	..
26 Ghana	29	33	2.7	4.1	22	7	27	22	7	7
27 Pakistan	25	33	4.4	4.6	1	0	44	42	10	13
28 Togo	13	26	6.4	6.6	55	14	..	..	..	..
29 Guinea	14	26	4.8	5.6	89	23	47	88	5	23
30 Nicaragua	47	60	4.4	3.9	46	28	36	44	15	26
31 Sri Lanka	22	22	1.5	1.5	17	4	..	..	..	..
32 Mauritania	14	48	10.4	7.3	83	39	..	..	..	..
33 Yemen, Rep.	13	30	7.0	7.3	11	3	..	..	..	..
34 Honduras	29	45	5.7	5.4	35	15	..	..	..	..
35 Lesotho	9	21	7.1	7.0	17	4	..	..	..	..
36 Indonesia	17	31	5.1	5.0	17	5	42	33	7	10
37 Egypt, Arab Rep.	42	47	2.5	3.2	37	17	53	52	22	24
38 Zimbabwe	17	28	5.6	5.8	31	9	..	..	..	..
39 *Sudan*	16	22	4.9	3.9	35	8	30	35	4	8
40 Zambia	30	51	5.9	6.0	25	12	..	..	..	..
Middle-income economies	**46** w	**62** w	**3.7** w	**3.2** w	**25** w	**14** w	**40** w	**40** w	**17** w	**24** w
Lower-middle-income	**41** w	**54** w	**3.6** w	**3.3** w	**28** w	**13** w	**36** w	**36** w	**13** w	**19** w
41 Bolivia	41	52	3.4	4.0	34	17	28	33	11	17
42 Côte d'Ivoire	27	41	7.5	4.7	45	18	30	45	7	18
43 Senegal	33	39	3.4	4.0	52	20	40	53	13	20
44 Philippines	33	43	3.8	3.7	32	14	28	32	9	14
45 Papua New Guinea	10	16	5.3	4.3	33	5	..	..	..	..
46 Cameroon	20	42	7.6	5.6	16	7	..	..	..	..
47 Guatemala	36	40	3.3	3.5	23	9	..	..	..	..
48 Dominican Rep.	40	61	4.9	3.9	52	31	46	51	16	31
49 Ecuador	40	57	4.8	4.4	21	12	50	49	19	28
50 Morocco	35	49	4.1	4.3	9	4	39	36	12	17
51 Jordan[b]	50	69	5.7	5.7	46	31	33	38	15	26
52 Tajikistan	..	32			..	..	..	..	..	..
53 Peru	57	71	4.0	3.1	41	29	37	41	19	29
54 El Salvador	39	45	2.9	2.1	26	11	..	..	..	..
55 Congo	33	41	4.0	4.7	68	28	..	..	..	..
56 Syrian Arab Rep.	44	51	4.1	4.1	34	17	58	60	23	30
57 Colombia	57	71	3.3	2.9	21	15	38	39	20	27
58 Paraguay	37	48	4.2	4.4	48	23	..	..	..	..
59 Uzbekistan	..	41			..	..	..	..	..	..
60 Jamaica	42	53	2.6	2.1	52	27	..	..	..	..
61 Romania	42	53	2.5	1.2	18	9	21	18	8	9
62 Namibia	19	28	4.9	5.1	36	10	..	..	..	..
63 Tunisia	44	55	4.1	2.8	37	20	35	37	14	20
64 Kyrgyzstan	..	38			..	..	..	..	..	..
65 Thailand	13	23	5.4	4.6	56	13	66	57	8	13
66 Georgia	..	56			..	..	..	..	..	..

Note: For data comparability and coverage, see the technical notes. Figures in italics are for years other than those specified.

		As a percentage of total population		Average annual growth rate (percent)		Population in capital city as a percentage of		Population in cities of 1 million or more in 1990, as a percentage of			
		1970	1991	1970-80	1980-91	Urban 1990	Total 1990	Urban 1965	Urban 1990	Total 1965	Total 1990
67	Azerbaijan	..	54	..	..	..	..	41	35	14	22
68	Turkmenistan	..	..	..	..	..	..	..	..	..	..
69	Turkey	38	63	3.7	5.8	8	5	32	28	16	18
70	Poland	52	62	2.0	1.3	9	6	21	19	10	13
71	Bulgaria	52	68	2.1	1.1	20	13	..	..	..	..
72	Costa Rica	40	48	3.6	3.7	72	34	62	72	24	34
73	Algeria	40	53	4.1	4.8	23	12	24	23	9	12
74	Panama	48	54	2.9	2.9	37	20	..	..	..	..
75	Armenia	..	68	..	..	..	..	..	..	..	..
76	Chile	75	86	2.4	2.2	42	36	39	42	28	36
77	Iran, Islamic Rep.	41	57	5.2	5.0	21	12	43	41	16	23
78	Moldova	..	47	..	..	..	..	..	..	..	..
79	Ukraine	..	67	..	..	..	..	..	..	..	..
80	Mauritius	42	41	1.7	0.5	36	15	..	..	..	..
81	Czechoslovakia	55	..	2.7	1.7	11	8	15	11	8	8
82	Kazakhstan	..	57	..	..	22	10	16	22	4	10
83	Malaysia	27	44	5.0	4.8	..	..	..	..	..	..
	Upper-middle-income	**53 w**	**73 w**	**3.9 w**	**3.0 w**	**21 w**	**15 w**	**46 w**	**44 w**	**23 w**	**32 w**
84	Botswana	8	29	10.0	10.0	37	10	..	..	..	..
85	South Africa	48	60	3.8	3.8	10	6	40	30	19	18
86	Lithuania	..	68	..	..	..	..	..	..	..	..
87	Hungary	46	62	2.0	1.1	33	20	43	33	19	20
88	Venezuela	72	85	5.0	2.7	25	21	34	29	24	27
89	Argentina	78	87	2.2	1.8	41	36	53	49	40	42
90	Uruguay	82	86	0.6	0.8	45	39	53	45	43	39
91	Brazil	56	76	4.1	3.3	2	2	48	47	24	35
92	Mexico	59	73	4.1	2.9	34	25	41	45	22	32
93	Belarus	..	66	..	2.3	..	..	..	..	..	..
94	Russian Federation	..	74	..	..	..	..	..	..	..	..
95	Latvia	..	71	..	..	..	..	..	..	..	..
96	Trinidad and Tobago	39	70	5.0	3.3	12	8	..	..	..	..
97	Gabon	26	47	8.3	6.0	57	26	..	..	..	..
98	Estonia	..	72	..	..	..	..	..	..	..	..
99	Portugal	26	34	2.6	1.4	48	16	44	46	11	16
100	Oman	5	11	8.0	8.3	41	4	..	..	..	..
101	Puerto Rico	58	75	3.1	1.9	53	39	46	54	24	40
102	Korea, Rep.	41	73	5.3	3.5	36	26	74	69	24	50
103	Greece	53	63	1.9	1.3	54	34	59	55	28	34
104	Saudi Arabia	49	78	8.4	6.1	17	13	23	29	9	23
105	*Yugoslavia*	35	..	3.6	2.8	12	7	11	12	3	7
	Low- and middle-income	**25 w**	**46 w**	**3.7 w**	**6.3 w**	**15 w**	**6 w**	**41 w**	**33 w**	**10 w**	**13 w**
	Sub-Saharan Africa	**16 w**	**29 w**	**5.8 w**	**5.8 w**	**33 w**	**9 w**	**30 w**	**30 w**	**4 w**	**9 w**
	East Asia & Pacific	**19 w**	**52 w**	**3.2 w**	**11.1 w**	**10 w**	**4 w**	**47 w**	**35 w**	**6 w**	**9 w**
	South Asia	**19 w**	**26 w**	**4.1 w**	**3.9 w**	**8 w**	**2 w**	**35 w**	**35 w**	**6 w**	**9 w**
	Europe and Central Asia	**44 w**	**64 w**	..	..	**16 w**	**9 w**	**31 w**	**28 w**	**12 w**	**16 w**
	Middle East & N. Africa	**41 w**	**55 w**	**4.5 w**	**4.5 w**	**26 w**	**14 w**	**43 w**	**41 w**	**17 w**	**22 w**
	Latin America & Caribbean	**57 w**	**72 w**	**3.7 w**	**2.9 w**	**24 w**	**16 w**	**44 w**	**44 w**	**24 w**	**33 w**
	Severely indebted	**54 w**	**68 w**	**3.7 w**	**3.0 w**	**21 w**	**14 w**	**41 w**	**42 w**	**21 w**	**29 w**
	High-income economies	**74 w**	**77 w**	**1.1 w**	**0.8 w**	**12 w**	**9 w**	**38 w**	**37 w**	**27 w**	**29 w**
	OECD members	**74 w**	**77 w**	**1.0 w**	**0.8 w**	**11 w**	**7 w**	**37 w**	**36 w**	**27 w**	**28 w**
106	Ireland	52	57	2.2	0.5	46	26	..	..	..	..
107	†Israel	84	92	3.2	2.3	12	11	43	45	34	41
108	New Zealand	81	84	1.4	0.8	12	10	..	..	..	..
109	Spain	66	79	2.0	1.1	17	13	26	28	16	22
110	†Hong Kong	90	94	2.6	1.5	101	95	90	99	81	93
111	†Singapore	100	100	2.0	1.7	101	101	73	100	73	100
112	United Kingdom	89	89	0.1	0.2	14	13	33	26	28	23
113	Australia	85	86	1.6	1.5	2	1	60	59	50	51
114	Italy	64	69	0.9	0.6	8	5	42	37	26	25
115	Netherlands	86	89	1.1	0.6	8	7	18	16	16	14
116	Belgium	94	97	0.3	0.3	10	10	..	..	..	..
117	Austria	52	59	0.7	0.9	47	27	51	47	26	28
118	France	71	74	0.9	0.6	20	15	30	26	20	19
119	Canada	76	77	1.2	1.2	4	3	37	39	27	30
120	United States	74	75	1.0	1.1	2	1	49	48	35	36
121	Germany	80	..	0.3	..	..	1	19	15	15	13
122	Denmark	80	87	0.9	0.4	31	27	38	31	29	27
123	Finland	50	60	2.1	0.4	34	20	27	34	12	20
124	Norway	65	75	1.3	1.0	21	16	..	..	..	..
125	Sweden	81	84	0.6	0.4	23	19	17	23	13	20
126	Japan	71	77	1.8	0.6	19	15	37	36	25	27
127	Switzerland	55	60	0.4	1.1	7	4	..	..	..	..
	World	**35 w**	**51 w**	**2.7 w**	**4.7 w**	**14 w**	**6 w**	**40 w**	**34 w**	**14 w**	**16 w**
	Fuel exporters	**35 w**	**52 w**	**5.6 w**	**4.9 w**	**25 w**	**13 w**	**30 w**	**31 w**	**10 w**	**16 w**

Table 32. Women in development

		Health and welfare							Education							
		Under-5 mortality rate (per 1,000 live births)		Life expectancy at birth (years)				Maternal mortality (per 100,000 live births) 1988	Percentage of cohort persisting to grade 4				Females per 100 males			
				Female		Male			Female		Male		Primary		Secondary[a]	
		Female 1991	Male 1991	1970	1991	1970	1991		1970	1986	1970	1986	1970	1990	1970	1990
	Low-income economies	**96** w	**104** w	**54** w	**58** w	**53** w	**61** w	**308** w	..	..	..	..	..	**78** w	..	**65** w
	China and India	**75** w	**80** w	**57** w	**60** w	**57** w	**64** w	**115** w	..	..	..	..	..	**79** w	..	**65** w
	Other low-income	**135** w	**148** w	**47** w	**57** w	**46** w	**54** w	**587** w	**65** w	**66** w	**74** w	**70** w	**61** w	**76** w	**44** w	**66** w
1	Mozambique	265	294	42	48	39	45		..	..	..	..	..	76	..	61
2	Tanzania	153	171	47	49	44	46	342	82	90	88	89	65	98	38	74
3	Ethiopia	185	204	44	50	43	47		57	56	56	56	46	64	32	67
4	Uganda	175	195	51	47	49	46	550					65		31	
5	Bhutan	200	188	41	49	39	47	1,305	..	..	..	..	5	59	3	41
6	Guinea-Bissau	236	262	36	39	35	38		..	..	..	..	43	56	62	53
7	Nepal	139	125	42	53	43	54	833	..	..	..	..	18	47	16	..
8	Burundi	169	189	45	50	42	46		47	84	45	84	49	84	17	57
9	Chad	197	219	40	49	37	46		..	77	..	81	34	44	9	22
10	Madagascar	156	174	47	52	44	50	333	65	..	63	..	86	97	70	99
11	Sierra Leone	341	377	36	45	33	40		..	..	..	..	67	70	40	56
12	Bangladesh	136	130	44	52	46	53	600	..	43	..	43	47	81	..	49
13	Lao PDR	153	172	42	52	39	49	561	..	..	..	..	59	77	36	66
14	Malawi	185	205	41	45	40	44	350	55	67	60	72	59	81	36	54
15	Rwanda	209	234	46	48	43	45	300	63	76	65	75	79	99	44	56
16	Mali	180	205	41	50	40	47	2,325	52	68	89	75	55	58	29	48
17	Burkina Faso	189	209	42	50	39	46	810	71	86	68	84	57	62	33	50
18	Niger	303	337	40	48	37	44		75	93	74	78	53	57	35	42
19	India	125	123	49	60	50	60		42	..	45	..	60	71	39	55
20	Kenya	97	113	52	61	48	57		84	78	84	76	71	95	42	78
21	Nigeria	177	195	43	53	40	50	800	64	..	66	..	59	76	49	74
22	China	37	48	63	71	61	67	115	..	76	..	81	..	86	..	72
23	Haiti	145	164	49	56	46	53	600	..	..	..	..	..	93	..	96
24	Benin	157	175	45	52	43	49	161	71	..	75	..	45	..	44	37
25	Central African Rep.	122	136	45	50	40	45		67	81	67	85	49	63	20	38
26	Ghana	122	140	51	57	48	53	1,000	77	..	82	..	75	82	35	63
27	Pakistan	139	137	47	59	49	59	270	56	..	60	..	36	52	25	41
28	Togo	131	149	46	56	43	52		85	78	88	86	45	65	26	34
29	Guinea	215	239	37	44	35	44	1,247	..	77	..	87	46	46	26	31
30	Nicaragua	59	72	55	68	52	64	300	48	62	45	59	101	104	89	138
31	Sri Lanka	19	25	66	74	64	69	80	94	97	73	99	89	93	101	105
32	Mauritania	188	209	41	49	38	45	800	..	83	..	83	39	69	13	45
33	Yemen, Rep.	148	166	42	52	41	52	330	..	..	..	..	..	..	..	..
34	Honduras	54	66	55	68	51	63	221	..	..	..	..	99	98	79	..
35	Lesotho	146	167	50	58	48	55	220	87	87	70	76	150	121	111	149
36	Indonesia	102	120	49	61	46	58	450	67	82	89	99	84	93	59	82
37	Egypt, Arab Rep.	82	96	52	62	50	60		85	..	93	..	61	80	48	76
38	Zimbabwe	50	63	52	62	49	59	77	74	81	80	81	79	99	63	88
39	Sudan	156	176	43	53	41	50		..	..	..	..	61	75	40	80
40	Zambia	166	186	48	50	45	47		93	..	99	..	80	91	49	59
	Middle-income economies	**44** w	**54** w	**62** w	**71** w	**58** w	**65** w	**107** w	**78** w	**87** w	**76** w	**90** w	**86** w	**91** w	**94** w	**104** w
	Lower-middle-income	**50** w	**60** w	**61** w	**69** w	**57** w	**64** w	**111** w	**79** w	**87** w	**80** w	**88** w	**80** w	**90** w	**89** w	**104** w
41	Bolivia	117	127	48	61	44	57	371	..	..	..	..	69	90	64	..
42	Côte d'Ivoire	144	163	46	53	43	50		77	83	83	88	57	71	27	45
43	Senegal	140	160	44	49	42	46		..	90	..	94	63	72	39	51
44	Philippines	53	68	59	67	56	63	74	..	85	..	84	..	94	..	..
45	Papua New Guinea	67	81	47	56	47	55	700	76	..	84	..	57	80	37	62
46	Cameroon	112	130	46	57	43	54		59	85	58	86	74	85	36	68
47	Guatemala	76	84	54	67	51	62		33	..	73	..	79	..	65	..
48	Dominican Rep.	66	72	61	69	57	65	300	55	..	13	..	99	98	..	..
49	Ecuador	56	62	60	69	57	64	156	69	..	70	..	93	..	76	..
50	Morocco	66	79	53	65	50	61		78	80	83	81	51	66	40	69
51	Jordan	30	33	..	70	..	66		90	97	92	99	78	94	53	96
52	Tajikistan	60	66	..	72	..	67	39	..	..	..	..	..	..	..	..
53	Peru	62	76	56	66	52	62	165	..	..	..	..	85	..	74	..
54	El Salvador	46	50	60	68	56	63	148	61	..	62	..	92	98	77	95
55	Congo	159	177	49	54	43	49		86	90	89	98	78	87	43	72
56	Syrian Arab Rep.	37	47	57	69	54	65	143	92	93	95	95	57	87	36	71
57	Colombia	23	29	63	72	59	66	200	57	74	51	72	101	98	73	100
58	Paraguay	38	46	67	69	63	65	300	70	77	71	77	89	93	91	102
59	Uzbekistan	47	59	..	73	..	66	43	..	..	..	..	..	..	..	..
60	Jamaica	16	20	70	76	66	71	115	..	100	..	98	100	99	103	..
61	Romania	28	38	71	73	67	67		90	..	89	..	97	106	151	174
62	Namibia	85	97	49	60	47	56		..	..	..	..	..	108	..	127
63	Tunisia	40	51	55	68	54	67	127	..	91	..	94	64	85	38	77
64	Kyrgyzstan	45	58	..	70	..	62	43	..	..	..	..	..	..	..	..
65	Thailand	30	40	61	72	56	66	37	71	..	69	..	88	95	69	97
66	Georgia	18	23	..	77	..	69	55	..	..	..	..	..	..	..	..

Note: For data comparability and coverage, see the technical notes.   Figures in italics are for years other than those specified.

300

		Health and welfare							Education							
		Under-5 mortality rate (per 1,000 live births)		Life expectancy at birth (years)				Maternal mortality (per 100,000 live births) 1988	Percentage of cohort persisting to grade 4				Females per 100 males			
				Female		Male			Female		Male		Primary		Secondary[a]	
		Female 1991	Male 1991	1970	1991	1970	1991		1970	1986	1970	1986	1970	1990	1970	1990
67	Azerbaijan	34	45	..	75	..	67	29	..	..	..	..	..	..	..	..
68	Turkmenistan	68	83	..	70	..	62	55	76	98	81	98	73	89	37	63
69	Turkey	70	77	59	70	55	64	146	99	..	97	..	93	95	251	266
70	Poland	15	21	74	75	67	67	..	91	91	100	93	94	93	..	198
71	Bulgaria	18	23	74	75	69	68	..	93	91	91	90	96	94	111	103
72	Costa Rica	13	16	69	78	65	74	18	90	95	95	97	60	81	40	79
73	Algeria	77	85	54	67	52	65	..	97	88	97	85	92	93	99	103
74	Panama	24	28	67	75	64	71	60	..	..	..	..	..	..	..	..
75	Armenia	24	30	..	75	..	68	35	..	..	..	..	..	..	..	..
76	Chile	18	22	66	76	59	68	40	86	..	83	..	98	95	130	115
77	Iran, Islamic Rep.	83	91	54	65	55	65	120	75	92	74	93	55	86	49	74
78	Moldova	24	32	..	72	..	65	34	..	..	..	..	96	..	127	..
79	Ukraine	18	26	74	75	67	66	33	97	99	97	99	94	98	66	100
80	Mauritius	22	28	65	73	60	67	99	96	97	98	97	96	97	183	132
81	Czechoslovakia	12	17	73	76	67	68	..	..	..	..	..	..	..	..	..
82	Kazakhstan	33	44	..	73	..	64	53	..	..	..	..	..	..	..	..
83	Malaysia	15	21	63	73	60	68	26	..	..	..	..	88	95	69	104
	Upper-middle-income	**36 w**	**46 w**	**64 w**	**72 w**	**59 w**	**65 w**	**104 w**	**75 w**	..	**70 w**	**94 w**	**94 w**	**95 w**	**101 w**	**102 w**
84	Botswana	36	44	51	70	48	66	..	97	96	90	97	113	107	88	114
85	South Africa	65	79	56	66	50	59	29	..	..	..	..	98	..	95	..
86	Lithuania	15	21	75	76	67	65	..	90	97	99	97	93	95	202	198
87	Hungary	17	23	73	74	67	66	..	84	91	61	81	99	99	102	137
88	Venezuela	35	44	68	73	63	67	55	92	..	69	..	98	103	156	..
89	Argentina	28	32	70	75	64	68	140	..	98	..	96	91	95	129	..
90	Uruguay	21	25	72	77	66	70	36	56	..	54	..	99	..	99	..
91	Brazil	60	73	61	69	57	63	140	..	73	..	94	92	94	..	92
92	Mexico	38	50	64	73	60	67	200	..	..	..	..	..	..	..	..
93	Belarus	15	21	76	76	68	66	25	..	..	..	..	..	..	..	..
94	Russian Federation	21	29	..	74	..	64	49	..	..	..	..	..	..	..	..
95	Latvia	17	23	..	75	..	64	57	..	..	..	..	..	..	..	..
96	Trinidad and Tobago	21	25	68	74	63	69	89	78	..	74	..	97	97	113	102
97	Gabon	144	163	46	55	43	52	..	73	80	78	78	91	..	43	..
98	Estonia	13	19	74	75	66	65	41	..	..	..	..	..	..	..	..
99	Portugal	11	15	71	77	64	70	..	92	..	92	..	95	91	98	116
100	Oman	33	43	49	71	46	67	..	..	97	..	100	16	89	..	82
101	Puerto Rico	16	20	75	80	69	72	21	96	100	96	100	92	94	65	87
102	Korea, Rep.	16	22	62	73	58	67	26	97	99	96	99	92	94	98	103
103	Greece	12	14	74	80	70	75	..	..	..	..	..	..	..	..	..
104	Saudi Arabia	33	44	54	71	51	68	..	93	..	91	..	46	84	16	79
105	*Yugoslavia*	19	25	70	76	65	70	..	91	..	99	..	91	94	86	98
	Low- and middle-income	**80 w**	**89 w**	**56 w**	**63 w**	**54 w**	**62 w**	**238 w**	**61 w**	**76 w**	**64 w**	**80 w**	**70 w**	**81 w**	**60 w**	**73 w**
	Sub-Saharan Africa	**167 w**	**186 w**	**45 w**	**52 w**	**42 w**	**49 w**	**686 w**	**66 w**	**71 w**	**69 w**	**72 w**	**60 w**	**76 w**	**40 w**	**67 w**
	East Asia & Pacific	**46 w**	**58 w**	**60 w**	**66 w**	**58 w**	**66 w**	**195 w**	..	**78 w**	..	**82 w**	..	**88 w**	..	**75 w**
	South Asia	**129 w**	**127 w**	**48 w**	**59 w**	**50 w**	**59 w**	**444 w**	**45 w**	..	**48 w**	..	**55 w**	**69 w**	**38 w**	**54 w**
	Europe and Central Asia	**28 w**	**35 w**	**69 w**	**74 w**	**64 w**	**66 w**	**60 w**	**90 w**	**97 w**	**92 w**	**98 w**	**54 w**	**79 w**	**41 w**	**72 w**
	Middle East & N. Africa	**73 w**	**84 w**	**54 w**	**65 w**	**52 w**	**63 w**	**151 w**	**83 w**	**90 w**	**87 w**	**92 w**	**96 w**	**97 w**	**101 w**	**103 w**
	Latin America & Caribbean	**48 w**	**58 w**	**63 w**	**71 w**	**58 w**	**65 w**	**162 w**	**66 w**	**76 w**	**60 w**	**85 w**	**87 w**	**88 w**	**109 w**	**115 w**
	Severely indebted	**55 w**	**66 w**	**62 w**	**69 w**	**58 w**	**64 w**	**171 w**	**75 w**	**80 w**	**73 w**	**89 w**	**87 w**	**88 w**	**109 w**	**115 w**
	High-income economies	**8 w**	**11 w**	**75 w**	**80 w**	**68 w**	**73 w**	..	**95 w**	**98 w**	**93 w**	**97 w**	**96 w**	**95 w**	**95 w**	**100 w**
	OECD members	**8 w**	**11 w**	**75 w**	**80 w**	**68 w**	**73 w**	..	**95 w**	**98 w**	**93 w**	**97 w**	**96 w**	**95 w**	**95 w**	**100 w**
106	Ireland	9	11	73	78	69	72	..	..	98	..	97	96	96	124	101
107	†Israel	10	14	73	78	70	74	..	96	97	96	97	92	98	131	116
108	New Zealand	9	13	75	79	69	73	..	..	98	..	98	94	94	94	98
109	Spain	9	11	75	80	70	74	..	76	98	76	97	99	93	84	102
110	†Hong Kong	5	7	73	80	67	75	4	94	..	92	..	90	..	74	..
111	†Singapore	7	9	70	77	65	72	10	99	100	99	100	95	96	94	96
112	United Kingdom	8	10	75	79	69	72	..	..	..	..	..	94	95	91	99
113	Australia	8	10	75	80	68	73	..	76	97	74	94	94	95	86	97
114	Italy	10	12	75	81	69	74	..	..	..	..	..	96	99	91	109
115	Netherlands	8	10	77	80	71	74	..	99	..	96	..	96	97	87	..
116	Belgium	10	12	75	80	68	73	..	..	87	..	85	94	97	95	94
117	Austria	9	11	74	80	67	73	..	95	99	92	98	95	95	107	106
118	France	8	10	76	81	68	73	..	97	..	90	..	95	94	95	96
119	Canada	8	10	76	81	69	74	..	95	97	92	93	95	93	95	96
120	United States	9	13	75	79	67	72	..	..	..	..	..	95	95	..	..
121	Germany[b]	8	10	74	79	67	73	..	97	99	96	97	96	96	93	98
122	Denmark	9	11	76	78	71	72	..	98	100	96	100	97	96	102	106
123	Finland	7	9	74	79	66	73	..	..	98	..	99	90	95	112	111
124	Norway	9	11	77	80	71	74	..	99	..	98	..	105	95	97	105
125	Sweden	7	9	77	81	72	75	..	98	..	96	..	96	95	92	109
126	Japan	5	7	75	82	69	76	..	100	100	100	100	98	96	93	99
127	Switzerland	8	10	76	81	70	74	..	94	..	93	..	98	96	93	99
	World	**69 w**	**77 w**	**60 w**	**65 w**	**57 w**	**64 w**	**237 w**	**67 w**	**78 w**	**70 w**	**82 w**	**77 w**	**84 w**	**68 w**	**76 w**
	Fuel exporters	**114 w**	**127 w**	**50 w**	**61 w**	**48 w**	**58 w**	**492 w**	**75 w**	**88 w**	**75 w**	**88 w**	**60 w**	**81 w**	**51 w**	**80 w**

a. See the technical notes.   b. Data refer to the Federal Republic of Germany before unification.

Table 33. Forests, protected areas, and water resources

		Forest area (thousands of sq. km)				Nationally protected areas (1992)			Freshwater resources: annual withdrawal (1970–89)				
		Total area 1980		Annual deforestation 1981–85		Area (thousands of sq. km)	Number	As a percentage of total area	Total (cubic kilometers)	As a percentage of total water resources	Per capita (cubic meters)		Industrial and agricultural
		Total	Closed	Total	Closed						Total	Domestic	
Low-income economies													
China and India													
Other low-income													
1	Mozambique	154	9	1.2	0.1	0.0	1	0.0	0.8	1	53	13	40
2	Tanzania	420	14	3.0a	..	130.0	28	13.8	0.5	1	36	8	28
3	Ethiopia	272	44	0.9	0.1	25.3	11	2.1	2.2	2	49	5	44
4	Uganda	60	8	0.5	0.1	18.7	32	7.9	0.2	0	20	6	14
5	Bhutan	21	21	0.0	0.0	9.1	5	19.3	0.0	0	14	5	9
6	Guinea-Bissau	21	7	0.6	0.2	0.0	0	0.0	0.0	0	11	3	8
7	Nepal	21	19	0.8	0.8	11.1	12	7.9	2.7	2	151	6	145
8	Burundi	0	0	0.0	0.0	0.9	3	3.2	0.1	3	20	7	13
9	Chad	135	5	0.8	..	29.8	7	2.3	0.2	0	34	5	29
10	Madagascar	132	103	1.6	1.5	11.1	36	1.9	16.3	41	1,642	16	1,626
11	Sierra Leone	21	7	0.1	0.1	0.8	2	1.1	0.4	0	96	7	89
12	Bangladesh	9	9	0.1	0.1	1.0	8	0.7	22.5	1d	211	6	205
13	Lao PDR	136	84	1.3	1.0	0.0	0	0.0	1.0	0	260	21	239
14	Malawi	43	2	1.5	..	10.6	9	8.9	0.2	2	20	7	13
15	Rwanda	2	1	0.1	0.0	3.3	2	12.4	0.2	2	23	6	17
16	Mali	73	5	0.4	..	40.1	11	3.2	1.4	2	162	3	159
17	Burkina Faso	47	3	0.8	0.0	26.6	12	9.7	0.2	1	18	5	13
18	Niger	26	1	0.7	0.0	97.0	6	7.7	0.3	1d	41	9	32
19	India	640	378	0.5a	..	138.4	332	4.2	380.0	18d	612	18	594
20	Kenya	24	11	0.4	0.2	34.7	36	6.0	1.1	7	50	14	37
21	Nigeria	148	60	4.0	3.0	28.7	21	3.1	3.6	1d	37	11	26
22	China	1,150	978	0.0	..	286.5	402	3.0	460.0	16	462	28	434
23	Haiti	0	0	0.0	0.0	0.1	3	0.3	0.0	0	7	2	5
24	Benin	39	0	0.7	0.0	8.4	2	7.5	0.1	0	26	7	19
25	Central African Rep.	359	36	0.6	0.1	61.1	13	9.8	0.1	0	25	5	20
26	Ghana	87	17	0.7	0.2	10.7	8	4.5	0.3	1	35	12	23
27	Pakistan	25	22	0.1	0.1	36.6	53	4.6	153.4	33d	2,053	21	2,032
28	Togo	17	3	0.1	0.0	6.5	11	11.4	0.1	1	28	17	11
29	Guinea	107	21	0.9	0.4	1.6	3	0.7	0.7	0	140	14	126
30	Nicaragua	45	45	1.2	1.2	9.5	21	7.3	0.9	1	370	93	278
31	Sri Lanka	17	17	0.6	0.6	7.8	43	11.9	6.3	15	503	10	493
32	Mauritania	6	0	0.1	0.0	17.5	4	1.7	0.7	10d	494	59	435
33	Yemen, Rep.	0	0	0.0	..	0.0	0	0.0	1.5	147	179	7	172
34	Honduras	40	38	0.9	0.9	5.0	35	4.4	1.3	1	510	20	490
35	Lesotho	0	0	..	..	0.1	1	0.2	0.1	1	31	7	24
36	Indonesia	1,169	1,139	10.0a	..	193.4	186	10.2	16.6	1	95	12	83
37	Egypt, Arab Rep.	0	0	..	..	8.0	13	0.8	56.4	97d	1,213	85	1,128
38	Zimbabwe	198	2	0.8	0.0	30.7	25	7.9	1.2	5	138	19	119
39	Sudan	477	7	5.0	0.0	93.6	14	3.7	18.6	14d	1,092	11	1,081
40	Zambia	295	30	0.7	0.4	63.6	20	8.5	0.4	0	86	54	32
Middle-income economies													
Lower-middle-income													
41	Bolivia	668	440	1.2	0.9	98.6	27	9.0	1.2	0	184	18	166
42	Côte d'Ivoire	98	45	2.6a	..	19.9	12	6.2	0.7	1	66	15	51
43	Senegal	110	2	0.5	..	21.8	9	11.1	1.4	4d	202	10	192
44	Philippines	95b	95	1.4a	1.4a	5.7	27	1.9	29.5	9	693	125	568
45	Papua New Guinea	382	342	0.2	0.2	0.3	6	0.1	0.1	0	28	8	20
46	Cameroon	233	165	1.9a	1.0a	20.5	14	4.3	0.4	0	37	17	20
47	Guatemala	45	44	0.9	0.9	8.3	17	7.6	0.7	1	139	13	126
48	Dominican Rep.	6	6	0.0	0.0	9.7	18	19.9	3.0	15	443	22	421
49	Ecuador	147	143	3.4	3.4	107.5	18	37.9	5.6	2	567	40	527
50	Morocco	32	15	0.1	..	3.6	10	0.8	11.0	37	499	30	469
51	Jordan	1	0	..	..	1.0	8	1.1	0.5	41d	173	50	123
52	Tajikistan	..	..	..	..	0.9	3	0.6	..	..	..	..	..
53	Peru	706	697	2.7	2.7	27.0	22	2.1	6.1	15	301	57	244
54	El Salvador	1	1	0.1	0.1	0.2	5	0.9	1.0	5	245	17	228
55	Congo	213	213	0.2	0.2	11.8	10	3.4	0.0	0	19	12	7
56	Syrian Arab Rep.	2	1	0.0	..	0.0	0	0.0	3.3	9d	434	30	404
57	Colombia	517	464	8.9	8.2	90.5	41	7.9	5.3	0d	172	71	101
58	Paraguay	197	41	4.5a	..	12.0	14	3.0	0.4	0d	110	17	94
59	Uzbekistan	..	..	..	..	2.4	10	0.5	..	..	..	..	..
60	Jamaica	1	1	0.0	0.0	0.0	1	0.1	0.3	4	159	11	148
61	Romania	67	63	..	..	10.9	40	4.6	25.4	12d	1,144	92	1,052
62	Namibia	184	..	0.3	..	103.7	11	12.6	0.1	2	84	5	79
63	Tunisia	3	2	0.1	..	0.4	6	0.3	2.3	52d	317	41	276
64	Kyrgyzstan	..	..	..	..	2.0	5	1.0	..	..	..	..	..
65	Thailand	157	92	2.4a	1.6a	56.6	92	11.0	31.9	18d	600	24	576
66	Georgia	..	..	..	..	1.9	15	2.7	..	..	..	..	..

Note: For data comparability and coverage, see the technical notes.   Figures in italics are for years other than those specified.

302

		Forest area (thousands of sq. km)				Nationally protected areas (1992)			Freshwater resources: annual withdrawal (1970–89)				
		Total area 1980		Annual deforestation 1981–85		Area (thousands of square kilometers)	Number	As a percentage of total area	Total (cubic kilometers)	As a percentage of total water resources	Per capita (cubic meters)		
		Total	Closed	Total	Closed						Total	Domestic	Industrial and agricultural
67	Azerbaijan	..	..	..	..	1.8	11	2.0	..	..	..	..	..
68	Turkmenistan	..	..	..	..	11.1	8	2.5	..	..	..	..	..
69	Turkey	202	89	..	..	2.7	18	0.3	23.8	18[d]	434	104	330
70	Poland	87	86	..	..	22.4	80	7.2	16.8	30[d]	472	76	396
71	Bulgaria	37	33	..	..	2.6	50	2.4	14.2	7[d]	1,600	112	1,488
72	Costa Rica	18	16	0.4[a]	0.4[a]	6.3	27	12.4	1.4	1	780	31	749
73	Algeria	18	15	0.4	..	127.0	18	5.3	3.0	16[d]	160	35	125
74	Panama	42	42	0.4	0.4	13.2	14	17.2	1.3	1	744	89	655
75	Armenia	..	..	..	..	2.2	4	7.4	..	..	..	..	..
76	Chile	76	76	0.5	..	137.2	65	18.1	16.8	4	1,623	97	1,526
77	Iran, Islamic Rep.	38	28	0.2	..	79.8	62	4.8	45.4	39	1,362	54	1,308
78	Moldova	..	..	..	..	0.0	0	0.0	..	..	..	..	..
79	Ukraine	..	..	..	..	4.6	17	0.8	..	..	..	..	..
80	Mauritius	0	0	0.0	0.0	0.0	0	0.0	0.4	16	410	66	344
81	Czechoslovakia	46	44	..	..	20.6	65	16.1	5.8	6[d]	379	87	292
82	Kazakhstan	..	..	..	..	8.4	8	0.3	..	..	..	..	..
83	Malaysia	210[b]	210	2.7[a]	..	14.9	48	4.5	9.4	2	768	177	591

Upper-middle-income

84	Botswana	326	0	0.2	..	102.3	9	17.6	0.1	1[d]	100	5	95
85	South Africa	3	3	..	..	73.9	229	6.1	9.2	18	410	66	344
86	Lithuania	..	..	..	..	0.0	0	0.0	..	..	..	..	..
87	Hungary	16	16	..	..	5.8	54	6.2	5.4	5[d]	502	45	457
88	Venezuela	339	319	2.5	1.3	275.3	104	30.2	4.1	0	387	166	221
89	Argentina	445	445	1.8[a]	..	93.9	112	3.4	27.6	3[d]	1,042	94	948
90	Uruguay	5	5	..	..	0.3	8	0.2	0.7	1[d]	241	14	227
91	Brazil	5,145	3,575	13.8[a,b]	..	257.6	186	3.0	35.0	1[d]	248	107	141
92	Mexico	484	463	10.0[d]	..	98.1	60	5.0	54.2	15	875	53	823
93	Belarus	..	..	..	..	2.4	4	1.1	..	..	..	..	..
94	Russian Federation	..	..	..	..	200.3	75	1.2	..	..	..	..	..
95	Latvia	..	..	..	..	1.7	21	2.6	..	..	..	..	..
96	Trinidad and Tobago	2	2	0.0	0.0	0.2	13	3.9	0.2	3	148	40	108
97	Gabon	206	205	0.2	0.2	10.5	6	3.9	0.1	0	57	41	16
98	Estonia	..	..	..	..	3.2	36	7.1	..	..	..	..	..
99	Portugal	30	26	..	..	5.5	22	6.0	10.5	16[d]	1,075	161	914
100	Oman	0	0	..	..	0.5	2	0.3	0.4	22	561	17	544
101	Puerto Rico	..	..	..	..	0.4	29	4.0	..	..	..	..	..
102	Korea, Rep.	49	49	..	..	7.6	26	7.6	10.7	17	299	33	266
103	Greece	58	25	..	..	1.0	18	0.8	7.0	12[d]	720	58	662
104	Saudi Arabia	2	0	..	..	212.0	9	9.9	2.3	106	321	144	177
105	*Yugoslavia*	105	91	..	..	7.9	61	3.1	8.8	3[d]	393	63	330

Low- and middle-income
Sub-Saharan Africa
East Asia & Pacific
South Asia
Europe and Central Asia
Middle East & N. Africa
Latin America & Caribbean

Severely indebted

High-income economies
OECD members

106	Ireland	4	3	..	..	0.4	6	0.6	0.8	2	235	38	197
107	†Israel	1	1	..	..	2.1	21	10.0	1.9	86[d]	441	71	370
108	New Zealand	95	72	..	..	29.0	124	10.7	1.9	0	585	269	316
109	Spain	108	69	..	..	35.0	161	6.9	45.9	41[d]	1,184	142	1,042
110	†Hong Kong	..	..	..	..	0.4	12	36.3	..	..	..	..	..
111	†Singapore	0	0	..	..	0.0	1	4.4	0.2	32	84	38	46
112	United Kingdom	22	20	..	..	46.3	131	18.9	14.5	12	253	51	202
113	Australia	1,067	417	..	..	812.4	733	10.6	17.5	5	1,280	832	448
114	Italy	81	64	..	..	20.1	143	6.7	56.2	30[d]	984	138	846
115	Netherlands	4	3	..	..	3.5	67	9.4	14.5	16[d]	993	50	943
116	Belgium	8	7	..	..	0.8	3	2.5	9.0	72[d]	917	101	816
117	Austria	38	38	..	..	21.2	187	25.3	2.1	2[d]	279	53	226
118	France	151	139	..	..	53.6	79	9.7	43.7	24[d]	783	125	658
119	Canada	4,364	2,641	..	..	494.5	411	5.0	43.9	2	1,684	303	1,381
120	United States	2,960	2,096	1.6[a]	..	984.6	937	10.5	467.0	19	1,952	234	1,718
121	Germany	72[c]	70[c]	..	..	87.8	472	24.6	44.6[c]	28[c,d]	729[c]	73[c]	656[c]
122	Denmark	5	5	..	..	4.1	65	9.5	1.2	9[d]	228	68	160
123	Finland	232	199	..	..	8.1	34	2.4	3.0	3[d]	605	73	532
124	Norway	87	76	..	..	14.9	80	4.6	2.0	0[d]	490	98	392
125	Sweden	278	244	..	..	29.2	189	6.5	3.0	2[d]	356	128	228
126	Japan	253	239	..	..	46.7	685	12.3	89.3	16	733	125	608
127	Switzerland	11	9	..	..	7.5	112	18.2	1.1	2[d]	170	39	131

World
Fuel exporters

a. Data are for the periods as follows: Tanzania 1989, India 1983–87, Indonesia 1982–90, Côte d'Ivoire 1981–86, Philippines 1981–88, Cameroon 1976–86, Paraguay 1989–90, Thailand 1985–88, Costa Rica 1973–89, Malaysia 1979–89, Argentina 1980–89, Brazil (Legal Amazon only) 1989–90, Mexico 1981–83, United States 1977–87. b. See the technical notes for alternative estimates. c. Data refer to the Federal Republic of Germany before unification. d. Total water resources include river flows from other countries in addition to internal renewable resources.

Table 1a. Basic indicators for other economies

		Population (thousands) mid-1991	Area (thousands of square kilometers)	GNP per capita[a] Dollars 1991	GNP per capita[a] Average annual growth rate (percent) 1980-91	Average annual rate of inflation[a] (percent) 1970-80	Average annual rate of inflation[a] (percent) 1980-91	Life expectancy at birth (years) 1991	Adult illiteracy (percent) Female 1990	Adult illiteracy (percent) Total 1990
1	Cambodia	8,790	181	200	..	..	..	50	78	65
2	Equatorial Guinea	427	28	330	2.8	..	-0.9	47	63	50
3	Gambia, The	902	11	360	-0.1	10.6	18.2	44	84	73
4	São Tomé and Principe	118	1	400	-3.3	4.0	21.5	67	..	..
5	Guyana	802	215	430	-4.5	9.8	35.0	65	5	4
6	Maldives	221	b	460	6.7	..	..	62	..	..
7	Comoros	492	2	500	-1.0	..	..	56	..	..
8	Solomon Islands	325	29	690	3.5	8.4	12.4	65	..	..
9	Kiribati	73	1	720	..	10.6	5.4	56	..	..
10	Cape Verde	380	4	750	2.3	9.4	9.4	67	..	..
11	Western Samoa	161	3	960	..	..	11.6	66	..	..
12	Swaziland	828	17	1,050	3.1	12.3	10.3	57	..	..
13	Vanuatu	151	12	1,150	..	..	5.0	65	..	..
14	Tonga	100	1	1,280	..	..	..	67	..	..
15	St. Vincent	108	b	1,730	5.2	13.8	4.4	71	..	..
16	Fiji	741	18	1,930	-0.2	12.8	6.1	71	..	..
17	Belize	194	23	2,010	2.5	8.7	2.9	68	..	..
18	Grenada	91	b	2,180	..	..	..	70	..	..
19	Dominica	72	1	2,440	4.7	16.8	6.0	72	..	..
20	St. Lucia	153	1	2,490	..	..	..	72	..	..
21	Suriname	457	163	3,630	-4.5	11.8	9.0	68	5	5
22	St. Kitts and Nevis	39	b	3,960	5.8	..	7.2	70	..	..
23	Antigua and Barbuda	80	b	4,430	3.8	..	6.9	74	..	..
24	Seychelles	69	b	5,110	3.2	16.9	3.5	71	..	..
25	Barbados	258	b	6,630	1.3	13.5	5.2	75	..	..
26	Bahrain	516	1	7,130	-3.8	..	-0.3	69	31	23
27	Malta	357	b	7,280	3.8	4.2	2.1	76	..	..
28	Cyprus	710	9	8,640	4.9	..	5.5	77	..	..
29	Bahamas, The	259	14	11,750	1.3	6.4	5.9	69	..	..
30	Qatar	506	11	14,770	-12.2	..	..	70	..	..
31	United Arab Emirates	1,629	84	20,140	-6.3	..	1.1	72	..	..
32	Iceland	258	103	23,170	1.8	35.1	30.0	78	..	..
33	Luxembourg	385	3	31,780	3.5	6.9	4.2	75	..	..
34	Afghanistan	20,979	652	f	..	..	..	43	86	71
35	Albania	3,301	29	e	..	..	-0.4	73	..	..
36	American Samoa	40	b	c	..	..	..	..	..	..
37	Andorra	58	b	c	..	..	..	..	..	..
38	Angola	9,461	1,247	e	..	..	..	46	72	58
39	Aruba	61	b	d	..	..	..	..	..	..
40	Bermuda	61	b	c	..	8.4	..	..	..	..
41	Brunei	265	6	c	..	..	..	74	..	..
42	Channel Islands	145	b	c	..	..	..	77	..	..
43	Cuba	10,736	111	e	..	..	..	76	7	6
44	Djibouti	452	23	e	..	..	..	49	..	..
45	Faeroe Islands	47	1	c	..	..	..	..	..	..
46	Fed. Sts. of Micronesia	105	b	e	..	..	..	..	..	..
47	French Guiana	123	90	d	..	..	..	..	..	..
48	French Polynesia	202	4	c	..	..	..	68	..	..
49	Gibraltar	30	b	d	..	..	..	..	..	..
50	Greenland	56	342	c	..	..	..	..	..	..
51	Guadeloupe	395	2	c	..	..	..	74	..	..
52	Guam	145	1	c	..	..	..	72	..	..
53	Iraq	18,578	438	d	..	17.9	10.3	65	51	40
54	Isle of Man	70	1	c	..	..	..	..	..	..
55	Korea, Dem. Rep.	22,191	121	e	..	..	..	71	..	..
56	Kuwait	1,460	18	c	..	21.9	-2.7	75	33	27
57	Lebanon	3,708	10	e	..	..	..	66	27	20
58	Liberia	2,639	111	f	..	9.2	..	55	71	61
59	Libya	4,706	1,760	d	..	18.2	0.2	63	50	36
60	Macao	476	b	e	..	..	..	73	..	..
61	Marshall Islands	48	b	e	..	..	..	..	..	..
62	Martinique	363	1	d	..	..	..	76	..	..
63	Mayotte	76	b	d	..	..	..	..	..	..
64	Mongolia	2,250	1,567	e	..	..	1.0	63	..	..
65	Myanmar	42,758	677	f	..	..	..	59	28	19
66	Netherlands Antilles	192	1	c	..	..	..	77	..	..
67	New Caledonia	171	19	d	..	..	..	70	..	..
68	Reunion	602	3	d	..	..	..	72	..	..
69	San Marino	23	b	c	..	..	..	..	..	..
70	Somalia	8,051	638	f	..	15.2	49.7	48	86	76
71	Viet Nam	67,679	332	f	..	..	..	67	16	12
72	Virgin Islands (U.S.)	99	b	c	..	12.5	3.9	74	..	..
73	Zaire	38,631	2,345	f	..	31.4	60.9	52	39	28

a. See the technical note for Table 1.   b. Less than 500 square kilometers.   c. GNP per capita estimated to be in the high-income range.   d. GNP per capita estimated to be in the upper-middle-income range.   e. GNP per capita estimated to be in the lower-middle income range.   f. GNP per capita estimated to be in the low-income range.

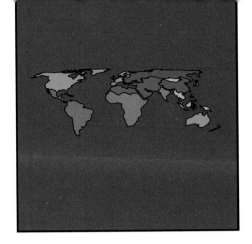

Technical notes

The main criterion for country classification is gross national product (GNP) per capita. With the addition of the recently independent republics of the former Soviet Union, the main tables now include country data for 127 economies, listed in ascending GNP per capita order. A separate table, showing basic indicators for economies with sparse data or with populations of less than 1 million, Table 1a covers a further seventy-three economies. Other changes are outlined in the Introduction.

Data reliability

Considerable effort has been made to standardize the data, but full comparability cannot be ensured and care must be taken in interpreting the indicators. Many factors affect availability and reliability; the statistical systems in many developing economies are still weak, statistical methods, coverage, practices, and definitions differ widely among countries, and cross-country and cross-time comparisons involve complex technical problems that cannot be unequivocally resolved. For these reasons, while the data are drawn from the sources thought to be most authoritative they should be construed only as indicating trends and characterizing major differences among economies rather than offering precise quantitative measures of those differences. In particular, data issues have yet to be resolved for the fifteen economies of the former Soviet Union. Coverage is sparse, and the data are subject to more than the normal range of uncertainty.

Most social and demographic data from national sources are drawn from regular administrative files, although some come from special surveys or periodic census inquiries. In the case of survey and census data, figures for intermediate years have to be interpolated or otherwise estimated from the base reference statistics. Similarly, because not all data are up-dated, some figures—especially those relating to current periods—may be extrapolated. Several estimates (for example, life expectancy) are derived from models based on assumptions about recent trends and prevailing conditions. Issues related to the reliability of demographic indicators are reviewed in the U.N.'s *World Population Trends and Policies*. Readers are urged to take these limitations into account in interpreting the indicators, particularly when making comparisons across economies.

Base years

To provide long-term trend analysis, facilitate international comparisons and include the effects of changes in intersectoral relative prices, constant price data for most economies are partially rebased to three base years and linked together. The year 1970 is the base year for data from 1960 to 1975, 1980 for 1976 to 1982, and 1987 for 1983 and beyond. These three periods are "chain-linked," to obtain 1987 prices throughout all three periods.

Chain-linking is accomplished for each of the three subperiods by rescaling; this moves the year in which current and constant price versions of the same time series have the same value, without altering the trend of either. Components of gross domestic product (GDP) are individually rescaled and summed to provide GDP and its subaggregates. In this process a rescaling deviation may occur between the constant price GDP by industrial origin and the constant price GDP by expenditure. Such rescaling deviations are absorbed under the heading *private consumption, etc.* on the assumption that GDP by industrial origin is a more reliable estimate than GDP by expenditure.

Because private consumption is calculated as a residual, the national accounting identities are maintained. Rebasing does involve incorporating in private consumption whatever statistical discrepancies arise for expenditure. The value added in the services sector also includes a statistical discrepancy, as reported by the original source.

Summary measures

The summary measures are calculated by simple addition when a variable is expressed in reasonably comparable units of account. Economic indicators that do not seem naturally additive are usually combined by a price-weighting scheme. The summary measures for social indicators are weighted by population.

The World Development Indicators, unlike the *World Tables*, provide data for, usually, two reference points rather than annual time series. For summary measures that cover many years, the calculation is based on the same country composition over time and across topics. The World Development Indicators permit group measures to be compiled only if the country data available for a given year account for at least two-thirds of the full group, as defined by the 1987 benchmarks. As long as that criterion is met, noncurrent reporters (and those not providing ample history) are, for years with missing data, assumed to behave like the sample of the group that does provide estimates. Readers should keep in mind that the purpose is to maintain an appropriate relationship across topics, despite myriad problems with country data, and that nothing meaningful can be deduced about behavior at the country level by working back from group indicators. In addition, the weighting process may result in discrepancies between summed subgroup figures and overall totals. This is explained more fully in the introduction to the *World Tables*.

Sources and methods

Data on external debt are compiled directly by the World Bank on the basis of reports from its developing member countries through the Debtor Reporting System. Other data are drawn mainly from the United Nations and its specialized agencies, the International Monetary Fund, and country reports to the World Bank. Bank staff estimates are also used to improve currentness or consistency. For most countries, national accounts estimates are obtained from member governments through World Bank economic missions. In some instances these are adjusted by Bank staff to provide conformity with international definitions and concepts, consistency, and currentness.

Growth rates

For ease of reference, only ratios and rates of growth are usually shown; absolute values are generally available from other World Bank publications, notably the 1993 edition of the World Tables. Most growth rates are calculated for two periods, 1970-80 and 1980-91, and are computed, unless otherwise noted, by using the least-squares regression method. Because this method takes into account all observations in a period, the resulting growth rates reflect general trends that are not unduly influenced by exceptional values, particularly at the end points. To exclude the effects of inflation, constant price economic indicators are used in calculating growth rates. Details of this methodology are given at the beginning of the technical notes. Data in italics indicate that they are for years or periods other than those specified—up to two years earlier for economic indicators and up to three years on either side for social indicators, since the latter tend to be collected less regularly and change less dramatically over short periods of time.

All growth rates shown are calculated from constant price series and, unless otherwise noted, have been computed using the least-squares method. The least-squares growth rate, r, is estimated by fitting a least-squares linear regression trend line to the logarithmic annual values of the variable in the relevant period. More specifically, the regression equation takes the form $\log X_t = a + bt + e_t$, where this is equivalent to the logarithmic transformation of the compound growth rate equation, $X_t = X_o(1 + r)t$. In these equations, X is the variable, t is time, and $a = \log Xo$ and $b = \log(1 + r)$ are the parameters to be estimated; e is the error term. If b^* is the least-squares estimate of b, then the average annual percentage growth rate, r, is obtained as $[\text{antilog}(b^*)] - 1$ and multiplied by 100 to express it as a percentage.

Table 1. Basic indicators

For basic indicators for economies with sparse data or with populations of less than 1 million, see Table A.1.

Population numbers for mid-1991 are World Bank estimates. These are usually projections from the most recent population censuses or surveys; most are from 1980–91, and, for a few countries, from the 1960s or 1970s. Note that refugees not permanently settled in the country of asylum are generally considered to be part of the population of their country of origin.

The data on *area* are from the Food and Agriculture Organization (FAO). Area is the total surface area, measured in square kilometers, comprising land area and inland waters.

GNP per capita figures in U.S. dollars are calculated according to the *World Bank Atlas* method, which is described below.

GNP per capita does not, by itself, constitute or measure welfare or success in development. It does not distinguish between the aims and ultimate uses of a given product, nor does it say whether it merely offsets some natural or other obstacle, or harms or contributes to welfare. For example, GNP is higher in colder countries, where people spend money on heating and warm clothes, than in balmy climates, where people are comfortable wearing light clothes in the open air.

More generally, GNP does not deal adequately with environmental issues, particularly natural resource use. The World Bank has joined with others to see how national accounts might provide insights into these issues. The possibility of developing "satellite" accounts is being considered; such accounts could delve into practical and conceptual difficulties, such as assigning a meaningful economic value to resources that markets do not yet perceive as "scarce" and allocating costs that are essentially global within a framework that is inherently national.

GNP measures the total domestic and foreign value added claimed by residents. It comprises GDP (defined in the note for Table 2) plus net factor income from abroad, which is the income residents receive from abroad for factor services (labor and capital) less similar payments made to nonresidents who contributed to the domestic economy.

In estimating GNP per capita, the Bank recognizes that perfect cross-country comparability of GNP per capita estimates cannot be achieved. Beyond the classic, strictly intractable index number problem, two obstacles stand in the way of adequate comparability. One concerns the GNP and population estimates themselves. There are differences in national accounting and demographic reporting systems and in the coverage and reliability of underlying statistical information among various countries. The other obstacle relates to the use of official exchange rates for converting GNP data, expressed in different national currencies, to a common denomination—conventionally the U.S. dollar—to compare them across countries.

Recognizing that these shortcomings affect the comparability of the GNP per capita estimates, the World Bank has introduced several improvements in the estimation procedures. Through its regular review of member countries' national accounts, the Bank systematically evaluates the GNP estimates, focusing on the coverage and concepts employed and, where appropriate, making adjustments to improve comparability. As part of the review, Bank staff estimates of GNP (and sometimes of population) may be developed for the most recent period.

The World Bank also systematically assesses the appropriateness of official exchange rates as conversion factors. An alternative conversion factor is used (and reported in the *World Tables*) when the official exchange rate is judged to diverge by an excep-

tionally large margin from the rate effectively applied to foreign transactions. This applies to only a small number of countries. For all other countries the Bank calculates GNP per capita using the *World Bank Atlas* method.

The *Atlas* conversion factor for any year is the average of a country's exchange rate for that year and its exchange rates for the two preceding years, after adjusting them for differences in relative inflation between the country and the United States. This three-year average smooths fluctuations in prices and exchange rates for each country. The resulting GNP in U.S. dollars is divided by the midyear population for the latest of the three years to derive GNP per capita.

Some sixty low- and middle-income economies suffered declining real GNP per capita in constant prices during the 1980s. In addition, significant currency and terms of trade fluctuations have affected relative income levels. For this reason the levels and ranking of GNP per capita estimates, calculated by the *Atlas* method, have sometimes changed in ways not necessarily related to the relative domestic growth performance of the economies.

The following formulas describe the procedures for computing the conversion factor for year t:

$$(e^{\star}_{t-2,t}) = \frac{1}{3} \left[e_{t-2} \left(\frac{P_t}{P_{t-2}} \middle/ \frac{P_t^{\$}}{P_{t-2}^{\$}} \right) + e_{t-1} \left(\frac{P_t}{P_{t-1}} \middle/ \frac{P_t^{\$}}{P_{t-1}^{\$}} \right) + e_t \right]$$

and for calculating per capita GNP in U.S. dollars for year t:

$$(Y_t^{\$}) = (Y_t / N_t \div e^{\star}_{t-2,t})$$

where

Y_t = current GNP (local currency) for year t
P_t = GNP deflator for year t
e_t = average annual exchange rate (local currency to the U.S. dollar) for year t
N_t = midyear population for year t
$P_t^{\$}$ = U.S. GNP deflator for year t

Because of problems associated with the availability of comparable data and the determination of conversion factors, information on GNP per capita is not shown for some economies.

The use of official exchange rates to convert national currency figures to U.S. dollars does not reflect the relative domestic purchasing powers of currencies. The U. N. International Comparison Programme (ICP) has developed measures of real GDP on an internationally comparable scale, using purchasing power of currencies (PPCs) instead of exchange rates as conversion factors. Table 30 shows the most recent PPC estimates. Information on the ICP has been published in four studies and in a number of other reports. The most recent study is Phase VI, for 1990, a part of which has already been published by the Organization for Economic Cooperation and Development (OECD).

The ICP figures reported in Table 30 are preliminary and may be revised. The United Nations and its regional economic commissions, as well as other international agencies, such as the EC, the OECD, and the World Bank, are working to improve the methodology and to extend annual purchasing power comparisons to all countries. However, exchange rates remain the only generally available means of converting GNP from national currencies to U.S. dollars.

Average annual rate of inflation is measured by the growth rate of the GDP implicit deflator for each of the periods shown. The GDP deflator is first calculated by dividing, for each year of the period, the value of GDP at current values by the value of GDP at constant values, both in national currency. The least-squares method is then used to calculate the growth rate of the GDP deflator for the period. This measure of inflation, like any other, has limitations. For some purposes, however, it is used as an indicator of inflation because it is the most broadly based measure, showing annual price movements for all goods and services produced in an economy.

Life expectancy at birth indicates the number of years a newborn infant would live if prevailing patterns of mortality at the time of its birth were to stay the same throughout its life. Data are World Bank estimates based on data from the U.N. Population Division, the U.N. Statistical Office, and national statistical offices.

Adult illiteracy is defined here as the proportion of the population over the age of fifteen who cannot, with understanding, read and write a short, simple statement on their everyday life. This is only one of three widely accepted definitions, and its application is subject to qualifiers in a number of countries. The data are from the illiteracy estimates and projections prepared in 1989 by UNESCO. More recent information and a modified model have been used; therefore, the data for 1990 are not strictly consistent with those published in last year's World Development Indicators.

The summary measures for GNP per capita, life expectancy, and adult illiteracy in this table are weighted by population. Those for average annual rates of inflation are weighted by the 1987 share of country GDP valued in current U.S. dollars.

Tables 2 and 3. Growth and structure of production

Most of the definitions used are those of the *U.N. System of National Accounts* (SNA), Series F, No. 2, Revision 3. Estimates are obtained from national sources, sometimes reaching the World Bank through other international agencies but more often collected during World Bank staff missions.

World Bank staff review the quality of national accounts data and in some instances, through mission work or technical assistance, help adjust national series. Because of the sometimes limited capabilities of statistical offices and basic data problems, strict international comparability cannot be achieved, especially in economic activities that are difficult to measure, such as parallel market transactions, the informal sector, or subsistence agriculture.

GDP measures the total output of goods and services for final use produced by residents and nonresidents, regardless of the allocation to domestic and foreign claims. It is calculated without making deductions for depreciation of "manmade" assets or depletion and degradation of natural resources. Although SNA envisages estimates of GDP by industrial origin to be at producer prices, many countries still report such details at factor cost. International comparability of the estimates is affected by differing country practices in valuation systems for reporting value added by production sectors. As a partial solution, GDP estimates are shown at purchaser values if the components are on this basis, and such instances are footnoted. However, for a few countries in Tables 2 and 3, GDP at purchaser values has been replaced by GDP at factor cost.

The figures for GDP are U.S. dollar values converted from domestic currencies using single-year official exchange rates. For a few countries where the official exchange rate does not reflect the rate effectively applied to actual foreign exchange transactions, an alternative conversion factor is used (and reported in the *World Tables*). Note that this table does not use the three-year averaging technique applied to GNP per capita in Table 1.

Agriculture covers forestry, hunting, and fishing as well as agriculture. In developing countries with high levels of subsistence farming, much agricultural production is either not exchanged or not exchanged for money. This increases the difficulty of measuring the contribution of agriculture to GDP and reduces the reliability and comparability of such numbers.

Industry comprises value added in mining; manufacturing (also reported as a separate subgroup); construction; and electricity, water, and gas. Value added in all other branches of economic activity, including imputed bank service charges, import duties, and any statistical discrepancies noted by national compilers, are categorized as *services, etc.*

Partially rebased, chain-linked 1987 series in domestic currencies, as explained at the beginning of the technical notes, are used to compute the growth rates in Table 2. The sectoral shares of GDP in Table 3 are based on current price series.

In calculating the summary measures for each indicator in Table 2, partially rebased constant 1987 U.S. dollar values for each economy are calculated for each year of the periods covered; the values are aggregated across countries for each year; and the least-squares procedure is used to compute the growth rates. The average sectoral percentage shares in Table 3 are computed from group aggregates of sectoral GDP in current U.S. dollars.

Table 4. Agriculture and food

The basic data for *value added in agriculture* are from the World Bank's national accounts series at current prices in national currencies. Value added in current prices in national currencies is converted to U.S. dollars by applying the single-year conversion procedure, as described in the technical note for Tables 2 and 3.

The figures for the remainder of this table are from the Food and Agriculture Organization (FAO). *Cereal imports* are measured in grain equivalents and defined as comprising all cereals in the *Standard International Trade Classification* (SITC), Revision 2, Groups 041-046. *Food aid in cereals* covers wheat and flour, bulgur, rice, coarse grains, and the cereal component of blended foods. The figures are not directly comparable because of reporting and timing differences. Cereal imports are based on calendar-year data reported by recipient countries, and food aid in cereals is based on data for crop years reported by donors and international organizations, including the International Wheat Council and the World Food Programme. Furthermore, food aid information from donors may not correspond to actual receipts by beneficiaries during a given period because of delays in transportation and recording or because aid is sometimes not reported to the FAO or other relevant international organizations. Food aid imports may also not show up in customs records. The time reference for food aid is the crop year, July to June.

Fertilizer consumption measures the plant nutrients used in relation to arable land. Fertilizer products cover nitrogenous, potash, and phosphate fertilizers (which include ground rock phosphate). Arable land is defined as land under temporary crops (double-cropped areas are counted once), temporary meadows for mowing or for pasture, land under market or kitchen gardens, and land temporarily fallow or lying idle, as well as land under permanent crops. The time reference for fertilizer consumption is the crop year, July to June.

Average growth rate of food production per capita has been computed from the index of food production per capita. The index relates to the average annual growth rate of food produced per capita in 1979-91 in relation to the average produced annually in 1979-81 (1979-81 = 100). The estimates are derived by dividing the quantity of food production by the total population. For the index, food is defined as comprising nuts, pulses, fruits, cereals, vegetables, sugar cane, sugar beet, starchy roots, edible oils, livestock, and livestock products. Quantities of food production are measured net of annual feed, seeds for use in agriculture, and food lost in processing and distribution.

Fish products are measured by the level of daily protein supply derived from the consumption of fish in relation to total daily protein supply from all food. This estimate indirectly highlights the relative importance or weight of fish in total agriculture, especially since fish is not included in the index of food production.

The summary measures for fertilizer consumption are weighted by total arable land area; the summary measures for food production are weighted by population.

Table 5. Commercial energy

The data on energy are primarily from U.N. sources. They refer to commercial forms of primary energy—petroleum and natural gas liquids, natural gas, solid fuels (coal, lignite, and so on), and primary electricity (nuclear, geothermal, and hydroelectric power)—all converted into oil equivalents. Figures on liquid fuel consumption include petroleum derivatives that have been consumed in nonenergy uses. For converting primary electricity into oil equivalents, a notional thermal efficiency of 34 percent has been assumed. The use of firewood, dried animal excrement, and other traditional fuels, although substantial in some developing countries, is not taken into account because reliable and comprehensive data are not available.

Energy imports refers to the dollar value of energy imports—Section 3 in the *Standard International Trade Classification*, Revision 1—and are expressed as a percentage of earnings from merchandise exports. Because data on energy imports do not permit a distinction between petroleum imports for fuel and those for use in the petrochemicals industry, these percentages may overestimate the dependence on imported energy.

The summary measures of energy production and consumption are computed by aggregating the respective volumes for each of the years covered by the periods and applying the least-squares growth rate procedure. For energy consumption per capita, population weights are used to compute summary measures for the specified years.

The summary measures of energy imports as a percentage of merchandise exports are computed from group aggregates for energy imports and merchandise exports in current dollars.

Table 6. Structure of manufacturing

The basic data for *value added in manufacturing* are from the World Bank's national accounts series at current prices in national currencies. Value added in current prices in national currencies is converted to U.S. dollars by applying the single-year conversion procedure, as described in the technical note for Tables 2 and 3.

The data for *distribution of manufacturing value added* among industries are provided by the United Nations Industrial Development Organization (UNIDO), and distribution calculations are from national currencies in current prices.

The classification of manufacturing industries is in accordance with the U.N. *International Standard Industrial Classification of All Economic Activities* (ISIC), Revision 2. *Food, beverages, and tobacco* comprise ISIC Division 31; *textiles and clothing,* Division 32; *machinery and transport equipment,* Major Groups 382–84; and *chemicals,* Major Groups 351 and 352. *Other* comprises wood and related products (Division 33), paper and related products (Division 34), petroleum and related products (Major Groups 353–56), basic metals and mineral products (Divisions 36 and 37), fabricated metal products and professional goods (Major Groups 381 and 385), and other industries (Major Group 390). When data for textiles, machinery, or chemicals are shown as not available, they are also included in *other.*

Summary measures given for value added in manufacturing are totals calculated by the aggregation method noted at the beginning of the technical notes.

Table 7. Manufacturing earnings and output

Four indicators are shown—two relate to real earnings per employee, one to labor's share in total value added generated, and one to labor productivity in the manufacturing sector. The indicators are based on data from the United Nations Industrial Development ment Organization (UNIDO), although the deflators are from other sources, as explained below.

Earnings per employee are in constant prices and are derived by deflating nominal earnings per employee by the country's consumer price index (CPI). The CPI is from the International Monetary Fund's *International Financial Statistics.*

Total earnings as a percentage of value added are derived by dividing total earnings of employees by value added in current prices to show labor's share in income generated in the manufacturing sector. *Gross output per employee* is in constant prices and is presented as an index of overall labor productivity in manufacturing, with 1980 as the base year. To derive this indicator, UNIDO data on gross output per employee in current prices are adjusted using the implicit deflators for value added in manufacturing or in industry, taken from the World Bank's national accounts data files.

To improve cross-country comparability, UNIDO has, where possible, standardized the coverage of establishments to those with five or more employees.

The concepts and definitions are in accordance with the *International Recommendations for Industrial Statistics,* published by the United Nations. Earnings (wages and salaries) cover all remuneration to employees paid by the employer during the year. The payments include (a) all regular and overtime cash payments and bonuses and cost of living allowances; (b) wages and salaries paid during vacation and sick leave; (c) taxes and social insurance contributions and the like, payable by the employees and deducted by the employer; and (d) payments in kind.

The term "employees" in this table combines two categories defined by the U.N., regular employees and persons engaged. Together these groups comprise regular employees, working proprietors, active business partners, and unpaid family workers; they exclude homeworkers. The data refer to the average number of employees working during the year.

"Value added" is defined as the current value of gross output less the current cost of (a) materials, fuels, and other supplies consumed; (b) contract and commission work done by others; (c) repair and maintenance work done by others; and (d) goods shipped in the same condition as received.

The value of gross output is estimated on the basis of either production or shipments. On the production basis it consists of (a) the value of all products of the establishment; (b) the value of industrial services rendered to others; (c) the value of goods shipped in the same condition as received; (d) the value of electricity sold; and (e) the net change in the value of work-in-progress between the beginning and the end of the reference period. In the case of estimates compiled on a shipment basis, the net change between the beginning and the end of the reference period in the value of stocks of finished goods is also included.

Tables 8 and 9. Growth of consumption and investment; structure of demand

GDP is defined in the note for Tables 2 and 3, but here it is in purchaser values.

General government consumption includes all current expenditure for purchases of goods and services by all levels of government. Capital expenditure on national defense and security is regarded as consumption expenditure.

Private consumption, etc. is the market value of all goods and services, including durable products (such as cars, washing machines, and home computers) purchased or received as income in kind by households and nonprofit institutions. It excludes purchases of dwellings but includes imputed rent for owner-occupied dwellings (see the technical note for Table 10 for details). In practice, it includes any statistical discrepancy in the use of resources. At constant prices, it also includes the rescaling deviation from partial rebasing, which is explained at the beginning of the technical notes.

Gross domestic investment consists of outlays on additions to the fixed assets of the economy plus net changes in the level of inventories.

Gross domestic savings are calculated by deducting total consumption from GDP.

Exports of goods and nonfactor services represent the value of all goods and nonfactor services provided to the rest of the world; they include merchandise, freight, insurance, travel, and other nonfactor services. The value of factor services, such as investment income, interest, and labor income, is excluded. Current transfers are also excluded.

The *resource balance* is the difference between exports of goods and nonfactor services and imports of goods and nonfactor services.

Partially rebased 1987 series in constant domestic currency units are used to compute the indicators in Table 8. Distribution of GDP in Table 9 is calculated from national accounts series in current domestic currency units.

The summary measures are calculated by the method explained in the note for Tables 2 and 3.

Table 10. Structure of consumption

Percentage shares of selected items in total household consumption expenditure are computed from details of GDP (expenditure at national market prices) defined in the *U.N. System of National Accounts* (SNA), mostly as collected from the International Comparison Program (ICP) Phases IV (1980) and V (1985). For countries not covered by the ICP, less detailed national accounts estimates are included, where available, to present a general idea of the broad structure of consumption. The data cover eighty-four countries (including Bank staff estimates for China) and refer to the most recent estimates, generally for 1980 and 1985. Where they refer to other years, the figures are shown in italics. *Consumption* here refers to private (nongovernment) consumption as defined in the SNA and in the notes for Tables 2 and 3, 4, and 9, except that education and medical care comprise government as well as private outlays. This ICP concept of ''enhanced consumption'' reflects who uses rather

than who pays for consumption goods, and it improves international comparability because it is less sensitive to differing national practices regarding the financing of health and education services.

Cereals and tubers, a major subitem of *food*, comprise the main staple products: rice, flour, bread, all other cereals and cereal preparations, potatoes, yams, and other tubers. For high-income OECD members, however, this subitem does not include tubers. *Gross rents, fuel and power* consist of actual and imputed rents and repair and maintenance charges, as well as the subitem *fuel and power* (for heating, lighting, cooking, air conditioning, and so forth). Note that this item excludes energy used for transport (rarely reported to be more than 1 percent of total consumption in low- and middle-income economies). As mentioned, *medical care* and *education* include government as well as private consumption expenditure. *Transport and communication* also include the purchase of *automobiles*, which are reported as a subitem. *Other consumption*, the residual group, includes beverages and tobacco, nondurable household goods and household services, recreational services, and services (including meals) supplied by hotels and restaurants; carry-out food is recorded here. It also includes the separately reported subitem *other consumer durables*, comprising household appliances, furniture, floor coverings, recreational equipment, and watches and jewelry.

Estimating the structure of consumption is one of the weakest aspects of national accounting in low- and middle-income economies. The structure is estimated through household expenditure surveys and similar survey techniques. It therefore shares any bias inherent in the sample frame. Since, conceptually, expenditure is not identical to consumption, other apparent discrepancies occur, and data for some countries should be treated with caution. For example, some countries limit surveys to urban areas or, even more narrowly, to capital cities. This tends to produce lower than average shares for food and high shares for transport and communication, gross rents, fuel and power, and other consumption. Controlled food prices and incomplete national accounting for subsistence activities also contribute to low food shares.

Table 11. Central government expenditure

The data on central government finance in Tables 11 and 12 are from the IMF's *Government Finance Statistics Yearbook* (1992) and IMF data files. The accounts of each country are reported using the system of common definitions and classifications found in the IMF's *Manual on Government Finance Statistics* (1986).

For complete and authoritative explanations of concepts, definitions, and data sources, see these IMF sources. The commentary that follows is intended mainly to place these data in the context of the broad range of indicators reported in this edition.

The shares of *total expenditure* and *current revenue* by category are calculated from series in national currencies. Because of differences in coverage of available data, the individual components of central government expenditure and current revenue shown in these tables may not be strictly comparable across all economies.

Moreover, inadequate statistical coverage of state, provincial, and local governments dictates the use of central government data; this may seriously understate or distort the statistical portrayal of the allocation of resources for various purposes, especially in countries where lower levels of government have considerable autonomy and are responsible for many economic and social services. In addition, "central government" can mean either of two accounting concepts: consolidated or budgetary. For most countries, central government finance data have been consolidated into one overall account, but for others only the budgetary central government accounts are available. Since all central government units are not always included in the budgetary accounts, the overall picture of central government activities is usually incomplete. Countries reporting budgetary data are footnoted.

Consequently, the data presented, especially those for education and health, are not comparable across countries. In many economies, private health and education services are substantial; in others, public services represent the major component of total expenditure but may be financed by lower levels of government. Caution should therefore be exercised in using the data for cross-country comparisons. Central government expenditure comprises the expenditure by all government offices, departments, establishments, and other bodies that are agencies or instruments of the central authority of a country. It includes both current and capital (development) expenditure.

Defense comprises all expenditure, whether by defense or other departments, on the maintenance of military forces, including the purchase of military supplies and equipment, construction, recruiting, and training. Also in this category are closely related items such as military aid programs. Defense does not include expenditure on public order and safety, which are classified separately.

Education comprises expenditure on the provision, management, inspection, and support of preprimary, primary, and secondary schools; of universities and colleges; and of vocational, technical, and other training institutions. Also included is expenditure on the general administration and regulation of the education system; on research into its objectives, organization, administration, and methods; and on such subsidiary services as transport, school meals, and school medical and dental services. Note that Table 10 provides an alternative measure of expenditure on education, private as well as public, relative to household consumption.

Health covers public expenditure on hospitals, maternity and dental centers, and clinics with a major medical component; on national health and medical insurance schemes; and on family planning and preventive care. Note that Table 10 also provides a measure of expenditure on medical care, private as well as public, relative to household consumption.

Housing, amenities; social security and welfare cover expenditure on housing (excluding interest subsidies, which are usually classified with *other*) such as income-related schemes; on provision and support of housing and slum-clearance activities; on community development; and on sanitation services. These categories also cover compensation for loss of income to the sick and temporarily disabled; payments to the elderly, the permanently disabled, and the unemployed; family, maternity, and child allowances; and the cost of welfare services, such as care of the aged, the disabled, and children. Many expenditures relevant to environmental defense, such as pollution abatement, water supply, sanitary affairs, and refuse collection, are included indistinguishably in this category.

Economic services comprise expenditure associated with the regulation, support, and more efficient operation of business; economic development; redress of regional imbalances; and creation of employment opportunities. Research, trade promotion, geological surveys, and inspection and regulation of particular industry groups are among the activities included.

Other covers interest payments and items not included elsewhere; for a few economies it also includes amounts that could not be allocated to other components (or adjustments from accrual to cash accounts).

Total expenditure is more narrowly defined than the measure of general government consumption given in Table 9 because it excludes consumption expenditure by state and local governments. At the same time, central government expenditure is more broadly defined because it includes government's gross domestic investment and transfer payments.

Overall surplus/deficit is defined as current and capital revenue and official grants received, less total expenditure and lending minus repayments.

Table 12. Central government current revenue

Information on data sources and comparability is given in the note for Table 11. Current revenue by source is expressed as a percentage of *total current revenue,* which is the sum of tax revenue and nontax revenue and is calculated from national currencies.

Tax revenue comprises compulsory, unrequited, nonrepayable receipts for public purposes. It includes interest collected on tax arrears and penalties collected on nonpayment or late payment of taxes and is shown net of refunds and other corrective transactions. *Taxes on income, profit, and capital gains* are taxes levied on the actual or presumptive net income of individuals, on the profits of enterprises, and on capital gains, whether realized on land sales, securities, or other assets. Intragovernmental payments are eliminated in consolidation. *Social security contributions* include employers' and employees' social security contributions as well as those of self-employed and unemployed persons. *Domestic taxes on goods and services* include general sales and turnover or value added taxes, selective excises on goods, selective taxes on services, taxes on the use of goods or property, and profits of fiscal monopolies. *Taxes on international trade and transactions* include import duties, export duties, profits of export or import monopolies, exchange profits, and exchange taxes. *Other taxes* include employers' payroll or labor taxes, taxes on property, and taxes not allocable to other categories. They may include negative values that are adjustments, for instance, for taxes collected on behalf of state and local governments and not allocable to individual tax categories.

Nontax revenue comprises receipts that are not a compulsory nonrepayable payment for public purposes, such as fines, administrative fees, or entrepreneurial income from government ownership of property. Proceeds of grants and borrowing, funds arising from the repayment of previous lending by governments, incurrence of liabilities, and proceeds from the sale of capital assets are not included.

Table 13. Money and interest rates

The data on monetary holdings are based on the IMF's *International Financial Statistics* (IFS). *Monetary holdings, broadly defined,* comprise the monetary and quasi-monetary liabilities of a country's financial institutions to residents but not to the central government. For most countries, monetary holdings are the sum of money (IFS line 34) and quasi money (IFS line 35). Money comprises the economy's means of payment: currency outside banks and demand deposits. Quasi money comprises time and savings deposits

and similar bank accounts that the issuer will readily exchange for money. Where nonmonetary financial institutions are important issuers of quasi-monetary liabilities, these are also included in the measure of monetary holdings.

The growth rates for monetary holdings are calculated from year-end figures, while the average of the year-end figures for the specified year and the previous year is used for the ratio of monetary holdings to GDP.

Nominal interest rates of banks, also from IFS, represent the rates paid by commercial or similar banks to holders of their quasi-monetary liabilities (deposit rate) and charged by the banks on loans to prime customers (lending rate). The data are, however, of limited international comparability, partly because coverage and definitions vary and partly because countries differ in the scope available to banks for adjusting interest rates to reflect market conditions.

Because interest rates (and growth rates for monetary holdings) are expressed in nominal terms, much of the variation among countries stems from differences in inflation. For easy reference, the Table 1 indicator of recent inflation is repeated in this table.

Table 14. Growth of merchandise trade

The main data source for current trade values is the U.N. Commodity Trade (COMTRADE) data file supplemented by World Bank estimates. The statistics on merchandise trade are based on countries' customs returns.

Merchandise *exports* and *imports,* with some exceptions, cover international movements of goods across customs borders; trade in services is not included. Exports are valued f.o.b. (free on board) and imports c.i.f. (cost, insurance, and freight) unless otherwise specified in the foregoing sources. These values are in current U. S. dollars.

The growth rates of merchandise exports and imports are based on constant price data, which are obtained from export or import value data as deflated by the corresponding price index. The World Bank uses its own price indexes, which are based on international prices for primary commodities, and unit value indexes for manufactures. These price indexes are country-specific and disaggregated by broad commodity groups. This ensures consistency between data for a group of countries and those for individual countries. Such consistency will increase as the World Bank continues to improve its trade price indexes for an increasing number of countries. These growth rates can differ from those derived from national practices because national price indexes may use different base years and weighting procedures from those used by the World Bank.

The *terms of trade*, or the net barter terms of trade, measure the relative movement of export prices against that of import prices. Calculated as the ratio of a country's index of average export prices to its average import price index, this indicator shows changes over a base year in the level of export prices as a percentage of import prices. The terms of trade index numbers are shown for 1985 and 1991, where 1987 = 100. The price indexes are from the source cited above for the growth rates of exports and imports.

The summary measures for the growth rates are calculated by aggregating the 1987 constant U.S. dollar price series for each year and then applying the least-squares growth rate procedure for the periods shown.

Tables 15 and 16. Structure of merchandise imports and exports

The shares in these tables are derived from trade values in current dollars reported in the U.N. trade data system and the U.N.'s *Yearbook of International Trade Statistics*, supplemented by World Bank estimates.

Merchandise *exports* and *imports* are defined in the technical note for Table 14.

The categorization of exports and imports follows the *Standard International Trade Classification* (SITC), Series M, No. 34, Revision 1. For some countries, data for certain commodity categories are unavailable and the full breakdown cannot be shown.

In Table 15, *food* commodities are those in SITC Sections 0, 1, and 4 and Division 22 (food and live animals, beverages and tobacco, animal and vegetable oils and fats, oilseeds, oil nuts and oil kernels). *Fuels* are the commodities in SITC Section 3 (mineral fuels, and lubricants and related materials). *Other primary commodities* comprise SITC Section 2 (inedible crude materials, except fuels), less Division 22 (oilseeds, oilnuts, and oil kernels) and Division 68 (nonferrous metals). *Machinery and transport equipment* are the commodities in SITC Section 7. *Other manufactures*, calculated residually from the total value of manufactured imports, represent SITC Sections 5 through 9, less Section 7 and Division 68.

In Table 16, *fuels, minerals, and metals* are the commodities in SITC Section 3 (mineral fuels, and lubricants and related materials), Divisions 27 and 28 (crude fertilizers and crude minerals, excluding coal, petroleum and precious stones, and metalliferous ores and metal scrap), and Division 68 (nonferrous metals). *Other primary commodities* comprise SITC Sections 0, 1, 2, and 4 (food and live animals, beverages and tobacco, inedible crude materials, except fuels, and animal and vegetable oils and fats), less Divisions

27 and 28. *Machinery and transport equipment* are the commodities in SITC Section 7. *Other manufactures* represent SITC Sections 5 through 9, less Section 7 and Division 68. *Textiles and clothing*, representing SITC Divisions 65 and 84 (textiles, yarns, fabrics, made-up articles, and related products and clothing), are a subgroup of *other manufactures*.

The summary measures in Table 15 are weighted by total merchandise imports of individual countries in current U.S. dollars and those in Table 16 by total merchandise exports of individual countries in current U.S. dollars. (See the technical note for Table 14.)

Table 17. OECD imports of manufactured goods: origin and composition

The data are from the United Nations, reported by high-income OECD economies, which are the OECD members excluding Greece, Portugal, and Turkey.

The table reports the value of *imports of manufactures* of high-income OECD countries by the economy of origin, and the composition of such imports by major manufactured product groups. These data are based on the U.N. COMTRADE database—Revision 1, SITC for 1970, and Revision 2 SITC for 1991.

The table replaces one in past editions on the origin and destination of manufactured exports, which was based on exports reported by individual economies. Since there was a lag of several years in reporting by many developing economies, estimates based on various sources were used to fill the gaps. Until these estimates can be improved, the current table, based on up-to-date and consistent but less comprehensive data, is included instead. Manufactured imports of the predominant markets from individual economies are the best available proxy of the magnitude and composition of the manufactured exports of these economies to all destinations taken together.

Manufactured goods are the commodities in the *Standard International Trade Classification* (SITC), Revision 1, Sections 5 through 9 (chemical and related products, basic manufactures, manufactured articles, machinery and transport equipment, and other manufactured articles and goods not elsewhere classified), excluding Division 68 (nonferrous metals). This definition is somewhat broader than the one used to define exporters of manufactures.

The major manufactured product groups reported are defined as follows: *textiles and clothing* (SITC Sections 65 and 84), *chemicals* (SITC Section 5), *electrical machinery and electronics* (SITC Section 72), *transport equipment* (SITC Section 73), and *others*, defined as the residual. SITC Revision 1 data are used for the year 1970, whereas the equivalent data in Revision 2 are used for the year 1991.

Table 18. Balance of payments and reserves

The statistics for this table are mostly as reported by the IMF but do include recent estimates by World Bank staff and, in rare instances, the Bank's own coverage or classification adjustments to enhance international comparability. Values in this table are in U.S. dollars converted at current exchange rates.

The *current account balance after official transfers* is the difference between (a) exports of goods and services (factor and nonfactor) as well as inflows of unrequited transfers (private and official) and (b) imports of goods and services as well as all unrequited transfers to the rest of the world.

The *current account balance before official transfers* is the current account balance that treats net official unrequited transfers as akin to official capital movements. The difference between the two balance of payments measures is essentially foreign aid in the form of grants, technical assistance, and food aid, which, for most developing countries, tends to make current account deficits smaller than the financing requirement.

Net workers' remittances cover payments and receipts of income by migrants who are employed or expect to be employed for more than a year in their new economy, where they are considered residents. These remittances are classified as private unrequited transfers and are included in the balance of payments current account balance, whereas those derived from shorter-term stays are included in services as labor income. The distinction accords with internationally agreed guidelines, but many developing countries classify workers' remittances as a factor income receipt (hence, a component of GNP). The World Bank adheres to international guidelines in defining GNP and, therefore, may differ from national practices.

Gross international reserves comprise holdings of monetary gold, special drawing rights (SDRs), the reserve position of members in the IMF, and holdings of foreign exchange under the control of monetary authorities. The data on holdings of international reserves are from IMF data files. The gold component of these reserves is valued throughout at year-end (December 31) London prices: that is, $37.37 an ounce in 1970 and $353.60 an ounce in 1991. The reserve levels for 1970 and 1991 refer to the end of the year indicated and are in current U.S. dollars at prevailing exchange rates. Because of differences in the definition of international reserves, in the valuation of gold, and in reserve management practices, the levels of reserve holdings published in national sources do not have strictly comparable significance. Reserve holdings at the end of 1991 are also expressed in terms of the number of months of imports of goods and services they could pay for.

The summary measures are computed from group aggregates for gross international reserves and total imports of goods and services in current dollars.

Table 19. Official development assistance from OECD and OPEC members

Official development assistance (ODA) consists of net disbursements of loans and grants made on concessional financial terms by official agencies of the members of the Development Assistance Committee (DAC) of the Organization for Economic Cooperation and Development (OECD) and members of the Organization of Petroleum Exporting Countries (OPEC) to promote economic development and welfare. Although this definition is meant to exclude purely military assistance, the borderline is sometimes blurred; the definition used by the country of origin usually prevails. ODA also includes the value of technical cooperation and assistance. All data shown are supplied by the OECD, and all U.S. dollar values are converted at official exchange rates.

Total net flows are net disbursements to developing countries and multilateral institutions. The disbursements to multilateral institutions are now reported for all DAC members on the basis of the date of issue of notes; some DAC members previously reported on the basis of the date of encashment.

The nominal values shown in the summary for ODA from high-income OECD countries were converted at 1987 prices using the dollar GDP deflator. This deflator is based on price increases in OECD countries (excluding Greece, Portugal, and Turkey) measured in dollars. It takes into account the parity changes between the dollar and national currencies. For example, when the dollar depreciates, price changes measured in national currencies have to be adjusted upward by the amount of the depreciation to obtain price changes in dollars.

The table, in addition to showing totals for OPEC, shows totals for the Organization of Arab Petroleum Exporting Countries (OAPEC). The donor members of OAPEC are Algeria, Iraq, Kuwait, Libya, Qatar, Saudi Arabia, and United Arab Emirates. ODA data for OPEC and OAPEC are also obtained from the OECD.

Table 20. Official development assistance: receipts

Net disbursements of ODA from all sources consist of loans and grants made on concessional financial terms by all bilateral official agencies and multilateral sources to promote economic development and welfare. They include the value of technical cooperation and assistance. The disbursements shown in this table are not strictly comparable with those shown in

Table 19 since the receipts are from all sources; disbursements in Table 19 refer only to those made by high-income members of the OECD and members of OPEC. Net disbursements equal gross disbursements less payments to the originators of aid for amortization of past aid receipts. Net disbursements of ODA are shown per capita and as a percentage of GNP.

The summary measures of per capita ODA are computed from group aggregates for population and for ODA. Summary measures for ODA as a percentage of GNP are computed from group totals for ODA and for GNP in current U.S. dollars.

Table 21. Total external debt

The data on debt in this and successive tables are from the World Bank Debtor Reporting System, supplemented by World Bank estimates. That system is concerned solely with developing economies and does not collect data on external debt for other groups of borrowers or from economies that are not members of the World Bank. The dollar figures on debt shown in Tables 21 through 25 are in U.S. dollars converted at official exchange rates.

The data on debt include private nonguaranteed debt reported by twenty-seven developing countries and complete or partial estimates for an additional twenty others that do not report but for which this type of debt is known to be significant.

Public loans are external obligations of public debtors, including the national government, its agencies, and autonomous public bodies. *Publicly guaranteed loans* are external obligations of private debtors that are guaranteed for repayment by a public entity. These two categories are aggregated in the tables. *Private nonguaranteed loans* are external obligations of private debtors that are not guaranteed for repayment by a public entity.

Use of IMF credit denotes repurchase obligations to the IMF for all uses of IMF resources, excluding those resulting from drawings in the reserve tranche. It is shown for the end of the year specified. It comprises purchases outstanding under the credit tranches, including enlarged access resources, and all special facilities (the buffer stock, compensatory financing, extended fund, and oil facilities), Trust Fund loans, and operations under the enhanced structural adjustment facilities. Use of IMF credit outstanding at year-end (a stock) is converted to U.S. dollars at the dollar-SDR exchange rate in effect at year-end.

Short-term debt is debt with an original maturity of one year or less. Available data permit no distinctions between public and private nonguaranteed short-term debt.

Total external debt is defined here as the sum of public, publicly guaranteed, and private nonguaranteed long-term debt, use of IMF credit, and short-term debt.

Total arrears on LDOD denotes principal and interest due but not paid.

Present value is the discounted value of the future debt service payments.

Table 22. Flow of public and private external capital

Data on disbursements, repayment of principal (amortization), and payment of interest are for public, publicly guaranteed, and private nonguaranteed long-term loans.

Disbursements are drawings on long-term loan commitments during the year specified.

Repayments of principal are actual amount of principal (amortization) paid in foreign currency, goods, or services in the year specified.

Interest payments are actual amounts of interest paid in foreign currency, goods, or services in the year specified.

Table 23. Aggregate net resource flows and net transfers

Net flows on long-term debt are disbursements less the repayment of principal on public, publicly guaranteed, and private nonguaranteed long-term debt. *Official grants* are transfers made by an official agency in cash or in kind in respect of which no legal debt is incurred by the recipient. Data on official grants exclude grants for technical assistance.

Net foreign direct investment is defined as investment that is made to acquire a lasting interest (usually 10 percent of the voting stock) in an enterprise operating in a country other than that of the investor (defined according to residency), the investor's purpose being an effective voice in the management of the enterprise. *Aggregate net resource flows* are the sum of net flows on long-term debt (excluding use of IMF credit), plus official grants (excluding technical assistance) and net foreign direct investment. *Aggregate net transfers* are equal to aggregate net resource flows minus interest payments on long-term loans and remittance of all profits.

Table 24. Total external debt ratios

Total external debt as a percentage of exports of goods and services represents public, publicly guaranteed, private nonguaranteed long-term debt, use of IMF credit, and short-term debt drawn at year-end, net of repayments of principal and write-offs. Throughout this table, goods and services include workers' remittances. For estimating *total external debt as a percentage of GNP*, the debt figures are converted into U.S. dollars from currencies of repayment at end-of-year official exchange rates. GNP is converted from national currencies to U.S. dollars by applying the conversion procedure described in the technical note for Tables 2 and 3.

Total debt service as a percentage of goods and services is the sum of principal repayments and interest payments on total external debt (as defined in the note for Table 21). It is one of several conventional measures used to assess a country's ability to service debt.

Interest payments as a percentage of exports of goods and services are actual payments made on total external debt.

The summary measures are weighted by exports of goods and services in current dollars and by GNP in current dollars, respectively.

Concessional debt as a percentage of total external debt conveys information about the borrower's receipt of aid from official lenders at concessional terms as defined by the DAC, that is, loans with an original grant element of 25 percent or more.

Multilateral debt as a percentage of total external debt conveys information about the borrower's receipt of aid from the World Bank, regional development banks, and other multilateral and intergovernmental agencies. Excluded are loans from funds administered by an international organization on behalf of a single donor government.

Table 25. Terms of external public borrowing

Commitments refer to the public and publicly guaranteed loans for which contracts were signed in the year specified. They are reported in currencies of repayment and converted into U.S. dollars at average annual official exchange rates.

Figures for *interest rates, maturities,* and *grace periods* are averages weighted by the amounts of the loans. Interest is the major charge levied on a loan and is usually computed on the amount of principal drawn and outstanding. The maturity of a loan is the interval between the agreement date, when a loan agreement is signed or bonds are issued, and the date of final repayment of principal. The grace period is the interval between the agreement date and the date of the first repayment of principal.

Public loans with variable interest rates, as a percentage of public debt refer to interest rates that float with movements in a key market rate; for example, the London interbank offered rate (LIBOR) or the U.S. prime rate. This column shows the borrower's exposure to changes in international interest rates.

The summary measures in this table are weighted by the amounts of the loans.

Table 26. Population growth and projections

Population growth rates are period averages calculated from midyear populations.

Population estimates for mid-1991 and estimates of fertility and mortality are made by the World Bank from data provided by the U.N. Population Division, the U.N. Statistical Office, and country statistical offices. Estimates take into account the results of the latest population censuses, which in some cases are neither recent nor accurate. Note that refugees not permanently settled in the country of asylum are generally considered to be part of the population of their country of origin.

The projections of population for 2000, 2025, and the year in which the population will eventually become stationary (see definition below) are made for each economy separately. Information on total population by age and sex, fertility, mortality, and international migration is projected on the basis of generalized assumptions until the population becomes stationary.

A stationary population is one in which age- and sex-specific mortality rates have not changed over a long period, and during which fertility rates have remained at replacement level; that is, when the net reproduction rate (defined in the note for Table 27) equals 1. In such a population, the birth rate is constant and equal to the death rate, the age structure is constant, and the growth rate is zero.

Population projections are made age cohort by age cohort. Mortality, fertility, and migration are projected separately, and the results are applied iteratively to the 1990 base-year age structure. For the projection period 1990 to 2005, the changes in mortality are country specific: increments in life expectancy and decrements in infant mortality are based on previous trends for each country. When female secondary school enrollment is high, mortality is assumed to decline more quickly. Infant mortality is projected separately from adult mortality. Note that the data reflect the potentially significant impact of the human immunodeficiency virus (HIV) epidemic.

Projected fertility rates are also based on previous trends. For countries in which fertility has started to decline (termed "fertility transition"), this trend is assumed to continue. It has been observed that no country where the population has a life expectancy of less than 50 years has experienced a fertility decline; for these countries, fertility transition is delayed, and the average decline of the group of countries in fertility transition is applied. Countries with below-replacement fertility are assumed to have constant total fertility rates until 1995–2000 and to regain replacement level by 2030.

International migration rates are based on past and present trends in migration flows and migration policy. Among the sources consulted are estimates and projections made by national statistical offices, international agencies, and research institutions. Because of the uncertainty of future migration trends, it is assumed in the projections that net migration rates will reach zero by 2025.

The estimates of the size of the stationary population are very long-term projections. They are included only to show the implications of recent fertility and mortality trends on the basis of generalized assumptions. A fuller description of the methods and assumptions used to calculate the estimates is contained in *World Population Projections, 1992–93 Edition.*

Table 27. Demography and fertility

The *crude birth rate* and *crude death rate* indicate respectively the number of live births and deaths occurring per thousand population in a year. They come from the sources mentioned in the note to Table 26.

Women of childbearing age are those in the 15–49 age-group.

The *total fertility rate* represents the number of children that would be born to a woman if she were to live to the end of her childbearing years and bear children at each age in accordance with prevailing age-specific fertility rates. The rates given are from the sources mentioned in the note for Table 26.

The *net reproduction rate* (NRR), which measures the number of daughters a newborn girl will bear during her lifetime, assuming fixed age-specific fertility and mortality rates, reflects the extent to which a cohort of newborn girls will reproduce themselves. An NRR of 1 indicates that fertility is at replacement level: at this rate women will bear, on average, only enough daughters to replace themselves in the population. As with the size of the stationary population, the assumed year of reaching replacement-level fertility is speculative and should not be regarded as a prediction.

Married women of childbearing age using contraception are women who are practicing, or whose husbands are practicing, any form of contraception. Contraceptive usage is generally measured for women age 15 to 49. A few countries use measures relating to other age groups, especially 15 to 44.

Data are mainly derived from demographic and health surveys, contraceptive prevalence surveys, World Bank country data, and Mauldin and Segal's article ''Prevalence of Contraceptive Use: Trends and Issues'' in volume 19 of *Studies in Family Planning* (1988). For a few countries for which no survey data are available, and for several African countries, program statistics are used. Program statistics may un-

derstate contraceptive prevalence because they do not measure use of methods such as rhythm, withdrawal, or abstinence, nor use of contraceptives not obtained through the official family planning program. The data refer to rates prevailing in a variety of years, generally not more than two years before the year specified in the table.

All summary measures are country data weighted by each country's share in the aggregate population.

Table 28. Health and nutrition

The estimates of *population per physician* and *per nursing person* are derived from World Health Organization (WHO) data and are supplemented by data obtained directly by the World Bank from national sources. The data refer to a variety of years, generally no more than two years before the year specified. Nursing persons include auxiliary nurses, as well as paraprofessional personnel such as traditional birth attendants. The inclusion of auxiliary and paraprofessional personnel provides more realistic estimates of available nursing care. Because definitions of doctors and nursing personnel vary—and because the data shown are for a variety of years—the data for these two indicators are not strictly comparable across countries.

Data on *births attended by health staff* show the percentage of births recorded where a recognized health service worker was in attendance. The data are from WHO, supplemented by UNICEF data. They are based on national sources, derived mostly from official community reports and hospital records; some reflect only births in hospitals and other medical institutions. Sometimes smaller private and rural hospitals are excluded, and sometimes even relatively primitive local facilities are included. The coverage is therefore not always comprehensive, and the figures should be treated with extreme caution.

Babies with low birth weight are children born weighing less than 2,500 grams. Low birth weight is frequently associated with maternal malnutrition. It tends to raise the risk of infant mortality and lead to poor growth in infancy and childhood, thus increasing the incidence of other forms of retarded development. The figures are derived from both WHO and UNICEF sources and are based on national data. The data are not strictly comparable across countries since they are compiled from a combination of surveys and administrative records that may not have representative national coverage.

The *infant mortality rate* is the number of infants who die before reaching one year of age, per thousand live births in a given year. The data are from the U.N. publication *Mortality of Children under Age 5: Projections, 1950–2025* as well as from the World Bank.

The years of life lost (per 1,000 population) conveys the burden of mortality in absolute terms. It is composed of the sum of the years lost to premature death per 1,000 population. Years of life lost at age *x* are measured by subtracting the remaining expected years of life, given a life expectancy at birth fixed at 80 years for men and 82.5 for women. This indicator depends on the effect of three variables: the age structure of the population, the overall rate of mortality, and the age structure of mortality.

Child malnutrition measures the percentage of children under five with a deficiency or an excess of nutrients that interfere with their health and genetic potential for growth. Methods of assessment vary, but the most commonly used are the following: less than 80 percent of the standard weight for age; less than minus two standard deviation from the 50th percentile of the weight for age reference population; and the Gomez scale of malnutrition. Note that for a few countries the figures are for children of three or four years of age and younger. The summary measures in this table are country data weighted by each country's share in the aggregate population.

Table 29. Education

The data in this table refer to a variety of years, generally not more than two years distant from those specified; however, figures for females sometimes refer to a year earlier than that for overall totals. The data are mostly from UNESCO.

Primary school enrollment data are estimates of children of all ages enrolled in primary school. Figures are expressed as the ratio of pupils to the population of school-age children. Although many countries consider primary school age to be 6 to 11 years, others do not. For some countries with universal primary education, the gross enrollment ratios may exceed 100 percent because some pupils are younger or older than the country's standard primary school age.

The data on *secondary* school enrollment are calculated in the same manner, but again the definition of secondary school age differs among countries. It is most commonly considered to be 12 to 17 years. Late entry of more mature students as well as repetition and the phenomenon of "bunching" in final grades can influence these ratios.

The *tertiary* enrollment ratio is calculated by dividing the number of pupils enrolled in all post-secondary schools and universities by the population in the 20-24 age group. Pupils attending vocational schools, adult education programs, two-year community colleges, and distance education centers (primarily correspondence courses) are included. The distribution of pupils across these different types of institutions varies among countries. The youth population—that is, 20 to 24 years—has been adopted by UNESCO as the denominator since it represents an average tertiary level cohort even though people above and below this age group may be registered in tertiary institutions.

Primary net enrollment is the percentage of school-age children who are enrolled in school. Unlike gross enrollment, the net ratios correspond to the country's primary-school age group. This indicator gives a much clearer idea of how many children in the age group are actually enrolled in school without the numbers being inflated by over- or under-age children.

The *primary pupil-teacher ratio* is the number of pupils enrolled in school in a country, divided by the number of teachers in the education system.

The summary measures in this table are country enrollment rates weighted by each country's share in the aggregate population.

Table 30. Income distribution and PPC estimates of GDP

The first six columns of the table report distribution of income or expenditure accruing to percentile groups of households ranked by total household income, per capita income, or expenditure. The last four columns contain estimates of per capita GDP based on purchasing power of currencies (PPCs) rather than exchange rates (see below for the definition of PPC).

The first six columns of the table give the shares of population quintiles and the top decile in total income or consumption expenditure for 36 low- and middle-income countries, and 20 high-income countries. The rest of this note refers to the former set of countries. The data sets for these countries refer to different years between 1981 and 1991, and are drawn from nationally representative household surveys. The data sets have been compiled from two main sources: government statistical agencies (often using published reports), and the World Bank (mostly data originating from the Living Standards Measurement Study). In cases where the original unit record data from the household survey were available, these have been used to calculate directly the income (or expenditure) shares of different quantiles; otherwise, the latter have been estimated from the best available grouped data. For further details on both the data and the estimation methodology, see Chen, Datt, and Ravallion, 1993.

There are several comparability problems across countries in the underlying household surveys, though these problems are diminishing over time as survey methodologies are both improving and becoming more standardized, particularly under the initiatives of the United Nations (under the Household Survey Capability Program) and the World Bank (under the Living Standard Measurement Study and the Social Dimensions of Adjustment Project for Sub-Saharan Africa). The data presented here should nevertheless be interpreted with caution. In particular, the following three sources of noncomparability ought to be noted. First, the surveys differ in using income or consumption expenditure as the living standard indicator. For 17 of the 36 low- and middle-income countries, the data refer to consumption expenditure. Typically, income is more unequally distributed than consumption. Second, the surveys differ in using the household or the individual as their unit of observation; in the former case, the quantiles refer to percentage of households, rather than percentage of persons. Third, the surveys also differ according to whether the units of observation are ranked by household income (or consumption) or by per capita income (or consumption). The footnotes to the table identify these differences for each country.

The 1987 indexed figures on PPC-based GDP per capita (US=100) are presented in the seventh column. They include: (i) results of the International Comparison Programme (ICP) Phase VI for 1990 for OECD countries extrapolated backward to 1987; (ii) results of ICP Phase V for 1985 for non-OECD countries extrapolated to 1987; (iii) the latest available results from either Phase IV for 1980 or Phase III for 1975 extrapolated to 1987 for countries that participated in the earlier phases only; (iv) World Bank estimates for the economies of the Former Soviet Union (FSU) based on partial and preliminary ICP data for the former U.S.S.R. for 1990 extrapolated to 1987; (v) a World Bank estimate for China; and (vi) ICP estimates obtained by regression for the remaining countries that did not participate in any of the phases. Economies whose 1987 figures are extrapolated from another year or imputed by regression are footnoted accordingly.

The blend of extrapolated and regression-based 1987 figures underlying the seventh column is extrapolated to 1991 using Bank estimates of real per capita GDP growth rates and expressed as an index (US=100) in the eighth column. For countries that have ever participated in ICP, as well as for China and the economies of the FSU, the latest available PPC-based values are extrapolated to 1991 by Bank estimates of growth rates and converted to current "international dollars" by scaling all results up by the U.S. inflation rates; these are presented in the ninth column. Footnotes indicate which year PPC-based data were extrapolated. Regression estimates of all countries except FSU economies, whether or not they participated in ICP, extrapolated from 1987 to 1991

and expressed in 1991 international dollars, are presented in the tenth column. The adjustments do not take account of changes in the terms of trade. The observed figures should be used wherever available. Where both observed and regression numbers are available a comparison between the two indicates the range of errors associated with the regression estimates. For countries that do not have PPC-based observed data, there is no alternative to the use of regression estimates, but the extent and direction of errors cannot be inferred in these cases.

ICP recasts traditional national accounts through special price collections and disaggregation of GDP by expenditure components. ICP details are prepared by national statistical offices, and the results are coordinated by the U.N. Statistical Division (UNSTAT) with support from other international agencies, particularly the Statistical Office of the European Communities (Eurostat) and the Organization for Economic Cooperation and Development (OECD). The World Bank, the Economic Commission for Europe, and the Economic and Social Commission for Asia and the Pacific (ESCAP) also contribute to this exercise. A total of sixty-four countries participated in ICP Phase V. For one country (Nepal), total GDP data were not available, and comparisons were made for consumption only. Luxembourg and Swaziland are the only two economies with populations under 1 million that have participated in ICP; their 1987 results, as a percentage of the U.S. results, are 83.1 and 15.0, respectively. The figures given here are subject to change and should be regarded as indicative only.

The next round of ICP surveys for 1993 is expected to cover more than eighty countries, including China and several FSU economies.

The "international dollar" (I$) has the same purchasing power over total GDP as the U.S. dollar in a given year, but purchasing power over subaggregates is determined by average international prices at that level rather than by U.S. relative prices. These dollar values, which are different from the dollar values of GNP or GDP shown in Tables 1 and 3 (see the technical notes for these tables), are obtained by special conversion factors designed to equalize the purchasing powers of currencies in the respective countries. This conversion factor, the Purchasing Power of Currencies (PPC), is defined as the number of units of a country's currency required to buy the same amounts of goods and services in the domestic market as one dollar would buy in the United States. The computation involves deriving implicit quantities from national accounts expenditure data and specially collected price data and then revaluing the implicit quantities in each country at a single set of average prices. The average price index thus equalizes dollar prices in every country so that cross-country comparisons of GDP based on them reflect differences in quantities of goods and services free of price-level differentials. This procedure is designed to bring cross-country comparisons in line with cross-time real value comparisons that are based on constant price series.

The ICP figures presented here are the results of a two-step exercise. Countries within a region or group such as the OECD are first compared using their own group average prices. Next, since group average prices may differ from each other, making the countries in different groups not comparable, the group prices are adjusted to make them comparable at the world level. The adjustments, done by UNSTAT and Eurostat, are based on price differentials observed in a network of "link" countries representing each group. However, the linking is done in a manner that retains in the world comparison the relative levels of GDP observed in the group comparisons, called "fixity."

The two-step process was adopted because the relative GDP levels and rankings of two countries may change when more countries are brought into the comparison. It was felt that this should not be allowed to happen within geographic regions; that is, that the relationship of, say, Ghana and Senegal should not be affected by the prices prevailing in the United States. Thus overall GDP per capita levels are calculated at "regional" prices and then linked together. The linking is done by revaluing GDPs of all the countries at average "world" prices and reallocating the new regional totals on the basis of each country's share in the original comparison.

Such a method does not permit the comparison of more detailed quantities (such as food consumption). Hence these subaggregates and more detailed expenditure categories are calculated using world prices. These quantities are indeed comparable internationally, but they do not add up to the indicated GDPs because they are calculated at a different set of prices.

Some countries belong to several regional groups. A few of the groups have priority; others are equal. Thus fixity is always maintained between members of the European Communities, even within the OECD and world comparison. For Austria and Finland, however, the bilateral relationship that prevails within the OECD comparison is also the one used within the global comparison. But a significantly different relationship (based on Central European prices) prevails in the comparison within that group, and this is the relationship presented in the separate publication of the European comparison.

To derive ICP-based 1987 figures for countries that are yet to participate in any ICP survey, an estimating equation is first obtained by fitting the following regression to 1987 data:

$$\ln (r) = .5603 \ln (\text{ATLAS}) + .3136 \ln (\text{ENROL}) + .5706;$$
$$\quad\quad (.0304) \quad\quad\quad (.0574) \quad\quad\quad\quad (.1734)$$

RMSE = .2324; Adj.R-Sq = .95; N = 78.

where all variables and estimated values are expressed as US = 100;

r = ICP estimates of per capita GDP converted to U.S. dollars by PPC, the array of r consisting of extrapolations of the most recent actual ICP values available for countries that ever participated in ICP;

ATLAS = per capita GNP estimated by the *Atlas* method;

ENROL = secondary school enrollment ratio; and

RMSE = root mean squared error.

ATLAS and ENROL are used as rough proxies of intercountry wage differentials for unskilled and skilled human capital, respectively. Following Isenman (see Paul Isenman, "Inter-Country Comparisons of 'Real' (PPP) Incomes: Revised Estimates and Unresolved Questions," in *World Development*, 1980, vol. 8, pp.61-72), the rationale adopted here is that ICP and conventional estimates of GDP differ mainly because wage differences persist among nations due to constraints on the international mobility of labor. A technical paper providing fuller explanation is available on request (Sultan Ahmad, "Regression Estimates of Per Capita GDP Based on Purchasing Power Parities," Working Paper Series 956, International Economics Department, World Bank, 1992. For further details on ICP procedures, readers may consult the ICP Phase IV report, *World Comparisons of Purchasing Power and Real Product for 1980* (New York: United Nations, 1986).

Table 31. Urbanization

Data on urban population and agglomeration in large cities are from the U.N.'s *World Urbanization Prospects*, supplemented by data from the World Bank. The growth rates of urban population are calculated from the World Bank's population estimates; the estimates of urban population shares are calculated from both sources just cited.

Because the estimates in this table are based on different national definitions of what is urban, cross-country comparisons should be made with caution.

The summary measures for urban population as a percentage of total population are calculated from country percentages weighted by each country's share in the aggregate population; the other summary measures in this table are weighted in the same fashion, using urban population.

Table 32. Women in development

This table provides some basic indicators disaggregated to show differences between the sexes that illustrate the condition of women in society. The measures reflect the demographic status of women and their access to health and education services. Statistical anomalies become even more apparent when social indicators are analyzed by gender, because reporting systems are often weak in areas related specifically to women. Indicators drawn from censuses and surveys, such as those on population, tend to be about as reliable for women as for men; but indicators based largely on administrative records, such as maternal and infant mortality, are less reliable. More resources are now being devoted to develop better information on these topics, but the reliability of data, even in the series shown, still varies significantly.

The *under-5 mortality rate* shows the probability of a newborn baby dying before reaching age 5. The rates are derived from life tables based on estimated current life expectancy at birth and on infant mortality rates. In general, throughout the world more males are born than females. Under good nutritional and health conditions and in times of peace, male children under 5 have a higher death rate than females. These columns show that female-male differences in the risk of dying by age 5 vary substantially. In industrial market economies, female babies have a 23 percent lower risk of dying by age 5 than male babies; the risk of dying by age 5 is actually higher for females than for males in some lower-income economies. This suggests differential treatment of males and females with respect to food and medical care.

Such discrimination particularly affects very young girls, who may get a smaller share of scarce food or receive less prompt costly medical attention. This pattern of discrimination is not uniformly associated with development. There are low- and middle-income countries (and regions within countries) where the risk of dying by age 5 for females relative to males approximates the pattern found in industrial countries. In many other countries, however, the numbers starkly demonstrate the need to associate women more closely with development. The health and welfare indicators in both Table 28 and in this table's maternal mortality column draw attention, in particular, to the conditions associated with childbearing. This activity still carries the highest risk of death for women of reproductive age in developing countries. The indicators reflect, but do not measure, both the availability of health services for women and the general welfare and nutritional status of mothers.

Life expectancy at birth is defined in the note to Table 1.

Maternal mortality refers to the number of female deaths that occur during childbirth per 100,000 live births. Because deaths during childbirth are defined more widely in some countries to include complications of pregnancy or the period after childbirth, or of abortion, and because many pregnant women die from lack of suitable health care, maternal mortality is difficult to measure consistently and reliably across countries. The data in these two series are drawn from diverse national sources and collected by the World Health Organization (WHO), although many national administrative systems are weak and do not record vital events in a systematic way. The data are derived mostly from official community reports and hospital records, and some reflect only deaths in hospitals and other medical institutions. Sometimes smaller private and rural hospitals are excluded, and sometimes even relatively primitive local facilities are included. The coverage is therefore not always comprehensive, and the figures should be treated with extreme caution.

Clearly, many maternal deaths go unrecorded, particularly in countries with remote rural populations; this accounts for some of the very low numbers shown in the table, especially for several African countries. Moreover, it is not clear whether an increase in the number of mothers in hospital reflects more extensive medical care for women or more complications in pregnancy and childbirth because of poor nutrition, for instance. (Table 28 shows data on low birth weight.)

These time series attempt to bring together readily available information not always presented in international publications. WHO warns that there are inevitably gaps in the series, and it has invited countries to provide more comprehensive figures. They are reproduced here, from the 1991 WHO publication *Maternal Mortality: A Global Factbook.* The data refer to any year from 1983 to 1991.

The *education* indicators, based on UNESCO sources, show the extent to which females have equal access to schooling.

Percentage of cohort persisting to grade 4 is the percentage of children starting primary school in 1970 and 1986, respectively, who continued to the fourth grade by 1973 and 1989. Figures in italics represent earlier or later cohorts. The data are based on enrollment records. The slightly higher persistence ratios for females in some African countries may indicate male participation in activities such as animal herding.

All things being equal, and opportunities being the same, the ratios for *females per 100 males* should be close to 100. However, inequalities may cause the ratios to move in different directions. For example, the number of females per 100 males will rise at secondary school level if male attendance declines more rapidly in the final grades because of males' greater job opportunities, conscription into the army, or migration in search of work. In addition, since the numbers in these columns refer mainly to general secondary education, they do not capture those (mostly males) enrolled in technical and vocational schools or in full-time apprenticeships, as in Eastern Europe.

All summary measures are country data weighted by each country's share in the aggregate population.

Table 33. Forests, protected areas, and water resources

This table on natural resources represents a step toward including environmental data in the assessment of development and the planning of economic strategies. It provides a partial picture of the status of forests, the extent of areas protected for conservation or other environmentally related purposes, and the availability and use of fresh water. The data reported here are drawn from the most authoritative sources available. Perhaps even more than other data in this Report, however, these data should be used with caution. Although they accurately characterize major differences in resources and uses among countries, true comparability is limited because of variation in data collection, statistical methods, definitions, and government resources.

No conceptual framework has yet been agreed upon that integrates natural resource and traditional economic data. Nor are the measures shown in this table intended to be final indicators of natural resource wealth, environmental health, or resource depletion. They have been chosen because they are available for most countries, are testable, and reflect some general conditions of the environment.

The *total area* of forest refers to the total natural stands of woody vegetation in which trees predominate. These estimates are derived from country statistics assembled by the Food and Agriculture Organization (FAO) in 1980. Some of them are based on more recent inventories or satellite-based assessments performed during the 1980s. In 1993 the FAO will complete and publish an assessment of world forest extent and health that should modify some of these estimates substantially. The total area of *closed* forest refers to those forest areas where trees cover a high proportion of the ground and there is no continuous ground cover. Closed forest, for members of the Economic Commission for Europe (ECE), however, is defined as those forest areas where tree crowns cover more than 20 percent of the area. These natural stands do not include tree plantations. More recent estimates of total forest cover are available for some countries. Total forest area in the Philippines was es-

timated to be between 68,000 and 71,000 square kilometers in 1987. The most recent estimate for Malaysia is 185,000 square kilometers.

Total annual deforestation refers to both closed and open forest. Open forest is defined as at least a 10 percent tree cover with a continuous ground cover. In the ECE countries, open forest has 5–20 percent crown cover or a mixture of bush and stunted trees. Deforestation is defined as the permanent conversion of forest land to other uses, including pasture, shifting cultivation, mechanized agriculture, or infrastructure development. Deforested areas do not include areas logged but intended for regeneration, nor areas degraded by fuelwood gathering, acid precipitation, or forest fires. In temperate industrialized countries the permanent conversion of remaining forest to other uses is relatively rare. Assessments of annual deforestation, both in open and closed forest, are difficult to make and are usually undertaken as special studies. The estimates shown here for 1981–85 were calculated in 1980, projecting the rate of deforestation during the first five years of the decade. Figures from other periods are based on more recent or better assessments than those used in the 1980 projections.

Special note should be taken of Brazil—the country with the world's largest tropical closed forest—which now undertakes annual deforestation estimates. The estimate of deforestation is the most recent. Brazil is unique in having several assessments of forest extent and deforestation that use common methodology based on images from Landsat satellites. Closed forest deforestation in the Legal Amazon of Brazil during 1990 is estimated at 13,800 square kilometers, down from the 17,900 square kilometers estimated in 1989. Between 1978 and 1988, deforestation in this region averaged about 21,000 square kilometers per year, having peaked in 1987 and declined greatly thereafter. By 1990, cumulative deforestation (both recent and historical) within the Legal Amazon totaled 415,000 square kilometers. Deforestation outside the Legal Amazon also occurs, but there is much less information on its extent. A 1980 estimate, that open forest deforestation in Brazil totaled about 10,500 square kilometers, is the most recent available.

Nationally protected areas are areas of at least 1,000 hectares that fall into one of five management categories: scientific reserves and strict nature reserves; national parks of national or international significance (not materially affected by human activity); natural monuments and natural landscapes with some unique aspects; managed nature reserves and wildlife sanctuaries; and protected landscapes and seascapes (which may include cultural landscapes). This table does not include sites protected under local or provincial law or areas where consumptive uses of wildlife are allowed. These data are subject to variations in definition and in reporting to the organizations, such as the World Conservation Monitoring Centre, that compile and disseminate these data. Total surface area is used to calculate the percentage of total area protected.

Freshwater withdrawal data are subject to variation in collection and estimation methods but accurately show the magnitude of water use in both total and per capita terms. These data, however, also hide what can be significant variation in total renewable water resources from one year to another. They also fail to distinguish the variation in water availability within a country both seasonally and geographically. Because freshwater resources are based on long-term averages, their estimation explicitly excludes decade-long cycles of wet and dry. The Département Hydrogéologie in Orléans, France, compiles water resource and withdrawal data from published documents, including national, United Nations, and professional literature. The Institute of Geography at the National Academy of Sciences in Moscow also compiles global water data on the basis of published work and, where necessary, estimates water resources and consumption from models that use other data, such as area under irrigation, livestock populations, and precipitation. These and other sources have been combined by the World Resources Institute to generate (unpublished) data for this table. Withdrawal data are for single years and vary from country to country between 1970 and 1989. Data for small countries and countries in arid and semiarid zones are less reliable than those for larger countries and those with higher rainfall.

Total water resources include both internal renewable resources and, where noted, river flows from other countries. Estimates are from 1992. Annual internal renewable water resources refer to the average annual flow of rivers and of aquifers generated from rainfall within the country. The *total* withdrawn and the *percentage* withdrawn of the total renewable resource are both reported in this table. Withdrawals include those from nonrenewable aquifers and desalting plants but do not include evaporative losses. Withdrawals can exceed 100 percent of renewable supplies when extractions from nonrenewable aquifers or desalting plants are considerable or if there is significant water reuse. *Total per capita* water withdrawal is calculated by dividing a country's total withdrawal by its population in the year that withdrawal estimates are available. *Domestic* use includes drinking water, municipal use or supply, and uses for public services, commercial establishments, and homes. Direct withdrawals for *industrial* use, including withdrawals for cooling thermoelectric plants, are combined in the final column of this table with withdrawals for *agriculture* (irrigation and livestock production). Numbers may not sum to the total per capita figure because of rounding.

Data sources

Production and domestic absorbtion	U.N. Department of International Economic and Social Affairs. Various years. *Statistical Yearbook*. New York. ———. Various years. *Energy Statistics Yearbook*. Statistical Papers, series J. New York. U.N. International Comparison Program Phases IV (1980), V (1985), and Phase VI (1990) reports, and data from ECE, ESCAP, Eurostat, OECD, and U.N. FAO, IMF, UNIDO, and World Bank data; national sources.
Fiscal and monetary accounts	International Monetary Fund. *Government Finance Statistics Yearbook*. Vol. 11. Washington, D.C. ———. Various years. *International Financial Statistics*. Washington, D.C. U.N. Department of International Economic and Social Affairs. Various years. *World Energy Supplies*. Statistical Papers, series J. New York. IMF data.
Core international transactions	International Monetary Fund. Various years. *International Financial Statistics*. Washington, D.C. U.N. Conference on Trade and Development. Various years. *Handbook of International Trade and Development Statistics*. Geneva. U.N. Department of International Economic and Social Affairs. Various years. *Monthly Bulletin of Statistics*. New York. ———. Various years. *Yearbook of International Trade Statistics*. New York. FAO, IMF, U.N., and World Bank data.
External finance	Organization for Economic Cooperation and Development. Various years. *Development Co-operation*. Paris. ———. 1988. *Geographical Distribution of Financial Flows to Developing Countries*. Paris.
Human and natural resources	IMF, OECD, and World Bank data; World Bank Debtor Reporting System. Bos, Eduard, Patience W. Stephens, and My T. Vu. *World Population Projections, 1992–93 Edition* (forthcoming). Baltimore, Md.: Johns Hopkins University Press. Chen, S., G. Datt, and M. Ravallion. 1993. ''Is Poverty Increasing in the Developing World?'' Working Paper Series 1146. World Bank, Policy Research Department, Washington D.C. Institute for Resource Development/Westinghouse. 1987. *Child Survival: Risks and the Road to Health*. Columbia, Md. Mauldin, W. Parker, and Holden J. Segal. 1988. ''Prevalence of Contraceptive Use: Trends and Issues.'' *Studies in Family Planning* 19, 6: 335-53 Sivard, Ruth. 1985. *Women—A World Survey*. Washington, D.C.: World Priorities. U.N. Department of International Economic and Social Affairs. Various years. *Demographic Yearbook*. New York. ———. Various years. *Population and Vital Statistics Report*. New York. ———. Various years. *Statistical Yearbook*. New York. ———. 1989. *Levels and Trends of Contraceptive Use as Assessed in 1988*. New York. ———. 1988. *Mortality of Children under Age 5: Projections 1950-2025*. New York. ———. 1991. *World Urbanization Prospects 1991*. New York. ———. 1991. *World Population Prospects: 1990*. New York. ———. 1992. *World Population Prospects: 1992 Revision*. New York. U.N. Educational Scientific and Cultural Organization. Various years. *Statistical Yearbook*. Paris. ———. 1990. *Compendium of Statistics on Illiteracy*. Paris. UNICEF. 1989. *The State of the World's Children 1989*. Oxford: Oxford University Press. World Health Organization. Various years. *World Health Statistics Annual*. Geneva. ———. 1986. *Maternal Mortality Rates: A Tabulation of Available Information*, 2nd edition. Geneva. ———. 1991. *Maternal Mortality: A Global Factbook*. Geneva ———. Various years. *World Health Statistics Report*. Geneva. World Resources Institute data (unpublished). FAO and World Bank data World Conservation Monitoring Center data (unpublished).

Part 1 Classification of economies by income and region

Income group	Subgroup	Sub-Saharan Africa[a]		Asia		Europe and Central Asia		Middle East and North Africa		Americas
		East & Southern Africa	West Africa	East Asia and Pacific	South Asia	Eastern Europe and Central Asia	Rest of Europe	Middle East	North Africa	
Low-income		Burundi Comoros Ethiopia Kenya Lesotho Madagascar Malawi Mozambique Rwanda Somalia Sudan Tanzania Uganda Zaire Zambia Zimbabwe	Benin Burkina Faso Central African Rep. Chad Equatorial Guinea Gambia, The Ghana Guinea Guinea-Bissau Liberia Mali Mauritania Niger Nigeria São Tomé and Principe Sierra Leone Togo	Cambodia China Indonesia Lao PDR Myanmar Solomon Islands Viet Nam	Afghanistan Bangladesh Bhutan India Maldives Nepal Pakistan Sri Lanka			Yemen, Rep.	Egypt, Arab Rep.	Guyana Haiti Honduras Nicaragua
Middle-income	Lower	Angola Djibouti Mauritius Namibia Swaziland	Cameroon Cape Verde Congo Côte d'Ivoire Senegal	Fiji Kiribati Korea, Dem. Rep. Malaysia Marshall Islands Micronesia, Fed. Sts. Mongolia Papua New Guinea Philippines Thailand Tonga Vanuatu Western Samoa		Albania Armenia Azerbaijan Bulgaria Czecho-slovakia[b] Georgia Kazakhstan Kyrgyzstan Moldova Poland Romania Tajikistan Turkmenistan Ukraine Uzbekistan	Turkey	Iran, Islamic Rep. Iraq Jordan Lebanon Syrian Arab Rep.	Algeria Morocco Tunisia	Belize Bolivia Chile Colombia Costa Rica Cuba Dominica Dominican Rep. Ecuador El Salvador Grenada Guatemala Jamaica Panama Paraguay Peru St. Lucia St. Vincent
	Upper	Botswana Mayotte Reunion Seychelles South Africa[a]	Gabon	American Samoa Guam Korea, Rep. Macao New Caledonia		Belarus Estonia Hungary Latvia Lithuania Russian Federation Yugoslavia[c]	Gibraltar Greece Isle of Man Malta Portugal	Bahrain Oman Saudi Arabia	Libya	Antigua and Barbuda Argentina Aruba Barbados Brazil French Guiana Guadeloupe Martinique Mexico Netherlands Antilles Puerto Rico St. Kitts and Nevis Suriname Trinidad and Tobago Uruguay Venezuela
No. of low- & middle-income economies: 162		26	23	25	8	22	6	9	5	38

Part 1 *(continued)*

| Income group | Subgroup | Sub-Saharan Africa[a] | | Asia | | Europe and Central Asia | | Middle East and North Africa | | |
		East & Southern Africa	West Africa	East Asia and Pacific	South Asia	Eastern Europe and Central Asia	Rest of Europe	Middle East	North Africa	Americas
High-income	OECD countries			Australia Japan New Zealand			Andorra Austria Belgium Denmark Finland France Germany Iceland Ireland Italy Luxembourg Netherlands Norway San Marino Spain Sweden Switzerland United Kingdom			Canada United States
	Non-OECD countries			Brunei French Polynesia Hong Kong Singapore OAE[d]			Channel Islands Cyprus Faeroe Islands Greenland	Israel Kuwait Qatar United Arab Emirates		Bahamas Bermuda Virgin Islands (US)
Total no. of economies: 201		26	23	33	8	22	28	13	5	43

a. For some analysis, South Africa is not included in Sub-Saharan Africa.
b. Refers to the former Czechoslovakia; disaggregated data are not yet available.
c. Refers to the former Socialist Federal Republic of Yugoslavia; disaggregated data are not yet available.
d. Other Asian economies—Taiwan, China.

Definitions of groups

These tables classify all World Bank member economies, plus all other economies with populations of more than 30,000.

Income group: Economies are divided according to 1991 GNP per capita, calculated using the *World Bank Atlas* method. The groups are: low-income, $635 or less; lower-middle-income, $636–2,555; upper-middle-income, $2,556–$7,910; and high-income, $7,911 or more.

The estimates for the republics of the former Soviet Union should be regarded as very preliminary; their classification will be kept under review.

Part 2 Classification of economies by major export category and indebtedness

| | Low- and middle-income | | | | | | | High-income | |
| | Low-income | | | Middle-income | | | | | |
Group	Severely indebted	Moderately indebted	Less indebted	Severely indebted	Moderately indebted	Less indebted	Not classified by indebtedness	OECD	non-OECD
Exporters of manufactures			China	Bulgaria Poland	Hungary	Czecho-slovakia[a] Korea, Dem. Rep. Korea, Rep. Lebanon Macao Romania	Armenia Belarus Estonia Georgia Kyrgyzstan Latvia Lithuania Moldova Russian Federation Ukraine Uzbekistan	Belgium Canada Finland Germany Ireland Italy Japan Luxembourg Sweden Switzerland	Hong Kong Israel Singapore OAE[b]
Exporters of nonfuel primary products	Afghanistan Burundi Equatorial Guinea Ethiopia Ghana Guinea-Bissau Guyana Honduras Liberia Madagascar Mauritania Myanmar Nicaragua Niger São Tomé and Principe Somalia Tanzania Uganda Viet Nam Zaire Zambia	Guinea Malawi Rwanda Togo	Chad Solomon Islands Zimbabwe	Albania Argentina Bolivia Côte d'Ivoire Cuba Mongolia Peru	Chile Costa Rica Guatemala Papua New Guinea	Botswana French Guiana Guadeloupe Namibia Paraguay Reunion St. Vincent Suriname Swaziland	American Samoa	Iceland New Zealand	Faeroe Islands Greenland
Exporters of fuels (mainly oil)	Nigeria			Algeria Angola Congo Iraq	Gabon Venezuela	Iran, Islamic Rep. Libya Oman Saudi Arabia Trinidad and Tobago	Turkmenistan		Brunei Qatar United Arab Emirates
Exporters of services	Cambodia Egypt, Arab Rep. Sudan	Benin Gambia, The Haiti Maldives Nepal Yemen, Rep.	Bhutan Burkina Faso Lesotho	Jamaica Jordan Panama	Dominican Rep. Greece	Antigua and Barbuda Barbados Cape Verde Djibouti El Salvador Fiji Grenada Kiribati Malta Martinique Netherlands Antilles Seychelles St. Kitts and Nevis St. Lucia Tonga Vanuatu Western Samoa	Aruba	United Kingdom	Bahamas Bermuda Cyprus French Polynesia
Diversified exporters	Kenya Lao PDR Mali Mozambique Sierra Leone	Bangladesh Central African Rep. Comoros India Indonesia Pakistan Sri Lanka		Brazil Ecuador Mexico Morocco Syrian Arab Rep.	Cameroon Colombia Philippines Senegal Tunisia Turkey Uruguay	Bahrain Belize Dominica Malaysia Mauritius Portugal South Africa Thailand Yugoslavia[c]	Azerbaijan Kazakhstan Tajikistan	Australia Austria Denmark France Netherlands Norway Spain United States	Kuwait

Part 2 *(continued)*

| Group | Low- and middle-income | | | | | | | High-income | |
| | Low-income | | | Middle-income | | | Not classified by indebtedness | OECD | non-OECD |
	Severely indebted	Moderately indebted	Less indebted	Severely indebted	Moderately indebted	Less indebted			
Not classified by export category							Gibraltar Guam Isle of Man Marshall Islands Mayotte Micronesia, Fed. Sts. New Caledonia Puerto Rico		Andorra Channel Islands San Marino Virgin Islands (US)
No. of economies 201	30	17	7	21	16	47	24	21	18

a. Refers to the former Czechoslovakia; disaggregated data are not yet available.
b. Other Asian economies—Taiwan, China.
c. Refers to the former Socialist Federal Republic of Yugoslavia; disaggregated data are not yet available.

Definitions of groups

These tables classify all World Bank member economies, plus all other economies with populations of more than 30,000.

Major export category: Major exports are those that account for 50 percent or more of total exports of goods and services from one category, in the period 1987–89. The categories are: nonfuel primary (SITC 0,1,2, 4, plus 68), fuels (SITC 3), manufactures (SITC 5 to 9, less 68), and services (factor and nonfactor service receipts plus workers' remittances). If no single category accounts for 50 percent or more of total exports, the economy is classified as *diversified*.

Indebtedness: Standard World Bank definitions of severe and moderate indebtedness, averaged over three years (1989–91) are used to classify economies in this table. Severely indebted means either of the two key ratios is above critical levels: present value of debt service to GNP (80 percent) and present value of debt service to exports (220 percent). Moderately indebted means either of the two key ratios exceeds 60 percent of, but does not reach, the critical levels. For economies that do not report detailed debt statistics to the World Bank Debtor Reporting System, present-value calculation is not possible. Instead the following methodology is used to classify the non-DRS economies. Severely indebted means three of four key ratios (averaged over 1988–90) are above critical levels: debt to GNP (50 percent); debt to exports (275 percent), debt service to exports (30 percent); and interest to exports (20 percent). Moderately indebted means three of four key ratios exceed 60 percent of, but do not reach, the critical levels. All other low- and middle-income economies are classified as less-indebted.

Not classified by indebtedness are the republics of the Former Soviet Union and some small economies for which detailed debt data are not available.

How to order
World Development Report

CUSTOMERS IN THE UNITED STATES:

Complete this coupon and return to:

World Bank Publications
Box 7247-8619
Philadelphia, PA 19170-8619, U.S.A.

To have your order shipped faster, call (202) 473-1155 to charge by credit card, or send this completed order coupon by facsimile by dialing (202) 676-0581.

CUSTOMERS OUTSIDE THE UNITED STATES:

Contact your local World Bank publications distributor or branch of Oxford University Press for information on prices in local currency and payment terms. If no distributor is listed for your country, use this order form and return it to the U.S. address. Orders from countries with distributors that are sent to the U.S. address will be returned to the customer.

Order number	Title	Quantity	Unit price	Total amount ($)
60890	World Development Report 1993: Investing in Health		19.95	
60876	World Development Report 1992: Development and the Environment		19.95	
60868	World Development Report 1991: The Challenge of Development		19.95	
60851	World Development Report 1990: Poverty		19.95	

Other language editions are available. Please contact customer service or your local distributor for languages and availability.

*   SHIPPING AND HANDLING charges are US$3.50 if paying by check or credit card. If purchase order is used, actual shipping and handling costs will be charged. For air mail delivery outside the U.S., include an additional US$6.00 per item. Allow 6–8 weeks for delivery by surface mail outside the U.S.

Subtotal US $_____

Shipping and handling* US $_____

Total US $ _____

CHECK METHOD OF PAYMENT

❑ Enclosed is my check, payable to World Bank Publications.

❑ Charge my   ❑ VISA   ❑ Mastercard   ❑ American Express

_____   _____   _____

Credit card number   Expiration date   Signature

❑ Bill me. (Institutional customers only. Purchase order must be included.)

PLEASE TYPE OR PRINT. Legible information ensures prompt and correct delivery.

Date_____

Name _____

Firm_____

Address _____

_____

City _____State _____

Postal code_____Country _____

Telephone (_____) _____

Ship to: (Enter if different from purchaser.)

Name_____

Firm _____

Address_____

_____

City _____ State _____

Postal code _____ Country _____

Telephone (_____) _____

Thank you for your order.

Distributors of World Bank Publications

ARGENTINA
Carlos Hirsch, SRL
Galeria Guemes
Florida 165, 4th Floor-Ofc. 453/465
1333 Buenos Aires

AUSTRALIA, PAPUA NEW GUINEA, FIJI, SOLOMON ISLANDS, VANUATU, AND WESTERN SAMOA
D.A. Information Services
648 Whitehorse Road
Mitcham 3132
Victoria

AUSTRIA
Gerold and Co.
Graben 31
A-1011 Wien

BANGLADESH
Micro Industries Development
  Assistance Society (MIDAS)
House 5, Road 16
Dhanmondi R/Area
Dhaka 1209

Branch offices:
Pine View, 1st Floor
100 Agrabad Commercial Area
Chittagong 4100

76, K.D.A. Avenue
Kulna 9100

BELGIUM
Jean De Lannoy
Av. du Roi 202
1060 Brussels

CANADA
Le Diffuseur
C.P. 85, 1501B rue Ampère
Boucherville, Québec
J4B 5E6

CHILE
Invertec IGT S.A.
Americo Vespucio Norte 1165
Santiago

CHINA
China Financial & Economic
  Publishing House
8, Da Fo Si Dong Jie
Beijing

COLOMBIA
Infoenlace Ltda.
Apartado Aereo 34270
Bogota D.E.

COTE D'IVOIRE
Centre d'Edition et de Diffusion
  Africaines (CEDA)
04 B.P. 541
Abidjan 04 Plateau

CYPRUS
Center of Applied Research
Cyprus College
6, Diogenes Street, Engomi
P.O. Box 2006
Nicosia

DENMARK
SamfundsLitteratur
Rosenoerns Allé 11
DK-1970 Frederiksberg C

DOMINICAN REPUBLIC
Editora Taller, C. por A.
Restauración e Isabel la Católica 309
Apartado de Correos 2190 Z-1
Santo Domingo

EGYPT, ARAB REPUBLIC OF
Al Ahram
Al Galaa Street
Cairo

The Middle East Observer
41, Sherif Street
Cairo

FINLAND
Akateeminen Kirjakauppa
P.O. Box 128
SF-00101 Helsinki 10

FRANCE
World Bank Publications
66, avenue d'Iéna
75116 Paris

GERMANY
UNO-Verlag
Poppelsdorfer Allee 55
D-5300 Bonn 1

HONG KONG, MACAO
Asia 2000 Ltd.
46-48 Wyndham Street
Winning Centre
2nd Floor
Central Hong Kong

INDIA
Allied Publishers Private Ltd.
751 Mount Road
Madras - 600 002

Branch offices:
15 J.N. Heredia Marg
Ballard Estate
Bombay - 400 038

13/14 Asaf Ali Road
New Delhi - 110 002

17 Chittaranjan Avenue
Calcutta - 700 072

Jayadeva Hostel Building
5th Main Road, Gandhinagar
Bangalore - 560 009

3-5-1129 Kachiguda
  Cross Road
Hyderabad - 500 027

Prarthana Flats, 2nd Floor
Near Thakore Baug, Navrangpura
Ahmedabad - 380 009

Patiala House
16-A Ashok Marg
Lucknow - 226 001

Central Bazaar Road
60 Bajaj Nagar
Nagpur 440 010

INDONESIA
Pt. Indira Limited
Jalan Borobudur 20
P.O. Box 181
Jakarta 10320

IRELAND
Government Supplies Agency
4-5 Harcourt Road
Dublin 2

ISRAEL
Yozmot Literature Ltd.
P.O. Box 56055
Tel Aviv 61560

ITALY
Licosa Commissionaria Sansoni SPA
Via Duca Di Calabria, 1/1
Casella Postale 552
50125 Firenze

JAPAN
Eastern Book Service
Hongo 3-Chome, Bunkyo-ku 113
Tokyo

KENYA
Africa Book Service (E.A.) Ltd.
Quaran House, Mfangano Street
P.O. Box 45245
Nairobi

KOREA, REPUBLIC OF
Pan Korea Book Corporation
P.O. Box 101, Kwangwhamun
Seoul

MALAYSIA
Univ. of Malaya Coop. Bookshop, Ltd.
P.O. Box 1127, Jalan Pantai Baru
59700 Kuala Lumpur

MEXICO
INFOTEC
Apartado Postal 22-860
14060 Tlalpan, Mexico D.F.

NETHERLANDS
De Lindeboom/InOr-Publikaties
P.O. Box 202
7480 AE Haaksbergen

NEW ZEALAND
EBSCO NZ Ltd.
Private Mail Bag 99914
New Market
Auckland

NIGERIA
University Press Limited
Three Crowns Building Jericho
Private Mail Bag 5095
Ibadan

NORWAY
Narvesen Information Center
Book Department
P.O. Box 6125 Etterstad
N-0602 Oslo 6

PAKISTAN
Mirza Book Agency
65, Shahrah-e-Quaid-e-Azam
P.O. Box No. 729
Lahore 54000

PERU
Editorial Desarrollo SA
Apartado 3824
Lima 1

PHILIPPINES
International Book Center
Suite 1703, Cityland 10
Condominium Tower 1
Ayala Avenue, H.V. dela
  Costa Extension
Makati, Metro Manila

POLAND
International Publishing Service
Ul. Piekna 31/37
00-677 Warzawa

For subscription orders:
IPS Journals
Ul. Okrezna 3
02-916 Warszawa

PORTUGAL
Livraria Portugal
Rua Do Carmo 70-74
1200 Lisbon

SAUDI ARABIA, QATAR
Jarir Book Store
P.O. Box 3196
Riyadh 11471

SINGAPORE, TAIWAN, MYANMAR,BRUNEI
Information PublicationsPrivate, Ltd.
Golden Wheel Building
41, Kallang Pudding, #04-03
Singapore 1334

SOUTH AFRICA, BOTSWANA
For single titles:
Oxford University Press
  Southern Africa
P.O. Box 1141
Cape Town 8000

For subscription orders:
International Subscription Service
P.O. Box 41095
Craighall
Johannesburg 2024

SPAIN
Mundi-Prensa Libros, S.A.
Castello 37
28001 Madrid

Librería Internacional AEDOS
Consell de Cent, 391
08009 Barcelona

SRI LANKA AND THE MALDIVES
Lake House Bookshop
P.O. Box 244
100, Sir Chittampalam A.
  Gardiner Mawatha
Colombo 2

SWEDEN
For single titles:
Fritzes Fackboksforetaget
Regeringsgatan 12, Box 16356
S-103 27 Stockholm

For subscription orders:
Wennergren-Williams AB
P. O. Box 1305
S-171 25 Solna

SWITZERLAND
For single titles:
Librairie Payot
Case postale 3212
CH 1002 Lausanne

For subscription orders:
Librairie Payot
Service des Abonnements
Case postale 3312
CH 1002 Lausanne

THAILAND
Central Department Store
306 Silom Road
Bangkok

**TRINIDAD & TOBAGO, ANTIGUA
BARBUDA, BARBADOS,
DOMINICA, GRENADA, GUYANA,
JAMAICA, MONTSERRAT, ST.
KITTS & NEVIS, ST. LUCIA,
ST. VINCENT & GRENADINES**
Systematics Studies Unit
#9 Watts Street
Curepe
Trinidad, West Indies

TURKEY
Infotel
Narlabahçe Sok. No. 15
Cagaloglu
Istanbul

UNITED KINGDOM
Microinfo Ltd.
P.O. Box 3
Alton, Hampshire GU34 2PG
England

VENEZUELA
Libreria del Este
Aptdo. 60.337
Caracas 1060-A